LightWave 3D Applied
Version 5.6

Dave Jerrard
Joe Tracy
Scott Wheeler

ADVANSTAR

MARKETING SERVICES
A Division of Advanstar Communications Inc.

Cleveland, Ohio

Printed in the United States of America

10 9 8 7 6 5 4 3

ISBN 0-929870-48-4

Library of Congress Catalog Card Number 98-074172

Published by Advanstar Communications, Inc.

Advanstar Communications is a US Business information company that publishes magazines and journals, produces expositions and conferences, and provides a wide range of marketing services.

For additional information on any magazines or a complete catalog of Advanstar Communications books, please write to Advanstar Communications Customer Service, 131 West 1st Street, Duluth, MN 55802 USA.

Cover Design: Dave Crouch Graphics, Cleveland, OH
Interior Design: Lachina Publishing Services, Inc., Cleveland, OH
Product Manager: Danell M. Durica
CD-ROM: Michael Meshew
Cartoons: Willie Lloyd

LightWave 3D™ is a trademark of NewTek, Inc.

About the LightWave 3D Applied CD-ROM and Cartoons

THE CD-ROM

The CD-ROM that comes with this book is a free gift to you from the authors and Michael Meshew of Graphic Detail. When you first access the CD-ROM, you'll notice two folders, "Applied" and "Lightrom." The "Applied" folder contains material from the authors to you. The "Lightrom" folder contains bonus objects, scenes, backgrounds, and more, courtesy of Graphic Detail, which puts out the popular LIGHT-ROM CD sets. Graphic Detail can be reached at 502-363-2986, where you can request a brochure or more information about its products.

When you open the "Applied" folder, you will see it is divided into chapters. There are five folders, labeled "Chapter1," "Chaps2_7," "Chapter8," "Chapter9," and "Chaptr10." Note that the naming of the folders and files follows the eight-character structure so that the CD can work on all platforms. The authors have included material you need to complete the tutorials in these folders. In some cases, as in the folder called "Chaps2_7," you'll find quite a bit more bonus material, including two tutorials not in the book! You'll also find large color versions of the figures in these chapters. Best of all, it has been formatted in HTML so that it will display on your browser. To access all of this bonus material, open the "Chaps2_7" folder. Now open the file titled "La_index" (LightWave Applied Index). You now have a very cool and easy interface to work from in accessing the bonus material provided by

Dave Jerrard. You'll also find four popular LightWave 3D tutorials that Dave Jerrard wrote for *NewTekniques* magazine.

The "Applied" folder is only half of the bonus material you get on the CD-ROM. The other half is in the "Lightrom" folder. Here you will find hundreds of bonus objects that you can use in Light-Wave 3D or Inspire 3D. You'll find scenes, backdrops, DEM files, images, surfaces, and more! If you like this material, contact Graphic Detail about getting some of its other CD sets.

If at any time you come across a .txt file, be sure to read it. Each of these contain important information. In the "Applied" folder, be sure to read the "Changes.txt" files in the "Chapter8," "Chapter9," and "Chaptr10" folders, which will help you get the right files to complete the tutorials in those chapters.

For more detailed information about using the CD-ROM, check out the LightWave Applied Web site at **http://www.advanstarbooks.com/lightwave**. Hopefully you'll find this free CD bonus alone to be worth the price of the entire book. Enjoy!

THE CARTOONS

The cartoons that begin each tutorial were created by Willie Lloyd, a long-time LightWave 3D artist. Lloyd has done a lot of Light-Wave 3D work for television affiliate stations (mostly Warner Brothers) across the United States. In his free time, Lloyd does humorous LightWave sketches.

Contents

Introduction

Centuries ago, lords, ladies, kings, queens, princes, princesses, and knights roamed castles throughout the world in many medieval adventures. Centuries later, as we approach the year 2000, that age returns and you have the power to recreate it (and the future) through the applications you will learn in this book—applications that will help take your work to the next level.

LightWave 3D Applied—Version 5.6 is unlike any other book or manual you've ever stumbled across. That is because *LightWave 3D Applied—Version 5.6* is based on the notion that people learn best from hands-on projects. Therefore, instead of a list of button descriptions and quick tips, this book takes you into the world of actual model building and animation—a world where you will create castles, fountains, swords, and much more, including the *Mercury* Space Capsule.

The tutorials in *LightWave 3D Applied—Version 5.6* are some of the most in-depth tutorials ever written for any book. Take "Tutorial 6: The Sword in the Stone," for example. It has 121 steps and over 65 images! By working through these tutorials, you begin to get a real feel for approaching and mastering big projects, while advancing your learning abilities.

LightWave 3D Applied—Version 5.6 is very easy to follow, since each chapter is divided into a step-by-step format. The novice and advanced applications in Tutorials 2–10 may be intimidating for those just entering the 3D community with LightWave 3D or Inspire 3D. This is the reason for Tutorial 1, which gives those just starting out some of the basic knowledge, advice, and beginner tutorials needed to overcome the "intimidation factor."

It is our sincere hope that every page in this book will be a great benefit in advancing your work and career, as that was the reason for writing the book.

ABOUT THE AUTHORS

Dave Jerrard is the lead tutorial writer for *NewTekniques* magazine and has received much praise from *NewTekniques* readers for producing some of the best tutorials in the market. "The laser tutorial [by Dave Jerrard] is one of the best tutorials I've seen. I was able to put it to use in some of my projects immediately," says Tom Jordan, lead animator for the epic software group that was responsible for the tutorial CD-ROM that ships with Inspire 3D. *NewTekniques* magazine frequently receives such comments about Jerrard's work. In *LightWave 3D Applied,* Jerrard writes some of the most detailed and awesome tutorials ever for LightWave 3D users, including one on building a medieval castle from scratch!

Scott Wheeler is well-known within the Hollywood effects industry for his work on shows like *The X-Files, Dark Skies, Space: Above and Beyond,* and the Emmy-award-winning *From the Earth to the Moon.* In addition to his excellent effects work, Wheeler is the LightWave 201 columnist for *NewTekniques* magazine, where he shares his insight with readers through a university-like course program that advances every year. *NewTekniques* readers have voted LightWave 201 their favorite column in the magazine. Wheeler carries that success into this book, where he writes three tutorials detailing how to build the *Mercury* Space Capsule, create a parachute for it, and land it at sea.

Joe Tracy is editor in chief of *NewTekniques* magazine and the former editor in chief of *Video Toaster User* magazine. In addition, he is the author of the highly acclaimed *Flyer Mastery Guide* that NewTek considered replacing its own Flyer manual with because of its detailed step-by-step tutorials helping users master the Video Toaster Flyer. Now Tracy brings his passion for LightWave 3D into the print medium with a detailed tutorial aimed at getting those just starting out into the LightWave 3D arena. Tracy also wrote a tutorial for advanced users on how to break into the Hollywood effects arena.

THE AUTHORS' COMMITMENT TO YOU

The three *LightWave 3D Applied—Version 5.6* authors are each very responsive to questions posed in the LightWave 3D community. This commitment to readers is one of the reasons, outside of ability, that this particular team was assembled. Chances are that your learning won't stop after you've read this book, since the authors will be setting up an area on the LightWave Applied Web site to personally answer questions you may have regarding some of the book's tutorials and further tips/techniques.

ACKNOWLEDGMENTS

I want to thank Tom Clarke, for his invaluable input and error catching, and the advent of the spell checker, without which I'd be swimming in white-out. I'd like to also recognize Dave Adams, Bob Driskell, and Faisal Naqvi for their assistance and encouragement. I thank my family for locking me in the basement, safe from the sun all summer. Finally, I'd like to acknowledge both of my remaining friends who still remember who I am after only a dozen or so prompts. I dedicate this book to my aunt, Jean Black, an artist who left us before her time. You won't be forgotten.

—Dave Jerrard

I dedicate this book to Lana, for she makes everything possible.

—Scott Wheeler

In life there are instances when projects just wouldn't have been completed without the aid of another person. My wife, Vicki Tracy, was an invaluable assistant, not only by keeping everything in check but also by assisting in some of the writing itself! I'd also like to acknowledge Lee Worley for her assistance. Finally, I'd like to thank both Dave Jerrard and Scott Wheeler for the excellent jobs they did. I enjoyed working with both of them on this team project. I dedicate this book to my wife, Vicki, for her continued assistance, understanding, and companionship.

—Joe Tracy

All of the authors would like to thank the book's production manager, Danell Durica, for her hard and excellent work. Furthermore, we thank Advanstar Communications for seeing this as a good project and Lachina Publishing Services for the great job it did assembling the book.

The authors would also like to extend their deepest appreciation to Michael Meshew of Graphic Detail for assembling the CD-ROM and Willie Lloyd for his excellent cartoons!

Finally, the authors would like to acknowledge the LightWave 3D community and the dreams and visions each user strives for to achieve success.

1

Beginner Techniques for LightWave 3D and Inspire 3D

Joe Tracy

OVERVIEW

Many people who buy LightWave 3D or Inspire 3D as their first introduction into the 3D world find the program too intimidating to use. Some of these people re-sell the program to a friend while others let it sit on a shelf and collect dust.

The purpose of this chapter is to take those of you who are beginners in the world of LightWave 3D or Inspire 3D and introduce you to some introductory techniques that will help you overcome that intimidation and open the door to a broader experience. If you are already gifted in LightWave 3D or Inspire 3D, you'll want to move on to the next chapter, which begins the more advanced step-by-step tutorials. If this is your first experience into the world of 3D, then read on! The majority of our time in this chapter will be spent in Modeler, which for many is the more difficult of the two (Modeler and Layout) to learn.

In this chapter you will use:

- Many basic features and buttons in Modeler
- Many basic features and buttons in Layout

What you will need:

- LightWave 3D or Inspire 3D
- A couple of free hours

What you will learn:

- Three things your computer needs to enhance Modeler/Layout
- The general Interface structure of Modeler
- How to create and surface objects
- Effect uses of the Boolean command
- How to use Lathe, Mirror, and Extrude
- How to use Layers
- Effect use of the Volume button (Include and Exclude)
- How to create multiple surfaces on one object
- How to create 3D text
- How to cut, paste, and set the Perspective View
- How to change surfaces in Layout
- How to create keyframes
- How to create a lens flare
- How to use background Images
- How to move and rotate objects
- X, Y, Z, and H, P, B

OVERCOMING THE INTIMIDATION FACTOR

One of the authors of this book is Scott Wheeler. Wheeler is well known for the excellent LightWave 3D effects he has created for shows such as *Space: Above and Beyond, The X-Files, Buffy the Vampire Slayer,* and *From the Earth to the Moon.* Yet he was once in the exact position you are in today. Wheeler best explains his situation in the April 1997 issue of *NewTekniques* magazine. He had just been hired as a cable employee in Danvers, MA: "Soon after I arrived, we got a Video Toaster and I began playing with the Switcher, CG, and ToasterPaint," Wheeler says. "Occasionally I would hit the 3D button [which loads LightWave 3D] by accident and scream in horror at the alien nature of the module."

Wheeler wasn't alone. Many people who own Video Toaster systems have never even entered the LightWave 3D portion of the program more than once because it appears too intimidating. After all, words like Lathe, Boolean, Dithered Motion Blur, Edge Z Scale, Pivot Point, Rail Extrude, and Numeric Knife Parameters are not in most people's everyday vocabulary. But Wheeler decided to take the leap to learn the operations of a program that so many 3D artists had praised. He committed to learning: "Slowly, I began exploring more with the 3D button and eventually got to the point where I was making logo openings for shows we produced." It is important to note that Wheeler advanced slowly. He didn't become a LightWave 3D expert overnight, but rather over the period of a few years, learning a little at a time and becoming more advanced. Now he's a premier Hollywood artist!

Likewise, John Gross was just a swimming pool salesman when he started exploring LightWave 3D. Today Gross is the co-founder and co-owner of Digital Muse, a premier visual effects company in Hollywood that does work on shows such as *Star Trek: Deep Space Nine, Star Trek: Voyager, Beowulf,* and *Virus.*

Scott Wheeler and John Gross are no different from you. Like them, you have the power to reach for a dream in the world of 3D animation if that is what you really want. The hardest hurdle in reaching that dream is to overcome the initial fear and intimidation of LightWave 3D or Inspire 3D. Once you are beyond that point, the rest is a fun and interactive learning experience where you are the director, producer, and effects artist in a quest for animation excellence.

GETTING STARTED

You've purchased either LightWave 3D or Inspire 3D and you're ready to get started. If Inspire 3D is the program you purchased, all you have to do is to install the program and you're on your way! If LightWave 3D is the program you purchased, getting up and running is a little more tricky.

LightWave 3D comes with a hardware dongle that must be plugged into the Parallel Port of your computer in order for it to work. Furthermore, after 14 days you'll be required to enter a license number into the program or else it will cease to function! Follow these easy steps to get up and running in a quick manner and without worry that the program will suddenly quit on you.

STEP 1: On the back of the dongle hardware lock (and your CD case) is the program serial number for your copy of LightWave 3D. The serial number starts with an "LW" followed by 5 to 6 numbers. Write the serial number down in a safe place like the inside cover of your manual.

STEP 2: Turn off your computer. Plug the hardware dongle lock into the Parallel Port of your computer.

STEP 3: Turn your computer on. Install LightWave 3D. At the end of the installation, you will be given a hardware lock serial number that is different from the program serial number you wrote down in Step 1. Write the hardware lock serial number down next to the program serial number you wrote down in Step 1.

STEP 4: Call 1-888-438-5955. A NewTek customer service representative will answer the phone if it is during office hours. Tell the representative that you need to register your copy of LightWave 3D and obtain a license number.

STEP 5: The representative will walk you through the registration process, asking you a series of questions, then present you with a 16-digit license number that is very important. Write this number down next to the other two numbers so that you have all three in the same place. The representative should instruct you on how to enter the number. If not, the next step does.

STEP 6: You want to run the program called **License.exe** and type in the 16-digit license number you were given, so that your program will run without limitations. There is one important note here. An apparent bug on Intel systems will not recognize the license number if you register by going to the Start button and selecting the License option from your Programs directory. Instead you must do it the long way:

1. Double-click on the My Computer icon on your desktop window.

2. Double-click on the drive letter that contains LightWave 3D (most likely this is drive "C:").

3. Double-click on the NewTek folder.

4. Double-click on the Programs folder.

5. You will see an icon that says **License.exe**. Double click on it.

6. A window will open asking you to enter your registration code (Figure 1-1). Enter your 16-digit license code and click OK.

FIGURE 1-1 The LightWave License window. Type in the 16-digit number you receive from NewTek into this window, then click OK.

STEP 7: You have successfully installed LightWave 3D and have it properly registered and set up so that it won't quit on you after 14 days! Keep all your numbers (program serial number, hardware lock serial number, and 16-digit license number) in a very safe place as you will need the numbers if you ever reinstall LightWave 3D or need technical support assistance.

Three Things to Simplify Life

Before you start using the program, there are three things you should strongly consider obtaining that will simplify your life while using Inspire 3D or LightWave 3D:

1. *RAM.* RAM is cheap and makes a major difference in the amount of resources and memory you have when operating LightWave 3D, Inspire 3D, or any other program on your computer. I would very strongly recommend that you have at least 128 MB of RAM installed in your computer. While this is well above the minimum you need to run LightWave 3D or Inspire 3D, it is a mandatory number when you consider the low cost of RAM and amount of frustration it will save you later on. Many aspects of LightWave 3D and Inspire 3D heavily depend on RAM. You may even want to go beyond 128 MB.

2. *OpenGL card.* There are many excellent display features within LightWave 3D and Inspire 3D that you simply won't be able to use unless you have an OpenGL card installed in your computer. There are many OpenGL cards that work well with LightWave 3D and Inspire 3D, including the Oxygen 402 OpenGL Accelerator by Dynamic Pictures, which is the card I use. It seems that every month newer and faster OpenGL cards are being introduced to the marketplace. Publications such as *NewTekniques* cover such introductions, as do a few Light-Wave 3D Web sites.

3. *Updates.* Check NewTek's Web site to see if an update (i.e., bug fix) to your program has been released. Go to **www.newtek.com** and select Service and Support from the left-hand navigation

menu. Now select Software Updates. You will now see a list of product updates and the dates the updates were made. If the date of the update is recent, you will want to download and install it.

MODELER SIMPLIFIED

Now that all the formalities are out of the way, let's have some fun! This chapter has been set up to explain some beginning process techniques to you in the most simplistic form possible. Once you've mastered these techniques, you should feel confident to begin experimenting on your own and following the more advanced tutorials in chapters 2–10 to increase your knowledge. Keep in mind that there are literally dozens of ways to accomplish the same task in Modeler. Therefore, experimentation is extremely important.

In the most basic form possible, Modeler represents two ideas:

1. Shapes make objects.

2. Points are dots and Polygons are the connection of the dots.

You might be surprised to learn that some of the most detailed 3D objects you see on videos and television are simple shapes that have been manipulated into objects. Remember when you were a kid playing with Legos? You would take the shaped pieces and put them together to make some inventive and cool creations. That is Modeler simplified!

A Look at the Interface

Load up the Inspire 3D or LightWave 3D Modeler. Your Inspire 3D interface should look like Figure 1-2 (with much richer colors than the LightWave Modeler interface). If you're using LightWave 3D 5.6, it should look like Figure 1-3.

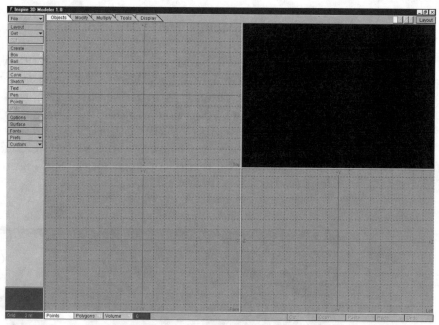

FIGURE 1-2 Inspire 3D Modeler 1.0 interface shot. The look and feel are the same as the LightWave 3D 5.6 interface, but the colors are much more rich (see the LightWave 3D Applied Web site for color version).

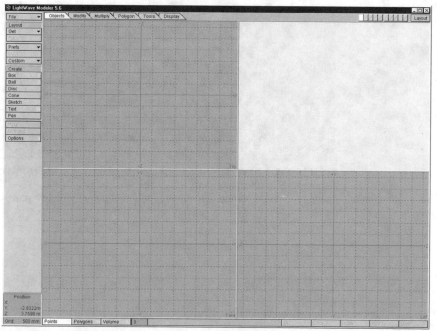

FIGURE 1-3 LightWave 3D Modeler 5.6 interface shot.

When you first enter Modeler, you are greeted by a workspace divided by four screens. Three of the screens are for you to work in and a fourth screen is where you view the results of your work. The top left-hand window is the Top View. The bottom left-hand window is the Face View. The bottom right-hand window is the Left View. It is in these three windows that you will create. Whenever you make a modeling change to your creation in one of the windows, the other two will automatically be updated. The top right-hand window is the Perspective View where you see the results of your work. See Figure 1-4 to easily identify the four windows.

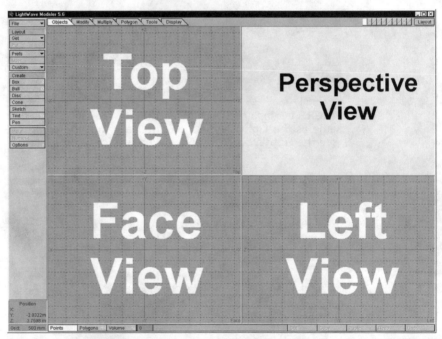

FIGURE 1-4 I have labeled in big letters each window in this LightWave 3D Modeler 5.6 interface shot. I like to refer to the Perspective View as simply the Preview Screen, since it is where you see the results of your work.

At the top of the Modeler, you have different tabs that access special menus to aid you in your work. Both Inspire 3D and Light-Wave 3D 5.6 have the following tabs: Objects, Modify, Multiply, Tools, Display. For LightWave 3D 5.6 users there is an additional tab labeled Polygon. Each tabbed section has its own set of options and buttons. Refer to your Reference Manual for a complete description.

Understanding Layers

One of the most important aspects of Inspire 3D and LightWave 3D are Layers. These are the buttons in the upper right-hand corner of the Modeler interface. With Inspire 3D there are 4 sets of Layer buttons to the right of the Layout button, as shown in Figure 1-5. With LightWave 3D 5.6, you get 10 sets of Layer buttons to the right of the Layout button, as shown in Figure 1-6.

FIGURE 1-5 Inspire 3D Layer buttons. There are four sets.

FIGURE 1-6 LightWave 3D 5.6 Layer buttons. There are 10 sets.

Notice that each Layer button has a top portion and a bottom portion. A diagonal line going through each Layer button separates the top from the bottom. Many people explain Layers in different terms. For the sake of simplicity, I like to look at Layers as separate pieces of onion skin paper with cool computer options optimized for the digital age. This includes the ability to cut, copy, paste, interact, and merge one Layer with another. Hands-on practice is the best way to understand this concept, so let's try a quick tutorial. This tutorial uses the Inspire 3D interface, but is done the exact same way in LightWave 3D 5.6.

STEP 1: Open Modeler.

STEP 2: Place your cursor over the File button. The black arrow on this button signifies that it is a pull-down menu so that when you click and hold your mouse cursor over this button, more options appear. With your cursor over the File button, click and hold down the left mouse button. A menu screen will pop up (Figure 1-7). Move your cursor over Load Object (Figure 1-8) and let go.

FIGURE 1-7

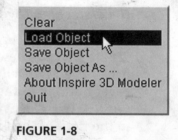

FIGURE 1-8

STEP 3: The Load Object window will open, as shown in Figure 1-9, which is displaying the Windows version. You must now navigate to your Inspire 3D folder then Objects folder if using Inspire 3D or NewTek folder directory, then Objects folder if using LightWave 3D 5.6. When you get there, it should be similar to Figure 1-10.

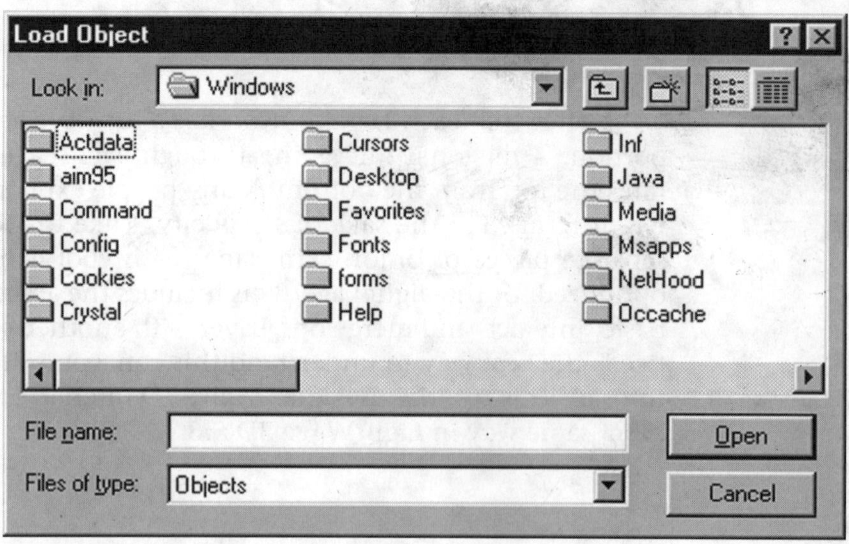

FIGURE 1-9

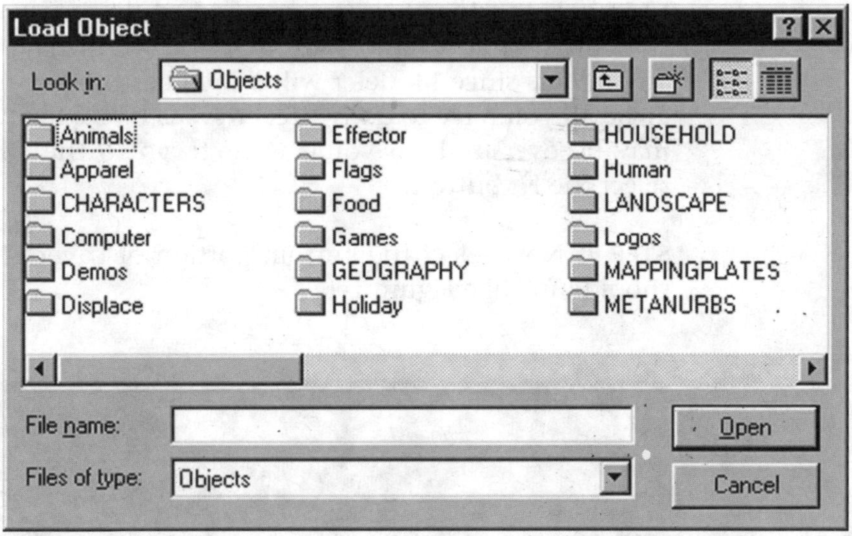

Load Object

Look in: 📁 Objects

📁 Animals
📁 Apparel
📁 CHARACTERS
📁 Computer
📁 Demos
📁 Displace

📁 Effector
📁 Flags
📁 Food
📁 Games
📁 GEOGRAPHY
📁 Holiday

📁 HOUSEHOLD
📁 Human
📁 LANDSCAPE
📁 Logos
📁 MAPPINGPLATES
📁 METANURBS

File name: [   ]   **Open**

Files of type: Objects   Cancel

FIGURE 1-10

STEP 4: Find the GEOGRAPHY folder and double-click on it. Now double-click on THEUNITEDSTATES folder. Click once on **CALIFORNIA.LWO**, then click Open.

STEP 5: The state of California will load into Modeler! You may, however, not be able to see it because of the size parameters. This is easily solved. Select your Display Tab in the upper part of the Modeler screen. A new set of buttons will appear to the left. From the menu on the left, select the Fit button. Now you'll see the full state of California!

STEP 6: Here's where we get to Layers. The state of California loaded into your first Layer and you'll notice that the first Layer button is highlighted in yellow. Click on the second Layer button to highlight it like in Figure 1-11.

FIGURE 1-11

STEP 7: Following the same methods as in Steps 2 to 4, load the state of Nevada. Chances are that you won't have to navigate to any folders since Modeler will remember the last folder you were at. So all you have to do is select **Nevada.LWO**, then Open. Again, it may be oversized, so you'll want to go to the Display Tab and select the Fit button.

STEP 8: Now select the bottom portion of Layer one. Your image should look like Figure 1-12.

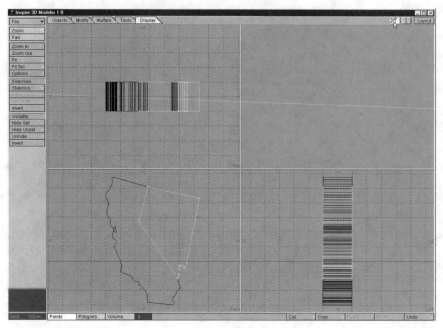

FIGURE 1-12

Notice that the state of Nevada is outlined in white and the state of California is outlined in black. When you selected the bottom portion of Layer one, it lets you see through to that Layer. Yet any changes you make on this screen will affect only the state of Nevada, outlined in white. The bottom portion of the Layers are for reference. For example, say that the two states weren't aligned properly. The way you have it set up now, you'd be able to easily align Nevada to California. There are, of course, many other uses of foreground and background Layers as we will learn in another tutorial. But first, notice that there is nothing showing in the Perspective View window because we have not yet set our Display options. We'll do that next.

Setting the Display

Here we'll learn how to set the Display options so that you can see the results of your work in the Perspective View window.

STEP 1: Select the Display Tab.

STEP 2: From the menu to the left, select the Options button.

STEP 3: The Display Options panel as shown in Figure 1-13 will open.

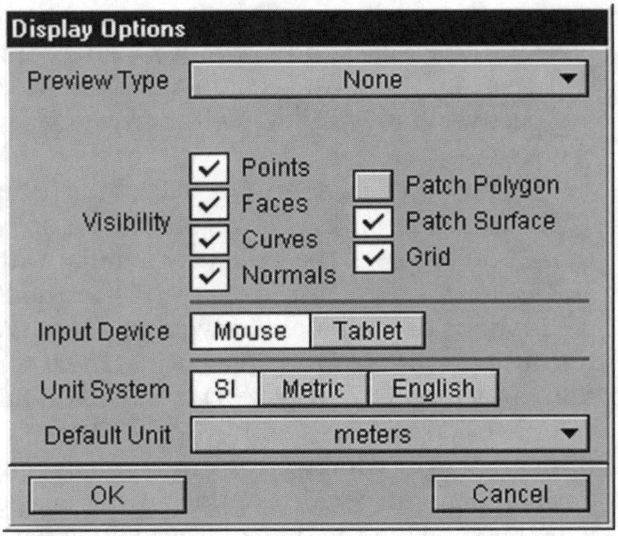

FIGURE 1-13

STEP 4: Next to Preview Type is a scroll-down button. Drag your cursor over this button and hold down the left mouse button. A menu similar to that on Figure 1-14 will open. The reason I say "similar" is because different options will appear on different platforms.

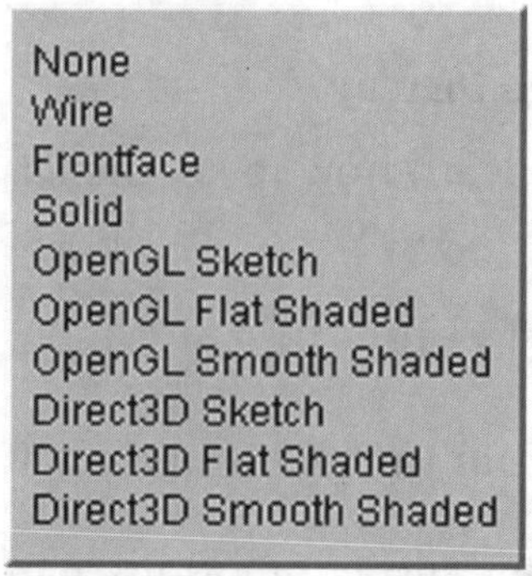

None
Wire
Frontface
Solid
OpenGL Sketch
OpenGL Flat Shaded
OpenGL Smooth Shaded
Direct3D Sketch
Direct3D Flat Shaded
Direct3D Smooth Shaded

FIGURE 1-14

STEP 5: If you have an OpenGL card and lots of RAM, your preference in the Preview Type will be OpenGL Smooth Shaded, which will give you the most accurate representation of your object. The Perspective View window will always display what is shown on the active Layer.

If you don't have an OpenGL card, try using the Solid view. There are some things you can see and do on certain views that you cannot on others, so become very familiar with all views. If you are an Inspire 3D user, turn to page 19.4 in the Reference Manual for descriptions of each menu. If you are a LightWave 3D 5.5/5.6 user, turn to page 24.5 in the Reference Manual for a complete description of each option. Inspire 3D users should furthermore pop in the tutorial CD that comes with Inspire 3D and run the Modeler walkthrough script, which gives great visuals. Figure 1-15 shows the OpenGL Smooth Shaded option in the Perspective View window, which is showing the state of Nevada that we loaded in the preceding tutorial.

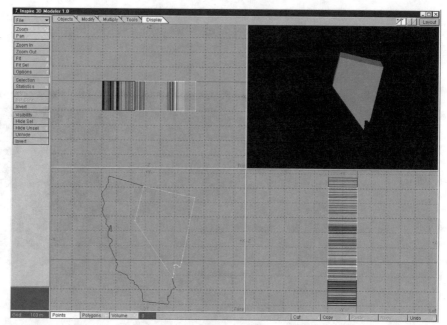

FIGURE 1-15

Cut and Paste

You should still have California and Nevada loaded into Modeler with your screen looking like Figure 1-12 if you don't have a Preview Type selected, or like Figure 1-15 if you do. In this example we are going to learn how to take something from one Layer and place it into another so that it becomes one object. Right now the states of California and Nevada are two separate objects. California is in the first Layer and Nevada is in the second Layer. Our goal is to remove Nevada from the second Layer and paste it into the first Layer. Let's see how long this will take.

STEP 1: On the bottom bar in Modeler you will find 5 buttons, the first 3 being Cut, Copy, and Paste. Select the Cut button. The state of Nevada will disappear! This is only temporary.

STEP 2: Go up to the Layer buttons and select the top portion of Layer one. Your screen should look like Figure 1-16.

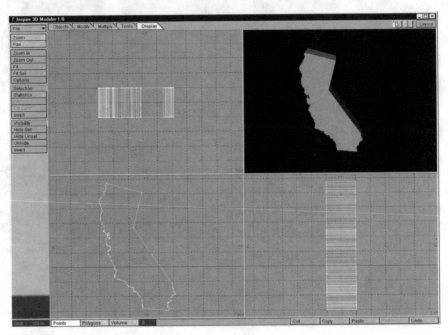

FIGURE 1-16

STEP 3: Now select the Paste button (on the bottom menu bar). The state of Nevada is now connected to California! You're done! The end result should look like Figure 1-17.

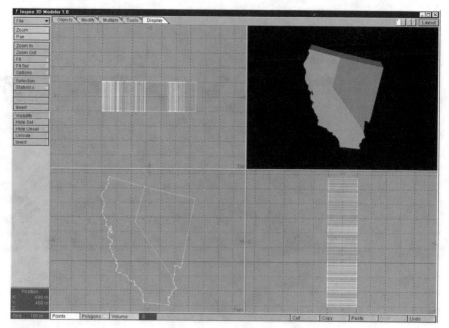

FIGURE 1-17

Erasing Mistakes

One of the 5 buttons at the bottom of the screen (the last one) is called Undo. Both Inspire 3D and LightWave 3D have Undo options. Inspire 3D will allow you to undo up to 8 levels. Light-Wave 3D 5.6 allows up to 15. The Undo levels heavily depend on memory, which is another (of dozens) of reasons that you should have a lot of RAM installed in your computer. Because the Undo levels are user definable (to preserve memory, you can tell the program to allow less than the maximum), you will need to set the number. Here's how.

STEP 1: Select the Object Tab at the top of the Modeler screen.

STEP 2: From the menu on the left, click on the Options button.

STEP 3: A Data Options panel will open (Figure 1-18 for Inspire 3D users and Figure 1-19 for LightWave 3D 5.6 users).

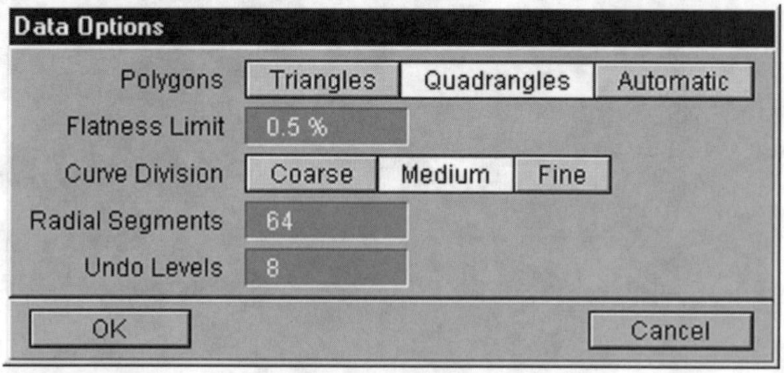

FIGURE 1-18 Inspire 3D Data Options panel.

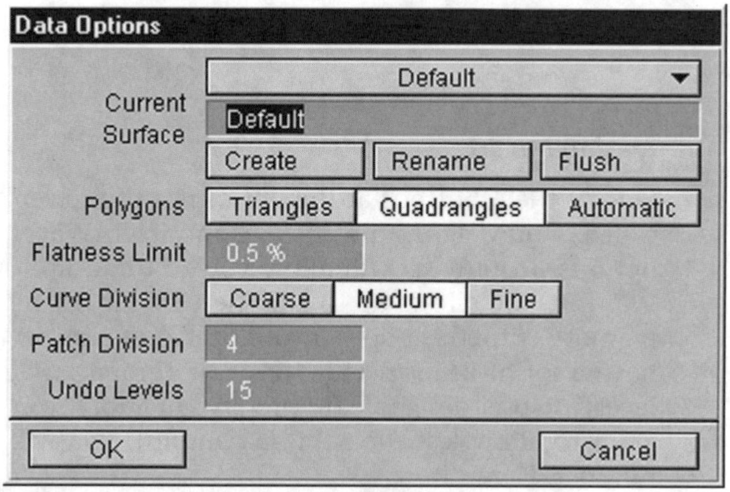

FIGURE 1-19 LightWave 3D 5.6 Data Options panel.

STEP 4: You can enter the number of Undo levels you want in the box next to Undo Levels.

STEP 5: Click OK. You're done! Notice that next to the Undo button is a Redo button. The Redo button becomes active only after you have applied the Undo button to something so that you can undo the Undo!

Clearing a Project

In a second, we're going to step into a whole new direction—using text in Modeler. First, however, we must clear the last project we were working on. To do this, follow these 2 simple steps.

STEP 1: The first button in the upper left-hand corner of Modeler, which remains there no matter what tab area you are in, is the File button. Hold down the left mouse button over the File button to access the File menu options. Select Clear.

STEP 2: A Warning panel will come up saying that all material will be lost if you proceed. Since we have no reason to save California and Nevada, select OK.

Loading Text in Modeler

Before you can work with text in Modeler, you must first load fonts. The following 2 steps will help you achieve this.

STEP 1: If you are using Inspire 3D, from the main Modeler screen, select the Fonts button. The Edit Fonts List panel will open (Figure 1-20). Proceed to the next step. If you are using LightWave 3D 5.6, click on the Text button. Now click on the Numeric button. A Make Text string panel will open (Figure 1-21). Proceed to the next step.

FIGURE 1-20 The Inspire 3D Edit Font List panel where you will select fonts you want to load and use in Modeler.

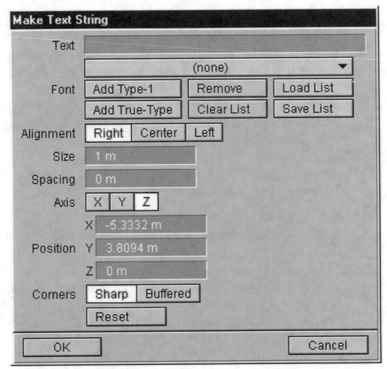

FIGURE 1-21 The LightWave 3D 5.6 Make Text String panel where you will select fonts you want to load and use in Modeler.

STEP 2: Select the Add True-Type button. This will bring up a Fonts panel where you can select the fonts you want to use in Modeler. For now simply select Arial and click OK. If you don't have Arial, then select another font. The Arial font is now installed for you to use in Modeler.

You can use the above 2 steps to load as many fonts as you want. In this case, we'll stick with Arial.

Using Text and Surfaces in Modeler

Now that we've cleared the screen and have loaded a font, we are ready to experiment with a few quick text effects. Modeler makes working with text fun and easy as you will soon see.

STEP 1: Make sure the Objects tab is selected near the top of the screen. From the buttons on the left, select the Text button.

STEP 2: Move your cursor into the Face screen, near the center, and click down once. You'll see a red mark appear.

STEP 3: Type in the word "Water" without the quotes. One of 3 things will happen:

1. You will see the word "Water" appear perfectly on the screen.

2. You will not see anything except a red cross on the screen.

3. You will see the word "Water," but it will be upside down.

Naturally you prefer to see the word "Water" appear perfectly on the screen, but the last 2 "problems" are easily rectified. Modeler makes adjusting the size and position of text very easy. Therefore, if you have the second problem, move your cursor over the cross hairs, like in Figure 1-22a, and hold down the left mouse button while dragging the cross upward (Figures 1-22b and 1-22c). You'll see the word "Water" appear!

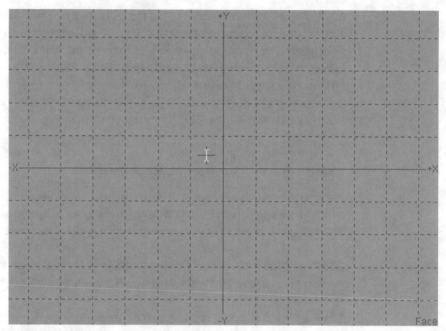

FIGURE 1-22A

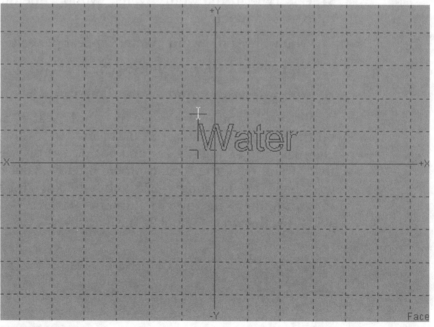

FIGURE 1-22B

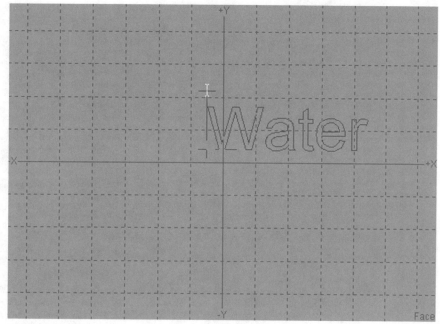

FIGURE 1-22C

STEP 4: Move your cursor over the red cross-hairs in the bottom left of the text like in Figure 1-23. If you hold down the mouse button here, you can drag the entire word anywhere on the screen! Position and size the word so that appears exactly the same as Figure 1-24.

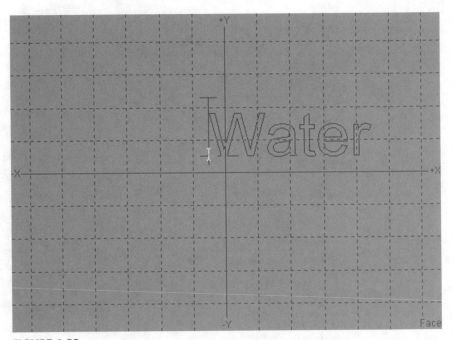

FIGURE 1-23

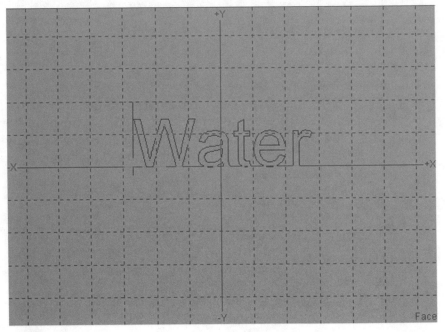

FIGURE 1-24

STEP 5: From the buttons on the left, select the Make button. Your screen will now look like Figure 1-25.

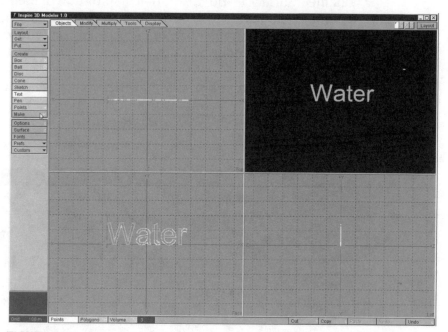

FIGURE 1-25

Congratulations, you have made your first text! From here the options are endless. You can extrude the text to give it a 3D look, Bevel it, and so on. Only your imagination and effort are the limits. Let's continue on and experiment with creating a reflection of this text. First, we'll want to create a Surface for the current text we have.

Importance of Naming Surfaces: Naming surfaces, to various aspects of your objects in Modeler, is of the utmost importance. A surface is a predetermined area of your object that you want to apply a texture or color to. Take, for example, your eye. If you were creating an eye, you'd want three different surfaces. One would be the white part of the eye, which is called the sclera. The next would be the iris and finally the pupil. Each one of these you'd want to give a different Surface name in Modeler so that you could apply separate textures to each part in Layout.

STEP 6: From the buttons on the left, select the Surface button. The Change Surface panel will open. In this panel, you'll see the name "Surface" and next to it a pull-down menu to choose a name and a text box to enter your own surface name. Since this is the first surface we are naming for this object, you won't have any other names in your pull-down menu. So we'll create one.

STEP 7: In the text box that has the word Default in it, erase that word and type in "Front" (without the quotes). Your panel should look like Figure 1-26, which was taken from Inspire 3D.

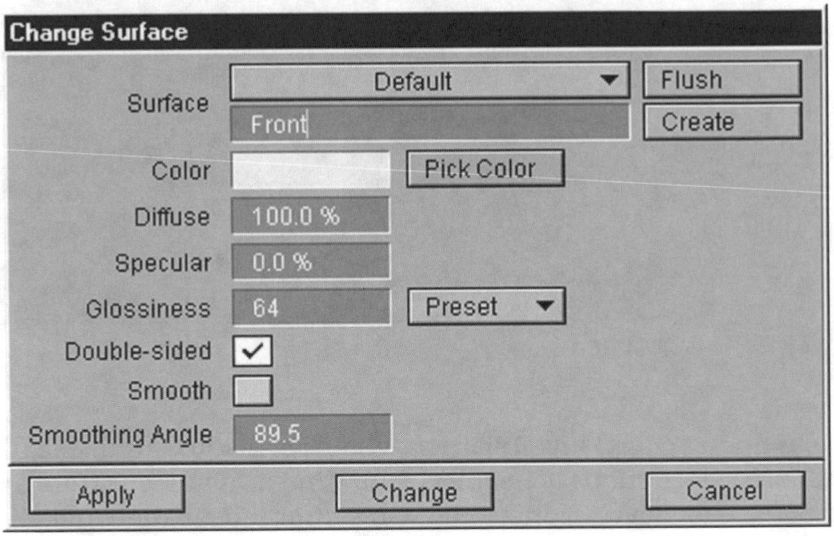

FIGURE 1-26

STEP 8: Click the Apply button at the bottom of the Change Surface panel. What you have done is given this object its own surface name called "Front." In Layout, when you load this object, it will have the surface name of "Front" that you can adjust, as you'll discover in one of our Layout tutorials. Now let's save this object.

Saving Objects

STEP 1: In the top left-hand corner of the Modeler screen is the File button. Hold your mouse button down over this button to bring up the file menu. Select Save Object As. . . . The Save Object As panel will open.

STEP 2: Navigate to the Objects directory and type in the name "Water1" (without the quotes), as shown in Figure 1-27.

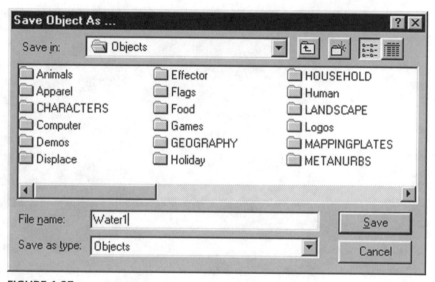

FIGURE 1-27

STEP 3: Click the Save button to save the object. Now let's have some more fun with it.

Using the Mirror Tool and Volume Button

Continuing with our tutorial, we are going to create another "Water" word, but this time we are going to turn it upside down, give it a different Surface name, and create a reflection. Here we go.

STEP 1: You should still have the word "Water" on your screen. From the top tabs, select the Multiply Tab. A new list of buttons will appear to the left.

STEP 2: Select the Mirror button. Move your cursor into the Face window. Hold down the left mouse button and a red line will appear. Keep holding the button and drag the red line under the word "Water," leaving a little space, so that it looks like Figure 1-28.

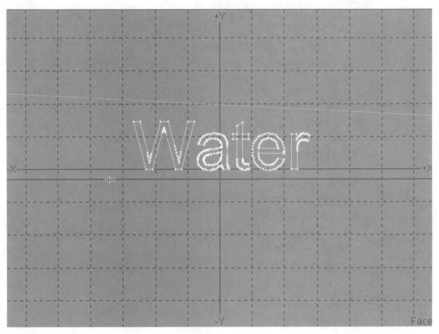

FIGURE 1-28

STEP 3: Let go of the mouse button. A mirrored version of the word "Water" will appear! Your screen should now look like Figure 1-29.

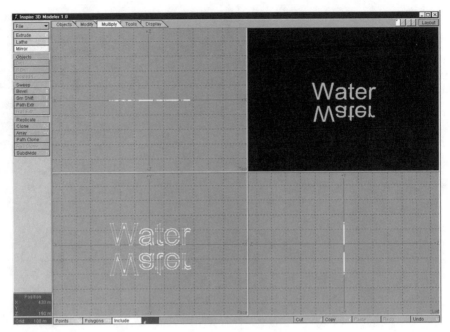

FIGURE 1-29

Now our goal is to give this upside-down "Water" a different surface name from the original one. To do this we will use the Volume button. At the bottom, near the left, of your screen are three buttons: Points, Polygons, and Volume.

Understanding Points and Polygons: Points and Polygons are the foundation building blocks for creating 3D objects. Points are much like the dots in dot-to-dot coloring books we used to do as children. A Polygon is the shape that the Points make after all the dots are connected. Once a Polygon is made, we can texture (color) it.

STEP 4: Click the Volume button once. You will see it change to the word "Exclude." Click it one more time and you will see it change to "Include." Your screen should now look like Figure 1-30.

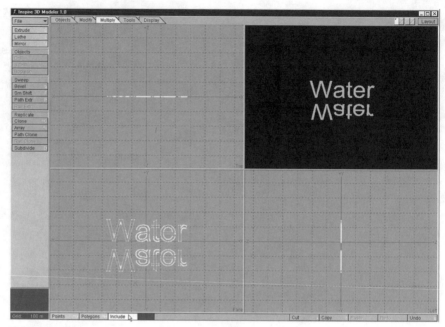

FIGURE 1-30

Understanding Include and Exclude: When you draw a box (using the Volume button) around a certain area of an object, "Include" (which draws a solid red line) will select both what is inside the red box and any points and polygons immediately attached along the outside border of the red box. When you draw a box using "Exclude" (which draws a dotted red line), it will select only those points and polygons on the inside of the red box. These commands are especially helpful when you need to make important changes or additions while working with numerous objects or surfaces in one Layer.

STEP 5: Move your cursor to the Face window and while holding down the left mouse button, draw a box around the upside-down "Water" object. Your Face View should look like Figure 1-31.What we have done is to tell Modeler to make changes only to the "Water" word that is upside down. If our 2 words had been touching as one object, we would have had to use the Exclude technique (as we do in the area on creating 3D Text later on) to get the desired result since Include affects Polygons that straddle the box's border.

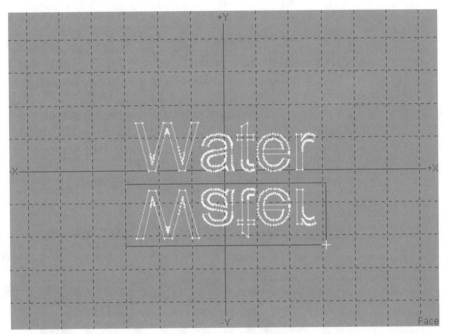

FIGURE 1-31

STEP 6: From the top tabs, select the Objects Tab. Now select the Surface button from the buttons on the left. The Change Surface panel will open. In the text box, type in the word "Reflection" (without the quotes). Click Apply.

Changing Surface Colors: If your Perspective View window is set to show one of the Flat Shaded or Smooth Shaded options, then you can see your different surfaces in color! Simply open the Change Surface tab, select the surface that you want to apply a color to, and then click on Pick Color. Once you select a color and click OK then Apply, that surfaced portion of your object will be displayed in the color you selected!

STEP 7: All that's left to do is saving the object! Go to the File menu and select Save Object As. . . . Navigate to your Objects directory (it may already be there) and type in the name Water2. Click Save.

A Sneak Peak at Layout Surfacing

To complete the project we've been working on, we're going to take a quick sneak peak at LightWave's Layout. If you have plenty of RAM, then you can load Layout, with Modeler remaining open, simply by selecting the button on the top right of Modeler, called Layout. Otherwise, you'll have to close down Modeler and load Layout separately. Go ahead and load Layout. If you are using Inspire 3D, it should look like Figure 1-32. If you are using Light-Wave 3D 5.6, it should look like Figure 1-33.

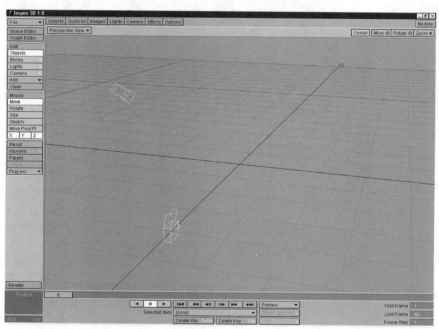

FIGURE 1-32 Inspire 3D Layout Interface.

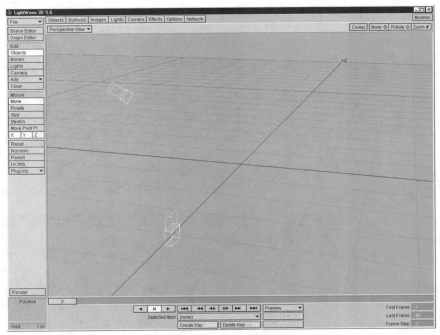

FIGURE 1-33 LightWave 3D 5.6 Layout Interface.

Loading Layout: Inspire 3D and LightWave 3D are made up of two programs, Modeler and Layout. However, the buttons can be a little deceiving. While the icon to open Modeler is appropriately called Inspire Modeler or LightWave Modeler, the button to open Layout is simply called Inspire or LightWave. So when you want to load Layout, load Inspire or LightWave depending on which program you are using. If you already have a program open, you can quickly go to the other by selecting the button in the top right-hand corner (labeled Layout if you're in Modeler or labeled Modeler if you're in Layout).

On the top menu of Layout there will be 7 buttons across the top of Inspire 3D (Objects, Surfaces, Images, Lights, Camera, Effects, and Options). LightWave 3D 5.6 Layout has the same top menu buttons as Inspire 3D, plus one more called Network. Our interest for now is only in the Objects and Surfaces buttons.

STEP 1: Select the Objects button. The Objects Panel will open. The Objects Panel of Inspire 3D and LightWave 3D are virtually identical, except that the LightWave Objects Panel allows you to load 4 Displacement Map plugins versus the 2 that Inspire 3D allows.

STEP 2: Click the Load Object button. The Load Object File requester will open. Navigate to your Objects directory and find the object we saved earlier called **Water2.LWO**. When you've found it, select it and then click Open. Click the Close Panel button to exit the Objects Panel. You will see your object in the main Layout screen like in Figure 1-34 (Inspire 3D view).

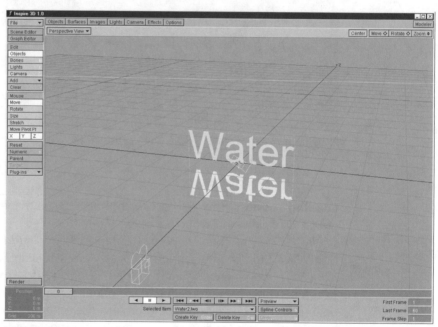

FIGURE 1-34

STEP 3: Hit F9 on your keyboard to render the object to see what it looks like now! After you've viewed the rendered version, click the "Continue" or "Done" button to exit. Our goal is to now give the top and bottom "Water" names separate surfaces.

STEP 4: Click on the Surfaces button. The Surfaces Panel will open.

STEP 5: Next to Current Surface you'll see a pull-down menu that most likely has the word "Front" in it. Press down your left mouse button over this to also see the other surface you created, "Reflection." As shown in the Inspire 3D Layout, the menu should look like Figure 1-35.

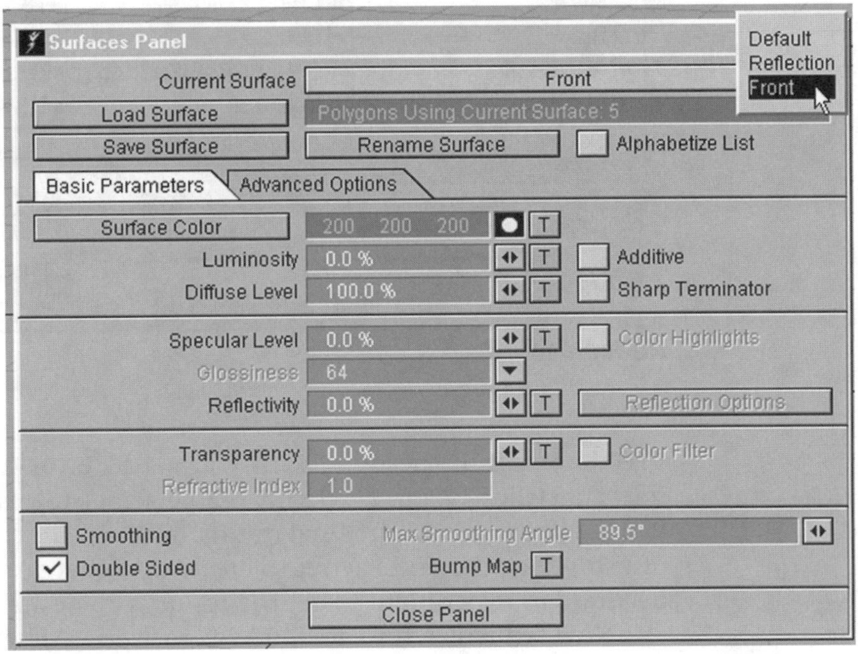

FIGURE 1-35

STEP 6: Make sure that Front is selected, then let go of the mouse button. Select the Load Surface button. Double-click on the folder called Flat to open it. Now select **Flatblue.srf** and click Open. Now click the Close Panel button to exit the Surfaces Panel and you'll notice the top "Water" word is now a flat blue.

STEP 7: Open the Surfaces Panel again and change the Current Surface setting to Reflection. Now select Load Surface and navigate to the main Surfaces folder as shown in Figure 1-36 (Windows 95).

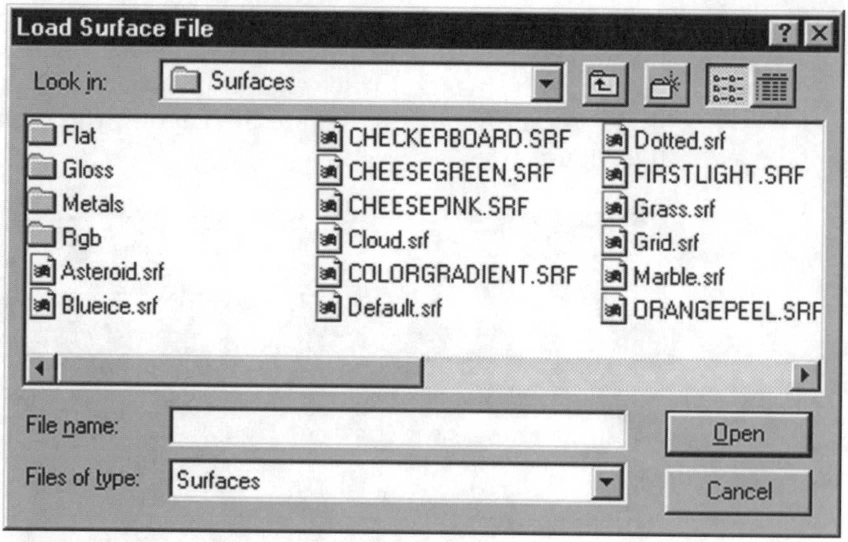

FIGURE 1-36

STEP 8: Scroll to the right until you get to **UNDERWATER.SRF** and select it. Click Open. Now click Close Panel to exit the Surfaces Panel. Hit F9 to view the final results. You've learned the essentials of using Modeler and Layout to create and change Surfaces. Don't be afraid to experiment to get the results you desire.

Now we will return to Modeler to learn a few more goodies before we make a return trip here to Layout to teach you a few more beginner techniques. If you made the smart decision to install a high amount of RAM into your computer, you can quickly jump to Modeler by selecting the Modeler button in the upper right-hand corner of the Layout screen.

Quick 3D Text

If you have something already in your Modeler screen, clear the screen (File then Clear), as you learned earlier. Also make sure that the Objects Tab is highlighted. Now we will use a quick method to make 3D text and I'll also show you a quick way to separate the front part from the side so that you can assign them different surfaces.

STEP 1: Both Inspire 3D and LightWave 3D have a scroll-down menu button called Custom. If you select this button, a number of options come up. If you are using Inspire 3D, these options all start with IN_. If you are using LightWave 3D, the options all start with LW_. Figure 1-37 shows what appears when the Inspire 3D Custom button is selected. Figure 1-38 shows what appears when the LightWave 3D 5.6 Custom button is selected. Our interest is in the option called TextCompose. When you select it, a Compose Text Panel like that of Figure 1-39 opens.

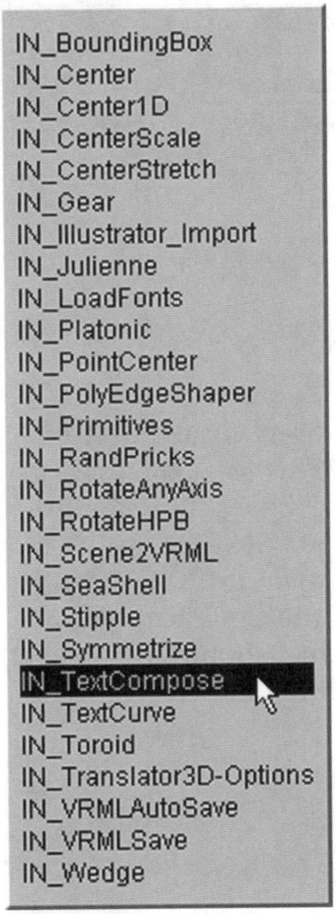

```
LScript
LScript-RT
LScriptCompiler-MD
LW_AllBGLayers
LW_BoundingBox
LW_Cage
LW_Calculate
LW_Center
LW_Center1D
LW_CenterScale
LW_CenterStretch
LW_CutCurves
LW_Envelopes
LW_Gear
LW_Illustrator_Import
LW_Julienne
LW_LightSwarm
LW_LoadFonts
LW_MathMotion
LW_NextEmptyLayer
LW_ParametricObj
LW_PathToMotion
LW_Platonic
LW_Plot1D
LW_Plot2D
LW_PointCenter
LW_PolyEdgeShaper
LW_Primitives
LW_Quadric
LW_RandPricks
LW_RotateAnyAxis
LW_RotateHPB
LW_Scene2VRML
LW_SeaShell
LW_Stipple
LW_Symmetrize
LW_TextCompose
LW_TextCurve
LW_Throw
LW_Toroid
LW_Translator3D-Options
LW_VRMLAutoSave
LW_VRMLSave
LW_Wedge
```

```
IN_BoundingBox
IN_Center
IN_Center1D
IN_CenterScale
IN_CenterStretch
IN_Gear
IN_Illustrator_Import
IN_Julienne
IN_LoadFonts
IN_Platonic
IN_PointCenter
IN_PolyEdgeShaper
IN_Primitives
IN_RandPricks
IN_RotateAnyAxis
IN_RotateHPB
IN_Scene2VRML
IN_SeaShell
IN_Stipple
IN_Symmetrize
IN_TextCompose
IN_TextCurve
IN_Toroid
IN_Translator3D-Options
IN_VRMLAutoSave
IN_VRMLSave
IN_Wedge
```

FIGURE 1-37

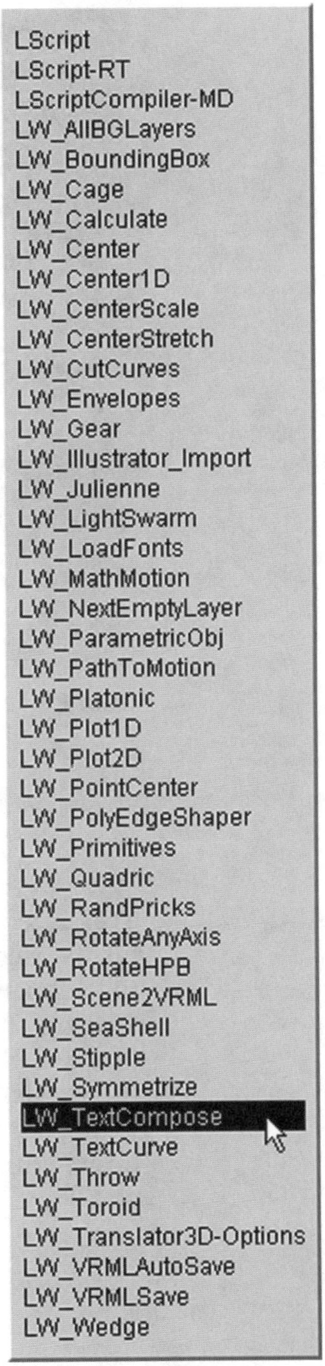

FIGURE 1-38

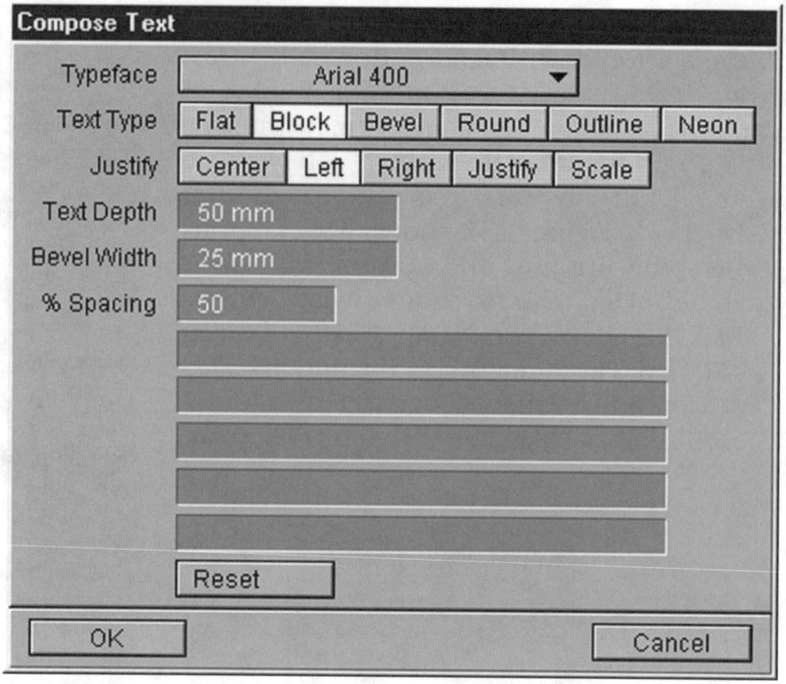

Compose Text

Typeface	Arial 400 ▼

| Text Type | Flat | Block | Bevel | Round | Outline | Neon |

| Justify | Center | Left | Right | Justify | Scale |

Text Depth	50 mm
Bevel Width	25 mm
% Spacing	50

Reset

OK   Cancel

FIGURE 1-39

STEP 2: For Typeface select Arial. For Text Type, select Bevel. For Justify, select Center. Next to Text Depth, type in 500 mm and hit the Tab key on your keyboard. Bevel Width should read 25 and % Spacing should read 50. Next are 5 lines where you can type in text. On the first line type in "Cool"; on the second line type in the words "3D Effect" (both without quotes). When you are done, your Compose Text Panel should look like Figure 1-40. Remember to experiment with different settings to see what kind of results you'll get.

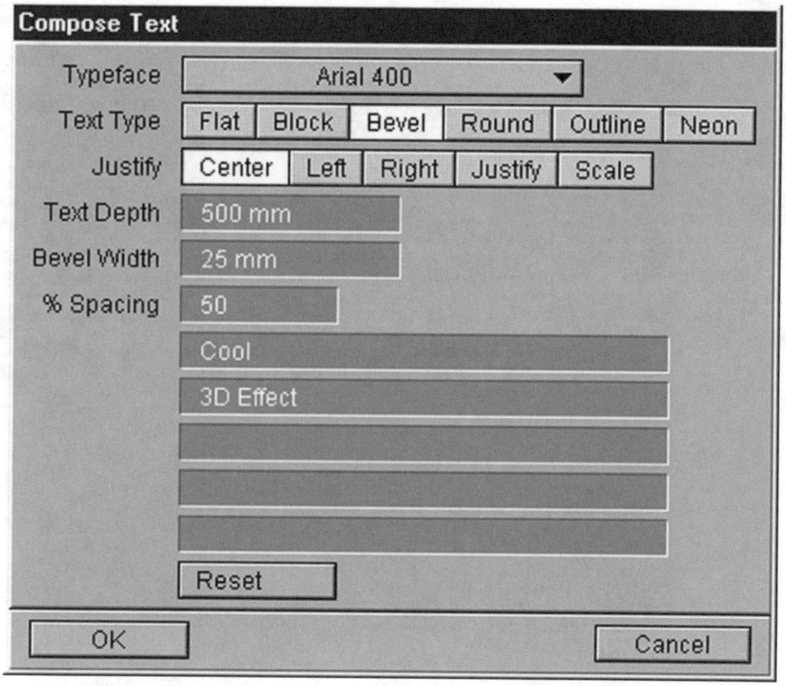

Compose Text

Typeface	Arial 400 ▼

Text Type: Flat | Block | Bevel | Round | Outline | Neon

Justify: Center | Left | Right | Justify | Scale

Text Depth: 500 mm

Bevel Width: 25 mm

% Spacing: 50

Cool

3D Effect

Reset

OK | Cancel

FIGURE 1-40

STEP 3: Click the OK button. Initially you may see only a little dot on your screen. You must get the text to fit the screen by changing the Display settings.

STEP 4: Click the Display Tab. A new set of buttons will appear to the left. Select the Fit button. Your text will appear in all the windows and should look similar to Figure 1-41.

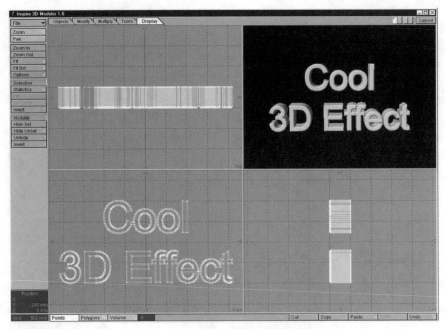

FIGURE 1-41

STEP 5: Select the Objects Tab to bring up the Object button selections. Now select the Surface button. Delete the word "Default" and type in "Side" (without the quotes). Pick a color (like blue) if you wish and then click Apply.

Now our goal is to separate the front of the text from the side so that you can make it a different color. We will use the Exclude command (Volume button) to accomplish that task.

STEP 6: From the bottom bar, select the Volume button once so that it changes to Exclude.

STEP 7: Go to the Top View and draw a box around the front solid white portions of the text. Your screen should look like Figure 1-42.

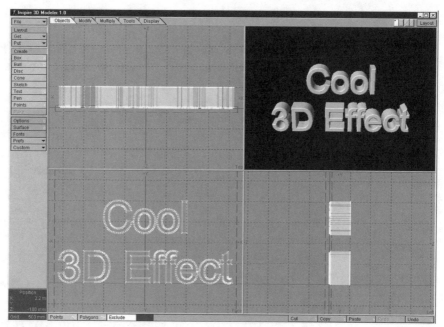

FIGURE 1-42

STEP 8: Select the Surface button again. The Change Surface panel will open. In the Surface text box, type in "Front" (without the quotes). Pick another color to represent the front if desired. Hit the Apply button. You now have 3D text with separate face and side surfaces.

Now follow the same techniques we used to apply surfaces in Layout with the Water object to this object. Be sure to save it first, however, before exiting Modeler. When you're done experimenting, return to Modeler and reload the 3D text example for our next lesson.

The Ultra-Cool Boolean Operation

Now it's time to introduce you to my personal favorite command in all of Modeler, *Boolean*. In short, Boolean will take something in a background Layer and add or subtract it to something in the foreground Layer. Since hands-on is the best example, let's get right to it!

Make sure the 3D text you created is loaded. Hopefully you have OpenGL or Direct3D as seeing this example in color will make a lot of difference.

STEP 1: To start, we need to make sure that the Surface colors for the front and side of the 3D text are the same. So with the 3D Text open, make sure the Objects Tab is selected, then press the Surface button. In the drop-down menu next to Surface select Front. Now click the Pick Color button and select a yellow color. Click OK.

STEP 2: While still in the Surface panel, access the drop-down menu next to Surface and select Side. Now click the Pick Color button and select the same yellow color. Click OK. Now click Apply. Your entire 3D text should be yellow.

STEP 3: Go to your second Layer, then select the bottom portion of the first Layer so that you can see the 3D Text object. Your screen should look like Figure 1-43.

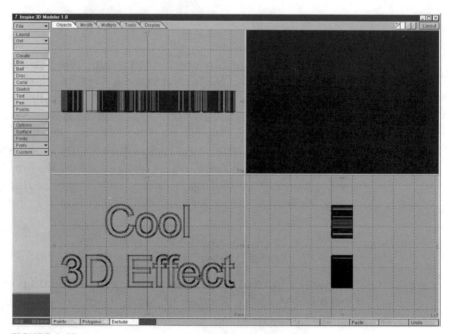

FIGURE 1-43

STEP 4: Make sure the Objects Tab at the top is selected, then press the Box button. Your cursor will turn into a tiny white cube. Move the cursor to the Face View and draw a box around your entire object. It should look like Figure 1-44.

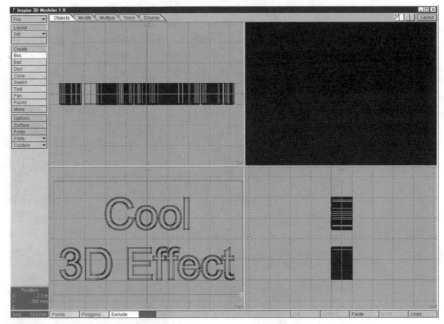

FIGURE 1-44

STEP 5: Now move your cursor to the Left View window. Click just to the right of the red line, but before reaching the end text like in Figure 1-45. Now, remaining in the Left View, do the exact same thing on the other side, like in Figure 1-46.

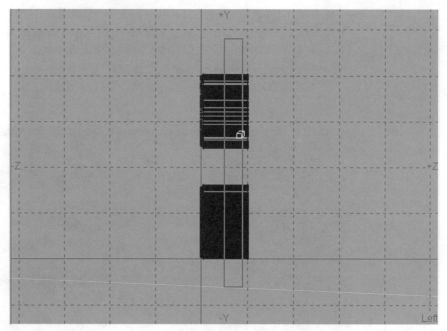

FIGURE 1-45

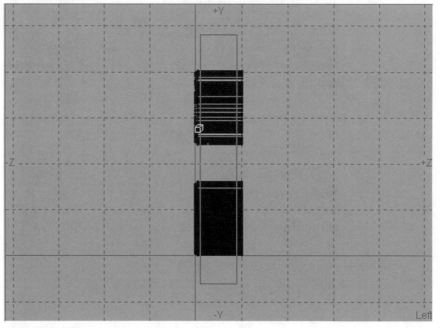

FIGURE 1-46

STEP 6: From the buttons on the left-hand side, click the Make button. A box will be made. The box should be yellow, but if it isn't, then select Surface and give it a name, then pick the color yellow for it. Your screen should now look like Figure 1-47.

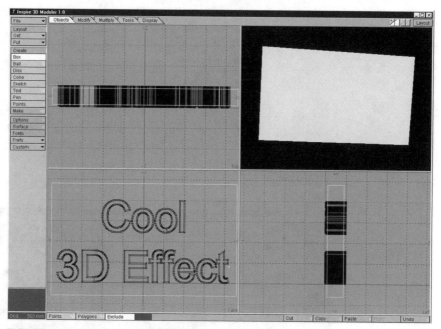

FIGURE 1-47

STEP 7: Save this object as BooleanTest.

STEP 8: Here's where the fun begins! From the top tabs, select the Multiply Tab. A new set of buttons will appear on the left, one named Boolean. Select the Boolean button. A Boolean CSG panel will open like in Figure 1-48.

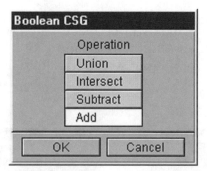

FIGURE 1-48

STEP 9: Select the Subtract button inside this Boolean CSG panel. It will highlight. Now click the OK button and wait a few seconds (or minutes). When it is done the box will have a cutout of your text on it like in Figure 1-49.

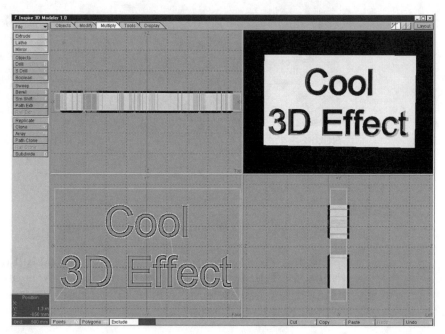

FIGURE 1-49

Tip: Changing Cutout Color. The surface color you have for your text object will determine what color the cutout in the box is. So if our text had been all blue then wherever the letters were cut out you'd see the color blue around the edges.

STEP 10: Click the Undo button. The Boolean we just created will disappear. Now select the Boolean button again. This time click Add followed by OK. When it is done, the text will be embossed on the box like in Figure 1-50! Your possibilities with Boolean are endless, so do a lot of experimenting (not just with text either) for some very cool results.

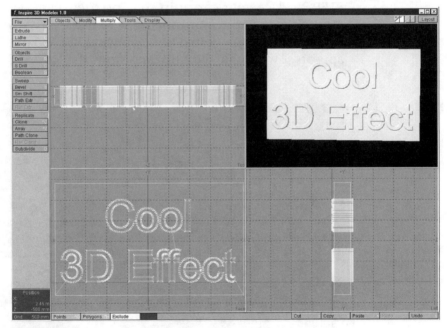

FIGURE 1-50

The 6-Sided Cube

You've learned quite a bit so far about many of the basic operations of Modeler and how those operations work. One of the things we learned was how to apply two surfaces to an object that you can texture separately in Layout. Now we're going to go a step further and create a 6-side cube with each side having its own surface!

STEP 1: From the File scroll-down menu, select Clear. If the Object Tab is not selected, select it now.

STEP 2: Click on the Box button. Your cursor will turn into a tiny white cube.

STEP 3: Place your cursor in the Top View window and drag your mouse down and toward the right to make a box the same size as Figure 1-51. When you're done drawing it, a red outline of the box appears. Two single red lines appear in the Face and Left Views.

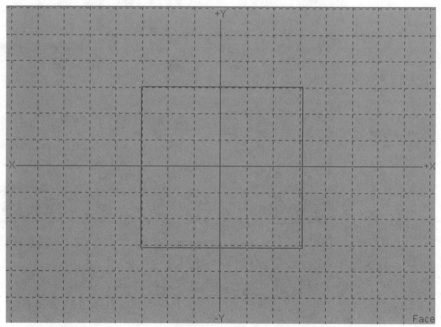

FIGURE 1-51

STEP 4: Move over to the Left View. Move the cursor about 3 squares to the left of the middle red line and click once. The box will encompass that area like Figure 1-52.

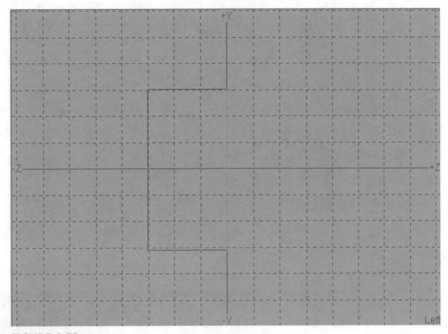

FIGURE 1-52

STEP 5: Now move the cursor about 3 squares to the right of the middle red line and click once. The box in the Left View will now look like Figure 1-53. The box will now look the same in all 3 views. Click the Make button (or hit the Return key) to make the box. Your whole screen should now look like Figure 1-54. Congratulations, you've made a 6-sided cube! Now we have to give it 6 separate surfaces.

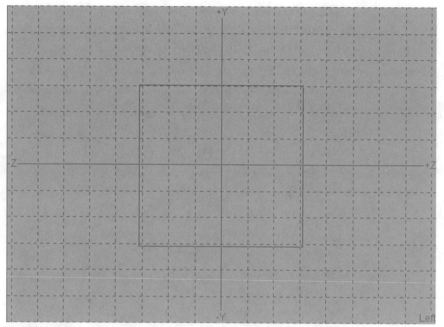

FIGURE 1-53

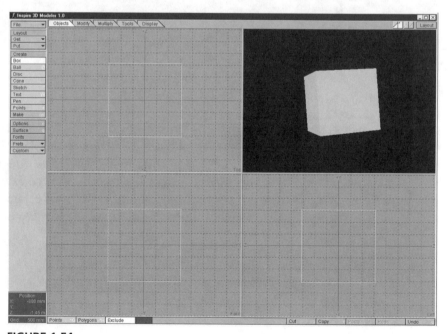

FIGURE 1-54

STEP 6: At the bottom of the screen, select the Polygon button. The box lines will turn white.

Perspective View Tip: The Perspective View isn't just for watching. You can place your mouse button into that window, click down, and rotate the object in all directions to see it from all sides!

STEP 7: Move your cursor to the Left View window. Position your cursor just before the top part of the box and hold down the **right** mouse button (note that we are using the right, not left, mouse button). Hold it down and draw a circle around the top of the box exactly like Figure 1-55. When you make a circle, let go and the top line will turn yellow (highlight).

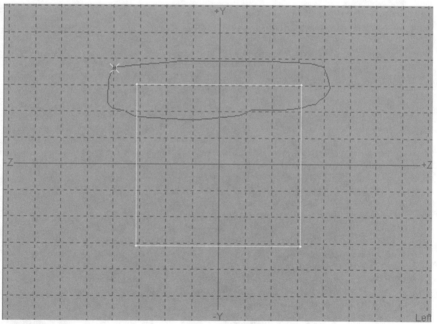

FIGURE 1-55

STEP 8: Click on the Surface button. Type in "Side1" (without the quotes). Now select Pick Color and pick a yellow color. Click OK then Apply. Now move your cursor to the Perspective View (preview window) and move the cube around until you see the yellow side. You've created your first of 6 sides!

STEP 9: Return to the Left View and by using the right mouse button again, draw a circle in the exact same area as before. This time the highlight will disappear. You have deselected it.

STEP 10: Now draw a circle (right mouse button) around the bottom line in the Left View like in Figure 1-56. Let go and the bottom line will highlight. Click the Surface button and type in Side2. Now click Pick Color and select Red. Click OK followed by Apply. Now you have a red side that appears opposite of the yellow side.

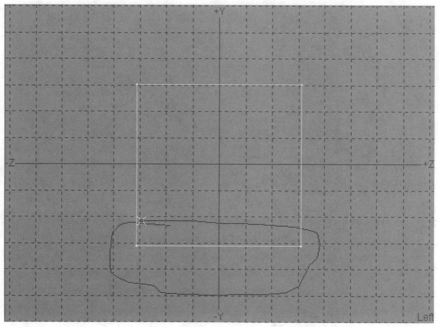

FIGURE 1-56

STEP 11: We'll remain in the Left View. Using the right mouse button, draw another circle around the bottom line to deselect it.

STEP 12: Now draw a line around the left side of the box in the Left View (using the right mouse button), like in Figure 1-57. Let go and the left line will highlight. Click the Surface button and type in Side3. Now click Pick Color and select Green. Click OK followed by Apply. You are halfway done!

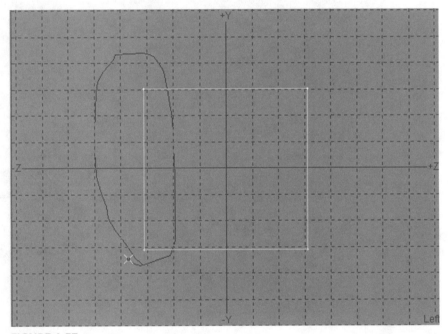

FIGURE 1-57

STEP 13: We are still working in the Left View. Using the right mouse button again, draw another circle around the left line to deselect it.

STEP 14: Now, still in the Left View, draw a line around the right side of the box using the right mouse button like in Figure 1-58. Let go and the right line will highlight. Click the Surface button and type in Side4. Now click Pick Color and select Pink. Click OK followed by Apply. We've now done 4 surfaces!

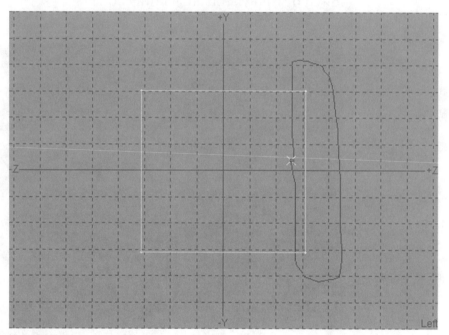

FIGURE 1-58

STEP 15: Return to the Left View and, using the right mouse button, draw another circle around the right line to deselect it.

STEP 16: Now we are going to the Top View for the final 2 sides. From the Top View, use the right mouse button to draw a circle around the left side of the box like in Figure 1-59. Let go and the left line in the Top View will highlight. Click the Surface button and type in Side5. Now click Pick Color and select a Dark Blue. Click OK followed by Apply. One more to go!

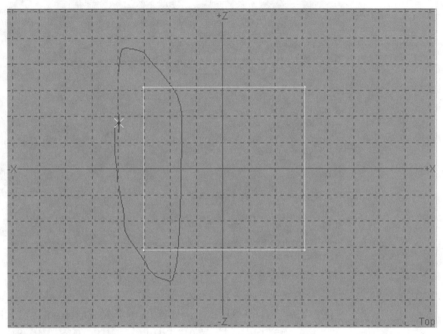

FIGURE 1-59

STEP 17: Return to the Top View and, using the right mouse button, draw another circle around the left line to deselect it.

STEP 18: From the Top View, use the right mouse button to draw a circle around the right side of the box like in Figure 1-60. Let go and the right line in the Top View will highlight. Click the Surface button and type in Side6. Now click Pick Color and select a Light Blue (or Aqua). Click OK followed by Apply.

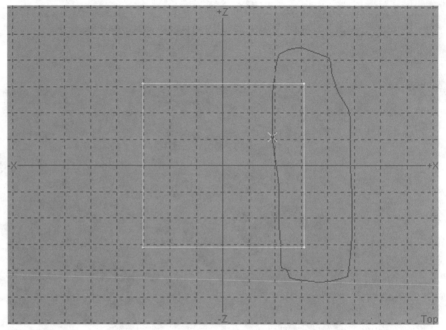

FIGURE 1-60

STEP 19: From the scroll-down File button, select Save Object As. . . . Navigate to your Objects directory and give it the name Cube. Click Save.

You're done! You have successfully created a 6-sided box with 6 different surfaces. You could even paste a different image on each surface in Layout and animate it. Again, the possibilities are endless.

Modeling a Game Piece

Now we'll turn our attention to the Pen button and how to use Points/Polygons, Lathe, and Layers to create a simple game piece. You will also begin learning about the Generic Information Display (bottom left-hand corner of Modeler), which I like to simply refer to as the Position Box (a much easier and nonintimidating name). The information will show up in the box only when you put your cursor in one of the View windows.

When you finish this simple tutorial, you should have a good starting point to begin experimentation on doing your own modeling. Within minutes of completing this tutorial you should be able to start creating your own objects, such as a wine glass.

STEP 1: Select Clear from the File menu.

STEP 2: Select the Objects Tab from the top tabs menu.

STEP 3: For this tutorial, we will be starting in the second Layer. So from the top Layer buttons, click on the top portion of the second Layer so that it looks like Figure 1-61 (Inspire 3D Modeler screen grab).

FIGURE 1-61

STEP 4: From the buttons on the left, select the Disc button. This button is different from the Ball button in that it lets you make a flat circle polygon.

STEP 5: Working in the Face View, place your cursor on the upper Y axis until the Position Box reads X = 0 m, Y = 1 m (Figure 1-62).

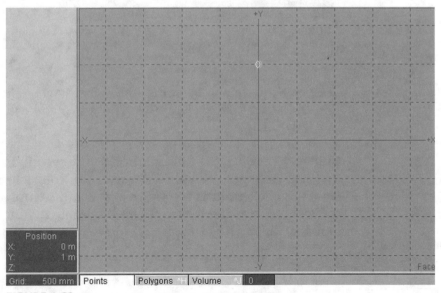

FIGURE 1-62

STEP 6: Hold down the left mouse button and drag your mouse down to the right until the Position Box reads X = 750 mm and Y = 500 mm (Figure 1-63). Let go of the left mouse button and click the Make button (or hit the return key). It will make a small circle! To get rid of the red outline, move your mouse to the blank gray area (under the buttons to the left) and click once. The red outline will disappear and be out of our way.

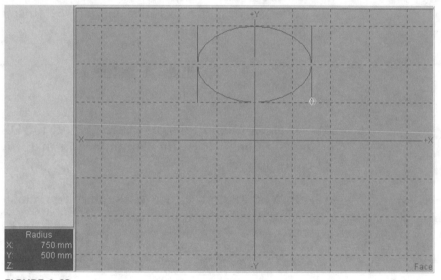

FIGURE 1-63

STEP 7: Now we will be going to the first Layer. Click the top portion of the first Layer. The circle you just made will disappear, but it is safe in Layer two.

STEP 8: Now click the lower button of the second Layer. The circle that just disappeared will reappear in the color black, telling us it is in the background. We will use this as a template for drawing the top of the game piece. Before proceeding, your screen should look like Figure 1-64 (Inspire 3D Modeler screen grab).

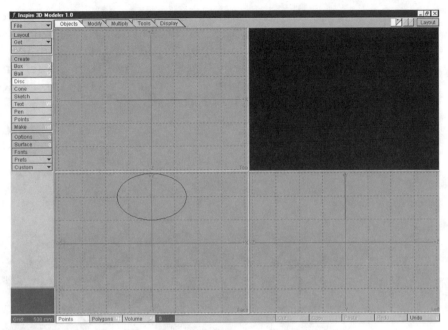

FIGURE 1-64

STEP 9: Select the Pen button. The cursor will turn into a tiny white pen. Working in the Face View again, place your cursor on the Y axis on the black line on top of the circle (Figure 1-65). Click once. A red dot will appear in that position.

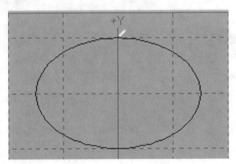

FIGURE 1-65

STEP 10: Now follow the black curve on the left side of the circle, strategically placing pen dots like in Figure 1-66. Remember, you do have an Undo button if you need it. Continue to place dots so that it looks exactly like Figure 1-66. Your full screen will look like Figure 1-67 (Inspire 3D Modeler screen grab). Notice that we are drawing only half of our object.

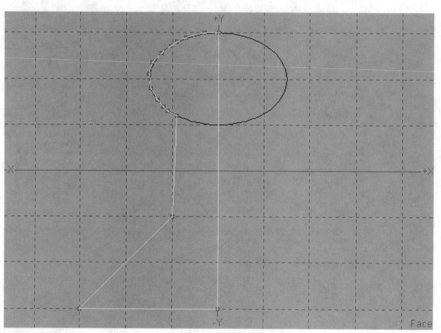

FIGURE 1-66

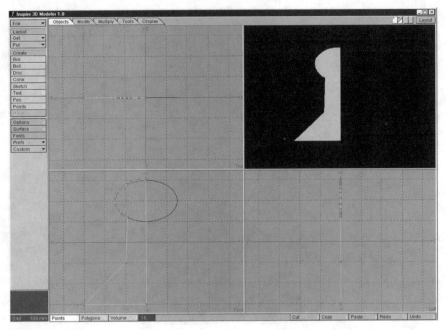

FIGURE 1-67

STEP 11: Click on the blank gray area under the buttons on the left-hand side to get rid of the red highlights around the dots. Your Face View should now look like Figure 1-68.

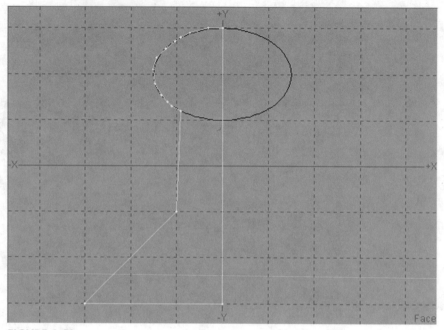

FIGURE 1-68

STEP 12: From the top tabs menu, select the Multiply Tab. From the new buttons that appear on the left, select the Lathe button. Your cursor will turn into a tiny white stick with an arrow circling it.

STEP 13: Move the cursor to the Top View so that it is right in the middle of the lines (X = 0 m and Z = 0 m). See Figure 1-69. Click once.

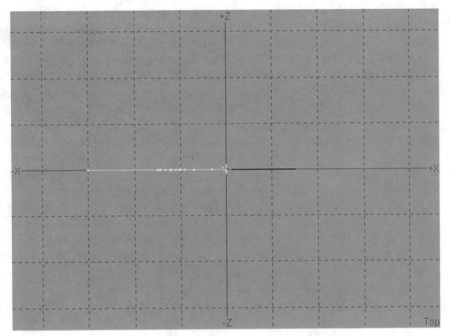

FIGURE 1-69

Instantly, your creation turns into a 3D game piece! You now have a 3D game piece for your game. Be sure to give it a surface name, surface, and so on, and do some more experimenting with it. See Figure 1-70 for the finished result. Practice the same techniques taught to you, except to make your own shapes. See Figure 1-71 to see what the final game piece on a game board looks like after being given a texture in Layout!

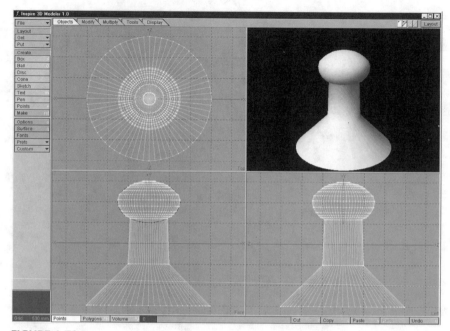

FIGURE 1-70

FIGURE 1-71

Continuing Your Exploration of Modeler

We have just touched a few basics of Modeler that, I hope, have given you the enthusiasm to explore further. There are lots of tabs to select, buttons to push, and discoveries to be made! But before you go diving in, take a quick trip with me into Layout.

LAYOUT SIMPLIFIED

In its simplest form, the secret to animating is to move or rotate an object and to create a key. You then move or rotate the object again and create another key. That's the basic concept of animation in a nutshell—*move or rotate an object and create a key*. As you will soon find out, this process is almost as simple as it sounds!

Earlier in this chapter we snuck into Layout to surface an object, so you've already had a sneak peak at the Layout interface. The Layout is used for many purposes, including lighting, surfacing, morphing, and animating. In short, the Layout is a stage and you are the director. Everything is at your disposal. It is a place where you can make movie magic. All you have to do is give the orders (and press some buttons, of course)!

A Basic Overview of Layout

Just like in Modeler, you'll find a File menu button in the upper left-hand corner where you can Clear, Load, and Save your Layout scenes. Instead of 4 different windows, like in Modeler, you only have one large view in Layout. This is your stage where you will direct your objects, lights, and camera. By default, Layout automatically starts with one light and one camera set up on your stage and ready to go, as seen in the Figure 1-72 interface picture, which is taken from LightWave 3D 5.6.

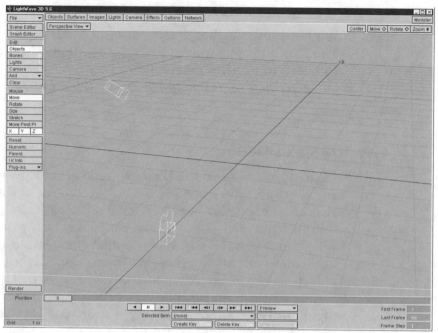

FIGURE 1-72

To the immediate right are 7 smaller buttons if you're using Inspire 3D, and 8 if you're using LightWave 3D. Figure 1-73 shows all 8 buttons in LightWave 3D 5.6. Inspire 3D has the same buttons, except for the last button called Network.

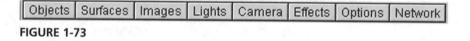

FIGURE 1-73

Directly below the Objects and Surfaces buttons is the View scroll-down button that defaults to Perspective View. As director, it is from this button that you can choose how you want to view your stage. Do you want to view the whole stage at once (Perspective View)? Perhaps you'd prefer a view looking straight down on your scene (Top View). You can view it from the side (Side View), from the perspective of a light View, or even from the lens of the camera (Camera View). It is this final view in which your scene will be recorded.

The very bottom of your Layout screen contains your animation controls, which are exactly the same in Inspire 3D and LightWave 3D (Figure 1-74). We'll look more closely at these controls in the tutorial Learning Basic Animation in 15 Minutes.

FIGURE 1-74

On the left-hand side of the Layout screen are your direct Layout command buttons, divided mainly into two key areas of Edit and Mouse selections. The buttons are exactly the same in Inspire 3D and Light-Wave 3D except for one difference. The second-to-the-last button in Inspire 3D (Figure 1-75) is Target. In LightWave 3D (Figure 1-76) it is IK Info. This is because Inspire 3D doesn't have IK functions like Light-Wave. However, LightWave 3D does have a Target function. When you select the Lights or Camera button under the edit area, the IK Info button will change to a Target button.

In the bottom left corner you'll find the Render button that you use to render and record your final scenes. Enough of the browsing. Let's get right into the hands-on experiments that are the best teaching aids. And to make life interesting, let's take a trip to a rural area where you never know what might be in the middle of a road—including a cow!

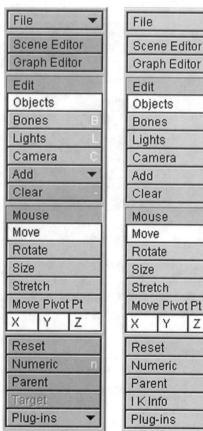

FIGURE 1-75   **FIGURE 1-76**

A Cow in the Road

STEP 1: From the top set of buttons, click the Objects button (to the left of the Surfaces button). The Objects Panel will open. Now click Load Object. Navigate to your Objects directory where you will see a series of folders that contain numerous objects. The first folder (in both Inspire 3D and LightWave 3D) is called Animals. Double-click it. Click on **Cow.lwo** once, then click the Open button. Click Close Panel to close the Objects Panel. There's Betsy with a rather unpleasant view of her backside (Figure 1-77). We'll change that soon.

FIGURE 1-77

STEP 2: Remember the scroll-down View button just below the Objects and Surfaces button? The default says Perspective View, but we want to change it to Camera View so that we see everything from the camera's eye. Go ahead and access this menu. Select each view, one at a time, to see the different perspectives that it gives you.

When you're done, select Camera View from this menu. Your screen should look like Figure 1-78 (taken from Inspire 3D interface).

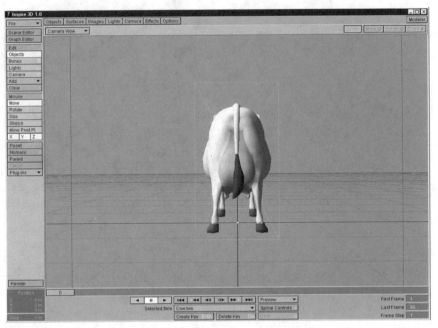

FIGURE 1-78

STEP 3: Now we are going to load a background image for Betsy to interact with. From the top set of buttons, select Images. The Images Panel will open. Click on Load Image. A Load Image File requester will pop up. It should default to the Images folder. Believe it or not, the backdrop we want to load is only on the Inspire 3D program! That's right, Inspire 3D users have something LightWave users don't! If you are using Inspire 3D, you can double-click on the BACKDROPS folder (LightWave 3D doesn't have this folder) and then **scene100.iff**. Click Open. Your images panel should look like Figure 1-79. LightWave 3D users, see the sidebar "But wait, I use LightWave 3D!"

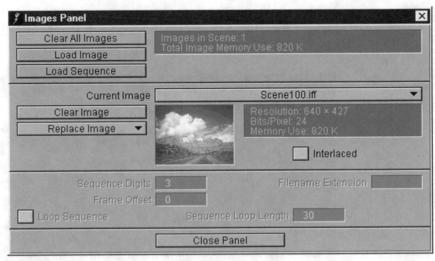

FIGURE 1-79

But Wait, I Use LightWave 3D! No need to fret. I've included the **scene100.iff** file on the CD-ROM! However, this is for educational purposes only, meaning you cannot reuse this scene in any actual projects without licensing permission from NewTek since it doesn't appear on your Light-Wave CD-ROM. Follow Step 3 until you have the Load Image File requester. Put the LightWave Applied CD-ROM into your CD-ROM drive. Double-click on the Applied folder. Now double-click on the Chap1 folder. There is the **scene100.iff** file! Select it and click Open. Like in Figure 1-79, you will see the image in the preview box. Now continue to Step 4!

STEP 4: Click the Close Panel button to exit the Images Panel. You won't see any changes yet because we haven't told LightWave to make the image the background scene. That is next.

STEP 5: From the top set of buttons, select the Effects button. The Effects Panel as shown in Figure 1-80 will pop up (picture from Inspire 3D). In this panel, click the Compositing tab. New options will appear, the first one being Background Image. Access the scroll-down menu next to Background Image and select **scene100.iff**. You'll see our background picture appear in the little preview window. Click the Close Panel button to exit the Effects Panel.

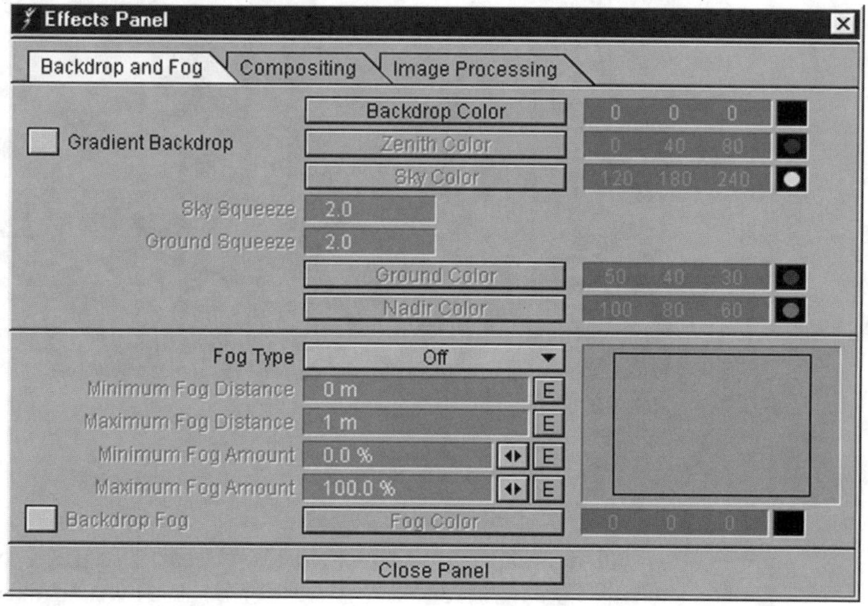

FIGURE 1-80

You still won't see any changes yet to your scene, even though the image has been applied to the background. However, you can see that it has been applied to the background by hitting F9 on your keyboard. Layout will render the image and it should look identical to Figure 1-81.

FIGURE 1-81

Now everyone knows that cows can't fly (unless we give Betsy wings), so we need to "bring her back down to earth." Being able to see the background image in Layout would be very helpful in achieving this goal, which we'll do next.

STEP 6: Make sure you are back on the Layout screen. In the top set of buttons is one called Options. Click it once to open the Options Panel (Figure 1-82). From this panel, click the Layout View tab. It should look like Figure 1-83 (picture from Inspire 3D). Next to Layout Background, you'll see that Blank is highlighted. Click BG Image. After a few seconds the image will load into the background of your scene! Click Close Panel to exit the Options Panel. Your screen should look like Figure 1-84 (picture from Inspire 3D). "Fly, Betsy, Fly!"

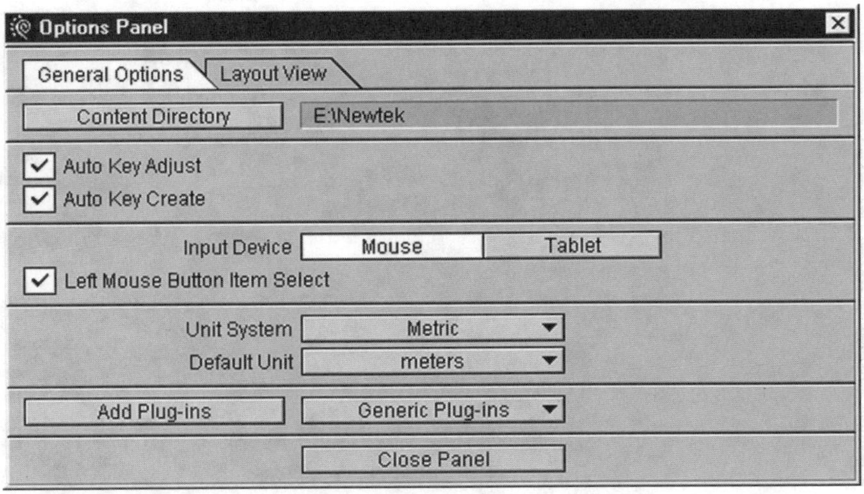

FIGURE 1-82

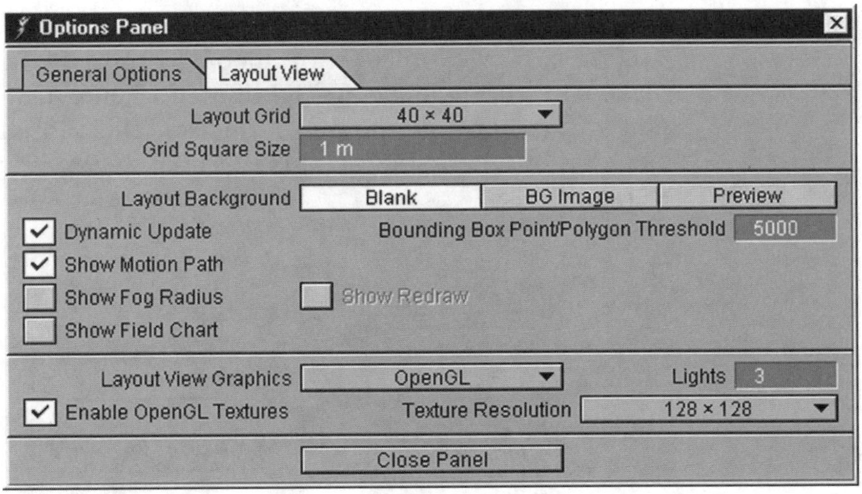

FIGURE 1-83

FIGURE 1-84

STEP 7: Now we will use the menu to the left. In the Edit area, make sure that Objects is highlighted (Figure 1-85). Now, in the Edit area (still on the menu to the left) select Rotate (Figure 1-86). Notice that when you did this the small X, Y, Z buttons changed to H, P, B.

FIGURE 1-85

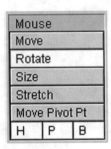

FIGURE 1-86

Move, Rotate, and the Three Little Buttons: When the Move button is highlighted in the Mouse Edit area, you'll notice three smaller buttons highlighted (below the Move Pivot Pt button) that have an X, Y, and Z. These buttons represent the axis (X, Y, and Z) in which you can move your Object (or Camera, Light, etc.) in the Layout view. X represents moving an item sideways (left and right). Y represents moving an item up and down. Z represents moving an item back and forth (toward you and away from you). The great thing about these buttons is that you can deselect buttons you don't want to use! This means that if I just wanted to move Betsy up and down, I can deselect the X button and Z button and the only direction Layout will allow me to move the cow is up and down. There is a tricky aspect to this scenario, however. Items moved along the X and Z axis are done so by holding down the *left* mouse button. To move on the Y axis, you must hold down the *right* mouse button.

When the Rotate button is highlighted in the Mouse Edit area, the three small buttons change to reflect an H, P, and B. These represent your rotation angles. H represents rotating your item to the left and right. P represents rotating your prop up and down (in a rotation manner). B represents rotating your item side to side (like a boat rocking side to side in the ocean). Like with the X, Y, and Z, there is a tricky aspect to this scenario. Items rotated via H and P use the *left* mouse button. Items rotated via B use the *right* mouse button.

STEP 8: Deselect the small P and B buttons (by clicking on each one time) so that only H is highlighted.

STEP 9: Move your cursor over Betsy. Hold down the left mouse button and drag it to the right. Don't panic when you see Betsy disappear into just a highlighted box. The box represents her. Angle the box sideways so that it looks like Figure 1-87. Now we want to bring poor Betsy down from the sky so that she can innocently stand in the middle of the road.

FIGURE 1-87

STEP 10: In the Mouse Edit area, select Move. The three little buttons will now change to X, Y, and Z. We want to move the cow down (remember that Y represents up and down) and further away from us (remember that Z represents back and forth). Click once on the X button to deselect it since our interest is only in moving Betsy along the Y and Z axis.

STEP 11: Move your cursor over Betsy and hold down the *right* mouse button. Slowly drag her (the box) downward toward the road. When you get low enough, let go. Now hold down the *left* mouse button over Betsy and drag the cursor up to move her further into the distance. Stop when it looks like the whole box is on the road. Use Figure 1-88 as a guide for her final placement.

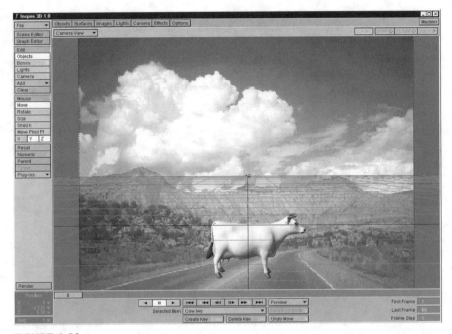

FIGURE 1-88

Cow Placement Tip: If your cow looks too big, then move it back farther (Z axis) and then down (Y axis). You can effectively decrease the size, while still making it look close to the camera.

Now we need to tell Layout to save this position. You do this with the Create Key button at the very bottom of Layout (to the left of the Delete Key and Undo buttons).

STEP 12: Click the Create Key button once. The Create Motion Key panel will open (Figure 1-89). Since this is a still picture (and not an animation), we will accept the Default keyframe of 0. So simply click OK. Betsy is now saved (but not safe) on the road!

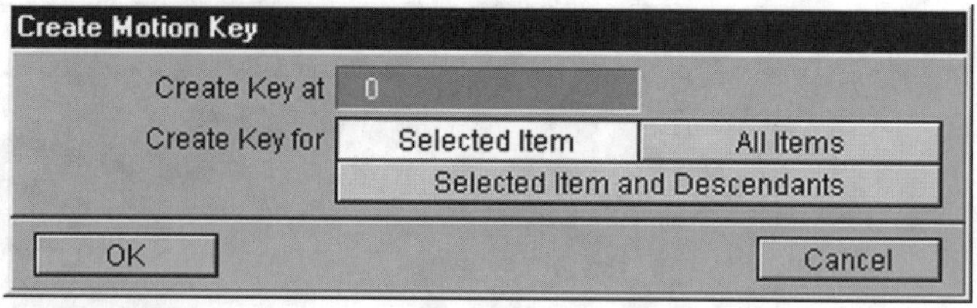

FIGURE 1-89

Create Key: The Create Key button is one of the most important buttons in Layout because it is where you save the settings of all the moves and rotations you make to Objects, Cameras, and Lights throughout your animation. If you are creating a still scene, you only have to worry about creating a key at the default setting of 0. But if you were animating, you would follow the rule of 30 frames equals 1 second of video. Let's say that when Betsy was in the air, we clicked on Create Key and changed the default number 0 to number 1 (first frame, where the animation begins). Now let's say that we moved her into the position on the road (as outlined in the steps we've completed) and clicked Create Key and made the number 30. What would happen? Well, you would have created a 1-second animation in which Betsy would have flown down from the sky onto the road!

OK. It's a beautiful day in the country. No cars are in sight. Betsy is admiring the view from the road. What can we do to improve this scene? No, adding a car coming toward Betsy at 75 mph is not the answer! How about a sun in the sky?

STEP 13: Select the Lights button in the upper row of buttons. A Lights Panel window appears, as shown in Figure 1-90 (picture from Inspire 3D). Click on the Add Light button once. Notice that next to Current Light, the scroll-down menu changed by adding the number 2 in parentheses. This tells you that you are working with the second light in your scene.

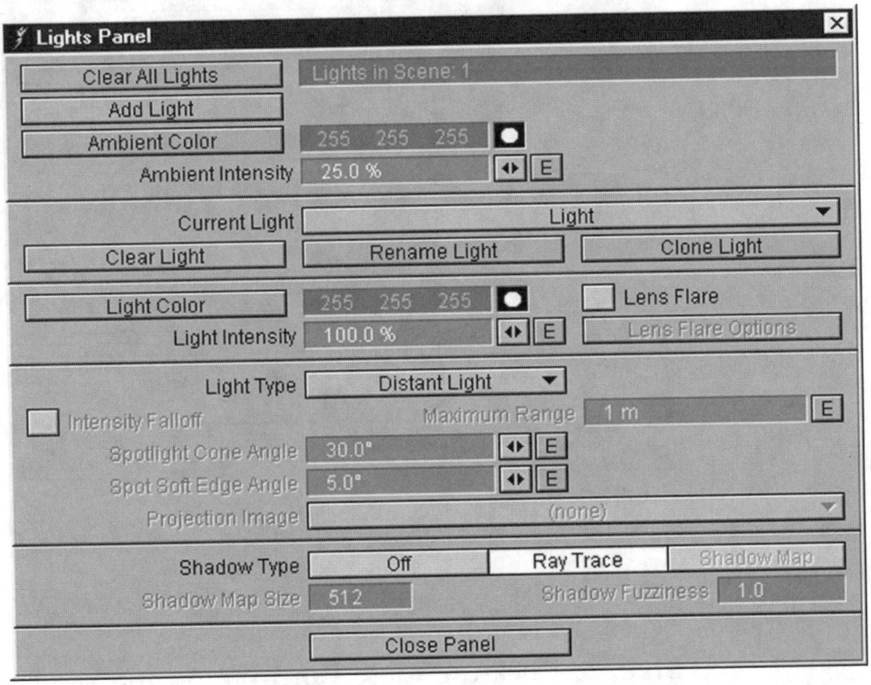

FIGURE 1-90

STEP 14: Next to the Light Color options is a little square button called Lens Flare. Click the box next to the name (Figure 1-91) A new button under it, Lens Flare Options, becomes available. We won't go here for this tutorial, but you may want to come back later and select it to edit your settings for the flare.

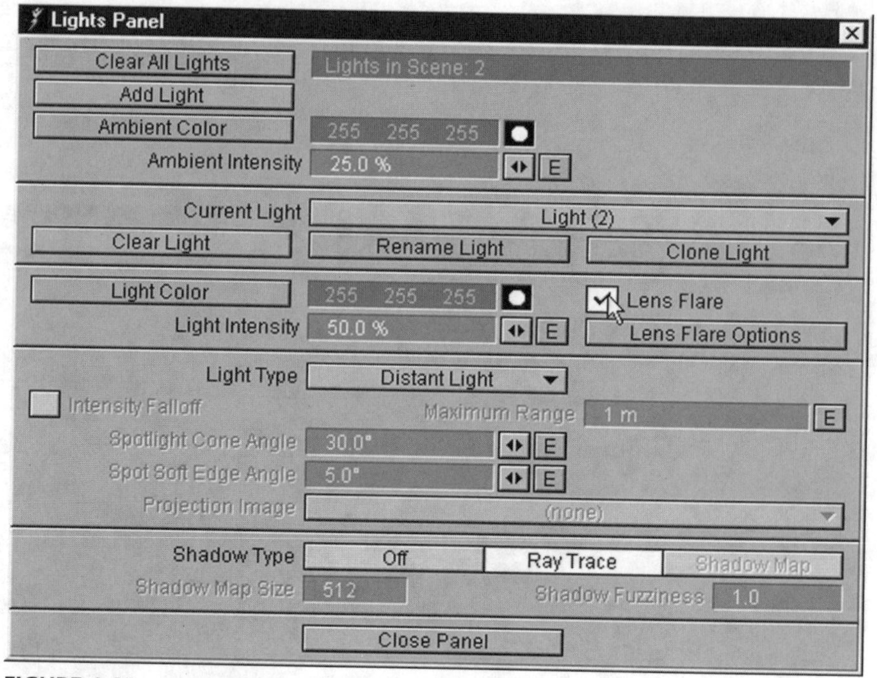

FIGURE 1-91

STEP 15: Click the Close Panel button to exit. The second light you added now appears in front of the camera's view in a gray color.

STEP 16: Move the Light the same way you moved Betsy, but instead of selecting the Objects button (left set of buttons) you now select the Lights button directly below it. Notice that the light turns yellow. Your screen should look like Figure 1-92 (picture from Inspire 3D). Move this light into the upper-right corner, as shown in Figure 1-93.

FIGURE 1-92

FIGURE 1-93

STEP 17: Create a keyframe again (Create Key button in lower screen). Then render it out (F9). Your Scene should look something like Figure 1-94.

FIGURE 1-94

Congratulations, you're done! Now you can experiment on your own. Go ahead and add a car to the scene on your own, but whatever you do, don't hit Betsy (or at least give her wings).

Learning Basic Animation in Fifteen Minutes

When you complete this short 15-minute tutorial, you will have basic animation under your belt with the power of experimentation increasing your skills even further. And still, you will be using only 5% of Layout's total power! Be sure that you've first mastered the techniques in the preceding tutorial (A Cow in the Road), then start your stopwatch and let's get going.

STEP 1: Load Layout. If it is already loaded, clear the scene by selecting the File button and highlighting Clear Scene.

STEP 2: Hold down your left mouse button over the View Menu (just under the Objects and Surfaces button). Select Camera View. The view menu button will now read Camera View, and the view in your main Layout window will change. You will no longer see the light or camera, because you are looking through the camera!

STEP 3: It's time to load an object to animate. From the top menu, select the Objects button. The Objects panel will open. Click on the Load Object button. A Load Object File window will come up. Navigate to the Objects drawer. Find the folder called "Space" and double-click on it. If you are using LightWave 3D you can just next select **PLANETHOPPER.lwo** then click Open. Proceed to Step 4. If you are using Inspire 3D you need to double-click on the SPACE-CRAFT folder then select **PLANETHOPPER.lwo** and click Open. Proceed to STEP 4.

STEP 4: Click the Close Panel button to exit the Objects Panel. You'll see the back of your spacecraft like in Figure 1-95 (picture from LightWave 3D 5.6 interface). Hit F9 on your keyboard to see what it looks like.

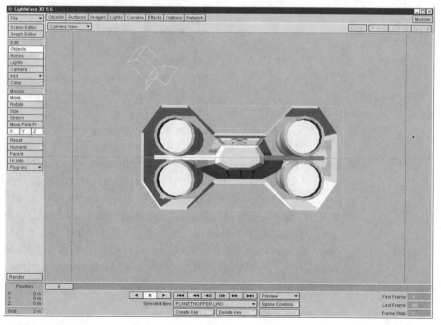

FIGURE 1-95

STEP 5: Return to the main Layout screen after viewing the rendered image. What we want to do is to turn the spacecraft around so that it is facing us. As you learned in the last tutorial, we do this with the Rotate command on the left-hand side. Click the Rotate button.

STEP 6: Since we want to simply spin the ship around to face us, click once on the P and B buttons so that they are deselected, leaving only H highlighted. Move your cursor over the spacecraft and hold down the left mouse button. Drag your cursor to the right and the spacecraft outline box will begin to move toward you. While you rotate the box, keep an eye on the Direction box in the lower left-hand corner until you see that H = 180.00 (Figure 1-96). Let go of the mouse button. The spacecraft is now facing you! Now we want to move the spacecraft into its starting position, where we will create the first keyframe for our animation.

FIGURE 1-96

STEP 7: From the Mouse area on the left-hand side, select Move (just above Rotate). Click once in the X and Y boxes, leaving only Z highlighted because we are going to move the spacecraft back into a starting point where we will animate it zooming toward the camera. Place your cursor over the spacecraft and hold down the left mouse button. Drag it up and the plane will start to move into the distance on the Z axis. Watch your Direction box again and stop when Z = 50 m. Your screen should look like Figure 1-97 (picture from Inspire 3D interface). This is our starting point!

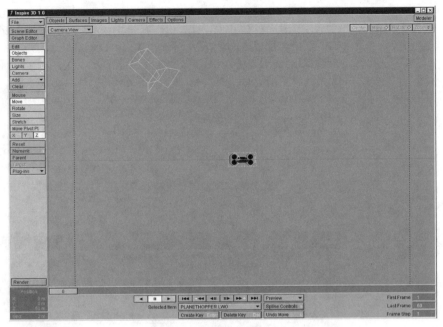

FIGURE 1-97

STEP 8: Click the Create Key button and change the 0 to a 1. Click OK.

STEP 9: We still have the Move and the Z buttons highlighted, so we can easily move the spacecraft toward us. Place your cursor over the spaceship and hold down the left mouse button. Drag your cursor downward. The plane will come toward you. Watch the Direction box until it reads Z = −6 m (negative six). This is our ending point!

STEP 10: Click the Create Key button and change the 0 to 30. Click OK. You have just told Layout to start the ship far back and bring it up close in 30 frames. Remember that in video (NTSC) 30 frames equals 1 second. Therefore, the ship will travel from your starting point to the end point in 1 second and look like it is about to crash through your screen! Let's make a preview.

STEP 11: In the menu on the bottom of the screen there is a scroll-down button called Preview. Hold your mouse button over it and highlight Make Preview. The Make Preview panel will appear. The defaults will have the First Frame as 1 and Last Frame as 60. Change the Last Frame to say 30 and hit the tab key so that it registers the change. Now click the Wireframe button. Your panel should look like Figure 1-98.

Click OK. Layout will proceed to create a preview and when it is done it will bring up a Preview Playback Controls panel that you can use (like a VCR) to watch your wireframe model fly toward the screen! After you are done viewing it, click the End Preview button.

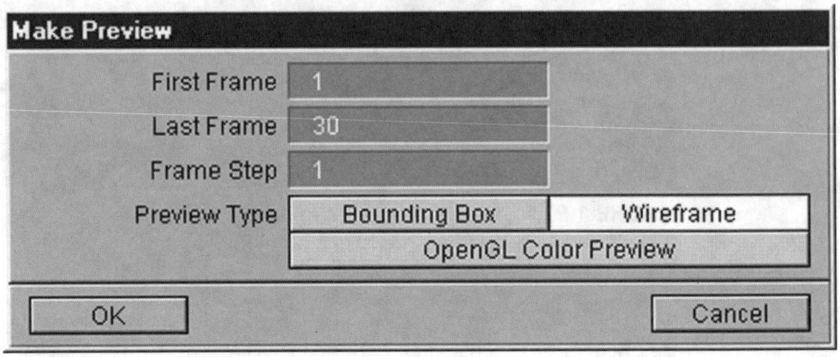

Make Preview

First Frame	1
Last Frame	30
Frame Step	1
Preview Type	Bounding Box	Wireframe
	OpenGL Color Preview

OK   Cancel

FIGURE 1-98

Congratulations on making your first animation! It would be mean of me, however, if I didn't show you how to render it! We'll turn it into an AVI file that you can view on your computer screen.

STEP 12: From the top menu select the Camera button. The Camera Panel will open. Next to Basic Resolution is where you will select the type of resolution you want your finished animation to play back in. For the sake of this tutorial, access the scroll-down menu and select Medium Resolution. Click the Close Panel button.

STEP 13: Click the Render button in the bottom left-hand corner of Layout. The Render Panel will come up. For Rendering mode, make sure Realistic is selected. If you want to see the rendering in progress, make sure to place a check next to Show Rendering in

Progress. I prefer to leave this unchecked as having it checked slows down the rendering time. But for this example, let's check it. You will get a warning message. Click Continue. Place a check in the box next to Automatic Frame Advance. Just below this option is a Save Animation button. Under it is an Animation Type scroll-down menu. Select the scroll-down menu and highlight IN_AVI_256. Now select Save Animation. Navigate to the drive you want to save the animation to and type in the name **test.avi** without the quotes. Be sure that you add the **.avi** after the word test! Click the Save button. Next to the Render Display, set it to None. Your panel should look like Figure 1-99.

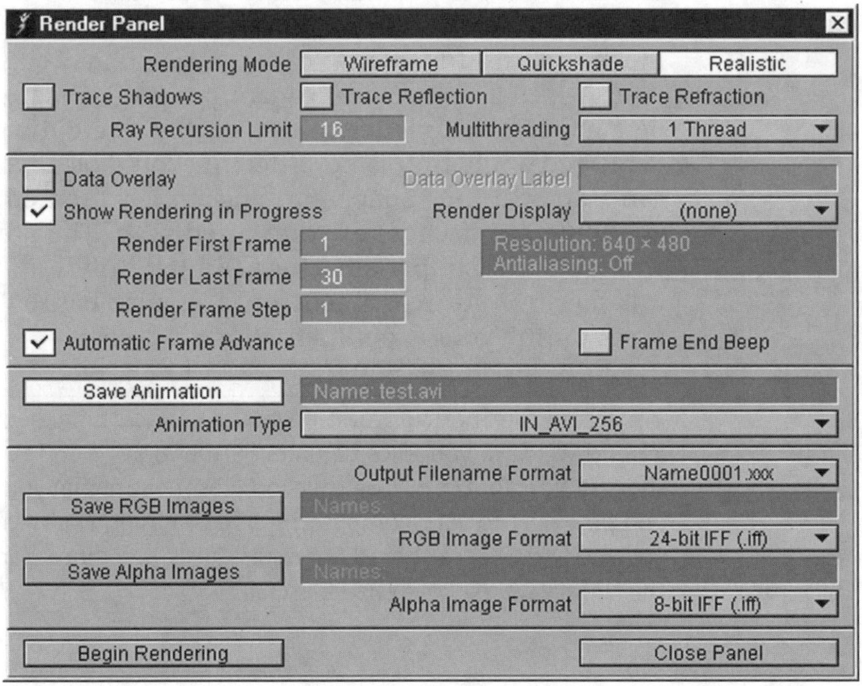

FIGURE 1-99

STEP 14: Click on Begin Rendering. When it is done, exit the program and go find your AVI file and play it back!

Congratulations on mastering the basics of animation in 15 minutes, with a couple to spare! Now you can practice rotations, space maneuvers, and laser battles. Before you know it, you'll be animating on the next *Star Trek* spin-off series!

EXPERIMENTATION IS ESSENTIAL

To learn the full power of Inspire 3D and LightWave 3D, experimentation is essential. This means that you need to set aside a 5- to 10-hour block at least once a week in which you do nothing but experiment with the different buttons in Modeler and Layout to see how changes you make effect your object or work. You will be amazed not only by the power you discover, but also by how much fun it is! In a matter of seconds you may accidentally turn a button into a vortex or a square box into a planet. Some of the best medical discoveries of this century were discovered by accident, and animation is no different. You'll be amazed at how you can start with one shape and end up with something inconceivably different from what you started with. The power of Modeler and Layout is simply amazing, and the only way to discover the full power is to experiment on a regular basis. Be sure to keep notes during your experimentation sessions!

Tip: Learn the Shortcut Keys! Keyboard shortcuts make your life much easier and will save you a lot of time. Furthermore, NewTek has provided the shortcut keys for LightWave users on glossy pages that you can easily detach and post next to your computer! If you are using LightWave 3D 5.5 or 5.6, you will find the "Keyboard Shortcuts Quick Reference Card" in the back of the LightWave 3D Reference Manual.

CONCLUSION

As stated earlier, there are dozens of ways to accomplish each task in Modeler and Layout. In this chapter you have learned only one way. Find a way that best meets your needs and go with it, but always keep an open mind to other ways of accomplishing tasks.

You still have many areas to cover and explore. In this chapter we haven't even covered one thousandth of the possibilities of Modeler and Layout. To cover such, simply from a beginning perspective, would take two or three entire books! We have only touched on the tip of the iceberg with quick methods to get you up and running, while having some fun along the way.

The chapters ahead are much more advanced and in-depth, but feel free to jump in and try them out. Dave Jerrard and Scott Wheeler have structured their tutorials in a step-by-step fashion that should make the task a little easier. I'll touch base with you again in the final chapter of this book that talks about Breaking into Hollywood.

Be sure to check out the bonus area on the LightWave 3D Applied book Web site where there are dozens of links to Inspire 3D and LightWave 3D tutorials for you to learn more! The Web site is located at **http://www.advanstarbooks.com/lightwave**.

2

Planet Earth

Dave Jerrard

OVERVIEW

One of the earliest animations created in LightWave, which many of the old-timers out there will remember, was the Paradigm Shift animation that kicked off NewTek's "Revolution" Toaster demo tape. It featured an old-style earth globe being circled by a sun, reminiscent of the artwork of da Vinci, which then was transformed to a more accurate animation of the earth orbiting the sun. In the years after that animation was created, nearly every LightWave artist has tried his hand at creating an earth in shape or form. In a tribute to that animation, which helped start the desktop video industry 8 years ago, we'll start this book with a study of the earth, from the past to the present.

We'll start this tutorial by creating a simple, old-style desktop globe and then move way up, for a look at the real world as seen from space.

In this tutorial you will use:

- Texture Reference objects
- Steamer
- Fast Fresnel shader
- Thin Film shader

What you will need:

- Texture images and Earth Maps included on CD
- Installed Layout plugins: Interfere.p, Steamer.p
- Installed Common plugins: Png.p, Jpeg.p

What you will learn:

- Creative surfacing techniques
- Use of Texture Layers
- Object layering to create clouds
- How to create an atmosphere with Steamer

STEP 1: One of the first things we need is a globe. Open Modeler and click the Ball button under the Tools menu. We'll build a relatively large globe here, half a meter in diameter, so type "n" to open the Ball's Numeric panel. We'll make this sphere as smooth as possible, so change the Ball Type to Tessellation. This will create our sphere out of evenly distributed triangles, like a geodesic sphere. Raise the Level to a value of 3 to 5 so the sphere is very smooth. Make sure the three Center values are all set to zero, and then enter a value of 250 mm for each of the three Radii values. Click OK, then hit Enter to make the sphere. Keep in mind, the higher the Tessellation Level, the more polygons will be created. A level of 5 will create 20,480 polygons, using 10,242 points, and it is extremely unlikely you will ever need to use a level of 6, which is currently the maximum level that can be loaded into Layout.

STEP 2: Type "q" to open the Change Surfaces panel and type in a new surface name. We'll call this one Earth—Oldstyle. Click the Apply button, and that's it for the earth! Save this object as **EarthGlobe.lwo.**

STEP 3: Start up Layout and load the earth we just created. It won't look like much yet since it's missing a few details, like a map. In the Earth directory on the accompanying CD, you will find a selection of various earth maps. Open the Images Panel and load the map named **Earth-Alpha.iff.** This is a simple black-and-white image that depicts landmasses in solid white and water as black, which we'll use to create our surface. Close this panel and open the Surface Panel. Select the Earth-Oldstyle surface and click the "T" button beside the Diffuse Level. On the Texture Panel that opens, click the button labeled Texture Type and select Spherical Image Map from the popup list. Just below that, there's another popup list labeled Texture Image. Click this and select the Earth-Alpha image we just loaded. You'll also notice there's a load image option at the bottom of that list, which we'll be using quite a bit from now on. The default values for this texture are all we'll need for now, with one exception. Turn off the Texture Antialiasing since that is somewhat less than friendly with spherical images (Figure 2-1).

FIGURE 2-1 Texture Antialiasing tends to smear details at the poles of a spherical image map. Another artifact that appears is the small dot at the pole, which is caused by pixels from the top edge of the image blending with those of the bottom edge.

Tip: Texture Antialiasing is rarely needed when normal frame antialiasing is used. It can, however, be used for special texture effects by increasing the strength higher than 1, particularly on bump maps, where it can be used to soften the edges of otherwise sharp images, giving a gentler slope to the bumps.

This texture will currently make all our water areas pure black, which is a bit too severe for the look we're after, which is similar to an old parchment or vellum look. We can reduce the intensity of this by simple lowering the Texture Opacity at the top of the panel. Lower this to 40% to allow this texture to blend with the base value. A test sample will show that the water areas are now much lighter than before. Close this panel by clicking the Use Texture button. While we're on the main Surface Panel, activate Smoothing, raise the Specularity to 20%, and reduce the Glossiness to Low.

STEP 4: Our globe is currently a bit bland, so let's add that old parchment look. We'll do this with a couple of layered color textures, but first, we need to set a base color. Click the Surface Color button and change the color to R: 190 G: 130 B: 100, which gives a rich tan color. Next, click the Texture button (T) beside the Surface Color and select Fractal Noise from the Texture Type popup in the Texture Panel that appears. Here, we'll change the color to R: 220 G: 180 B: 110 to add a lighter, less saturated tan color. Click the Texture Size button and enter a value of 5 cm for each axis so this texture shows up as a small mottled appearance on the surface. Finally, we'll increase the Frequencies to 4 and raise the Small Power to 1 to further increase the randomness of the pattern. Click the Render button on the preview strip to see the effect of this noise texture.

We could leave this surface as it stands, but we'll add a third color for a little more variation. Click the Add Texture button at the top of this panel, and once again select Fractal Noise from the Texture Type popup list. Change the color of this texture layer to R: 180 G: 190 B: 150 and click the Texture Size button. This time, we'll change the values to 10 cm each so the two texture layers cover the surface differently. This will give a good mix of the three colors, giving a more organic appearance to the surface. Again, we'll raise the Frequencies to 4 and the Small Power to 1. This time, we'll lower the Texture Opacity to 50% so this layer gets blended with the colors below it. Click the Use Texture button and then type F9 to see a test render of the surface thus far (Figure 2-2).

FIGURE 2-2 The globe starts to take on an ancient appearance with a couple of layers of colored fractal noise.

STEP 5: This earth is nearly done, but a few details remain to be added. Most globes will have a grid marking out lines of latitude and longitude, so why should we be any different? We can add the entire grid by simply adding a single square outline and tiling it across the surface (Figure 2-3). We'll apply a black grid, so we only need to apply it to the Diffuse channel. Click the Diffuse channel's Texture button to open the Texture Panel. We already have our earth map in this layer, so click the Add New Texture button to start a new layer. Select Spherical Image Map from the Texture Type popup list, then click the Texture Image button. This time, select the Load Image option at the bottom of the list. Included on the CD, in the Earth directory, is an image named **GridSquare.iff,** which is simply a 100- × 100-pixel image consisting of a white background and a thin black border. This will provide our grid when it's tiled, which we'll do by increasing the Height and Width

Tiling options. On globes lines of latitude and longitude are usually placed in 10-degree increments, so we'll follow suit. There are 360 degrees in a circle, so we'll need to tile this image 36 times to mark off every tenth longitude, which is the number we'll use for the Width Wrap Amount. Latitudes are measured from the equator, which is 0, to the poles, which are 90 degrees. This gives us 180 degrees pole to pole, meaning we need to tile the image 18 times for the Height Wrap Amount. Again, turn off the Texture Antialiasing, and make sure the Mapping Axis is set to the Y Axis.

FIGURE 2-3 Simply tiling a single square creates an instant grid.

As this texture is set up currently, it will overwrite the earth map we applied in the layer before it, as a sample preview will show. We only want to apply the black border of this image and make the white background transparent. To do this, we'll use the Texture Alpha Image, just below the Texture Image option. When using these alpha images, the Texture Image will be applied according to the luminosity of the alpha image. White areas of the alpha image will apply the Texture image at 100% opacity, whereas darker areas will blend it with the underlying surface. Select the **GridSquare.iff** image for the Texture Alpha Image, and then click the Negative Alpha Image option below its thumbnail. This will invert the alpha image so now the black areas apply the Texture Image while the white center prevents it from being added.

If the lines this grid creates seem a bit dark, feel free to lighten them by lowering the Texture Opacity for this layer. Seventy-five percent will give a good blend of the lines with the underlying surface, making them look as though they were drawn on with a semitransparent pigment.

STEP 6: Another common marking on globes is the equatorial line, which is frequently a dashed line, with each dash marking off a degree of longitude. Again, we can apply this detail by tiling a smaller image of a single dash, which is also supplied on the CD. Once again, we'll apply this image on the Diffuse channel, so click the Diffuse Texture button if that panel isn't already open. This image will have to be applied on top of the two current layers, so if you're not already on the grid layer, click the Next Texture button to advance to it, then click the Add New Texture button. Click the Texture Image button and select the Load Image option. Load the **Equatorial.iff** image from the CD, then click the Texture Type button. This time, instead of using a spherical map, we'll apply this image using Cylindrical mapping on the Y axis since we're only mapping it in a thin strip around the center of the globe. This image is small, being only 16 x 8 pixels, so to keep it from looking blurred, turn off Pixel Blending and Texture Antialiasing.

We want our equatorial line to be a few millimeters thick, so click the Texture Size button and change the size to 4 mm on the Y axis. This image consists of a yellow square on one side with a black background, which, when tiled, will create an alternating pattern that will become our dashed line. If you think of it as a yellow and a black dash, then we'll need to set the Width Wrap Amount to 180 for each dash to indicate a single degree of longitude. Finally, to keep this line from tiling vertically as well, turn off the Height Repeat, then click the Use Texture. This will be hard to see in a preview sample, but a test render by hitting F9 will show a line similar to the one in Figure 2-4.

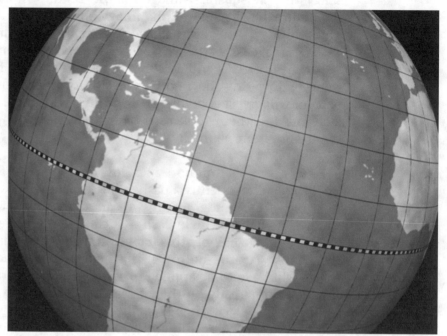

FIGURE 2-4 A cylindrical image, with the Height Repeat deactivated, allows the application of an equatorial line.

STEP 7: Most of our surfacing is complete here, but for an old-style globe, ours is just a bit too smooth. Let's roughen it up a bit by adding some bumps. Close the Texture Panel for the Diffuse channel and click the Bump Map button at the bottom of the Surface Panel. We'll use the same earth image we used on the Diffuse channel to make the land masses appear raised, so click the Texture Image button and select the Earth-Alpha image. Change the Texture Type to Spherical Image Map, and once again turn off the Texture Antialiasing. Raise the Texture Amplitude to 100% and make sure the Texture Axis is set to the Y Axis.

While we're here, we'll add some more surface irregularities by adding a second bump layer. Click the Add New Texture button and change the Texture Type to Fractal Bumps. Click the Texture Size button and change the size to 10 mm for each axis. Click the use Texture button and type F9 to do a test render, which will now look almost as though the earth was made from two types of leather or thick parchment (Figure 2-5). This globe can be considered finished now, so save it again to preserve the textures.

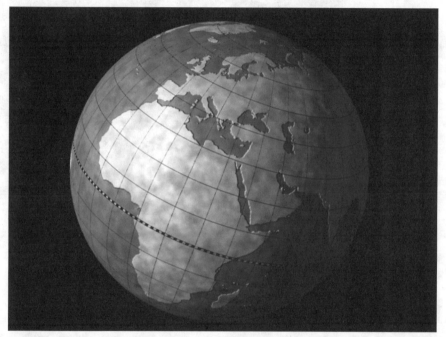

FIGURE 2-5 The fully textured globe takes on a leathery appearance.

STEP 8: Since we're building a desk globe, we need a stand for it. Go back to Modeler and switch to an empty layer. The first thing we'll build here is the ring that will support the globe itself. The first thing we need to decide on is what kind of ring to use. Some globes will use a complete ring whereas others use a partial ring that just reaches past the poles. We'll cover both here, starting with the simpler full ring. In the Top view, use the Pen tool to draw out a polygon like the one in Figure 2-6. The following coordinates were used to create the polygon in the image.

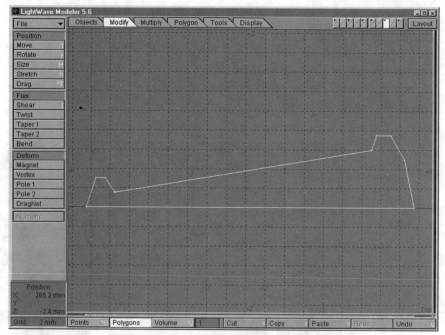

FIGURE 2-6 The profile polygon that we will use to lathe the globe's ring. Note the inclined side, which will play an important role in the texturing phase.

Point #	X (mm)	Z (mm)
1	257.5	0
2	258.5	3
3	259.5	3
4	260.5	1.5
5	287	6
6	287.5	7.5
7	289	7.5
8	290.5	5
9	291.5	0

These coordinates place the polygon just a few millimeters outside of the globe's radius, ready for lathing. Before we do that, however, we'll need to mirror this polygon since it's only half the ring profile. Click the Multiply tab and select the Mirror tool, then click the Numeric button just below it. Change the Plane to the Z axis and make sure the position is 0, click OK, then hit the Enter key to actually perform the Mirror.

We'll now have two polygons that need to be merged so we don't end up with a ring of polygons inside the ring. Select both polygons, then hit the "m" key to open the Merge Points panel. Select the Automatic mode and click OK. You should see a message stating that two points were eliminated. Click the OK button on that panel, and then click the Polygon tab. In the Revise section, click the Merge button, which will actually merge the two polygons into one. This polygon may very well be facing downward right now, which can be checked by looking at the surface normal for it in the Face or Side view. If the normal is pointing down, we'll need to flip it by typing "f". Otherwise, our lathe will produce an object with inward facing polygons. We're ready to lathe this polygon now.

STEP 9: Copy this polygon and paste it into a new layer so we have a backup copy. We'll cover the full ring in this step, so click the Multiply tab and select the Lathe tool. We're going lathe this around the Z axis, so click the Numeric button to open the Lathe tool's options. First of all, under the Axis section, click the Z button and make sure the center values all read 0. Also make sure the Start Angle is 0 and the End Angle is 360. Finally, raise the number of Sides to 100 so we have a very smooth ring. Click the OK button, then hit the Enter key to perform the lathe (Figure 2-7).

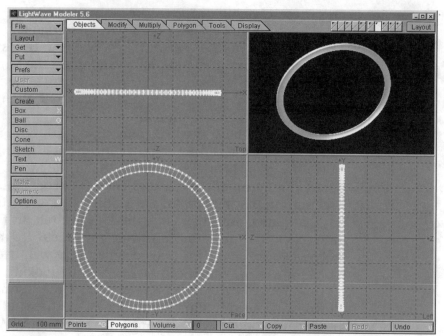

FIGURE 2-7 A simple lathed ring.

STEP 10: Now we'll create the second type of frame for the globe, so go back to the layer with the original polygon you created in Step 8. The process is similar, but a little more intricate. We'll create a partial ring that reaches from pole to pole and overshoots each by 25 degrees. We already know that there are 180 degrees from pole to pole, and now we're adding an extra 25 at each end, for a total of 230 degrees. While we're doing this math, we might as well figure in the tilt of the earth's axis, which is 23.5 degrees. Click the Lathe tool again, and open the Numeric panel for it. With the Start Angle field, we're able to define an alternate starting angle for the lathe, other than where the polygon is currently located. If we use a value of 0, the lathe will start where our polygon is, but instead we'll back that up a bit so it starts at the top. That means we need to back up 90 degrees to place our starting point at the top of the arc, and then a further 25 degrees to allow for the overshoot. Finally, we'll add in the earth's tilt. Modeler actually allows us to enter mathematic equations such as this one, so let's do that. In the Start Angle field, type $-90-25+23.5$ followed by the Enter key. The equation will be replaced with the solution, which is -91.5 degrees.

The same holds true for the End Angle, only this time, it's a bit simpler. Just enter the range of the arc we want, which is 230 degrees, and then subtract the 91.5 degrees, and you should see the value 138.5 degrees appear in the field after hitting Enter.

Click the OK button then hit Enter to perform the lathe. You should see a partial ring already tilted to match that of the earth's axis (Figure 2-8).

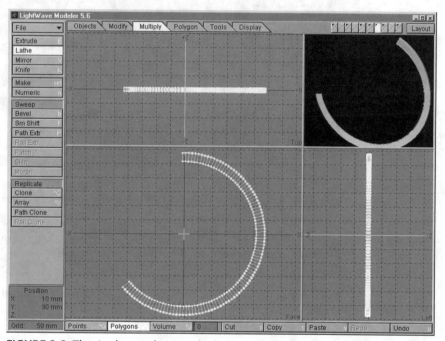

FIGURE 2-8 The Lathe tool can calculate angles to lathe a polygon to form arcs with precise start and end points.

STEP 11: Now for the tedious part; setting the surface names for this ring. (This step applies to both ring types.) Drag the Face view to full screen and fit the ring to the new size. We need to select the large polygons that make up the main sides of the ring, so make sure you're in Polygon Edit mode by clicking the Polygons button at the bottom of the screen. Now, simply drag the pointer over the wide polygons making sure only the large ones are selected (Figure 2-9). You should have 200 polygons selected when you're done. Type "x" to cut these polygons, then switch to an empty layer and paste them there by typing "v". Now we can name the new surfaces.

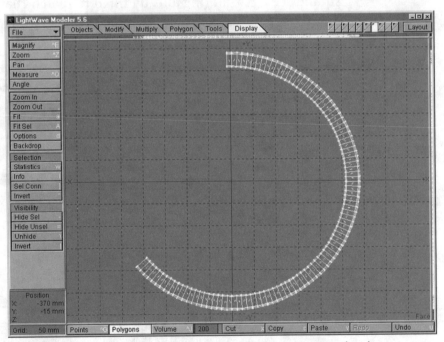

FIGURE 2-9 The polygons that we will need to move to another layer temporarily.

STEP 12: Widen out the Side view and select a polygon or two on the left side of the ring in that view, then type "]" to select the connected polygons. This will select all the polygons on the front side of this ring (Figure 2-10). Type "q" to open the Change Surface panel and then call this surface, "Scale—Front," then click the Apply button. Next, type "Shift-apostrophe" to invert the selection and open the Surface Panel again. This time, create a surface called "Scale-Back" and click Apply. Now, switch back to the original layer we just cut these polygons from and open the Surface Panel again. Create another surface named "Scale-Rim," and click Apply once again. Finally, cut these polygons by typing the "x" key and switch back to the layer containing the two sides we just named. Paste the "rim" polygons here by typing "v" and then type "m" to merge points.

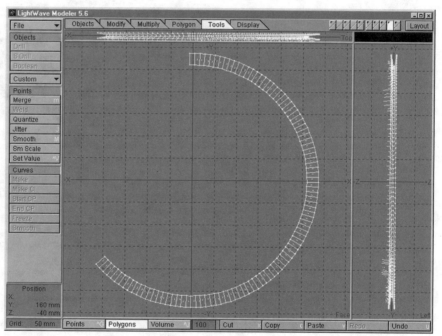

FIGURE 2-10 The side polygons, with the front side selected.

STEP 13: (This step applies to the partial ring only.) This partial ring is pretty much complete, but it could do with a couple of caps on its ends. This is easily accomplished by applying a few bevels to them. Type "w" to open the Polygon Statistics panel, and click the + button beside the entry labeled ">4 Vertices," which will show that 2 polygons currently have more than 4 points. This will select the two end polygons for us and set us up for the bevels. Close this panel and zoom in on one of the ends so you can see exactly what's happening (Figure 2-11). Type "b" to open the Bevel tool. We'll apply a total of 5 bevels to these polygons to create the end caps. For the first bevel, change the Inset to 0, and enter 1 mm for the shift. Make sure the Edges are set to Inner and the Surface is set to Source, and then click OK. This first bevel merely extended the end slightly, adding space between the end and the side surfaces we created earlier.

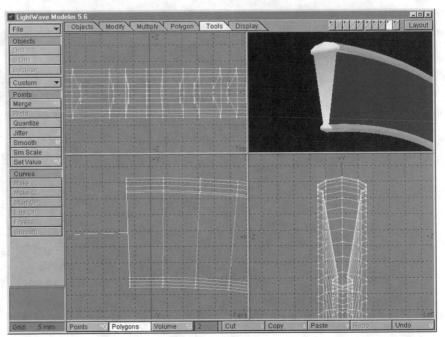

FIGURE 2-11 A closeup of the unfinished end of the partial ring. The side polygons have been darkened.

Type "b" again, and this time, change the Inset value to −1 mm and leave the Shift value at 1 mm, then click OK. This will cause the beveled polygons to bevel outward slightly. Type "b" again, and change the Inset value to 0 once again, then click OK. Apply another Bevel, this time with an Inset value of 1 mm, which will return the selected polygons to their original size. Finally, for our last bevel, which we'll add to prevent smoothing errors later, change the Inset value to 0.5 mm and change the Shift value to 0 (Figure 2-12). This will surround the irregularly shaped end polygons with co-planar polygons so the end polygons won't try to smooth into the angled polygons we just created, which would normally cause smoothing errors in the form of weird streaks in renders.

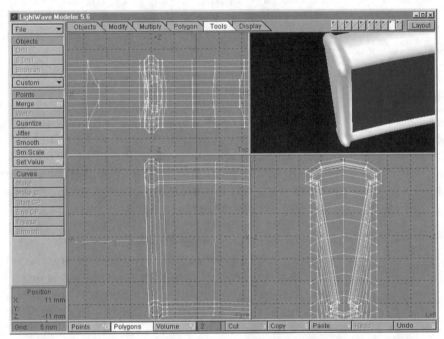

FIGURE 2-12 The same section after the application of 5 Bevel operations.

Tip: When using the Put command, the object is only saved under the filename when you use the <<NEW>> option. If you use it to replace an object that is already in Layout, only a temporary file is written to disk, leaving the original object file untouched, until you specifically save the object. This allows you to repeatedly change the object in Layout without having to save multiple files everywhere. This is handy in cases where you want to work on small sections of an object, where you can transfer the parts back and forth, then save the completed object when all the adjustments have been made.

Note: The rest of this tutorial applies equally to both ring types.

STEP 14: Our end caps are now complete, so let's surface this thing in Layout. Under the Objects menu, click the Put button, and select the <<NEW>> entry in the popup list. A requester will open asking for a filename. We'll call this **GlobeStand.lwo** and click the Save button. Next, click the Layout button to switch over to Layout. If you still have the Earth globe loaded, select it and type the minus key to remove it from the scene so it's not in the way.

STEP 15: We'll start off with the simple surface first, so open the Surface Panel and select the surface we called "Scale-Rim." We'll make this a silver surface, which will highlight the brass sides we'll add later, so we need a good metal color. Click the Surface Color button and change the color to R: 150 G: 160 B: 170. Next, we'll add a slight color variation to help define the presence of this surface, which is so often missing in reflective surfaces in 3D imagery. Click the Texture button beside the Surface Color and select Fractal Noise as the Texture Type. We'll add a slightly darker tint of the color here, so change this color to R: 130 G: 150 B: 170. Next, raise the Small Power to 1.0 to randomize the fractal pattern more, then click the Texture Size button. This arc is nearly 2 cm thick in the Z axis, so if we squeeze a fractal texture on that same axis, it will take on the appearance of streaks, or grain, running along the curve of the arc. To create this effect, we'll use a value of 4 cm for the X and Y axes, and a value of 0.1 mm for the Z axis. Click the Use Texture button to accept this texture.

STEP 16: We'll raise the Specularity to 200% to create a very bright highlight and to lower the Glossiness to Low. We can now give this surface a more metallic look by reducing the Diffuse level to 30% and activating the Color Highlights option. We'll also make this surface reflective, so increase the Reflectivity to 50%, since metals tend to be less reflective than they are specular. Click the Reflection Options button to the right of this so we can specify how we want these reflections to behave. In the panel that opens, there will be two popup buttons. For the one labeled Reflection Type, click and select the last option in the list, which is Ray Tracing & Spherical Map. Obviously, since we've specified the Spherical Map, we'll need to use the second option, Reflection Image. Click this button and select the Load Image option at the bottom. NewTek supplies a little-known, but highly effective, image for creating metallic reflections, called **MetalRefMap.iff.** This image has been tucked away in the Images/Brushes directory for a few years now and is conveniently included on the CD that accompanies this book. Load the **MetalRefMap.iff** image, then close this panel. Finally, activate the Smoothing option at the bottom of the Surface Panel.

STEP 17: We'll add two last adjustments to this surface before we call it finished. The first will be to add a few marks to simulate scuff marks or smudges. These will be subtle and are easily created with Fractal Noise. Click the Texture button for the Diffuse channel and change the Texture Type to Fractal Noise. Next, click the Texture Size button and enter a size of 5 cm for each axis. Finally, set the Texture Value to 70% and raise the Small Power to 1.0. Click the Use Texture button, and then click the Advanced Properties tab on the Surface Panel. We'll add our last adjustment through the use of a shader plugin.

Click the first plugin slot and scroll down the list of plugins until you find the one named LW_FastFresnel. Select it and then click the Option button next to the slot. This plugin will change the value of up to 5 surface attributes according to the angle of the surface to the camera. Most surfaces tend to become more reflective when viewed at extreme glancing angles, and metals are no exception. In the Fast Fresnel panel, we'll be using only the Reflectivity and the Specular option, so make sure these are the only buttons that are highlighted. We'll increase the Reflectivity to 100% here and raise the Specularity to 400%. That's it for the rim, now let's do the tricky stuff.

STEP 18: We'll be making the sides of this ring a brass color, so select the surface named "Scale—Front" and change its color to R: 240 G: 200 B: 120. This will set up a good base color to create our brass siding from. Once again, since this is a metal, we'll set the Specularity to 50% and the Glossiness to Low. Activate the Color Highlights and reduce the Diffuse Level to 30%. Change the Reflectivity to 25% and click the Reflection Options button. Just as we set for the Rim surface, we'll use the Ray Tracing and Spherical Map method and the **MetalRefMap.iff** image. Since this surface is slanted slightly toward the axis it was lathed around, we'll need to apply smoothing to it. We don't want this to smooth into the rim surface, so lower the Maximum Smoothing Angle to 10 degrees.

Just as we did with the rim surface, we'll add a slight smudging to the surface. Click the Texture button for the Diffuse channel and select the Fractal Noise texture. We'll set the Texture Size to 5 cm on each axis and use the default Texture Value of 50%. Finally, increase the Small Power to 1.0 and click Use Texture.

STEP 19: We now have a good brass surface, but it would look better if it had a brushed surface. Normally, a curved surface like this would make using a procedural texture nearly impossible, but this surface has that incline toward the center, which opens up a couple of possibilities. The first possibility is that we can use that incline to "bend" a procedural texture to follow the curve of the surface. Click the Bump Map button and select Fractal Bumps as the texture. This angle of the polygons in this surface give it a thickness of 4.5 mm on the Z axis, which isn't much, but a texture with a small size on the Z axis would appear to stretch outward across the width of this ring. To see this demonstrated, give these Fractal Bumps a size of 10 mm on the X and Y axes, and a much smaller size of 0.01 mm on the Z axis. Increase the Texture Amplitude to 100% and click Use Texture. Close the Surface Panel and move the camera close to the ring so you have a closeup of the front surface, then type F9 for a test render. You will see that our Fractal Bumps have now aligned themselves to follow the curve of the ring (Figure 2-13).

FIGURE 2-13 A closeup of the top of our stand, showing the Fractal Bumps as they curve along the arc of the ring.

STEP 20: The other possibility is to apply an image to this surface and have that image bend to conform with the curve as well. In this case, we can add a latitude scale (hence the name we gave this surface), using a simple image, and have the surface bend it around in an arc for us. Click the Texture button for the Diffuse channel, then click the Add Texture button to create a second texture layer. Change this to a Cylindrical Image map and then click the Texture image button. Select the Load Image option at the bottom of the popup list, and load the image called **GlobeScale1.iff,** which is located in the Earth directory on the CD. Select this same image as the Alpha Image, and activate the Negative Alpha option. This is a simple image depicting a scale that ranges from −90 through 0 to 90, then back again. The negative Alpha works much like our grid texture on the globe did, by applying only the black lines of the image to the surface. Click the Automatic Sizing button to size this image to fit the surface, then click the Texture Center button. Make sure the X and Y values are both 0, but leave the Z value alone. Change the Texture Axis to the Z axis, and we now have a scale that wraps itself around the curve of the arc, even though the image is straight and horizontal. Finally, deactivate the Texture Antialiasing. Hit F9 again and you'll see the scale wrapping around the arc, with 90 placed at the very top (Figure 2-14). Now we need to fix that because it won't line up with the north pole when we add the earth at a 23.5-degree angle.

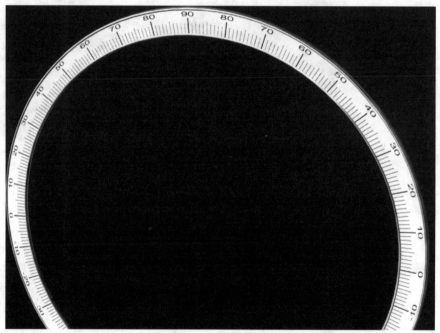

FIGURE 2-14 Just like the Fractal Bumps we applied, a simple, straight-scale image bends to conform to the shape of the ring.

Tip: When working with an object that you don't plan on moving during an animation, it's a good idea to turn off all the motion channel buttons for that object. This will prevent any accidental changes to the object's position from being made. Changes can still be made, but they must be made through the Numeric panel, the Motion Graph, or by activating the motion channel button again.

STEP 21: Turning this image used to mean re-editing it in an image processor by shifting it sideways enough to have the correct value at the top. A simpler method is included in LightWave, and that's the Texture Reference Object. Click the Add Reference Object button and the wide bar above it will show the current reference object is called Ref Obj, which is nothing more than a simple null object that has been added to the scene. Click the Use Texture button and close the Surface Panel. In the main Layout window, you'll see a null object in the center of the ring. Select this as the active object and rotate it on its bank to −23.5 degrees. If you have the OpenGL/DirectDraw3D texture active, you'll see that the scale itself also rotated. This null can serve an additional purpose for us now. It can be used not only to rotate the scale image, but also to tilt our earth the same amount. Before we add the earth, we should attach this null to the stand so it moves with it. Otherwise, if we attach our earth to this null, the earth will be left behind whenever we move the stand. Click the Parent button on the left side of the screen and a panel will appear asking for a parent object. Select the Stand and click OK.

Now, if we move the ring upward so it's above the ground plane, the reference object will move with it. Select the stand and move it upward about 50 cm. Again, if Layout texture is active, you will notice something happening to the scale image. Hit F9 again to see exactly what happened (Figure 2-15). Reference objects generally add their position and orientation only to the texture coordinates they affect. The texture itself is still attached to the surface it's applied to, so moving the surface will move the texture with it, just as with normal textures. However, since we moved the reference object as well, its new position is added to the texture's center, so by moving the stand upward by 50 cm, we inadvertently moved our texture center a full meter in the same direction since the null was also moved 50 cm. If we didn't have the null parented to the stand, the texture would still be mapped correctly. This could become a bit messy after a few more reference objects are created since they must be left in the center of the LightWave universe, leaving a hefty pile of nulls all packed into that one spot.

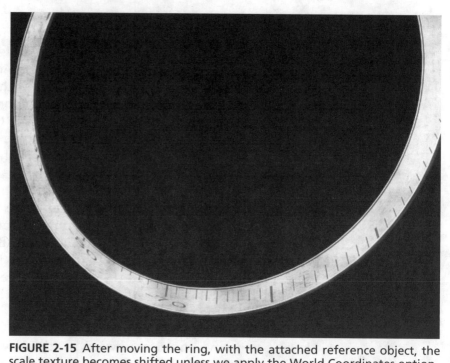

FIGURE 2-15 After moving the ring, with the attached reference object, the scale texture becomes shifted unless we apply the World Coordinates option.

There's a trick to parenting these reference objects to the surfaces they affect by using the World Coordinates option in the texture panel. Open the Texture Panel for this image again (Diffuse texture 2), and click the World Coordinates button. Now the texture will be attached to the "world" and then have the reference object's offsets applied. Since the "world" never changes, the texture will appear to be attached to the reference object, following it wherever it goes. Another render will show that our scale is now centered correctly again. We can now safely move this stand with the attached reference null anywhere we want. Click the Reset button on the side of the screen to reposition this object in the center of the universe.

STEP 22: We have our markings for the scale, but let's engrave them into the surface. To do that, we'll use this same texture as for a bump map. Type Ctrl-c to copy this current texture into memory. Before we leave, we'll reduce the intensity of this Diffuse texture by lowering the Texture Opacity to about 75%. This will allow some of the base color to show through the lines. Click the Use Texture button, and then click the Bump Map button.

We already have the Fractal Bumps in the first texture layer, so click the Add new Texture button, then type Ctrl-v to paste a copy of the scale texture here. We need to make only a minor adjustment here. We won't need the Texture Alpha Image for this layer, so remove it by clicking the popup list and selecting "none" at the top of the list. Click Use Texture, and this surface is virtually finished (Figure 2-16).

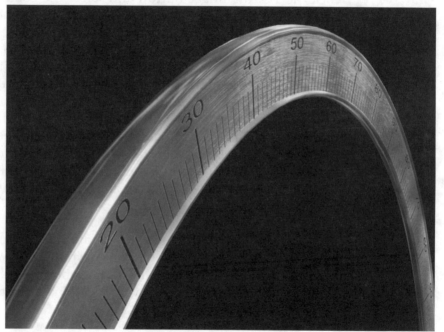

FIGURE 2-16 A closeup of the finished scale surface.

STEP 23: Let's add that Fast Fresnel Shader to this surface as well, so click the Advance Options tab and load the LW_FastFresnel plugin into the first slot. Click the Options button and make sure only the Specular and Reflectivity options are activated, and make these both 100%. Close the panel and this surface is done. Now for the other side.

STEP 24: Rather than go through all those steps again, simply click the Render button on the preview strip. This will generate a texture sample of this current surface. Next, select the Scale—Back surface from the surface list, then click the bottom texture sample we just created. A Copy Surface requester will appear. Click OK to accept, and we now have an identical copy of the front surface here. This also means that our scale image will be facing the wrong way, as well as being off-center for this side of the stand. Click the Basic Parameters tab and open the Diffuse Texture panel. Click the Next Texture button to advance to the scale texture. There is a second-scale image included on the CD for this side, so click the Texture Image button and select the Load Image option. Load the image called **GlobeScale2.iff.** Select this same image as the Texture Alpha Image, and then click the Automatic Sizing button to center this texture for this side. You will have to reactivate the World Coordinates button since the Automatic Sizing will deactivate this. Finally, make sure the Texture Center values for the X and Y axes are both 0, and then click Use Texture.

Click the Bump Map button and advance to the second texture layer. We'll need to make the same changes here, so change the Texture Image to **GlobeScale2.iff** and click Automatic Sizing. Reactivate the World Coordinates and make sure the Texture Center values for the X and Y axes are both 0. Close this panel by clicking the Use Texture button.

STEP 25: Let's finish this stand by creating the base for it. Switch back to Modeler, which should still have the ring we exported to Layout. Clear this layer and click the Get button. Select the Globe-Stand object and it will load back into Modeler, bringing with it the textures we applied to it.

STEP 26: Switch back to Modeler, which should still have the ring we exported to Layout. Clear this layer and click the Get button. Select the GlobeStand object and it will load back into Modeler, bringing with it the textures we applied to it. The first thing we'll add is an axis to place our globe on. Switch to a new layer and put the layer containing the ring in the background. Click the Disc tool and, working in the top view, drag out a disc from the center to a 2.5-mm radius. Next, working in the Face or Side view, stretch this disc to reach across the inside of the ring in the background layer. The ends of this disc should be positioned on the Y axis at 259 mm for the top and −259 mm for the bottom, which will place the ends inside the inner rim of the ring (Figure 2-17). Hit "n" to open the Numeric Panel to confirm the dimensions.

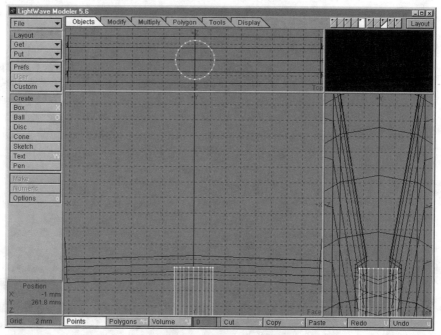

FIGURE 2-17 The top end of the globe axis, positioned where it will not poke through the ring, shown here in the background layer.

Sides:	24		Center (m)	Radii
Segments:	1	X	0	2.5 mm
Bottom:	−259 mm	Y	0	0 m
Top:	259 mm	Z	0	2.5 mm
Axis:	Y			

Click OK to accept the values and then hit Enter to create this cylinder. The ends of this cylinder will be buried inside the ring so we won't need the polygons at the ends. Type "w" to open the Polygon Statistics panel and click the + button beside the entry for ">4 Vertices," which will be our two end polygons. Close this panel and hit the Delete key to remove these.

STEP 27: Since this will be the axis our globe will spin on, we need to tilt it 23.5 degrees. Type a "y" to activate the rotate tool, then type "n" to open the Numeric Panel for it. On this panel, click the Z button to set the rotation axis, then enter a value of 23.5 for the Angle. Finally, make sure the three center values are all set to 0, then click OK. Our axis will now be tilted as shown in Figure 2-18. All we need to do now is to give this a surface name. Type "q" to open the Change Surface panel and select the Scale-Rim surface in the popup list. The values below will be updated to reflect that surface's settings. Under the Surface button, type in a new name, such as "Globe Axis." This will create a new surface. While this panel is open, we'll reduce the Specularity to 100%, so this isn't as shiny as the rim surface. Click Apply and this axis is finished. Copy this object, and then switch over to the background layer with the ring and paste the axis there. This completes our frame. Let's finish this stand by creating the base for it.

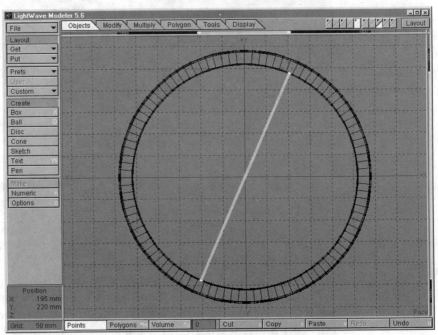

FIGURE 2-18 The final position of the earth's axis.

STEP 28: Switch to another empty layer and place the ring in the background once again. Under the Objects menu, select the Pen tool and draw out a shape similar to the one shown in Figure 2-19. It doesn't need to be exact since we'll be converting it to splines next. Drawing this polygon is just a quick-and-dirty way to create a few points while roughing out the shape of the profile we'll use to lathe the base of our stand.

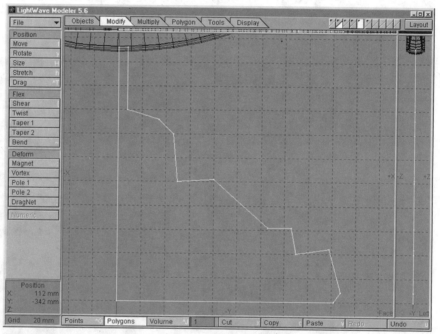

FIGURE 2-19 The Pen tool is excellent for roughing out designs before final tweaking.

STEP 29: We'll retrace these points and make spline curves from them, but there are a couple sections we don't want to make curves from. The first section is the top bar that will support the ring. This will be a simple cylinder, but we'll make that at the same time we lathe the base. Switch to Point Edit mode, zoom in to the top section, and select the two points that make the right edge of it. Type "p" to create a 2-point polygon from these points (Figure 2-20). Switch back to Polygon Edit mode and you will see this 2-point polygon highlighted. Make sure the top point of this polygon is located at −288 mm on the Y axis so it's within the widest area of the rim. Under the Tools menu, click the Set Value button. We'll need to make sure this polygon, when lathed, will not make a shaft that's thicker than the ring. When we created the ring profile in Step 8, the maximum X axis dimension was 7.5 mm, which means our polygon has to be less than that, otherwise it will poke through the ring. On the Set Value panel, set the Axis to X and type in a value of 7 mm, which will make this a half millimeter thinner than the ring. Click OK to accept this change. Since we applied this to the polygon, the two points that make it have been adjusted, so this polygon is perfectly vertical now.

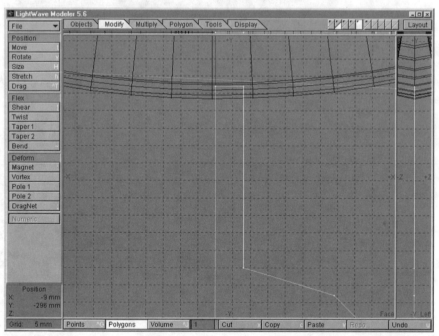

FIGURE 2-20 The location of the polyline that will form the supporting shaft. Note the location of the top edge compared to the background layer.

STEP 30: We'll do a similar procedure on the bottom of this stand to ensure that it's flat. Deselect everything by clicking in the blank area to the left, and then zoom in to the bottom of this rough polygon. Switch back to Point Edit mode by clicking the Points button at the bottom of the screen, and select the two bottom-most points, and once again, type "p" to create a second 2-point polygon (Figure 2-21). Switch to Polygon Edit mode and open the Set Value tool again. This time, we'll make sure our base is set to −50 cm on the Y axis, so change the Axis to Y and enter −50 cm in the numeric field, then click OK.

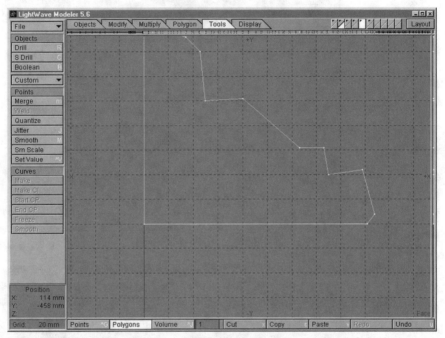

FIGURE 2-21 A second polyline will form the bottom surface of the base.

STEP 31: Switch back to Point Edit mode and select the remaining points in order from the bottom end of the top polyline to the right end of the bottom polyline. Click the Make button under the Curves section of the Tools menu to create a spline curve from them (Figure 2-22). Switch to the Modify menu and select the Drag tool. Use this to drag various points around until you have a curve that you like, taking care not to modify the two end points of this curve. If you want to add a sharp corner to this curve, select the point where you want a corner, then switch to Polygon Edit mode (Polygons button at the bottom of the screen or Ctrl-h) and select the curve. Then, under the Polygon menu, click the Split button. This will split the curve into two separate curves at that point (Figure 2-23).

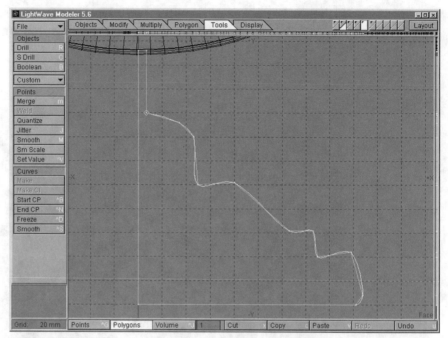

FIGURE 2-22 A spline curve begins to define the actual profile that will be lathed later.

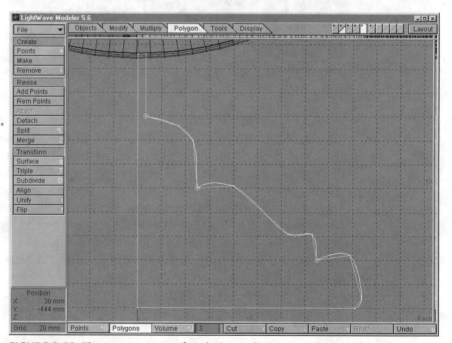

FIGURE 2-23 The same curve, after being split in two places, takes on a more intricate shape.

STEP 32: When you have a curve that you like, deselect everything, then select the original polygon by clicking the edge that runs along the left side, and hit the Delete key. This should leave you with the two polylines and the curves you just created. This object is ready to be lathed right now, but we'll apply a couple of surfaces first. We'll do the entire base first, so type "q" to open the Surface panel. We'll make this a brass base, so select the "Scale—Front" surface from the popup list, then type "Base" in the area below to create a new surface with the base values of the scale surface. For the shaft at the top, we'll apply the same surface we applied to the axis earlier. Select the top 2-point polygon and type "q" to open the Surface Panel. Select the Globe Axis surface, then click Apply. Now, when we lathe this profile, the finished object will have the appropriate surfaces already in place.

STEP 33: Under the Multiply menu, click the Lathe tool and open the Numeric Panel for it. Make sure the Start Angle is 0 and the End Angle is 360, and then change the number of Sides to 40. Finally, change the Axis to Y, and make sure the Center values are all set to 0. Click OK, then hit the Enter key to apply the lathe (Figure 2-24). Type "m" to open the Merge Points panel and set it to the Automatic method, then click OK. This way 160 points will be eliminated.

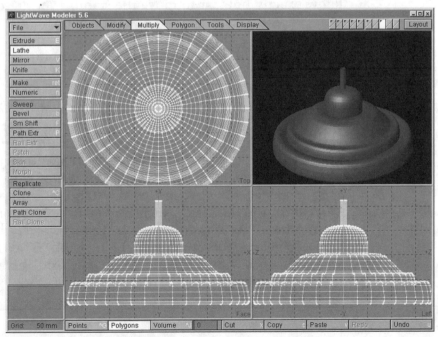

FIGURE 2-24 The finished base after lathing.

STEP 34: Modeler will create double-sided polygons whenever it lathes a 2-point polygon, so we'll clean these up now. Click the Polygon tab at the top of the screen, and then click the Unify button on the side panel. You should see a message appear, stating that 80 polygons have been removed. Close that requester, then click the Align button above Unify to make sure all the polygons face outward.

STEP 35: The bottom of this base is currently made of 40 triangles, which we don't really need. Type "w" to open the Polygon Statistics panel and click the + beside the entry for "3 Vertices" to select these bottom polygons. Close the panel and click the Merge button to the left. You should now be left with a single 40-sided polygon for the bottom. There will also be a single stray point at the center of this polygon, which we don't need. Select it and hit the Delete key.

STEP 36: Now we'll assemble this stand into a single object. Copy this base and paste it into the same layer as the ring and axis. The final step will be to move this entire assembly upward so the bottom of the base rests on the ground plane. Since we already know that the bottom polygon is located at −50 cm on the Y axis, we know exactly how far to move the stand. Type "t" to activate the Move tool, then type "n" to open the Numeric panel for it. Type 50 cm for the Y Offset and make sure the X and Z values are both 0, then click OK. Our Globe Stand is now complete and ready for Layout. Use the Put command to send this back to Layout, replacing the old object that is already there.

STEP 37: Switch back to Layout and move the camera back a bit so you can see the entire stand. Hit F9 to do a test render. You will notice that a slight problem has occurred again (Figure 2-25). The scale that we mapped earlier is now all out of whack once again. This happened when we moved the stand 50 cm up the Y axis in Modeler in the last step, which changed the location of its center point. The solution is quite simple, though. Merely select the reference object and move it up 50 cm on the Y axis as well. The scale will once again be correctly mapped on this surface. Now, let's polish up that base.

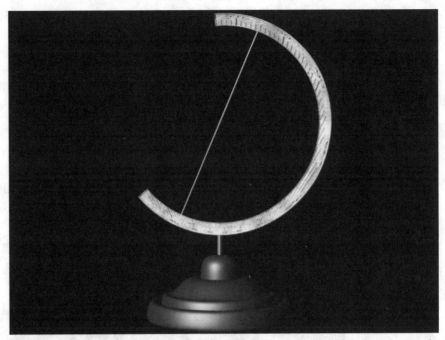

FIGURE 2-25 The completed stand in Layout, but with a slight mapping problem again.

STEP 38: Open the Surface Panel and select the Globe Axis surface from the surface list. Most of the settings have already been set when we used the Rim surface in Modeler. However, this only copied the base parameters and no textures were copied. We'll need to first reapply the Color Highlights to regain the metallic look, so activate that option once again. Next, we need to replace the missing reflections. Click the Reflection Options button and change the Reflection Type to Ray Tracing + Spherical Map, then select the **MetalRefMap.iff** and the Reflection Image. Close this panel, and then click the Advanced Options tab. Select the Fast Fresnel shader and click the Option button to access its controls. We'll be applying only the Specular and Reflectivity options, so turn off the Transparency button. Increase the Reflectivity level to 100% and the Specular level to 200% and click OK. Now we can work on the base.

STEP 39: Select the Base surface, which will need the same set of adjustments as the axis surface did. Repeat Step 38 on this surface, and then click the Basic Parameters tab. Since we "borrowed" the surface from the brass scale, it will have the same Maximum Smoothing Angle, which makes it look a little faceted in some areas. Increase this to about 40 degrees, which is a good general-purpose setting. Last, we'll add a slight smudginess to this surface. Click the Texture button for the Diffuse channel, and select the Fractal Noise texture. Change the size of this texture to 5 cm on each axis, and then raise the Small Power to 1.0. The remaining default values will suffice, so close this panel by clicking the use Texture button.

This completes our stand, so open the Objects panel and save this object to commit the textures to it (Figure 2-26). Also, save this scene as **EarthGlobe.lws** to save the reference object info.

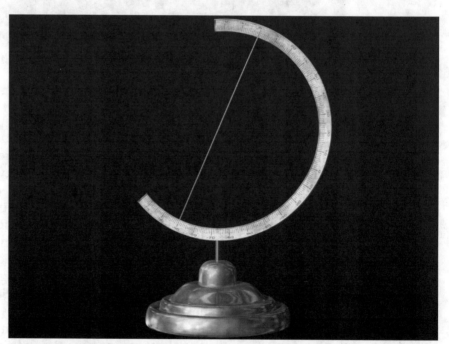

FIGURE 2-26 The same stand after all the surfacing has been completed, awaiting its globe.

STEP 40: Now, we'll add our globe to the stand, so click the Load Object button and select the **EarthGlobe.lwo** object we created earlier. Close the Objects Panel and you'll see the globe with the top part of the stand sticking through the top. The globe should be the active object right now, so let's put it in place. Since the reference object we created a while back for the scale defines not only the center for the scale texture but also the 23.5-degree tilt, it will serve well as a parent object for our globe. Click the Parent button on the side panel for the globe and select the Ref Obj from the popup list. Click OK and the globe will snap into place inside the ring (Figure 2-27).

FIGURE 2-27 The completed globe and stand assembly.

Tip: There are a handful of commercial, high-resolution earth maps available, some ranging in prices over $1000, and boasting resolutions of 25,000 × 12,500 pixels. At that size, each pixel covers one square kilometer of surface area at the equator, which is enough to make out some geographical landmarks, such as cities, airports, and strip-mining operations, and even some natural disasters, such as oil spills or fires. These maps would require enormous amounts of memory to load, making them impractical for general 3D animation. The maps included on the CD are a much more manageable size, being only 2000 × 1000 pixels, with a resolution of 12.5 km per pixel.

It would be a good idea to lock the motion channels for movement by deactivating the X, Y, and Z buttons on the side panel for this globe. Likewise, select the Rotate button under the Mouse edit section and deactivate the P and B buttons, leaving only the H button active. This will allow us only to rotate this globe on its heading, preventing any accidental rotations or movements in any of the other motion channels. You might even want to do this with the Scale and Move Pivot Point buttons as well. Save this scene again and our desk globe is ready to be used in other projects by simply using the Load From Scene button on the Objects Panel. Now, let's take a look at a more realistic earth.

STEP 41: Clear Modeler by clicking the File button and selecting Clear from the popup list. To keep our scale manageable, we'll create our realistic earth as a simple 1-meter sphere. The objects we create here can always be scaled up to the appropriate sizes later for other projects, if necessary. Since you will likely want to get close to this earth for those spectacular horizon-from-space scenes, we'll create a highly detailed globe. Select the Ball tool from the objects menu and click the Numeric button below it. In the panel that pops up, change the Ball Type to Tessellation, and increase the Level to 4 so we have a very smooth sphere. Make sure the Center values are all set to zero, and make the Radii values all 500 mm. Click OK and hit Enter to create this sphere. Once again, our modeling of the earth is done. Save this as **Earth.lwo**, then flip over to Layout.

STEP 42: If you haven't done so already, clear the scene in Layout and load the **Earth.lwo** we just created. We're going to need a few images to make this surface look realistic, so open the Images Panel and load the following images that are supplied on the CD:

Earth-Map

Earth-Lights

Earth-Specular

Earth-Bump

EarthClouds

EarthClouds-clip

EarthClouds-top

(The JPEG version of the Earth-Map image requires 6 megabytes of RAM to load into LightWave since it's a full 24-bit image. If your system is low on memory, use the 8-bit IFF version instead, which only requires 2 megabytes.)

STEP 43: Open the Surface Panel, which should have the surface we created our sphere with already selected as the Current Surface. Rename this surface as Earth, and then click the Texture button for the Color Channel. Change the Texture Type to Spherical Image Map and select the Earth-Map image. Be sure to deactivate the Texture Antialiasing to avoid the blurring that happens at the poles, and then click Use Texture. This just applied the main imagery we needed for our earth. Click the Render button on the Sample strip to the right to see how our globe looks so far.

STEP 44: Water tends to be a bit reflective, even when seen from space, so we should give our oceans a little gloss. We can't just raise the Specularity since that would make the land look shiny as well, which isn't exactly realistic. Instead, leave the Specularity at 0% and click the Texture button for the Specular channel. Once again, select Spherical Image Map, and this time, choose the Earth-Specular image, which is a 16-level grayscale map that shows the water bodies as pure white and the land masses as black. When applied as a Specular texture, the white area will make the surface 100% specular whereas the black areas will prevent any highlight from appearing. Once again, deactivate the Texture Antialiasing, which we'll do for every surface we create here. Render a texture sample and you'll see our specular highlight (Figure 2-28).

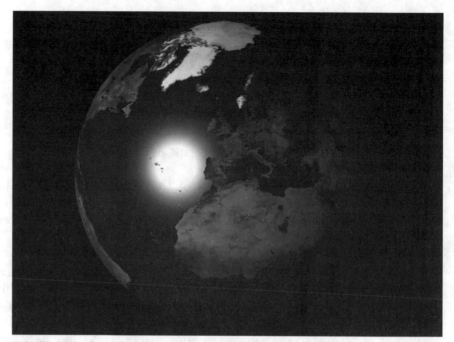

FIGURE 2-28 The Earth-Specular image applies a highlight to the oceans while keeping the landmasses dull. Note that this highlight is a little too intense.

Tip: The Texture Opacity can be used as a sort of dynamic range for texture maps. A high-contrast black-and-white image can be darkened by making the base value black or lightened by making the base value white, then using the Texture Opacity to control the amount of blend between the two. Used this way, the Texture Opacity defines the texture's dynamic range.

Remember that the white areas of the map apply a 100% specularity to the surface, which is why the highlight is a bit intense in that sample. Satellite photos never show this highlight at such an intense level, so we'll need to tone ours down. One way to do this would be to bring the image we're using into a paint program and adjust its intensity, but that would mean actually changing the image. There's a safer way to do this directly within this Texture Panel that doesn't require editing the image at all. All we need to do is lower the Texture Opacity, which will blend this texture with the underlying base value. Since our base Specularity is 0, or "black," this will have the effect of darkening our texture, thus reducing the intensity of our highlight. Lower the Texture Opacity to 30%, which will lower the highlight's intensity to 30% as well. Close this panel and set the Glossiness to Low. Create another texture sample to see that change.

STEP 45: The surfacing of our home planet is nearly finished. If you've ever looked out a window, which is a rarity for 3D animators, you'll notice that land is not very flat or smooth. If we're going for realism, we can't have smooth land on our globe either. Click the Bump Map button, and once again select Spherical Image Map. This time we'll use the Earth-Bump image, which is a grayscale image that approximates the surface elevations of the landmasses. This will mainly give our mountainous regions better shading near the terminator. Set the Texture Amplitude to 20%, then click Use Texture.

STEP 46: Speaking of the terminator, activate the Sharp Terminator button. Also activate Smoothing, or our globe will look faceted. The last texture we'll apply will be readily noticeable only on the dark side and will show that there is life on this planet, intelligent or otherwise. Open the Luminosity Texture Panel, and select the Earth-Lights image. Again, this will be a spherical map, which will make small areas of the globe luminous, simulating city lights as seen from space. These will also need to be toned down, just as with the specular map, or they'll be bright enough to see in daylight. Lower the Texture opacity to 50%, which will be enough to hide them in the sunlight.

STEP 47: Open the Lights Panel and lower the Ambient Intensity to 5% (or lower), so we have extremely dark shadow areas, just like in space. Close this panel, then move the camera to a position where you can see the earth lit up from about a 90-degree angle, then hit F9 for a test render. So far, so good, but people on this planet would be suffering from a severe air shortage! We need to add an atmosphere now.

STEP 48: Go back to Modeler, which should still have our original sphere sitting there. We'll need to use additional spheres to create our atmosphere, and this one is just about the right size already. Type "q" to open the Surface Panel and rename this surface as Clouds. While this panel is open, activate both the Smoothing and the Double Sided options, and then click Apply. This will become our cloud layer, but right now, it's the same size as the earth, which will only give us mere ground fog. We need to increase the size of this object very slightly. Type Shift-h to activate the Scale tool, then hit "n" to open its Numeric Panel. Make the center values all 0, then increase the Scale Factor to 100.1%, and click OK. This doesn't seem to do much, but we just increased the diameter of this sphere by an entire millimeter. On our earth's scale, this will place our cloud surface pretty high up in the atmosphere.

STEP 49: Use the Put command to send this object directly into Layout, using the <<NEW>> option and naming this object **Earth-Clouds.lwo.** Switch over to Layout, where you'll see the new Earth-Clouds object where our earth used to be. The earth is still there—it's just hidden under that severe cloud cover. Let's clear that sky a bit now. Open the Surface Panel, which should now have the cloud surface selected. We don't have to do a lot here, just open the Transparency Texture Panel. Change this to a Spherical map, and select the EarthClouds image that we loaded earlier. This image will need to be inverted to look right as a transparency map, so activate the Negative Image option. Again, make sure that the Texture Antialiasing is turned off, and then click Use Texture. We'll make these clouds almost a pure white, so change the color to R: 230 G: 230 B: 230, then activate the Sharp Terminator.

There is one tiny quirk you can run into when rendering shadows between polygons as close as our clouds are to the earth. In solid areas of the texture, some polygons may cast solid shadows, showing up as hard-edged black triangles in the shadow areas. To avoid these, simply make sure there are not fully opaque areas in the surface. We can do this by raising the base Transparency Level to 100%, then lowering the Texture Opacity to 80%. This will ensure that the texture is never less than 20% transparent.

STEP 50: Close the Surface Panel, and click the Render button in the lower left of the screen. Activate Trace Shadows, then open the Objects Panel. Click the Appearance Options tab, and deactivate the Self-Shadow option for both objects since they're spheres and spheres can't exactly cast shadows on themselves. This will also speed up the rendering process since each object has one less shadow to worry about. Click the Save All Objects button so you don't lose any surface settings, then close this panel. Finally, select the cloud object and parent it to the Earth. Hit F9 for a new test render and sit back.

STEP 51: This render will take a little longer since there's now a Transparency Mapped surface casting shadows on the Earth (Figure 2-29). We can speed this rendering process up a little more by not tracing shadows for the completely transparent areas of the cloud surface, where there won't be any. What we need is a way to get rid of the completely transparent sections of this surface so there will be nothing to cast a shadow from. Open the Objects Panel again, and select the Earth-Clouds object. Under the Appearance Options tab, click the Clip Map button. A familiar texture panel will open, so once again, select Spherical Image Map as the Texture Type. This Clip Map is similar to a Transparency texture, but this will actually remove parts of an object from the rendering process, taking with it any highlights. Anything in this clipped area is considered nonexistent by LightWave as it renders, and is ignored. This means that clipped areas will not be figured into the shadow calculations.

FIGURE 2-29 Earth with a simple layer of clouds passing over the Atlantic Ocean.

Tip: Polygons only cast ray-traced shadows on their visible side. This is due to the method LightWave uses to trace a ray from the camera to the object, and then to a light. This ray needs to be able to "see" a polygon's visible side to know whether a polygon is between it and a light source, and thus, if there should be a shadow. If viewed from the light's point of view, it's possible to see a shadow cast by an invisible polygon.

Click the Texture image button and select the EarthClouds-clip image. This image is a high-contrast version of the cloud image, which will remove the transparent areas between our clouds. As with the transparency map, we'll need to activate the Negative Image option. Accept this texture and do another test render. This time the earth will render a bit faster.

STEP 52: Our clouds look all right the way they are, but they lack depth. We could add a bump map to them, but that would only show up along the terminator since the Sharp Terminator option will wash them out everywhere else. Instead, we'll add real depth to them. Flip back over to Modeler, where our unsurfaced cloud object should still be loaded. Select the Scale tool again and open its Numeric Panel. Scale this object up by 100.05% and then open the Surface Panel. Create a new surface called Cloud-Tops and click Apply. Use the Put command to send this object to Layout as well, but name this one **Earth-Cloudtops.lwo** (Figure 2-30).

FIGURE 2-30 A secondary cloud layer adds a sense of depth and volume to the cloud without resorting to a Bump Map.

STEP 53: Switch back to Layout, and once again you'll see a white ball where our earth used to be. This new object will be basically a copy of the first cloud object, but with a different map. Open the Surface Panel, and select the Clouds surface we finished earlier. Click the Render button on the Sample strip to the right, then select the newer Cloud-Tops surface. Click on the texture sample we just created and click OK on the requester that pops up. This just copied the Clouds surface to this new one, saving a few extra steps. Click the Texture button for the Transparency Level and click the Texture Image button. Select the image called Earth-Clouds-Top then click Use Texture. This image is a slightly modified version of the EarthClouds image, but with thinner cloud patterns to simulate the tops of large clouds.

STEP 54: Open the Objects Panel and select this new object. Click the Clip Map button and apply the EarthClouds-Clip image as a Spherical Map, just as we did with the first cloud object. Make sure the Negative Image option is set, and then click Use Texture. Deactivate the Self-Shadow option for this object as well. This not only helps speed up rendering, but also prevents render errors that can occur with self-shadowing, double-sided polygons, which can show up as random black dots or as black polygons. Close this panel and parent this object to the **EarthClouds.lwo** object, then do another test render. This time, the clouds will appear to have thickness to them since the top layer of clouds is now casting shadows on the layer below, providing a slightly volumetric look. This effect can be further enhanced by adding more layers, but at a severe cost in render times.

We could simply combine these two spheres into a single object, but there is a drawback. Doing so would mean we would have to reactivate the Self-Shadow option, and likely reintroduce those render errors. By keeping the two layers as separate objects, we can "turn off" one layer for quick tests by raising the object's Dissolve level to 100%, then turn it back on for the final render.

STEP 55: Save the Cloud-Tops object again, and then save this scene to preserve the object hierarchy and Clip Map information. Again, switch back to Modeler, where we'll build our sky.

STEP 56: There are two ways we can build a sky, but we'll cover the simpler one first. Generally, a sky is done in much the same way as the one on the planet that appears in the SpaceFighters scene we've all seen by now. That's simply a sphere with Edge Transparency applied. The technique is used quite often, but we'll improve on it a little here. But first, we need our sky object, and wouldn't you know it, there already happens to be a sphere sitting in Modeler. Select the Scale tool, and scale this by a factor of 103% to make it a fair bit larger than our CloudTops, then open the Surface Panel. Name this surface Sky, then export this as a new object to Layout called **Earth-Sky.lwo** by clicking the Put button under the Objects menu.

STEP 57: Flip back to Layout once again and open the Surface Panel there. Select the Sky surface and change the color to R: 95 G: 110 B: 170 and activate both the Sharp Terminator and the Additive options. Also raise the Transparency to 90% and make sure the Smoothing and Double Sided options are active. Click the Advanced Options tab and click the Opaque button to set the Edge Transparency. This now creates a transparent "shell" around our earth that is nearly invisible when viewed straight on, but becomes brighter toward the horizon (Figure 2-31). Unfortunately, the outer edge of this atmosphere is quite hard, so let's fix that. Click the top Shader Plugin slot and select the LW_FastFresnel shader. Click the Option button beside it, and when the interface opens turn off all the options except the Transparency button. Raise the Transparency value to 1000% (it can take values outside the normal 0–100 range), and increase the Minimum Glancing Angle to 74. This will make the very edge of the sphere become transparent again, softening the outer edge.

FIGURE 2-31 The same earth, this time with an atmospheric shell, gets an additional intensity boost.

STEP 58: While we're here, we can change the color of sky as its angle changes to better simulate a real atmosphere. Click the second plugin slot and select the LW_ThinFilm shader. Click the Options button to open its interface and you will see a thin color gradient across the top of the panel. Clicking anywhere in this gradient will change the value for the Primary Wavelength immediately below. This is the color that will be applied to the parts of a surface that face directly at the camera, and the color will gradually shift to the left on this gradient, the distance specified by the Angle Variation, as the surface angle increases to a glancing angle. We want our surface to be a very light blue, like we already have, and have this shift towards the purple end of the spectrum at the horizon. Change the Primary Wavelength to 500 nm, and then set the Angle Variations to −75 nm. This negative amount will shift the color to the right instead of the left. We'll keep the Blend button active and leave the percentage set to 50% so these colors don't become too intense. Click OK, then render a test to see these effects on our planet (Figure 2-32).

FIGURE 2-32 The same atmosphere after having the edges made more transparent and receiving a slight color shift from the Thin Film shader.

STEP 59: You'll notice that this time, the atmosphere didn't appear as a thick band around the planet. However, this surface is a bit bright, so let's tone that down a bit. Click the Basic Parameters tab on the Surface Panel and lower the Diffuse Level to 50% (or lower). This will darken the entire sky, and since this surface is additive, it will affect the surfaces behind equally less.

STEP 60: Finally, we'll speed this up a bit by switching to the Objects Panel and deactivating the Self Shadow and the Cast Shadow options for this sky object. Click the Save Object button to preserve the sky surface, then close the panel. Parent the Sky to the Earth, and then save this scene once again. A new test render will show a much better sky, which makes the earth's surface almost appear to glow.

This sky works best for the more distant shots of Earth, but it does hold up relatively well for the many closer views as well. Unfortunately, these closer views may tend to start revealing the atmosphere for what it is, a thin polygonal surface floating just above the ground. This surface also doesn't react to the light the way a real atmosphere does. By now, we've all seen images of a sunrise from behind a planet, where the atmosphere first begins to brighten in an intense arc just before the sun appears. This is caused by sunlight scattering through the atmosphere, and this polygonal surface just isn't capable of that effect—but Steamer is!

STEP 61: Go back to modeler and switch to an empty layer. We'll create our improved sky by creating a very small cube. This might sound a bit strange, but if you ever looked closely at how Steamer works on particles, you'll see that a Steamer "sphere" shrouds each particle. If we were to place just one of these spheres inside our earth and make it slightly larger than the earth's diameter, it should poke through the surface and surround the planet. So, why are we creating a cube instead of using a simple null object? Steamer doesn't like nulls. Instead, it seems to require that an object have at least two points before it will apply its effects to it. We'll use a cube, which is made from eight points, to create a good, evenly spaced group of points that we'll apply Steamer to. Select the Box tool and open its Numeric Panel. We'll create a very small box so that the Steamer effects will all overlap into one seamless sphere. The following values will create that box:

	Low (mm)	High (mm)	Segments
X	−0.1	0.1	1
Y	−0.1	0.1	1
Z	−0.1	0.1	1

Click the OK button to accept these values, then hit the Enter key to create the box. We don't need the polygons on this box, so type "k" to remove them without losing the points they're connected to. That's it for this object, so click the Put button once again, and save this object as **SteamerAtmosphere.lwo**.

STEP 62: Go back to Layout and open the Objects Panel. We can remove the old sky object we just surfaced and select the new SteamerAtmosphere object instead. Click the Deformations tab and a set of 4 plugin slots will appear. Click on the first one and select the LW_SteamyParticles plugin. Close this panel and open the Effects Panel next. Click the Image Processing tab, then click the top Pixel Filter plugin slot and select the Steamer plugin. Click the Options button next to it to open the Steamer interface. Click the Edit Object button, which is the third button down the left side of the panel, and select the SteamerAtmosphere object in the drop-down list. Click the Activate button, and then click OK to close the panel for now. Close the Effects Panel and parent this steamer object to the Earth. Render a low-resolution test image so Steamer "knows" what the scene looks like for its internal preview.

STEP 63: When the test render is done, open the Steamer Panel again. The first thing we'll do is to select an active light so our sky knows where the sunlight is coming from. Click the Active Light button and select the only light we currently have in the scene. Now we'll set the size of our atmosphere. We built our globe with a radius of a half-meter, so our atmosphere will have to be slightly larger. Deactivate the Automatic Sizing option and change the radius to 0.53 meters.

STEP 64: If you click the Refresh button below the Preview window, you won't see much of a sky appear yet. The current falloff setting has the sky become nearly invisible before it even reaches the surface. To fix that, lower the Falloff value to −4, which will give the Steamer spheres a harder edge. We'll leave the Mode set to Additive since this is the most intense of the four possible settings. The preview will show a slight improvement, but we're not quite finished. We still need to make this sky blue, so, in the next section, change the color to H: 150 S: 150 V: 255 and raise the Luminosity to 400%. Now we're done.

By raising the Luminosity, we increased the sharpness of the edge of the Steamer spheres even more. This effect would normally render as a pure white with a very thin bluish edge, which can be seen in the Preview by deactivating the Use Z-Buffer option. When we render this for real, the earth's surface renders just above this "hot" area, allowing only the thin blue surface of the Steamer spheres to be visible. You'll also notice that Steamer adds a gradual intensity change toward the horizon, similar to the one we used the Fast Fresnel shader for (Figure 2-33). Since this sky is a volumetric effect, we could fly our camera through it, but being that close to the surface would make the planet's surface look blurred and chunky because of the relatively low resolution of the map we used.

FIGURE 2-33 The earth again, this time with a Steamer Atmosphere. Notice how the atmosphere gradually lightens the surface toward the horizon, similar to the sky object we created earlier.

STEP 65: There is one last thing to be aware of. If you render a view in which the clouds are prominent, you may notice that they seem to have developed a dark outline (Figure 2-34). Since Steamer is a post process, it's not normally visible through transparent surfaces, like our cloud surfaces. The camera cannot look through the cloud surface to see the Steamer effects below. It can, however, see through the clip mapped sections fine. One solution would be to apply the Steamy Shader plugin to the cloud surfaces, but this can drastically increase render times. The better solution is to open the Object Panel again, and remove the clip maps from the two Cloud objects. This won't make the sky visible through the clouds, but it will spread the darkening effect over the entire sphere, thus eliminating the outline. A final test render will show a marked improvement (Figure 2-35).

FIGURE 2-34 A closeup of the clouds through the Steamer atmosphere. Notice the dark edge that appears, tracing the outline of the clip map that's applied.

Tip: If you wish to use the Steamer atmosphere on planets with a different size, simply multiply Steamer's radius by the appropriate size factor (i.e., a 100-meter-diameter planet would require a 53-meter Steamer Radius). In addition, the Luminosity value will need to be *divided* by that same factor. This means our 100-meter planet would have a Steamer luminosity of only 4% (400/100).

FIGURE 2-35 The same earth, this time backlit, showing a sunrise from space. Notice how the atmosphere along the horizon is much more intense in this image.

Since this sky is created entirely by Steamer, this small SteamerAtmosphere object can be used to create an atmospheric haze for virtually any planet, just by altering the Steamer parameters. By changing the color to a greenish gray, we can make the earth look like it was invaded by the Borg. Red would give it a more Martian appearance, or we could make it look as if World War III just happened.

In addition, through the use of the supplied maps, many styles of globes are possible, from simple black-and-white ones to more intricate "floating continents." The Specular and Alpha maps are ideal for use as Texture Alpha Images, opening a wide range of possibilities through creative texture layering. Feel free to experiment since that is an excellent way to learn and to develop techniques.

Tip: Spheres, although they are among the simplest objects, are also the most finicky and tend to require a higher level of subdivision than other objects. Polygon corners tend to be more apparent along the edges of spheres, particularly when viewed up-close, which is quite frequent when dealing with planets. When building planets, model them with the viewing distance in mind. The closer the camera will get, the higher the level of detail. A tessellation level of 3 is good for average shots, but for anything close, consider using a level of 4. A level 5 tessellation is better for extreme closeups, but at this level, the polygon count starts getting extremely high. At this point, it's a good practice to model only the part of the globe that will be visible in the animation.

Building a Castle, Part I

Dave Jerrard

OVERVIEW

Castles have always inspired wonder and instilled a sense of awe. They seem to show up everywhere in literature and film, from the famous Camelot to the infamous Nottingham. They come in all shapes and sizes, from boxy-looking keeps to vast, sprawling palaces, like the Palace of Versailles, to the majestic multi-spired castle at Disney World. Even Jabba the Hut had his own castle in *Return of the Jedi*, so why can't we? Well, we can.

These next two chapters will cover the basics of designing and building a castle, starting with the simple layout and construction in this chapter, then continuing on with the more advanced surfacing and scene setup in the next chapter. While it's beyond the scope of this book to cover every detail or design, we will cover the basic design elements, which can then be assembled to create an endless variety of castles. Castles are quite large; many contained entire villages and towns within their walls. For simplicity's sake, we'll focus on the castle proper, which most people visualize when they think of castles.

In this tutorial you will use:

- LightWave Modeler
- Boolean operations

What you will need:

- Moderate modeling skills
- Some free time
- Installed Modeler Plugins: Dublside.p

What you will learn:

- Basic to advanced modeling techniques
- Advanced use of Bevel and Smooth Shift

STEP 1: Load Modeler and zoom the grid size to 2 meters to give enough space to work in. Most of our work will be done using two surfaces. Type "q" to open the Surface Panel and create a new surface name called "Walls," then click Apply. We'll start our castle by creating one of its best known features, a tower. These can be of endless shapes, but the most common is the round tower with a flanged top studded with battlements. The first thing we'll do then is to create a cylinder. Select the Disc tool and type "n" to open the Numeric panel. Increase the number of Sides to 40 and set the Axis to Y. We'll be resting this on the ground, so make the Bottom 0 meter and the top 18 meters. This gives us a tower approximately 6 stories tall. Make the Radius of this tower 6 meters and click OK. Hit the "Enter" key to create the cylinder. This just created the main body of the tower, so let's add the top.

STEP 2: Flip to an empty layer and place the tower body in the background for reference. We're going to draw out a profile polygon, which we'll lathe to form the top of the tower. Drag the Face view to full screen and zoom in to the top of the tower body in the background. Select the Pen tool from the Objects menu and trace out a shape like the one in Figure 3-1, using the following coordinates:

Point #	X (m)	Y (m)
1	0	19
2	6	19
3	6	20
4	6.5	20
5	6.5	18
6	5.5	16
7	0	16

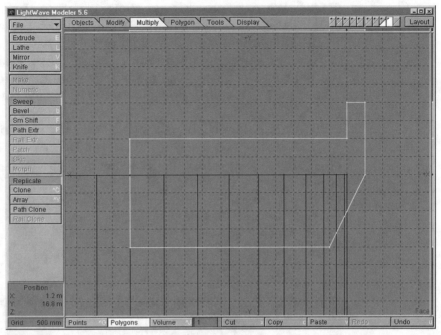

FIGURE 3-1 The lathe template for the top of our first tower. The rest of our towers will be based on this first one.

Fact: These towers were exceptional defensive systems of the time, providing an elevated platform for fighting the enemy while shielding defenders from arrows with their trademark stone battlements. Below these were small holes in the floor called machicolations, which led through to the underside of this platform, through which castle defenders would drop rocks and pour boiling oil upon the enemy below without exposing themselves to enemy fire.

STEP 3: When this polygon is created, click the Multiply tab and select the Lathe tool. We'll lathe this so it has the same number of sides as the main body, so open the Numeric panel and enter 40 in the Sides field. Set the Axis to Y and set the center values to 0. Click OK and hit "Enter" to lathe this polygon. There is a reason why we didn't just create the tower and this top at the same time, which will become clear later.

STEP 4: We currently have a short 1-meter-tall wall around the edge of this platform, which is a bit short to use as an effective shield again enemy archers. We'll place our battlements on top of this by first selecting all the top polygons of this wall. Simply use the right mouse button to drag a lasso around the top edge in the Face view. Next, resize the views so the Top view is full screen and type Shift-a to fit the selected polygons to this view. Now, deselect every other polygon, so you have 20 selected polygons alternating with 20 unselected ones, as shown in Figure 3-2. These selected polygons will become our battlements. Type Shift-f to open the Smooth Shift tool. We'll make these battlements 3/4 of a meter taller than the wall, so enter a value of 0.75 for the Offset and click OK. You should now have a ring of 20 battlements along the top of this wall.

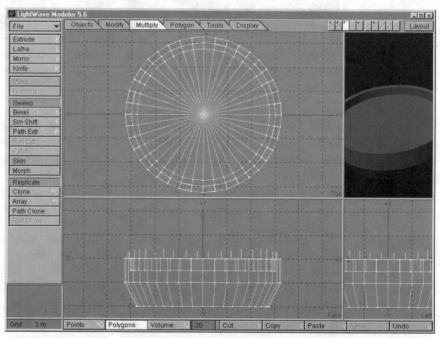

FIGURE 3-2 The selected polygons ready to be Smooth Shifted to form the battlements.

STEP 5: These battlements, as they are right now, could prove quite hazardous, so let's round off those corners a bit by adding a bevel. The top polygon of each battlement should still be selected, so type "b" to open the Bevel tool. Enter a value of 0.05 to 0.2 m (experiment) for both the Inset and the Shift. Make sure the Edges are set to Inner and that the Surface is set to Source. Click OK and you will have safer-looking battlements, like those in Figure 3-3.

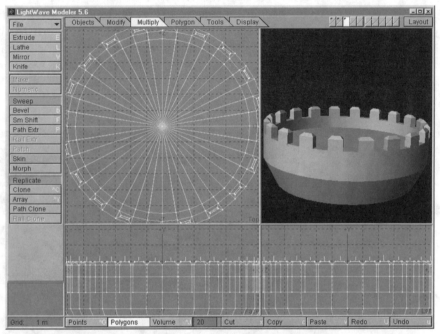

FIGURE 3-3 While the Smooth Shifted polygons are still selected, they're beveled to round off the sharp corners.

STEP 6: To finish off our battlements, we'll round the sides in a similar fashion. Holding the Shift key and working in the top view, we'll select more polygons. This time we want only the polygons that form the spaces between the battlements, so drag the pointer through the center of the outermost ring of polygons, taking care not to select any polygons that form the inner or outer wall. Note, however, that you will end up selecting the polygons that form the tapered surface below, as well as the beveled top we just created, which is fine. These will be deselected later. Resize the views so you can see the bottom of this section from the side and drag out a lasso around the bottom half of this section to deselect the tapered polygons. Do the same around the top, to deselect the polygons we created with the bevel in the previous step, leaving only 60 polygons selected (Figure 3-4). Type the "b" key again to open the Bevel tool and enter a value of 5 cm for both the Inset and the Shift, then click OK. You should now have a series of nicely beveled battlements, as in Figure 3-5.

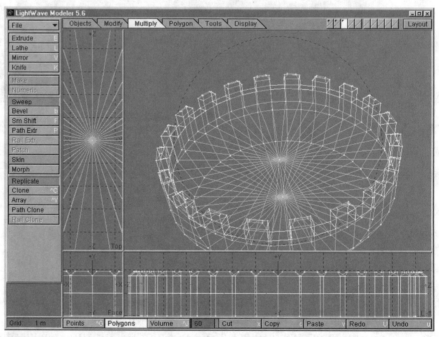

FIGURE 3-4 A 3D wireframe shows the selected polygons that we'll be beveling to finish off the battlements.

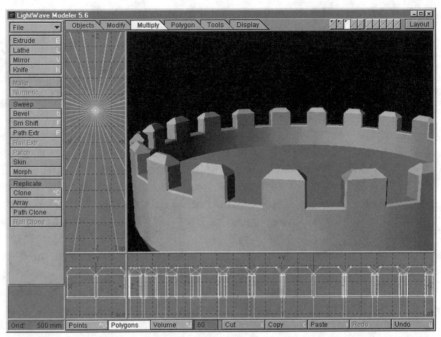

FIGURE 3-5 The completed battlements ready to shield bold castle defenders.

STEP 7: Here's why we built this top as a separate object. We're going to use Booleans to create machicolations, or holes, in the underside of this platform, at the same time creating a ring of decorative arches. To do this, we need a "cutter," so flip to a new layer and place this platform in the background. Select the Disc tool again, and open its Numeric Panel. Click the Reset button to erase the previous settings and enter the following values:

Sides:	24		Center (m)	Radii (m)
Segments:	1	X	0	0.8
Top:	−7 m	Y	17	0.8
Bottom:	−5 m	Z	0	0.8
Axis:	Z			

Click OK and hit Enter to create a small horizontal cylinder that passes through the slanted edge of our tower platform. Since we're going to cut an arch, we'll need to extend one half of this cylinder downward to get the additional height we'll need.

STEP 8: Click the Polygons button at the bottom of the screen both to drop the Disc tool and be sure we're in Polygon Edit mode. In the Face view, use the right mouse button to drag a lasso around the 12 polygons that make up the lower half of this cylinder. Click the Polygon tab at the top of the screen and then click on the Merge button in the Revise section. This will merge the selected polygons, creating what is now a very distorted polygon. Don't worry about it for now, since it will be corrected next. Click the Points button at the bottom of the screen to switch to Point Edit mode. Once again, drag a lasso around the 22 points that form the bottom half of the cylinder, and then hit the Delete key. We have now effectively cut this cylinder in half and kept it as a solid object in doing so. Now we can extend that bottom a bit.

STEP 9: Switch back to Polygon Edit mode, and you should see the bottom polygon already highlighted. Type Shift-f to activate the Smooth Shift tool again. This time, enter a value of 0.5 m for the Offset and click OK (Figure 3-6). Our "cutter" is ready for action—almost.

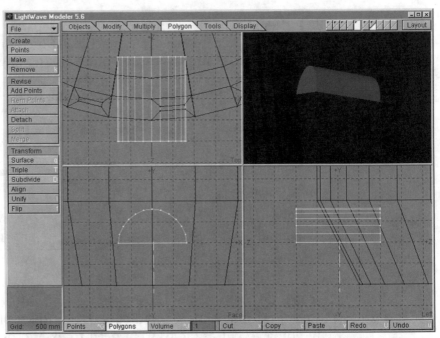

FIGURE 3-6 Our decorative arches will start with a very basic shape.

STEP 10: We're going to place 20 of these arches around the tower, one for each battlement above. Rather than cut them one at a time, we'll do them all at once. Deselect everything and click the Multiply tab. Select the Array button and then click the Radial button in the panel that opens up. This is similar to using the Rotation values of the Clone tool, but simpler. We want 20 of these cutters, all evenly spaced around the tower, so enter 20 for the Number. The Axis should be set to Y and the center values should all be set to 0. Click OK and you should have what appears to be a circle of pup tents (Figure 3-7).

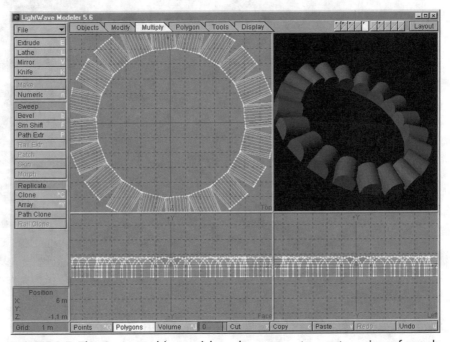

FIGURE 3-7 The Array tool is a quick and easy way to create a ring of evenly spaced copies of an object.

STEP 11: Finally, rotate these slightly so they line up directly under the battlements above. Type the "y" key and hit "n" to open the Rotate tool's Numeric panel. Enter a value of 4.5 degrees and set the Axis to Y. The Center values should all be 0, then hit OK.

STEP 12: Since we put the tower in the background, type the apostrophe key to swap layers. This will put the pup tents in the background, where we need them. Type Shift-b to open the Boolean panel and select the Subtract button. Click OK and in a few seconds, a series of arches will be cut into the sides of the tower (Figure 3-8).

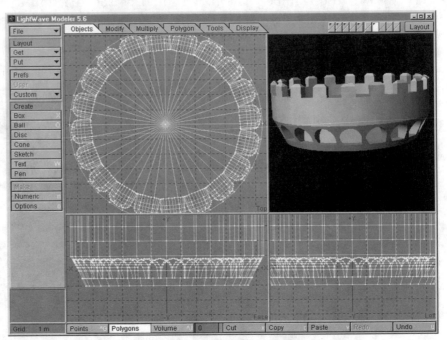

FIGURE 3-8 The top of the tower after subtracting the pup tents.

STEP 13: Now we can attach this section to the main tower body. Select the layer that contains the main body we created in Step 1 as the background layer, with the tower top as the foreground. Since we just did a Boolean operation on this section, and we're about to do another one, be sure to merge points by typing "m". Booleans always leave the new polygons they create detached from the rest of the object. Now, type Shift-b again, and this time, click the Union button, then click OK (Figure 3-9).

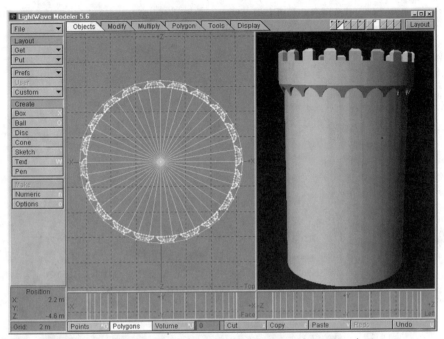

FIGURE 3-9 The tower top, in its final position atop the tower base.

To make these arches, properly called machicolations, stand out a bit more later, drag a lasso around this entire tapered section to select the polygons, then open the Surface panel. Enter a new surface name of Stone and click Apply. Deselect everything and Merge Points again, then save this object as **Tower.lwo.**

These towers are typically placed at every corner of the outer walls of a castle complex, where they give archers stationed on them a clear line of sight along the walls, thereby making it impossible for attackers to hide against them. Some towers would even have flared bottoms or wedges that would force attackers rounding the tower do so several feet from the main wall, where they would be open to attack from both the tower above them and the adjoining walls and neighboring towers. These wedges were a very simple defense mechanism, and they're easy to create here as well.

STEP 14: Place this tower in a background layer, then select the Box tool and drag out a box across the bottom of the tower. This box should be 6 meters tall and 13 meters in both the X and Z dimensions.

	Low (m)	High (m)
X	−6.5	6.5
Y	0	6
Z	−6.5	6.5

Hit Enter to create this box (Figure 3-10). Click the Modify tab and select the Taper 1 tool. In the Top view, place the pointer in the center of the tower and drag to the left to taper the top of this box inward until its Scale Factor is 65% (Figure 3-11). Type "q" to open the Change Surfaces panel and change the surface of this box back to the "Walls" surface, then click Apply.

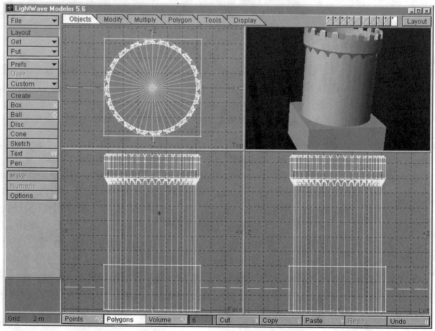

FIGURE 3-10 The position of the box that will become the defensive wedges at the bottom of the tower.

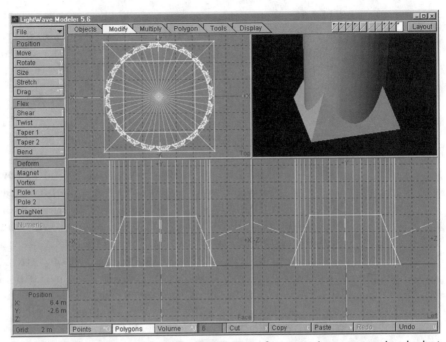

FIGURE 3-11 The same box as in Figure 3-10 after tapering creates simple, but effective, barriers that prevent enemies from seeking shelter against the tower wall.

STEP 15: We'll use Booleans to attach this wedge to the tower, so swap layers by typing the apostrophe key. We'll need to make one small adjustment first. Boolean operations don't work well when they have to deal with polygons that share the same plane, which we have here. The base of the tower is on the plane as the bottom polygon of the wedge. This will cause some confusion for Modeler since it won't be able to tell which of these two surfaces to consider as the outside surface. We can prevent that confusion by simply selecting the bottom polygon of this tower and raising it slightly. Make sure this is the only polygon that's selected and type "t". Then simply drag this polygon up on the Y axis about half a meter. This will ensure that Modeler makes no mistake that this surface is "inside" the object in the background layer. Deselect everything, then type Shift-b to activate the Boolean panel. Click the Union button and click OK. When the Boolean is completed, hit "m" to merge points. This tower is finished for now. We'll add windows and arrow slits later, after we've put it in place on the rest of the castle.

STEP 16: Save this as **Tower-Wedged.lwo** so we have it for later.

Many castles were built over the span of centuries, with some construction dating as far back as the 11th century while surrounded by more recent additions. This has the effect of multiple styles being incorporated into the castle design, representing the latest in castle defense technology appearing alongside much older designs. Why should our castle be any different? We'll include a second tower design into this castle.

STEP 17: Switch to an empty layer and load the **Tower.lwo** object we saved in Step 13. This tower will be a simpler design that uses a flared base instead of the wedges. Select the bottom polygon of this tower and hit "t" to activate the Move tool. Drag this polygon upward 3 meters, then type "b" to activate the Bevel tool. Enter a value of −1 meter for the Inset and 3-meter for the Shift. Click OK and the tower will once again rest on the ground plane, but this time, with a slightly wider base (Figure 3-12). This flare would have had the same effect as the wedges, keeping invaders away from the wall, where they were open to archer fire from above. Save this tower as **Tower-Flare.lwo.**

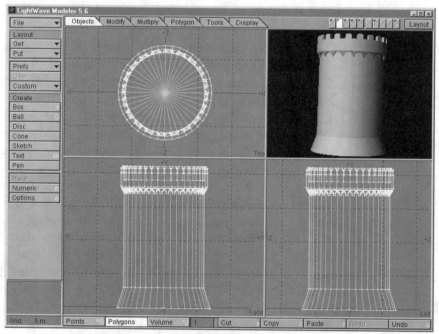

FIGURE 3-12 An alternative design, equally effective and simple to create.

Before we build our main structure, we should mark out the area our castle will encompass. Just as with a real castle, we'll do this by placing the outer walls to define the castle's perimeter. These walls provided not only a defensive barrier, but also an efficient platform to post men at arms, who would be able to counterattack the enemy before they could reach the wall. In fact, many castles would have a network of walls, each becoming taller and more difficult to pass as they neared the main structures. This network also served to help trap the invading enemy in tight quarters while providing the defenders an unobstructed line of fire. Our castle won't be quite so grandiose, but the design elements we'll cover here will also apply to much larger castles as well.

STEP 18: For simplicity, we'll build a rectangular wall around our castle site. This wall will have a walkway along the top with shielding battlements on either side to make this wall an effective defense platform. We'll also decorate this wall a bit by adding machicolations along the outward facing of the wall, so we'll need a slight overhang. Since this is a simple four-sided structure, we can draw a profile and simply lathe it with four sides. Switch to an empty layer and use the Pen tool to draw out a polygon in the Face view. The following values will create our wall profile (Figure 3-13):

Point #	X (m)	Y (m)
1	40	0
2	40	14.75
3	40.5	14.75
4	40.5	13
5	42.5	13
6	42.5	14.75
7	43	14.75
8	43	12.5
9	42.5	12
10	42.5	0

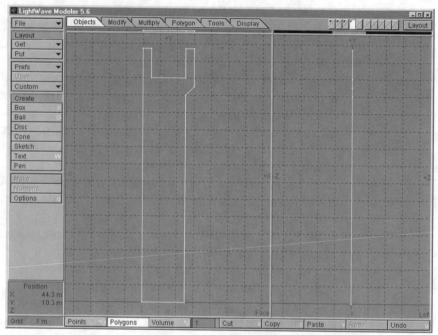

FIGURE 3-13 A simple profile, which will become the outer wall.

STEP 19: We're going to lathe this profile to form a square wall 86 meters across, but we want the sides to be aligned with the X and Z axes. If we were to lathe this profile as it exists now, we would have walls that are all at 45 degrees. This polygon will also be used to create the corners of the walls, and since it will be at a 45-degree angle to them, they would tend to be thinner than we want. We'll fix that by shearing our polygon to where we'll place a corner. Under the Modify menu, click the Shear tool. To turn this polygon so it's at a 45-degree angle, we'll need to shear the outer edge a distance equal to the polygon's width. This polygon is 3 meters wide, but we'll also need to position it after shearing. We can accomplish both steps with the Shear operation and shear the polygon from the center of what will become our courtyard. Type "n" to open the Shear tool's Numeric panel. The first thing to set here is the Shear Axis, which will be the X axis. Next, change the Range to Fixed. Since we'll be shearing this from the center, set the Low value to 0 and the high value to 43, which is the same as the right-most edge of our profile polygon. Make sure the Preset curve is Linear, then set the Offset amount, which will be the same as the range, 43 m on the Z axis. The X and Y offset values should both be 0. Click OK and you should end up with a polygon that's sheared to a 45-degree angle (Figure 3-14).

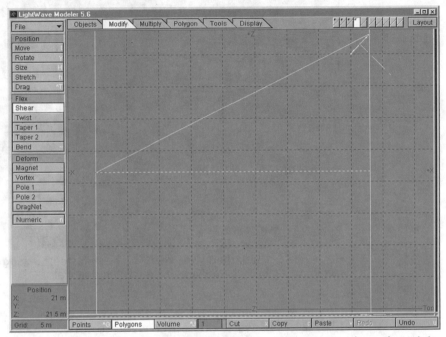

FIGURE 3-14 After Shearing, the profile is at a 45-degree angle to the origin, ready to be lathed.

Tip: We could have used any pair of matching values for the Shear tool's Range and Offset amounts, as long as they were equal to or greater than the right edge of the polygon.

STEP 20: Now we're ready to lathe this profile. Under the Multiply menu, click the Lathe tool and then type "n" to open its Numeric panel. Click the Reset button to make sure the tool is centered at the origin. Since we're going to make a 4-sided castle wall, the first thing we should do is to lower the number of sides to 4 here as well. Click the Y axis button, and then click OK. Hit the Enter key to perform the lathe. We'll now have a simple 4-sided wall with a walkway along the top (Figure 3-15).

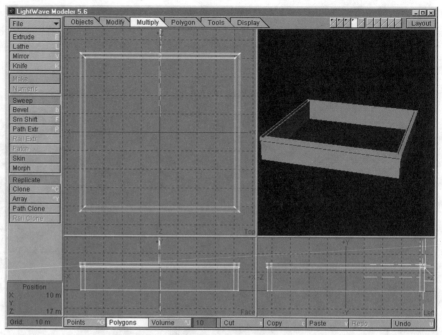

FIGURE 3-15 The lathed wall, ready to be adjusted for length. The selected section will merely be moved to stretch the side walls.

STEP 21: We want our outer walls to form a rectangular area, so drag a lasso around the polygons of one of the end walls, as shown in Figure 3-15. Select the Move tool by typing "t" and drag this wall 20 meters out from the center. Hold the CTRL key down to constrain the movement to the Z axis. Deselect everything, then click the Custom button under the Objects menu and select the Center 1D plugin. In the panel that opens, click the Z axis, then click OK. This will immediately recenter this wall on the Z axis for us.

STEP 22: Now that we have our wall all laid out, let's start adding the details. First, open the Change Surface panel and make sure the surface we're working with is the "Walls" surface, then click Apply. This will be the surface we'll be using for most of the exterior geometry, with most of the other exterior details being done with the "Stone" surface. Select the 4-angled polygons that form the overhang near the top of the wall and open the Surface Panel again. Change this to the Stone surface, then click Apply. This strip will become another set of machicolations, which we'll build next.

STEP 23: Switch to a new layer and place the outer walls in the background for now. We'll use Booleans to cut the holes into the walls, just as we did with the tower, but these will be slightly different. Select the Pen tool from the Objects menu and zoom into the corner of the wall in the background until the angled polygon fills the Face view. Draw out a simple shape that cuts across this polygon, which will define the shape of the holes we'll make. The following values were used to create the shape shown in Figure 3-16.

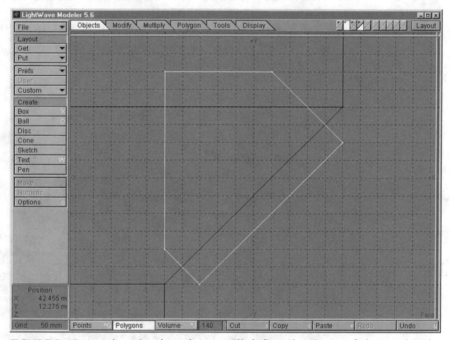

FIGURE 3-16 Another simple polygon will define the shape of the machicolations that will line the outer wall.

Point #	X (m)	Y (m)
1	42.5	12.6
2	42.8	12.6
3	43	12.4
4	42.6	12
5	42.5	12.1

STEP 24: Once the shape is drawn, we'll need to make it a solid. Click the Extrude button under the Multiply menu and open its numeric panel. Set the Axis to Z and change the Extent to 0.4 meters. Click OK and hit the Enter key to finish the extrusion. We now have the shape of our "cutter" object. All we need now is about 400 more to cover the 4 walls.

STEP 25: Click the Clone button under the Multiply menu, which we'll use to make several evenly spaced duplicates of this cutter. In the panel that opens, set the number of clones to 99, which will give us a total of 100 of these cutters, including the original. Finally, set the Offset for the Z axis to 1.5 meters, then click OK. This will create a row of evenly spaced cutters (Figure 3-17).

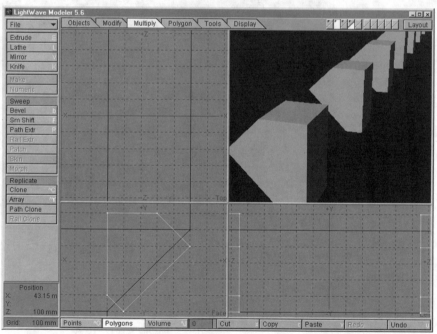

FIGURE 3-17 After cloning, we have a long row of identical "cutter" objects.

STEP 26: This row of cutters needs to be centered against the wall before we actually use it, so go back to the Objects menu and click the Custom button. Select the Center 1D plugin, which should be right under the mouse since we just used it in Step 21, and again, we'll center on the Z axis. Click OK and the cutters will extend along the length of the wall and a bit past. This is fine since we just wanted to be sure we'd have enough for the job. Now we need to make a similar set for the opposite wall.

STEP 27: Under the Multiply menu, select the Mirror tool. Type "n" to open the tool's Numeric panel and set the Plane to the X axis and the position to 0. Click OK and then hit Enter. This will give us 2 rows of cutters, but we still need 2 more for the shorter walls. Copy these by typing "c" and switch to a new layer. Paste the cutters in this layer, and delete the left row. In the Top view, place the mouse pointer over the very center, so its X and Z values are both 0, then type the "e" key. This will rotate everything 90 degrees counterclockwise centered on the pointer's location.

Now we just have to line these cutters up with the shorter wall. We moved one of the shorter walls 20 meters out earlier, then centered everything, so that means we'll need to move these cutters 10 meters to match up. Place the layer containing the walls in the background and zoom in toward the cutters in the Side view. Type "t" to select the Move tool and drag these cutters 10 meters on the Z axis. They should now line up, just as the first set did. Mirror these cutters on the Z axis, then copy them to the previous layer with the first set of cutters. All that remains is to trim off the excess cutters that extend past the walls. Use the Lasso to select the cutters at each corner, then type the "]" key to be sure no polygons were missed, then hit the Delete key. Your corners should now look like those in Figure 3-18.

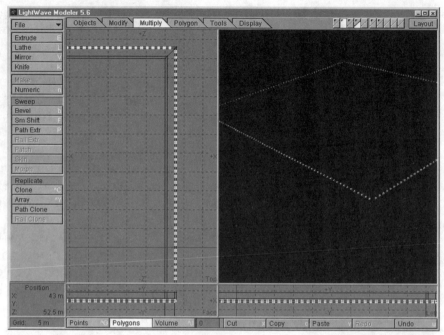

FIGURE 3-18 All our cutters are ready for action. Note that the excess cutters have been removed at the corners.

STEP 28: Now we're ready to cut the holes into the walls. Switch back to the layer with our outer walls and place the cutters into the background. To speed things up, select the 4 polygons that have the Stone surface again, then type Shift-b. Select the Subtract button on the Boolean Panel, then click OK. In a few seconds, the angled ledge of the wall will have a series of evenly spaced holes (Figure 3-19). The last thing we need to do here is merge points, so type "m" and then click OK.

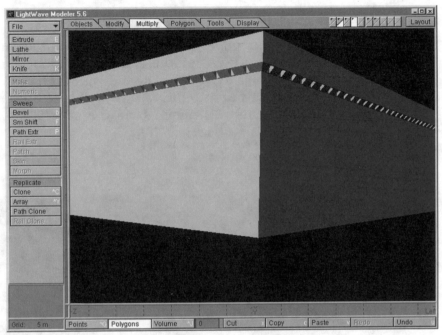

FIGURE 3-19 The wall after the Boolean Subtract.

STEP 29: Now that we have the machicolations built, we need to add the battlements on the tops of these walls. Switch to a new layer and place the layer with the walls in the background. Open the Surface panel and change the current surface to "Walls" and click Apply. We're going to create another series of objects that we'll use to cut the slots between the battlements, so click the Box tool under the Objects panel, then open its Numeric panel. Enter the following values, which will create a long thin box that will span the width of the walls.

	Low (m)	High (m)
X	−60.0	60.0
Y	14.0	16.0
Z	−0.3	0.3

Click OK, then hit the Enter key to create this box. Now we need several more copies to cover the length of these walls. Click the Clone tool under the Multiply menu. In the panel that opens, enter a value of 24 for the Number of Clones and Offset of 4 meters on the Z axis. Click OK and you will have what appears to be a series of beams. Once again, we'll need to center these, so open the Center 1D plugin from the Objects menu, and center this on the Z axis (Figure 3-20).

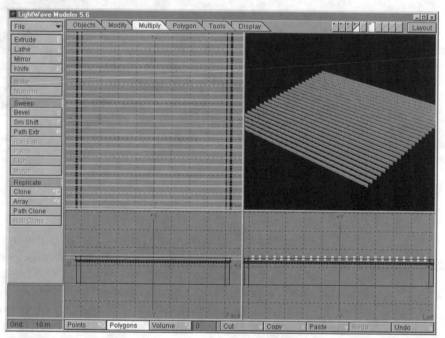

FIGURE 3-20 The first set of "beams" that we'll use to cut the slots between the battlements.

STEP 30: Now we're ready to cut our battlements, so type the apostrophe key to swap layers. In the side view, select the top edge of the walls, which will select 12 polygons, then type Shift-b to open the Boolean panel. Select the Subtract button and click OK.

In a few seconds, you will have the first set of battlements built along the tops of the long walls (Figure 3-21). Type "m" to merge points since these new polygons will not be attached to the rest of the walls yet, and we're about to do another Boolean.

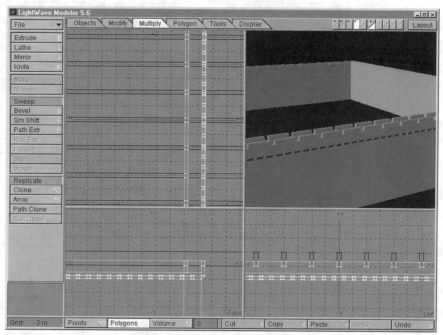

FIGURE 3-21 After another Boolean operation, we have the familiar battlement block design along the walls.

STEP 31: Type the apostrophe key again to swap back to the layer with the beams. Using the Top view, place the mouse pointer at the origin and type the "e" or the "r" key to rotate the beams 90 degrees. Since the walls we're about to cut are shorter, we can delete a few beams we don't need. Select the 3 beams at each end (Figure 3-22) and delete them. Swap layers once again so the beams are in the background.

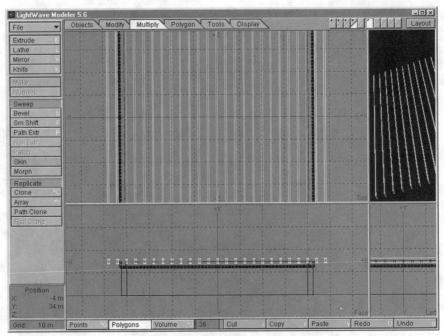

FIGURE 3-22 The beams we are about to use to cut the shorter walls. Note the selected beams on either end, which we don't need for these walls.

STEP 32: In the Face view, select the top edge of the walls, so once again, 12 polygons are selected, then type Shift-b. Click OK and in a few more seconds, our battlements will all be created. Again, follow this with a Merge Points.

STEP 33: All we have left to do on these battlements is to smooth them out with a slight bevel. In the Face view, use the lasso to select the polygons that form the tops and the spaces between the battlements (Figure 3-23). Type "b" to open the Bevel tool and enter a value of 0.05 meters for both the Inset and the Shift, then click OK. You will now have a series of nice wide, beveled battlements along the tops of the walls (Figure 3-24).

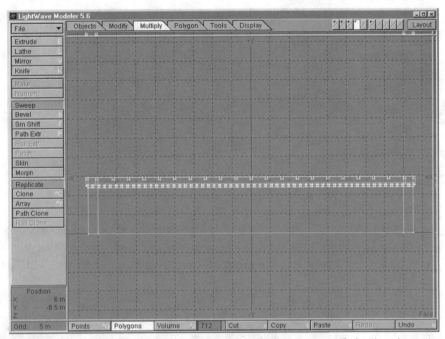

FIGURE 3-23 The polygons that form the sides and tops of the battlements are selected, ready to be beveled.

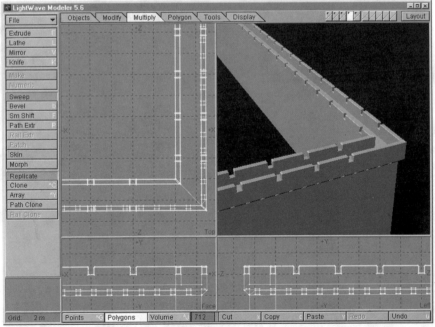

FIGURE 3-24 A closeup of the corner after the bevel operation.

STEP 34: The last thing we have left to do on this wall is to create an opening for our gates, which we'll be creating later. This opening will also be created with a Boolean operation. Switch to an empty layer and select the Box tool from the Objects menu. Open the Numeric panel and enter the following values, which will create a box where we'll be placing a gatehouse a bit later.

	Low (m)	High (m)
X	−8	8
Y	−5	20
X	−60	−45

Click OK and hit the Enter key to create this box (Figure 3-25). Swap layers again and do another Boolean Subtract on the walls to create the opening. Merge points to keep this wall as a solid.

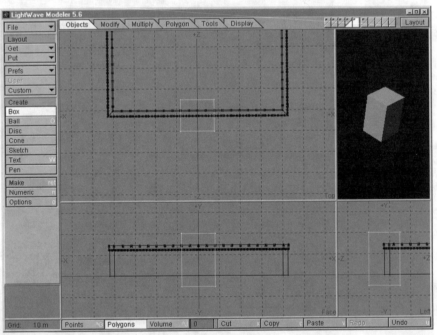

FIGURE 3-25 The placement of the block that we will use to cut an opening in the wall.

STEP 35: All that remains now is to position a tower at each corner. Swap layers again, and delete the box we created in the last step. Load the **Tower-Wedged.lwo** object that we created a while back and resize the Top view to full screen. Fit the contents to the view by typing "a", then type "t" to activate the Move tool. Move the tower to one of the corners, which will be 42.5 meters along the X axis and 52.5 meters on the Z axis. Select the Mirror tool and create a Mirror plane along the center of the Z axis and hit Enter to create a duplicate of this tower on the opposite side. Drag another Mirror Plane along the center of the X axis and hit Enter to create 2 more towers at the remaining corners. Finally, copy these towers to the same layer as the walls and save this as **OuterWall.lwo** (Figure 3-26).

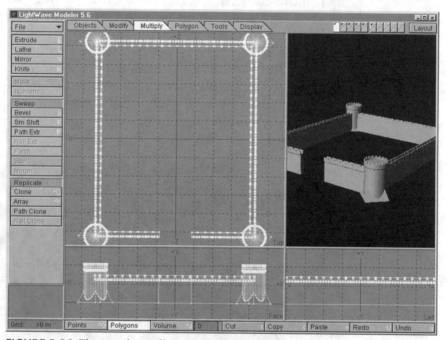

FIGURE 3-26 The castle wall, now with an opening where we will place a gatehouse later.

Now that we have our outer defense wall, we should really have something inside for it to defend. That would be our main building, which we'll design and build next. Again, these castle structures can be of any shape and size, but they tend to have the same general set of features, most notably, the towers, many with a large central tower. Our castle will have a fairly large base structure, which usually housed the smithy, stables, kitchens, and armories, as well as living quarters for the guards and other servants. In the floors above ground level will be the living quarters for the higher class, such as the nobility and knights, as well as the main hall, where they would feast and be entertained. This structure would be capped off with a series of battlements, just as with the outer walls and towers. In fact, it would frequently have its own towers, usually taller than the outer towers, to serve as additional backup defense.

We'll also place a smaller central structure on top of this main building to provide a base for our crowning central tower. We'll also circle this tower with a series of smaller towers. Not many castles had all these towers, but this is *our* castle, so we're going to splurge!

The first thing we need to do is to design a floor plan for the main structure. We won't go into any kind of interior details since most of these would not likely be seen. Instead, we'll just build the exterior walls and add external details as needed. This gives us greater freedom to play around with the design later. We'll place this main structure against the rear wall of the courtyard, though this isn't the only place it could be located. Figure 3-27 shows the design we'll be tackling.

FIGURE 3-27 The general design of our castle, which is created using the various elements we will build in this chapter.

STEP 36: Clear Modeler by clicking the File button in the top left corner and selecting the Clear option. Load the **OuterWall.lwo** object we just created, which we'll use as a background template for our main structure. This will also load in the 2 surfaces we've been using so everything will be consistent. Switch to an empty layer and place this Outer Wall in the background. Open the Surface Panel and set the Current Surface to "Walls."

STEP 37: We'll place this structure in the center of the rear wall to keep things simple. Drag the Top view to full screen and zoom in to the back wall in the background layer. Select the Pen tool and draw out a polygon like the one in Figure 3-28. The following values will duplicate this exactly.

Point #	X (m)	Z (m)
1	10	55
2	20	40
3	20	20
4	10	20
5	10	10
6	−10	10
7	−10	20
8	−20	20
9	−20	40
10	−10	55

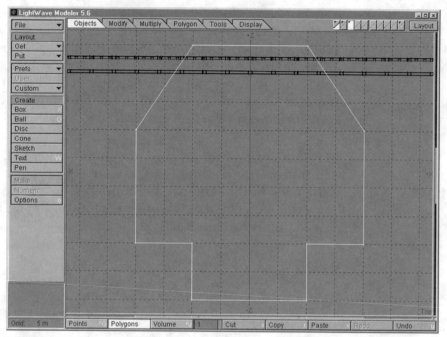

FIGURE 3-28 The basic floor plan of our main structure.

This polygon should be resting on the ground plane, so open the Set Value tool under the Tools menu and set the Axis to Y and enter 0 for the Value, then click OK. Now that we have the basic plan of the structure, we can extrude this to form the outer walls.

STEP 38: Under the Multiply menu, select the Extrude tool, then click on the Top view. This will set the Extrude Axis to Y and allow us to interactively adjust the amount of the extrusion, which will set the height of our building. We'll make this about 3 to 4 stories tall, so let's set the extent to 12 meters. Open the Numeric panel for this tool and ensure that the number Segments is set to 1 and click OK. Hit Enter to create the extrusion. Since our polygon was facing upward when we extruded it, the walls of our building will be facing inward. Type "f" to flip these so they face outward. This gives us a good representation of our main building (Figure 3-29).

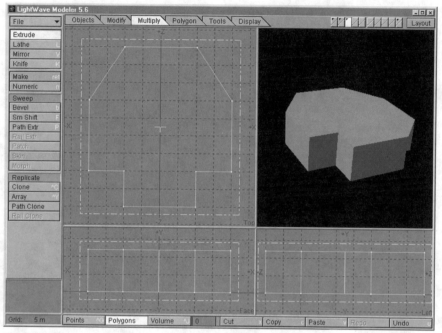

FIGURE 3-29 A simple extrusion turns a floorplan into a 3D structure.

We could start working on the roof details, like the machicolations and the battlements, but we'll do this later, when we can build 2 roofs for the price of 1. Let's move onto the second structure, which we'll use as a base for our central tower.

STEP 39: In this same layer, we'll build our upper structure, which will be in the form of a hexagon. Working in the Top view, use the Disc tool to create a 6-sided disc. Use the Numeric panel to enter the following values, which will place this disc on the same plane as the "roof" of our lower structure (Figure 3-30).

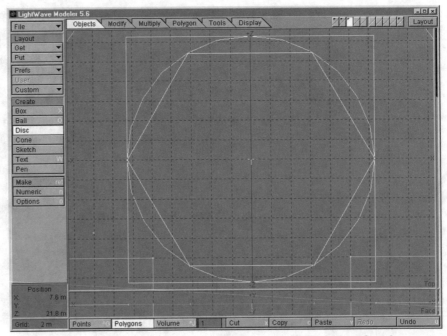

FIGURE 3-30 A 6-sided disc creates the hexagonal floorplan for the upper structure.

Sides:	6		Center (m)	Radii (m)
Segments:	1	X	0	12.5
Bottom:	12 m	Y	12	0.0
Top:	12 m	Z	30	12.5
Axis:	Y			

Once again, we'll extrude this shape to 12 meters on the Y axis to create another 3-to-4-story section. Select this disc polygon then activate the Extrude tool again, and click on the Top view. The previous settings will still be set, so just hit Enter to extrude this upward. Since the disc tool created this disc facing downward, when we extruded it, the walls were created already facing outward (Figure 3-31).

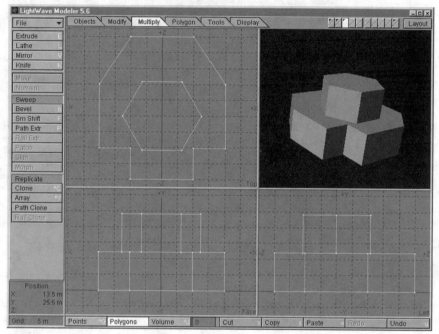

FIGURE 3-31 The two structures combined.

STEP 40: Now that we have the walls in place, we can start adding details such as the machicolations. We'll also be able to do these details on both roofs at the same time, which will save a lot of work. To do this, select the 2 polygons that form the current roofs, as shown in Figure 3-32.

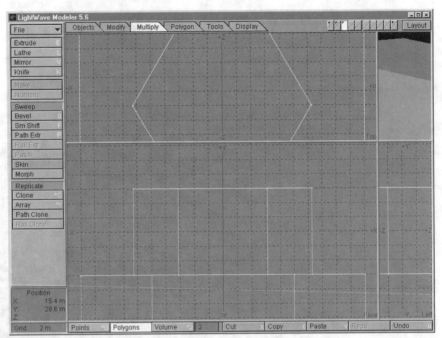

FIGURE 3-32 The two "roof" polygons to which we will be adding new points.

Most of the details will be created through the use of the Bevel tool, but before we can start that, we'll need to subdivide the edges of these polygons a bit so our beveled sides will be comprised of several smaller polygons. There is no simple Subdivide Edge tool, but we do have a Subdivide Polygons tool. This will create the necessary points along the edges that we'll need. To use this, however, we'll need to Triple these 2 polygons. Type Shift-t and our roofs will now be created out of triangles, which we can subdivide. Don't worry if it looks like a mess since this will only be temporary. Type Shift-d to open the Subdivide Polygons panel. Use the Faceted option and make sure the Fractal value is set to 0, then click OK. This will divide every polygon into 4 smaller ones, adding additional points as it does so. We need a few more points, so subdivide these polygons 3 more times using the same settings.

STEP 41: This should give you a fine mesh of 3,072 polygons that make up these 2 roofs now. We don't need this mesh; we only needed the additional points along the edges, which this mesh created for us. Type Shift-z to Merge Polygons, which will basically return us to the original two polygons we started with, but with a mess of additional points (Figure 3-33). Switch to Point Edit mode and type "w" to open the Point Statistics panel. Click the + button on the second line, which shows the number of points that are attached to 0 Polygons, then close the panel. There should be 1,410 points selected now, so hit the Delete key to get rid of them. This will leave us with the original polygons, but with many additional, evenly spaced points along the edges.

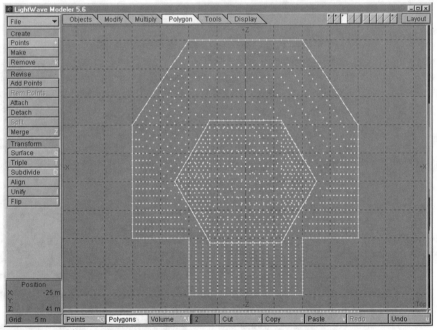

FIGURE 3-33 After 4 subdivisions and polygon merging, we are left with the original shapes and a lot of extra points.

STEP 42: Switch back to Polygon Edit mode, which should reveal that the 2 roof polygons are still selected, then type "q" to open the Surface Panel. Change to the "Stone" surface and click Apply. Now we're ready to create the roof details.

STEP 43: The first little detail we'll create will be the angled over-hang that will become our machicolations. Type "b" to open the Bevel tool and enter an inset of −0.5 meters and a Shift value of 0.5 meters. Click OK and we'll have a small 45-degree outward bevel around both roof polygons (Figure 3-34). We changed the surface here to make it easier to select these polygons later when we actually turn them into the machicolations. The rest of the roof details will all be done using the original surface, so open the Surfaces panel again and change the surface back to "Walls."

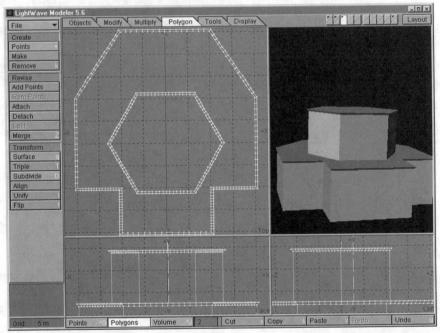

FIGURE 3-34 The next Bevel creates multiple polygons along each edge, thanks to the additional points.

STEP 44: The next thing we need is the base for our battlements. To create this short wall, type Shift-f to open the Smooth Shift panel. Enter an Offset value of 1.5 meters, and leave the Maximum Smoothing Angle at the default 89.5 degrees, then click OK. This will create an outer wall, which will become a railing, around the edge of the roof (Figure 3-35). All we need to do now is to create the inner side of this wall. Type "b" to open the Bevel tool again, and enter an Inset value of 0.5 meters and a Shift value of 0. This will simply shrink the roof polygons, leaving a half-meter border around them. Finally, type Shift-f to open the Smooth Shift panel again. This time, we'll "push" these roof polygons down into the roof, so enter a value of −1 meter for the Offset and click OK. This will leave a 1-meter-tall railing around the edge of both rooftops, which we'll place our battlements on next (Figure 3-36).

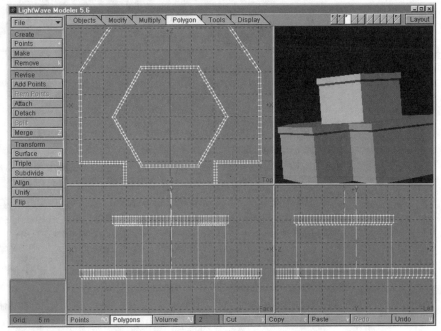

FIGURE 3-35 A Smooth Shift creates a smaller wall segment on top of the main structures.

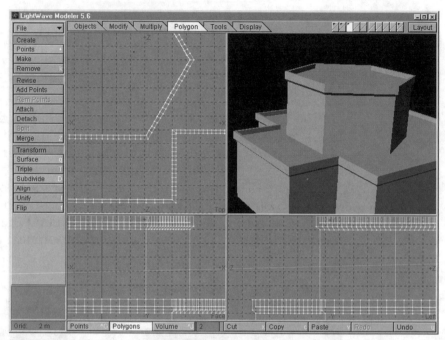

FIGURE 3-36 The completed upper wall, ready for the battlements and the machicolations.

STEP 45: Our battlements will be placed on top of this small wall we just created, and once again, we can do both levels in one shot. To make things easier, we'll do these battlements in a fresh layer. Deselect everything and then use the lasso to select the top polygons of these 2 walls. This is easier if you select the tops of one section, then hold the Shift key and drag a second lasso around the remaining wall top. Cut the polygons and switch to a new layer, then paste the polygons in this empty layer. Select all the polygons, then drag the Top view to full screen, and fit the objects to the view by typing "a". What we'll do here is to deselect polygons wherever we want to have a space between the battlements. Keep in mind that we will be placing towers at the outer corners of this structure, so there's no need to add additional detail near these corners. There's no hard-and-fast rule for the placement of these gaps, but they should generally be at least 1 meter (or more) apart and at least a half meter wide, meaning that you can deselect pairs of polygons, particularly in the areas where the polygons are smaller. Figure 3-37 shows one possible pattern of deselection.

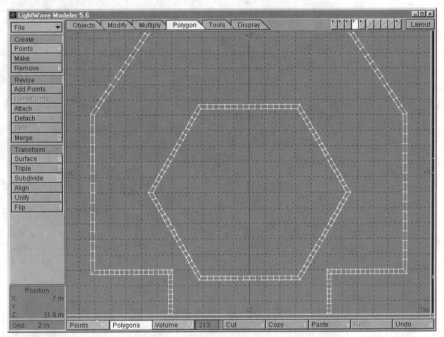

FIGURE 3-37 A sample pattern to use for the placement of the battlements.

STEP 46: Once you have all the polygons you want deselected, merge the remaining selected ones by typing Shift-z. This will allow us to bevel the tops of the battlements later, in long continuous bevels instead of multiple segments. Hit the double-quote key to invert the selection and type Shift-z again to merge the remaining polygons for the same reason. Invert the selection again to return to the original selection pattern (Figure 3-38). Type Shift-f to open the Smooth Shift panel and enter a value of 0.75 meters for the Offset, then click OK. You will now have a series of battlements for both levels (Figure 3-39).

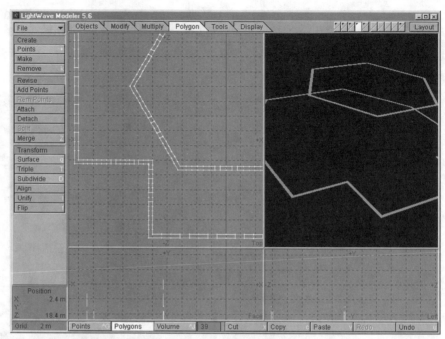

FIGURE 3-38 After merging polygons we are left with an object that is a bit easier to work with.

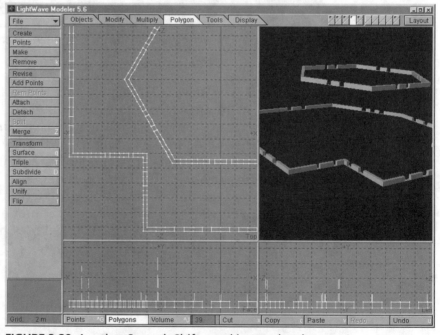

FIGURE 3-39 Another Smooth Shift—and instant battlements!

STEP 47: Just as we did with the tower and the walls, we'll add a bevel to these battlements as well. This means another session of selecting the polygons between the battlements, but this time, it will be a bit easier since that's all we have in this layer. Just as described in Step 6, select the polygons that form the spaces between these battlements. If you happen to accidentally select a side polygon, simply drag a lasso around it without holding the Shift key to deselect it, then continue on, holding the Shift key again to continue selecting new polygons until all the spaces are selected. Type "b" once again to activate the Bevel tool. As before, add a value of 0.05 meters for both the Inset and Shift values, then click OK. This will finish off the battlements so we can place them back on the main structure (Figure 3-40).

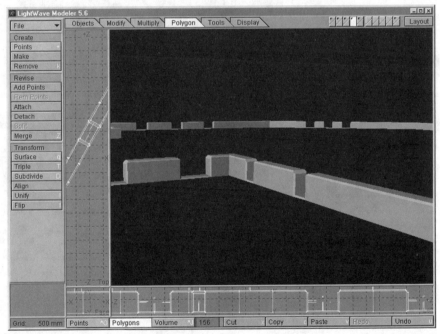

FIGURE 3-40 Another bevel on the tops and sides finishes the battlements off nicely.

STEP 48: Deselect everything and then cut these polygons. Switch back to the layer where the rest of our castle is sitting and paste the polygons here. Merge points to actually attach the battlements to the building. Now we can move on to the machicolations.

STEP 49: This will be a bit easier than the battlements since we already made the selection process simple. Type "w" to open the Polygon Statistics panel and select the Stone surface in the popup list near the bottom of the panel. Click the + button immediately above it to select all the polygons that use that surface name, which we set up in Step 42. Close this panel and you'll see that all the polygons that are on a 45-degree slope are now highlighted. Before we go any further, working in the Top view, deselect the polygons that are located at the corners (Figure 3-41).

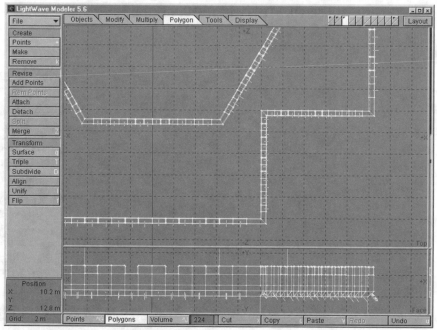

FIGURE 3-41 The angled polygons under the ledges are selected, except for the corners.

STEP 50: Now that these polygons are selected, we'll simply bevel them into the wall to create the openings. If we were to do this right away, we'd have extremely sharp edges between the openings, which wouldn't look quite right. Instead, we'll use one bevel to simply reduce the size of the selected polygons to add some space between them. Activate the Bevel tool and enter a value of 0.1 meters for the Inset, but set the Shift to 0, then click OK. This will shrink the polygons slightly, creating a border around each in the process. Now we can bevel them into the wall. Activate the Bevel tool again and this time set the Inset to 0.1 meters and the Shift to −0.2 meters. Click OK and you will have a series of machicolations that surround both structures. The final modification will be to move these upward to make the holes a bit deeper. Type "t" to activate the Move tool and drag these selected polygons upward on the Y axis 0.4 meters (Figure 3-42).

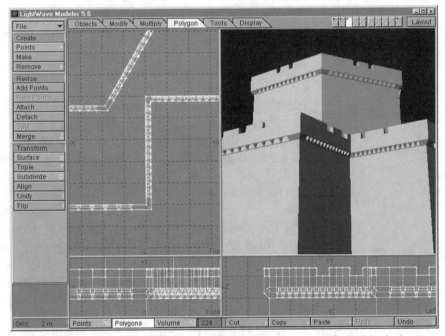

FIGURE 3-42 Another application of Bevels creates a set of machicolations on two different levels simultaneously.

This finishes off the base structure for now. Save this as **Castle-Base.lwo** since we'll be adding a few things to it later. But to do that, we'll need to build those things, which is what we'll do next.

STEP 51: The first tower we built is a little too wide for placing at each corner of this structure, so we'll need to build a narrower one. Before we do anything, open the Surface Panel and set the Current Surface to "Walls," then click Apply. As before we'll start with the disc tool and create a cylinder. This time, our cylinder will be 20 meters tall, so open the Numeric panel and enter the following values:

Sides:	40		Center (m)	Radii (m)
Segments:	1	X	0	3
Bottom:	0 m	Y	0	0
Top:	20 m	Z	0	3
Axis:	Y			

Click OK, then hit the Enter key to create the main body of the tower. This might seem a bit narrow for such a tall tower, but this tower will be positioned at the corners of the main building, where it would gain additional support from the surrounding structure.

STEP 52: Now that we have the basic body, let's create the parapet. This time, we'll create it much the same way we created the battlements of the main building, and just "grow" them by using the Bevel and Smooth Shift tools. The first bevel will form the taper where we'll place the machicolations, so to follow the pattern, we've set with the outer walls and main structure, we'll build this with the Stone surface. Select the top polygon and open the Surface panel, then change the Current Surface to "Stone" and click Apply. Next, activate the Bevel tool and enter a value of −0.5 meters for the Inset and 1 meter for the Shift. Click OK, then open the Surface panel again. Change the Current Surface back to the Walls surface, then click Apply again. Now we can finish off this tower.

STEP 53: Activate the Smooth Shift tool and enter a value of 1.5 meters for the Offset and click OK. Follow this with another Bevel, this time with an Inset of 0.5 meters and a Shift value of 0. Finally, we'll do another Smooth Shift, this time with an Offset of −1 meter. This should leave you with a tower like the one in Figure 3-43. Now it's time to add those little details again.

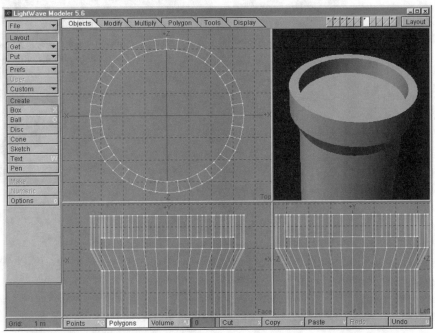

FIGURE 3-43 Another series of Bevels and Smooth Shifts creates a similar wall for our smaller tower.

STEP 54: Once again, we'll need to select the polygons that form the very top edge of this tower. Cut these and paste them into a fresh layer. Since this tower is much thinner than the first one we created, we'll create only half as many battlements. Working in the Top view, deselect alternating pairs of polygons, as shown in Figure 3-44, then type Shift-z to merge the selected polygons. Invert the selection by hitting the double-quote key and merge these polygons as well. This will leave you with 11 selected polygons separated by 11 unselected polygons.

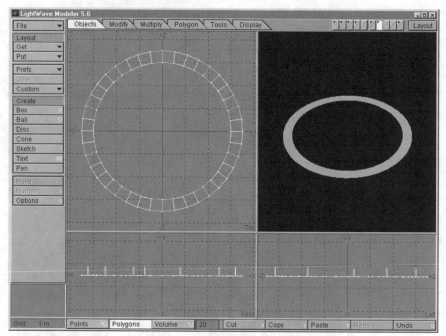

FIGURE 3-44 The top polygons selected and ready to be turned into more battlements.

STEP 55: We'll create our battlements using the Smooth Shift tool, with an Offset of 0.75 meters again. Finally, to finish these off, we'll need to select the polygons between these battlements, then apply a Bevel, using a value of 0.05 meters for both the Inset and the Shift. Deselect everything and cut this object. Switch back to the original layer and past the battlements back on the tower. Be sure to merge points before moving on to the next step.

STEP 56: Use the Polygon Statistics panel to select the 40 polygons that have the Stone surface, and close that panel. Once again, apply a Bevel with an Inset of 0.1 meters and a shift of 0 to add some space between the polygons, which we'll Bevel into the tower. Apply a second Bevel, this time with a value of 0.1 meters for the Inset and a Shift of −0.1 meters. Type the "t" key to activate the Move tool and move these polygons upward 1 meter, as shown in Figure 3-45. This completes our smaller tower, so save this as **SmallTower.lwo,** since we'll be using it a bit later.

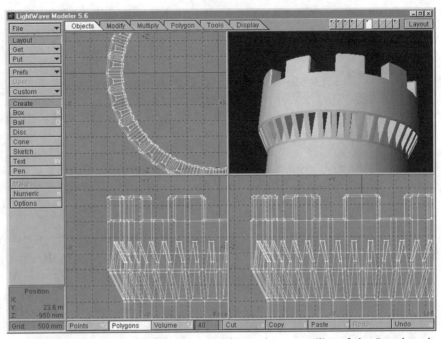

FIGURE 3-45 More machicolations, thanks to the versatility of the Bevel tool.

STEP 57: Now we'll build the main central tower, which will look a bit different from the other towers we've built. We could simply draw a profile polygon and lathe that to create this tower, but instead, we'll "grow" this tower from a simple disc. Having said that, let's create that disc. Select the disc tool and enter the following values into the Numeric panel for this tool:

			Center (m)	Radii (m)
Sides:	40			
Segments:	1	**X**	0	7
Bottom:	20 m	**Y**	0	0
Top:	20 m	**Z**	0	7
Axis:	Y			

Click OK and hit Enter to create this disc. Again, this disc will be created facing down, so type "f" to flip it over. Open the Surface Panel and change this to the "walls" surface.

STEP 58: Select this polygon and activate the Bevel tool. We'll give this tower a slight taper on the main body, so enter an Inset of 1 meter and a Shift of 17 meters. Click OK and we'll have the base of our central tower. We'll place a wider section on top of this base, so let's set the width of that section next. Apply a second Bevel, this time with an Inset of −1 m and a Shift of 0. Follow this with a Smooth Shift of 8 meters, which will give us a roomy 2-story living space. Now we need a roof.

STEP 59: Before we add a roof, we'll need a slight overhang, and we'll use the Stone surface for this. Open the Surface Panel and change the Current Surface to "Stone" and click Apply. Bevel this polygon again, this time using an Inset of −1 m and a Shift of 1 m to create a 45-degree flare. This will become the support structure for the roof, which we'll decorate later, in much the same way we created the machicolations earlier. Open the Surface Panel again, and create a new surface called "roof." Click Apply, then activate the Bevel tool again. Give this a value of −0.5 meters for the Inset and a shift of 0, which will give our roof an added overhang.

STEP 60: We'll finish off the basic shape of this tower with 3 more bevels, then top it off with a flag pole. The next bevel will create the lower flare of the roof, so open the Bevel panel and give this a value of 2 meters for both the Inset and the Shift. Click OK, and activate the Bevel tool again. This time, we'll create the main slope of the roof. Give this an Inset value of 6.25 m and a Shift of 12 m. The last Bevel will round off the top and provide a place to stick a flagpole. Activate the Bevel tool one more time, and give this one an Inset of 0.21 meters and a Shift of 0.1 meters. This will leave a small disc at the very top of this roof, about the right diameter for a flagpost (Figure 3-46).

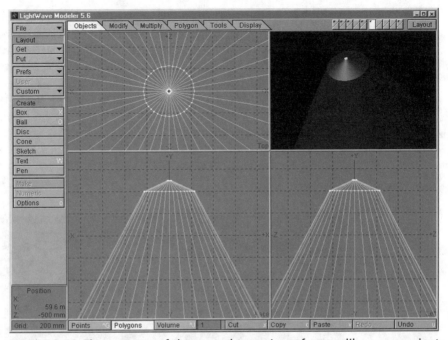

FIGURE 3-46 The very top of the central tower's roof seems like a convenient place to put a flagpole.

STEP 61: Open the Surface Panel again, and create a new surface called "Flagpoles," then click Apply. Our last main detail now is to create this flagpole. Type Shift-f to open the Smooth Shift panel. Enter a value of 8 meters for the Offset and lower the Maximum Smoothing Angle to about 20 degrees. The polygons around the disc are at an angle that would normally cause the Smooth Shift to create a flared extension, looking more like a funnel. This lower Smoothing Angle will prevent that from happening and let us create a normal pole. Click OK and you will have the basic structure of our central tower.

STEP 62: Now we'll select the Stone surface just below the roof, and create some interesting recesses. Use the Polygon Statistics panel and select all the polygons using the surface of Stone, then close that panel. The first thing we'll do again is to create some space between these polygons, so activate the Bevel tool and give these an Inset of 0.1 meters and a Shift of 0. Follow this with a second Bevel. This one will use an Inset of 0.4 meters and a Shift of −1 meter (Figure 3-47).

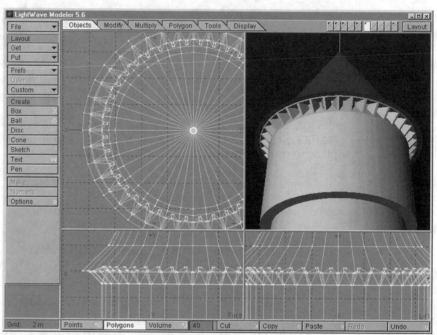

FIGURE 3-47 The same process for creating machicolations works well for adding vents under the roof.

STEP 63: This tower's looking pretty good so far, but let's add a little bit of detail around that first overhang. We'll add a simple ledge around the base of this upper section, but to do that, we'll need to add some more polygons to work with. Deselect everything, then under the Multiply menu select the Knife tool. Resize the Face view to full screen and zoom into the neck section of the tower. Using the Knife tool, drag a line across the tower at 37.5 meters up the y axis. This will give us a half-meter-wide band at the base of the upper section of the tower (Figure 3-48).

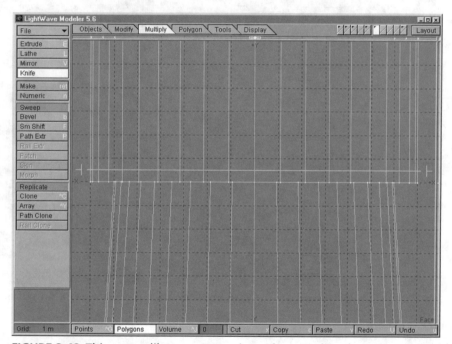

FIGURE 3-48 This seems like an appropriate place to slice the tower to add more detail.

STEP 64: Now for the details. After seeing how well the bevel tool works for adding details for other sections of the castle, we'll use it here as well. Click the Polygons button to be sure we're in Polygon Edit mode, then select the polygons we just created in this strip. Type "b" to activate the Bevel tool and apply a value of 0.1 meters to both the Inset and the Shift, then click OK. This will create what will appear to be a ring of cut blocks around the base of this upper section (Figure 3-49).

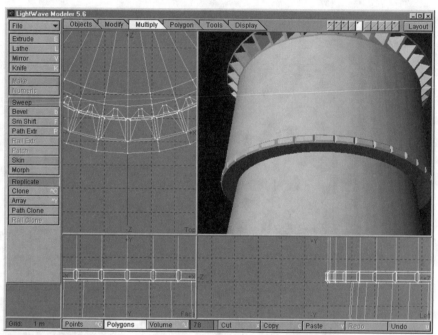

FIGURE 3-49 Another application of Bevel creates a ring of brick-like details.

STEP 65: While we're working on this section, and it *is* the center-piece of the castle, let's further decorate it with some ornamental supports. Switch to a new layer and place this tower in the back-ground. Select the Pen tool and draw out an interesting shape, similar to the one shown in Figure 3-50. Be creative, but don't create details that are too small. Try to keep adjacent points no closer than 200 mm to each other since we'll apply a few bevels to this.

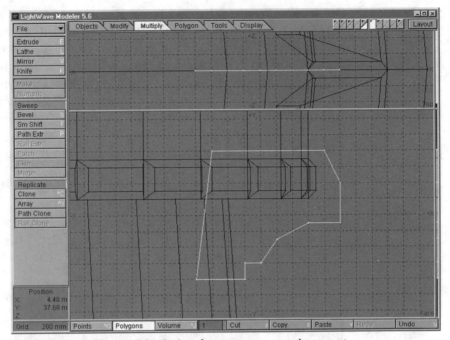

FIGURE 3-50 One possible design for an ornamental support.

STEP 66: Once we have a design we're satisfied with, we'll need to give it some thickness. Open the Surface panel and change this to the Stone surface so it matches the block ring we just created a couple of steps ago. Rather than extrude this shape and then recenter it and possibly flip polygons, we'll use another trick. Under the Tools menu, click the Custom popup button and select the LW_Make-DoubleSided plugin. Now you should have two identical polygons selected. Type Shift-f to open the Smooth Shift panel, and enter a value of 0.25 meters. Click OK and you will have a solid object, extruded in both directions and centered already. Now we can continue with the bevels. The first bevel will use a value of 0.1 meters for both the Inset and the Shift to give us a nice 45-degree edge. Apply this Bevel again, this time with a Shift of 0 so we only reduce the size of the polygon. Click OK and check the polygon for any corners that might be crossed. This will tend to show up in the solid preview as a flipped polygon. If points are crossing, Undo the bevel and try it again with a smaller Inset. Finally, our last bevel will push this polygon back into the object. Try a value of 0.05 meters for the Inset and a Shift of −0.1 meters. Again, check for any crossed corners, which may or may not appear, depending on your design. This is the main reason to avoid placing points too close to one another on polygons that will be beveled.

STEP 67: To finish this main tower off, deselect everything and activate the Array tool under the Multiply menu. Clear any previous setting by clicking the Reset button. Change the Array Type to Radial and enter 6 for the Number (other values will work as well, so feel free to adjust this). Since we just reset this tool, the Center values will already be set for us, so click OK. This will create a series of evenly spaced supports that encircle the neck of our tower (Figure 3-51).

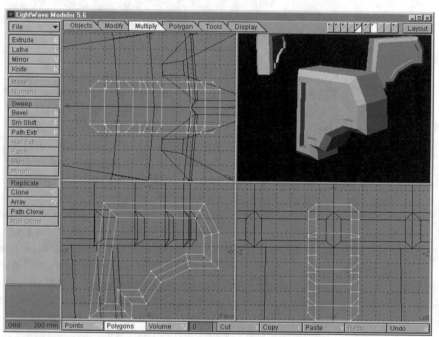

FIGURE 3-51 The finished support, arrayed and ready to be added to the tower.

Note: By Smooth Shifting a double-sided polygon, we can actually perform the same function as the Extrude tool, but we can extrude the profile in any direction. We could also create these same supports by applying the Array tool before we did the smooth shift.

STEP 68: Copy these supports, then switch to the layer with our central tower and paste them here. The last step we'll do will be to position this tower where it will be located on the base structure. This will be placed in the middle of the hexagonal section, which, you might remember, was centered at 30 meters on the Z axis. Use the Move tool to move this tower 30 meters on the Z axis, then save this object as **MainTower.lwo.** Now we can start on the smaller towers that will surround this one.

STEP 69: Clear Modeler once again, and load the **CastleBase.lwo** we created a while back in Steps 37–50. Switch to a new layer and load the **SmallTower.lwo** we created in Steps 51–56. This tower will become the basis from which we'll create the upper towers.

STEP 70: These upper towers, if you remember from Figure 3-27, also have a roof, much like the central tower. This Small Tower doesn't. Well, not yet, but it will, and very quickly. The first thing we need to do is to lose the battlements. We could just chop the top off, but we want to save the machicolations we built. Here's the fast way to lop the top and keep the other details while keeping this tower as an enclosed solid. Resize the Face view to full screen, and then zoom in on the battlements of this tower. Drag a lasso around the battlements and the parapet floor to select them. This is easily done by drawing the lasso, starting at the side, at a height of 21.4 meters, and arcing over the top to the opposite side. An imaginary line will connect the two ends of this lasso, running right under the floor, through the inner polygons of the machicolations below. This is fine, since none of the machicolation polygons will be entirely inside this selection area, so none of them will be highlighted. This will select only the polygons that make up the battlements and the floor they surround (Figure 3-52).

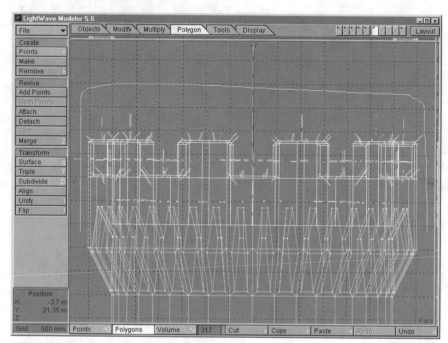

FIGURE 3-52 The top of our small tower, showing the top polygons that we will turn into one single flat disc again.

STEP 71: Now we'll quickly get rid of these battlements and prepare for the roof by typing Shift-z. This will merge all the selected polygons into one, which will be a simple disc, located where the bases of our battlements were. Switch to Point Edit mode and type "w" to open the Point Statistics panel and select the 336 points that belong to 0 polygons. Close this panel and hit the Delete key to remove them. Switch back to Polygon Edit mode and you see that the new disc is still selected.

STEP 72: Activate the Move tool by hitting "t" and move this polygon up 2 meters on the Y axis to position it where we'll start our roof (Figure 3-53). Open the Surface Panel and create a new surface called Tower Roof, then click Apply. Select the Bevel tool again, and enter a value of −0.5 meters for the Inset and a Shift of

0.1 meters. Click OK and this will create a small overhang using the Tower Roof surface. Activate the Bevel tool again, and this time enter a value of 1 meter for both the Shift and Inset to create a short 45-degree outer slope, much like the roof of the central tower. Activate the Bevel tool again and apply an Inset of 2.75 meters and a Shift of 5 meters to create the main slope or the roof (Figure 3-54). We'll round off this top with one more bevel. This time, we'll use an Inset of 0.2 meters and a Shift of 0.1 meters.

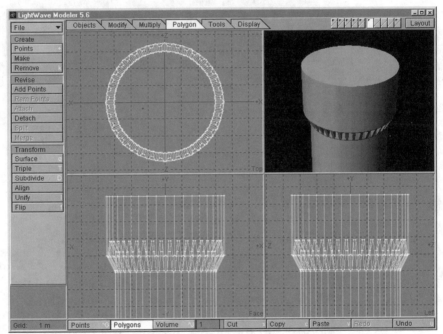

FIGURE 3-53 The new flat disc is raised, ready to form the roof.

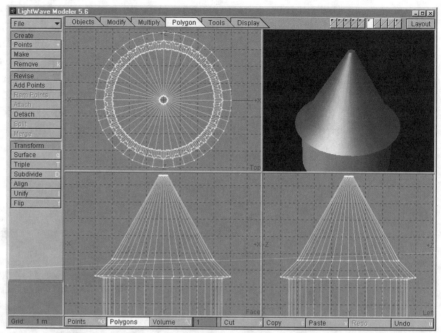

FIGURE 3-54 Just as we did with the central tower, we have grown another roof for the smaller towers.

STEP 73: Since this is pretty much a smaller version of the larger central tower's roof, we might as well add a flagpole to this one as well. Open the Surface Panel and change the Current Surface to FlagPoles, then click Apply. Finally, type Shift-f to open the Smooth Shift tool. Give this an Offset of 8 meters and set the Maximum Smoothing Angle to 20 degrees. Click OK and you will have a tower similar to the one in Figure 3-55.

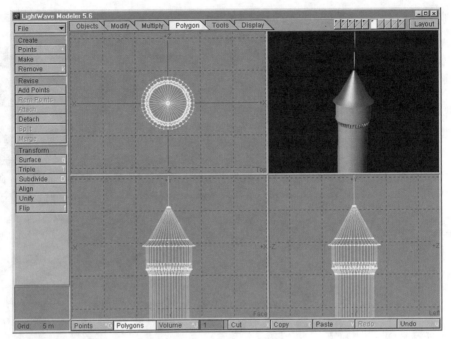

FIGURE 3-55 The completed tower top.

STEP 74: We're almost done with this tower. Since this will be one of the upper towers, we need to raise it a bit. Place the CastleBase in the background layer as a guide, and deselect everything. Activate the Move tool and move this tower 9 meters up the Y axis. Let's also get this tower into position in relation with the CastleBase, so resize the Top view to full screen and fit the view by typing "a". Move this tower to the left-side corner of the upper section of the CastleBase. This will place the center of this tower at X: −12.5 m Z: 30 m (Figure 3-56).

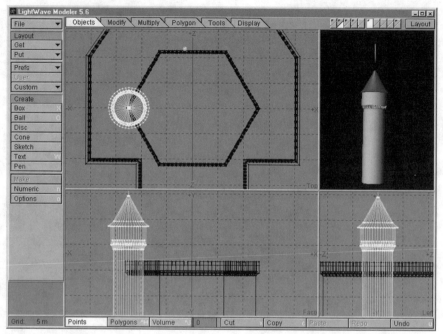

FIGURE 3-56 The upper tower moved into position against the main structure in the background.

STEP 75: We could leave this tower as it is, with the base coming out of the lower structure, but we'll be fancy about it and make this a suspended tower. Select the bottom polygon of this tower, and select the Move tool again. Move this polygon 13 meters up the Y axis, which will place it 9 meters up the wall it will be attached to. This doesn't exactly give it much support, so we'll fix that next. Activate the Bevel tool again, and enter a value of 2.75 meters for the Inset and give it a Shift of 3 meters. Click OK and you will now have a tapered base, which would provide a fair amount of support for a tower like this (Figure 3-57). Save this tower as **UpperTower.lwo,** since we're done with it for a while.

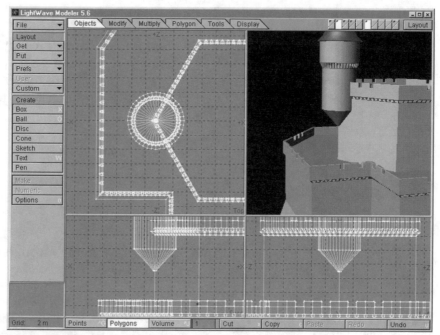

FIGURE 3-57 The finished tower, with the beveled base, shown here in its final position on the main structure.

STEP 76: We're almost done building the main elements of this castle. Now we'll create the last major detail for the main structure. This small upper tower will be quite close to the main central tower, so it would be convenient to have a short access path between the two, rather than have to climb to the bottom of one tower, cross over, and climb up the next. Load the **MainTower.lwo** object into this layer with the upper tower and you'll see that they're only a few short meters apart. Not too far apart to add a small bridge.

Switch to an empty layer and place these two towers in the background so we have a visual reference of where our bridge will go. We'll create a single bridge for now, and then duplicate it a bit later so we have a bridge going out to each of the 6 upper towers. Open the Surface panel and change the Current Surface to "Walls" again.

STEP 77: We already have these two towers placed in their final locations, so we'll build our bridge in place as well. This will be a simple bridge, with an arched underside. To create this, we'll start out with a simple box that spans the distance between these towers. Activate the Box tool from the Objects menu and open its Numeric panel. Enter the following dimensions to create a 2-meter-wide box.

	Low (m)	High (m)
X	−11	−5
Y	27	32
Z	29	31

Click OK and then hit Enter to create a rough shape for the bridge (Figure 3-58).

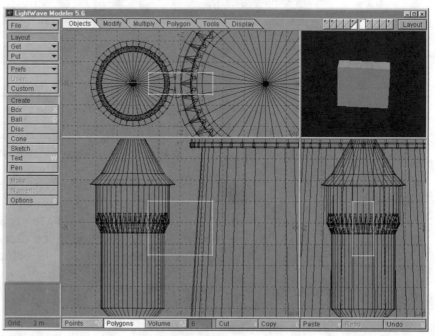

FIGURE 3-58 The location of our small bridge.

STEP 78: Switch to a new layer, and place this box in the background. Now we'll create a disc, which we'll use to carve the bottom of the bridge, so activate the Disc tool. Open its Numeric panel and enter the following values to make the disc, which will be an oval shape:

Sides:	40
Segments:	1
Bottom:	28 m
Top:	32 m
Axis:	Z

	Center (m)	Radii (m)
X	−8.1	1.4
Y	27.0	3
Z	30.0	1

STEP 79: Swap layers so the disc is in the background, then type Shift-b to open the Boolean panel. Select the Subtract button, and then hit OK. In a second or two, an arch will be cut from the bottom of the box (Figure 3-59). The bridge is about half-finished now.

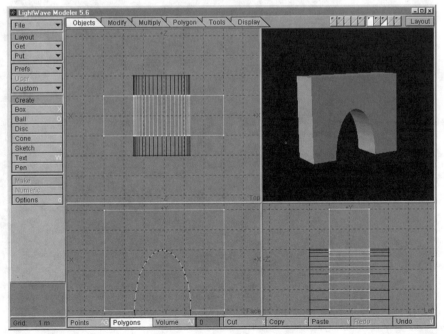

FIGURE 3-59 A simple Boolean Subtract creates the basic shape of the bridge.

STEP 80: Let's give this bridge some additional support by having this arch continue all the way down to the building below, creating a frame along the tower walls. Merge points, and then select the two bottom polygons of this bridge. Type Shift-f to open the Smooth Shift tool, and enter a value of 4 meters, then click OK. Right now, the support on the right will disappear inside the main tower about halfway down because of the slight taper of the tower's base. Deselect the polygon on the left side so only the right one is active, then use the Move tool to adjust the right leg. Move this polygon −0.25 meter on the X axis, which will shear this leg to match the slope of the main tower (Figure 3-60). Deselect everything again, and then select the 3 polygons on each side of this bridge by clicking on the seam across each leg. Type Shift-z to merge these polygons so we only have one polygon on each side.

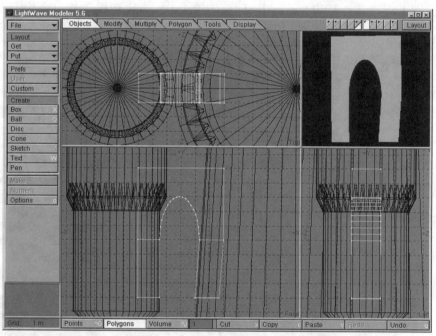

FIGURE 3-60 After extending the legs, we need to move one under the bridge to allow for the slope of the main tower wall.

STEP 81: Keeping these 2 polygons selected, activate the Bevel tool, and set the Inset to 0.2 meters and the Shift to 0.1 meters. This will widen out the bridge slightly, creating a nice beveled archway in the process. Let's spice that arch up a little more before we finish this off.

STEP 82: Deselect everything, then select the beveled polygons that line this arch. Rename them to the Stone surface, and then activate the Bevel tool again. Enter a value of 0.05 meters for both the Shift and the Inset and click OK. This will create what will appear to be a strip of stone blocks that frame the archway (Figure 3-61).

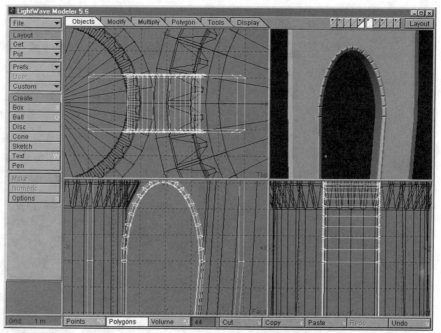

FIGURE 3-61 Another bevel on a strip of polygons creates a decorative arch.

STEP 83: Now we'll create the actual walkway along the top of this bridge. For safety reasons, we'll need a railing on each side, much like we did with the outer walls. Since the ends of this bridge will be hidden inside the towers, we can simply use the Bevel tool to create a wall all around the walkway, and we won't have to worry about seeing this wall at the ends. Deselect everything once again, then select the very top polygon of this bridge. Open the Surface panel and change the Current Surface to "Walls" again, then activate the Bevel tool. Inset this bevel 0.1 meters, but use a shift of 0. This will simply shrink this top polygon, creating a flat border around it. Activate the Bevel tool again, and this time, change the Shift value to −1 meter, leaving the Inset alone. Click OK, and the top polygon will now be pushed down into the bridge, which, when combined with the two towers, will create a nice little walled walkway (Figure 3-62). Save this object as **Bridge.lwo** and we're done building the major elements.

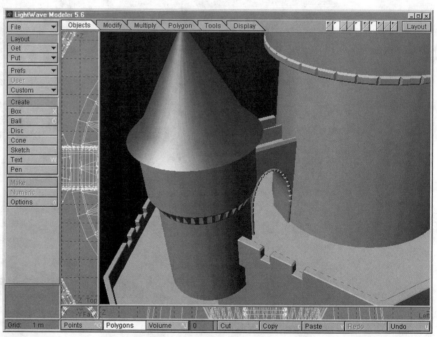

FIGURE 3-62 The completed bridge, shown here with the two towers it connects.

When creating large models like this one, it's much easier to work on a section at a time to get the basic shapes built, then add the smaller details later, much like you would do with a physical model kit. In the next chapter, we'll assemble these individual elements into a full-blown castle, as well as add all the finer details, such as textures, windows, arrow slits, and doors. We'll also build the main entrance to this castle, the gatehouse, where we'll create a working portcullis.

For fun, you can apply most of these same construction techniques on your own designs, especially the Smooth Shift and Bevel method of "growing" a building from a simple polygon. In fact, that's exactly how we'll build our gatehouse in the next tutorial!

4

Building a Castle, Part II

Dave Jerrard

OVERVIEW

In Tutorial 3 we built most of the major elements for our castle. We'll continue in this tutorial by constructing the gatehouse and then finally assembling everything for rendering. We'll explore some interesting uses for LightWave's textures, including the Natural Shaders, to create a realistic-looking castle. Let's finish the main construction first. Our castle still needs a gatehouse, so let's get that done.

In this tutorial you will use:

- Booleans
- Natural Shaders
- SkyTracer

What you will need:

- Objects created in Tutorial 3
- Image maps provided on CD
- Installed Modeler plugins; Dublside.p, Reduce.p
- Installed Layout plugins; NaturalShaders.p, Png.p, SkyTracer.p

What you will learn:

- Basic to advanced modeling techniques
- Realistic surfacing

STEP 1: Clear Modeler and load the **OuterWall.lwo** we created in Tutorial 3. Switch layers and place this object in the background so we have a reference while we build the gatehouse. In this current layer, we'll design the basic shape of the gatehouse (Figure 4-1) by laying out a floorplan. Drag the Top view to full screen and zoom in to the opening in the wall that's in the background layer. Open the Surface Panel and set the Current Surface to "Walls," which we've used quite a bit in the last chapter.

FIGURE 4-1 The basic design of the gatehouse, showing four connected towers and the main entryway.

Tip: One of the keys to becoming a good modeler is to learn to see the basic shapes that form them. Cans, glasses, computer cases, and many everyday objects are made from simple shapes. Larger objects, such as cars, houses, boats, and planes, are basically little more than collections of smaller objects, which are usually made from even simpler shapes. Pick up an object nearby and study the surface and in time you will start to see the simple shapes that form it. A lot of the time, that simple shape is so obvious, most people overlook it.

This gatehouse will have two large towers at the front, and these towers, as seen in Figure 4-1, are integrated into the design of the rest of the building, with battlements flowing from the straight walls to the towers and back. We could attempt to attach a couple premade towers with Booleans, but we would still be faced with the task of removing the battlements where the tops of the 2 objects overlap. This would not be a fun task. There is a much simpler process, and we've already used it a few times in Tutorial 3. If you look closely at the basic shape of the gatehouse, minus the 2 rear towers, you'll see that it's basically an extruded box with a disc at 2 corners. Well, that's simple enough to build!

STEP 2: Use the Box tool to create a box with the following dimensions:

	Low (m)	High (m)
X	−10	10
Y	0	0
Z	−65	−45

This will be the basic cubic structure that will create the flat walls. Now for those attached towers. Select the Disc tool, and open the Numeric panel for it. Set it up with the following values, which will center the disc on the front right corner of the box we just made.

Sides:	40
Segments:	1
Bottom:	0 m
Top:	0 m
Axis:	Y

	Center (m)	Radii (m)
X	10	6
Y	0	0
Z	−65	6

Click OK and hit the Enter key to create this disc. Now we need one for the other corner. The Disc tool will still be active, so click the crosshair in the center of it in the Top view. Drag it to the left, placing the crosshair over the bottom left corner of the box, then hit Enter again. You should have something identical to Figure 4-2.

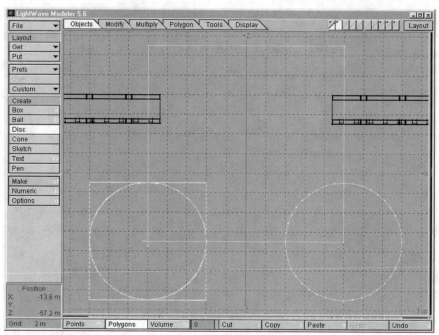

FIGURE 4-2 Three shapes form the basis for the gatehouse.

If we were to extrude these shapes now, we'd have several polygons that form the sides of the towers trapped inside the box, where they won't be seen. We'll also have the same problem with the tops of the towers if we try to create the battlements, which would be that they intersect those of the box instead of being one continuous row. Before we extrude this shape, then, we'll have to turn it into a single polygon. The obvious way to do that would be to just trace out all the points, in order, and hit "p". Not too troublesome for this shape, but tedious, and even more so with more complex shapes. Here's a quicker method.

STEP 3: Switch to an empty layer and place this plan in the background. Drag out a box in the Top view that's large enough to contain the plan in the background layer. Hit Enter to create this box, then type Shift-R to open the Drill tool's panel. Select the Y axis and set the drill's Operation to Slice, then click OK. In a second, you'll see the layout of the gatehouse sliced into this polygon (Figure 4-3). Now, the reason we did this will become clear. Much like we did with the small tower in Tutorial 3, where we merged the top polygons, which were facing in many directions, into one single polygon, we can now merge these polygons into one single polygon. That sure beats tracing over all those points one at a time.

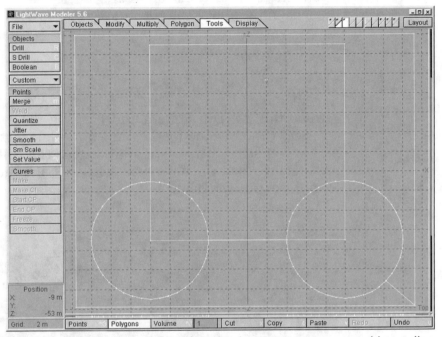

FIGURE 4-3 The Drill tool's Slice function is a great way to assemble a collection of various 2D shapes.

Tip: For the logo builders out there, this drill technique is a charm for creating fast 2D characters. You can slice spline curves and polylines as well as polygons into a flat plane, then delete the plane, leaving the characters as flat polygons. These polygons can then be merged and otherwise readied for beveling and extruding. It makes splines much easier to integrate with normal polygons.

STEP 4: Naturally, there is some cleanup involved, but it's nothing too intense. First, select the original box we sliced these shapes into (Figure 4-3), and delete it, leaving only the gatehouse plan.

Next, select all the remaining polygons (there should be 5) and type Shift-Z to merge them. Finally, to quickly get rid of the remaining unattached points, type the three key sequence of, "X", "Z", and "V". Did you catch what happened?

Since the merged polygon was still selected, when we hit the "X" key, we copied only the polygon and removed it from the layer. The "Z" key, by default, is also a delete key, which removed the remaining points, and then the "V" key pasted back the polygon we cut, without the excess points! Now we're ready to build this up into a gatehouse.

STEP 5: Since this polygon was originally created with the box tool, its surface normal will be pointing down. This means we can extrude this polygon upward and have the sides created facing out. Select the Extrude tool and open its Numeric panel. Set the Axis to Y and give it an extent of 17 meters. This will make it a few meters taller than the outer wall. Click OK and hit Enter to perform the extrusion (Figure 4-4).

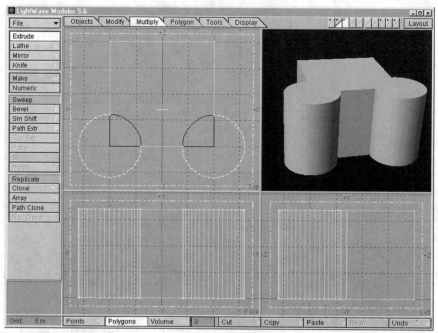

FIGURE 4-4 A simple extrusion quickly generates the basic structure of the gatehouse.

Tip: When extruding polygons, watch the surface normal. If it points outward from the Extrude tool's bounding box, all the new polygons that it creates will also point outward, creating a nice solid. If they point inward, then the extrusion will create the new polygons also facing inward, which works fine if you're building the interior of an object, like a room.

STEP 6: Now we're at a fairly familiar stage again, much like the CastleBase object from Tutorial 3. What we'll do now is set up for the battlements and the machicolations again, but there's one thing we need to do here. We have 4 straight wall sections, each one a single polygon in length. If we plan on using the Bevel tool to create these details like we did before, we're going to need more polygons. Select the very top polygon of this object and drag the Top view to full screen if it isn't already. Zoom in on this view until you have a grid size of 1 meter. Click the Polygon tab at the top of the screen and select the Add Points button on the side. The pointer will turn into a tiny arrow with the word "to" beside it. Now, click along the straight edges of this highlighted polygon at 1-meter intervals. This will add new points to this polygon without altering its shape, giving us the additional points we need for the next few steps. Don't worry if they're not exactly at 1-meter intervals, as that will be taken care of next.

STEP 7: When you have all the points added, switch to Point Edit mode by clicking the Points button at the bottom of the screen. Select the points that we just added by dragging a lasso around them, taking care not to select any that are part of the two towers (Figure 4-5). Click the Tools tab and then click the Quantize button on the left side panel. In the panel that pops up, enter a value of 1 meter for each axis, and then click OK. This will have the effect of "snapping" all the selected points to a 1-meter grid, ensuring that these are now all evenly spaced. Now we can continue on with the roof details.

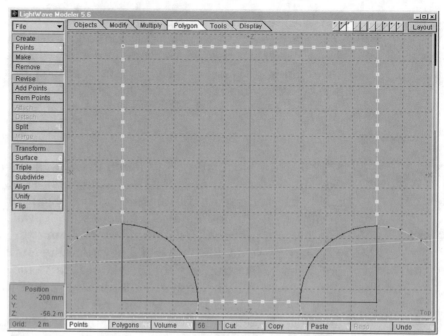

FIGURE 4-5 The selected points that will be Quantized to ensure they are evenly spaced.

STEP 8: Switch back to Polygon Edit mode and the roof polygon will still be highlighted. The first detail we'll add will be the machicolations, which we'll create the same way we did with the CastleBase. Open the Surface panel and change the Current Surface to "Stone" and click Apply. Next, activate the Bevel tool and enter an Inset of −0.5 meters and a Shift of 1 meter. You will see a tapered strip of evenly spaced polygons that completely circle the perimeter of the roof. Let's continue on with the battlements now. Open the Surface panel again and change the Current Surface back to Walls. Type Shift-F to open the Smooth Shift panel and enter a value of 2 meters for the Offset. Click OK and you will have a smaller outer wall over the Stone strip. Activate the Bevel tool once more, this time with an Inset of 0.5 meters and a Shift of 0 to add the ledge. Smooth Shift this polygon −1 meter to create the insides of the wall and we're ready for the battlements (Figure 4-6).

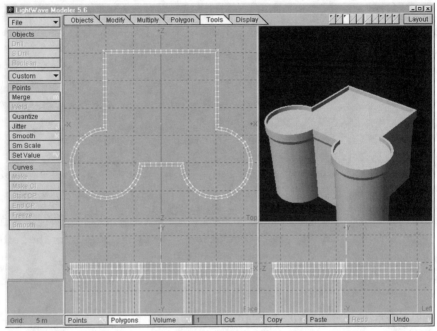

FIGURE 4-6 The roof after a series of Bevels and Smooth Shifts acquires a small wall that follows the shape of the building.

STEP 9: Deselect that roof polygon since we're done with it. What we need now are the polygons that form the top of the short wall that surrounds it. Drag the Lasso around these in the Face view and cut them by typing "X". Switch to a new layer and paste them here. Select all the polygons again, then deselect the ones where you want to have a gap between battlements. This will work out best if each battlement is made from 2 polygons, using the pattern shown in Figure 4-7.

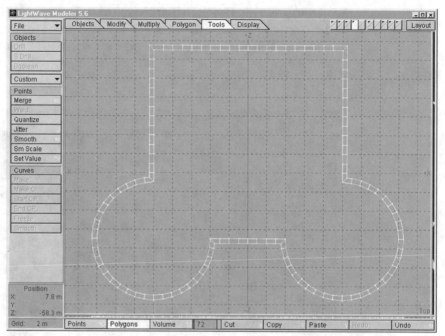

FIGURE 4-7 Just one of several possible patterns for the battlements.

STEP 10: Before we create these battlements, let's reduce the polygon count by merging these selected polygons. This will improve the results of the Bevel we'll add later. Type the double-quote key to invert the selection and then merge these polygons as well. Invert the selection again, then type Shift-f to activate the Smooth Shift tool. Enter a value of 0.75 m and click OK. This gives us our battlements. Now for the tedious part, again. Working in the Top view, select the polygons that form the spaces between the battlements. When these are all selected, apply a bevel with an Inset and Shift of 0.1 m to create a nice 45-degree beveled edge to the battlements (Figure 4-8).

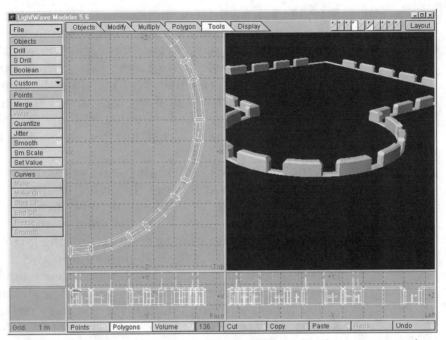

FIGURE 4-8 After Smooth Shifting and Beveling, the battlements are ready to be placed back onto the gatehouse.

STEP 11: Deselect the beveled polygons, then copy this entire object and paste it back on top of the gatehouse in the other layer, then merge points. Now for the machicolations, which we'll start off with by typing "w" to open the Polygon Statistics panel. Select the polygons with the Stone surface and close the panel. Before we go any further, deselect the two polygons in each corner where the towers meet the flat walls. Apply a bevel with an Inset of 0.1 meters and a Shift of 0 to add a little space between these polygons, then follow that with a second bevel, this time with an Inset of 0.3 m and a Shift of −0.2. Finally, select the Move tool and move these polygons up 1 meter on the Y axis to make the machicolations a bit deeper (Figure 4-9).

STEP 12: You might have noticed in Figure 4-1 that the gatehouse had a flared base. This is entirely optional, but the process is simple. Select the bottom polygon of the gatehouse and use the Move tool to move the bottom up 3 meters along the Y axis. Activate the Bevel tool and enter a value of −1 meter for the Inset and 3 meters for the Shift. Click OK and the gatehouse will suddenly have a flared base to keep attackers out in the open. Now it's time to build the actual gateway itself, but first, save this as **Gatehouse.lwo**, just to be safe.

The main gate is where the castle would be most vulnerable. If the enemy was to charge through this, then all the men at arms stationed on the outer walls and towers would become highly ineffective since now, the enemy would be behind the walls, which in many cases, were behind the guards. This meant they either had to leave their post to join the melee or stay at their post and sit this one out, hoping their fellow warriors will survive without them. To prevent this, the gatehouse was born, which provided living quarters for the men stationed there, as well as an extremely lethal defense platform. A huge portcullis usually protected the gateway itself. Sometimes two or more of these were found along the fairly lengthy tunnel, which would do a great job at delaying any attempts to invade. Meanwhile, above this entrance were the machicolations, placed right where rocks and boiling oil could be dropped on anyone foolish enough to try to lift or squeeze through the portcullis. Even if an invader successfully passed the portcullis, he then found himself facing a long dark tunnel, lined with murder holes and arrow slits from which hundreds of arrows could be loosed before he reached the other side, where, in all likelihood, was another portcullis to trap him.

These gatehouses, while providing access in and out of the castle grounds, were deathtraps to the enemy, who often had to resort to finding other ways into the castle or just find another castle to conquer. These are just a few points to keep in mind as we build our gateway.

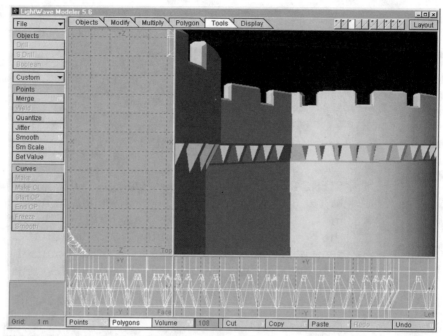

FIGURE 4-9 A series of machicolations is quickly created with the Bevel tool. Note the areas in the corners that were not beveled.

Tip: When using Booleans, speed things up by placing the object with higher detail in the foreground and select only the polygons you want to have affected by the Boolean. Since you can't select polygons in the background layer, this is the next best way to reduce the number of polygons that will be used.

STEP 13: Switch to an empty layer and place the gatehouse in the background. We'll build our gate in this layer, but as a solid, which we'll use to cut into the gatehouse later. Open the Surface panel and change the Current Surface to "Walls" if it isn't already set to that. The typical gateway was an arch, so let's start with that. Select the Disc tool and open the Numeric panel for it. Enter the following values to create a cylinder that passes through the entire length of the gatehouse.

Sides:	40		Center (m)	Radii (m)
Segments:	1	**X**	0.0	2.5
Bottom:	−70 m	**Y**	2.5	2.5
Top:	−40 m	**Z**	0.0	0.0
Axis:	Z			

Click OK and hit Enter to create this cylinder.

STEP 14: We only need to top off this cylinder, so, just like we did in Tutorial 3, we'll merge the bottom half to make it flat. Working in the Face view, drag a lasso around the 20 polygons that form the bottom half of this cylinder, then type Shift-z to merge them. Switch to Points edit mode and select the points that also form the bottom half, and delete them. This will leave us with a perfect half-cylinder (Figure 4-10).

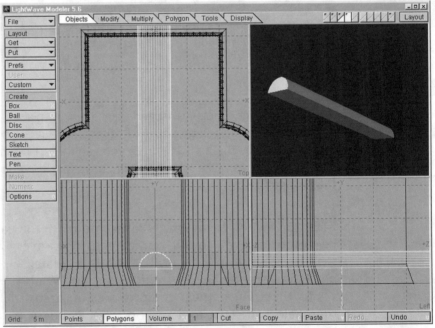

FIGURE 4-10 The cylinder after being halved, shown against the gatehouse in the background.

STEP 15: Switch back to Polygon Edit mode and you should find that the bottom polygon is selected. Apply a Smooth Shift to this polygon, with an Offset of 3 meters. Deselect the bottom polygon and we're ready to add a few details to this gateway.

Note: Remember, as we work on this archway, what we see in the solid preview is a negative of what the object will look like when we're finished. We will be cutting this shape out of the gatehouse later, which will leave a tunnel that this object would fit into. To see what the tunnel would look like from the inside, simply type "f" to flip the polygons. Be sure to flip them back before doing anything else, though, or you could end up with a mess.

STEP 16: We're going to place a wide arch high above the front gate, which will cover a second, lower machicolation that targets the gate itself. The first thing we'll do is to add the additional polygons that we need to do this. Select the Knife tool from the Multiply Menu, then zoom in to the front part of the gate and, working in the Top view, drag the Knife across the tunnel at −64.5 meters on the Z axis. Do this again, but this time at the −64-meter mark so we have a half-meter-wide arch cut into the tunnel (Figure 4-11).

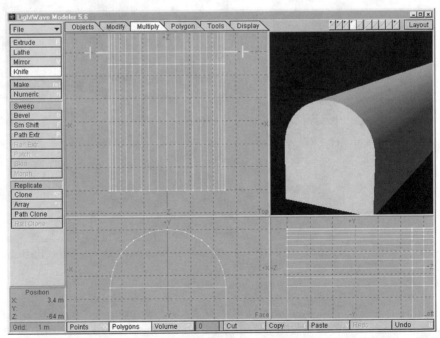

FIGURE 4-11 The tunnel object, showing the locations of the two slices that we'll make with the Knife tool.

STEP 17: Select the top 20 polygons in this thin strip. We'll use these to create a slot in the ceiling of this tunnel. Activate the Smooth Shift tool and enter a value of 0 for the offset. Yes, that's right, 0! Click OK and you should see that apparently nothing happened. Well, something *did* happen.

We want to make a vertical slot above these polygons. Extruding them would leave polygons on where these are, meaning we'd have to go in later to get rid of them. Smooth Shift will perform the same extrusion, but without leaving any polygons where it started. However, Smooth Shift would also spread these out in a wide arc, so it only half-does what we're after. An Offset of 0 still did the Smooth Shift, creating the side polygons, but the end polygons haven't moved yet. Click the Tools tab and open the Set Value panel. Enter a value of 6 meters and set the Axis to Y, then click OK. There are our side polygons for the Smooth Shift (Figure 4-12).

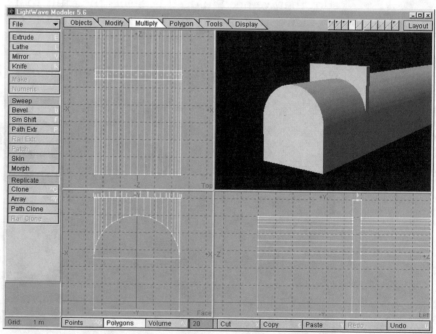

FIGURE 4-12 The Set Value tool quickly extrudes and flattens the polygons of the top of the small arch.

Tip: By applying a Smooth Shift with an Offset of 0 to selected polygons, then deleting them, you can quickly create a series of 2-point polygons. Simply merge points after deleting the shifted polygons, and each side will automatically become a polyline.

STEP 18: We currently have a few more polygons than we need, so let's clean this up a bit. Deselect everything, then click the Custom button under the Tools menu to select the LW_Reduce-Polygons plugin. The default values will suffice for this, so just click the OK button and our tunnel will be all cleaned up and ready for the next step.

If you view this tunnel against the gatehouse in the background layer, you'll notice that this slot is behind the front wall by half a meter. What we want to do now is to raise this slot a few meters higher and have it behind an arch that is also higher up above the tunnel. We just built an arch, so. . . .

STEP 19: Working in the Side view, drag a lasso around the 20 polygons that form the short section of ceiling, as well as the front and top polygons of the slot we just created, as shown in Figure 4-13. Next, use the Move tool to move these polygons up 5 meters along the Y axis (Figure 4-14). Now, when we cut this shape from the gatehouse, this raised section will cut a taller archway through that half-meter-thick section of wall in front of the large machicolation we created here. In fact, let's do this now.

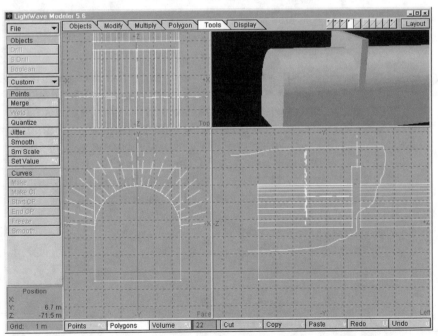

FIGURE 4-13 A selection showing the polygons that we'll be moving.

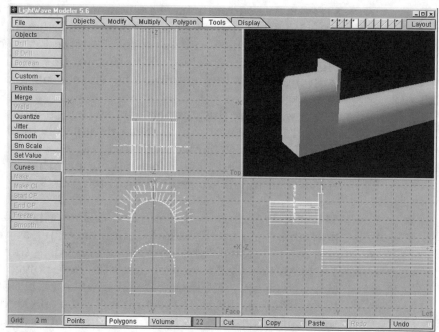

FIGURE 4-14 The final tunnel object, which will be used to cut a tunnel through the gatehouse.

STEP 20: Swap layers by typing the apostrophe key and select the polygons that form the front, back, and bottom of the gatehouse, as shown in Figure 4-15. This will help to speed up the Boolean that we're about to do. Next, open the Boolean tool by typing Shift-B. Since we'll be cutting a chunk out of this object, select the Subtract button, and then click OK. In a few seconds, our gatehouse will have a tunnel (Figure 4-16). Merge Points to attach these new polygons to the gatehouse.

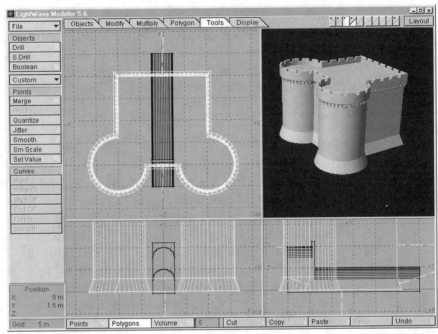

FIGURE 4-15 To speed the Boolean operation, only the affected polygons are selected.

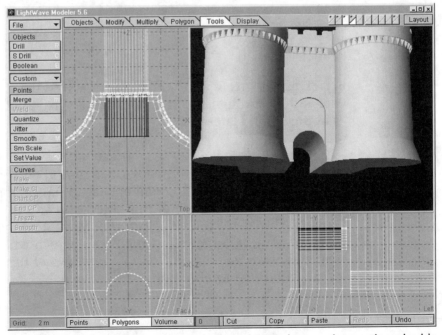

FIGURE 4-16 After the Boolean, the gatehouse has an interesting double archway at the entrance.

Note: We positioned the bottom of the tunnel object below the bottom of the gatehouse to avoid trouble with the Boolean operation. Booleans do not like it when both layers have polygons that are coplanar. This is confusing to the Boolean operation and usually results in either one of the polygons being left over, but it can be as bad as having large holes appear in the object.

STEP 21: While we're working on this tunnel, let's add a few more interior details. The first thing we need is a socket for the portcullis, or this castle isn't going to be very secure. Since the portcullis is essentially a large heavy gate that is raised and lowered, it will need some form of guides along the sides of the tunnel, which we'll create along with the socket. Switch to an empty layer, and again, place this gatehouse in the background. Zoom into the front of the tunnel and select the Box tool. We're going to create a simple box that will be used to cut some grooves and a socket for the gate, so open the Numeric panel and enter the following values, then click OK.

	Low (m)	High (m)
X	−3	3
Y	−1	7
X	−63	−62.5

This will create a thin box that runs into the sides of the tunnel and up through the arch, creating a very simple guide for the gate we'll build later.

STEP 22: All we need is a second gate at the other end. Select all the polygons in this layer, copy them, and then paste them right back down again. Nothing will appear to have happened, but we now have a selected copy of this object and an unselected one sitting in the same place. Select the Move tool and move this selected copy 16.5 meters on the Z axis, which will place it at the rear end of the gatehouse. We now have two of these boxes, ready to cut into the tunnel.

STEP 23: Swap layers and select the bottom 2 polygons (when we created the tunnel, we split the original bottom polygon into 2), as well as the polygons that make up the tunnel. This is easily accomplished by running the pointer along the edge of the tunnel in the Face view. Type Shift-b and once again, we'll use the Subtract Operation. Click OK and you will see 2 slots in the tunnel, just the right size for a pair of gates (Figure 4-17). Merge points once again to remove the duplicates that the Boolean caused.

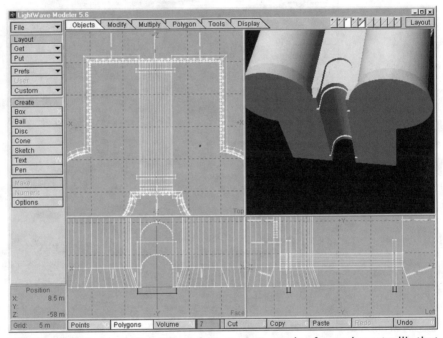

FIGURE 4-17 A second Boolean Subtract creates a slot for each portcullis that we'll add later.

STEP 24: We could consider this tunnel finished, but let's add a few more details in here, like additional support arches. Deselect everything, then resize the Top view to full screen. Drag the lasso around the middle polygons of the tunnel to select that section, then activate the Knife tool from the Multiply menu. What we'll do now is cut a few more half-meter-wide strips across the tunnel to place our support arches (Figure 4-18). Just make a slice somewhere on the tunnel, then make a second slice a half-meter to the side of that, then repeat this where you want another archway. Don't worry too much if you don't like where these are right now since they can easily be moved later. Since we selected only the polygons that form the inside of the tunnel, these are the only polygons that the Knife tool will cut.

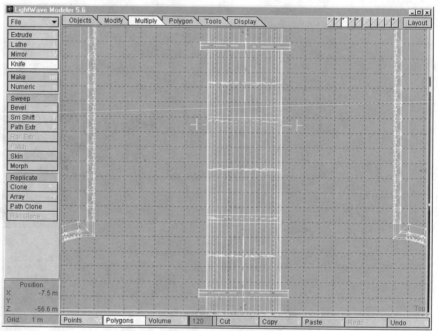

FIGURE 4-18 Another set of slices is made to the tunnel for support arches.

STEP 25: Drop the Knife tool and deselect everything again. We're going to work on just these archways that we created, so select the polygons that form them by dragging a lasso around each (hold the Shift key to keep the previous selections while dragging a new lasso). Open the Surface Panel and change the Current Surface back to Stone, then type Shift-F to activate the Smooth Shift tool, and enter a value of 0.3 meters for the Offset. Click OK and you will now have thick frames along the archways (Figure 4-18).

STEP 26: Let's make these a little more impressive. You might remember that we used the Bevel tool to create a ring of stone blocks around the central tower in one easy step. Well, we can do pretty much the same here and make these arches look like they were made from cut stone blocks. Before we do that, we'll need to subdivide the vertical sections of these arches. Once again, use the lasso to select all the polygons in each arch since the sides will currently not be selected. Now, in the Face or Side view, use the Knife tool to cut the vertical sections into smaller segments, roughly the same size as the segments that make up the curved tops, about half-meter intervals. Five segments should be all that you really need (Figure 4-19).

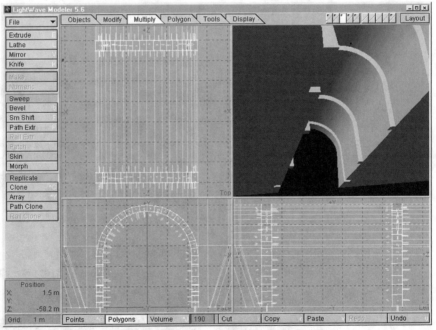

FIGURE 4-19 The arches are Smooth Shifted, and then the vertical sections are sliced into smaller segments.

STEP 27: Now we'll create the brick look. Open the Bevel tool and enter an Inset of 0.05 meters and a Shift of 0.025 meters. This will create a double bevel around the inner edges of these arches, which will look close to cut stone blocks. Not too bad, but let's make them a little less uniform. Undo that bevel by typing "u", then activate the Bevel tool again. This time, we'll use the two extra fields labeled +/−. These will randomize the bevels up to the amount we specify here, either adding or subtracting to the base values we give. A good rule of thumb when using these is to keep the values to about half the base values. This will ensure that no bevel ends up being adjusted backward into the surface or flaring outward when it should taper inward. We'll set the first value to 0.025 meters and the second to 0.01 meters. Click OK again and this time you should see blocks that are all different, as seen in Figure 4-20. This is a little more interesting than having them all the same.

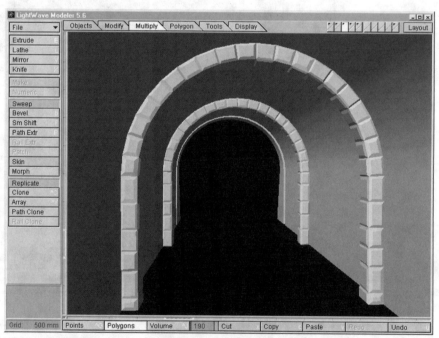

FIGURE 4-20 A randomized Bevel quickly creates an archway of cut blocks.

STEP 28: Save this gatehouse again, then switch to an empty layer. It's time to add those rear towers that we see in Figure 4-1, so load the **SmallTower.lwo** object. Place the gatehouse in the background layer and type "a" to fit the view. The SmallTower will be several meters behind the gatehouse, so select the Move tool and move it forward so it's positioned at one of the rear corners of the gatehouse. Moving it −45 meters on the Z axis and 10 meters on the X axis will place it exactly on the right rear corner.

STEP 29: If you look in the Face or Side view, you see that the parapet of this tower is a bit close to the roof of the gatehouse. This should be raised since these towers would serve as a backup defense for the 2 front towers, and thus, they had to be able to "see" out in front. Select the polygons that form the top of this tower by dragging a lasso around them. Select the Move tool again and move this section 8 meters or more up the Y axis. Now for the bottom of the tower. If you chose to flare the bottom of the gatehouse back in step 12, then you should add the same flare to this tower since we'll be attaching it to the gatehouse. Deselect everything, the select the bottom polygon of the tower. Use the Move tool to drag this 3 meters up the Y axis, then activate the Bevel tool. Click the Reset button to clear the random values, then enter a value of −1 meter for the Inset, and 3 meters for the Shift. Click OK and the tower will have a matching flared base.

STEP 30: Now we'll place a matching tower on the other corner. Deselect everything once again, then select the Mirror tool. Open the Numeric Panel and set the Plane to X and enter 0 for the position. Click OK and then hit Enter. This will create a tower at the opposite corner of the gatehouse (Figure 4-21).

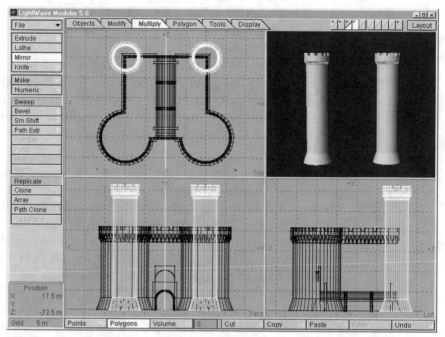

FIGURE 4-21 After mirroring, we have two identical towers, ready to be added to the rear wall of the gatehouse.

Tip: Any time you're about to create new geometry, it's a good idea to open the Surface Panel to be sure you're using the appropriate surface. This can save a lot of tedious polygon selection later on.

STEP 31: Now it's time to attach these towers to the gatehouse. To speed things up, select the polygons for the vertical sides and the flared bottoms of these towers since these are the only polygons that pass through the same space as the gatehouse. Since we're not selecting the two bottom polygons of these towers, they won't be affected by the Boolean, so we avoid the problem of having two coplanar polygons in the Boolean operation. Finally, type Shift-B to open the Boolean Panel. Select the Union button and click OK. In a few seconds, the gatehouse will appear in this layer, with the 2 rear corners cut to fit with the 2 towers (Figure 4-22). Deselect everything once again and Merge Points.

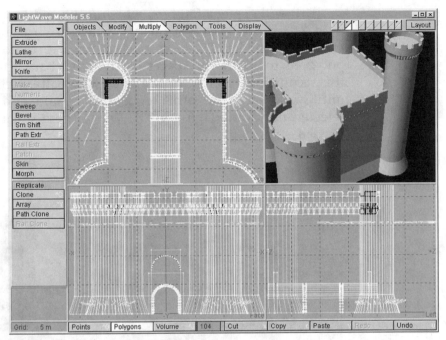

FIGURE 4-22 The assembled gatehouse.

STEP 32: Save this gatehouse again since we're now finished with the main construction of it.

STEP 33: We've done a fair amount of work to create a space to put a portcullis, so it's about time we built the portcullis. Clear Modeler and zoom in until you have a grid size of half a meter. A portcullis is simply a large heavy gate, usually with huge beams, about the size of railroad ties. We'll start off with the vertical beams. We could build one beam and then clone it to create the others, but we can save a step or two and build them all at the same time. Create a box, using the settings below, to set up a quick template for the gate.

	Low (m)	High (m)	Segments
X	−2.75	2.75	21
Y	0.0	0.0	1
Z	−0.15	0.15	1

This will create a flat box, which is the width of our gateway, with 21 evenly spaced segments, which we'll use to create the vertical members. To do this, we'll have to remove half these polygons to create the spaces between the bars, so starting with the second polygon from the end, select alternating polygons, until you reach the other end. You should end up with 10 selected polygons (Figure 4-23). Delete these since they are not needed.

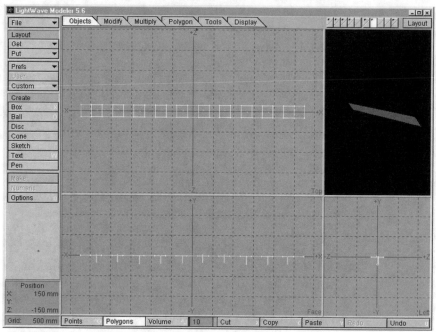

FIGURE 4-23 A segmented Box showing the polygons that we'll be deleting.

STEP 34: Now we'll extrude the remaining 11 polygons, so select the Extrude tool and open the Numeric Panel for it. Enter 5.4 meters for the Extent and set the Axis to Y. Make sure the Segments are set to 1, then click OK and hit Enter to create the extrusion. This will create a series of evenly spaced square bars. The two outer bars will be the main frame of the gate and thus they should be a bit thicker than the rest. Their current thickness is good, so let's make the other bars a bit thinner instead. Select the polygons of the 9 inner bars, then click the Tools tab at the top of the screen. Click the button labeled Smooth Scale on the side and a small panel will open. Enter a value of –0.05m and click OK. What this just did is similar to the Smooth Shift, but this only moved the selected polygons along their normals without creating extra geometry along the sides. In effect, we just reduced each polygon's size by 5 cm on each side, making these bars thinner by 10 centimeters.

STEP 35: As often portrayed in movies, the portcullis had large spikes at the bottom which would sink into the ground when it was dropped, making it difficult to try to dig under, as well as more dangerous. Not many people would want to be under these spikes when the gate was lowered! We'll create our spikes here, by first deselecting everything *except* the bottom polygons of these inner bars. We won't be placing a spike on the 2 end members, which will be inside the grooves in the inner wall when we position this gate in the gatehouse. In the Side view, simply drag the pointer across the tops of the selected bars. This will deselect the tops and sides, leaving only the bottom polygons selected. Now, activate the Bevel tool (what would we do without it?) and enter a value of 0.075 m for the Inset and give it a Shift of 0.3 m. Click OK and you will see that the bottoms of these bars are now all adorned with crude spikes. Let's finish these off by smoothing them out a bit. Deselect everything, then activate the Smooth Shift tool. Enter an Offset of 0.02 meters and lower the Max. Smoothing Angle to 20 degrees. Click OK and you will see that every sharp corner of these bars has become a 45-degree bevel (Figure 4-24).

FIGURE 4-24 A closeup of the spikes after the application of a Smooth Shift, showing the beveling that occurred.

STEP 36: Now we'll create the cross-members of this portcullis. The process will be quite similar, so let's get started by switching to a new layer and placing the vertical members in the background. Select the Box tool again, and this time, we'll create a vertical box, subdivided to set the vertical spacing. The following values will create that box:

	Low (m)	High (m)	Segments
X	0.0	0.0	1
Y	0.0	5.5	16
Z	−0.25	0.25	1

Click OK and hit Enter to create this box, which will be located in the center of the bars in the background.

STEP 37: Once again, select each alternate polygon, this time starting with the bottom (Figure 4-25). Delete these polygons since these were only created for spacing. Click the Tools tab and select the LW_Make-DoubleSided plugin from the Custom popup list. Now we can stretch these polygons across the width of the gate by using the Smooth Shift tool. Type Shift-f and then enter an Offset of 3 meters, then click OK. We just extruded those polygons in both directions, creating our horizontal crossbeams.

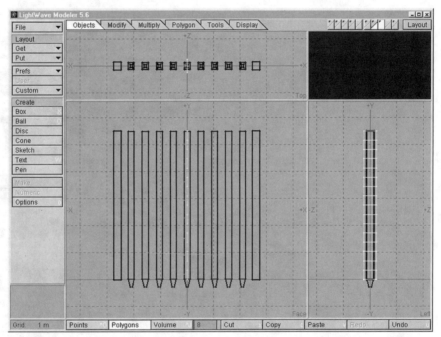

FIGURE 4-25 Another segmented box for the cross members, with the selected polygons that we don't need.

STEP 38: These beams are a bit thick right now, but the top and bottom bars are just about right. Select the polygons of the middle bars, then type "h" to activate the Stretch tool. Open the Numeric Panel for it and click the Reset button to quickly set the Center values for all to 0, then enter a value of 90% for the X-axis scale factor and 30% for the Z-axis scale factor. Click OK and the middle bars will become narrower, more like thick planks. This also moved the ends of the crossbeams to a point where they're inside the vertical beams in the background. Once again, activate the Smooth Scale tool and use the same Offset we used before, −0.05 meters, which should still be in the panel. This will narrow the beams a bit more and increase the spacing between them slightly. Finally, we'll add beveled edges to these beams, too, so deselect everything, then open the Bevel tool and apply an Inset of 25 mm and a Shift of 10 mm. Click OK and these cross-members will now have slightly rounded corners (Figure 4-26). Our last step will be to combine these 2 sections into one object.

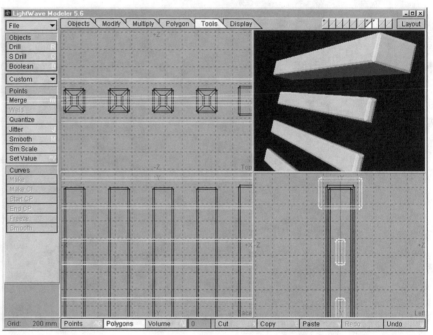

FIGURE 4-26 The final cross beams, ready to be added to the vertical members.

STEP 39: Well, that portcullis is pretty well finished. Before we assemble the two parts, let's apply some surface names. Open the Surface Panel and create a new surface name called Portcullis—Horizontal, then click Apply. This gives our horizontal beams their own surface apart from the vertical ones. Swap layers and open the Surface Panel again, and this time create a surface called Portcullis—Vertical. Click Apply and the portcullis is finished, with one last step. Type Shift-B to open the Boolean Panel and select the Union button. Click Apply, and in a few seconds, both sections of our portcullis will be combined. Merge points to get rid of the duplicates (1704 points should be eliminated), then save this object as **Portcullis.lwo**.

This completes the construction of the major elements of our castle (Figure 4-27). We can now assemble these elements to complete the construction, so let's do that. Much of this final construction will involve Booleans, but these aren't mandatory. The elements, in their individual layers, may simply all be saved in one shot, with intersecting polygons to save a bit of time, but the Booleans will tend to create models that will render faster, saving much more time in the long run.

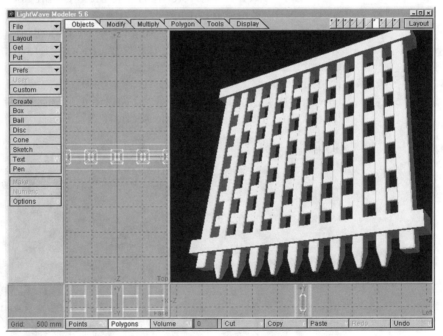

FIGURE 4-27 Our finished portcullis.

STEP 40: The first object we'll assemble will be the main castle itself. Clear Modeler and load the **CastleBase.lwo** object into the first layer. Select a polygon on the top section of this object, then type the "]" key to select the connected polygons. This will select the rest of this upper part since we never actually attached the two objects. Cut these polygons, then switch to the second layer and paste them here. When we originally created this base, we did it in two smaller, separate sections, and now we can take advantage of that for the Booleans we're about to do. Before we do those Booleans, we can simplify this object a bit more. Click the Custom button under the Tools menu and select the LW_Reduce-Polygons plugin. Again, we'll use the default values and click OK, and in a few seconds a few hundred polygons will be removed. Most of these polygons were the smaller ones that formed the battlements and machicolations, which have now been merged into larger flat faces, greatly simplifying the object.

STEP 41: Switch to the third layer and load the **MainTower.lwo** object. Put the second layer into the background and you'll see that this tower is centered on the hexagonal section, and sinks through the top a few meters (Figure 4-28). Select the 40 polygons that form the base of this central tower, then type Shift-B to activate the Boolean tool. We'll use the Union operation, so click that, then click OK. In a few seconds, the hexagonal section will appear in this layer. Merge points to actually connect the base to the tower. This should get rid of 40 duplicate points. Swap layers and delete the original hexagonal section since we're done with it now.

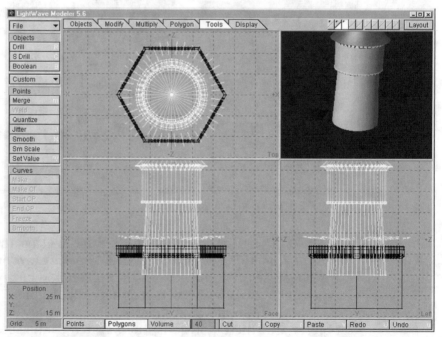

FIGURE 4-28 The central tower with the bottom polygons selected prior to the Boolean operation.

Tip: Objects that will be used in a Boolean operation do not always have to be enclosed solids. As long as the areas that will be affected follow the general rule of having aligned polygons, merged points, and no double sided or nonplanar polygons, the Boolean operations will tend to work. Be sure to remove any single- or two-point polygons and any duplicate polygons that may exist as these usually end up wreaking havoc on the Boolean results.

As objects increase in complexity, they take longer for the Boolean operations to process. It's always a good idea to try to group Boolean operations into simpler collections. Our castle, for instance, will have 6 towers that ring the main central tower. These will each be connected to the main tower with a bridge, which we also have as a separate object. There's a few ways we can get all these connected with Booleans. We could add each tower, one at a time, and then do the same with each bridge, requiring a total of 12 Boolean operations and a fair amount of object manipulation to place each object. Unfortunately, this will also gradually increase the complexity for each additional Boolean. We could add all the towers at once, then add all the bridges, in a simpler two-pass operation. Again, the first Boolean will leave us with a much more complicated object to add the bridges to. Keeping in mind that we should try to keep the processes as simple as possible, we can group these towers and bridges into two simpler Boolean operations.

STEP 42: To start off, load the **UpperTower.lwo**, then switch to the fourth layer. Load the **Bridge.lwo** object into this layer, then set the second layer as the background layer. Since we'll be repeating both of these objects 6 times around the main tower, it doesn't make a lot of sense to also repeat the same Boolean operation 6 times as we add them to the main structure. Instead, we'll do this very simple Boolean once. Type Shift-B to activate the Boolean tool, which should still have the Union button selected, then click OK. This bridge is a simple enough object that it would actually take longer to select the polygons we want affected than it will take to just do the Boolean process on the entire object. In a second, or less, you will have the small upper tower attached to one end of this bridge (Figure 4-29). As usual after most Boolean operations, follow up with a Merge Points.

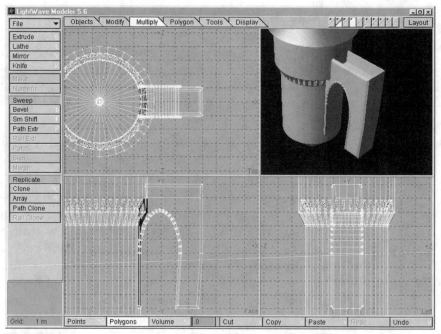

FIGURE 4-29 A small upper tower is attached to a bridge.

Tip: It is not always required that you merge points right after a Boolean operation. There are times where you will want to work on the new geometry that was created. By not immediately merging points, you can easily select the new geometry by selecting a new polygon and then typing "]" to select all the connected polygons. From this point, you can move the new polygons to another layer for further editing.

Another thing to watch out for after any Boolean operation is stray points. Occasionally, seemingly random points will be created, not attached to any polygons. Switch to Point Edit mode and type "w" to open the Points Statistics panel and check the second row that reads "0 Polygons." If this is not 0, click the + button beside it and close the panel. Since these points are unattached, they have no effect on the model, so delete them. They could actually interfere with other operations later on, so check for them often.

STEP 43: Now that we have this first Boolean done, we can make the other towers and bridges, with the 2 objects already combined. Under the Multiply menu, click on the Array button and set the Array Type to Radial. We want 6 of these towers spaced evenly around the main central tower, so enter a value of 6 for the Number, and set the Axis to Y. The center of the Main tower is located at 30 meters on the Z axis since we moved that in the last chapter, and since we're placing these smaller towers around the main one, we'll use the same center point. Make sure the X value is 0 and enter 30 meters for the Z value. (The Y value has no effect since this is the axis our array will be centered on.) Click OK and you will have 6 identical towers, each with a short bridge spanning toward the center (Figure 4-30).

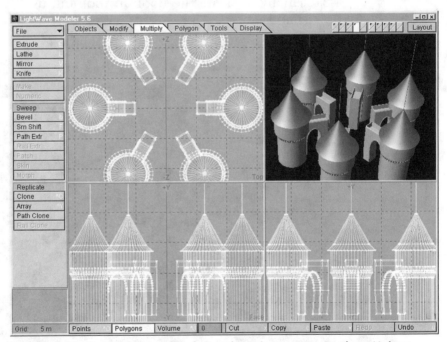

FIGURE 4-30 The Radial Array is faster than six separate Boolean Unions.

STEP 44: We now have our 6 towers, so let's connect them to the main tower. Select the third layer, which has our main tower assembly, as the foreground layer and select the fourth layer as the background. Normally, we'd place the less complicated object in the background and select the appropriate polygons of the object in the foreground to speed the Boolean process, but in this case, selecting the necessary polygons of these 6 towers would take longer. It's easier this time to put the towers in the background and to select the necessary polygons of the main tower. Resize the Face view to full screen and zoom in to the lower half of the main tower assembly. The bridges in the background will be joining into the sloped sides of the main tower while each of the 6 towers will be merging with a corner of the hexagonal base, intersecting the battlements, machicolations, and the floor and outer walls. Knowing this, we can simply select these polygons by dragging a lasso around the lower half of this assembly, as shown in Figure 4-31. Finally, activate the Boolean tool and use the Union function again.

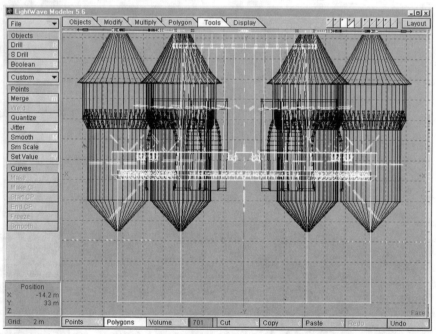

FIGURE 4-31 The central tower assembly showing the selected polygons that will be joined with the upper towers.

Even though we've optimized the object for this Boolean, it can still take up to 2 minutes to complete, depending on the speed of your machine. This is preferable to the 3 to 4 minutes that it would take to add the towers and then the bridges.

When this is done, you will still have a few polygons selected. Deselect everything, then merge points. We now have the completed upper section of the main castle (Figure 4-32).

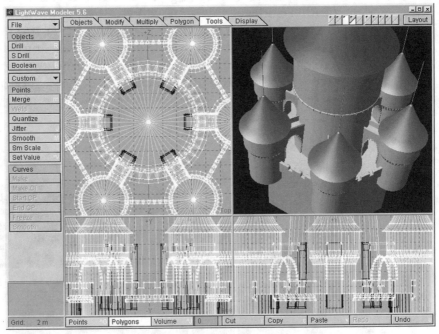

FIGURE 4-32 The completed tower assembly.

Before we go any further, we should plan ahead for surfacing. In Tutorial 3 we created the main tower and gave the roof a surface name of Roof. We called the roof of the smaller tower Tower Roof. This was fine for just two rooftops, which can be mapped independently of one another. However, we now have 6 rooftops with the surface name of Tower Roof. If we plan on surfacing these independently, we'll need to give each of these roofs its own surface name.

STEP 45: Type "w" to open the Polygon Statistics panel and select all the polygons with the surface name Tower Roof. Close this panel and then cut these polygons. Switch to an empty layer and paste them here. Now we have them isolated from the rest of the castle so they're easier to work with. Working in the top view, drag a lasso around one of these roofs to select it, then type "q" to open the Surface Panel. Create a surface name of Tower Roof 1, then click Apply (Figure 4-33). Deselect this roof, then drag a lasso around another roof. Open the Surface Panel again and create another surface, this time called Tower Roof 2. Continue doing this until you've created 6 surfaces numbered 1 to 6. It will be convenient to do this in a clockwise order, starting at the top of the screen. Now, when we apply textures to these roofs, we can do each one independently. Finally, deselect everything, then cut these objects and paste them back onto the towers in the third layer, and merge points.

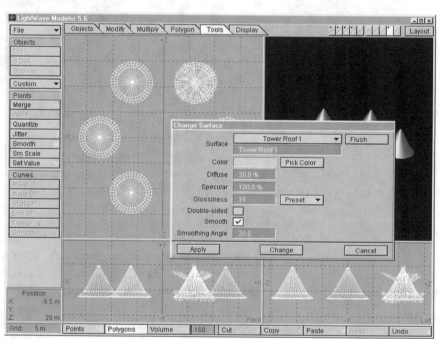

FIGURE 4-33 The first of six smaller roofs gets its own surface name.

STEP 46: Save this object as **Castle.lwo** so we have it for later. Now we'll work on the bottom half, which will mainly be the addition of towers at the corners, but also attaching this castle to the outer wall.

STEP 47: Clear Modeler, then load the CastleBase object into the first layer. Once again, select the top hexagonal section and this time delete it. All we want this time is the bottom section of the castle. We'll be doing a series of Boolean operations on this as well, so it'll help speed things up if we reduce the amount of polygons on this object. Click the Custom button under the Tools menu and select the LW_Reduce-Polygons plugin again. We'll use the default setting once more, so just click OK. This should remove a thousand or more polygons (depending on the placement of your battlements and machicolations), roughly half of the original polygon count.

STEP 48: Switch to the second layer and load the **OuterWall.lwo** object. As with the CastleBase, this outer wall is comprised of objects that are not actually connected to one another. Select a polygon along the length of one of the walls, then type the "]" key to select the connected polygons. This will select the rest of the wall, so type "X" to cut these polygons, then switch to the third layer and paste them here. We now have the base of the castle in one layer, the corner towers in layer 2, and the outer walls in the third layer. Since we're about to perform Boolean operations to this wall, it would be a good idea to run the LW_Reduce-Polygons plugin on it first.

STEP 49: Before we do anything further, we should decide if we want to add a flared base to this wall and the castle base like we did with the gatehouse in Step 12. If so, then select the bottom polygon and move it 3 meters up the Y axis, then apply a Bevel with an Inset of −1 meter and a Shift of 3 meters (Figure 4-34). This is still optional and doesn't necessarily need to be added to both the castle base and the walls.

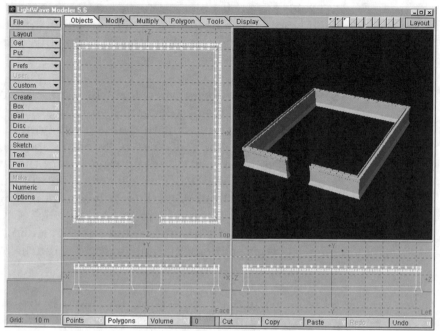

FIGURE 4-34 The outer wall with a defensive flare added.

STEP 50: Now we're nearly ready to finish with the Booleans. It's always a good idea to check how the 2 objects will look together before actually combining them, so hold the Shift key, select both layers 1 and 3 as the foreground, and check the 3D preview. In this case we see that the rear wall passes through the back section of the castle base, but looking closer, we see a slight problem. These objects are the same height, and across the top where the 2 combine, we now have 3 rows of battlements (Figure 4-35)!

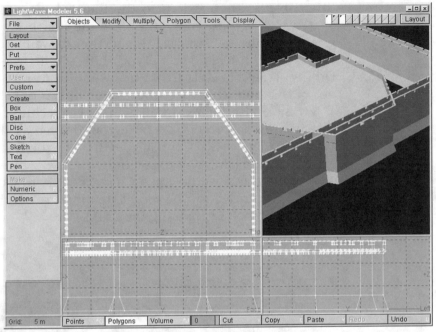

FIGURE 4-35 An unwanted triple row of battlements appears where the main structure passes through the outer wall.

This causes two problems for us. The first is that the roof polygons behind the battlements are on the same plane, and this is confusing to Boolean operations. The second problem is that even if the Boolean works we still have those extra rows of battlements. We will be placing a large tower in the corners where the wall meets the base, but we'll still have the extra walls. We could make the wall or the castle base taller so the battlements of one are buried in the other, but that could very well require that some other elements, like the upper towers, also be adjusted. This sounds bad, but all is not lost yet.

STEP 51: Click on the first layer button so we see only the castle base, then select the large top polygon that forms the roof. Copy this polygon, then switch to the fourth layer and paste it here. Switch to the third layer and place the fourth layer in the background (Figure 4-36). Since this section of wall will be a problem for us, we'll just remove it. Type Shift-R to activate the Template Drill tool. Set the Axis to Y since we want to take a vertical slice out of this wall, and select the Tunnel operation. Click OK and in a few seconds the rear wall will have a chunk removed that matches the polygon in the background layer, as viewed from the Top view (Figure 4-37). If you were to view the first and third layers together again, you'll see that the two objects fit together much better and we no longer have a triple row of battlements. Again, this process can be accelerated if we select the polygons of the rear wall before applying the drill.

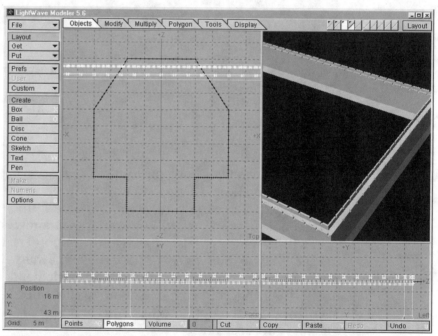

FIGURE 4-36 The outer wall about to be sliced using the template polygon in the background.

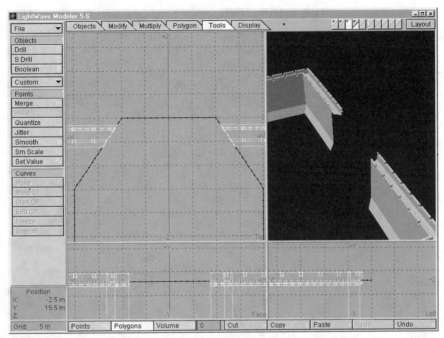

FIGURE 4-37 After slicing, we have eliminated the unwanted section of battlements.

STEP 52: Switch to the fourth layer again and delete the polygon that we placed here since it's done its job. Load the **Tower-Flared.lwo** object we created in Tutorial 3 and once again run the Reduce-Polygons plugin on this object since we'll be using it in a Boolean operation. Place the first and third layers in the background and select the move tool. We'll place two of these towers at the rear of the castle base, where it intersects with the rear wall. Move this tower 10 meters on the X axis and 52.5 meters on the Z axis to position it (Figure 4-38). We need a second matching tower for the other side, so select the Mirror tool and mirror this tower on the X plane.

STEP 53: Now that the 2 towers are in position, let's attach them to the castle. Again, to speed things up, we'll select only the polygons of these towers that share the same space as the objects in the background. Dragging the pointer across the towers in the side view, selecting polygons along the edge of the flare and the tower wall will select the polygons we need. Now we need to decide which objects to Boolean first, the wall or the base? Why not both? They both intersect the towers, so just leave these two layers in the background and type Shift-B. Again, use the Union operation and click OK. This Boolean will do two things: it will give you some time to stretch your legs, and it will actually add the objects in both background layers to these towers, saving us an extra step (Figure 4-39). Deselect everything and once again Merge Points.

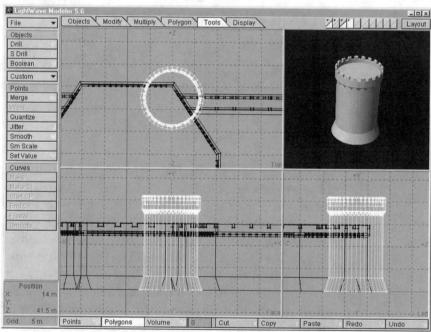

FIGURE 4-38 One of the large towers is moved into place.

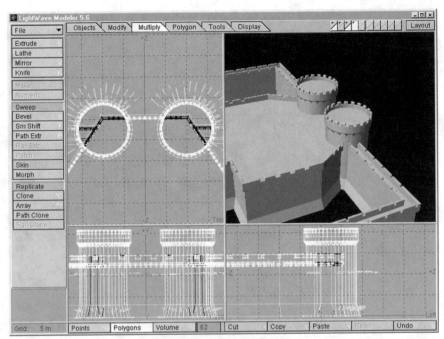

FIGURE 4-39 Two large towers are joined with the walls and the main structure, from two separate background layers.

STEP 54: OK, let's add those other towers and finish this section off. Switch to the fifth layer and load the **SmallTower.lwo** object. As before, run the Reduce-Polygons plugin on this tower to simplify it a bit. Resize the Top view to full screen and select the fourth layer as the background. Adjust the view so that the castle base fills the window, then select the Move tool. Move this tower to the first corner on the right, which is located at 10 meters on the X and Z axes. Now, drag a lasso around this tower, then type "C" and then "V", which will create an unselected copy under this selected one. Now, move this selected tower to the next corner, which is located at 20 meters on X and 20 meters on Z. This will leave a copy of the tower at the first corner. Type the "C" and "V" keys again and move the selected tower 20 meters along the Z axis to the last corner before the outer wall (Figure 4-40).

Finally, deselect everything and use the Mirror tool again to make copies of these three towers on the other side of the castle base (Figure 4-41).

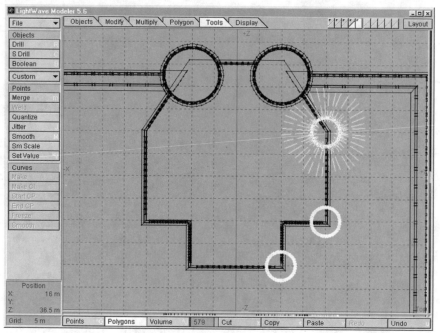

FIGURE 4-40 The positions of the three thin towers.

STEP 55: These towers don't have a flared base, but if you did add the flare to the castle, then it should also be applied to these towers. Select the bottom polygons of these towers and use the Move tool to raise these polygons 3 meters on the Y axis. Follow this with the Bevel tool, using the Inset of −1 m and a Shift of 3 meters. Deselect the bottom polygons, then continue on to the next step.

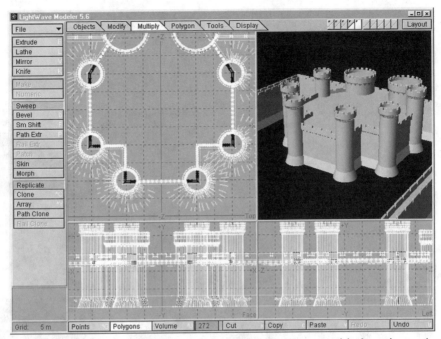

FIGURE 4-41 After being mirrored, the small towers are added to the main building.

STEP 56: Now we're ready to attach these towers. Select the side polygons of these towers to accelerate the Boolean process, then activate the Boolean tool. Click OK and get a little exercise as this Boolean processes since it could take a while.

As you can see, the time it takes to process Boolean operations can get quite high as the model becomes more detailed. Luckily, we're nearly finished. Now would be a good time to Merge Points and check for any stray points that may have been created.

STEP 57: Select the second layer and place the fifth layer in the background. Now we'll add the 4 large towers to the outer wall, so once again run the Reduce-Polygons plugin on these towers to simplify them. Next, select the polygons that form the vertical sides and the wedges, then activate the Boolean tool again. This model is quickly becoming very complicated, so this Boolean operation could take several minutes. When it's done, Merge Points again (Figure 4-42).

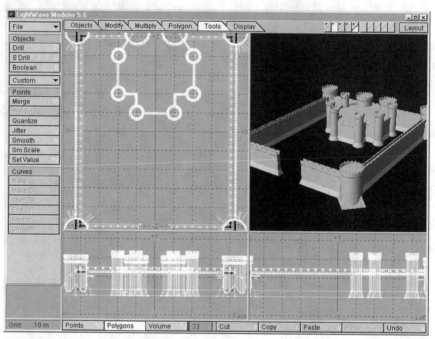

FIGURE 4-42 Finally, the four outer towers are added to the walls.

STEP 58: Select the sixth layer and load the **Gatehouse.lwo** object. Again, we'll run this through the Reduce-Polygons plugin, which will remove 1030 polygons, so it's a little simpler for the Boolean operation. Place the second layer in the background, then select the polygons that make the sides of this gatehouse, where the outer wall intersects them, then activate the Boolean tool again. Use the union option, then click OK and wait.

STEP 59: Wait some more. OK, had enough? Click the abort button to stop this. There's got to be a faster way to do this. Well, there is! Switch to the second layer, where we have the majority of our castle. In the Top view, drag a lasso around the two front walls (Figure 4-43), then cut these polygons. Switch to an empty layer and paste them there. Go back to the gatehouse and place the front walls we just moved into the background, then select the side walls of the gatehouse to isolate the Boolean operation to just those polygons (Figure 4-44). Now that we have a much simpler object in the background, this shouldn't take too long. Perform the Boolean Union again and you should notice a big speed difference. When this is done, we'll have 2 short wall sections sticking out the sides of the gatehouse (Figure 4-45). Deselect everything and merge points.

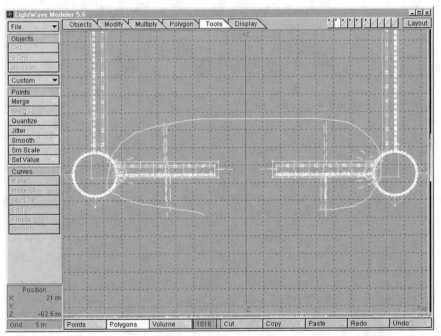

FIGURE 4-43 Rather than wait an eternity, cut these two walls and place them in their own layer for the next Boolean.

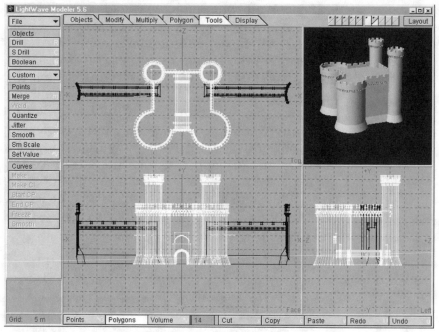

FIGURE 4-44 To speed thing up more, the side walls of the gatehouse are selected prior to the Boolean.

STEP 60: Now we need to replace the missing walls in the second layer. Cut the polygons in this layer, and then switch to the second layer. Type "V" to paste them here and you'll notice that they're a perfect match. Once again, Merge Points and check for stray points.

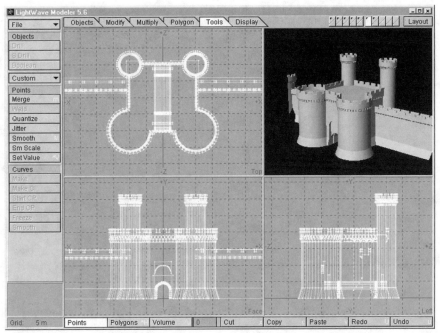

FIGURE 4-45 The assembled gatehouse and walls. Note the tower polygons in the background. This is harmless and they'll be returned soon enough.

STEP 61: Now it's time to add the last major section to complete our castle. That last section will be the upper half of the castle itself, which will be joined with the roof of the castle base. We already know that the roof is a single polygon, and it's the only one that the upper section has any contact with, so select that polygon and cut it, then paste it in an empty layer. Switch to a new layer again, then load the **Castle.lwo** object. The first thing we'll do is to run the Reduce-Polygons plugin on it. After that, select the 7 polygons at the very bottom that form the 6 large walls and the bottom face (Figure 4-46). Place the single roof polygon we just moved into the background, and perform another Boolean Union. This one will go by very fast. Finally, cut all these polygons and switch back to the second layer, where the rest of our castle site is located, then paste this final section (Figure 4-47). Merge points and check for stray points.

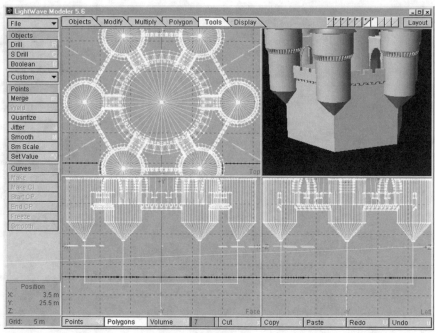

FIGURE 4-46 Preparation for the last of the large Booleans. The bottom seven polygons of the tower assembly are selected for speed.

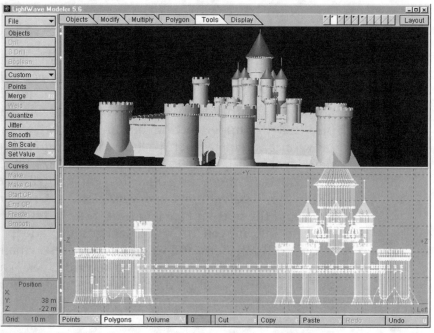

FIGURE 4-47 The fully assembled castle, ready for detailing.

STEP 62: Our final step will be to clean up the bottom of this castle. During these Booleans, we always selected the polygons that form the sides and tops of the structures, but not the bottom polygons. Since these bottom polygons all lie on the same plane, they would tend to cause problems during the Boolean process, either by causing flipped or unwanted polygons or simply by canceling the operation because of a "polygon partitioning error." If you look closely, you'll notice that we still have the original bottom polygons of these objects sitting at the bottom. Use the Lasso to select all the polygons that rest on the ground plane, then cut them. Switch to an empty layer and paste them here. You might find that this situation is similar to how we started the gatehouse at the beginning of this chapter. Switch to another empty layer and place the bottom polygons in the background. Create a box on the ground plane, large enough to contain the polygons in the background layer (Figure 4-48).

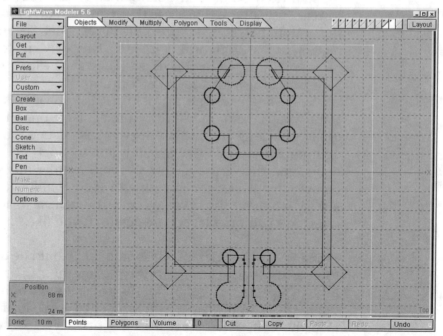

FIGURE 4-48 Another flat box will be used to simplify the bottom polygons of this castle.

STEP 63: Type Shift-R to activate the Template Drill tool and set the Axis to Y. Use the Slice operation again and click OK. In a second, all the polygons in the background layer will have their outlines sliced into this object. Select the outer edge of this box, which will select the outer polygon, then delete it. This will leave us with a set of polygons that match the bottom of the castle. Run the Reduce-Polygons plugin on this object to combine everything into one polygon. Finally, Cut this polygon and paste it back into the layer with the rest of our castle, then Merge Points.

STEP 64: Finally, we'll prepare this castle for placement on a ground surface. Since the ground is rarely ever level, especially in medieval times, we need to allow for variations in the ground surface. A very simple way to do this is to just extend the bottom of the castle down below the ground plane a short distance. We can't just drag the bottom polygon lower since that will disrupt the flatness of some of the sides, mainly the wedges of the corner towers. Instead, we'll just use that familiar Bevel tool again. Select the bottom polygon and open the Bevel panel. Set an Inset of −0.5 meters and a Shift of 1.5 meters. This will create a slope that matches the angle of the flared bases we created for the towers. Now we can save this again as **Castle.lwo**.

This completes the major construction of this castle. If you want, you can add more towers, like a large one in the middle of each of the long outer walls, or even just change the heights of the existing towers. All that's really left to do is to add windows, doors, and the various arrow slits and murder holes. Rather than go over the placement of each and every window and door, we'll just cover the steps involved and the general placement guidelines, and you can place these details as you like.

STEP 65: The first details we should add would be doorways. Like the castles themselves, doorways come in all shapes and sizes, from simple rectangular portals to majestic arched entrances. We'll create ours with a simple arched top. Clear Modeler and load the **Castle.lwo** object into the first layer. Switch to the second layer and zoom in until you have a grid size of a half-meter.

A typical doorway is approximately 2 meters tall and about 1 meter wide, so we'll start with a shape of those dimensions. In the Face view, use the Pen tool to draw out a polygon similar to the one in Figure 4-49. This should be about 3 meters wide and 4 meters tall, since we're allowing for a frame. This will become the template for the main doors that will be placed at ground level. Type "q" to open the Surfaces panel and change the Current Surface to Stone, then click Apply. Extrude this polygon to an Extent of 5 meters, and then select the two end polygons. Open the surface panel again, and create a new surface called Doors, then click Apply. Deselect everything and copy this object to another layer.

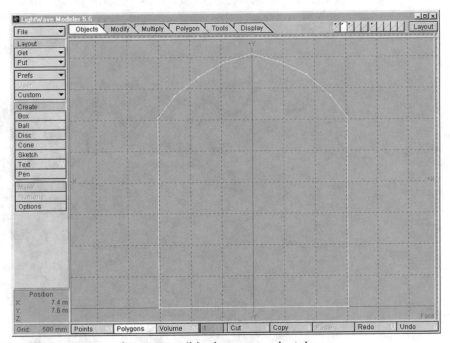

FIGURE 4-49 One of many possible doorway arch styles.

Note: This object should be set up so that the base is just slightly above the ground plane. This will help prevent partitioning errors that can occur during the Boolean operations since the castle itself has polygon edges that are also in line with this plane.

STEP 66: We'll be using this object to cut the main doors into the castle through the use of Booleans. Place the Castle in the background, then move this object so it intersects with the base of the main castle structure, as shown in Figure 4-50. Swap layers and select the polygons of the castle that this object intersects, then activate the Boolean tool. Use the Subtract method and click OK. In a second or two, this wall will have an indentation, which will be the main entrance (Figure 4-51). This time, we will not merge points right away. Instead, select a couple of these new polygons, type "]" to select the connected polygons, and then move them to a new layer.

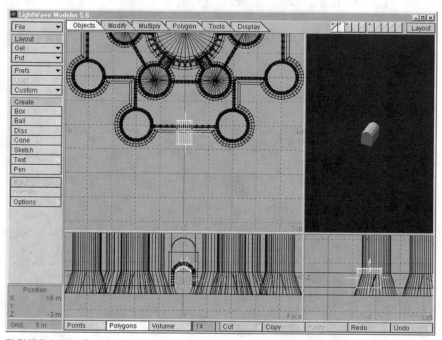

FIGURE 4-50 The doorway cutter in position against the main castle structure.

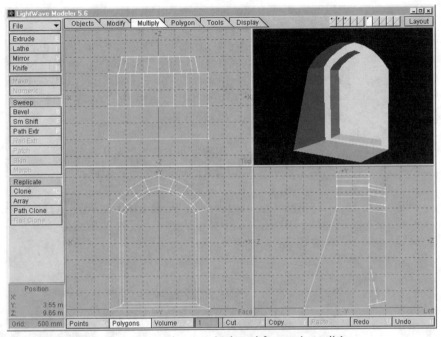

FIGURE 4-51 The doorway polygons, isolated for easier editing.

STEP 67: This door, being the main entrance, will be a slightly different design from the rest. The first thing we'll do is to set the surface of all these polygons to the Walls surface. Next, select the end polygon and change its surface to Stone. Now we'll create a frame for the door. Activate the Bevel tool and apply an Inset of 0.3 meters and a Shift of 0. This will set the thickness of the frame, so now we need the depth. Apply a second Bevel, this time with an Inset of 0.1 meter and a Shift of −0.5 meter. Change the surface once more, this time back to the Doors surface so our end polygon is a door again. This creates a basic arched frame for our main entrance (Figure 4-51).

STEP 68: We'll decorate this frame a bit more, but first select the polygon that now serves as the top of the step, shown highlighted in Figure 4-52. Select the Move tool and move this polygon down −0.2 meter on the Y axis so we don't have such a steep step. Open the Polygon Statistics Panel and select all the polygons that use the Stone surface and close that panel again. As we did with the arches inside the tunnel of the gatehouse, use the Knife tool to slice the long vertical polygons that form the sides of this frame. About 5 to 10 slices are all that's needed, keeping them fairly evenly spaced. When this is done, apply one last Bevel, this time with the following settings:

Inset: 0.05 m +/− 0.025 m

Shift: 0.025 m +/− 0.01 m

Click OK and you'll have another archway that looks like cut blocks (Figure 4-52).

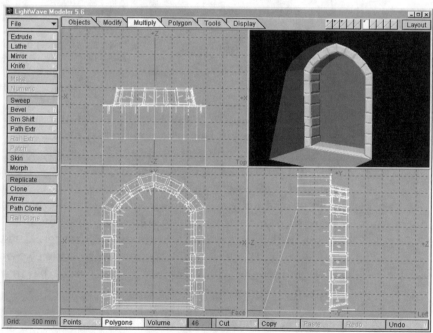

FIGURE 4-52 Once again, the randomized Bevel makes great cut blocks.

STEP 69: Deselect everything and cut these polygons. Go back to the Castle in the first layer and paste these polygons. Now we can Merge Points (Figure 4-53).

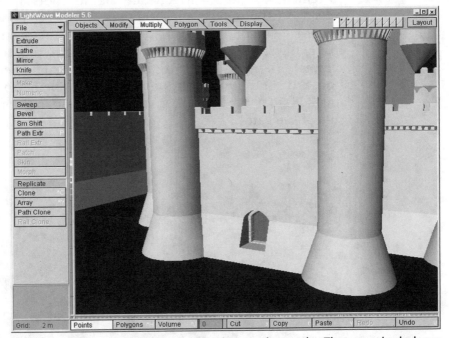

FIGURE 4-53 The doorway is replaced onto the castle. That seemingly large step will actually be underground.

Note: If you want to create another large entrance like this one somewhere else on the castle, just repeat Steps 66 to 69. You can do more than one of these large doors at the same time. Just perform the Booleans to get all the doors cut, then move all these cut sections to a new layer, then continue with Steps 67 and 68 on all these frames simultaneously.

STEP 70: Now we'll create a set of doors for the gatehouse. These will also be large doors, but not as large as those of the main entrance. Switch back to the second layer, and scale the doorway template we have there by 75%, then copy this template to an empty layer and place the castle in the background. It's important to remember there will generally be no doors anywhere on the outside of the outer walls. The doors to the gatehouse will be to either side of the main gate, but these will be on the wall facing inside toward the courtyard, so use the Move tool to position this template between the gate and a small rear tower of the gatehouse. It should intersect the rear wall by about a half-meter (Figure 4-54). Use the Mirror tool to create a duplicate on the opposite side of the gate.

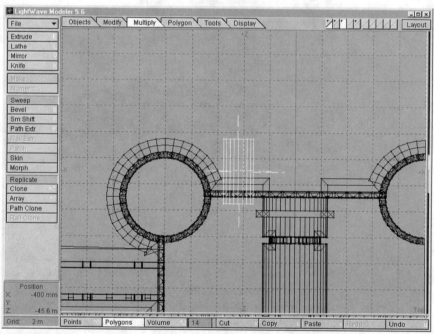

FIGURE 4-54 A doorway to the gatehouse is created the same way.

STEP 71: Swap layers and select the polygons that form the rear wall of the gatehouse and perform a Boolean Subtract. The rest of this procedure is virtually identical to the main entrance, following Steps 66 to 69, with one exception. Since this doorway is smaller, use lower values on the first two Bevels that we used to create the arched frame. (Hint: add the equation "*0.75" after the values used in Step 67).

This will create two matching doors for the gatehouse (Figure 4-55). This same door template may also be used to add additional doors to the main castle itself, including the second level, providing access to the lower roof (Figure 4-56).

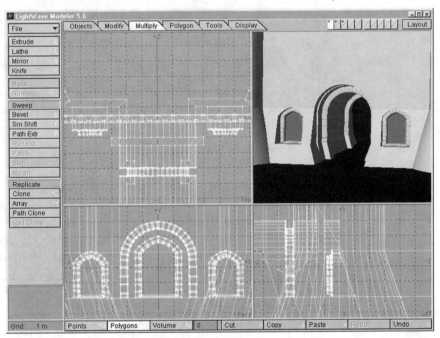

FIGURE 4-55 Two completed gatehouse doors.

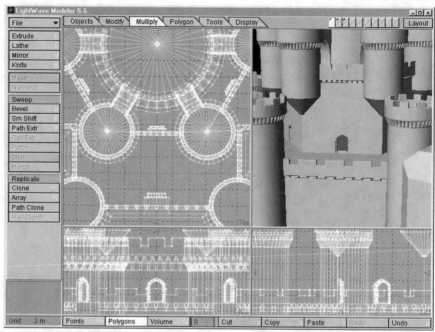

FIGURE 4-56 Similar doors are added to the hexagonal structure, leading out to the first parapet.

STEP 72: Now we'll create our smaller doors, which will provide access to the walls, towers, and bridges. These may be arched or just simple rectangular openings. These doorways need to be only about 2 meters tall and about 1 meter wide. If you're using the archway we created in Step 65, simply scale it to the appropriate height and width. Just make sure that the extruded sides use the surface name of Stone and the ends are called Doors since we'll be calling these up later.

There will be several of these doors, mainly placed on the towers, and some towers have 2 doorways. Most of these doorways will be placed wherever a wall or roof meets a tower, so they won't be at ground level, though there's no reason you can't place doors at ground level as well. In fact, the large towers at the corners of the outer wall could do with a door at their base, on the inner side of the walls.

Take your time, and just work on one tower at a time, but since these doors are simpler, the process will be a bit different. We'll use a bridge door as an example here.

STEP 73: To make things easier to navigate, we'll temporarily be copying sections of the castle to other layers to work on them. Let's start off with the bridges. Switch to the first layer and zoom in on the main tower in the Top view. Use the Lasso to select the polygons that form the central tower, the bridges, and the walls of the smaller towers these bridges are connected to (Figure 4-57). Copy these polygons and place them into an empty layer.

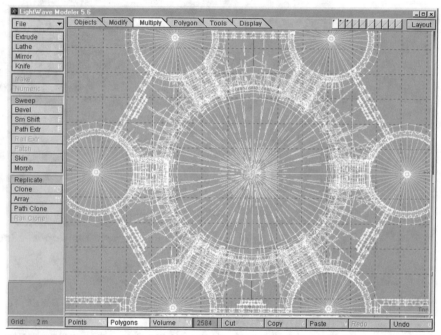

FIGURE 4-57 To simplify things, this section of the castle will be temporarily moved to another layer.

STEP 74: Switch to the layer with the door template and place the walls in the background. Move the template into place along one of the bridges as shown in Figure 4-58. Select all the polygons of this object, then copy and paste it to create a duplicate. Move the selected object down below this bridge so we can place another set of doors at the base. You might need to adjust the ends of these two templates to ensure that they are approximately half a meter inside the tower walls in the background (Figure 4-58).

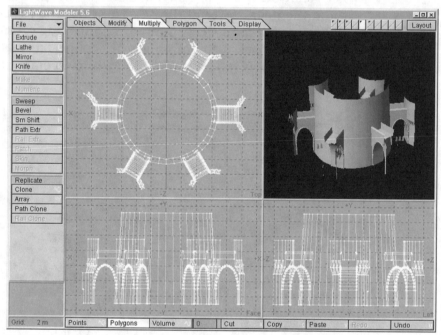

FIGURE 4-58 The removed polygons, ready to have doors added.

STEP 75: Since we used a Radial Array to make 6 copies of the small upper towers and bridges earlier, we can do the same thing to set up the rest of our doors. Deselect everything, then activate the Array tool under the Multiply menu. Make sure the Axis is set to Y and the Number is set to 6. Set the center value for the Z axis to 30 meters, and then click OK. This will create 12 objects that align with the bridges in the background. Now we're ready to make those doorways.

STEP 76: Switch to the first layer and place the door templates in the background. Once again, select the polygons that form the surfaces we'll be using in this Boolean operation, just like we did in Step 73, so this Boolean operation won't take all day. Finally, type Shift-B to open the Boolean tool, select the Subtract button, then click OK. In a few seconds, there will be a doorway at each end of each bridge, as well as two more doorways below each bridge (Figure 4-59).

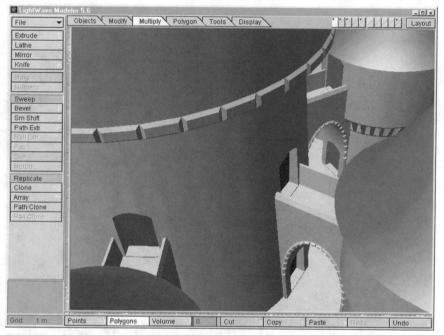

FIGURE 4-59 The doors around the bridges start to make this castle look like a livable place.

STEP 77: We'll finish off these doors by enhancing the frames. There will still be some selected polygon on this castle after the Boolean, so type the "]" key to select all the connected polygons. This will select everything except for the doors we just created since we haven't merged points yet. Type the double-quote key to invert the selection, then cut these doorways and paste them in a new layer. Use the Polygon Statistics Panel to select the polygons with the surface name of Stone, then use the Knife tool to slice the long vertical polygons that form the sides of these doorways, just like we did with the main entrances. Finally, activate the Bevel tool and apply the following values to form these polygons into a cut block pattern (Figure 4-60).

Inset: 0.05 m +/− 0.025 m

Shift: 0.025 m +/− 0.01 m

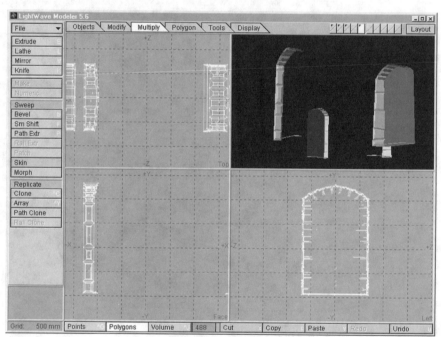

FIGURE 4-60 The doorframes look much better with that familiar cut block look.

STEP 78: Deselect everything again, then cut these polygons and paste them back onto the castle in the first layer, then Merge Points.

STEP 79: Create the doors for the other towers in much the same way; select a tower, copy it to another layer, then use that as a guide to position the door template. Switch to the first layer and select the polygons you're about to cut into, then perform the Boolean. Next, move the new doorway polygons to a new layer and repeat Steps 77 and 78 on these doorways. Keep in mind that this castle is symmetrical, which means that you need to place the doorways for only one side, then Mirror them before performing the Boolean Subtract.

When we have our doors placed, it's time to give some thought to the windows. The process will be very similar, but we'll be altering the procedure a bit. Glass windows were extremely rare in medieval times, so windows were often little more than openings in the walls, with wooden shutters to close them at night. Since we won't be adding glass to ours, we'll generally be able to see inside, without having our view obscured by reflections. This means we'll need to have something behind the windows so we don't end up looking through the opposite walls and out into the rest of the scene. We'll accomplish this by building a fake room, which will be little more than a box with inward-facing polygons. We'll then place this box behind a wall before we cut our windows, which will end up giving the window frame some thickness, as well as some interior detail. This will add another degree of realism to the castle. We'll use the gatehouse as an example, and then you can just repeat the process wherever you want windows.

STEP 80: Clear all the layers except the first one, which is where our castle is. We'll be keeping that since we need it for the window placement. This would also be a good time to save it again.

STEP 81: Our windows can be any shape, but windows generally followed the same design as the doors, being either rectangular or arched. They were also typically tall and narrow, so use the Pen tool in an empty layer to draw out your window, keeping it less than a meter wide and no more than 1.5 meters tall (Figure 4-61). When you have a shape you like, simply extrude it to about 2 meters in length. Open the Surface Panel and change the surface to the Stone surface and click Apply. Copy this object to another layer so we always have the original shape.

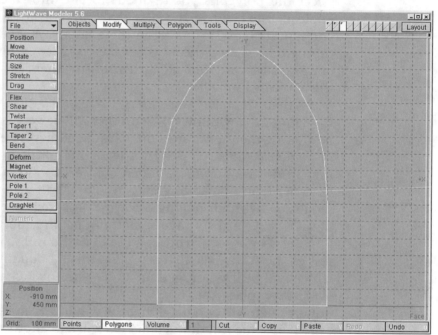

FIGURE 4-61 A basic window template.

Before we place any windows, there are a couple of guidelines we should follow. First, castles almost never had windows on the ground level of the towers. This was usually reserved for arrow slits, which would provide hidden archers an excellent line of fire. Instead, windows would generally begin to appear only at around the third story, but these could be placed along the outer walls as well as the ones facing the courtyard. The second point is to keep in mind where the various floors would be. If we keep our windows aligned at about 4-meter intervals, then we've given ourselves enough room to allow for floors and relatively high ceilings inside, even though we won't be adding these for real.

STEP 82: In the first layer, select the polygons that form the front wall of the gatehouse and copy these to a new layer. Switch over to the layer with the extruded window and place the gatehouse wall in the background. Select the window template, and position it so it passes through the wall in the background, much like we did with the doors, but in this case, we want it to extend about 1 meter or so into the wall. Place more copies of this window along this wall, as in Figure 4-62.

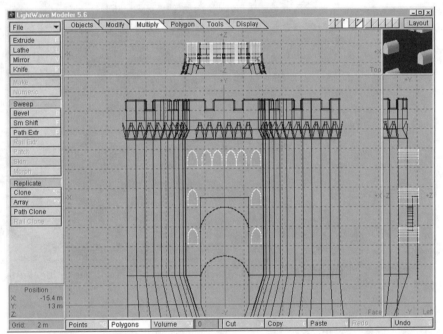

FIGURE 4-62 A typical window placement for the front of the gatehouse.

STEP 83: Switch to a new layer and place both the gatehouse wall and the window templates in the background. Select the Box tool and drag out a box that will fit about a half-meter behind the gatehouse wall, which will be used to create a room behind the windows. Place one of these boxes behind each window, or group of windows, if there are any that are close together, as in Figure 4-63. When you have a box behind each window, type "f" to flip the polygons so they face inward. Open the surface panel and create a new surface called "Interiors" and apply this to these boxes.

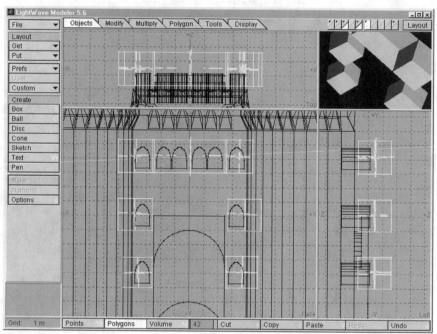

FIGURE 4-63 Simple inward-facing boxes will make ideal interior facades.

STEP 84: Now we're about ready to cut these windows into the real castle. First, cut these boxes and paste them into the first layer so they're inside the gatehouse. Place the window templates in the background and then select the front wall and the boxes. Open the Boolean Panel and select the Subtract operation, then click OK. In a few seconds, you will have a set of windows cut into the front of the gatehouse, revealing rooms inside (Figure 4-64).

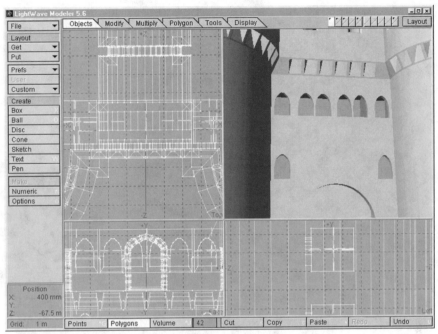

FIGURE 4-64 The gatehouse front, after cutting the first windows, reveals the fake rooms inside.

STEP 85: Let's make these windows a little more visible. Select a polygon of the main castle and type the "]" key to select all the connected polygons. Since we haven't merged points, the new polygons we created will not be selected, so type the double quote key to invert the selection, which should leave only the window frames selected. Cut these and paste them into an empty layer. We'll create a nice stone block frame for these windows by applying a Smooth Shift to them. Use an Offset of 0.1 meters and increase the Max Smoothing Angle to 100 degrees, then click OK. This will create a simple frame around the windows.

Note: You may need to increase the Max Smoothing Angle more, depending on your window designs. If the corner polygons of the windows cross each other after Smooth Shifting, then Undo it and increase the value, then try again.

STEP 86: To create the stone block look, apply a Bevel to these frames. Use an Inset of 20 mm, with a random value of 10 mm. Use a value of 10 mm for the Shift with a random amount of 5 mm, and then click OK. You will now have cut a block window frame for each window (Figure 4-65). Finally, cut these frames and paste them back onto the castle in the first layer and merge points.

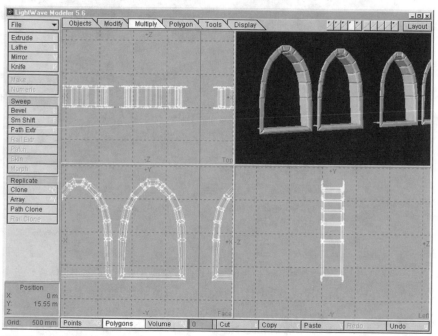

FIGURE 4-65 After being moved to a new layer, the window frames also get the stone block look.

STEP 87: Continue on, selecting various walls and adding windows to them using this same procedure. Occasionally, you may need to drag a box around a bit to make it fit behind a wall, such as the angled walls of the base and the towers. Also keep in mind that towers usually had spiral staircases and these windows were used to illuminate them, so their placement on the towers should imply a spiral pattern. Most of the windows should appear on the main castle itself, and the rear wall of the gatehouse would have a similar pattern as the front. The main outer wall would not have any windows and the same is true for the angled base of the buildings, if you chose to add that defensive flare. When you're done adding windows, save the castle again.

Note: This castle can get extremely complex, so keep an eye on the number of points that it contains. The LightWave object format can currently only contain up to 65535 points in any object (except the special saved layers format), although you can build objects in Modeler with a point count far in excess of this number. Each window we add will increase the number of points by about 200. At this point, it's a good idea to cut the castle into separate sections. This will give us two (or more) objects with a fraction of the total number of points each. The entire central tower assembly, from the base of the hexagonal part and up, makes an ideal place to cut the object. Just use the lasso to select the central tower and the 6 surrounding towers and bridges, then move these to another layer. Save these towers as **Castle-Top.lwo** and the rest of the castle would use the **Castle.lwo** filename. Don't worry about the hexagonal hole in the roof of the lower section. When both of these objects are loaded into Layout, they will load back into place with one another, and the towers will once again cover that hole. Another benefit of this is now you will have a separate bounding box for the central towers, making camera navigation around the castle easier. You might also want to separate the gatehouse in the same way.

All we have left to build now are the arrow slits and murder holes. Arrow slits are simply tall, narrow slots cut into the walls through which an archer could loose arrows at the enemy. These were about 2 meters in height and only about 20 centimeters wide. Most often they were placed near the bases of towers, though they also made appearances in the centers of long battlements as well.

Murder holes are a similar device, being a simple hole about 50 centimeters square. They were usually placed within the first two stories, tending to be near entryways. They were also commonly found lining the ceiling of the gatehouse tunnel, where castle defenders could ambush invaders with little risk to themselves.

STEP 88: To create these features, simply create a box using the values below. Give these a surface name of Default, then, just as with the doorways, position copies of these boxes where you want them, then use the Boolean Subtract to cut them into the castle. Use the provided samples on the accompanying CD for reference on where to place these holes (Figure 4-66).

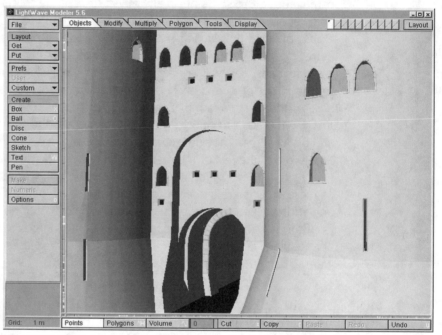

FIGURE 4-66 The completed gatehouse front, showing the positions of the arrow slits on the towers and the murder holes above the main gateway.

	Arrow Slits		Murder Holes	
	Low	High	Low	High
X	−100 mm	100 mm	−250 mm	250 mm
Y	−1 m	1 m	−250 mm	250 mm
Z	−1 m	1 m	−1 m	1 m

Once the Boolean has been performed, select only the surfaces with the name of Default, then move these to a new layer. Here we can bevel the opening a bit to make it look better. Select all the polygons and change the surface to Stone, then apply a bevel using an Inset and Shift of 0.05 meters. This will move the inside surfaces toward each other, making the slot thinner. It will also leave doubled polygons along the corner, sticking out like small fins. First, while the beveled polygons are still selected, apply a new surface name of Holes to them.

STEP 89: Now we can get rid of those beveled edges that are behind these holes. Select all polygons, then, working in the Top view, use the Lasso to deselect the bevels that form the open ends of the holes, where they would attach to the walls. Next, use the Polygons Statistics panel to deselect the polygons with the Holes surface. The remaining selected polygons may now be deleted. Finally, move these holes back to the layer with the castle and perform a Merge Points.

STEP 90: Save this castle again and we're done! Well, for now. You can always add more details to the castle later, but we've covered a lot of construction. It's about time for a change of pace. On to the texturing!

STEP 91: Run Layout, then load in the castle sections that we've just finished constructing. The first thing we'll need to do is to set up a texture for the Walls surface. We'll need a color, so let's get that out of the way. Castles were built of stone, so they tended to be colored in shades of grey or tan. We'll cover a couple of different looks here, starting with the grey. Open the Surfaces Panel and select the Walls surface. Click the Surface Color button and enter the RGB values of 155, 150, 140. This gives us a good slate grey color as a start. Now we need to make it look like stone. Click the Bump Map button at the bottom of this panel and select the Crumple texture. Castles are built from the bottom up, so they'll have slight horizontal strata to their surfaces, which we'll simulate by merely stretching our texture. Click the Texture Size button and enter 50 cm for each axis, except the Y axis, which we'll reduce to 10 cm. We'll give this a finer texture by increasing the Number of Scales to 6 and raising the Small Power to 1.0. This will give a pretty good stony surface now, as a test sample will reveal.

STEP 92: Our towers, as well as the straight walls, all use the same surface, so right now, they'll render with a faceted appearance. We'll need to smooth these out, but without affecting the straight walls they're attached to. Activate the Smoothing button and then lower the Max Smoothing Angle beside it to 10 degrees. This is enough to let the 40 sides of the towers smooth together, but not enough for them to smooth into other structures, which are generally at angles of 30 degrees or higher. Now we're ready for a test render. Close the Surfaces Panel and position the camera relatively close so you have a good view of a tower, then hit F9.

STEP 93: Not too bad, but a bit flat looking. We need to add a little more variation to the surface since very few surfaces in the real world have perfectly even shades to them. Open the Surfaces Panel again and click the "T" button beside the Diffuse channel. Select the Fractal Noise texture and increase the size to 5 meters on all axes. The rest of the values may be left at their defaults for now. Hit F9 again to see a new render of this castle. This Diffuse texture helps break up the even shade, giving a greater sense of depth to the castle, particularly with the towers.

We can add to this even more by altering the color a bit. Click the "T" button beside the Color channel and once again, select the Fractal Noise Texture Type. The effect we'll add here will be very subtle, but it's these subtleties that help avoid that "Computer Generated look" that so many 3D renders have in common. Click the Texture Color button and enter RGB values of 130, 135, 140. This will add a darker, cooler grey to the surface. Finally, give this a Texture Size of 4 meters for X and Z and 2 meters for the Y axis. This will squeeze the texture vertically, helping it blend in with the bump map. We'll also increase the Small Power to 1.0 to break up the texture even more. F9 will show a very slight difference, which is just what we were after.

Our castle will have been outside, exposed to the elements for a long time since castles did take quite a while to build. While the fractal textures help give it a weathered look, we can enhance that look further. Right now, this thing looks more like it was made of poured concrete since the walls look quite smooth. Let's wear some of that smoothness away and reveal the underlying stone-work. Castles were built of materials that were readily available, mostly stone, flagstone being quite common. Cut stone blocks and cobble were used on some castles as well. We could apply an image of stone blocks to this castle, but we would have to do so in many steps, a process almost as tedious as adding the windows, since we have wall surfaces facing in several directions, making mapping difficult. To do that, we would have to give each tower, as well as some of the battlements, a unique surface name. Also, unless we use a huge image map, a repetitive pattern could become quite apparent, spoiling the whole effect. We need a texture that can give us a stone look without worrying about which way the walls are facing—something procedural.

STEP 94: Flagstone was mentioned a short time ago, and Light-Wave just happens to have a procedural texture that can simulate flagstone quite well. Click the "T" button for the Color channel and click the Add New Texture button. On this panel, select the Veins texture. This creates a good approximation of flagstones all placed tightly together, especially if we use a negative Bump Strength. If we compressed this texture on the Y axis like we did with the Crumple texture, the pattern will resemble stacked flag-stones. Set this texture up using the setting below, then hit F9 again.

Texture Size (cm)		Texture Color:	0, 0, 0
X	50	Coverage:	0.01
Y	10	Ledge Level:	0.01
Z	50	Ledge Width:	0.5
		Bump Strength:	−0.25

A test render now will show a surface that is an amazing match to the stonework of some real-life castles. Not only does this texture look good no matter which way the walls are facing, but also when seen from above, it creates a good flagstone "floor" for the parapets of the castle. The negative Bump Strength reverses the normal bump texture of the veins, and gives the illusion of grooves between the "stones."

STEP 95: After several years of exposure to the elements, our castle would begin to exhibit other signs of wear, such as water stains in the corners, while the more exposed areas would be bleached by the sun. To do this, we'll use a Shader Plugin. Click the Advanced Options tab on the Surfaces Panel and click on the first plugin slot. Scroll down the list that appears and select the plugin named LW_Rust. This is one of the Natural Shaders collection, and this shader uses the shape of the object to determine how it will affect the surface.

Before it can do this, it needs to know what the objects look like, so render a low-resolution test before moving on. Don't worry about what this image looks like for now since this is just the shader using its default settings, which we'll be changing. When this is done, click the Options button for this plugin and a large panel will open.

It's a pretty safe bet that stone doesn't tend to rust, but it can get wet and wet rock will become darker. We can use this shader to simulate this effect by simply deactivating the Change Rust Colors button at the bottom. Now the shader will simply modify the surface using the four Rust Shading parameters in the middle of the right side of the panel. To get a good water-stained look, lower the Diffuse level to about 25% to 50%. If you want a wet look, as though it had just rained and the tower is slowly drying, raise the specularity to 25% to 40%; if not, lower it to 0. You'll see the small preview to the left update as you make these changes.

Now we'll modify the area of the shader's effects. Make sure the Mode is set to Drops, which will place the effects under any kind of overhang, where the sun is unlikely to shine. Leave the Rust Amount set to 10% and use a Rust Grain between 10% and 30% for some good water trails. This effect is a bit tight right now, so let's extend this down the walls a bit more. Increase the Min Radius to 1 meter and the Max Radius to 2 meters. The Preview window will show some very dark marks along the corners of the castle now, which will be just a bit too severe. In the top left corner, activate the Use Slope button, and the texture will look much better. This last option lowered the effect on vertical surfaces while keeping it more pronounced on level surfaces, where water would tend to sit longer, leaving darker stains.

Click OK and do another test render. This time, you will have dark, wet-looking streaks under the various overhangs, including the frames around our windows, adding greatly to the rustic appearance of our castle. Feel free to play with different values for the Diffuse and Specularity levels as a variety of looks can be generated.

STEP 96: We can make this castle look even older by adding a slight moss covering to it. Click the Basic parameters tab and then open the Texture Panel for the Color channel. Since moss grows on top of a surface, we'll need to place our moss texture on top of the other textures we already have in place. Click the Next Texture button to advance to the second texture layer, which is our veins texture, then click the Add New Texture button. This creates a third texture that will be placed on top of the previous ones. We'll use the Fractal Noise texture again, this time with a Texture Size of 3 meters. Give this texture a dark green color for the moss using RGB values of 65, 85, 40. Lower the Contrast to 0.5, and raise the Small Power to 2.0. This will create a soft mottled clumping pattern to the walls. Moss tends to grow closer to the ground, where it can find shade, so we don't want ours to be growing all over the upper towers. Click the Texture Falloff button and enter a falloff of 5% to the Y axis. Now our moss will gradually fade over 20 meters of altitude, being most evident at ground level. Finally, lower the Texture Opacity to 50% to 75% to thin the moss out a little more at ground level. Click Use Texture, and then hit F9 to render a test image (Figure 4-67).

Now that we've done a grey wall, let's try a tan color. Our basic settings will remain the same since we're only changing the color, so click the Surface Color button and change the RGB values to 200, 180, and 135. Click the Texture button beside this and change the color of the first texture layer to a similar shade. RGB values of 190, 165, 130 work well for this. Click Use Texture, and then hit F9.

FIGURE 4-67 A view of the castle from the second portcullis, showing the stone texture, complete with moss patches.

STEP 97: Now that the main walls are textured, let's work on the Stone surface, which we used for the trim around the machicolations and window and door frames. This should closely match the Walls surface, so we'll copy this surface to use as a base, which we'll modify for the Stone surface. Create a texture sample of the walls, then select the Stone surface from the surface list. Now, click on the bottom texture sample, which we just created. A panel will appear to confirm that we want to copy these settings, so click the Yes button to accept this. Now the Stone surface will be identical, so let's add a few changes. Since this surface is mainly used for the trim of the castle, we don't need the rough stone block look. Open the Texture Panel for the Surface color and then click the Next Texture button. This will be the Veins texture, which we no longer need, so click the Remove Texture button at the bottom. The rest of the settings will be fine, though you might want to change the Texture Size of the Crumple bump map to 50 cm for each axis.

Another thing to try is to lower the color saturation of this surface or to give it a lighter shade, which will help set the trim apart from the rest of the castle. These can both be done by either lowering the saturation amount or raising the value, which are settings that are included on the new Color Picker plugin.

STEP 98: Now that we have most of the stonework done, let's finish up with the interiors. These were built to give a sense of depth behind the windows, which looks better than using a simple flat polygon as is so often the case on architectural renders. Interior castle walls were usually of finer workmanship, so we should follow suit here. Again, create a test sample of the Stone surface, then select the Interiors surface. Copy the Stone surface to this one by clicking the bottom sample so we have the basic settings already in place. Open the Texture Panel for the Surface Color and click the Next Texture button. This will take us to the green fractal noise we set up as our moss. Moss is unlikely to grow in such a dark area, so just click the Remove Texture button to get rid of it, and then click the Use Texture button for the remaining fractal noise.

Open the Texture Panel for the Diffuse level and change the Texture Type to Cubic Image Map. We'll just quickly set up a brick pattern on these walls that will pass for interior construction if we happen to look inside a window. On the CD there is an image called **RandomBrick-lines.iff**, so click the Texture Image button and select the Load Image option to load this image. Give this a texture size of 3 meters for both the X and Z axes and 2 meters for the Y axis to create a good-size brick pattern on the walls. Since this is a cubic map, the same pattern will appear on the floor and ceiling, which is fine for our purposes. Finally, type Ctrl-C to copy these texture settings, then click the Use Texture button.

We'll add a similar pattern to the Bump Map, so click that button and then click the Add New Texture button on the Texture Panel. Type Ctrl-V to paste the diffuse settings here. Now, we'll change the image we are using. Click the Texture Image button and select the Load Image option again. This time, we'll load the image called **RandomBrick-lt.iff**. Increase the Bump Amplitude to 100% and click Use Texture.

This gives us a very acceptable brick wall texture, which allows us to actually place the camera inside one of these rooms and still render a half-decent image. There is one problem, though, and that is that our Rust shader will make a real mess on these walls.

STEP 99: Click the Advanced Options tab and open the Rust Shader's panel. We'll still use this shader, but this time it will be used to darken the corners of the room, which will add even more depth. Change the Mode to Grooves, so the effect is concentrated in the corners. Increase the Rust Amount to 20% and the Rust Grain to 50%. We'll tighten the effect to the corners a bit more by lowering the Min Radius to 0.1 meters and the max Radius to 0.5 meters. Finally, set the Diffuse value to 25% and leave the other Rust Shading parameters set to 0%. Make sure the Use Slope button is highlighted and that the Change Rust Colors is not, then click OK. If you were to place the camera inside a room and render, you would have an image similar to Figure 4-68.

FIGURE 4-68 Inside one of the gatehouse rooms, showing the rust shader at work, darkening the corners of the walls.

Tip: Occasionally during rendering, some of the interior surfaces will render before being covered by the exterior polygons, which can severely add to the render times. We can fix this by tricking LightWave into rendering these polygons last. This is done by simply clicking the Texture button for the Transparency channel and clicking Use Texture *without* actually applying a texture. Now, LightWave has this surface flagged as a transparent surface, even though it isn't, which means it will be rendered after all the nontransparent surfaces. This is not recommended for interior views, however, since LightWave would render the nontransparent surfaces that are behind these walls first, then cover them with the walls themselves, wasting even more time in most cases.

STEP 100: We'll finish off the stonework of this castle with the Holes surface, which is the inside of the arrow slits and murder holes. Again, we'll just copy the Stone surface here, but this time, we'll remove the Rust Shader since we won't be able to see its effects. We can also remove the Fractal Noise textures from the Color and Diffuse channels for the same reason. Finally, lower the Diffuse Level to about 30% so these holes will always look dark.

STEP 101: Now we can move on to the roof textures. We'll just cover the main roof here since the other 6 roofs will all use the same setup, but with different texture centers. Castle roofs were often made with metal plates, typically copper, which when oxidized would become a light pale bluish-green. We'll start out by creating the copper base color, then adding the oxidation later. Select the Roof surface and click the Surface Color button. We'll create an old copper color by setting the RGB values to 200, 160, 120 and lowering the Diffuse level to 30%. Raise the Specularity to 100% and activate Color Highlights, then lower the Glossiness to Low. Since the roofs are made of two different angles, we'll want to keep a sharp edge between them, but keep these two sections smooth. Activate Smoothing and lower the Max Smoothing Angle to 10 degrees. We now have a good basic copper color. Now we need to add the plates.

STEP 102: Included on the CD are two images, RoofPlates.png and RoofPlatesSpec.iff, which we'll use for the roof. Click the Bump Map button and select Cylindrical Image Map as the Texture Type. For the Texture Image, load the **RoofPlates.iff** image and then click the Automatic Sizing button. Increase the Texture Amplitude to 100% and raise the Width Wrap Amount to 3 or more so these panels don't appear too large. Remember the number you used because we'll be adding more cylindrical maps to the other texture channels and they'll need to have the same value or they won't match. Finally, turn off the Texture Antialiasing (or lower the strength to about 0.25).

Because our tower is centered 30 meters along the Z axis, the texture sample strip will be virtually useless to us for this surface. Instead, we'll have to rely on test renders, so position the camera where you have a good view of the top of the central tower, then hit F9. You should see a roof that looks like it's made with overlapping copper panels. Now we'll weather these panels to separate them from one another.

STEP 103: Click the Texture button for the Diffuse level and select Cylindrical Image Map for the Texture Type. For the Texture Image, load the **RoofPlatesSpec.iff** image, then click on Automatic Sizing. Set the Width Wrap Amount to the same number you used for the bump map and turn off the Texture Antialiasing. As this texture is now, the black parts of the image will make the surface completely black as well, although we'll still have copper-colored highlights. This will be a bit strong, so lower the Texture Opacity to 50%. This will give us an even blend of this texture and the base 30% diffuse level we applied earlier.

The dark areas of this image represent dirt streaks and oxidation, so these areas wouldn't be as shiny as the rest of the roof. Type Ctrl-C to copy this Diffuse texture, then click Use Texture. Open the Texture Panel for the Specularity channel and paste this texture there, using Ctrl-V. A test render now will show a more pronounced roof texture, looking a lot like bronze plates. Not quite the copper we were planning, but it doesn't look bad either.

OK, let's do that copper. We have the base copper color, so now we need the copper oxide, which is a light blue-green color. This oxide will be most intense in the crevasses between the plates where water would collect for an extended time and gradually thin out to the underlying copper surface. The RoofPlatesSpec image already defines those areas, but in shades of grey. We want shades of green with this same pattern. This is easily accomplished by using the Spec image as an Alpha image and applying it to a green image.

STEP 104: Open the Color Texture Panel and select the Roof-PlatesSpec image as the Texture Alpha Image. For the Texture Image itself, load the CopperOxide.png image that's also included on the CD. Almost there, but the way we're set up right now, our green color will be visible wherever there's white in the alpha image, which places it away from the crevasses. Activate the Negative Alpha option to correct this. Now we have our green oxide, but it's a bit dark, as a test render will show.

While metals are generally not very diffuse, the oxides they produce are usually the opposite. We'll have to set the Diffuse channel a bit differently now. Open the Diffuse Texture panel and activate the Negative Image button, then click Use Texture. Now the black areas of the image will render brighter. This texture is still being blended evenly with the base Diffuse level, which we set to 30%. Now that we've made the texture a negative, our copper areas are now a bit dark. We can compensate for this by inverting the base level. Previously, we had white image areas blending with the 30% base level for the copper. Now that we've made the Texture Image a negative, we have black areas blending with that base. Raise the Diffuse Level to 70%, which effectively inverts the base value, so once again, we have the same copper look in these areas.

STEP 105: Finally, oxides are almost never shiny, so we need to eliminate the specular highlights from ours. We already have the specular texture set up, but it's only 50% opaque. Open the Specular Texture Panel and raise the Texture opacity to 100%, then close the panel. Hit F9 to do another test render, which will now have nice green copper oxide streaks running down the roof (Figure 4-69).

FIGURE 4-69 The copper roof showing the oxide streaks around the edges of the panels.

Tip: Feel free to change the Width Wrap Amount for the various roofs to make each one look different.

STEP 106: When you have a roof texture to your liking, create a texture sample of it. Next, select the Tower Roof 1 surface and click the last texture sample to copy the settings over to this surface. Open each Texture Panel and click the Automatic Sizing button to fit this texture to the new roof. Do this with the other 5 Tower Roof surfaces as well.

STEP 107: While we're working so high up, we might as well paint our flagpoles. Select the Flagpoles surface and activate Smoothing, using a Max Smoothing Angle of 40 degrees, which will prevent the pole from trying to smooth into the roof below it. These poles would usually be white, but there's no rule about it and they may just as easily be black or any other color. As usual, a slight fractal color variation will help them appear real. Use a Texture Size of 10 cm for the X and Z axes and 1 meter for the Y axis to stretch the texture into a vertical streaking pattern. Raise the Small Power to 1.0 and keep the Texture Color close to the base color you chose. Keep each of the RGB values within about 30 of the base color for best results. Since these poles will rarely be seen up close, we don't really have to worry about them too much.

STEP 108: We have only one surface left on this castle, which are the doors. We'll just give these a generic wooden plank texture, which will be applied to every door at the same time. First, we'll start with the color, so select the Doors surface and set the Surface Color to 70, 60, 50, which gives us a dark chestnut brown. Now we'll weather this a bit by clicking the Texture button for the Diffuse channel. Select Fractal Noise for the texture and give this a size of 10 cm for the X and Z axes and 1 meter for the Y axis, which will give our doors a sense of wood grain. The rest of the default values will be fine, except for the Small Power, which we'll raise to 2.0 to break up the pattern more and sharpen it.

To create the wooden planks, we'll use another image map, which is provided on the CD. Click the Add New Texture button to create a second Diffuse texture, then select Cubic Image Map. For the Texture Image, load the **Planks-Vert.iff** image. Give this texture a size of 5 meters so our planks don't look like thin strips. Since this is a Diffuse texture, the white area of the image will make the surface 100% diffuse, which will overwrite the previous texture we just applied. All we want are the dark lines of this image and to do that, click the Texture Alpha Image and select the same image, but apply the Negative Alpha to it. A test sample will now show the fractal wood pattern sliced by dark lines. The final step for this texture is to deactivate the Texture Antialiasing.

STEP 109: Wood that has been put through a lot of use tends to become shiny in areas, so we'll add a 20% level of Specularity to our doors. This Specularity shouldn't be even across the entire door, so open the Texture Panel for this channel and once again, select Fractal Noise. Give this texture a size of 10 cm, and a Small Power of 1.0. Finally, we'll give this a Texture Value of 0 so we have some areas of the doors that are not specular at all. Click Use Texture and change the Glossiness to Low.

STEP 110: The final step for the doors will be to roughen them up a bit. Open the Bump Map Panel and select the Crumple texture. The default values will do just fine, but we'll change the size to 10 mm on the X and Z axes and 50 cm for the Y axis. This gives a good approximation of an old wooden surface. Now we need to give our "boards" some depth. Click the Add New Texture button and select Cubic Image Map again. Use the **Planks-Vert.iff** for the Texture Image and give this a Texture Size of 5 meters. Deactivate the Texture AA again and give this a Bump Amplitude of 100%. This second texture will add grooves between the individual boards that we mapped on the Diffuse channel. Click Use Texture and the surfacing of the main castle is complete.

STEP 111: All that remains now is our portcullis, so, if you haven't already, load the portcullis and open the Surface Panel again. We'll use the same basic color as the doors since these gates were also made of heavy wooden beams. Select the Portcullis-Horizontal surface and set the Surface Color to 70, 60, 50 for that dark brown again. We'll lower the Diffuse level to 50% this time to make these gates a bit darker than the doors. Raise the Specularity to 20% and change the Glossiness to Low. These gates were often exposed to dirt that would fall from the mechanism above that was used to lift it, so we'll simulate this dirt by opening the Texture Panel for the Diffuse Channel and selecting the Fractal Noise texture. Set the Texture Value to 10% here and raise the Small Power to 1.0. The rest of the settings can remain at their defaults, so click Use Texture.

To finish the dirt texture, we'll add some noise to the specularity as well, so click the Texture button for the Specular channel and select Fractal Noise again. Give this texture a size of 10 cm and a Texture Value of 0%. Finally, raise the Small Power to 1.0 and close this panel. This gives us a good dark mottled surface, so let's add our wood bump texture.

Click the Bump Map button and select the Crumple texture. The default values will give us a good wood look, but we need to adjust the size of this texture. Since we're working on the horizontal beams, we want the wood grain to be horizontal as well. We can do this by simply lowering the Y and Z axis sizes to 10 cm. Close this panel and do a test render to see a set of very weathered wooden crossbeams.

STEP 112: We can make this surface even more rustic by adding the Rust Shader to it. Click the Advanced Options tab and select the LW_Rust plugin. Open the shader's interface and, under the Drops mode, increase the Rust Amount to 20%. We'll break up this texture a bit more by increasing the Rust Grain to 200%. Set the Min Radius to 0.1 meters and the Max Radius to 3.

Next, in the Rust Shading section, lower the Diffuse level to 25% and the Specular level to 5%. This will keep our rust looking dark and dirty as well. We'll roughen up the rust as well, so activate the Fractal Bumps button and give this a Scale of 0.005 meters and amplitude of 2. Finally, activate the Use Slope option. We'll keep the default Rust Colors, so click OK to accept these settings.

STEP 113: Our vertical beams will be the same texture, but this time, the crumple will be stretched vertically. Create a texture sample of the horizontal surface, then select the Portcullis-Vertical surface. Copy the previous surface settings to this one by clicking the last texture sample. Next, open the Bump Map panel for this surface and change the Texture Size. This time, we want 10 cm for the X and the Z axes and the Y axis will be 1 meter. Position the camera so you have a view of the portcullis, which will be located in the middle of the courtyard right now, then do a test render (Figure 4-70). We're done with the surfacing of our castle now, so close the surface panel.

FIGURE 4-70 Our fully textured portcullis, complete with rust stains.

Tip: Included on the CD is a tutorial for creating trees, which was originally published in the April–May 1998 issue of *NewTekniques* magazine. A mini-tutorial for creating an incredibly realistic ground surface is also included.

STEP 114: Open the Objects panel and click the Save All Objects button to save all these surfaces with our objects.

STEP 115: While we have these objects loaded, we might as well set up a scene with them. To start off, parent all the castle elements to the **Castle-Bottom.lwo** object so we can move everything easily later if need be. The next thing to do is to position our portcullis in the gatehouse. Select the **Portcullis.lwo** and open the Motion Graph for it by typing "m". Select the Z Position channel and enter a value of −62.75 meters. This will place the gate at the first slot in the tunnel of the gatehouse. Click the Use Motion button to accept this value.

STEP 116: Now we need a second gate for the rear of this tunnel. Click the Clone Object button to create a duplicate of this portcullis, complete with the parent information intact. Select the **Portcullis.lwo** (2) object and open its Motion Graph. The Z Position should already be displayed, so just enter a value of −46.25 meters to position this gate at the rear gate slot, then click Use Motion. Now that our gates are in position we can easily lower and raise them by moving them up and down on the Y axis. Save this scene to preserve this hierarchy and we're done with the castle! Now, let's render some images.

STEP 117: Load the **Ground.lwo** object from your Landscape directory, or use the one that's described in the mini-tutorial that's included on the CD. One of the first things you'll notice is that part of our castle is now buried underground. This is intentional since we added this extension to allow for irregular ground surfaces so we don't run into the problem of "gopher" holes under our buildings.

STEP 118: Now that we have a ground for our castle to sit on, we need a sky. Open the Effects Panel and click the Image processing tab. Click the top Pixel Filter plugin slot and select the SkyTracer plugin. There's an endless variety of sky images that can be created with this plugin and you can spend days playing with different settings. The following settings will create a sky that resembles a typical outdoor photograph or snapshot, being quite bright and less saturated than a typical computer rendition.

	Atmosphere	Haze
Quality	50	20
Thickness	40 km	1000 m
Luminosity	400	10
Opacity	90	0
Falloff	120	0

Cloud Edit	Cumulus	Stratus
Type	Cumulonimbus	Cirrus
Grain	50	7000
Altitude	1000 m	50 m
Big Scale	2 km	4 km
Small Scale	50 m	30 m
Cover	50%	35%
Contrast	150	180
Luminosity	20	15
Opacity	100	20

Of course, this is just one sky possibility. Feel free to try out others.

STEP 119: Our castle is a pretty large structure, but it lacks a sense of scale. One solution to this is to add other objects to the scene. Vegetation is always a good way to convey a sense of scale, as is the addition of people and other common objects. Placement of the camera is another major contributing factor. If we render our castle from 30 meters above the ground, it will always appear smaller. To put the castle in the correct perspective, keep the camera about 1.5 to 2 meters above the ground (or other surface the camera is positioned over), which is about eye level for most people. This creates an upward perspective that is more familiar to the eye and also serves to make the images more dramatic than looking down on the castle. We get a far greater sense of scale and mass when we have to look up at this castle, as seen in Figure 4-67.

STEP 120: Another way to infer size is through the use of aerial perspective, which is the result of haze in the atmosphere "bluing" objects in the distance. We can do this in LightWave quite easily through the use of fog. Open the Effects Panel again and click the Backdrop and Fog tab. Set the Fog Type to Nonlinear 1 and set a Maximum Fog Distance of 1 km. For the Maximum Fog Amount, we'll use a value of 75% so we don't completely eliminate distant details. Finally, set the Fog Color to the RGB values of 215, 250, 255, which is a very light bluish white. Figure 4-71 shows the effects of this fog as well as how a low camera angle makes the castle look huge.

FIGURE 4-71 Outside the castle walls, from a standing position several meters away, we see the effects of the haze on the castle in this "snapshot."

Tip: What good are flagpoles without flags? Try the short flag tutorial on the LightWave Applied Web site to create some gently fluttering flags atop the castle.

Now that we have a simple scene set up, we can create some nice renders. For best results, use the Trace Shadows option on the Render Panel. If you can spare the render time, the use of LightWave's area lights is recommended since these excel at simulating sunlight. Just be sure to place the light at least a few hundred meters from the castle and scale it up by a factor of 30 so it's approximately the same size that the sun would be in the sky. It will take a lot longer to render, but the images will look much more realistic.

Experiment with various lighting setups. Add lights inside the windows and render a nighttime scene. Add a cliff face (Figure 4-72). Or place this castle in the middle of a desert somewhere.

We've put a lot of work into this castle, so it's time to have some fun with it. Try out your own designs or try to recreate existing castles. Be sure to look over the included CD-ROM as there are a few additional techniques to try, which will help flesh out this castle.

FIGURE 4-72 Another view of the castle, bordering on fantasy . . . and a cliff face.

Fact: Although this castle is purely fictional, much of its design is based on photographs of the Welsh castles Chepstow, Pembroke, and Kidwelly, as well as several others built between the 11th and the 15th centuries.

Fountain in the Courtyard

Dave Jerrard

OVERVIEW

Water has always been a challenge to recreate in 3D animation because of the number of factors involved, such as environmental reflections, water clarity, surface disturbances, lighting, and viewing angles. Although these can be successfully tackled by using the Fresnel and Water shaders, there remains one final aspect of water that is still difficult, or at least was, up until now.

With the inclusion of Particle Storm Lite and the new HyperVoxels, we can now add realistic splashing and other liquid effects (among others) to our scenes. In fact, these two plugins work very well together, so let's use them to create a simple water fountain. We won't get too fancy here, though the techniques covered can be very easily modified and duplicated to create virtually any type of fountain. We'll get started by creating the actual fountain itself, then add the pool later.

In this tutorial you will use:

- HyperVoxels
- Particle Storm Lite

What you will need:

- Texture images included on CD
- Prebuilt objects included on CD
- Installed Layout plugins: PSCreateLite.p, PSPlay.p, HyperVoxels.p, NaturalShaders.p
- Installed Modeler plugins: Reduce.p
- Installed Common plugins: Png.p, Jpeg.p

What you will learn:

- Basic Particle Storm usage
- Use of HyperVoxels to simulate water
- Advanced mapping techniques

STEP 1: Start LightWave and click the Plugins button at the bottom of the edit controls on the left-hand side of the Layout screen, then select the ParticleStormLite plugin from the popup list. A large panel will open with a smaller Layout window on the right half. This is where we'll design the look of our fountain (Figure 5-1).

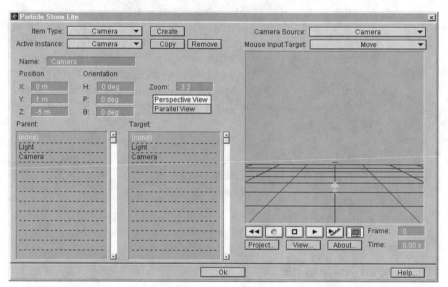

FIGURE 5-1 The main Particle Storm interface showing the Camera controls.

STEP 2: Before we can really do anything in this panel, we need to set up a Particle Group, which is simply an object comprised of single-point polygons, which we'll create within this plugin. Click the Item Type button in the top left and select the Particle Group option, which will be second from top in the popup list. Since we're building a fountain here, let's rename this group to something more appropriate. In the Name field, enter the name, "Fountain," then hit Enter. The Active Instance button above will replace the PSGROUP label it had with the new name. This will be the name of our particle object when we create it. Before we do that, we should set up a path for the files that will be created.

STEP 3: Click the Project button under the VCR controls below the perspective view. In the small panel that opens, use the Browse button to select a directory for the files to be stored. For the sake of this tutorial, we'll create a directory called PS-files inside the New-

Tek directory. This could be placed anywhere, but it's a good idea to keep it within the Content Directory. When the path is entered, click OK to return to the main Particle Storm interface.

Make sure the Total particles is set to 1000, then click the Create Object Now button. We need to do this only once since we won't be changing the number of particles. There will now be an object file called **Fountain.lwo** saved in the PS-files directory we created. Also be sure that Recycle Particles is active, or our fountain will run out of water pretty quickly.

STEP 4: The next thing we need to do is to define our fountain. Click the Item Type button again and select the (aptly named) Fountain Emitter. Now we can actually play with how this fountain works, but first let's get it moving. Under the perspective view, click the play button (the one with the black triangle) and several white specks will begin to move through a large sphere inside the window (Figure 5-2). That large sphere defines the size of the emitter, and right now, it's a bit large. In the middle of the left half of this panel is a section for positioning and sizing this emitter. Change the Size values to 0.04 meters for both X and Y and 0.1 meters for Z. You will now see what appears to be a wireframe airhorn with particles spraying out the end (Figure 5-3).

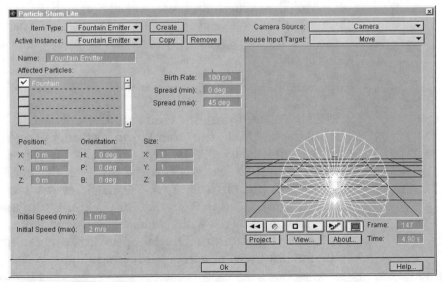

FIGURE 5-2 The default Fountain Emitter, showing the emitter size as a large yellow sphere.

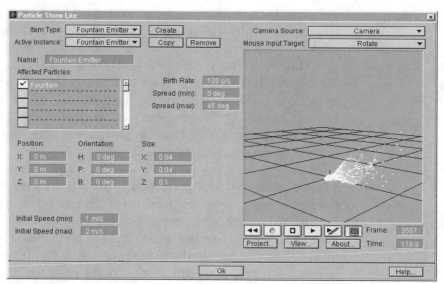

FIGURE 5-3 Scaling the emitter down creates a better-looking spray.

Tip: We made the emitter size longer on the Z axis to help randomize the distances of the particles as they shoot out. If we used a small point, particles would seem to strobe near the emitter as each successive particle would appear at the same position the previous particle did when it appeared. This could make them appear to be stationary, or even move backward depending on the speed, much like helicopter blades seem to change direction when seen on video.

STEP 5: Water fountains tend to shoot upward, so let's get ours to do likewise. Under the Orientation section, change the Pitch angle of this emitter to −90 degrees. This is a bit better, but our water looks more like feathers floating away. Let's speed it up a bit by increasing the Birth Rate to 750 particles per second. We'll also narrow the Spread to 2 degrees for the minimum and 3 degrees for the maximum. This will give us a slightly widening spray. Finally, increase the minimum Initial Speed to 5 meters per second and the maximum to 6 meters per second (Figure 5-4).

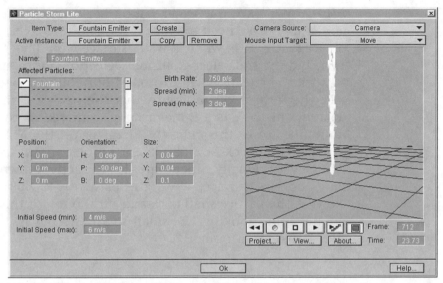

FIGURE 5-4 The fountain begins to take shape after being tilted upward.

Tip: This fountain is about the same height as an average person. If you want to make it taller, simply increase the Initial Speed values of the Fountain Emitter.

STEP 6: What goes up must come down, so let's get our water to come back as well. Click the Item Type button again, and select the Gravity option. This option wasn't actually active when we started Particle Storm, so click the Create button at the top. Nothing will appear to happen to the fountain itself since we haven't told this gravity instance which Particle Group to affect. Our Fountain should be the only one listed in the Affected Particles list, so click the check box beside it. In a second or two, the fountain will start to show the effects of gravity and will start to fall back to earth, looking more like a fountain should. We don't need to modify anything else on this panel, so let's move on to the next attribute.

STEP 7: We have our water falling back down, but it just keeps going down. We need to block it somehow, so let's add a collision object at the base, where a water surface would be. Click the Item Type button and select Collision Detection. Once again, we need to click the Create button to build our collision object. This will take the form of a simple box that the particles will land on. By default, this box is a 2-meter cube, centered at the base of our fountain. Lower this cube to −1 meter on the Y axis, and then activate the check box beside our particle group in the Affected Particles list. Finally, since water isn't exactly known for having a hard, bouncy surface, lower the Elasticity to 30% (Figure 5-5). Now, as the particles fall back and hit the top of this cube, they'll bounce a bit, looking like small splashes. That is, they would, if they lasted long enough.

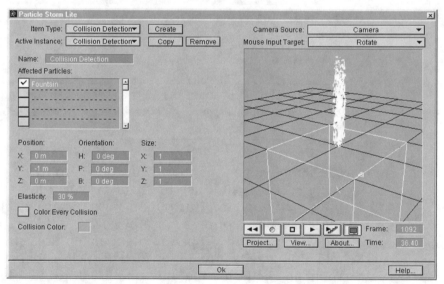

FIGURE 5-5 The application of Gravity and a Collision Object finish off the look of the fountain.

Tips: Raising the Death Value higher can create an interesting pulsing effect. This will keep particles around longer and the emitter will temporarily run out of particles until the oldest bounced particles expire, then the fountain will spring to life once again. A similar effect can be achieved by increasing the Birth Rate as well. With a Birth Rate of 750, the fountain will intermittently run out of particles for the first few seconds, until their collisions get spaced apart by the range we gave with the Initial Speeds. Let the preview play for a few seconds until the particles have a chance to get more evenly distributed before you record their paths if you want to avoid this "sputter." When applying the HyperVoxel Pixel Filter, it's a good practice to leave the first plugin slot empty, just in case you want to add SkyTracer later. This order is important since SkyTracer will overwrite the effects of the HyperVoxel filter if it's applied after HyperVoxels. In addition, HyperVoxels should be added before Steamer if these two filters are to be used together as well, since Steamer blends its effects with the rendered image, rather than replace the affected areas. Thus the ideal order would be SkyTracer first, HyperVoxels second, and Steamer third.

STEP 8: Our particles currently only have a short lifespan before they disappear and get launched into the air again. Click the Item Type once again and select Death Wish. Now we can control how long each particle will remain visible before being recycled. In our case, we'd like them to last long enough to give one good bounce so they look like a splash. We can make sure they stick around long enough to do this by setting the Method of Death to Collision Age and setting the Death Value to 0.5 seconds. Now, each particle will stick around for half a second after it hits the water, which is enough time for it to bounce once, then appear to sink into the water for good.

STEP 9: Click the Item Type one more time and select Particle Shader. We won't be using any special shading information for these particles since we won't actually be seeing them, so we can remove this item by clicking the Remove button.

STEP 10: Now that we have our fountain particles working, it's time to turn them into something we can use within LightWave. This is done by recording a motion path for each particle and saving these paths as a PSM file. Under the preview is a set of VCR style controls, complete with a Rewind button (2 triangles), followed by a Record button (the round dot). Click the rewind button to reset the animation to the beginning, and watch the animation from the start since this is generally where we'll start recording.

You'll notice that around frame 60 our fountain seems to run out of water momentarily. It did, but it will happen only twice, once more around frame 120. With a Birth Rate of 750, the fountain will have shot all 1000 particles by frame 45 and will be waiting for the first particles to collide and die before it can shoot any more. At frame 60, the last of that first volley has reached the top of the fountain as the first particles begin to die off. After this point, the particles will be spread out by the differences in their Initial Speeds since the slower particles will be the ones to bounce first (they don't go as high as the faster particles).

We can start recording these paths at any frame, so if you like this "sputter," then click the Stop button (the square symbol) and click the Rewind button again. Click the Record button, which will turn into a red dot to show that you're recording, then click the play button again. If you don't want the sputter, then let the animation play for a while until it's had a chance to even out (around frame 150). Then at any time, click the Record button, followed by the Play button again.

We'll record about 10 seconds worth of particles, so just keep an eye on the frame number to the right. To speed this up, you can turn off the preview by clicking the last button with the blue monitor screen. The particles will still be recorded, but the recording process will no longer be slowed down by the preview display.

STEP 11: When you have about 300 frames of particles recorded, click the Stop button. Now we need to save this information. Click the Project button again to open the Project Options panel. The first thing we'll do here is to save this project, so click the Save Project button and save this as **Fountain.prj** in the PS-files directory. When we saved this **.prj** file, we also saved the PSM file, which contains the actual motion paths for our particles. This is the file that will be used within LightWave.

While we're here, we can create a scene that we can start working with. Click the Create Scene for Particle Groups button and save this as **Fountain.lws** in the Scenes directory. This scene will have our **Fountain.lwo** object already set up and ready to use.

Finally, click the OK button to close this panel and then close the Particle Storm panel as well.

STEP 12: Load the **Fountain.lws** scene that we just created in Particle Storm, then open the Objects Panel. Under the Deformations tab, you'll notice there's a plugin already added in the first plugin slot, labeled Particle Storm "Fountain.psm". Click the Options button beside this and check the number of frames that are actually in the PSM file this plugin has loaded. Right below this is a frame range for Usage. This should range from 0 to the total number of frames, minus 1. Clicking the Load PSM File button and manually loading the **Fountain.psm** file will usually insert the correct values here. If you don't see any particle movement in Layout, it's likely because this Usage range is not set correctly.

The rest of the settings in this panel we don't need to worry about since they'll have no effect on our fountain's appearance, so click the OK button.

STEP 13: Now we'll set up for our HyperVoxels by clicking the second Displacement plugin slot and selecting the LW_Hyper Voxel_Particles plugin. This plugin is needed for the HyperVoxel filter to know where to apply its effects. We don't need to worry about the options for this plugin, so we're done here. Finally, to avoid having our particles show up in renders, click the Appearance Options and lower the Polygons Size to 0%. This will make the particles invisible during renders, but unlike using a 100% Object Dissolve, they will remain visible in the Layout window.

STEP 14: Open the Effects Panel and click the Image Processing tab to access the Pixel Filter Plugin slots. Click the second or third plugin slot and select the LW_HyperVoxel plugin, then click the Options button beside it. At the top of the right section of the HyperVoxel panel, select the **Fountain.lwo** object from the Object popup list, and then click the purple Activate button below it. Now we can turn these particles into water droplets.

STEP 15: The first thing we need to do is to set the sizes of these drops. In the second section of the right half of this panel, change the Sizing Method to Absolute, then enter a Particle Size of 0.01 meters. This will create some nice small droplets, but they'll all be the same size. To create a range of droplet sizes, increase the Size Variation to 500%. This will randomly scale up each droplet to 5 times its original size of 0.01 meters, giving us droplets ranging from 1 to 5 centimeters in size. Click the Refresh button under the Preview window to see how these look (make sure the fountain is visible in the Camera in Layout).

STEP 16: We have our droplets the right size, so let's make them look like water now. In the Surface Shading Options, enter the following values, which will create a basic watery appearance.

Surface Color:	230, 255, 230
Luminosity:	0
Diffuse:	5%
Specular:	100%
Glossiness:	10
Reflectivity:	100%
Transparency:	100%
Refractive Index:	1.333

STEP 17: Before checking the Preview to check this surface, we should add some sort of backdrop for these particles to interact with. Transparent blobs on a black background reflecting a black environment tend to look a bit dark and uninteresting. Click the OK button to close this panel, then click the Backdrop and Fog tab on the Effects Panel. Here we'll just activate the Gradient Backdrop, which will give us something for the HyperVoxels to reflect and allow us to see what we're doing. However, this backdrop will show up in the HyperVoxel Preview only if we render a frame, so hit F9 to create a test render (Figure 5-6). This will also let us get a closer view of our fountain in progress.

FIGURE 5-6 After adding HyperVoxels to the fountain, we have a nice watery-looking spray.

Tip: Although the HyperVoxel preview will show the effects of refraction on other HyperVoxels, it will not account for other objects in the scene. This means that a test render could look quite different from the preview. When working with transparent HyperVoxels, it's always a good idea to do a "real" test render from time to time so you don't get tricked into doing a lot of unnecessary adjustments.

STEP 18: Go back to the HyperVoxel panel and click the Advanced Parameters tab. The first thing we need to fix is the reflectivity of these particles. Right now, they look more like chrome blobs than water. We'll fix this by activating the Fresnel Effect and setting the Minimum Reflectivity to 25%. This controls the reflection amount at a perpendicular viewing angle, which on a sphere would be the center.

Next, set the Minimum Transparency to 25% as well. This will reduce the transparency of the droplets at glancing angles, or along the edges of these drops, just the opposite of the Reflectivity. (The manual incorrectly states that both of these options affect the perpendicular viewing angle.) Another preview render will appear much more watery.

STEP 19: Finally, to finish these HyperVoxels off, change the Ray-Trace Mode to Full Refraction. This will make our fountain look much more realistic. Click OK and then hit F9 for another test render so we can see the full effects of these settings (Figure 5-7). Save this scene so we don't lose these settings while we move on to the next steps.

FIGURE 5-7 The Fresnel shading and full raytrace recursion add the finishing touches to the HyperVoxel water.

Tip: Remember that water's appearance is mainly defined by its surroundings. Change the surroundings and the water's appearance will change also.

Now that we have a fountain of water, we need a place to put it. Fountains like ours are typically located in, or near, the center of a pool of water, so that seems like a good place to put ours. That means we need a pool.

STEP 20: We'll create a typical round pool, so start up Modeler and Type "q" to open the Change Surface Panel. Create a new surface called Pool Wall and click OK. Next, select the Pen tool, and working in the Face view, draw out a polygon like the one in Figure 5-8. This will be a profile that we'll lathe to form the pool. Keep it about 1.2 meters tall, and make sure the distance from the inner edge at the top to the center is 2 meters, since we're going to make our pool 4 meters in diameter. Make sure the 2 points on the left side of this polygon are on the X-axis centerline. Don't create too many points since we'll be smoothing this out later.

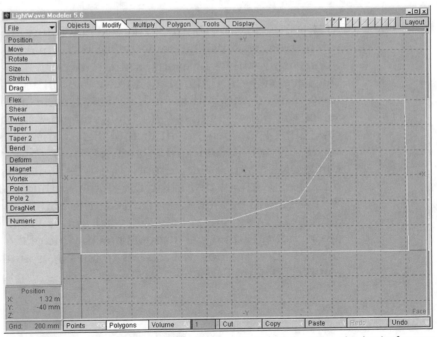

FIGURE 5-8 A very simple-profile polygon that will become the basin for our fountain.

STEP 21: Once the polygon is drawn, click the Multiply tab and select the Lathe tool. Type "n" to open the Numeric Panel for it and click the Reset button to make sure there are no old values still kicking around. These default values are all we need, but change the Axis to Y, then click OK. Make sure you're in Polygon Edit mode (Ctrl-H), then hit Enter to perform the Lathe.

STEP 22: We now have a rough version of our pool, so let's smooth it out. Type Shift-D to open the Subdivide tool and select Metaform. Lower the Max Smoothing Angle to 80 degrees, then click OK. This smoothed the curves of the pool while leaving the sharp edges along the top and base since these are greater than 80 degrees. You'll notice that the pool's basin is now much rounder, which saved on a lot of point editing when we created the profile polygon.

STEP 23: A smooth bottom like we have now isn't really that interesting, so let's add some detail to it, making it look like a liner with wrinkles or even a sediment-covered rocky surface. In the Face view, use the right mouse button to drag a selection lasso around the bottom half of this basin, taking care not to select the polygons that form the outer sides of this pool. Next, type Shift-J to open the Jitter tool. Select the Gaussian method, set the X and Z values to 0, and set the Y value to 0.1 meters. Click OK and the selected polygons will be jittered in a vertical direction, without distorting the shape of the pool walls (Figure 5-9). This will be a bit too angular at the bottom though, so type Shift-D to open the Subdivide Panel again. We'll use Metaform again, but this time, we'll add a Fractal value of 0.5. Click OK and the base of our pool will lose its harsh edges and become more rounded (Figure 5-10).

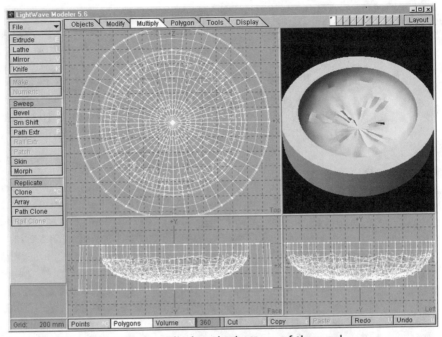

FIGURE 5-9 A slight jitter applied to the bottom of the pool.

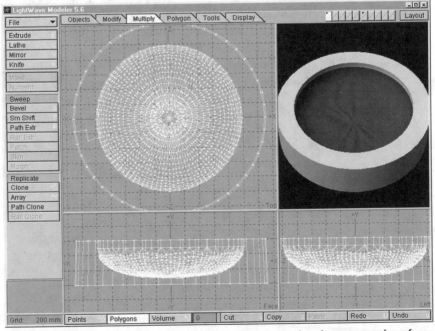

FIGURE 5-10 The finished pool object, with a smoother bottom and surfaces defined.

STEP 24: Since we've just jittered a bunch of 4-point polygons, they're unlikely to remain flat. Nonplanar polygons don't render very well, and they render even worse when they're being reflected or refracted by raytracing. To fix this, type "w" to open the Polygon Statistics panel. At the very bottom, where the Non-Planar label is, click the + button, then close this panel again. This just selected every polygon that Modeler has determined to be nonplanar, which should be every polygon that was adjacent to the ones we jittered and Metaformed.

STEP 25: While we have these selected, type "q" to open the Surface Panel and create a new surface called Pool Bottom, then click Apply. Now we'll finish off this bottom by typing Shift-T to Triple all these selected polygons, turning them into triangles, which are always flat.

STEP 26: We can clean this object up a bit by removing unnecessary polygons. Under the Tools tab, click the Custom button and select the LW_Reduce-Polygons plugin. We don't need to change anything in the panel that pops up, so click OK. Click the Polygon tab, and then click the Align button since occasionally some polygons can accidentally get flipped during these last few steps. Finally, save this object as **FountainPool.lwo**.

Now that we have our pool, let's fill it with water. We could simply use a flat disc and apply a water texture to it, which would be the common method, but since we will have a fountain in the middle of our pool, our water will be a little more agitated. Instead, we'll use a mesh for our water surface, which will allow us to add displacement effects.

STEP 27: Switch to a new layer and select the Box tool from the Objects menu. Open its Numeric Panel and enter the following values, which will create a fine mesh that's suitable for our needs.

	Low	High	Segments
X	−2 m	2 m	200
Y	−10 mm	−10 mm	1
Z	−2 m	2 m	200

Click the OK button then hit Enter and our mesh will be made.

STEP 28: We now have a square mesh that we need to fit into a round pool. We're going to have to get rid of a few corners, so switch to an empty layer and select the Disc tool. Working in the Top view, place the pointer at 0, 0 and drag out a disc with a radius of 2 meters for both the X and the Z axes. Hit Enter to create this disc, then switch back to the layer with our mesh.

STEP 29: Put the layer with the disc in the background, then type Shift-R to open the Template Drill tool. In the panel that opens, select the Y axis and set the Operation mode to Core, then click OK. In a few seconds our square mesh will be cropped to a circle (Figure 5-11).

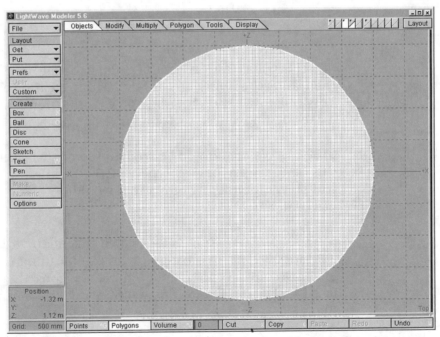

FIGURE 5-11 Our fine mesh after it has been cut with the Drill tool.

STEP 30: Now we'll do a slight adjustment, which will allow for some advanced surfacing techniques. What we're going to do is to pull the center of this mesh upward slightly, leaving the edges right where they are, so select the Magnet tool under the Modify tab. Open the Numeric Panel and enter the following values:

			Radius	Center
Axis:	Y			
Preset:	Bell			
Range:	Fixed	**X**	2 m	0 m
		Y	0 m	0 m
		Z	2 m	0 m

Offset	
X	0 m
Y	10 mm
Z	0 m

This will create an Area of Influence that fits our disk exactly, then shifts the center upward by 10 mm, creating a smooth bulge. This bulge will not be noticeable during rendering, but it will make a few advanced surfacing tricks possible.

STEP 31: We're going to be applying some displacement effects to this object in Layout, so type Shift-T to triple the polygons. This will prevent rendering errors that would normally occur with displaced quads.

STEP 32: Since we originally created this mesh with the Box tool, all our polygons are facing downward, meaning they'll be invisible from above. Type "f" to flip these polygons, then open the Surface Panel again. Create a new surface called Water, and then click Apply.

STEP 33: Our water object is finished now, so let's save that as **Water.lwo**, then head over to Layout again.

STEP 34: If you don't already have it loaded, load the **Fountain.lws** scene since we'll be using the fountain again. Next, load the **FountainPool.lwo** and the **Water.lwo** objects we created. We'll set up a small hierarchy here so we can move this fountain without its falling apart. Select the **Fountain.lwo** and click the Parent button on the left side of the screen. Select the **Water.lwo** object as the fountain's parent, then click OK. Next, select the Water object and parent this to the FountainPool.

STEP 35: Now we just have to raise our water object since it's currently sitting at the bottom of the pool. Move this about 1 meter up the Y axis, depending on how full you want your pool. The Fountain object will move right along with the water surface, so there's no need to worry about sinking it.

STEP 36: Let's texture that pool object so we have something for the water to interact with when we start on it. To speed things up, open the Objects Panel and click the Appearance Options tab. Increase the Object Dissolve to 100% for the water object so we can see the inside of the pool better. Close this panel and then move the camera so you have a good view of the pool.

STEP 37: We'll texture the outside of this pool first, so open the Surface Panel and select the Pool Wall surface. We won't get fancy with this surface so we'll just do a quick simple stone texture. Activate the Smoothing option and lower the Max Smoothing Angle to 10 degrees, then click the Bump Map button. Select the Crumple texture and click the Texture Size button. Our pool is approximately 1 meter tall, so let's make this texture 25 cm on the Y axis and stretch it to 50 cm for the X and Z axes. Finally, increase the Number of Scales to 6 and raise the Small Power to 1.0, which almost always creates a good stone surface. Click the Use Texture button, and then render a small texture sample to see how the surface looks so far.

STEP 38: We now have an acceptable light grey stone surface, but it's a bit too evenly shaded. Click the Texture button for the Diffuse Level and select the Fractal Noise texture. We'll make this a small texture, so click the Texture Size button and enter a size of 10 cm for all 3 axes. Raise the Texture Amplitude to 75% and the Small Power to 1.0, and then click Use Texture. Finally, hit F9 for a test render (Figure 5-12).

FIGURE 5-12 A very simple stone texture applied to the Pool Wall surface.

STEP 39: Now it's time to do the bottom of this pool. We'll use the same basic surface as the outer wall, so select the PoolBottom surface and then click the last Texture Sample we made for the Pool-Wall. A requester will appear asking if we're sure we want to copy this surface, which we do, so click OK. Since this surface is quite lumpy at the bottom, increase the Max Smoothing Angle to 80 degrees so we have very few sharp edges, if any. Now we'll take advantage of that rough surface.

STEP 40: Although it might be common these days for pools to be quite clean, it's more interesting to have a dirty-looking object in 3D imagery. We'll dirty our pool bottom a bit by adding some algae.

Click the Advanced Options tab and then click the first Shader Plugin slot. Select the LW_Snow shader from the list, then click the Options button beside it. The first thing we'll do is to change the color of this snow, turning it into green algae. At the bottom of the Snow Shader panel, set the following colors for the snow:

Color 1:	R:	40	G:	100	B:	40
Color 2:	R:	100	G:	100	B:	40

In the top right corner, we'll leave the Snow Amount set to 10% and lower the Start Slope Angle to 10 degrees, so we get a good spread of the two colors. Lower the Smoothness to −50 to even out the coverage of the 2 colors more.

Since algae don't tend to grow as well in deep water, raise the Y End value to 0.5 meters. Finally, lower the Diffuse and Specular settings to 0%, then click OK. A new test render will show a fairly dirty pool bottom (Figure 5-13).

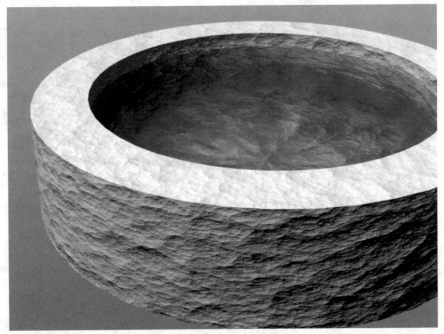

FIGURE 5-13 A copy of the stone texture applied to the basin, then covered in green snow, looks like a coating of algae.

STEP 41: We can add a little more detail to the bottom and make it look like a rock-covered bottom. Click the Basic Parameters tab, and then click the Texture button for the Surface Color. Select the Veins texture and give it a Texture Size of 40 cm. Lower the Coverage and Ledge Level to 0.01 and increase the Ledge Width to 0.5. Apply a Bump Strength of −1.0 and then change the Texture Color to black (0, 0, 0). Click Use Texture and the next render will look like algae-covered rocks (Figure 5-14).

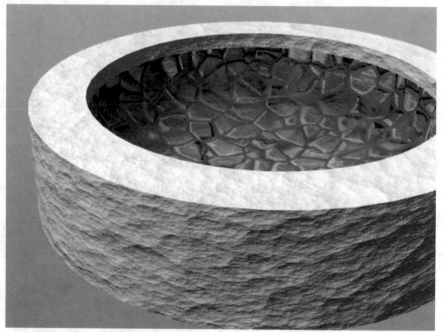

FIGURE 5-14 An inverted Veins texture does a great job of simulating a flagstone pattern. Note how the bumps modify the effect of the Snow Shader.

Tips: When creating objects with transparent surfaces, such as windows or water, it's often a good idea to save these transparent surfaces as separate objects, then parent them to the main object in Layout. This will allow you to turn off the shadow options for these surfaces to allow for the use of Shadow Maps and to increase render speed. Since Planar Image Maps only displace points along their Texture Axis, the points of our water surface will be displaced only vertically. This makes it ideal for creating waves in an aquarium or other container with thin sides, without having the displaced surface poke through the sides.

Note: These last 2 steps are entirely optional since the bottom surface can be virtually anything from a simple white surface to psychedelic patterns if desired.

STEP 42: Now it's time to bring our water to life. Open the Objects Panel and select the **Water.lwo** object. Click the Appearance Options tab and return the Object Dissolve to 0% again so we can see our water. While we're on this section, deactivate the Cast Shadow option. This will not only speed up renders with raytraced shadows, but also allow us to use Shadow Mapped spotlights. Transparent surfaces will always cast solid shadows with this type, so a Shadow Mapped light would cause the water to appear very dark since the water surface would be casting a solid shadow on the pool bottom.

STEP 43: Click the Deformations tab on this panel, then click the Displacement Map "T" button. This is where we'll create our displacement magic. The first thing we'll do is to create a splashing effect around the base of the fountain. We'll need to isolate this to just the immediate area around the base of the fountain and keep the rest of the surface relatively calm.

Normally, a procedural displacement would be used, but those modify the object in 3 dimensions, which can result in the water surface pulling away from the sides of the pool, as well as distorting surface textures. We want to limit our displacements to the Y axis, leaving the other two alone. To do that, we'll use a simple Planar Image Map, which is what we have selected on this texture panel already. We just need an image now. Click the Texture image button and select the **Splashing.iff** image that's included on the CD-ROM. Set the Texture Axis to the Y axis and give this a Texture Amplitude of 0.05.

Right now, the entire water surface will be highly displaced, as in Figure 5-15, which is not what we want. We need to apply a falloff to our displacement, but we run into another problem here. LightWave uses a linear falloff, starting at the texture's center and falling off along each axis it's applied to. With two or more falloff directions, we end up with a diamond-shaped falloff pattern, as shown in Figure 5-16. This not only looks strange, but also limits the rate of the falloff. What we really want is a radial falloff with a nonlinear curve, a curve like the one we put into the water object.

FIGURE 5-15 The effect of the first displacement on the water surface before we apply any falloff.

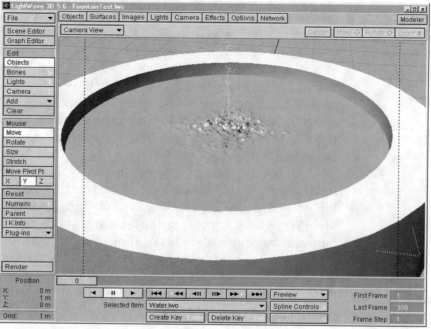

FIGURE 5-16 A falloff on both the X and Z axes results in this diamond-shaped zone.

The center of this water object is 10 mm higher than the outer edge, being exactly at 0 on its Y axis. The object also has a curved slope that radiates outward to the edge, which is located at −10 mm on its Y axis. If you were to scale this object on its Y axis, you will see that it has a bell-shaped curve to it (Figure 5-17). If we center a texture at the top or bottom of this object, then apply a falloff on the Y axis, that falloff would be adjusted by this curve and would disperse in a radial fashion.

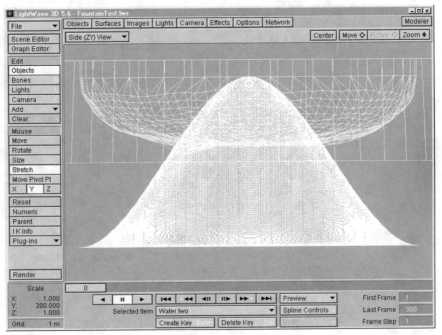

FIGURE 5-17 Scaling the water object on the Y axis reveals the secret curve that will make our mapping techniques possible.

STEP 44: Click the Texture Falloff button and apply a falloff of 50,000% to the Y axis. This texture is already centered at the very top of this curve, and the high falloff value will make our displacement completely dissipate over a couple of millimeters along the

Y axis. Those couple of millimeters cover the very top portion of the water object and the result is a radial falloff effect, as seen in Figure 5-18.

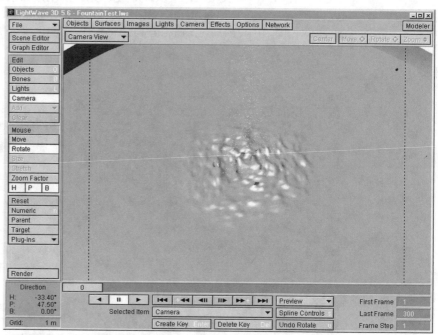

FIGURE 5-18 A Y axis falloff of 50,000% limits the displacement to the top of the water object, resulting in a smooth, round falloff shape.

Tips: The falloff does not have to be radial all the time. In fact, it can be made to follow the contours of irregular shapes just as easily by using the Bevel tool. To simulate a ring of splashing that would occur with a bell foun-tain, simply change the texture's Y axis center to −5 mm. Since the texture falls off equally in both directions on the Falloff Axis, we can have it disap-pear before reaching the top and bottom, leaving only a ring-shaped effect. At frame 0, the two displacement layers will be identical and the object will appear to have only twice the displacement amplitude it should. After frame

0, the two layers will have moved slightly and will no longer line up with one another, creating a constantly changing displacement. If you were to use a negative amplitude on one of these layers, the two textures would cancel each other out on frame 0, leaving the surface completely smooth.

As you can see, this slightly sloped surface allows for very powerful texturing techniques, which we'll explore in Tutorial 7.

STEP 45: Well, we have some nice displacements for our splashes, but they're no good if they don't move. To add movement, click the Texture Velocity button and set a value between 5 mm and −5 mm for the X axis. Do the same for the Z axis, but use a different value. Since this texture will be repeating, these two differing values will help to hide that repetition.

STEP 46: Now we just need to hide the texture's movement direction, which when animated will simply appear as a series of waves moving across the surface as opposed to a bunch of random splashes. To do this, we'll apply a second displacement, to which we'll give a different direction and velocity. With the current displacement settings open, type Ctrl-c and then click the Add New Texture button. Type Ctrl-p to paste an exact copy of the texture in this second layer. Now click the Texture Velocity button and change the values here, preferably exchanging positives and negatives so this second texture moves in the general reverse direction of the first. As these two textures overlap, their effects will combine in some places, doubling the amplitude momentarily, which will greatly enhance the splash effect.

STEP 47: While we are working on displacements, let's add a slight overall displacement to the entire surface to break up the rigid flat edge we have around the edge of our pool. Click the Add New Texture button again to create a third displacement layer. Once again, we'll use the Planar Image Map, but this time we'll use a different image for more subtle waves. Load the **Rock.iff** image from the CD and set the Texture Axis to the Y axis. Lower the Texture Amplitude to −0.015, which will have the effect of pushing this texture down into the surface rather than pulling it up like the previous textures. Finally, give this texture a velocity of around −15 mm to 15 mm for the X and Z axes, then click Use Texture.

The effect this creates is subtle, but it helps add a bit of chaos to the surface, particularly the edges, where the water will be seen to dip and swell against the pool wall (Figure 5-19).

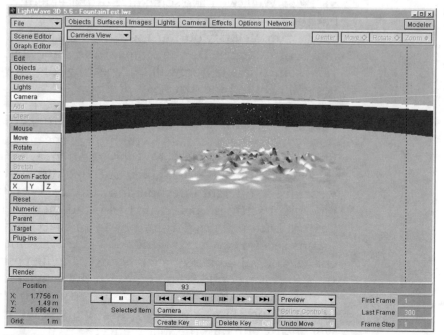

FIGURE 5-19 The third displacement adds a subtle disturbance that is visible along the edge of the water surface, as is seen along the far edge here.

Tips: Since the fountain particles are parented to the water object, you can scale the water on the Y axis to adjust the height of the fountain and also adjust the amplitude of the displacement maps at the same time. This will let you turn off the fountain with a Y-scale factor of 0, which will also make the water much calmer. You can alter the apparent Wavelength of each

Wave Source by increasing the Texture Size on the Y axis. This will have the effect of spreading the sources apart vertically and cause each set of waves to affect the surface from different distances. The farther a source is from the surface, the wider its waves will appear.

STEP 48: Click the Save All Objects button so we have all the current textures saved, then save the scene so we don't lose our parenting and displacement settings. Now it's time to make our water look like water.

STEP 49: Open the Surface Panel and select the Water surface from the popup list. Water has a slight green tint to it, so click the Surface Color button and change the RGB values to 240, 255, 240, which gives us a very light greenish white color. This surface will be transparent, so we don't want a lot of diffuse shading on it. Lower the Diffuse Level to 10%, which will leave just enough diffusion to let shadows remain visible on the surface, then increase the Reflection Level to 10%. Finally, activate the Smoothing option, and then click the Advanced Options tab.

STEP 50: To make our water look as realistic as possible, we'll use the Water Shader that's included with LightWave 5.6. Before we apply that shader, we need to remember that we're using Hyper-Voxels to create our fountain. If we want these to be reflected in the water surface, then we'll need to also apply the HyperVoxels Shader. Just as with the Pixel Filters, order is important with this shader. For the HyperVoxels to reflect in the water surface, the HyperVoxel Shader must be applied *before* the Water Shader. Click the first Plugin slot and select the LW_HyperVoxels_Shader, then click the Options button.

In the panel that opens, we only need to activate the Reflect HyperVoxels option. There is another option to Refract HyperVoxels, which is necessary if we want to see them through transparent surfaces. In the case of our fountain, we don't want that. By leaving that option off, as soon as any HyperVoxel sinks below the water surface, it's no longer visible. This makes it look more like the "water drop" has joined with the rest of the water again.

A word of warning: Reflecting HyperVoxels can take an extremely long time, so you might want to deactivate the shader for test renders. Then, when you're ready for a final render, just open the shader again and click the Enable Shader button.

STEP 51: Click on the second plugin slot and select LW_Water from the list, then click the Options button for it. The default values are almost all we need, with three changes. The first change is to deactivate the Wavelets option. Next, increase the Min Reflection Value to 10%, and finally, for the Depth Attenuation, increase the Fog Distance to 5 meters. Click OK to close this panel and then click the Basic Parameters button again.

STEP 52: Our water surface is nearly complete. All that's missing is a set of soft ripples. Just as with our displacement mapping, we can use the curve of this surface to control how our ripples behave. With the splashing that we have in the center, there should be a series of ripples radiating outward from it, gradually decreasing in intensity. Click the Bump Map button and select the Ripples bump map. Increase the Bump Amplitude to 100% and lower the Wave Sources to 2. Give these ripples a Wavelength of 0.1 meters and a Wave Speed of 0.015. Now we'll set the falloff, so click the Texture Falloff button and enter a value of 10,000% for the Y axis. This will make the ripples decrease in intensity all the way out to the outer edge of the surface. Finally, give this a Texture Size of 0.5 meters so the ripples start near the center of the pool.

STEP 53: To further enhance our ripples, we'll make a second set with a slightly different wavelength and speed. Click the Add New Texture button and select the Ripples texture again. This time we'll use a Texture Size of 25 cm and a Falloff of 20,000%. Last, lower the Wavelength to 0.08 and give this texture a Wave Speed of 0.008. This will create a set of smaller ripples that move slightly more slowly than the previous set and have a faster Falloff rate (Figure 5-20).

FIGURE 5-20 The ripples are more intense near the center of the water surface and gradually dissipate at they approach the edge.

Tip: When using the HyperVoxel shader, be sure to have the HyperVoxel pixel filter plugin set up in one of the plugin slots on the Effects Panel. It doesn't need to be active, only present. If this isn't present in the scene when the shader is called, LightWave will almost certainly crash. Although the Water Shader has its own reflection settings, we still need to set a base Reflection Level in the Basic Parameters section to tell the HyperVoxels Shader how much to reflect, since it can't get this information from the Water Shader.

STEP 54: Let's add one last Ripple texture, this time along the edge of the pool to simulate the effects of the Pool Wall on the water surface. We'll use a Texture Size of 25 cm and a Texture Amplitude of 50%. We'll use a Wavelength of 0.05 and a Wave Speed of

−0.005, which will cause these ripples to move backward, toward the center.

To get these ripples to start at the edge of the pool and fade off toward the center, we need to lower the Texture Center for it. Click the Texture Center button and change the Y value to −10 mm. Finally, open the Texture Falloff panel and enter a value of 200,000%. This will keep this set of Ripples tight against the edge of the pool, creating the illusion of ripples bouncing off the pool wall (Figure 5-21).

FIGURE 5-21 The third set of ripples is restricted to the edge of the water surface, showing that an inverse falloff is possible through the use of a curved surface.

STEP 55: Save All Objects again and our fountain is done. All that's left to do is to use the Load From Scene button to load this fountain into your scenes. There is one more little problem to fix, though.

This fountain is currently an above-ground pool. Suppose we wanted to turn it into an in-ground pool or pond. It's a simple matter to just move the FountainPool object down the Y axis, through the ground, but this is where we run into a problem. The first thing that we'll notice is that the ground or floor will now fill the pool because LightWave's objects are able to pass through one another. What we need to do is dig a hole for our pond.

STEP 56: Load the Courtyard object from the CD, which we'll use for this example. Position the FountainPool inside this courtyard, then move it down on the Y axis so the top is nearly level with the floor. If you were to do a render now, you would see this floor passing right through the pool (Figure 5-22).

FIGURE 5-22 Without a clip map, the ground object fills our fountain basin as we lower it into the floor.

STEP 57: To dig our hole, we'll use a simple Clip Map on the Courtyard object. Open the Objects Panel and click the Appearance Options tab, then click the Clip Map button. We'll use a Planar Image Map, which will be a simple black-and-white image that matches the shape and size of our pool as seen from above, which, in our case, is a simple disc shape. Click the Texture image button and select the Load image option. Load the **WhiteDisc.iff** image from the CD, then give this a Texture Size of 4 meters, which is the same size as our water surface. Next, deactivate the Width and Height Repeat options since we only want one hole, not an array of them.

This will now create a round hole in the courtyard object, but since this is a Planar Image, this hole will pass through the entire object, which could be trouble if our courtyard had a roof or other details that were in the path of this Clip Map. Click the Texture Falloff button and apply a Falloff of 50% to the Y axis. This will limit the effect of the Clip Map to within 1 meter above and below the texture's center. Now we just need to match the position of this texture to the pool itself.

This is as simple as clicking the Texture Reference Object button and selecting the **Water.lwo** object. It's also a good idea to activate the World Coordinates option as well. Now, wherever the water goes, so does the clip map, so we can freely place this fountain anywhere and not have to worry about the ground filling it up (Figure 5-23). Just make sure to apply this clip map to any object that you'll be using under the fountain.

We've covered the basics here, so feel free to try these techniques on your own designs. Be sure to browse through the CD for other sample images of what's possible with these techniques. Above all, have fun. Now, wouldn't a fountain look good in front of the castle?

FIGURE 5-23 The finished fountain.

The Sword in the Stone

Dave Jerrard

OVERVIEW

Swords have been a part of historical and fantasy lore since the first warrior ever wielded one in battle. Nearly every fantasy painting contains at least one sword, and they've played roles as important as any leading character, as evidenced in the classic legends of King Arthur, Camelot, and Excalibur, known to most as *The Sword in the Stone*. Swords can be as plain as a simple sharpened steel strip and a handle to an ornate, bejeweled symbol of stature. It's only fitting that we should include one in our journey. This chapter will cover a lot of ground, from basic modeling skills to very detailed surfacing techniques, which are applicable to more than just swords.

In this tutorial you will use:

- MetaNurbs
- Fast Fresnel shader
- Ray Tracing
- Interference shader
- Thin Film shader
- Snow Shader
- Steamer

What you will need:

- Texture images included on CD
- Installed Layout plugins: Interfere.p, Steamer.p, LWFresnel.p, NaturalShaders.p
- Installed Common plugins: Png.p, Jpeg.p

What you will learn:

- Intermediate modeling techniques
- Modeling with MetaNurbs
- Advanced surfacing techniques
- Steamer lights and fog

STEP 1: We'll start off just like any blacksmith, by building the blade. In Modeler, create a box in the Face view, 50 mm wide and 10 mm tall. This should be centered and subdivided once, so the following values will take care of that.

	Low	High	Segments
X	−25 mm	25 mm	2
Y	−5 mm	5 mm	2
Z	0 m	0 m	1

STEP 2: This will be our cross-section, but it's currently a bit blunt for a sword (Figure 6-1). Switch to Points mode by clicking the Points button at the bottom left of the screen, then select the 4 corner points and delete them. This should leave you with a diamond shape, as in Figure 6-2.

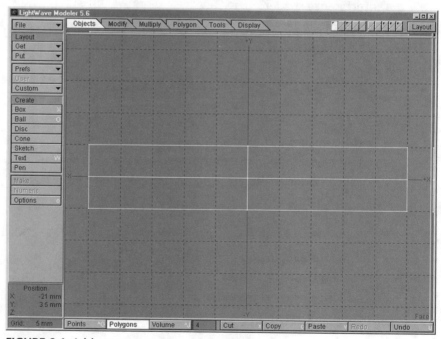

FIGURE 6-1 A blunt cross-section of our blade.

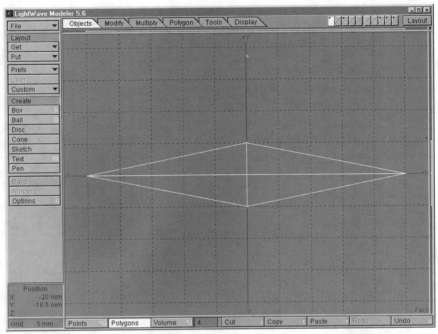

FIGURE 6-2 Remove the 4 corner points and you have a diamond.

STEP 3: We could now extrude this to get the main body of the blade, but we'll add a little more detail first. Instead of just giving it a simple straight bevel on the edge, we'll give it a nice concave edge. To do this we need to subdivide the surface a bit. First, click the Polygons button at the bottom of the screen and then select the two polygons on the left-hand side and delete them. We don't need them since we'll be mirroring the right side when we're done.

STEP 4: Now that we have only one edge to work on, we can start the subdividing. Type Shift-d to bring up the Subdivide Polygons panel. We just want the Faceted option for now, so make sure it's selected and then click OK. Open the panel once more and click OK again, so we have 2 subdivisions performed on this triangle. You should have something very similar to Figure 6-3.

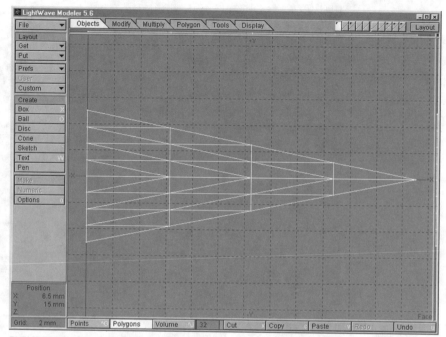

FIGURE 6-3 The blade cross-section after being cut in half and subdivided.

STEP 5: Here's where we'll give the edge a slight concave curve. Under the Modify menu, select the Taper 1 tool. Hit "n" to open the Numeric requester for it and enter a value of 50% for the Factor. Make sure the Center values are all zeros and click the X button for the Axis. The range should be Automatic, and the sense set to positive (+). Finally, set the Preset Curve to Ease Out, and click Apply.

			Center (m)	
Axis:	X			
Sense:	+	X	0	
Range:	Automatic	Y	0	
Preset:	Ease Out	Z	0	
Factor:	50%			

The Sense has set the taper tool's effective end at the point of our triangle. Since there's only a single point at that end, it will have no effect on the end, but as the Taper's influence travels toward the centerline, the triangle is widening and thus can be affected. Also, while the triangle widens, the taper's effects are also diminishing, so the area of greatest effect is the center of the triangle, giving the edges a slight inward curve (Figure 6-4). The base of the Taper tool's area of influence has no effect, so the points along the centerline remain unchanged.

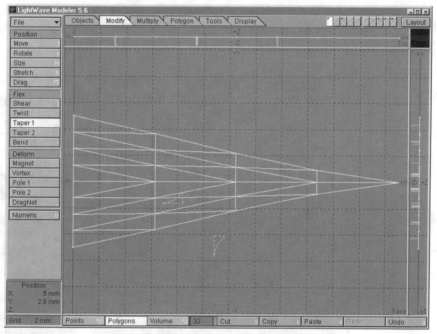

FIGURE 6-4 A 50% taper gives a slight inner curve to the edges.

STEP 6: Now that we have our edge defined for one side, we need to add the other side, since this is a double-edged sword. Click the Multiply menu button and then select the Mirror tool. In the Face view, click on the vertical centerline and drag up until the Mirror Line is vertical and aligned with the left edge of the triangle. Hit Enter when it is and you will once again have the diamond shape, but this time with slightly curved sides. Hit "m" to bring up the Merge Points tool since we will now have duplicate points along the center. Use the Automatic method and just hit the OK button.

STEP 7: We now have several polygons in excess of what we need, so let's get rid of most of them. Drag a lasso around the diamond using the right mouse button so we have all the polygons selected. Then, under the Polygon menu, click Merge, in the Revise section. You should now only have a single polygon, as in Figure 6-5, with several unattached points sitting around in the center. These are not needed any longer either, so we can get rid of them as well. Switch back to points mode and type "w" to bring up the Point Statistics panel. Click the + sign beside the "0 Polygons" entry (second row) and close the panel. Every point that is not connected to the remaining polygon will be selected, so hit the "Delete" key to remove them.

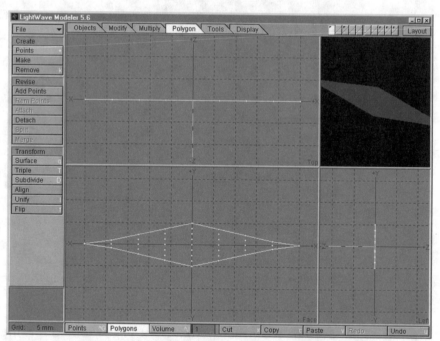

FIGURE 6-5 After mirroring and merging, we're left with a new diamond, with a few unwanted points remaining, highlighted here for deletion.

Tip: The steps outlined here, though specifically written for a generic longsword, may be adjusted for nearly any kind of sword by simply altering the measurements. Short swords are generally between 12 inches and 2 1/2 feet, while broad swords are about the same length as longswords, or longer, but with a much wider blade.

STEP 8: Now we're ready to extrude this shape into a sword blade, so click the Extrude button under the Multiply menu, then hit the "n" key to bring up the Numeric requester. Longswords are generally about 1 meter in length, which is what we're creating here, so we'll be extruding the blade to about that length. We'll have to allow for a handle yet, so we'll use an extrusion length of 87 centimeters. We're also going to subdivide this blade so we can add a tapered point in the next couple steps, so enter the following values into the numeric requester.

Axis:	Z
Segments:	20
Extent:	870 mm

Click the OK button then hit Enter to perform the Extrude. You'll be left with an object that's starting to resemble a sword, divided evenly into 20 segments (Figure 6-6).

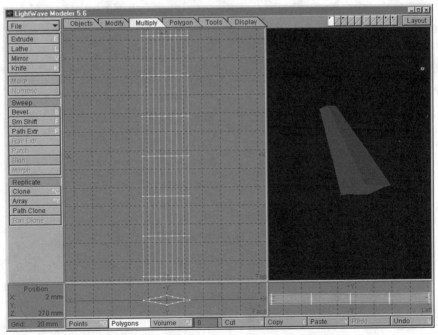

FIGURE 6-6 The blade begins to take shape after extruding.

Tip: We've built this sword with the blade extending in the Z axis so animating the rotation of the sword is easier to handle. Heading and Pitch are applied to the object first, and then Bank is applied after. This means that no matter how the first two rotation values are set, rotating the sword on its bank will always have the sword rotate on its long axis. It can easily be positioned to point in any direction, and then a bank angle applied, if needed, to make the sword blade horizontal, or vertical. This layout is least susceptible to Gimbal Lock.

STEP 9: We added the segments so we have enough polygons to create a smooth curve for the sword tip. To do this, we first need to move these points toward the tip. Switch to Point Edit mode, and then drag a lasso around all the points, except the originals that formed the diamond that we just extruded. Next, type "h" to activate the Stretch tool. We'll be using this to squeeze all these segments into a small area near the tip of the sword, which is located at 870 mm on the Z axis. Rather than try to do this manually, type the "n" key to bring up the Stretch Tool's numeric panel. Enter the following values, then click OK.

	Factors	Center
X	100%	0 m
Y	100%	0 m
Z	10%	870 mm

The segments will now all be concentrated at the tip (Figure 6-7), ready for the next steps.

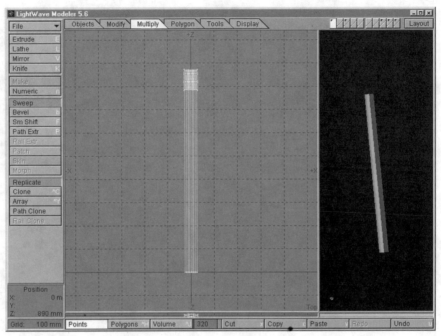

FIGURE 6-7 Concentrating the points near the tip with the stretch tool.

STEP 10: With the tip now nicely subdivided, we can round it to a point quite effectively. We'll use the Taper 1 tool again, this time tapering on the Z axis. Since we want a point, we'll use a taper factor of 0%, and we'll use the Ease Out curve settings to apply a nice smooth curve to the tip. You should still have all the points in the tip selected. If not, select them again (Figure 6-7) and type Shift-a to fill the views with the tip. Click the Taper 1 tool and hit "n" to open the numeric panel for it. Apply the following values to get a point like the one in Figure 6-8.

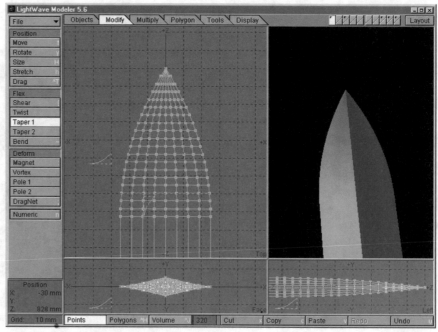

FIGURE 6-8 The tip after tapering.

Tip: Various other tip styles can be made by simply changing the center point of the Taper tool. By centering it a few centimeters off the X axis, a hooked tip can be made, giving a Middle Eastern look to the blade.

Axis:	Z		Center (m)
Sense:	+	X	0
Range:	Automatic	Y	0
Preset:	Ease Out	Z	0
Factor:	0%		

Note: Modeler may cause the polygons at the very tip to suddenly appear to flip. This is just a harmless quirk of Modeler and the flipped polygons will correct themselves in the next step. Occasionally, Modeler will create unwanted single and dual point polygons. Use the "w" key to check for these and remove them if any exist.

STEP 11: Deselect everything and type "m" to merge points. Since we had a 16-sided polygon at the tip that was created when we extruded, we'll now have a stray single-point polygon sitting there, left over from the point merge. Switch to Polygon Edit mode and drag a lasso around the very end polygon, then hit the Delete key.

STEP 12: We're almost done with the blade at this point, but it currently looks a bit hefty for a longsword. We need to thin this out a bit more. To do this, we'll taper it again. This time, we'll use the Taper 2 tool to narrow the blade along its width. Since we'll be tapering the entire blade, make sure that nothing is currently selected, and then click the Taper 2 button. Type "n" to open the numeric requester and enter the following values.

			Factors (%)	Center (m)
Axis:	Z			
Sense:	+	X	50	0
Range:	Automatic	Y	100	0
Preset:	Ease Out	Z	100	0

Try out various Taper Curve settings to find one that you like. The effects will be subtle from one another and won't impact the rest of this tutorial. In any case, you should have a more elegant-looking blade as in Figure 6-9.

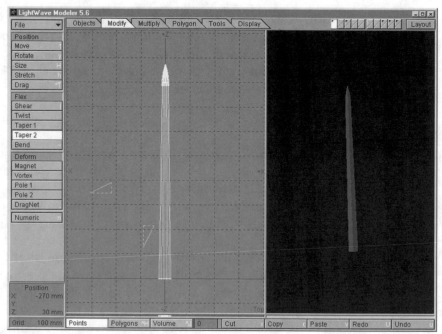

FIGURE 6-9 A 50% taper on the entire blade gives it a much more balanced look.

Tip: The Linear Taper curve will not cause affected polygons to become nonplanar. Other curve settings, however, will result in nonplanar polygons. Polygons that share edges with tapered polygons may end up being distorted as well, so after any taper operations, it's a good idea to check for nonplanar polygons.

STEP 13: To enhance the 3D preview, type "q" to open the Surfaces panel. Set the Diffuse value to 15%, the Specular to 75%, and Glossiness to Medium. Activate Smoothing and set the Smoothing Angle to 20 degrees. The 3D preview will now have a more metallic look to it. Also give this a surface name of SwordBlade.

STEP 14: Since we've tapered this object, we'll have a few nonplanar polygons sitting around, so it will be a good idea to Triple everything to avoid trouble later. Open the Polygons Stats panel and select all the 4-point polygons. Close the panel and then type Shift-t to triple these. Save this as **SwordBlade-Ridged.lwo.**

STEP 15: Our blade can be considered finished as it is now, but we can still dress it up a bit. For one, we can add some flat sides to it since it currently only has a ridge running along its length. To do this, we'll need to flip to an empty layer. Select the layer containing the blade as a background layer and click the Box tool under the Objects menu. Drag out a box that completely encompasses the blade, but make it slightly thinner on the Y axis (Figure 6-10). The following values will work well. Hit the Enter key to make the box.

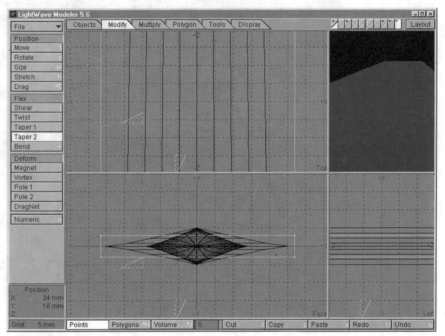

FIGURE 6-10 The blade in the background, ready to be cut by the box in the foreground.

	Low	High	Segments
X	−50 mm	50 mm	1
Y	−3 mm	3 mm	1
Z	−1 m	1 m	1

STEP 16: We'll use a Boolean operation to shave the ridge off each side of the blade so it had two flat sides to it. Type Shift-b to bring up the Boolean panel and select the Intersect option. This will remove everything in the current layer except the volume that is taken up by both the box and the blade. Click the OK button and in a few seconds you will have a blade similar to the one in Figure 6-11.

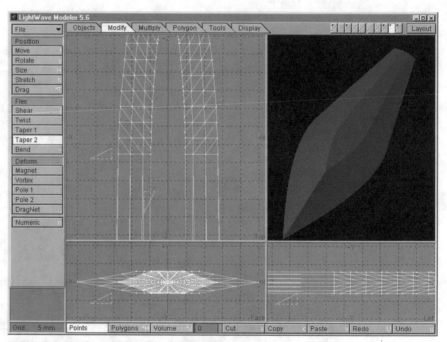

FIGURE 6-11 The blade after the Boolean operation.

STEP 17: Merge points to ensure the blade is a solid since Boolean operations always leave new geometry detached from the original. Save this as **SwordBlade-Flat.lwo.**

STEP 18: Another way we can dress the blade up is by adding a groove down the center. Switch to an empty layer and load the **SwordBlade-Ridged.lwo** object we saved in Step 14. Size the Face view up and fit the contents to it by typing Ctrl-a. Switch to another empty layer and put the blade layer in the background. Select the Disc tool and drag out a 12-mm-diameter disc while holding the Ctrl key. This will constrain the tool to a perfect circle. Position this disc so it just slightly clips the top of the blade in the background layer. 8.4 mm up on the Y axis is a good location. We're creating a cutter object to carve a groove along the sword so we need this disc to extend the length of the blade. Type "n" to open the Disc tool's numeric requester and enter the following values:

Sides:	40
Segments:	1
Bottom:	−10 mm
Top:	860 mm
Axis:	Z

	Center	Radius
X	0.0 m	6.0 mm
Y	8.4 mm	6.0 mm
Z	0.0 m	0.0 m

Click OK and then hit Enter to create the cylinder.

STEP 19: Select the Mirror tool and open its Numeric panel. Select the Y axis as the Mirror Plane, and enter 0 for the position. Click OK and then hit Enter. You should now have two identical cylinders, one above and one below the sword blade.

STEP 20: Type "q" to access the Change Surface panel. In the Surface field, type the name Groove, and then change the color to something noticeable, like yellow. Click the Apply button and then type the apostrophe key to swap layers. You should now have the sword blade in the foreground and the two cylinders in the background, as in Figure 6-12.

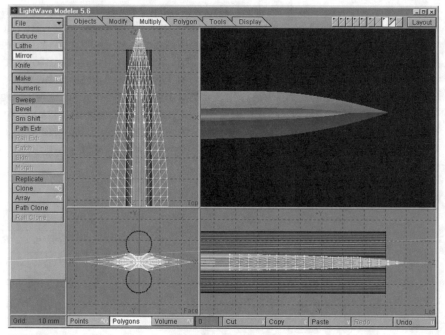

FIGURE 6-12 Another blade design, again done with Boolean.

Fact: The Samurai warrior typically carried a set of three swords, collectively known as the Daisho, which consisted of the famous longsword known as the Katana, the short sword called a Wakizashi, and the small dagger called a Tanto. Each had very specific functions, and they were a Samurai's highest badges of honor. Merely touching a Samurai's Katana without permission was an offense punishable by death.

STEP 21: Type Shift-b to bring up the Boolean options and select the Subtract button. Click OK, and in a few seconds, you should have a groove running from the base of the blade almost to the tip, where it will narrow and end before reaching the point. This groove will also have the surface we applied to the two cylinders, and will show up in the OpenGL (or QuickDraw 3D) preview in a different color than the rest of the blade. Once again, after a Boolean operation it will be necessary to Merge Points, so type "m" and hit the OK button.

STEP 22: Save this blade as **SwordBlade-Grooved.lwo.** Now we're ready to texture these blades, so click the Layout button in the top right corner.

STEP 23: Since all three blades will be the same material, we'll surface them all at the same time. Load all three blades into Layout and position them so they're beside each other. Adjust the camera so you have a good closeup view of at least one blade. They're all being surfaced the same way, so it doesn't matter which one you're looking at. Click the Surfaces button at the top of the screen and select the SwordBlade surface. We'll start off by setting up the base values, so enter the following settings:

Color:	240 250 255	**Glossiness:**	16 (Low)
Luminosity:	0%	**Reflectivity:**	25%
Diffuse:	25%	**Smoothing:**	On
Specular:	50%	**Max. Smoothing Angle:**	20
Color Highlights:	On		

These values will give a good basic steel look to the blades, but they still need some work. We'll start by adding a slight bumpiness to the blades to break up the reflections a bit. Click the Bump Map button and select the Fractal Bumps Texture Type. Set the Texture Size to 5 cm and the Bump Intensity to 5%. Leave the Frequencies set to 3 and click Use Texture.

STEP 24: We have set a Reflectivity value for this surface, but we still haven't set the Reflection Options, so click that and set the Reflection Type to Ray Tracing and Spherical Map. Click the Reflection Image button and select the "Load Image" option. We need a good image that will make a surface look metallic, and the Fractal Reflections image just doesn't work very well for that. NewTek does supply an excellent image for metallic reflections, but they hid it away in the Brushes directory. Look in the Images/Brushes for a file called **MetalRefMap.iff** and load that. Close the panel and click the Render button on the texture Samples panel. You should be getting a good steellike surface developing now.

STEP 25: Now we'll add a slight grain to the blade to give it a ground steel appearance. We'll do this by using a texture in the Diffuse channel, so click the Texture button beside Diffuse Level and select the Fractal Noise Texture Type. Enter the following values to add some fractal streaks along the length of the blade:

Texture Size			Texture Value:	40%
X	1 mm		Frequencies:	1
Y	50 um		Contrast:	1.0
Z	20 cm		Small Power:	1.0

Click the Options button on the Samples panel and enter a size of 0.005 m. This will scale the preview sample up enough that it's the same thickness as our blade and let us see the details we're adding.

STEP 26: Many ancient swords, notably the Japanese Samurai swords, had an slight blue color to the sharp edge of the blade called a temper line, caused by the process of tempering the edge under high heat to make it stronger. There's no reason our sword can't have the same detail, so let's add it. Click the T button for the Color channel and select the Marble texture. We're going to run a marble vein along the edge of the sword, so we need to position the texture carefully. The Marble texture is centered at exactly the halfway point between two veins, so we'll need to offset the texture by half of the Vein Spacing distance. We'll need to map the texture on the Y axis to line it up with the blade as well, and that axis will be the one we need to apply that offset to. Enter the following values for this texture:

Texture Color:	70 68 135			Texture Size	Texture Center
Frequencies:	3		X	1 mm	0 m
Turbulence:	0.05		Y	1 mm	3 mm
Vein Spacing:	0.006 (m)	Z	1 mm	0 m
Vein Sharpness:	8.0				

What we've done here is space the veins approximately 1 blade width apart (6 mm) and then shifted them along the Y axis to line one of these veins with the center of the blade (Figure 6-13). The blue color will be a bit intense, so let's tone that down a bit by lowering the Texture Opacity to 50%.

FIGURE 6-13 Adding a temper line by placing a marble vein through the center of the blade, as seen in this cross-section.

Fact: The temper line of Japanese swords, known as the "Ha" line, was integrated as a design element itself. Sword smiths would stylize these bluish lines into intricate patterns, from simple waves to floral shapes.

STEP 27: We can use a similar procedure to add a slight roughening along the blade edge to simulate the effects of sharpening the sword by grinding. We'll use the Fractal Bumps texture again, so click the Bump Map button. Click the Add New Texture button to add a second bump texture on top of the one we already have and then select Fractal Bumps Texture Type. The values below will provide a good brushed metal look and isolate this texture to the very edge of the blade due to the high Texture Falloff value (Figure 6-14).

Texture Amplitude:	50%
Frequencies:	3

	Texture Size	Texture Falloff
X	10 mm	0.0%
Y	10 mm	100,000.0%
Z	1000 nm	0.0%

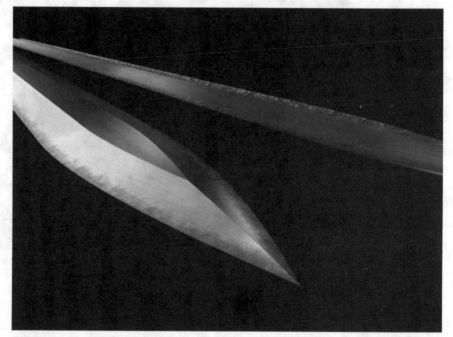

FIGURE 6-14 The blade begins to look very sharp after a slight bump map brushing along the edge.

STEP 28: The final touch to add to this surface is a Fresnel effect. Click the Advanced Options tab and click the first plugin slot. Select the LW_FastFresnel shader and click the Options button. Highlight the Reflectivity, Specular, and Diffuse buttons, and set their Glancing Levels to 75%, 0%, and 100%, respectively.

STEP 29: Our grooved blade has an additional surface we need to take care of. Click the Render button on the Samples panel to generate a preview of the SwordBlade surface with all the settings we just applied, then select the Groove surface. Click on the texture sample we just created and a requester will appear asking if you want to copy that surface to this one. Click the Yes button. There are a few things we don't need on this surface, so click the texture button for the Color channel and click Remove Texture. While we're here, change the color to R: 146, G: 152, B: 155. We'll also change the Bump Map for this surface, so open the bump panel. Click the Next Texture button, then the Remove Texture button since we only need one texture layer here and change the remaining Texture Type to Crumple. Enter the following values to create a good unpolished metal look (Figure 6-15):

			Texture Size	
Texture Amplitude:	20%			
Number of Scales:	6	X	5 mm	
Small Power:	1.0	Y	5 mm	
		Z	5 cm	

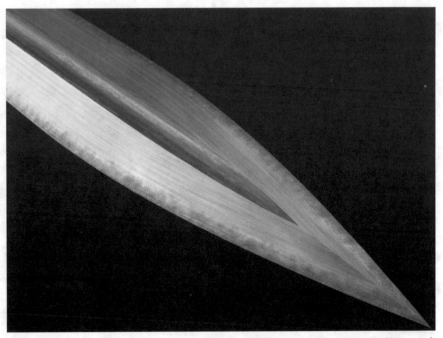

FIGURE 6-15 A darker color and a rougher surface give the groove an unpolished look.

Switch to the Objects Panel and click on the Save All Objects button followed by Clear All Objects. Let's get a handle on things now.

STEP 30: Switch back to Modeler and select an empty layer. In fact, you can safely clear everything by typing Shift-n and clicking OK. Drag out the Top view window and zoom in until you have a grid size of 10 mm. Switch to Polygon Edit mode again by clicking the Polygons button at the bottom of the screen. We're going to create a profile that we'll lathe to create the handle, so select the Pen tool from the Objects menu and draw out a shape as shown in Figure 6-16. The following values will duplicate the one in the figure:

Point #	X (mm)	Z (mm)
1	0	0
2	15	0
3	25	−70
4	15	−140
5	0	−140

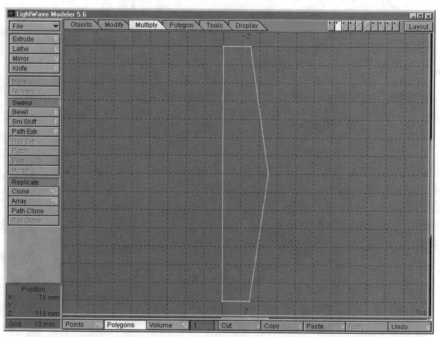

FIGURE 6-16 The Pen tool is a quick way to draw out a template for a Lathe operation.

Don't worry about how rough this looks now. It will be smoothed out later.

STEP 31: Under the Multiply menu, select the Lathe tool. Open the Numeric panel for it and click the Reset button. Change the number of Sides to 8 and the lathe axis to Z. Click OK and then hit Enter. This will create a very rough-looking handle, as in Figure 6-17.

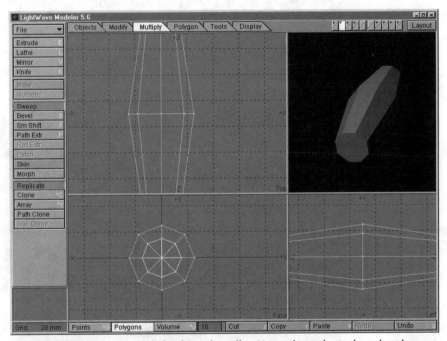

FIGURE 6-17 A very rough-looking handle. Note the selected end polygons, which will be moved to another layer for later.

STEP 32: Since we only need the outer sides of this shape, we can get rid of the polygons on the ends. We will be using the polygons at the lower end later, however, so let's just move these to another layer. In the Face view, click on the center of the handle to select these polygons and hit "x". Switch to another layer and paste them there using the "v" key. In fact, you might want to save these polygons for use later on, in case you exit Modeler at some point.

STEP 33: Switch back to the layer containing the handle and hit the Tab key to activate MetaNurbs. The handle will immediately smooth out giving the handle an elegant, rounded appearance. Sword handles are generally slightly thinner along the blade's shortest axis, so we'll squeeze the handle in a similar fashion. Select the Stretch tool by hitting the "h" key. Open its Numeric panel and click the Rest button, then change the scale factor for the Y axis to 80%. Click OK and the handle will squeeze slightly.

STEP 34: Type "o" to open the Data Options panel. If it isn't already, set the Patch Division level to 6 and click OK. Next, type Ctrl-d to freeze the MetaNurb handle into a polygonal object again (Figure 6-18).

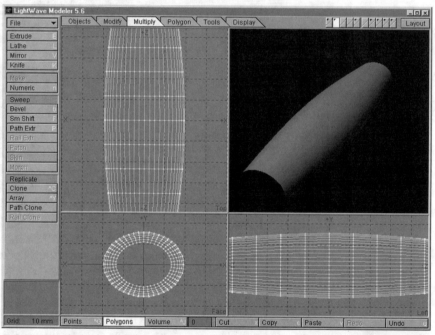

FIGURE 6-18 The rough handle object after applying MetaNurb and freezing.

STEP 35: Although this handle looks okay so far, it needs some collars on the ends to really set it off. In the Top view, zoom in on one end until you have a grid size of 2 mm. Hit Shift-k to activate the Knife tool and drag a line across the handle at a point 10 mm from the end. This will be almost 2 mm from the second segment. Hit OK then draw a second line at the 11-mm mark, right between the slice we just made and the second segment (Figure 6-19). Repeat this procedure on the opposite end.

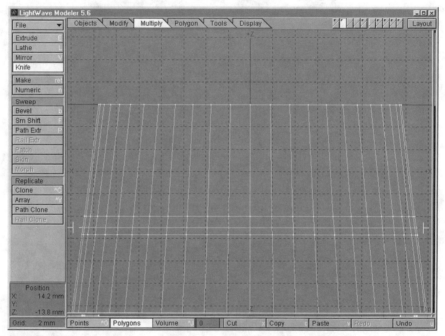

FIGURE 6-19 The Knife tool being used to cut the second slice through the handle.

STEP 36: Select all the polygons of this object, except for the last three segments on each end (Figure 6-20). A simple method would be to select all the polygons by dragging a lasso around the object, then deselecting the ends with the lasso again. Click the Tools menu tab and then click the Smooth Scale button. A requester will appear asking for a scale amount. Type in "−0.5 mm," and click OK. This will slightly shrink the selected polygons and taper the adjoining unselected segments, as seen in Figure 6-21.

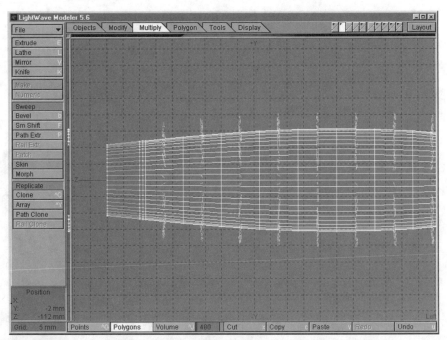

FIGURE 6-20 All but the three segments on each end are selected, ready for the next set of adjustments.

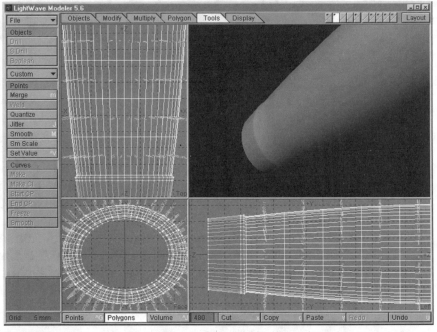

FIGURE 6-21 The Handle polygons after a slight Smooth Scale operation.

STEP 37: Keep the polygons selected and type Shift-f to bring up the Smooth Shift tool. Enter the same value here, "−0.5 mm," and click OK. The handle will reduce slightly again, this time leaving a sharp edge along the unselected segments, almost as though these were separate objects that were later attached (Figure 6-22).

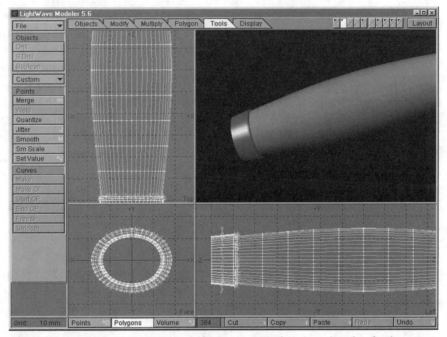

FIGURE 6-22 After the Smooth Shift, we can apply a rough color for later surfacing. Here, the end collars are given a gold color.

Tip: When changing Texture Types, the values for Texture Size, Center, Velocity, and Falloff will remain unchanged.

You will notice that the second segment on each end is not modified at all. This is intentional. If we just did one slice with the Knife tool, we would have a near-45-degree bevel between the Smooth Shifted segments and the ends. With smoothing applied, the end segments will attempt to smooth into this bevel, creating unrealistic reflections. This second segment is added to prevent this. Now, this second segment will try to smooth into the bevel, while the end segments will now be smoothing into this second segment, which is not angled to the ends. This lets the end segments smooth in a flatter fashion, and the second segment controls how wide the rounding effect will appear.

STEP 38: Type "q" to open the Change Surface panel and add a new surface named Handle. Click Apply and then hit the double quote key to invert the selection so the end segments are now selected. Type "q" again and add a surface named Gold and give this a yellow color. We will have a few nonplanar polygons sitting around as a result of the Smooth Scale and Smooth Shift operations, so bring up the Polygon Statistics panel and click the – button beside Total Polygons to deselect everything. Next, click the + button at the bottom to select the nonplanar polygons and close the panel. Type Shift-t to triple these polygons.

Note: The Flatness Limit in the Data Options panel should be set to a very small number, like 0.01 or less, for best results.

STEP 39: Finally, save this as **Handle.lwo** by switching to the Objects menu and using the Put command. Click the Layout button in the top right corner to flip over to Layout.

STEP 40: In Layout, you should see the Handle object sitting in the center of the universe. If not, be sure you're using the Camera view by typing "6" and then type Shift-c to select the Camera as the Edit Item. Reset the Camera's position by selecting the Move button followed by Reset. Do the same for the Rotation. Finally, move the camera up and back slightly to see the handle.

We'll start off by texturing the handle itself. Sword handles come in an endless variety of textures, including wood, leather, ivory, cloth wrap, metal, and sometimes, stone. We'll explore a few of these texture ideas here, and we'll start off with one of the simpler ones, leather.

STEP 41: Open the Surfaces Panel and select the Handle surface from the popup list. The first thing to do is to change the name here. We'll call it Leather Handle, just to be real creative. Click on the smoothing button and leave the Max.Smoothing Angle at 89.5 degrees. Now we need a leather color. Again, leather comes in a variety of colors, the most common being tans and blacks, but nearly any color can be used. We'll start with tan leather, so a good base color here would be R: 160 G: 120 B: 85. Real-world surfaces are very rarely ever a perfectly continuous color, so we'll break this up slightly by adding a fractal color variation. Click the T button for the Color channel and select Fractal Noise from the Texture Type popup list. Enter the following values here to create a rustic-looking leather color:

Texture Color:	120, 95, 85	Texture Size (cm)	
Frequencies:	3	X	2
Contrast:	1.0	Y	2
Small Power:	1.0	Z	10

STEP 42: This has given us a leather color, but we're only about half done. We still need to make it look like leather, which usually has small creases in its surface. We'll add these by applying a Crumple texture. Click the Bump Map button and before doing anything else, we'll click the Automatic Sizing button. This will get the dimensions of our handle so we don't have to guess at them. Now, select the Crumple Texture and set the Number of Scales to 6 and the Small Power to 1.0. Currently this will look a lot like a rock surface, which we don't want. We can turn the Crumple texture into a much smoother looking surface by applying a negative amplitude. For the Texture Amplitude, we'll use a value of −10%. We will now have a much more leathery-looking surface (Figure 6-23).

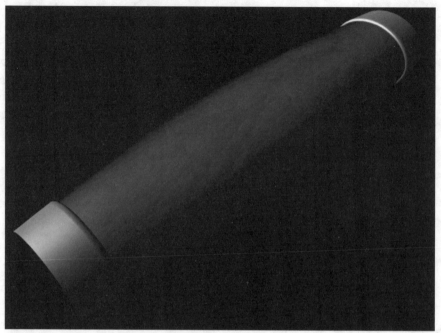

FIGURE 6-23 A slight Fractal Noise and a small inverted Crumple begin to make the handle look like leather.

STEP 43: We still need a slight specularity to this surface and we'll apply that with the Fast Fresnel shader. Click the Advanced Options tab and select the LW_FastFresnel plugin for slot 1, then click the Options button. First, we'll add the specularity by highlighting that option and supplying it with a value of 100%. We'll also activate the Diffuse button while we're here and make this a value of 0% so our surface becomes darker at glancing angles. This will help to enhance the Crumple texture near the edges by making the creases a bit darker as well. Everything else should be turned off here and the Minimum Glancing Angle should be 0 degrees. Click OK to accept these values. A test render here would show a very subtle improvement.

STEP 44: For our finishing touch, we'll add what every leather owner despises. Swords, in their heyday, were put through very harsh situations, and it's only natural that they would end up with scratches. Click the Bump Map button again and then click the Add New Texture button. Select Cylindrical Mapping and click the Automatic Sizing button. Now, click on the Texture Image button and select the Load Image option. Load the **Scratches.iff** image from the CD and set the Texture Axis to Z. Turn off the Texture Antialiasing and make sure the Texture Amplitude is set to 50%. This will add some random scratches to the bump texture, but leather scratches tend to collect dirt, especially in a surface that would be handled as often as a . . . handle. This can be quickly simulated by simply typing Ctrl-c while the scratch Bump Map panel is open. Click Use Texture, then click the T button for the Diffuse channel. When the Diffuse Texture Pane l opens, type Ctrl-v to paste a copy of the bump settings to this panel. Everything is all set, except we'll lower the Texture Opacity to 50%. This will prevent our scratches from looking solid black.

A test render now will show what looks like worn-down leather that's seen better days (Figure 6-24). Save this object as **Handle-Leather.lwo**.

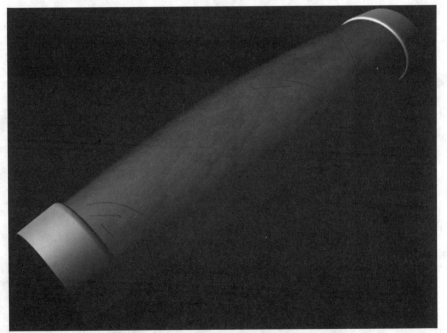

FIGURE 6-24 A subtle Fresnel effect and a few scratches add to the effect.

Tip: To further improve the look of the leather, try adding another Crumple bump map in a third layer, using much smaller sizes. This will add a slight grain to the surface.

STEP 45: Another common handle wrapping is cloth, usually a canvas, cotton, or other tough fabrics, including silk at times. Once again, the color can be virtually anything, so we'll focus on the texture of this fabric and not on color this time. Rename the surface to Handle—Cloth and clear this surface. A simple way to do this is to select the default surface (it's always present), render a sample of it, then switch back to the Handle—Cloth surface and click the last preview. This will copy the default surface back to the handle surface. Turn on Smoothing, then click the Bump Map button and select Cylindrical Image Map as the Texture Type. Click the Texture Image button and load the **WeaveBrush.iff** image from the Bumps directory. Change the Texture Axis to Z and the Texture Size on the Z axis to 3 mm. Since this is a cylindrical mapping method, only the size on the Texture Axis has any effect. Deactivate the Texture AA again, and raise the Texture Amplitude to 200%.

Increase the Width Wrap Amount to 40 and do a test render. You should have a very clean-looking white canvas texture (Figure 6-25).

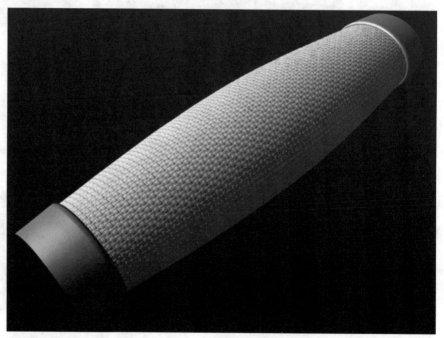

FIGURE 6-25 A simple repeating bump map has a drastic effect on a default surface.

STEP 46: Once again, we need to add a bit of wear to this surface, including some dirt between the threads, similar to the scratches in the leather. Copy these texture settings by typing Ctrl-c then clicking on the Use Texture button. Click the Texture button for the Diffuse channel and past the texture here by typing Ctrl-v. Everything will be set already, but once again, we'll reduce the Texture Opacity to reduce the intensity of this surface. We'll add a little more wear to this by clicking the Add New texture button and selecting the Fractal Noise Texture Type. The values below will finish this texture off.

			Texture Size (cm)	
Texture Value:	50%			
Frequencies:	3	**X**	5	
Contrast:	1.0	**Y**	5	
Small Power:	0.5	**Z**	1	

Click Use Texture and then switch to the Advanced Options tab. Select the Fast Fresnel shader again and activate only the Diffuse and Specular options. Lower the Diffuse value to 0% and leave the Specular at 100%. Switch back to the Basic Parameters tab and lower the Glossiness to 16 (Low), since cloth doesn't normally have much of a shine to it. This time, F9 will produce a dirty-looking, cloth-wrapped handle (Figure 6-26). Save this handle as **Handle-Cloth.lwo.**

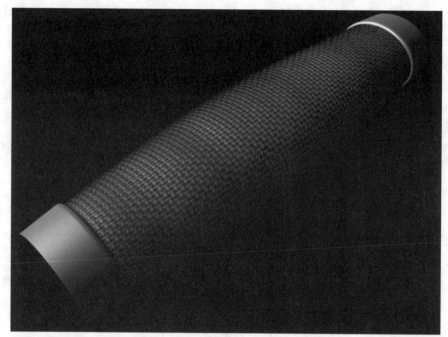

FIGURE 6-26 The same texture, when applied to the Diffuse channel as well, increases the texture's sense of depth. An additional fractal noise adds the illusion of frequent use.

STEP 47: With a very small modification, this canvas texture can be made to look like a wire mesh. To do this we need to add a reflective map to it. Copy the first Diffuse texture layer as we've done in Steps 44 and 46, and paste this into the Texture panel for Reflectivity. Lower the Texture Opacity here to 25% and click Use Texture. Click the Reflection Options button and select the **MetalRefMap.iff** image as the Reflection Image and use Ray Tracing + Spherical Image for the Reflection Type. Paste this same texture into the Texture panel for Specularity, but this time, set the Texture opacity to 100%. Now all our "raised" areas will have a more polished look to them than the rest of the surface area.

STEP 48: Raise the Glossiness to Medium and lower the Diffuse value to 0%. By lowering the Diffuse value, we've darkened the spaces between the threads in our Diffuse texture. Remember that the Texture Opacity for this is 50%, so half the base value will be blended with it. To make this look metallic, we need a metallic color. A light blue usually does this well, so click the Color button and change the values to R: 145, G: 145, B: 170 and click OK. Activate the Color Highlights option, then click the Advanced Options tab. Open the Fast Fresnel options again, activate the Reflective button, and enter a value of 75% here. Click OK and press F9. You will now have an image similar to Figure 6-27.

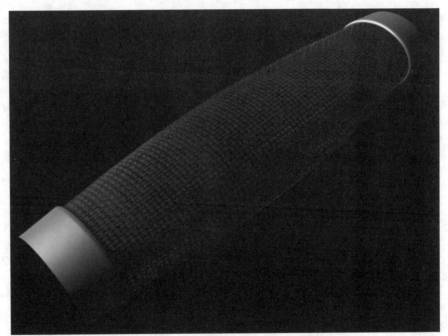

FIGURE 6-27 A slight change in reflection options turns a cloth surface into a metallic one.

Rename this surface to Handle—Wire Mesh, and save the object as **Handle-WireMesh.lwo.**

STEP 49: While we're doing wire textures, let's create a wire-wrapped handle. Clear this surface as we did in Step 45 and then click the Diffuse texture button. Select Cylindrical Mapping change the Texture Axis to Z. Click the Texture image button and select the Load Image option. Load the **WireWrap.iff** image from the CD and then change the Texture size on the Z axis to 1.5 cm. Turn the Texture Antialiasing off and change the Width Wrap Amount to 2. Finally, lower the Texture opacity to 30%. We're going to use this texture on a few other channels as well, so copy this before clicking Use Texture.

STEP 50: Click the Texture button for the Specular channel and paste the texture here. Raise the Texture Opacity to 100%, then click Use Texture. Do the same with the Reflectivity channel, but set the Texture opacity to 50%. Finally, click the Bump Map button and past the texture here as well. Increase the Texture Amplitude to 200%, and the Texture Opacity should be 100%. Click Use Texture, then activate the Smoothing option.

STEP 51: We need to set the Reflection Options, so set those the way we did in Step 47, then lower the diffuse value to 0%. Now we need a good wire color. We'll try a nice rustic bronze color, so click the Surface Color button and change this to R: 170, G: 135, B: 100. Once again, we'll add a slight variance to the color by clicking the T button and applying a Fractal Noise. Set this color to R: 150, G: 125, B: 95 and give it a Contrast of 2. Change the Texture Size to 5 cm for each axis, then click Use Texture. Finally, we'll add the Fresnel Shader again, so click the Advanced Options tab and load up the LW_FastFresnel plugin. Click the Options button and set Reflectivity to 75%, Diffuse to 0%, and Specular to 100%. Deactivate the Transparency button, then click OK. F9 will give you something similar to Figure 6-28. Rename this surface to Handle-WireWrap, then save it under a similar name.

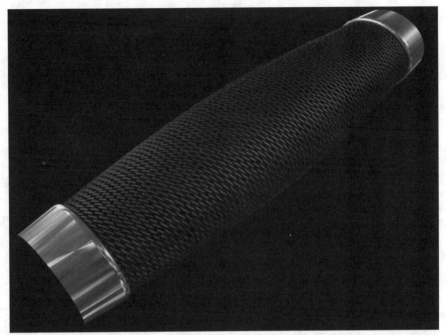

FIGURE 6-28 The **WireWrap.iff** image along with a rich brown color creates the illusion of a pair of twisted bronze wires wrapped around the handle.

We now have a small collection of sword handles to go with our blades, but these are still incomplete. We need to finish the hilt and add a pommel, so let's create those.

STEP 52: Enter Modeler again and select an empty layer. Click the Box tool under the Objects menu and type "n". We're going to rough out the side of our hilt, which we'll loosely base on the Excalibur sword that appeared in the 1981 movie of the same name. We'll be using MetaNurbs to smooth this out later so detail isn't important right now. We'll start off with a box with four segments, so enter the following values in the Numeric requester.

	Low (mm)	High (mm)	Segments
X	0	120	4
Y	−10	10	1
Z	0	20	1

Click OK, then hit Enter to create the box. This will form the beginnings of the right side of our hilt, which we'll mirror later. Now we'll smooth things out by hitting the Tab key to activate MetaNurbs. You should now have something that looks like a yellow hot dog wiener in the OpenGL display. For good results, the Patch Division in the Data Options Panel (type "o") should be set to at least 6.

STEP 53: We'll hammer this into a more suitable shape by tapering it. Click the Modify tab at the top of the screen and select the Taper 2 tool. We'll widen this along the Z axis at the same time we squeeze it vertically. In the Side view, place the cursor at the center of the "wiener," which will be located at 10 mm on the Z axis. Drag down and to the right to get an idea of how the shape will evolve. Click Undo, then type "n" to open the tool's Numeric requester. You will notice the center value is already set to 10 mm on the Z axis, and the other values show the amount of the taper we just applied. This is a handy way to plug in values quickly without having to memorize a bunch of numbers. The numbers we want to use are as follows:

Axis:	X
Range:	Automatic
Sense:	+
Preset:	Ease Out

	Factors	Center
X	100%	0 m
Y	50%	0 m
Z	200%	10 mm

Click Apply and the "wiener" will spread out as in Figure 6-29.

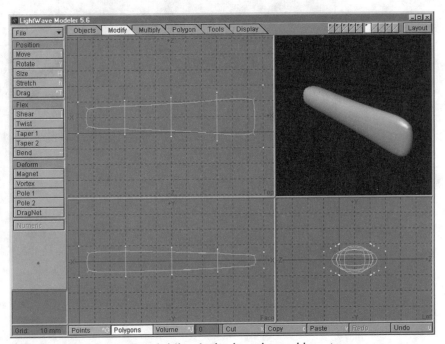

FIGURE 6-29 Our MetaNurb hilt, pinched on the end by a taper.

STEP 54: This is still just a bit too round-looking, so we'll add some corner detail. In the Face view, select the 8 patches that face along the Z axis. Type Shift-f to bring up the Smooth Shift options and enter an Offset of 1 mm. You should now have some squared-off corners along the long edges of this hilt, as in Figure 6-30.

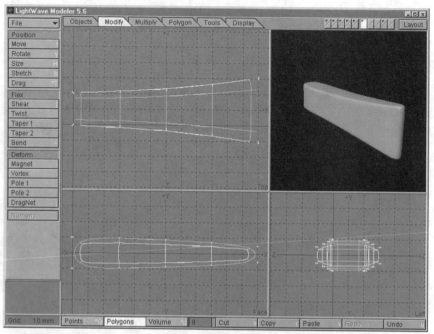

FIGURE 6-30 The addition of a slight Smooth Shift brings definition to the corners.

STEP 55: Deselect everything and then select the rightmost patches. This is easiest to do in the Face view by clicking on the small arc at the right end. Make sure there are only three patches selected, or the next operation could look messy. Type Shift-f again, and use the same values. Click OK and the end will now flatten itself, with thin, rounded corners (Figure 6-31).

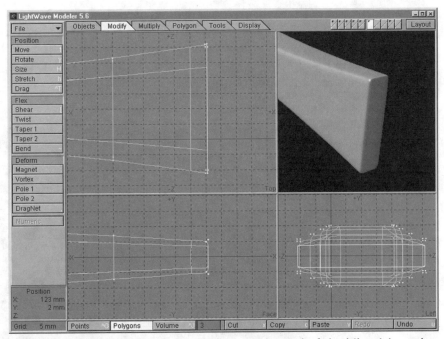

FIGURE 6-31 A second Smooth Shift flattens the end of the hilt, giving a less organic look to the hilt.

STEP 56: Our hilt has nearly taken shape in just a couple short steps, but it's still a bit bland looking. We'll add slight concavity to the wide sides to make it more interesting. Deselect everything by clicking in the gray area to the left, then select the row of polygons that run along the center of this object as seen in the Top view. Ten patches should be selected, 5 on top, and 5 on the bottom. Select the Taper 2 tool again, and type "n" to bring up the Numeric requester. We'll taper these selected patches inward slightly with the following settings:

Axis:	X		Factors	Center
Sense:	+	X	100%	0 m
Range:	Automatic	Y	50%	0 m
Preset:	Linear	Z	50%	10 mm

This will give our hilt a nice flare at the ends (Figure 6-32), which will make the gold surface we give it later look even better. When you're done, deselect everything by first clicking the Polygons button at the bottom to drop the Taper Tool, then clicking the blank area to the left.

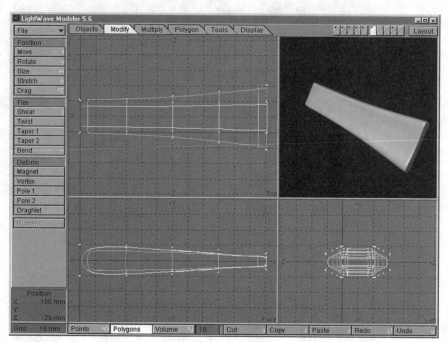

FIGURE 6-32 A slight inward taper of the inner patches creates a more elegant style.

STEP 57: Now we're almost ready to mirror this object, but before we do, we need to make sure the points on the left end are aligned with the centerline. Tap the Tab key to deactivate MetaNurbs for now, and select the 3 end polygons on the left edge. Type Ctrl-v to bring up the Set Value panel and set the X value to 0. Make sure the X axis is selected, then click OK. The 3 polygons will now be flattened on the X axis (Figure 6-33) and may now be deleted since they're no longer needed.

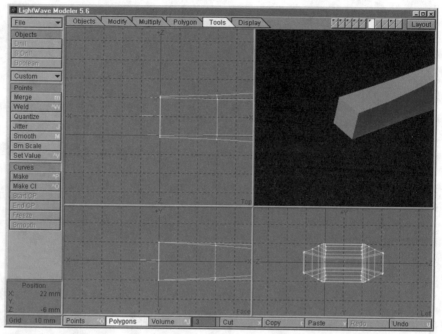

FIGURE 6-33 Flatten these polygons so the object mirrors correctly, then delete them.

STEP 58: Switch back to MetaNurbs mode (Tab) and click the Multiply tab at the top of the screen. Click the Mirror tool, and drag out a Mirror plane on the X axis, making sure it's centered. This should run through the points we just flattened in the previous step. Hit Enter to create a mirror copy of the hilt object. We will now have a fully formed hilt, but let's add one last little detail.

STEP 59: We'll add a central flare as well, so select all the points long the centerline of this object. Sixteen points should be selected since we didn't merge points after the mirror, and we're not going to. Type Shift-h to select the Scale tool, then type "n" to bring up the Numeric requester. We'll create a central ridge by scaling these points outward from the center, so enter a value of 150% for the Scale Factor and make sure the center values are all zeros. Click OK and you will have an object that looks like Figure 6-34.

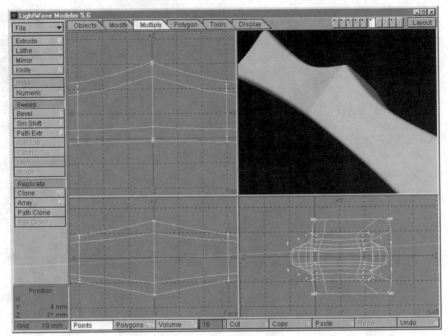

FIGURE 6-34 After Mirroring, a slight ridge is added, just for looks.

Tip: When MetaNurb patches contain points that could be merged with those of adjacent patches, as can happen when a patch is cut, then pasted back into place, point merging is not necessary. When freezing these patches, the frozen polygons will automatically merge across this "gap," but will not try to smooth into one another, retaining a sharp edge. Merging the points of the same patches before freezing will result in a standard rounded surface. By utilizing this fact, MetaNurb objects can be constructed with a greater degree of detail, including sharp corners.

STEP 60: The design work on our hilt is done, so we're ready to freeze these MetaNurbs. Before we do, copy this object to another layer and Merge Points on it. You will see the center ridge suddenly smoothed out into a graceful curve. Now flip back to the other layer with our ridged copy. Type Ctrl-d to freeze the patches. You will see the object subdivide into many more polygons, but the ridge will remain. Now type "m" to merge points. Select the Automatic method and click OK. In a second, a window will pop up saying "No points eliminated," even though we never merged the two halves while they were made of MetaNurbs. Switch to the second, Merged copy, and type Ctrl-d to freeze it. You now have two hilts to choose from, created from the same MetaNurb cage. Triple everything to remove the nonplanar polygons, then save both of these objects since you never know when you might want to change the look of your sword.

We're nearly finished with our sword. All that remains is the pommel, so let's get that done. Pommels come in all shapes and sizes, from simple flanges at the end of the handle to engraved discs to intricately carved animal heads and jewel settings. We'll keep ours simple, yet attractive, and go with an interesting jewel setting.

STEP 61: We already have the pommel started since we copied the end polygons off the handle when we started that back in Step 32. Switch to the layer that contains these polygons and delete the ones that are located at Modeler's center. Select the remaining polygons and hit the Tab key to turn them into MetaNurbs. Type "q" to bring up the Change Surface panel and select the gold surface, then click Apply. This will allow us to set the texture of both the pommel and the hilt at the same time in Layout.

STEP 62: With the MetaNurb patches selected, type Shift-f. This will bring up the Smooth Shift options, where we'll set the Offset to 3 mm. Click OK and the disc will become a bit thicker, with a rounded edge to it. Switch to point edit mode and select the single point in the center of this disc. Type "t" to activate the Move tool, then drag this point −15 mm along the Z axis. This will pull the center out into a smooth dome shape, as in Figure 6-35. We need to have this bulge so the bevels we do next will move out from the center.

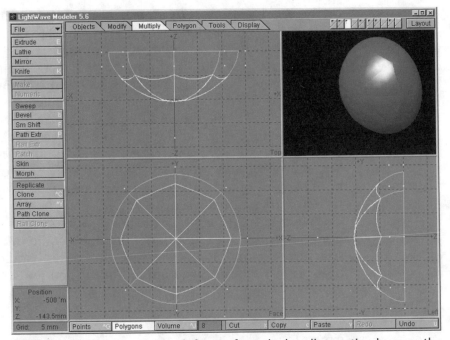

FIGURE 6-35 The old polygons left over from the handle creation become the basis for the pommel.

Optional: The pommel can be considered finished at the end of this step if you want to have a simple rounded knob. You can apply a Smooth Scale of 5 to 20 mm to these selected patches to increase the size of the knob if so desired. If you choose this option, skip ahead to Step 71.

STEP 63: Our pommel will take shape quite quickly now. We'll keep these MetaNurb patches selected throughout this process as we use them to grow fingers that will hold the gemstone we create later. Type "b" to open the Bevel Tool options. Enter an Inset value of 0 and a shift value of 15 mm. Make sure it's set to create Inner Edges and the Surface is set to Source. Click OK and you will suddenly have 8 fingers appear. Hit the "b" key again and apply a second bevel with these same settings. You should have something resembling some alien machine part, like the one in Figure 6-36.

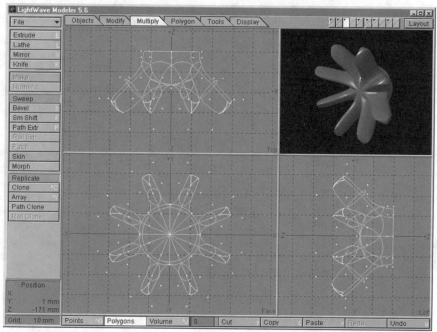

FIGURE 6-36 The pommel begins to take shape after two successive Bevels.

STEP 64: We now need to rotate the selected patches inward before we continue. To do this, we'll use the Set Value tool to flatten these patches on the Z axis. Type Ctrl-v to activate the Set Value tool, and click the Z axis button (Figure 6-37). Enter a value of −170 mm, then click OK. Now, any further bevels will be parallel to the Z axis, and each other.

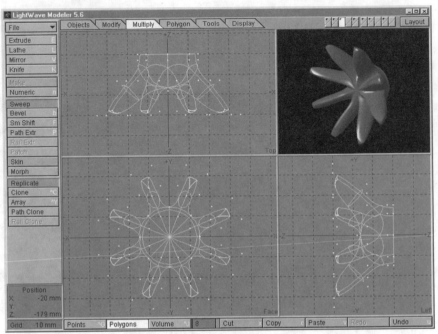

FIGURE 6-37 The end patches are rotated to face the same direction through the use of the Set Value tool.

STEP 65: Since we want these fingers to curve inward in order to hold a gem, we need to bring these ends in toward the center. Type Shift-h to activate the Scale Tool, then position the pointer at the –170 mm mark in the Side view. Make sure it's centered on the Y axis, then click and drag to the left to scale down the selected patches to 50%. This not only brings them closer together, but also tapers the fingers (Figure 6-38).

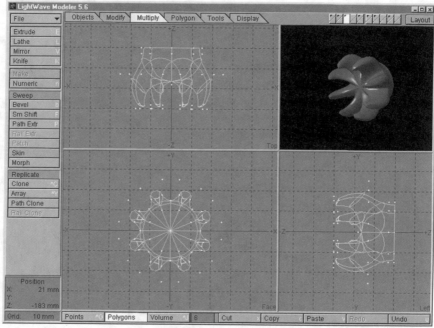

FIGURE 6-38 A 50% scale factor, centered between the finger tips, bend them inward in a smooth arc.

STEP 66: We'll create our last bevel here, again by typing "b" and using the same values as before. Click OK and the tips of the fingers will reach straight back, looking somewhat like a small squid (Figure 6-39).

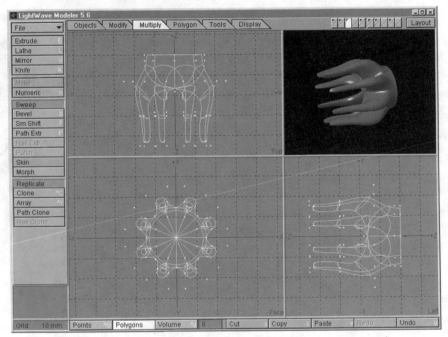

FIGURE 6-39 A third Bevel gives us the last finger segment we need.

STEP 67: Now we'll curve the fingers inward in a gripping fashion. Type Shift-h to activate the Scale Tool again. In the Side view, place the pointer at the −155 mm mark on the Z axis, right near the center point we dragged out earlier. Make sure the pointer is centered on the Y axis, the click and drag until the scale factor is 60%. We will now have 8 inward-arcing fingers, as in Figure 6-40.

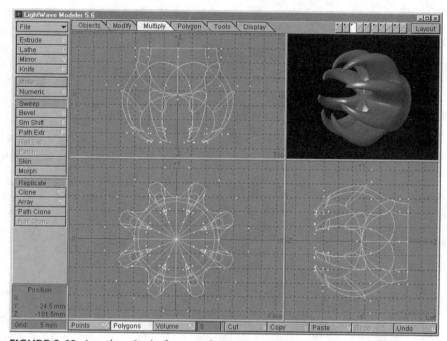

FIGURE 6-40 Another Scale factor of 60% completes the finger curves.

Optional: If you want a mean-looking set of claws instead of fingers, deselect everything, then select the middle portions of the fingers, as shown Figure 6-41. Type "b" to bring up the Bevel tool and enter 2 mm for both the Inset and the Shift. Click OK and the pommel will become much more menacing in appearance (Figure 6-42).

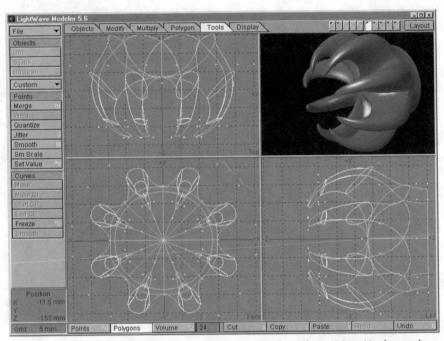

FIGURE 6-41 For a more evil-looking pommel, select these MetaNurb patches.

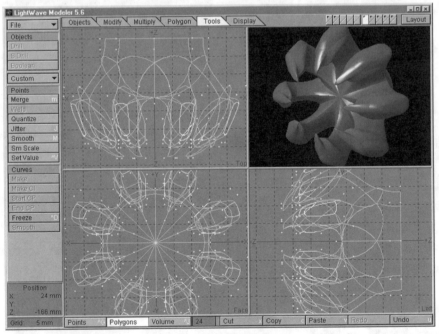

FIGURE 6-42 The same pommel, after Beveling the middle finger segments outward slightly, now seems to have developed talons.

STEP 68: All that remains is to match this pommel to the handle. When we created the handle, we scaled it by 80% on the Y axis, so we'll have to do the same here. Make sure nothing is selected, type "h", then type "n". In the Numeric panel, enter the following values:

	Factors (%)	Center (m)
X	100	0
Y	80	0
Z	100	0

Type Ctrl-d to freeze the MetaNurbs into polygons, then type Shift-t to triple them. Save this pommel, then load one of the handle objects we textured earlier. It should load into place with the pommel fitted to the end. Hit "m" to Merge Points and 48 points should be removed.

STEP 69: Next, load one of the hilts we just created, followed by a blade of your choice. These will both load into place, automatically assembling into a full sword (Figure 6-43).

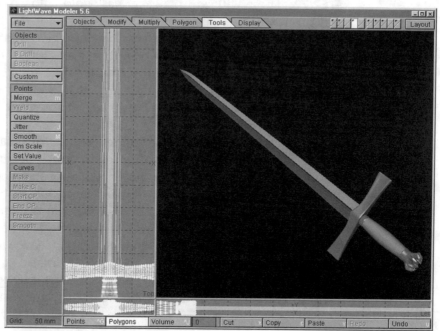

FIGURE 6-43 The assembled sword, ready to receive its gemstone.

STEP 70: Save this as **Sword.lwo,** then click the Layout button. In Layout, clear the scene, then load the sword we just saved in Modeler. Rotate this 90 degrees on its pitch so the sword blade points straight down. This will give us a good typical viewing angle to work with. We'll finish the surfacing of the sword here before we add the gemstone.

STEP 71: Open the Surfaces Panel and select the surface named Gold. The hilt, pommel, and the end collars of the handle will all have this surface name applied to them and it's the only surface we haven't textured yet. Since we've already named it gold, we might as well give it a good gold surface. The first thing to do is to set the base values:

Color:	240 220 120	**Glossiness:**	64 (Medium)
Luminosity:	0%	**Reflectivity:**	70%
Diffuse:	30%	**Smoothing:**	On
Specular:	100%	**Max. Smoothing Angle:**	89
Color Highlights:	On		

STEP 72: These will set up a good base gold color. Now we need to add the texturing. Click the Texture button for the Surface Color. Select Fractal Noise as the Texture Type and give this a Texture Size of 5 cm. We'll make this texture a slight variation of the base color, so click the Texture Color button and change the color to R: 245, G: 210, B: 145. Leave the Frequencies set to 3 and the Contrast set to 1.0. Finally, raise the Small Power to 1.0 and click Use Texture.

STEP 73: Now we'll add a simulated smudging that is common with shiny metals, either from finger prints or just wear. This smudging helps define where the surface appears to be, much like a handprint helps define where the surface of a mirror or window is. Click the Texture button for the Diffuse channel and once again, select the Fractal Noise Texture Type. Set the Texture Size to 2 cm this time, and set the Texture Value to 50%. Leave the Frequencies set 3 and raise the Contrast to 2.0. The Small Power can be left where it is. This higher Diffuse value will appear to be less polished areas of gold, giving a subtle shading variation across the gold surface. Click the Render button to generate a preview sample to see this in action. Click the Use Texture button to close this panel.

STEP 74: We need to set the Reflection Options to really get the gold to look right, so click that button next and set the Reflection Type to the fourth option in the list; Ray Tracing + Spherical Map. For the Reflected image, select the **MetalRefMap.iff**, which we also used for the blade. It does a great job for most metallic surfaces. Click the Close Panel button and we're done with the texturing. All that's left is a Fresnel enhancement.

STEP 75: Click the Advanced Options tab and select the LW_FastFresnel shader plugin. We'll be modifying the Reflectivity, Diffuse, and Specular options with values of 100%, 0%, and 200%, respectively. Luminosity and Transparency should be turned off. Click OK and our gold is complete. This calls for a test render!

STEP 76: Position the camera in a good viewing angle and press F9. For best results, turn on Trace Shadows and Trace Reflection in the Render Panel (Figure 6-44). Now is a good time to save the sword.

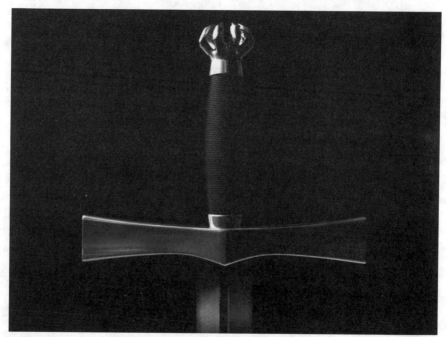

FIGURE 6-44 A closeup of the fully textured handle.

STEP 77: Switch back to Modeler and clear the current layer, which should have the sword we just assembled. We don't need this old version anymore, but we will want the one we just finished texturing. Flip to a new empty layer and place the sword layer in the background. Zoom in until the pommel fills the view. We'll create a very simple gemstone, so under the Objects menu, click the Ball tool. It's important to note that the measurements for this ball will vary depending on the method you used to create the pommel. The simple fingered pommel has more space for a larger stone than the taloned pommel, so type "n" and use the measurements below that fit your pommel.

Ball Type:	Tessellation
Level:	2

	Fingered		Taloned	
	Center	Radii	Center	Radii
X	0 m	14.5 mm	0 m	13 mm
Y	0 m	11.5 mm	0 m	10 mm
Z	−165 mm	10.0 mm	−164.5 mm	8 mm

Hit Enter to make this ball, then type "q" to open the Change Surface panel. We'll make this a generic gemstone, so pick any color you like. We'll name this surface "Gem" and make it 75% specular. Set the Glossiness to medium and turn the Smoothing off. The color preview should show something resembling a cut gemstone (Figure 6-45).

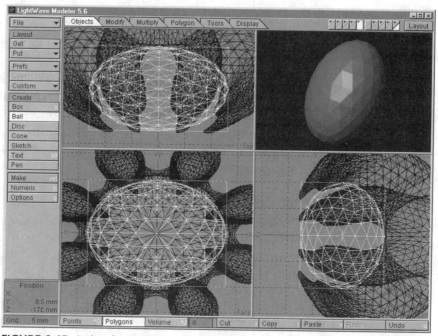

FIGURE 6-45 A simple tessellated ball without smoothing looks very gem-like.

Our gemstone is going to be one of the transparent kinds, such as diamond, ruby, or topaz. To do a stone like this correctly, we'll need to use refraction, which will bend the light as it enters the stone. However, we also need to bend the light back as it exits the stone. We can't simply make this surface double sided since that would end up having the light refract a certain amount when it hits the outside surface, then it would refract that same amount again as it hits the second surface as it exits. This effectively doubles the amount of refraction when we want to cancel it out. To do this we need a second, inward-facing surface to tell the exiting light that it is now entering air again. This inward-facing "air" surface is very important when trying to recreate anything that involves refraction accurately.

STEP 78: Hit the "c" key to make a copy of this object in memory, then type "f" to flip the polygons of the stone on the screen. Type "q" to open the Change Surface panel, and create a new surface called Air. Now, hit "v" to paste the copy we made into the layer. Type "m" to merge the points since we'll now have 162 duplicates we don't need. Now we're ready to make this stone sparkle.

STEP 79: Save this as **PommelStone.lwo** and switch over to Layout. Our sword should still be sitting there, but we don't need it right now. Rather than clear it out of the scene, open the Objects Panel and click the Appearance Options tab. Raise the Object Dissolve to 100%, so we don't see the sword for a while. Now, load the Pommel-Stone and position the camera so you have a good view of the gem.

STEP 80: Open the Surface Panel and select the Air surface. We'll need to make this transparent for our gem to look right, so raise the Transparency to 100%. Also, raise the Specularity to 100% and set the Glossiness to Low. Activate the Color Highlights button and raise the Reflectivity to 25%. This will set up our internal reflections, which will give the gem its sparkle. Click the Reflection Options and select the **MetalRefMap.iff** image as the Reflected Image. For the Reflection Type, we'll just use Spherical Reflection Map. We could use Ray Tracing, but that would drastically increase the render times due to the recursion of the internal reflections and the results would not be much different. Since this will be a cut gemstone, we don't want to add smoothing, so make sure that's off. Finally, make the Surface Color pure white.

You'll notice we activated the Color Highlights button, but there's no effect in the preview samples. Well, not yet. We'll get back to that a bit later.

STEP 81: Select the Gem surface now and set the transparency level to 100% as well. We'll start with a basic clear gemstone to get a feel for how it handles and then add color later. And what better clear gemstone than a diamond? Set the surface up with these base values to get started:

Color:	200 200 200	Glossiness:	64 (Medium)
Luminosity:	0%	Reflectivity:	20%
Diffuse:	10%	Transparency:	100%
Specular:	75%	Color Filter:	On
Color Highlights:	Off	Smoothing:	Off

These values will work for just about any gem type with a simple color change. We've applied a Color Filter to this surface that will only slightly darken anything seen through it due to light gray color we gave the surface, as will be seen in a preview sample with a patterned background. A pure white would have the effect of neutralizing the effects of the Color Filter, while any other color will show up. We'll need this Color Filter for gems such as ruby and emerald, so we might as well leave it on.

STEP 82: Finally, we need to set a Refractive Index. This determines how much the light is bent as it enters the gem and it varies depending on the material you want to simulate. We're doing a diamond, so we'll need a value of 2.417, as shown in the Refraction Index chart on page 4.12 of the LightWave Reference Manual. You might want to mark that page since we'll be using it a bit here. But first, let's see that refraction at work. Open the Render Panel and activate Trace Refraction in the upper right corner. Close this panel and then hit F9 (Figure 6-46). The gem is nearly finished but we'll add a few subtle improvements before we move on.

FIGURE 6-46 In just a couple of quick steps we have an attractive sparkly gemstone.

STEP 83: Our first improvement will be the addition of the Fast Fresnel shader. Although the effects it creates tend to be subtle, they will add that extra sparkle that's currently missing. We'll apply this effect to both the inside and outside surfaces, so open the Surface Panel and select the Gem surface. Click the Advanced Options tab and select the LW_FastFresnel plugin. We want the Reflectivity set to only 75% and Specularity set to 100%. Everything else for this shader will be turned off and the Minimum Glancing Angle should be 0 degrees. Click OK then select the Air surface. Once again, load the Fast Fresnel plugin and set the same two options, this time setting both Reflectivity and Specularity to 100% at a Minimum Glancing Angle of 0. We'll also add the Transparency to this one, making it 100% as well.

These two Fresnel effects will generate more intense reflections around the edges of the gemstone, both inside and out, adding some much-needed sparkle. However, there is still one thing missing. Physical gems tend to diffract light into its color components, creating brilliantly colored internal reflections. LightWave does not support this phenomenon, though it can be simulated.

STEP 84: When we created our Air surface, we applied the Color Highlights option to it, even though it had no color to add. We'll give it that color now, but in a much more dynamic way. For the second Shader Plugin slot, select the LW_Interference plugin. Click the Options button and make sure the Spectrum Scale is set to its default 100%. Click the check box for Single Band, then change the Angle Range values to span from a Minimum of 0 to a Maximum of 90 degrees. Finally, select the Blend button for the Color Mode and set the percentage to 100%. This will now color the inside surface according to its angle to the camera, covering the entire spectrum. Since the surface is 100% transparent, we won't see these colors, but they will affect the highlights and reflections that cross the surface. Another render will show a gem with more sparkle and colored highlights inside (Figure 6-47). Rename the Gem surface to Diamond, then save this object as **PommelStone-Diamond.lwo** since you might want to attach this to the sword later.

FIGURE 6-47 The same stone, this time with the addition of Fresnel shading and Interference effects.

STEP 85: Now that we have the basis for just about any gemstone we want, we can play with surface colors. Ruby is a very common sword decoration, at least in fantasy paintings, so let's try that. Select the Diamond surface and rename it to Ruby. The first thing to do is to change the color, so click the Surface Color button and change it to a deep red. RGB values of 180, 0, 0 give a good shade. Ruby is less dense than diamond is, and has a Refractive Index of 1.77, so that's our other main change. Since we have Color Filter activated on this surface, everything we see through the gem will now be colored in deep reds. On a black background, this stone will almost appear to be an opaque black, so let's brighten the backdrop a bit. Open the Effects Panel and click the Gradient Backdrop button. Now we'll have a better background to show off the gem. Hit F9 for another render (Figure 6-48).

FIGURE 6-48 A quick color change turns a diamond into a ruby.

STEP 86: Our ruby doesn't look too bad at all. We can still improve on it, though. One detail is still missing, and that's a sense of volume. A ruby, or any other gemstone, will absorb light as it travels though the crystal, becoming darker as the thickness increases. Right now, our ruby has the same constant opacity across the surface, so everything seen through it is filtered the same amount. In step 83 we added the Fast Fresnel shader to this surface, and at the same time, we activated the Transparency portion of it. Up until now, it has had no effect since both the Fresnel Transparency value and the base Transparency value have been identical. Open the Surfaces Panel and click the Basic Parameters tab. Lower the Transparency value to around 75%. This just made our gem less transparent to perpendicular rays, while the Fast Fresnel keeps the edges at 100% transparency. When rendered, this will make the gem appear to be darker in the center where it's thicker (Figure 6-49). Try other colors and experiment with the Transparency value. Remember to save the surface settings you like. You never know when you'll want to use them again.

FIGURE 6-49 Decreasing the base Transparency value adds a subtle change, making the center appear slightly darker than the edges.

Tip: When using the Thin Film shader, click on the spectrum to find the values of the two colors you want to use, then simply subtract the value of the color you want for the center from the edge value to find the Angle Variation amount.

STEP 87: There is another method of making a gem appear darker in the center, or even appear to be a different color altogether. Similar to the method we used to change the highlight colors of the Air surface; we can use another plugin to alter the colors of the outside surface. Click the Advanced Options tab and select the LW_ThinFilm plugin for slot 2. This is very similar to the Interference plugin, but much more selective. Click the option button and a small interface will open with a full color spectrum displayed across the top. Click anywhere in this spectrum to select a color, which will show up as a value measured in nanometers (nm) appearing in the Primary Wavelength field. This is the color that will appear on the surface when viewed at 90 degrees.

The second value, Angle Variation, tells the shader how much of the spectrum will be visible across the 90-degree arc, where the viewing angle becomes 0 degrees. Again, this is measured in nanometers and is added to the Primary Wavelength. This value may be negative, so you can have a range start with a dark red and span to light orange or go from dark blue to light blue.

The color can be applied in one of three ways, Add, Multiply, and Blend. We'll be using the Blend option, so click that button and increase the percentage value beside it to 100%. Now, the colors we select in this panel will completely overwrite the Surface Color.

We can recreate our ruby surface here by setting the Primary Wavelength to 780 nm and setting the Angle Variation to −150 nm. Be sure to raise the base Transparency value back to 100%, then hit F9. Figure 6-50 shows a ruby surface created with the Thin Film shader. Following are a few settings to create other gemstone surfaces. Feel free to play with various values.

FIGURE 6-50 Another ruby, this time courtesy of the Thin Film shader. Note the deeper red center without the cloudiness that appeared in Figure 6-49.

Gemstone	Primary	Angle
Ruby	780	−150
Sapphire	430	50
Topaz	620	−20
Amethyst	380	70

STEP 88: Now that we've created a few transparent gemstones, let's try some opaque ones. Go back into Modeler and activate the Ball tool. Open the numeric panel for the tool and raise the Tessellation Level to 3. The sizes you used for the gem should still be in memory, so click OK and then press Enter. Open the Surface Panel and create a new surface named clear, then click Apply. Copy this object by typing "c" and then open the Surface Panel again. This time, create a new surface called Stone, then click Apply. Under the Tools menu, click the Smooth Scale tool. A panel will open asking for an offset. Enter −0.1 mm here and click OK. The entire surface of this ball will now be moved inward by 1/10th of a millimeter. Now, paste the copy we made into the layer. You will now have two balls, one slightly smaller than the other, residing in the same layer. Each ball has its own surface, the smaller one called Stone and the outer one called Clear. This double surface will let us create even more interesting effects.

STEP 89: Save this object as **SmoothStone.lwo** and flip back to Layout. Open the Objects Panel and click the Replace Object button since we still have our gem sitting there. Select the SmoothStone we just created and then open the Surface Panel. We're going to create an iridescent stone here, similar to a black opal so select the surface named Stone and change its Surface Color to black (0, 0, 0), which we'll use as a base color. Our other base values will be a Diffuse Level of 20% and a Specular Level of 200%. Change the Glossiness to Low and activate the Color Highlights option. Finally, activate Smoothing, using the default Maximum Smoothing Angle of 89 degrees.

STEP 90: As this surface stands, it is completely black, including its highlights, making it very uninteresting. We'll add some points of interest by clicking the Texture button for the Color channel. Select the Fractal Noise Texture Type and give it a Texture Size of 5 mm. Make this surface a bright red and increase the Frequencies to 6. Drop the Contrast to 0.7 and raise the Small Power to 1.0. A preview sample will show a black sphere with a speckled red highlight. Let's add a little more color. Type Ctrl-c to copy this texture and then click the Add New Texture to paste the copy in this new layer and change the color to a bright green. A preview sample right now would show a green version of the last sample because our green texture is an exact copy of the red one and sits right on top of it.

In order to see the red texture, lower the Texture Opacity to 50%. Now a 50–50 mix of red and green is visible, but this now results in a yellow pattern because both textures still line up. Click the Texture Center button and type in some random number. This will offset the green texture so the red one can be seen around it. Click the Add New Texture button once again and type Ctrl-v to paste another copy of the red texture here. Change this to a rich blue color, and once again, give this a random Texture Center. Lower the Texture Opacity of this layer to 50% as well. We've just created a three-color fractal pattern that will show up only in the specular highlights of the surface. Click the Use Texture button to close this panel.

STEP 91: Select the surface we called Clear now, and raise its color to pure white (255, 255, 255). We'll also lower the Diffuse Level to 0% and increase the Specular Level to 100%. Increase the Glossiness to High and raise the Reflectivity to 20%. Click the Reflections Options and set the Reflection Type to Ray Tracing + Spherical Image and select the **MetalRefMap.iff** image as the Reflected image. Since this surface is called Clear, raise the Transparency to 100%. Increase the Refractive Index to 1.01 (or higher), then activate the Smoothing option.

STEP 92: This just created an outer clear coat around the Stone surface which allows us to keep a very smooth appearance to the gem, even if we apply bumps to the surface inside. Currently, the Stone surface has a wide intense, colored highlight, which will now have the smaller white highlight of the outer surface located in its center. Type F9 to see the two surfaces interacting with one another (Figure 6-51).

FIGURE 6-51 Layered surfaces can create incredible effects, including this colorful black opal.

STEP 93: We can make this stone look even more iridescent with the Interference shader. First, select the Stone surface again, and change the name to Fractal Opal, then switch over to the Objects Panel and save the object under that same name. Open the Surfaces Panel and click the Texture button for the Color channel and remove the three fractal textures. Next, raise the base color to a medium gray and lower the Specularity to 100%. Click the Advanced Options tab and select the LW_Interference plugin. We'll just use the values as they are, except we'll lower the Blend percentage to 20%. Since this plugin modifies the surface color, our specular highlights will be filtered according to the viewing angle. This surface is very smooth right now, so what we'll see is simply a series of spectral bands. What we want to do is disturb these bands a little. To do that, click the Basic Parameters tab and click the Bump Map button. Select the Fractal Bumps Texture and give it a size of 1 mm. Increase the Texture Amplitude to 100% and the Frequencies to 6.

Since a bump map changes the angle of the surface normal at each pixel in the image, the effects of the Interference plugin, or of any other plugin that reads the surface normal (Fast Fresnel, Water, Snow, Thin Film, etc.) will also be modified. A test render will show that the formerly even-spaced color bands are now distorted, resembling the patterns you would find on the inside of a seashell or on a pearl (Figure 6-52).

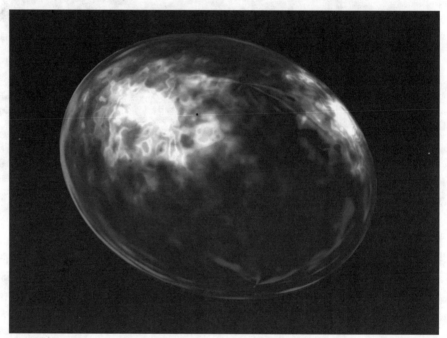

FIGURE 6-52 A variation, using the Interference shader and a fractal bump map on the inner surface, has a more dynamic coloring, which constantly changes with the viewing angle.

Things to try: Look through a jewelry catalogue, or even do a search on the web for gemstones, and try to recreate the various stones that you find. The techniques described here can be used to simulate about 90% of gemstones available.

STEP 94: With two specular highlights like these, endless effects can be created, from pearlescent swirls to crystalline sparkles. The final gemstone we'll cover here is a little more advanced, and is generally only thought possible through the use of Worley Laboratories' Gaffer plugin, until now. If you haven't done so, save this current gem, then rename the inner surface to Tiger's Eye. Tiger's Eye is a type of quartz crystal known for its signature highlight, called the "eye," which is an intense, elongated colored highlight that usually runs the length of the gem. Other gemstones have similar "eyes," but not quite as striking as those of a Tiger's Eye. We'll start by giving this surface a rich brown color, so click the Surface Color button and change the RGB values to 100, 65, 30. Click the Texture button next to it and select the Fractal Noise texture. We'll add some variation to the brown as well as add a few fibrous streaks, which are common in this type of stone. The following values will create those streaks (Figure 6-53).

FIGURE 6-53 A Tiger's Eye, without the "eye."

Fact: The elongated specular highlight in Tiger's Eye is caused in much the same way as streaks in a CD, radial highlights on records (remember those?), the many types of decorative highlights seen in metals, and thread- wrapped Christmas tree ornaments. This effect is known as anisotropy and is very common with metals like stainless steel and brushed aluminum. Worley Laboratories currently offers the only shader plugin that can recreate this effect and it is used extensively by some of the largest Hollywood effects houses.

Texture Color:	80 35 20		Texture Size (mm)	
Frequencies:	6	X	1	
Contrast:	1.0	Y	10	
Small Power:	1.0	Z	10	

Now that we have the colors, let's finish the rest of the surface and create that "eye." We need an intense highlight, so raise the Specular Level to 300% and set the Glossiness to 30. The Diffuse Level can be anywhere from 50% to 100%, but the highlight will look sharper with a lower level. We'll use 75% for now. Click the Advanced Options tab and remove the Interference shader since we won't need any plugins on this surface. A test render won't look very promising yet and will give just a standard round highlight.

Specular highlights are shaped by the contours of the surface that creates them. Spheres will create simple small points of light, flat surfaces create much wider highlights, and cylindrical objects create long and narrow highlights. How do we get a long and narrow highlight to appear on a round surface? Our gem is pretty much round, so it's creating a small rounded highlight. We want it to create the type of highlight a cylinder would create, so we need to somehow alter this round surface to a cylinder, without actually changing its shape. This sounds oddly like what a Bump Map does in LightWave. What we need is a bump map that will cancel out the gem's physical convex surface. We need a bump that will simulate a concave surface that we can apply to this convex one, and there just happens to be such a map on the CD.

STEP 95: Click the Bump Map button and select Cylindrical Image Map as the Texture Type. For the Texture Image, load the **SmoothRidge-v.iff** from the CD. This image is a grayscale with a luminosity curve that matches the curve of a sphere and this is what we'll use to cancel out the curve of our gemstone. Click the Negative Image button below this image since we need to apply an inverse bump to this surface. Click the Automatic Sizing button and set the Texture Axis to X Axis. This will wrap the image around the gemstone's long axis, canceling out the curve from side to side. Raise the Texture Amplitude to 100% and the magic is done. The tiger has its eye, so press F9 to see it. The effect, since it is really just a cheat, is best viewed within 45 degrees of the face of the stone. More acute angles can result in the eye splitting into two highlights, but since this gem will be placed in the sword handle, the viewing angle shouldn't be a problem. Our Tiger's Eye is done, so now would be a great time to save it (Figure 6-54).

FIGURE 6-54 The Tiger's Eye, the way it should appear.

Note: Unlike a real Tiger's Eye, this one will gain a new streak for every light source that shines on it. It will also appear inline with the normal specular highlights, where a real tiger's eye tends to appear anywhere within 90 degrees of the highlight.

STEP 96: Switch back to Modeler. We should still have our surfaced sword sitting in a background layer, so bring that up to the front by clicking the top half of the layer button (Figure 6-55). You will also have a small collection of gemstones on disk, so load one that you like into this same layer. When it loads, it will position itself in the claws of the pommel automatically since this is the location we created for it originally. Finally, save this new sword under whatever name you like. Remember that many historical swords had their own names, like Excalibur, Albion, etc., so you don't need to create a strange name like **Sword-Grooved-Leather-Gold-Talon-Opal.lwo** or **Sword-GLGTO.lwo.** Quite often, a real name will evoke a mental image of the object faster than some obscure labeling code. The steps we just followed can be used to create a virtual armory full of swords. By modifying the details in various steps, endless variations can be created; short swords, broadswords, two-handed swords, even Samurai swords. Feel free to experiment with other designs and surfaces. Now that we have a completed sword, let's show it off in an interesting setting.

FIGURE 6-55 The completed sword, or at least one of them.

Tip: We could alternatively assemble the sword in Layout, loading the parts we want, then parenting them all to a null object. We could then use the null to animate the entire assembly.

STEP 97: In homage to that classic tale, we will now thrust our sword into a stone! But first, we need a stone. In Modeler, select the Box tool and drag out a box about 1.5 meters long and about half a meter tall or more. Make it about as wide as it is tall. Type "n" to bring up the Box tool's numeric panel and increase the number of segments to 3 on each axis, then click OK. The following values were used for the rock in the examples.

	Low (mm)	High (mm)	Segments
X	−400	400	3
Y	0	600	3
Z	−600	600	3

Hit the Enter key to create this box.

STEP 98: To make this very geometric box look like an organically shaped rock, we'll first taper it to get the general shape. Select the Taper 2 tool from the Modify menu and click the Numeric button below it. Change the Curve setting to Ease Out and make sure the Sense is positive. We won't need to worry about numbers here since we'll be applying quite a bit of randomness to this object, so place the pointer somewhere over box in the Top view, preferably somewhere near the center. Click and drag to taper the top to about half its original size. This will give the box a slightly rounded dome shape (Figure 6-56).

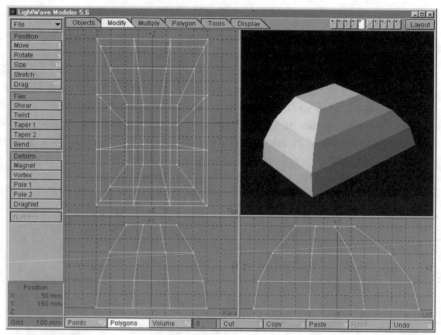

FIGURE 6-56 Our segmented box after tapering.

STEP 99: Now we'll turn this dome into a more rocklike object. Type Shift-d to bring up the Polygon Subdivide tool. Select Metaform and enter a 2 in the Fractal field. This will cause a jitter to be applied to the subdivided polygons, which will break up the neat geometric appearance our rock currently has. Click OK and the rock will look pretty messed up (Figure 6-57). This is fine since we'll be smoothing it out a bit later. First, apply a second Metaform, just like the first, again with a Fractal value of 2. This second Metaform will be less deformed than the first, but it's still quite rough.

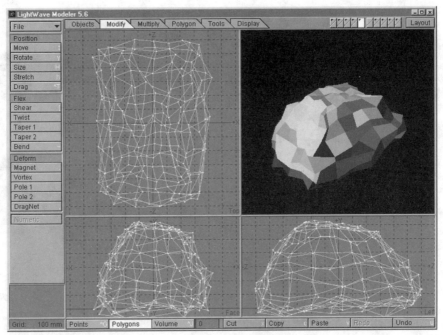

FIGURE 6-57 The same box after the first Metaform pass. The fractal value of 2 really distorts the shape.

Tip: Sometimes Modeler will exaggerate the effects of the Fractal variation, causing unwanted folds or intersecting polygons. If this happens, simply undo the previous Metaform and do it again. The Fractal effect is random and will be different each time it is applied.

STEP 100: Run the Metaform tool a third time, but this time, we'll drop the Fractal value to 1. Click OK and the rock will become much smoother. Do this one final time, again with a Fractal of 1 and our rock is nearly finished (Figure 6-58). All that remains is to fix it for rendering since it's highly unlikely it contains any planar polygons now. Type Shift-t to triple the polygons and then type "q" to open the Surface panel. Name this surface Rock, and save the object as **SwordStone.lwo** (Figure 6-59).

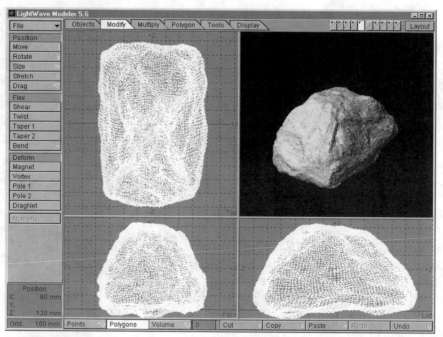

FIGURE 6-58 After three more Metaform passes, the rough shape is smoothed to a rocky surface.

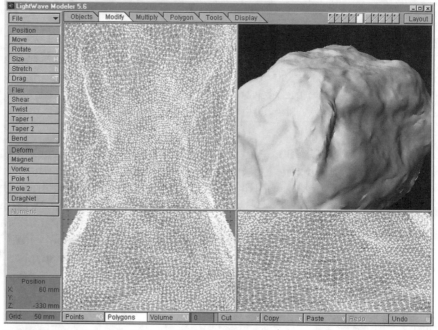

FIGURE 6-59 After Tripling and applying surface smoothing the rock is done and ready for texturing.

Tip: This same procedure can be modified easily to create asteroids, meteors, and other rough shapes you might need.

STEP 101: Switch to Layout and clear the scene. Load the Sword-Stone we just created, open the Surface Panel, and select the Rock surface. We're going to make this a big old weathered rock you would find in a forest, so the first step, as usual, would be to set the color. We'll go with a deep dark brown base color, which we can get with RGB values of 100, 80, 70. We'll keep the Diffuse level at 100% and raise the Specularity to 10%. Beat-up old rocks in a forest are rarely ever very shiny, so we'll lower the Glossiness to Low. Finally, activate the smoothing and set the Maximum Smoothing Angle to 50 degrees. This will round out most of the rock, but keep a few rough edges sticking around to look natural.

STEP 102: It would be very unlikely for a weathered old rock like ours to have a solid even color to it, so we'll break up the monotony of it with some Fractal Noise. Click the Texture button for the Color channel and select the Fractal Noise texture. We'll use this to create some horizontal bands to simulate rock strata so we'll compress this texture vertically. The following values will give us some random horizontal streaks of a darker color.

			Texture Size	
Texture Color:	80 60 35			
Frequencies:	6	X	1 m	
Contrast:	1.0	Y	2 cm	
Small Power:	1.0	Z	1 m	

We'll also add a few more streaks to simulate water stains, again through the use of Fractal Noise. This time, the streaks will be vertical, so click the Texture button for the Diffuse Channel and enter the following values for this Fractal Noise texture:

			Texture Size	
Texture Value:	25%			
Frequencies:	6	X	10 cm	
Contrast:	1.0	Y	1 m	
Small Power:	1.0	Z	10 cm	

Our stone will now look much stonier and a bit dirty now, as seen in Figure 6-60. However, it's still a bit too smooth, so let's rough it up a bit.

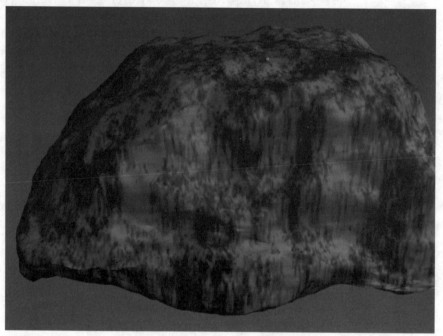

FIGURE 6-60 The rock with some fractal bands applied. It looks a little too smooth right now.

STEP 103: The Crumple bump texture has always been excellent at making rough surfaces, so it's only fair that we should use it for our rock. Click the Bump Map button and select the Crumple Texture. Our rock is about 1 meter in size, so we'll just leave the texture size alone. We'll also leave the Texture Amplitude set to 50%, but we will increase the Number of Scales to 8. This will break up the texture pattern quite a bit. We'll also increase the Small Power to 1.0, which will add even more detail and increase the apparent bump depth. A test render now will show a fairly rocklike surface, but still not quite as weathered as it could be.

STEP 104: Copy this Bump texture and then click the Add new Texture button. Paste this copy here, and this time change the Texture Amplitude to −100%. This will create the appearance of rounded lumps over the surface of the rock, but they're currently lined up to match the first bump layer. We'll need to give this second layer an offset so the two bump maps don't cancel each other out, so click the Texture Center, and just enter some random numbers so the two layers have different centers. A test render now will show a much more believable rock (Figure 6-61).

FIGURE 6-61 The rock with two layers of Crumple applied.

STEP 105: A rolling stone gathers no moss, but since ours isn't rolling, it's gathered a good coating of it. We'll create this moss with an unlikely sounding plugin called the Snow Shader. You might be wondering what the connection is between snow and moss. Well, for one, they both tend to accumulate on the upper surfaces of objects, and they both like to collect where there is little direct sunlight. In fact, if you turned snow green, and roughened it up a bit, it would look like moss, so that's what we'll do here. Click the Advanced Options tab and select the LW_Snow plugin. Before we go any farther, we'll need to render a test frame so this shader knows what the surface looks like. Hit F9 and in a minute or so, an image of our rock will appear, covered in snow.

Note: From this point on, do not use LightWave's built-in texture preview strip since this will immediately crash LightWave. The Snow Shader is part of the Natural Shaders collection, and each of these shaders uses the geometry of the object to determine how the effects are applied. The Preview Samples don't actually supply any geometry data for the shaders to use. Instead, we'll need to use the Shader's built-in preview display.

STEP 106: Click the Option button to open the Snow Shader interface. The first thing we'll do here is to turn the snow green. At the bottom of the panel are two Snow Colors. Color1 is the color that will appear where the effect is at its maximum, in this case, the thick areas of moss that we want to create. The second color is what will appear along the edges where the effect will blend into the surrounding surface. We want a rich green for Color1, so enter the RGB values of 15, 95, 40 for Color1. For the second color, we'll use a darker green, which is slightly brown as well. This will give our moss edges the appearance of dead or unhealthy growth. An RGB setting of 45, 55, 5 will create this olive color. If you have the Real Time update activated in the shader's preview area, you will now see a small version of the rock with a partial green cover. Now we just need to fine-tune this moss so it's not too intense.

STEP 107: We don't want the moss to cover the rock too much, so lower the Snow Amount to 5%. We'll spread its edges out to get more color variation by setting the Start Slope Angle to 0 degrees, which is a vertical surface. We'll set the End Slope Angle to 90 degrees so that as a surface becomes level, more and more moss will appear on it. Since we have a couple layers of bump maps on this surface, the effect will become mottled by these bump maps, adding to the illusion. Leave the Smoothing for this section at 0, then move down to the Snow Shading section. Everything here should be set to 0% with the exception of the Diffuse level, which we'll set at 50%. This will darken our moss and make the underlying surface appear darker as well, almost as though it were wet or caked with dirt.

STEP 108: Our last step here will be to add small bumps to the moss, so click the Fractal Bumps button, then set the Scale to 0.001 meters. We want this to be relatively strong, so increase the Amplitude to 2.0 and increase the Granulosity to 20 as well. This will add small details to the moss, making it look less like green paint (Figure 6-62). Save this object again so the surfacing information is saved with it.

FIGURE 6-62 By turning snow green we have given an excellent moss texture to our rock.

Optional: By activating the Use Shadows button, we can make this moss behave more like the real thing by avoiding direct sunlight. Unfortunately, if our light is moving, our moss will become unruly and continually try to hide from it, continually taking refuge on the dark side of the rock.

STEP 109: We've covered a lot of ground here, so let's wrap things up by finally thrusting our sword into the stone. We'll just do a simple, yet dramatic, scene consisting of only the sword and the stone, along with a little fog to fill in the background. Speaking of covering ground, let's do exactly that, with a thin layer of ground fog. Before we do, we'll set up our object and lights. We already have the rock loaded, so load the sword of your choice and place it in the stone. Leave the stone at its default position, and select the Sword as the Edit item. Each stone is different, but those differences will be small enough not to affect the sword positioning we'll use. For this scene, just use the following values, which will place the sword in the stone at a slight angle.

	Position (cm)		Rotation
X	−22	**H**	120
Y	90	**P**	60
Z	20	**B**	−120

We'll need to position our camera next, so let's move it to a point where we have a good view of the sword sticking out of the rock. We don't need to see the entire rock, so we'll move in close and crop the bottom of it. These values will give a good view, of both the rock, showing off the moss, and the sword.

Zoom Factor:	3.75

	Position		Rotation
X	−1.5 m	**H**	93
Y	65.0 cm	**P**	−5
Z	10.0 cm	**B**	0

STEP 110: Now we need to add lighting. Our main light will be an Area Light, which will give a good, even illumination on the rock surface. Area lights are excellent for making metal surfaces look more metallic as well, so this scene will be able to exploit this type of light very well. Open the Lights Panel and lower the Ambient Intensity to 0%. Change the default Distant Light to an Area Light

and rename it to Main Light. We'll be placing this light off to the side to get a good strong directional lighting throughout the scene while keeping shadows soft. Click the Add Light button to create a second light. This one will be a Spotlight, which we'll place almost directly above the sword as a key light, adding a few extra highlights across the upper surfaces. Change the Shadow Type to Shadow Map and leave the option for this at their defaults for now. Rename this light as Spotlight and increase its Intensity to 100%. The following values will set up the light positions and angles.

Cone Angle:	20
Soft Edge Angle:	5

	Main Light		*Spotlight*			
	Position	*Size*	*Position*		*Rotation*	
X	−4.5 m	0.1	**X**	2.0 m	**H**	−120
Y	12.0 m	0.1	**Y**	3.5 m	**P**	60
Z	−20.0 m	0.1	**Z**	1.0 m	**B**	0

The angle of our Area Light is not very important at this distance, but these lights do tend to shed virtually no light along their edge, so we'll angle this toward the sword to be sure we get the full effect. To do this, we'll simply use the sword as a target for this light. Select the Main Light as the Edit Item, then click the Target button. In the requester that opens up, select the sword object, then click OK.

We pointed the spotlight slightly off-center for a reason. We're going to be using this light with Steamer a bit later, and by pointing the light slightly behind the objects, we concentrate most of the steamer effects behind the objects instead of obscuring them with fog. There's enough light falling in front of the objects to add a slight amount of fog in front, as well as adding additional lighting to the objects themselves.

Click the Render button and turn on the 3 Ray Tracing options along the top of the Render panel. Hit F9 to see these lights in action (Figure 6-63).

FIGURE 6-63 With a powerful thrust, or at least a few keystrokes, we have our sword embedded in the stone. The background is a bit dull, but that's easily fixed.

Tip: A good habit to get into when using Steamer is to never apply it to the first slot since this will leave a blank slot to place SkyTracer if you should ever decide to use it after setting up Steamer. If SkyTracer is applied after Steamer, it will erase the Steamer effects. However, if Steamer follows SkyTracer, the effects of both will remain visible. If you plan to use SkyTracer Doubler, then leave slots 1 and 2 open by setting up Steamer in slot 3 or 4. Also, when setting up Steamer effects, start out with a low number of Samples to save time on the previews. When the effect is satisfactory, then raise the samples for the final output. This will save a lot of time during test renders.

STEP 111: Now we need to do something about the lack of ground. We'll cover this detail with a layer of ground fog. Open the Effects Panel and click the Image Processing tab. Click the second (or third) Pixel Filter plugin slot and select the Steamer plugin, then click the Options button beside it. The Steamer interface should open with the Edit Fog button highlighted. On the right half of the panel is a section containing all the fog controls. Click the On button at the top left corner of this section. Our fog is now active, but we'll need to adjust it a bit so it doesn't overpower the scene. In the next section down, we need to select an Active Light. This will be the light that is used to calculate how the fog is shaded and where shadows are rendered. Since this fog will accept shadows, we don't want to use an area light because soft-edged volumetric shadows would result in prohibitively long render times. Instead, we'll use the Spotlight we set up since it's using the much faster Shadow Mapped shadows. Select the light named Spotlight for the Active Light, then move to the section immediately below this.

STEP 112: We'll raise the Bottom of the fog to 0 meters to place it where our fictitious floor would be and lower the top of the fog to 0.6 meters, placing it just below the camera. Below this, we'll change the Falloff to 1, which will give a slow transition from 100% intensity at the bottom to 100% transparent at the top of this fog layer. We'll reduce the Clipping level to 10 since we don't need the fog stretching way off into the background. A Clipping level of 10 will constrain the fog effect to within 10 meters of the camera. Since we're applying the fog to a smaller area than usual, we can raise the number of Samples to a higher value for better results, so raise this to 40, which will provide higher-quality shadowing while keeping render times acceptable.

STEP 113: The next step is to give the fog its color. Currently it's white, but that will prove to be too bright for the scene, as a test sample will show when you click the Refresh button under the Preview window. We'll give our ground fog a slightly eerie quality by changing its color to a very dark blue-green. Steamer uses the Hue-Saturation-Value color model, so to set the color, we'll change the Hue (H) to 120. Next, we'll set the Saturation (S) to 50, which brings the color closer to white. Finally, we'll lower the

Value (V) to 100, which will darken the overall color, much like the Diffuse Level in the Surface Panel. We'll darken this even more by reducing the Luminosity to 25.

STEP 114: Our last step for now is to break this fog up into more interesting patterns, to make it look more realistic. Click the Fractal Noise check box to activate the options below it. We want a small, tight noise pattern, so change the Small Scale to 0.1 meters. We'll also increase the Grain to 50 to add a little more detail to the noise and raise the Amplitude to 1000. Finally, click the Filter button and select Smoky from the popup list.

STEP 115: Click the OK button at the bottom of the Steamer panel to accept these settings, then hit F9 to render a test. It's strongly advised to change the resolution to low for these Steamer tests since they can get quite lengthy. In a few minutes, you will have an image similar to Figure 6-64.

FIGURE 6-64 A simple Steamer setup creates a rolling ground fog around our stone.

Tip: Try not to place the camera inside the Steamer Fog volume. Strange artifacts can occur due to the nature of the volumetric rendering. These artifacts can make the fog look as though it were painted on the inside of a box, unless the samples are set to a much higher value.

STEP 116: We've covered the ground, so let's do something a little more dramatic with that black backdrop now. Our sword is a mystical one, so we'll put it in a misty setting by adding another steamer element behind it. Open the Steamer panel again, and this time, click the Edit Light button near the top left. Six new buttons will appear here, with a long one labeled Light. Click this and select the Spotlight we created earlier, then click the purple Activate button right beside it. This will make the options on the right side of the panel become active. Make sure the On button is highlighted, then proceed with the next steps.

STEP 117: The next section contains information about our light and will have the values set automatically to match our Spotlight. We'll just leave this section set to Automatic Sizing and move to the section below it. By default, the Falloff will be set to 2, which will once again cause a gradual falloff of intensity over the distance specified by the Height value in the section above it. We don't want any falloff here since we want the backdrop to be fairly evenly covered, so lower this to 0. While we're here, we'll raise the Samples to 30 to increase the detail.

STEP 118: If you were to click the Refresh button on the Steamer preview, you'll notice this light creates a pure white blob in the frame. We'll reduce this overexposure by decreasing the Luminosity to 10. We'll further decrease it by raising the Attenuation to 30. This will have the effect of filtering the light slightly as it travels through this fog, starting out white near the light source and gradually shifting toward either a red or blue color, as defined by the Red Shift value. To see this in action, we'll raise the Red Shift to 100, which will filter the light toward red. Finally, we'll make the fog itself white by raising the Value (V) to 255 and lowering the Saturation (S) to 0. The Hue will have no effect if either the Saturation or the Value is 0.

STEP 119: Finally, we'll add some Fractal Noise to the light to match our ground fog somewhat. Again, raise the Grain to 50, but drop the Small Scale to 0.075 meters. Increase the Amplitude to 300, so we have some strong fractal patterns and select the Smoky Filter. Click OK and do a test render by hitting F9. You will see the white light of our spotlight being changed to an intense red-orange color, as though a raging fire was nearby (Figure 6-65). Let's tone that down a bit and add a few streaks of light while we're at it.

FIGURE 6-65 A white Steamer light, attenuated severely toward red, gives the illusion of a fire nearby.

STEP 120: A Red Shift value of 0 will not filter the light to any color, resulting in only shades of the original color, in our case, shades of gray since our light is white. A Red Shift value of 50 would be an even blend of red and gray, so let's use that to get less saturated red. Close the Steamer Panel and open the Lights Panel. We're going to add some streaks of light to the fog as though our light was casting shadows into it.

In photography, a device known as a cookie would be used, which is little more than a transparent screen with opaque areas scattered over it, usually to simulate tree branches and leaves. We're using a Spotlight in this scene, and it would be fairly simple to create a cookie to place in front of it, but there's a simpler solution. Spotlights in LightWave can project an image, much like a film projector, so we can actually use this Projected Image as our cookie. The image can be anything, but best results are achieved with images containing high contrasting areas and very low color saturation. Many of the bump map images supplied with Light-Wave work well for this. We happen to be using one such image already, so let's save on memory and use it here.

Click the Projection Image button and select the **MetalRef-Map.iff** image. Our light will now be projecting this image through the Steamer fog and onto our objects, leaving streaks of varying intensity. Hit F9 once again to see this since the effect will not show up in the Steamer Preview (Figure 6-66).

FIGURE 6-66 The same light, this time with a projected image and less attenuated.

STEP 121: We'll finish this off by making this scene look as though the sword was in an alcove somewhere with blue skylight filtering down to it from above, possibly through thick foliage, or streaming through a hole in a ceiling in some dungeon or cavern. Open the Steamer panel again, and this time, change the Red Shift to −50 or lower, then close the panel. We'll also make the sword, which has reflective surfaces, reflect the Steamer effects to make it fit into the environment as much as possible. Open the Surface Panel and select the Gold surface of the sword.

Click the Advanced Options tab and select the Steamy_Shader plugin for slot 2. Click the option button to open the interface for this plugin and activate the Reflect Steamer Items check box. Under that, select the Reflect Lights option, then click OK. Do the same for the SwordBlade surface, then close the panel.

STEP 122: Open the Objects Panel and click Save All Objects to be sure we have the most recent versions on disk. Save the scene, then render the frame (Figure 6-67).

FIGURE 6-67 A Red Shift of −100 gives the illusion of blue skylight filtering down into the frame.

This image looks best when rendered at a resolution of at least 800 × 600, but at these higher resolutions, Steamer really starts to take its time. This can be sped up somewhat by adding the Steamer Doubler plugin, but at a slight cost in quality.

We've covered a lot of material so far, most of which can be applied to other projects. For practice, try creating your own sword designs, or create your own gemstones. Add some stone walls and a floor to the scene we just created, maybe even add a flaming torch in a sconce on the wall. Above all, play around and have fun. Just don't get fingerprints on the blades!

Catch a Wave

Dave Jerrard

OVERVIEW

One of the simplest-looking scenes to do in LightWave is also one of the most challenging and the most rewarding, the sea. Bodies of water come in endless colors and moods, from calm, glassy, mirrorlike pools to turbulent sprays. Their colors can be virtually pitch black or iridescent in intensity, and these moods can change from minute to minute. No wonder these are tough to recreate! It's common to use a photo for reference only to be discouraged when the LightWave render doesn't look like any other photo, and that's where many people go wrong. They try to match a variety of unique moods when they should be trying to create another unique mood. The photos should still be used for reference, but if you try to match one, make sure it's only one or you could drive yourself mad.

Here, we'll explore the creation of a seascape and then expand on that to include a beach with waves washing up on shore. To get started, let's get our feet wet.

In this tutorial you will use:

- Natural Shaders
- SkyTracer

What you will need:

- Texture images included on CD
- Premade objects included on CD
- Installed Layout plugins: LWFresnel.p. NaturalShaders.p, Interfere.p
- Installed Common plugins: Png.p, Jpeg.p

What you will learn:

- Various surfacing techniques to simulate natural effects
- Creative use of lighting to recreate nature

443

STEP 1: Start up Modeler and create a flat box that we'll use as our water. Click the Box tool, then type "n" to bring up the Numeric requester for the tool. Enter the following values in the requester and click OK:

	Low	High	Segments
X	−5 km	5 km	1
Y	0 m	0 m	1
Z	−5 km	5 km	1

Hit the Enter key to create the polygon and type "f" to flip this polygon so it faces upward, then save it as **Ocean.lwo** (Figure 7-1).

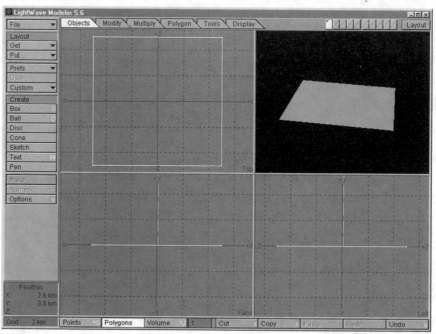

FIGURE 7-1 A very simple ocean.

Facts: Plankton, algae, and even stirred-up debris can make bodies of water look patchy. Water is not colorless, or blue as most people think. Pure water is actually tinted a very light green. The color of an ocean depends on several factors, including time of day, temperature, weather, depth, and location. Cold water will tend toward deeper blues, and warmer water is lighter, sometimes appearing green.

STEP 2: Load this object into Layout and open up the surface panel. Rename the surface "Water" and then click on the Surface color button. Oceans tend to be a shade of blue, so we'll start off with that by giving ours a deep blue color. Setting the values to R: 55 G: 75 B: 100 will get us started.

STEP 3: Position the camera a few meters above the surface of the water. You will probably have to reset the position first since the camera will likely have been moved a few kilometers away from the ocean object when we loaded it. About 2 to 3 meters above the water will give a nice eye-level view, as though we were viewing it from a small boat. Angle the camera so the water fills the lower two thirds of the frame. We won't do anything with the lighting for now.

STEP 4: Type F9 for a quick test render. Nothing very special yet, so let's give it some texture. Open the Surfaces panel again and click the Texture button for the color texture panel. Since water has various subtle shades to it in nature, we should add the same to ours. We'll add a slight green variance to ours by applying a slight fractal noise. Select the fractal noise texture and change the color to an almost olive drab. Values of R: 15 G: 60 B: 50 will do nicely here. Set the texture size to 3 meters to give some nice wide patches. Finally, give it a frequency setting of 4, a contrast of 1, and a small power of 1 as well. Another test render will give you something that's starting to look more like water.

STEP 5: We're getting close, but there's still a bit of work to do. Our water looks a bit dull, even murky, so let's fix that and give it some sparkle. Set the specularity to 100 and change the glossiness to medium. To see these changes, we'll need to turn the light so it shines more toward us. Since we're using a distant light, we don't need to worry about its location, only its angle, so select the light and change its heading to 180 degrees and its pitch to 20 degrees.

STEP 6: Hit F9 again to see the results. We're starting to get a watery look, though right now, it still looks a bit flat, almost like a countertop. We do, however, have a very nice specular highlight that will aid us in the next several steps (Figure 7-2).

FIGURE 7-2 A water surface in the making.

STEP 7: Before we go any farther, it's important that we have some atmosphere for the water to reflect. Open the Effects panel and turn on the Gradient Backdrop. For the Zenith color, we'll make the sky a rich blue. R: 0 G: 185 B: 255 will do nicely for this. Now change the Sky color to a lighter shade, like R: 155 G: 230 B: 255 since the sky near the horizon is always a bit lighter (Figure 7-3).

FIGURE 7-3 A sky makes a big difference! Next, waves!

STEP 8: Now that we have a sky, we can continue with the water. Open the Surface Panel again and set the water's Reflectivity value to 25%. Another test render by typing F9 will show some improvement over the previous render. Having a sky in the frame helps psychologically as well since we can better visualize this surface as a body of water instead of a simple textured polygon.

STEP 9: Now we're ready to start bringing life to this ocean. Open the Surface Panel again and click the Bump Map button. We'll use the Crumple texture to create our waves since it does an excellent job of it. Select the Crumple texture from the Texture Type popup. For the Texture Size, we'll use 3 meters. This will give us some nice, average-size waves. Set the Texture Amplitude to 100%, Number of Scales to 6, and the Small Power to 1. These last two settings will break up the larger waves by overlaying a variety of smaller ones on top. Other values may be used, but we'll stick with these for now. Note, however, that with higher values, render times will increase. Also note that higher values for the Small Power will increase the bump effects, so you may need to reduce the Texture Amplitude.

STEP 10: While we're here, we'll give this texture motion so it really starts to behave like the surface of water. Click the Texture Velocity button and enter the following values: X: 5 cm, Y: 3 cm, Z: 2 cm. This will cause our Crumple texture to move across the surface and up *through* it. Since Crumple is a procedural texture, it exists in 3 dimensions, but we only see it where it's intersected by a polygon. By moving the texture through the polygon like this, we'll see a slightly different "slice" of this texture rendered on each frame of an animation. When played back, this texture will appear to be small waves moving in all directions, forming and disappearing as they go. Alternatively, we could use a reference object to control the waves, but we'll leave those for now to keep things simple.

STEP 11: Hit F9 again to see the effect of Crumple on the surface. Now we're talking water! You'll also probably notice some mysterious brown specs in the water. We sure didn't put them there, so where are they coming from? (Figure 7-4).

FIGURE 7-4 Crumple applied to the surface suddenly changes the entire look. Note the appearance of brown in the waves.

Let's take a look at the backdrop colors again. We set the sky colors to nice blues, but look at the ground colors. There's our brown! Now, why is it showing up on top of the water? The answer is in the way bump maps work. Real bumps are physical protrusions on a surface, and in the case of reflective surfaces, light is often reflected from one bump to another before it reaches our eye. This is particularly true for waves, which are really just large bumps on a surface. Light hitting the side of a wave will be reflected, hit the surface of the water again on another wave, then continue on. Bump maps only simulate a bumpy surface without actually changing its physical shape. They work by tricking light into reflecting in a different direction as though the surface was angled, like the side of a wave. Since the actual surface is still flat and has no thickness at all, strange things can occur. Incoming light striking a flat surface at 90 degrees will normally be reflected straight back to the source.

A bump map alters the surface "normal" only slightly for each incoming light ray, simulating an angled surface. If this simulated angle is sufficient, say 45 degrees, the same incoming light will be reflected 90 degrees. Since the surface is physically flat, that light ray will travel along the same plane as the surface until it hits something else or vanishes in the distance. It could never hit another bump on this surface since it's flat (Figure 7-5). If the simulated bump angle is greater than 45 degrees, say, 50, the incoming ray will be reflected 100 degrees. If this was a real bump, the ray would bounce off it and hit the surface again, but it isn't. The light ray will be reflected in such a way that its new path is now 10 degrees below the surface! It will continue on this path as before, until it hits something else or is gone. This means that objects behind the surface may actually become visible in bump-mapped reflections, and this is exactly what happened with our water surface. Our line of sight was reflected enough by some waves that we were now able to see the ground gradient below the surface.

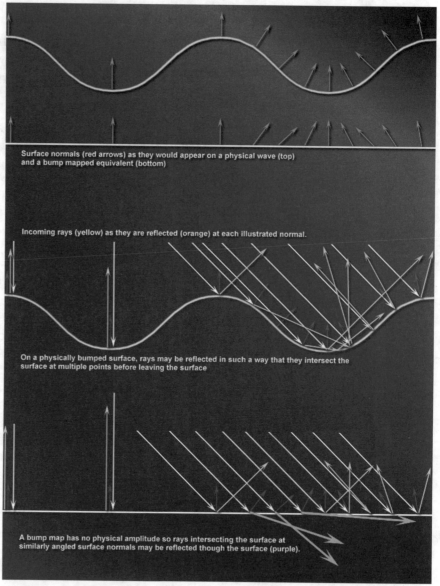

Surface normals (red arrows) as they would appear on a physical wave (top) and a bump mapped equivalent (bottom)

Incoming rays (yellow) as they are reflected (orange) at each illustrated normal.

On a physically bumped surface, rays may be reflected in such a way that they intersect the surface at multiple points before leaving the surface

A bump map has no physical amplitude so rays intersecting the surface at similarly angled surface normals may be reflected though the surface (purple).

FIGURE 7-5 Physical waves can reflect rays of light from one wave to another before the camera sees the ray. Bump maps only simulate the angles of the sides of waves and do not alter the surface itself. Incoming rays can never hit the surface a second time and may end up reflecting through it.

STEP 12: So, how do we avoid this little problem? Modeling every little wave is one way, but not exactly an ideal solution. A better solution is to simply hide the problem. We can do this by simply mirroring the sky gradient colors in the ground gradient. In the Effects Panel again, change the Ground color to the same values as the Sky color. Next, copy the Zenith color to the Nadir. Now, when we render, any stray rays will hit the same colors under the surface as exist above it, which looks a lot better (Figure 7-6).

FIGURE 7-6 Water, without the specks.

Tip: When rendering a procedural texture, try to use enhanced antialiasing whenever possible. Much of a procedural texture can be completely skipped during a single pass render, resulting in a deceptive preview image. Multiple render passes will bring out more of the real texture, possibly revealing that a texture might have more detail than is desired.

So far we have a nice ocean surface, but we can improve it a little more. For one, we've lost our bright specular highlight, so let's bring that back.

STEP 13: Open the Surfaces Panel and click the Bump Map button. Lower the Bump Amplitude to 50% and hit F9 again. This time you should have a very nice glistening gleam up to the horizon. It's a little on the flat side again, but that's easy to fix (Figure 7-7).

FIGURE 7-7 A better looking highlight, though maybe a bit too even.

STEP 14: While keeping the Bump Map panel open, click the Add New Texture button. What we want to create here is the look of soft ocean swells, so we'll pick the Fractal Bumps texture from the popup. Give this a Texture Size of 10 meters in all 3 directions and a Texture Velocity of 10 centimeters on all 3 as well. Set the Texture Amplitude to 100% and the Frequencies to 1 and we're ready for another test render. This time we should have an interesting wave running through the highlight (Figure 7-8).

FIGURE 7-8 The addition of a few swells breaks up the even look we had earlier.

Warning: When using any of the Natural Shaders, do not use the default texture preview. Use only the built-in preview on the shader's interface.

Very Cool Tip: The amplitudes of some bump textures can be adjusted by scaling the object they're applied to. In the case of the Ocean object, the amplitude of the Crumple texture can be animated over time by simply stretching the object on its Y axis. Since this object is flat, no change will be seen other than the Crumple texture getting more or less intense. This is due to a small bug that crept into LightWave with the addition of the following textures: Crumple, Crust, Bump Array, and Veins.

Tip: Typing F5 will reopen the last opened plugin interface.

Since we've added a texture velocity to these two bump layers, the water will change over time. The light angle will also play a big part in the look of the water. Light shining from high overhead will make the water look lighter and cut down on the specular highlights. Low light angles from behind the camera will create darker water, with almost no specular highlights at all.

What we have so far is a good simulation of an ocean surface, but it's still missing a couple of important factors. It's not transparent and the reflections don't quite behave like they should. Water is more reflective at glancing angles and less reflective when viewed from directly above. This is known as the Fresnel effect and there are several plugins for LightWave that incorporate various implementations of this factor. One of these is included with LightWave as part of the Natural Shaders collection and was designed specifically for water, so let's add that. First, save this object as **Ocean.lwo** so we have it for later.

STEP 15: Open the Surfaces Panel and click the Bump Map button again. Turn the Texture Opacity down to 0 for both bump layers. This will make it easier to see the effects of the next few steps without losing our bump settings (Figure 7-9).

FIGURE 7-9 The effect of the default Water Shader settings on our ocean. The Fresnel effect can be seen as the water lightens toward the horizon.

STEP 16: Click the Advanced Options tab to get to the Shader Plugin slots. Click the top slot and select the plugin labeled LW_Water. Click the Options button beside the slot to bring up the interface for the Water Shader. The first thing we need to do here is to activate the shader by clicking the button in the top left corner labeled Enable Shader.

STEP 17: Having done that, we need to provide the shader with information about the surface it's applied to. The Natural Shaders behave differently than other surfacing options in that they adjust to the underlying geometry of the surface they affect. To see a pre-view, we must first inform the shader what the geometry looks like by simply rendering a frame with the shader active. Close the shader panel and hit F9 again.

STEP 18: When the test render is done, you'll notice the water looks different from what we had earlier. That's simply the shader applying its default settings and nothing to worry about. Our orig-inal texture settings are still intact. Open the shader panel again by clicking the Options button. This time you'll see a small ver-sion of the test render in the preview area. We'll be using this for most of the visual feedback for this shader's effects. To start off, we'll leave most of the options off and apply them one at a time to better get a feel for how they work. Make sure the check boxes for Color Filter, Underwater, Wavelets, and Depth Attenuation are unchecked. What we're concerned with for now are the 8 options in the top right corner for transparency and reflection. These will have the greatest effect on the overall look of the water. The most noticeable will be the reflectivity, so let's take care of that first.

STEP 19: There are four options, grouped in two pairs here. Mini-mum Reflection Angle is the angle where reflections become the least intense, and is measured from the plane of the polygon. An angle of 0 degrees is parallel to the surface while a 90-degree value is perpendicular to it. Real water is least reflective when viewed at a perpendicular angle and becomes more reflective as that angle decreases, so let's set that first. For the Minimum Reflection Value, we'll use 0%. We'll also set our Minimum Reflection Angle to 80 degrees. This will reduce reflectivity to 0% for all viewing angles from 80 degrees to perpendicular. There may be a slight lag after applying these changes as the preview window updates to show their effects. This delay can be reduced by selecting the Draft Mode option located below the preview, or if you prefer, you can turn off the Real Time update option and use the Make Preview button to manually update it instead.

STEP 20: Now that we have our minimum reflection settings, let's set the maximum values. These will generally be the opposites of the minimum values, so for the Maximum Reflection Angle, we want 0 degrees and for the Maximum Reflection Value, we'll use the same values we used earlier, 25%. These values will affect the specularity as well, but they won't completely overwrite it like they do with the reflectivity.

STEP 21: The transparency of water behaves in pretty much the reverse of its reflectivity, being most transparent when viewed straight on and almost opaque when viewed at acute angles. This means our setting will be pretty much the reverse as well. Our Minimum Transparency Angle will be 0 degrees and we'll use 20% for the Minimum Transparency Value. Our Maximum Transparency Angle will be set to 80 degrees with a value of 150%.

STEP 22: Before we render this, we need to keep something in mind. Earlier, we used the Sky Gradient colors for the ground to avoid unwanted colors from showing up on the surface. Now that our surface is transparent, those backdrop colors will shine through, making our water a bit bright as we noticed when we first activated the Water Shader (Figure 6-9). We could simply make the ground colors darker, but we'll leave them for now. Instead, we'll use the Water Shader to fix this. Activate the Depth Attenuation option in the lower right of the panel. This will enable the fog two settings immediately below it. Set the Fog Distance to 30 meters and leave the Fog Value set to 100%. This will apply a fog effect, based on the water colors, to everything below the water surface so that anything beyond 30 meters from the surface will no longer be visible, including the backdrop colors. Smaller Fog Distances will create murkier waters while larger values can be used to create crystal-clear lakes.

STEP 23: Now we can do another test render to see the effects of our shader settings (Figure 7-10). Our new surface looks very similar to what we had earlier in Figure 7-3, but our specular highlight is now less intense. You'll notice the highlight appears more rounded and not as a long streak like we had earlier. That's just the shader modifying the highlight to more accurately simulate light reflecting off a transparent surface.

FIGURE 7-10 The same shader with the options we supplied.

STEP 24: It's a bit difficult to tell just how the transparency the shader applies is really affecting the surface without some sort of reference, so let's give it one. Load up the **LumpyGround.lwo** object from the CD. Position the camera a bit higher over the river that runs through this object so we're looking down into it. This will allow us to see not only the effects of the shader's reflective properties, but also how it affects submerged surfaces. Alter the light direction so we can see to the bottom of this river. A Heading of 135 degrees and a Pitch of 45 degrees will do nicely. A test render of this will show the bottom of this river fading into darkness under the surface. You'll also notice that the LumpyGround object is reflecting in the water (Figure 7-11), as well as being refracted under it. The Water Shader will trace both refraction and reflection, regardless of LightWave's Ray Tracing options set in the Render Panel, so you will see a bit of a slowdown when doing test renders. Luckily, the Water Shader's preview shows how the surface will affect objects seen through it.

FIGURE 7-11 Water looks much better when there's a sense of depth.

STEP 25: Thanks to our fractal noise, our river looks a bit blotchy, as though there was a layer of algae floating on the surface. We can reduce the intensity of that pattern by lowering the water's Diffuse value. The diffuse value of the surface can play a big part in setting the mood for the water surface. For rough seas, a high diffuse value will strengthen the color of the water, while a very low diffuse value is more suited to calm ponds and pools where the water would be much clearer. Try lowering the diffuse value to 0 and try another test. This time, the water should look very clear, but darker (Figure 7-12). This darkness is caused by the Depth Attenuation settings of the Water Shader. Increasing the Fog Distance will clear the water up, as will raising the Maximum Transparency value, which can go as high as 400%. Generally, you won't need anything beyond 200% since values higher than that will tend to make submerged surfaces appear to glow. Although the water may appear dark blue, it's actually colorless now. The blue is caused by the reflection of the sky above it. If you were to turn off the Gradient Backdrop and use a solid white as the backdrop color, the surface of the water would be virtually invisible without some form of surface disturbance like ripples or a reflected object.

FIGURE 7-12 Lower diffuse values make the water appear cleaner, but darker.

Tip: The apparent color of the water when the Diffuse setting is 0% is based on the environment it reflects and not the texture color. Unlike other texture channels, the Bump Map Texture Opacity has the same effect as the Bump Amplitude.

STEP 26: Right now our water looks like a pool you'd find in an underground cavern since it's so calm. Let's disturb the surface a bit, so let's return our waves we had earlier. We could use the

Wavelets feature of the Water Shader, which gives a slight gentle disturbance to the surface, but this cannot be animated at this time. Instead, we'll stay with the Bump Map method, which gives us a high degree of flexibility. Click the Bump Map button under the Basic Parameters tab and return the Texture Opacity values to 100% for both texture layers, then click Use Texture. We'll leave the Diffuse setting at 0% for the next few steps. The next render should look something like Figure 7-13.

FIGURE 7-13 A little bit of surface disturbance gives the water a sense of scale and depth.

Tip: By subdividing the ocean plane into a very fine mesh and applying an animated fractal bump displacement to it, we can add physical waves as well, but these can take hours to render when used with refraction and reflection.

As these last few frames rendered, you might have noticed that a fair amount of water surface was rendered, then covered up again by the Lumpy Ground object. That's not exactly efficient rendering and can really add up the hours on an animation. This is a result of LightWave's depth sorting, where it tries to figure out which polygons are closest to the camera so it can render those first. To do this, LightWave measures the distance from the camera to the center of each polygon. We don't want the ocean to be the first polygon rendered, or we'll have to wait for all the shadows, reflections, and other calculations to be done, which may end up being covered by other objects. One solution is to simply move the ocean back along the Z axis until its center point is farther from the camera than anything else. This will force it to be the last polygon rendered. Since the ocean is huge, the center could be anywhere and it would still look the same.

However, this solution isn't always possible, as would be the case for a large tabletop or the floor of a house. In these cases, the large polygon will be rendered before any background objects that sit behind the center point of the polygon. Another way to speed things up is to break these large polygons into smaller pieces. Simply subdividing a polygon in Modeler can drastically improve render times, since now only the foreground polygons will be rendered before any background objects. The background polygons will render a bit later, after the background objects have had a chance to fill some of the screen, meaning less of the floor surface will need to be rendered.

STEP 27: Start up Modeler and use the Get command to load the **Ocean.lwo** object from Layout. Under the Tools menu, select the Custom button, which will pop up a list of plugins. Scroll down to the LW_MetaFormPlus entry and let go. A requester with three options and a numeric field will appear. We're only concerned with the numeric value. Type in a value of 4 and click OK. This will subdivide the Ocean polygon into a grid of 16 polygons per side. Go back to the Objects menu and use the Put command to replace the **Ocean.lwo** object in Layout. Flip back to Layout and you'll see the new subdivided ocean in place and ready to render. This time, LightWave will render the frame a little more efficiently and you'll see that less of the submerged parts of the LumpyGround object will be rendered before being covered by the water surface. Save the ocean again since we'll be using it for the next scene.

Now that we got our feet wet, let's create a nice sunset beach scene. In fact, we'll incorporate our ocean into the castle scene for a nice moody image.

STEP 28: Clear Layout and load the **Ocean.lwo** object we've been working with. Next, load the **Cliff.lwo** from the CD. We'll need to move the camera in closer since it will now be pushed way back to fit the entire ocean in its view. What we want is a setup similar to the one in Figure 7-14, with a cliff face on the right side of the frame and the beach coming in from the lower left side. A test render will show one of the first things that will need work, the beach itself. A real beach usually has waves that move inland, crashing onto the sand in long rows of foam. Ours is pretty calm and uninteresting right now, so let's add a bit of surf.

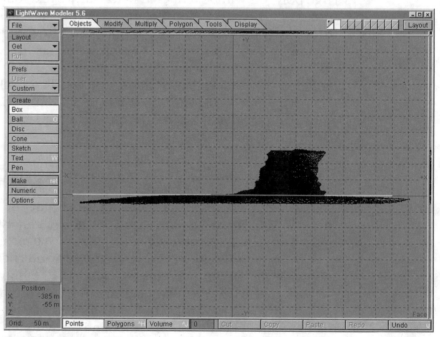

FIGURE 7-14 The cliff object in the background layer and our "cutter" object in the foreground.

STEP 29: Start Modeler and load the **Cliff.lwo** into layer 1. We need this to define the shape of our beach. Size the Front view to full screen and type "a" to fit the object to the view.

STEP 30: Switch to layer 2 and select layer 1 as a background layer by clicking the bottom half of its button. Select the Box tool and drag out a box that intersects the cliff at its base. We want our beach to be 1 meter tall, so type "n" to bring up the Numeric requester and enter the following values:

	Low (m)	High (m)	Segments
X	−500	500	1
Y	0	1	1
Z	−500	500	1

Click OK and tap the Enter key to make the box (Figure 7-14). We'll be using this box as a Boolean tool to create a special water surface for the beach.

STEP 31: Working in the same layer, type "B" to call up the Boolean tool. Since we want only the section of the cliff object that fits inside this box, we'll use the Intersect option. Click that and hit OK. After a few seconds, the box will be replaced by the polygons in the background layer that would fit inside it. There may also be a large square left over from the original box, but we don't need that. It can safely be removed by selecting it and typing the Delete key (Figure 7-15).

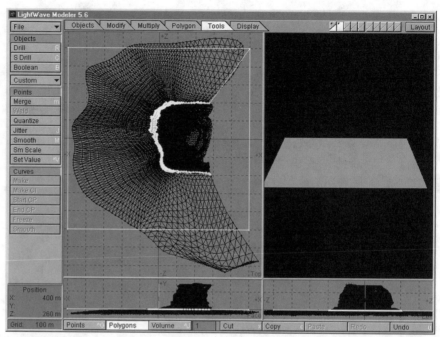

FIGURE 7-15 The section of beach we have after performing the Boolean operation. The large square polygon, highlighted here, may be deleted.

Tip: By default, Modeler recognizes both the z key and the delete key as shortcuts for the delete function. The Delete key cannot be remapped to another function, but the z key can, so you always have at least one keyboard shortcut for deleting in Modeler.

STEP 32: Copy this object to layer 3 and select layer 2 as the background layer. Now select the Taper 2 tool from the Modify menu and click the numeric button to access its options. Change the Sense to negative and make sure the Preset curve is set to Linear. Drag out the Top view so it fills the screen and type "a" to fit the view to the object. Position the cursor near the 200-meter mark on the X axis and start dragging up and to the left to apply the taper effect. Drag until the scale factors are about 130% for both X and Z directions. What we've just done is widen the base of this beach object without altering the top in any way. We have just created our surf surface (Figure 7-16).

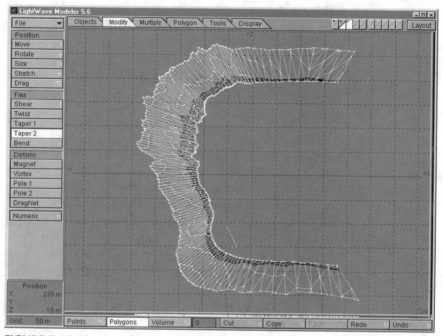

FIGURE 7-16 The beach after tapering the bottom outward by a factor of 130%.

STEP 33: Switch to an empty layer and load the **Ocean.lwo** we've been using earlier. This will add the water surface to the surface list and we can now apply that to this new object. Switch back to the surf object we just tapered and type "q" to bring up the Change Surface panel. Select the Water surface in the popup list and click Apply. Save this as **Waves.lwo** and switch back to Layout.

STEP 34: Open the Objects Panel and load the Waves object into Layout. You should still have the Cliff object loaded, so switch to that and click its Appearance Options tab. Make this object invisible by changing its Object Dissolve to 100%. We won't need to see it for the next few steps. While we're here we can clear the **Ocean.lwo** object since we won't need that.

STEP 35: Most of the work here will involve the Surface Panel, so let's open that. Select Water from the surface list and make sure the Diffuse value is set to 100%. Next, click the Advanced Options tab and open the Water Shader interface. Uncheck the Enable Shader check box in the top left corner of this panel and click OK. This will deactivate the shader and allow us to safely use the default texture previewer again.

STEP 36: We'll be using a simple little trick to create the illusion of waves moving inland. Since our beach is not exactly straight, these waves will have to somehow conform to the shape of the beach, but we've already solved that problem in Modeler when we built this object. Let's see what we did by first applying simple wave texture. LightWave's Marble texture will do an excellent job of this. Click the "T" button beside the Surface Color to open the Color Texture panel. The green Fractal Noise settings will appear here, which we want to keep. Click the Add New Texture button in the top right to start a new texture layer. Select Marble for the Texture Type and enter the following values:

			Texture Size (m)	Texture Center (m)
Texture Axis:	Y	**X**	3	0
Texture Color:	255 255 255	**Y**	3	1
Frequencies:	6	**Z**	3	0
Turbulence:	0.2		Texture Falloff	Texture Velocity
Vein Spacing:	0.25			
Vein Sharpness:	8.0	**X**	0%	0 m
		Y	100%	5 mm
		Z	0%	0 m

Change the Preview Samples Size to 2 meters to see what this texture is doing. The first thing you'll notice after clicking the pre-view Render button is that only the top half of the sample sphere (Figure 7-17) has the marble bands applied. This is because we applied the marble texture centered at 1 meter above the origin, which in the preview would be the very top of the sphere. The 100% falloff we applied on the Y axis then caused the texture to fade to nothing over a distance of 1 meter, so by the time the texture reaches the origin, it's no longer visible. Now let's see what it looks like on our beach object. Remember that this object is 1 meter in height, so the marble texture will be most intense at the top and fade to nothing at the bottom. Also remember that the bottom of this object is tapered outward, so we're mapping this marble texture on a very shallow incline. Type F9 to see how this taper affects the texture (Figure 7-18).

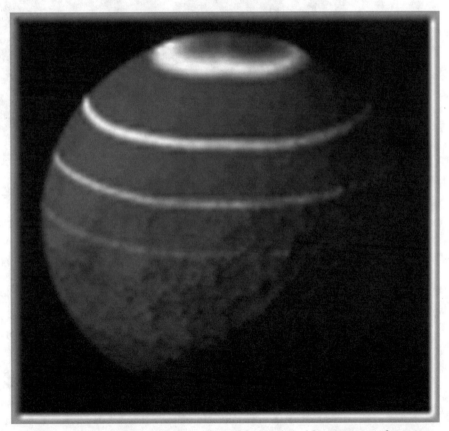

FIGURE 7-17 The first application of Marble on the older Water surface. Note how the intensity of the white bands fades to nothing at the middle of the sample.

FIGURE 7-18 The same texture as it appears on the beach object. By applying it to an inclined surface, the texture conforms to the contours of the object.

Tip: To better understand how the marble texture works, think of it as a stack of paper with a skewer pushed through it. Each sheet of paper would represent a marble vein and the skewer would be the texture axis. The turbulence would be how wrinkled the sheets are. We see only the part of this stack of paper that is intersected by a polygon that cuts through this stack, much like we see only the ring pattern of wood along the plane it is cut.

The marble texture we defined is a series of horizontal veins, one above the other. Viewed on a cylinder, they would appear as horizontal streaks that circle the sides, but if that same cylinder was tapered so it looks more like a cone, the streaks will still be horizontal, but will also appear to be concentric rings when viewed from above. Our beach object has a very wide taper to it, so as the marble texture is mapped from top to bottom, it's also stretched out over that tapered surface. Our 1-meter texture has been stretched over several meters in several directions, which has the effect of bending the texture to follow the contours of the surface.

STEP 37: This texture also has a velocity applied, making it move slowly upward along the Y axis. As the veins move upward, they will also appear to move inward as they approach the top edge of the object. Render a small test animation to see this in action. You'll notice that the veins also change shape as they move. They look very much like the foamy edges of waves as they come ashore. Now let's fill them in a little more.

STEP 38: The effect is a bit thin yet, so let's add some trailing turbulence to these waves. Open the Texture panel for the marble we just created, which should be labeled Color Texture 2. We'll make another texture layer using virtually identical settings as this one. Instead of having to manually set up all the settings again, simply type Ctrl-c to copy the values of this texture. Now, click the Add new Texture button to create a third texture layer. Type Ctrl-v to paste the marble settings into this new layer. We now have two texture layers with identical settings.

STEP 39: For the trailing effect, we want to have one of these textures lag a bit behind the other, and have less intensity. Our current settings simulate the foaming crest of the incoming waves, and we want the trailing effect to appear to be under this. Light-Wave places each successive texture layer over all the previous layers, so the higher the texture number, the closer it is to the top. We're currently on the top layer, so let's move back to the layer below it, which would be Color Texture 2. Click the Previous Texture button to get there. This texture is identical to the one we pasted into layer 3, so we have most of the setting we want. All we need to do is change the Vein Sharpness to 3.0 and the Frequencies to 4. This will soften the look of the veins in this layer. To place this texture slightly behind the top one, change the texture center to 0.96 meters on the Y axis. We'll also increase the Texture Falloff rate to account for the lower center by changing it to 105%. Next, drop the Texture Opacity for this layer to 75%. This will partially dissolve this texture so it blends with the base colors more, making the veins appear bluish. A test render will show the results of this additional texture, giving the illusion of submerged foam behind each wave crest (Figure 7-19).

FIGURE 7-19 A secondary texture gives the waves a sense of depth.

Tip: The number of visible waves can be adjusted by changing the Vein Spacing value for the marble textures. Higher values will decrease the number of waves while smaller values will make them more visible. Small velocities applied to the marble textures in the X and Z directions can give the water a sense of lateral movement.

Texture Axis:	Y
Texture Color:	255 255 255
Frequencies:	4
Turbulence:	0.2
Vein Spacing:	0.25
Vein Sharpness:	3.0

	Texture Size (m)	Texture Center (m)
X	3.0	0.0
Y	3.0	0.96
Z	3.0	0.0

	Texture Falloff	Texture Velocity
X	0%	0.0 m
Y	105%	5.0 mm
Z	0%	0.0 m

STEP 40: Now that we have our waves crashing up on shore, we need to have the water return to the sea somehow. To achieve that backwashing look, we simply create a third marble texture. Since a backwash normally runs under the incoming waves, we want this texture to appear under the other two marble textures. This doesn't mean that we have to now shuffle our existing textures to make room since we can simply create a new texture just about anywhere. Click the Previous Texture button to get back to the green fractal noise Color Texture 1. Now click the Add New Texture button. This just created a new Color Texture 2 and bumped all the other texture layers up a level for us. Since we still have the original texture settings in the clipboard from when we copied them, we can simply do another paste here by typing Ctrl-v again. This time, we want the textures to run in the opposite direction, so change the Y velocity to negative 5 mm. We also want this to be less intense than the other two, so we'll set the Texture Opacity to 50%. The complete list of texture settings should look like the following:

			Texture Size (m)	Texture Center (m)
Texture Axis:	Y	**X**	3.0	0.0
Texture Color:	255 255 255	**Y**	3.0	1.0
Frequencies:	3	**Z**	3.0	0.0
Turbulence:	0.2			
Vein Spacing:	0.25		Texture Falloff	Texture Velocity
Vein Sharpness:	3.0			
		X	0%	0.0 m
		Y	120%	−5.0 mm
		Z	0%	0.0 m

A simple test render with this additional texture applied won't look very impressive since its effects are most noticeable when they're animated. Then you'll see the top two layers of waves moving inland, and then a less intense wave will be seen rushing back out again, just in time to be covered by the next incoming wave. We've also made this layer falloff a little more quickly to simulate the increasing depth of the water as it travels farther off shore.

STEP 41: There are a few extra steps we can take to further improve the look of these waves yet. So far, we've only concerned ourselves with the color of the waves. Now we'll handle the other attributes to fix a few problems that still remain. First of all, we need to increase the transparency of the water as it moves inland. This can be accomplished easily by applying a simple vertical gradient grayscale to define the Transparency. Click the texture button for the Transparency channel. Leave the Texture Type set to Planar Image Map and click the Texture Image button to access the popup list. Select the Load Image option at the bottom and load the **Grayscale-Vert.iff** image from the CD.

Texture Axis: Z		Texture Size	Texture Center
	X:	1.0 m	0.0 m
	Y:	1.01 m	50.0 cm
	Z:	1.0 m	0.0 m

Since all we're trying to do here is ramp the transparency up over the height of the surface, a vertical grayscale, 1 meter tall, mapped on either the X or Z axis will do the trick. Since the transparency is proportional to the luminosity of the image used, we will have 100% transparency at the bottom of this gradient since that's where it's the lightest. By clicking the Negative Image button below the image preview, we can invert the effect of the gradient. Now the surface will be 100% transparent at the top and become fully opaque at the bottom. To prevent an unwanted side effect, we made the Y dimension 1.01 meters instead of just 1 meter. Often an image may not match up exactly with the edges of a surface and you will see a slight edge appear where it fell short. By making the image slightly wider, we make sure the image will cover the surface completely and no dark edges will appear. Since this is a gradient that spans all 256 levels of gray, we don't need to use the Pixel Blending feature, so we can turn that off to speed things up a bit. We can also deactivate the Texture Antialiasing as well.

STEP 42: We've made the water more transparent at the top now, but in doing so, we've also made the waves virtually disappear as well (Figure 7-20). We need to bring them back since we still want them to build up as they travel inland. To do this, we add another texture layer, this time applying a less transparent texture. What will work well is a copy of the Marble settings we used to create the original color textures. Close the Transparency Texture Panel and open the Color Texture Panel again (Figure 7-21). Click the Next Texture button until you reach Color Texture 4, which was the original Marble texture we assigned. Type Ctrl-c to copy this texture, click the Use Texture button, then go back to the Transparency Texture again. Click Add New Texture, and type Ctrl-v to paste the settings into this layer. They should be identical to the values in Step 36, with one exception. We don't need the texture falloff on the Y axis for this, so make that 0%. The other change we need to make is the Texture Value. Since we want this layer to define the nontransparent areas of the surface, a Texture Value of 0% will do the trick. You should now have a texture setting that looks like this:

			Texture Size (m)	Texture Center (m)
Texture Axis:	Y	**X**	3.0	0.0
Texture Value:	0.0%	**Y**	3.0	1.0
Frequencies:	6	**Z**	3.0	0.0
Turbulence:	0.2			
Vein Spacing:	0.25		Texture Falloff	Texture Velocity
Vein Sharpness:	8.0	**X**	0%	0.0 m
		Y	0%	5.0 mm
		Z	0%	0.0 m

FIGURE 7-20 A single transparency map eliminates the waves as they move ashore.

FIGURE 7-21 The waves with the first two transparency textures applied. Without the trailing Marble texture, the frontmost wave loses its effect and just looks like a marble vein again.

Tip: When working with multiple texture layers, use the Texture Opacity setting to turn various layers on and off to isolate the effects of a layer you're working on. It's easier to adjust a layer when it's the only one you see in test renders. When you're done, you can then raise the Opacity values again to reactivate the other layers. You can also use texture layers to store alternative surface settings that you like with your objects, instead of having to keep them as surface files. All the imagery that may be used by these alternative surfaces will be called on when the object is loaded, making it a bit easier to transport if the need arises.

STEP 43: This texture was originally used to create the crest of the waves, so it will be a bit thin. We'll need to copy the trailing texture as well (Figure 7-22). Go back the Color Texture Panel and skip up to the layer labeled "Color Texture 3" and copy those settings. Again, close that panel and open the Transparency Textures. To keep the Texture Layer order consistent with the Color Textures, this wider marble should be placed before the thinner one we just applied. We'll insert this one just like we did with the Color Texture before by Clicking the Add new Texture button while we're at layer number 1. This will insert a new Texture at layer 2 where we'll paste the values we just copied. Type Ctrl-v and you should have values like the ones below. Again, the Texture Value will be 0% and we won't need any Texture Falloff. The detail of this layer isn't critical, so we can also lower the frequencies value to 2 or 3.

Texture Axis:	Y
Texture Value:	0.0%
Frequencies:	3
Turbulence:	0.2
Vein Spacing:	0.25
Vein Sharpness:	3.0

	Texture Size (m)	*Texture Center (m)*
X	3.0	0.0
Y	3.0	0.96
Z	3.0	0.0

	Texture Falloff	*Texture Velocity*
X	0%	0.0 m
Y	0%	−5.0 mm
Z	0%	0.0 m

FIGURE 7-22 The same waves with the trailing marble transparency map applied.

Tip: You can use the Texture Opacity control to adjust the dynamic ranges of image maps to an extent.

We've controlled the transparency to account for the motion of the waves, but we still have a solid reflective and specular value. As soon as we add a sky or have the light at the right angle, we'll have a hard edge along the top of this object again. We could repeat Steps 42 and 43 for these channels as well, but that would add another 4 marble textures to the surface, and that can really slow down render times. Instead, we can cheat on this and just apply the grayscale gradient image to have both of these channels fade over distance like the first Transparency layer.

STEP 44: Open the Specular Texture Panel and select the **Grayscale-Vert.iff** image. Again the same values we used in the Transparency channel will be used here, with one exception. We won't need to use the Negative Image option this time.

Texture Axis: Z		Texture Size	Texture Center
	X	1.0 m	0.0 m
	Y	1.01 m	50.0 cm
	Z	1.0 m	0.0 m

Since the waves are created using a white texture that's 100% diffuse, any specular highlights will be virtually unnoticeable, so we don't need to add any additional texture layers here. If you do decide to add them, just repeat Steps 42 and 43, but use a Texture Value of 100% instead of 0%. Everything else will be identical to the Transparency channel.

STEP 45: We'll now control the reflectivity of this water the same way we did with the specularity in the previous step. Simply copy the Specular Texture and paste it into the Reflectivity Texture Panel. There is one important point to remember here. Our original Reflectivity value was only 25%. If we leave the texture as it is, the bottom end of the gradient will cause a Reflectivity value of 100%. We can control this with the Texture Opacity value. Reduce this to 25% to limit the total reflective range this texture can span to between 0% and 25%. Since this texture will now be blended with the base value, we'll need to change that to 0% to avoid any bleed-through that would occur in the lower reflective areas of this texture. Click the Use Texture button and then lower the Reflectivity base value to 0%.

Again, additional layers are not necessary here for the same reasons as for the Specularity.

STEP 46: A test render now will yield a much better-looking set of waves. All that is missing now, other than the sand, is some bumpiness to these waves. Let's add those bumps now. Click the Bump Map button and then click the Next Texture button in the panel to advance to the last texture. Click Add New Texture to create a third bump layer. This time, we'll use a Cylindrical Image Map to apply the bumps for the waves. Click on the Texture Image button and select the Load Image option. Load the **RandomNoise.iff** image from the CD. Next, click the Texture Alpha Image button and select Load Image once again. This time, load the **GreySine-Vert.iff** image. Click the Negative Image button for the alpha image. This will apply the texture effects to the top and bottom of the texture area and not the middle, similar to the way the Marble textures work.

Since this texture will be cylindrically mapped, we'll need to position it somewhere near the center of the wave surface. A value of 200 meters on the X axis will do nicely. The rest of the texture values are similar to those used for the marble textures:

			Texture Size	Texture Center
Texture Antialiasing:	off	**X**	1.0 m	200.0 m
Texture Axis:	Y	**Y**	25 cm	1.0 m
Texture Amplitude:	100%	**Z**	1.0 m	0.0 m
Width Wrap Amount:	100			

	Texture Falloff	Texture Velocity
X	0%	0.0 m
Y	100%	5.0 mm
Z	0%	0.0 m

What these settings will do is to apply a rough bumpiness to each wave, which increases in amplitude as the wave moves inland. The Texture Size of 25 cm on the Y axis matches the Vein Spacing of the Marble textures, and the alpha image restricts the bump effects to the top and bottom of this texture space. This aligns the bumpy areas with the marble veins while keeping it relatively smooth between the waves. The Texture Falloff constrains the bumps to the upper half of the surface, enhancing the rough, turbulent look of the waves as they grow in intensity.

Finally, the Texture Antialiasing is turned off since this texture is being mapped at a very narrow angle to the surface. This would result in the texture being blurred severely with the AA turned on, which we don't want. The effect will be subtle, but at certain lighting angles, it will add a nice sparkling effect that will look like water splashing. Save this object so you don't have to go through all that surfacing again (Figure 7-23).

FIGURE 7-23 The same waves, this time with bumps added.

Tip: The **GreySine-Vert.iff** image may also be used in another bump layer to make the waves look raised as well. The same settings would apply, but replace the RandomNoise image with the GreySine-Vert image, and remove the alpha image.

STEP 47: A test render will show that our entire surface still has a crumple texture applied. If we want smoother areas of water, we'll need to limit this crumple. We'll do that by setting a 100% falloff on the Y axis for both the Crumple texture in bump layer 1 and the Fractal Bumps texture in layer 2. Since both of these textures are centered at 0 on the Y axis, this will fade their effects over 1 meter above and below the origin.

STEP 48: Now we're ready to finish this off and add it to the ocean we created earlier. Switch back to Modeler and click on an empty layer. Load the subdivided ocean object we were working with earlier. Now switch to another empty layer and select the ocean layer as a background layer. Use the Get command to load the **Waves.lwo** object from Layout. We're going to cut a hole in the ocean so we can attach the beach waves to it for a nice seamless water surface. To do that, we'll use the Drill tool to cut the beach shape out. Swap layers by hitting the apostrophe key so we have the ocean in the foreground and the beach in the background. To make things go a bit faster, select the polygons that are in line with the waves object, as seen in Figure 7-24. This will restrict the Boolean operation to only the selected polygons, reducing the time the operation would take.

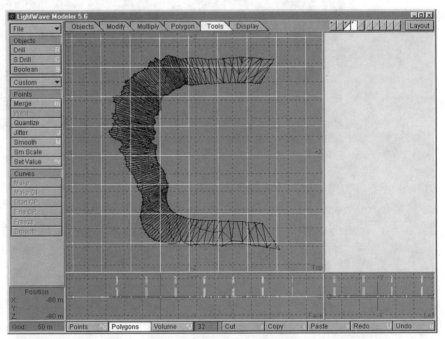

FIGURE 7-24 The waves object in the background, ready to be used as the cutting tool on the ocean object. Note the highlighted polygons that limit the effect of the Boolean, making it process faster.

STEP 49: Click the Tools tab and then click the Drill tool. A requester will appear asking for a drill method and a drill axis. We'll be drilling along the Y axis, and we want the Tunnel method. Click OK and in a few seconds, we'll have a beach-shaped hole in the ocean (Figure 7-25).

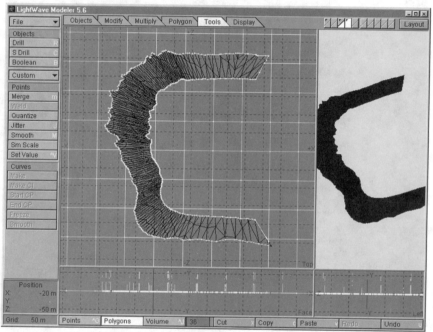

FIGURE 7-25 The ocean after cutting a beach out of it.

STEP 50: We should clean this up a bit to avoid trouble later. All we need to do is remove the polygons that will not be seen, which will be the ones that would end up underground when we add the cliff object later. Figure 7-26 highlights the unnecessary polygons. Simply select the polygons inside the beach area and type "z" to delete them.

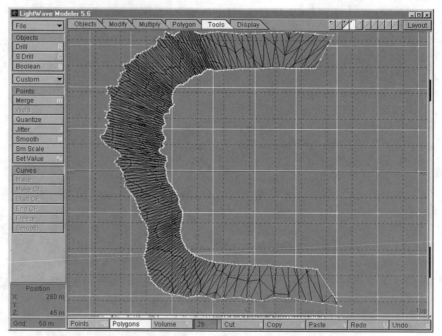

FIGURE 7-26 Simply remove the polygons in this highlighted area and we can join the two sections.

STEP 51: We're now ready to join these two sections. Deselect everything by clicking in the gray area to the left and then type "c" to copy the ocean object. Type the apostrophe again to swap layers and then type "v" to paste the ocean into the layer with the beach. Type "m" to Merge Points using the Automatic method, and finally, type "q" to bring up the Surfaces Panel. Make sure the Water surface is selected and click the Apply button. Save this object as **WavyBeach.lwo**.

STEP 52: Clear the scene in LightWave and load the **Cliff.lwo** object from the CD. This will shoot the camera back far from the object, so let's bring it back into a good viewing position. Give the Camera the following coordinates, which will provide us with an excellent view of the cliff for the surfacing we'll add to it.

	Camera Position		Camera Direction
X	−80	H	45.0
Y	50	P	0.0
Z	−270	B	0.0

STEP 53: Since we want to use this object as our beach, we're going to have to give it a beach surface. We still have an empty shader slot 1 available in the Advanced Options tab of the Surfaces Panel, so let's fill that. We're going to use the Snow Shader again, almost like we did before, but this time it will be used to create a sandy beach. The reason we kept this first plugin slot empty before will become apparent soon. Click the Options button for this slot and we'll start off by increasing the Snow Amount to 100%. Close the panel and do a low-resolution test render so the shader knows what our cliff looks like for its preview.

During this render, you'll see the reason we added the green snow in the second slot. Just like Texture Layers, the Snow Shader will apply its effect over the top of any previous surface information, and since it only applies a snow texture in specific areas, existing textures will show through the blank areas. This gives the effect of green vegetation growing on top of the snow we just applied (Figure 7-27).

FIGURE 7-27 With two Snow Shaders applied, the cliff looks like it just got hit by a frost. The beach area is just way too green, though.

STEP 54: Before we can add our sandy beach, we'll have to do some landscaping. Currently, we have a lot of greenery where our beach will be, so let's cut that back a bit. Open the interface for the Snow Shader in slot 2. We want the grass to start at a slightly higher elevation than the beach, which will keep it away from the water. To do this, we'll use the Y Start setting and plug in a value of 2 meters here. This specifies the lowest elevation the snow shader will apply its effects to. Now, if we just left it with that value, we'd end up with a very sharp grass line, as you will see in the Shader's preview window. We need to give it a gradual increase, so let's add a Y End value. Enter 30 meters here and we'll now have a span of 28 meters of elevation in which the grass will gradually increase in density. From 30 meters and up the grass will remain at its maximum density, which we specified in the Snow Amount value at the top of the interface. A test render will now show a snow-covered beach with nice greenery growing up on the hills (Figure 7-28).

FIGURE 7-28 The cliff after a quick landscaping job. Now we just need a snow-plow.

STEP 55: Now we need to do something about all that white snow. We want a nice, warm beach scene, not a wintery wilderness, so let's change the color. Right now the snow is piled up where we want sand, so let's give it a sand color. For Color 1 we'll give a light tan color and the second color will be just a bit darker. Enter the following values for a good generic beach:

Color 1	R: 210 G: 200 B: 180
Color 2	R: 190 G: 170 B: 150

The preview window will update to show the new look, which is starting to look sandy now (Figure 7-29).

FIGURE 7-29 Nice sand color, but it looks a bit rocky for a beach.

Tip: The Snow Shader not only uses the physical geometry of a surface to decide where to place snow, but also considers the amplitude of any bump maps as well. A strong bump map can be used to roughen the look of any snow area by breaking the effect into smaller patches.

STEP 56: Our beach is just a little bit on the rough side because of the Crumple bump map that covers this entire surface. We want to smooth out the beach area itself, but keep the roughness of the rest of the cliff. We could do the same thing here that we did with the waves and center the texture near the top of the cliff and use a texture falloff, but that would result in a smooth, continuous falloff that would also smooth the rock surface near the bottom. Another option is to add a second Crumple layer that has an inverse amplitude. This would effectively cancel out the previous texture, similar to how two inverted sound waves will result in silence. Well, almost. In the case of bump maps, a slight bumpiness will remain, although the entire effect will be reduced considerably. Switch to the Basic Parameters tab, click the Bump Map button, and copy this bump texture by typing Ctrl-c. Click the Add New Texture button and type Ctrl-v to paste an exact copy of the original bump texture here. Now, change the Texture Amplitude to −100%. To isolate this to just the beach area, we'll use a Texture Falloff of 10% on the Y axis. This will limit it to within 10 meters of sea level (Figure 7-30).

FIGURE 7-30 Now this is sand, although maybe a bit too much up on the cliff face.

STEP 57: We now have a lot of extra sand that's all over the cliff itself. Normally, that amount of sand would be blown off by wind or washed off by rain, so let's clean it up a bit. First of all, we want the beach to be full of sand, so let's increase the Snow Amount to 100%. The preview will now look like the cliff was caught in a sandstorm at this point. Unlike snow, sand collects only on more level surfaces. We'll set our Start Slope Angle to 50 degrees, remembering that these angles are measured from a level plane to the surface normal. Thus, an angle of 0 degrees indicates a vertical polygon and a value of 90 degrees indicates a perfectly level surface. We'll set our End Slope Angle, at which the snow would reach its maximum depth, to 90 degrees, indicating a level surface, since sand would have a hard time piling up on any inclined surface. We'll set the smoothness to 50 so we get a good blend of the two sand colors. A test render of this will show the sand is now less dense on the cliff, but much thicker on the beach area (Figure 7-31).

FIGURE 7-31 A change in the start and end slope angles reduces the amount of sand appearing up on the cliff.

Tip: A Camera Zoom Factor of 3.75 most closely duplicates the magnification of the human eye. It also approximates the properties of a standard 50-mm lens for a 35-mm SLR camera. Photography buffs may want to set the Film Type to 135 to feel more at home in Layout.

STEP 58: We don't want to isolate the sand to higher elevations, so we can leave the Y Start and Y End values at 0 meters. We don't want the sand to be shiny either, so under the Snow Shading section, everything should be set to 0 except the Diffuse values, which we'll set at 100%. Finally, we'll add some soft Fractal bumps to the beach. Click the check box and bump the scale up to 2 meters. Leave the Amplitude at 1 and set the Granulosity to 20. When you're finished, you should have settings like these:

Snow Amount:	100%		
Start Slope Angle:	50	Y Start:	0
End Slope Angle:	90	Y End:	0
Smoothness:	50	Smoothness:	0
Snow Shading		**Fractal Bumps**	
Luminous:	0%	Scale:	2
Diffuse:	100%	Amplitude:	1
Specular:	0%	Granulosity:	20
Reflection:	0%		

STEP 59: Close the Snow Shader panel and type F9 to see the new settings close up (Figure 7-32). Where we still had some of the sand texture on the cliff, we now have the green "snow" covering it. What little sand peeks out from under this greenery now looks like it belongs there, held in by vegetation. Now we're ready to just add water.

FIGURE 7-32 The second Snow Shader's effect covers remaining unwanted sand quite nicely.

Tip: One of the benefits the Water Shader gave us was the Fresnel effect. LightWave ships with two other plugins, which also provide Fresnel effects, Fast Fresnel, and Real Fresnel. Numerous third-party plugins offer these effects as well.

STEP 60: Open the Objects Panel and save this cliff object so we don't lose these settings. Now, while we're here, load the **Wavy-Beach.lwo** we spent an eternity on. If you haven't moved the cliff object, the water should load into place already matching the shoreline perfectly. Position the camera so you can see a good portion of the water on the beach and do a render to see how the waves look with sand under them. Note that we haven't reactivated the Water Shader. For a beach scene like this, the shader will produce less-than-desirable results since it overrides the transparency and reflectivity textures we assigned. We can use another shader to add the lost Fresnel effects, though.

STEP 61: Click on the Advanced Options tab for the Water Surface. We can keep the inactive Water Shader installed in the first slot as it won't interfere with anything while it's disabled. Click the second slot popup list and select the LW_FastFresnel plugin and click the Options button beside it. The default values are just about what we want to use, with one minor adjustment. We were using a Reflectivity value of 25% in the Water Shader, so we'll use that same value here as well. Figure 7-33 shows the interface with the settings we'll be using. Click OK and do a test render. For best results, the camera should be only a few meters above the water.

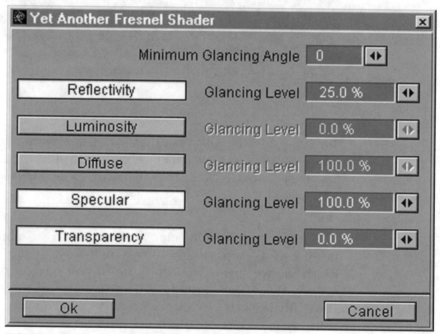

FIGURE 7-33 The Fast Fresnel interface, showing the values we'll be using.

STEP 62: OK, so the image is a bit dark without a sky. Open the Effects Panel and click the Image Processing tab. Click the top Pixel Filter slot and select the SkyTracer plugin. We'll just use the default values for now, but what we will change is the way SkyTracer is applied. Click the Options button and under the Render Controls heading, turn off the Overwrite Backdrop option. This will cause the clouds to be rendered over the backdrop colors we'll specify in the next step. You might also want to turn on the No Antialiasing option to speed things up. This will prevent SkyTracer from being rerendered in additional antialiasing passes, which is usually unnecessary. In the bottom right corner for Light1, select the only light we have in the scene (it should already be selected). Click the Refresh button under the preview to get an idea of what the sky will look like. The clouds may look a bit washed out, so you might want to reduce the Atmosphere Quality to 0. We'll also fix the flare for our sun by making both the Flare Intensity and the Boost values 100 and the Flare Size 20.

STEP 63: Since the SkyTracer sky does not reflect in surfaces, we'll fake it by using the old Backdrop Gradient in the Backdrop and Fog panel. Enter the following backdrop colors to get a simple blue sky:

Zenith Color:	45	140	200
Sky Color:	150	225	255
Sky Squeeze:	6		
Ground Squeeze:	6		
Ground Color:	150	225	255
Nadir Color:	10	95	125

Now our sky will be reflected in the surface of the water, with the exception of the clouds, but since the water surface is distorted by the waves, we wouldn't notice the clouds anyway. We should notice diffuse reflections of large objects, however, like the cliff, so open the Render Panel and turn on Trace Shadows and Trace Reflections. These options will result in longer renders, but the end results are usually well worth the wait. A new render will result in an image similar to Figure 7-34.

To add a slight haze on the horizon, add a Linear Fog in the Effects Panel. A Maximum Fog Distance of 5 km and a Maximum Fog Amount of 50% will do nicely. Set the Fog Color to a very light blue, such as R: 230 G: 255 B: 255 to create a good atmospheric haze effect on distant objects. This is known as Aerial Perspective and it provides a visual sense of depth on very distant objects such as buildings, hills, and mountains, giving them a slight blue tint. In some larger cities, this is also called smog, although it tends to be more of a gray brown in color.

STEP 64: Let's set up a simple composition while we're at it. Position the camera at the following coordinates to get a good view of the beach and the cliff from above the water surface.

	Camera Position (m)		Camera Direction
X	27	H	6.0
Y	16	P	−6.0
Z	−405	B	0.0

To match the human eye, set the zoom factor to 3.75. Now, to light this scene.

STEP 65: We'll use two lights to get a nice sunny feel to the scene. The first light, which we already have, will be our sun. It's a good idea to rename it as such, so open the Lights Panel and rename it to SUN. Sunlight is generally a slight yellow color, so change the color to R: 255 G: 255 B: 230. We'll make this a Distant light, with an intensity of 100%. Since SkyTracer will place a sun in the sky similar to the way a lens flare is created by using the position of the light, we'll have to move this light. To make things easier and to make sure our light angle matches the sun's position, click the Target button on the left side of the Layout screen. Select either the cliff or the ocean object since these are both at the same place and click OK. Now when we move the light, it will always be shining toward the center of the scene. Now, move the light to −20 km on the X axis, 25 km up the Y axis, and 90 km forward along the Z axis. This will put it up near the top left corner of the frame, where we don't have a lot of clouds from SkyTracer.

STEP 66: Now we'll create a second light to act as an ambient light source. Again, this will be a distant light, targeted to the Ocean or cliff object, and placed a fair distance away. Rename this to SKY and change its color to a light blue since we're simulating skylight filling in the shadowed areas. Dropping the blue component to 200 will be fine here. We'll also drop its intensity to 30% so it doesn't wash out the frame. While we're here, turn on the No Specular check box since we don't need this causing unwanted sparkling on the water surface. Move this light to −1 km on the X axis, −3.5 km back on the Z axis, and 5 km up the Y axis. This will put it somewhere over our right shoulder, aimed right into the dark shadows that the sun can't reach. Finally, in the Lights Panel again, turn the Ambient Intensity down to about 10%. Save this scene and we're ready to render (Figure 7-34).

FIGURE 7-34 A few clouds add to the mood.

For best results, Trace Shadows and Trace Reflection should be activated in the Render panel, but that's entirely optional. Another option, which will improve the look of the rendered image, is to change the lights to Area lights, giving the Sun a size of 1000 meters and the ambient light a size of 300 meters. This will size the area light to cover about the same amount of sky as the disk of the sun, with the appropriate softening of the shadows on the cliff. This will also improve the quality of the highlights on the water, making them more intense near the center. If you do use the area lights, be sure to lower the intensity values to about 75% of the original to adjust for the slight increase this light model adds.

STEP 67: Well, we've just created a nice sunny afternoon image, so let's try a setting with more mood. Everyone likes a sunset, so let's create one of our own. First of all, we need to change our sun to a nice deep orange red color. The lower we place the sun on the horizon, the redder it should be. Luckily, SkyTracer will take care of most of that for us, but we still need to color the light our sun is shining on the scene. Open the Lights Panel and change the SUN color to R: 255 G: 165 B: 0. Close the panel and move the light down closer to the horizon. The values below were used for Figure 7-35. Make sure the SKY light is about 30% intensity or lower and has the No Specular option activated.

Color		Position (km)	
SUN			
R	255	X	−15.0
G	165	Y	5.0
B	0	Z	90.0
SKY			
R	255	X	−15.0
G	165	Y	1.0
B	0	Z	−3.5

FIGURE 7-35 A change of lighting gives a whole new sense of time.

Tips: Linear Fog works well for creating aerial perspective, but nonlinear fog is recommended for scenes where a great deal of fog is needed. Lens reflections very rarely occur when the sun is even partially obscured by clouds. Generally, only direct sunlight will cause them to appear. Area Lights tend to render about 30% brighter than normal lights, depending on their size, so switching from a simple distant light could result in an image that looks overexposed or washed out. A good rule of thumb is to reduce their intensities to about 75% of the original value. An alternative method of creating soft shadows is included on the accompanying CD-ROM. It can be several times faster than the built-in area lights, but it works with the original distant, point-and-spot light types.

STEP 68: We could use the SkyTracer warp feature to create a sky object that will reflect in surfaces. However, if we wanted to have anything in the sky move, such as clouds change or even just have the sun sink below the horizon, we would have to manually render out an entire sequence and map those images on to the sky object. That could end up taking longer than just rendering the portion of the sky we'll see every frame. Instead, we'll use the Gradient Backdrop to cheat the reflections. The backdrop colors can always be reflected, whether SkyTracer covers them or not, and we can use that to our advantage. Open the Effects Panel and click the Backdrop and Fog tab. Enter the following values, then move on to the Fog controls.

Zenith Color:	5	75	120
Sky Color:	255	140	55
Sky Squeeze:	6		
Ground Squeeze:	6		
Ground Color:	255	140	55
Nadir Color:	5	75	120

Select the Nonlinear 1 Fog Type and make sure the Maximum Distance is 5 kilometers. Make the Maximum Fog Amount 50% and specify it to be a Backdrop Fog.

STEP 69: Finally, click the Image Processing tab and open the SkyTracer panel. This time, we'll use the Overwrite Backdrop option, so make sure that's checked. Also make sure the SUN is selected for Light 1 and the Sun button is selected for Type. Set the Flare Intensity to 100, Flare Size to 20, and Boost to 100. Finally, raise the Color Shift to 20. This will give our sky a nice round orange sun surrounded by a reddish glow.

The only adjustments to the Atmosphere settings are the Opacity and Falloff, which are 50 and 110, respectively. These lower values will keep the sky a nice orange color. Clouds may be set up any way you like, but the values used for Figure 7-35 were as follows:

	Atmosphere	Haze
Quality	10	0
Thickness	100 km	1000 m
Luminosity	100	10
Opacity	50	0
Falloff	110	0

	Cumulus	*Stratus*
Shadow:	100%	10%
Type:	Cumulonimbus	Cirrus
Grain:	40	50
Altitude:	1000 m	7000 m
Big Scale:	7 km	4 km
Small Scale:	150 m	44 m
Cover:	40%	20%
Contrast:	160	180
Luminosity:	20	15
Opacity:	80	20

STEP 70: Let's finish off with a very moody, ominous-looking image. Nothing says ominous quite like a dark cloudy sky, so open up the SkyTracer panel and click the Cumulus Clouds button. Activate the Edit mode for the Cumulus clouds and enter the following settings:

Clouds:	Cumulus
Shadow:	100%
Type:	Cumulonimbus
Grain:	100
Altitude:	1000 m
Big Scale:	100 km
Small Scale:	20 m
Cover:	110%
Contrast:	110
Luminosity:	20
Opacity:	100

	Atmosphere	*Haze*
Quality	5	0
Thickness	100 km	1000 m
Luminosity	100	10
Opacity	90	0
Falloff	120	0

Activate the Overwrite Backdrop option and click the Refresh button to see a wonderfully dismal sky. Since we have mainly shades of grey, we should make sure that's all our water will reflect as well. Click the Backdrop and Fog tab and create a grayscale gradient backdrop.

Zenith Color:	70	70	70
Sky Color:	120	120	120
Sky Squeeze:	6		
Ground Squeeze:	6		
Ground Color:	120	120	120
Nadir Color:	70	70	70

STEP 71: Since we have a very overcast sky, our lighting will need to be very soft. LightWave's Area Lights will be ideal for this. Select the SUN light and change it to an Area Light. Reduce its intensity to 50% and change its color to a light blue since we'll be using it to simulate the diffuse light filtering through the clouds. Again, R: 230, G: 255, B: 255 works well for this. While we're here, select the SKY light and change it to a darker blue, such as R: 200, G: 220, B: 255. Keep the intensity of this light to 20% or lower and make this an area light as well. Set the Shadow Options for this light to none since we'll be using it as a directional ambient light. Finally, lower the Ambient Intensity to 5% and we're done here (maybe even make it a slight blue as well). Close the panel and then position these two lights as shown below.

	Sun	Sky
X	−50.0 km	325.0 m
Y	50.0 km	7.0 km
Z	60.0 km	−12.5 km
Size	10,000	500

STEP 72: Well, this is getting pretty gloomy looking. All that's missing is some creepy ground fog. Why not? Open the Objects Panel and select the Cliff object. Under the Deformations tab,

click the top plugin slot and select the Steamy_Particles plugin. Next, open the Effects Panel again, click the third Pixel Filter slot, and select the Steamer plugin. Click the Edit Item button and select the Cliff object. Click the Activate button beside it and close the panel. Close the Effects Panel and simply move the current frame slider to update the scene information for Steamer. Type F5 to reopen the Steamer panel (if this doesn't work, then just get it through the Effects Panel again), and click the On button for the cliff settings. If you click the Refresh button under the preview window now, in all likelihood, you will eventually see a small version of the current frame with a bright red glow surrounding the cliff. This is normal since Steamer defaults to a red color initially. Before we do anything, we need to change this to a normal foglike white color. To the right of the preview is a small color swatch followed by three numbers in the HSV color model. Simply reduce the one labeled S (saturation) to 0 and you will have a pure white. Before we go farther, we need to set up a dedicated light for the Steamer effects, so close this panel.

STEP 73: Since we're using area lights for the scene, we need to create a faster light for the Steamer effect. An area light used for Steamer effects could easily take days to render. Open the Lights Panel and clone the light named SUN. Turn on the No Diffuse and No Specular options for this cloned light, and change it to a Spotlight. Reduce the Spotlight Cone Angle to 0.15 degrees and the Soft Spot Edge Angle to 0. This will focus the Shadow Map from this light to the cliff face. Change the Shadow Type to Shadow Map, rename this light to SteamerLight, and then close the panel. Shadow Maps are the fastest shadowing method in LightWave, so it only makes sense to use them for Steamer effects.

STEP 74: Open the Steamer Panel again, and click the check box at the top labeled No Antialiasing. Also, click the Affected By Fog button since we're using LightWave's internal fog feature on this scene. For the rest of the Steamer controls, the following values will give a soft rolling fog on our cliff object.

Dissolve:	80%	Var Scale:	10	Color (HSV):	0 0 255
Active Light:	Steamer Light	Falloff:	4	Clipping:	5000
Radius:	9 m	Mode:	Additive	Samples:	5
Automatic Sizing:	Off	Luminosity:	1	Opacity:	0
Variation:	0%	Attenuation:	0	Red Shift:	0

For test renders, I recommend reducing the Samples to 5 for the sake of speed. In fact, for distant shots like the one we've set up, 5 is all you will need, but if you plan on moving the camera up close, then a higher Samples value would be advised.

STEP 75: Type F9 and grab something to eat. The combination of Area Lights, Ray Tracing, and Steamer will add significantly to the render time, which is the reason we turned off the Antialiasing option for Steamer. In several minutes, you should have an image similar to the one in Figure 7-36.

FIGURE 7-36 Dark clouds, a little fog, and subdued lighting give the same setting an eerie mood. A few galleons and rowboats were added to complete a sense of mystery.

Now that you have a better understanding of how to simulate various types of water and how the lighting affects them, try adding other elements. You'll notice that the final frame in Figure 7-36 includes some ships, a couple of rowboats, and a distant mountainscape (borrowed from the Hummer scene included with Light-Wave). Populating a scene like this with signs of people adds a sense of intimacy, rather than just becoming another landscape image. Try adding a few campfires on the shore, a few tents, and maybe even the castle on the cliff top. All that would be missing, then, would be a dragon in the sky. But who needs dragons when we have space travel?

Mercury *Capsule*

Scott Wheeler

OVERVIEW

Ever since I was a kid I played with toy rockets and astronauts. I built models of the *Apollo* spacecraft. Even at the age of 8 I sat glued to the TV in our summer house at Carolina Beach watching as the space men returned from another mission. I waited and watched as the capsule splashed down while the other kids frolicked in the surf. This could explain why I cycle from burn to peel to pale whenever I get out in the sun, but that's another story.

Now you can imagine that when, 22 years later, I got the chance to help recreate some of those events for HBO's *From the Earth to the Moon* miniseries my toes were tapping indeed.

As the name of this tutorial states, we will be creating a *Mercury* capsule. More precisely, *Freedom 7,* the first *Mercury* capsule to carry a human, Alan B. Shepard, Jr., into space on May 5, 1961.

In the next few tutorials I will take you through the construction of some early Space Race hardware. We will be modeling the capsule at a level of detail that will be needed for a specific shot, so in many ways it will not be a difficult modeling assignment. However, if you love this stuff like I do, then there is nothing better than building spaceships.

After construction we will move on to surfacing our model. We will go over how to take a relatively low-detail model and spruce it up with some specific texture maps. We will then move to the construction of a parachute and finishing out with a shot of the capsule pre-splashdown from a rescue helicopter.

In this tutorial you will use:

- Modeler
- Layout

What you will need:

- Images from CD
- Time

What you will learn:

- Basic modeling techniques
- Applying multiple texture maps
- A handful of cheats and work arounds

STEP 1: Before we get into the modeling let's set the modeling environment so that we are all working with the same values. Open the Display Options (d) panel and make sure that your values match those of the panel below:

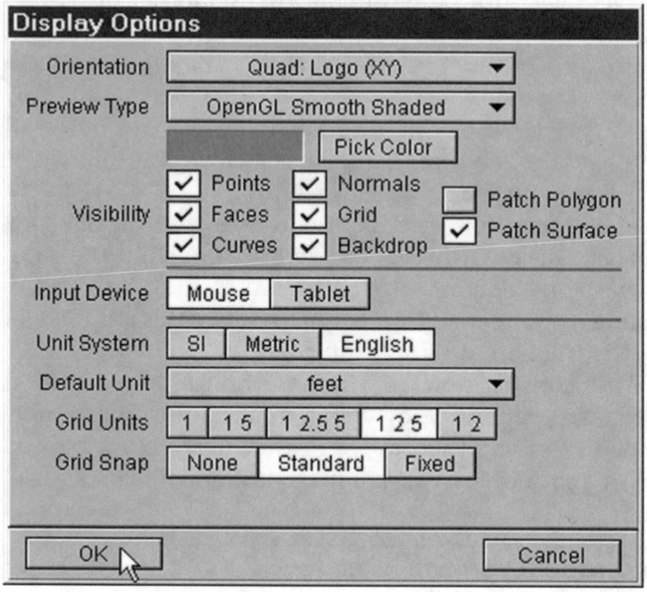

Display Options

Orientation	Quad: Logo (XY) ▼
Preview Type	OpenGL Smooth Shaded ▼

Pick Color

Visibility
- ☑ Points ☑ Normals
- ☑ Faces ☑ Grid
- ☑ Curves ☑ Backdrop
- ☐ Patch Polygon
- ☑ Patch Surface

Input Device	Mouse Tablet
Unit System	SI Metric English
Default Unit	feet ▼
Grid Units	1 1 5 1 2.5 5 1 2 5 1 2
Grid Snap	None Standard Fixed

OK   Cancel

"Inches?" you say. "Why Inches?" Well, in America in the 1960s metric was still a novelty and U.S. contractors weren't about to start building something in this new-fangled system. So, since all the reference is in inches and feet, then that's how we need to build our ship. On the CD I have provided a host of images from the Mercury program that I used to build the capsule. One of them is the simple blueprint in Figure 8-1. This gives us a good starting place for measurements on the capsule itself.

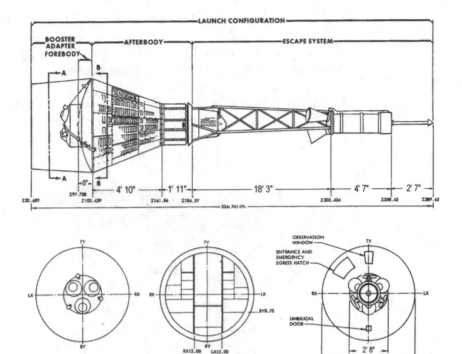

FIGURE 8-1

STEP 2: The first portion we will be building is the crew cabin. This gives us a good guide for adding the other pieces, and well, ya gotta start somewhere. We note from Figure 8-1 that the crew cabin is 4' 10" long and it tapers down from a width of 6' 2" to 2' 8" at the front.

What can't be seen in the blueprint but can be seen in the reference photos on the CD is that the surface of the crew compartment is not smooth but made up of a series of flat panels, 24 to be exact. To start we need to lay some points out (Shift-=) in the following order in the left view:

Point 1	(X: 0',	Y: 0',	Z: 2' 5")
Point 2	(X: 0',	Y: 1' 4",	Z: 2' 5")
Point 3	(X: 0',	Y: 3' 1",	Z: −2' 5")
Point 4	(X: 0',	Y: 0',	Z: −2' 5")

After all the points have been placed, Make a Polygon (p) out of them.

We have just created the profile of the crew compartment that we will use to lathe out the rest of the cabin.

STEP 3: In Polygon Selection Mode (Ctrl-h) activate the Lathe Tool (Shift-l). In Numeric Input (n) set the following values:

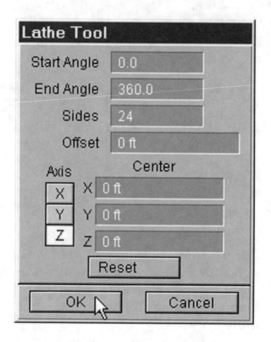

After setting those values Make (Return) the lathe. Your results should look like Figure 8-2.

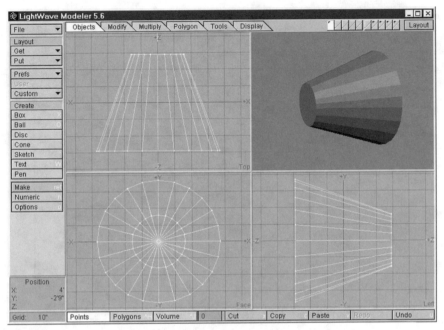

FIGURE 8-2

STEP 4: I know it's not a big deal as far as this model goes, but in the interest of being thorough we should reduce the polys on the top and bottom of our lathed section. Select the polygons as shown in Figure 8-3 and Merge (Shift-z) them. This has reduced the poly count from 48 to 2 on the top and bottom of our capsule. In this case it does not mean a lot as far as memory is concerned, but if you get in the habit you can really cut down the polys on more complicated models. The last part of this step is to remove the two now stray points from the layer. We do this by switching to Points Selection Mode (Ctrl-g) and bringing up the Point Statistics (w) panel. We want to select all points that are not associated with any polygons. We do this by clicking on the + next to the 0 Polygons field as shown:

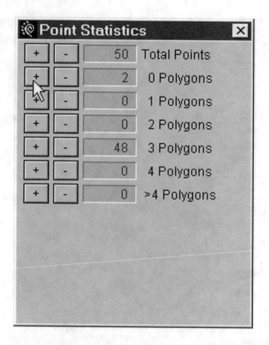

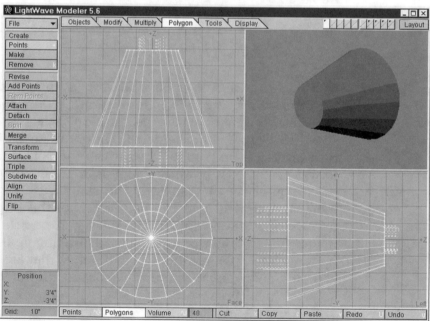

FIGURE 8-3

We can Cut (x) the points from the layer.

STEP 5: Before we go on to another portion of the model, let's name the surfaces we just created. Bring up the Change Surface Panel (q) and enter in these values:

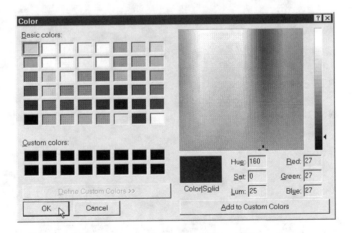

Before you hit Apply change the color in Pick Color to the values:

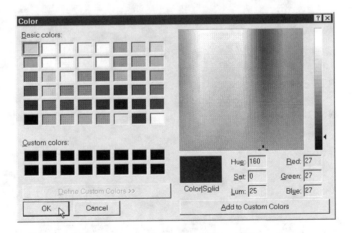

STEP 6: Now that we have a crew compartment ready, let's add a heat shield to the bottom of the craft. The shot we will finally create does not view the ship from below, so we need not spend a lot of time on it. We just need something to be there in the correct

shape and orientation. Let's make Layer 2 (2) our active layer and place layer 1 in the background (Alt-1). In the leftview plot out the following points:

Point 1	(X: 0',	Y: 0',	Z: −2' 5")
Point 2	(X: 0',	Y: 3' 1",	Z: −2' 5")
Point 3	(X: 0',	Y: −2' 9",	Z: −2' 8")
Point 4	(X: 0',	Y: 2' 0.5",	Z: −2' 10.5")
Point 5	(X: 0',	Y: 10'	Z: −3' 0.5")
Point 6	(X: 0',	Y: 0',	Z: −3' 1")

Make Them a Polygon (p). If all went as planned your screen should look like Figure 8-4.

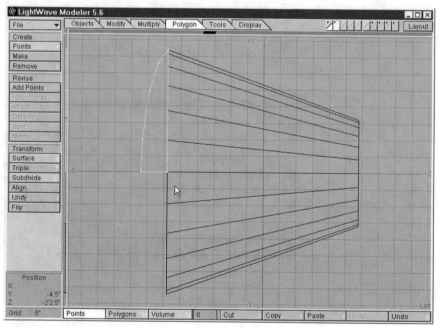

FIGURE 8-4

STEP 7: In Polygon Selection Mode (Ctrl-h) Lathe (Shift-l) the polygon with the following Numeric (n) values:

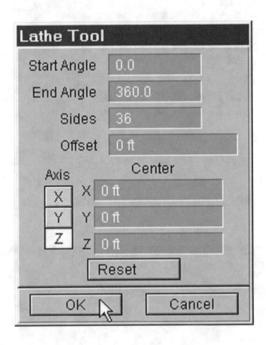

Surface the heat shield as follows:

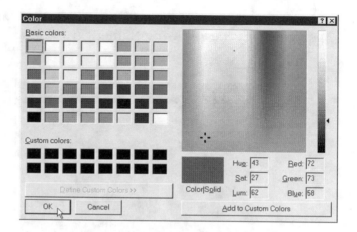

The finished result should be Figure 8-5.

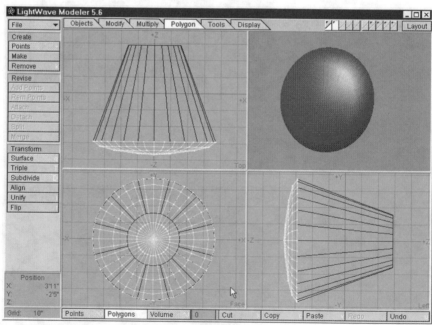

FIGURE 8-5

With that finished we can move to the nose cone section where the parachute is stored. But first we need to make Layer 3 (3) the active layer and put layer 1 and 2 in the background (Shift Alt-2-1). The nose cone section will be comprised of two parts, the nose itself and a silver collar on the end.

STEP 8: First we will construct the main nose section. To do this we need to make a Box (Shift-x) with the following Numeric Values (n):

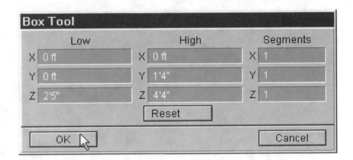

Next we should Lathe (Shift-l) the box with the following Numeric Values (n):

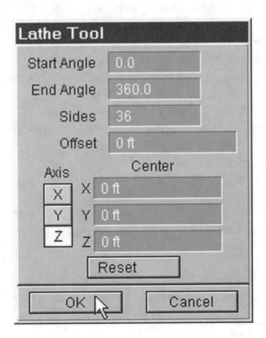

Since the object has the same extra amount of polygons on the top and bottom as did the crew compartment, we need to perform the same polygon reduction process that we applied in Step 4. When that is complete apply the following surface information to the nose:

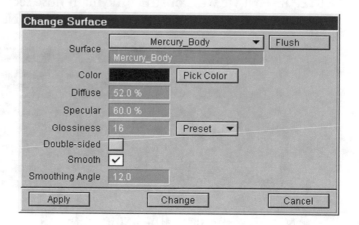

You will notice that the nose gets a smooth look while the crew compartment did not. We are using the Max Smoothing Angle to achieve this effect. Since we will be applying the same texture to both surfaces and we want one to be smooth and the other faceted, we needed a smoothing angle that would accomplish this. Since we Lathed the body 24 times and the nose 36 times we created a 5-degree difference between the angle of adjoining polygons. So, with a smoothing angle of 12 we will split the difference. This makes the nose smooth and the body faceted.

Note: Sometimes on more complicated models this is not possible. However, it is good practice to keep an eye on the smoothing angle of surfaces to help avoid rendering errors.

Our object should now look like Figure 8-6.

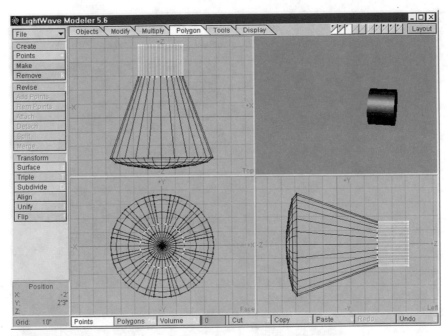

FIGURE 8-6

STEP 9: The next step is to add a silver ring to the nose of the capsule and some minor detail to the very top. Let's move up to Layer 4 (4) and put the other layers in the background (Shift-Alt-1-2-3). First let's create another profile Box (Shift-x) with the following Numeric Values (n):

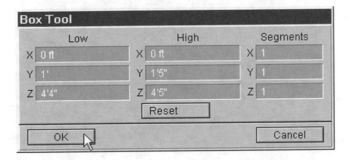

After we Make (Return) the box we need to Lathe (Shift-l) it with the following Numeric Values (n):

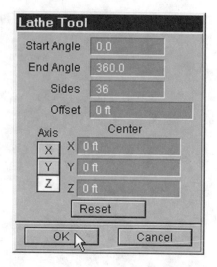

In the quad view Size To Fit (Shift-a) the view and your display should look like Figure 8-7.

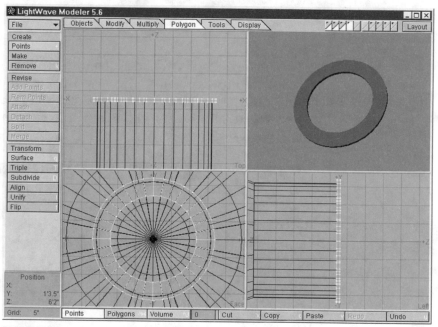

FIGURE 8-7

STEP 10: Since we are going to be using a cylindrical texture map on the body of the capsule we want to make sure we cover the top part with some minor detail to hide the texture map converging to the center point on the top. We are also not building the interior of the top where the parachute is deployed from, so we need to make sure the top is hidden in shadow. A simple way to do this is by adding two crossed boxes that stretch across the center of the top. Their exact size is not important, but use Figure 8-8 as a guide for them.

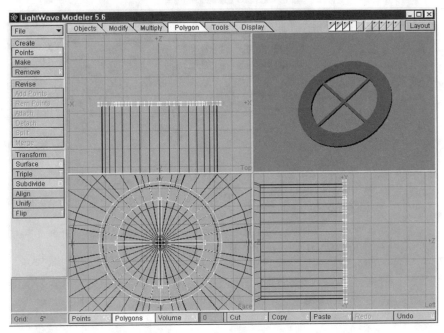

FIGURE 8-8

STEP 11: We will finish off our capsules modeling phase by applying the following Surface (q) values to the top ring:

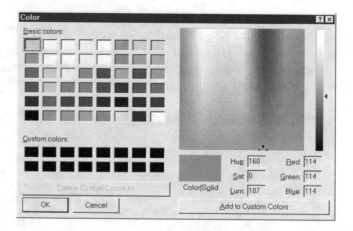

STEP 12: Select all the layers the objects we just built are in (Shift-1-2-3-4) and Put them to a fresh copy of LightWave as **MercuryCapsule.lwo.**

Now we move over to the LightWave side to finish the texturing of the Capsule.

STEP 13: The first thing we need to do is go to the Images Panel and load in the following images from the CD:

> Body_Color.iff
>
> Body_Diffusion.iff
>
> Body_Specular.iff
>
> Decals.iff
>
> Slats.iff

These are the images we will be applying to our capsule, and as you can see they are pretty easy to see where they will be applied.

STEP 14: We should change the background color in the Effects Panel under the Backdrop and Fog Tab from its default Black to a middle gray value of (R: 128, G: 128, B: 128) so that the predominantly black capsule will stand out.

STEP 15: Next we need to line up the Capsule in a position to begin texturing. Close down the Effects Panel (p) and change to Camera View (6). Currently our capsule is facing away from us. We can change that by moving it to following coordinates (X: 12.5 cm, Y: −41 cm, Z: −2 m) and rotating to (H: −7, P: −98, B: 67). If you set a KeyFrame (Return Return) at this point and Render a Frame (F9) your output should look like Figure 8-9.

FIGURE 8-9

STEP 16: Okay, now let's do a little surfacing. Open up the Surfaces Panel and select Mercury_Body as the active surface. Click on the T Button next to Surface Color. Since we know by looking at it that our capsule is a cylinder, we should change the texture Type to Cylindrical Image Map.

Now that we know that our surface is going to be mapped the proper way, we can assign the image we are going to use for the Surface Color. Since I named the maps what they will be used for, I am sure you will not be surprised to find that we are going to use the **Body_Color.iff** Image as our color map. Now that we have the image we want, let's set some important values. First, since we want the image to stretch across the whole surface click the Automatic Sizing Button to size the image to the size of the geometry. After hitting Automatic Sizing fill out the rest of the panel as in the following panel:

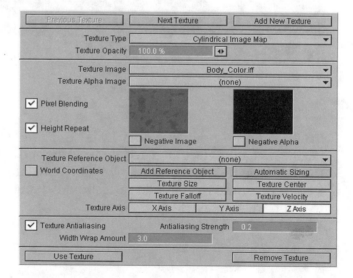

Note: Notice that the Antialiasing Strength is set to a low value. Texture antialiasing can be very helpful with texture maps, but a little bit goes a long way. Be careful not to make your setting too strong as images have a tendency to become blurry at stronger settings.

Once you have finished filling in the values Render (F9) a frame. It should look like Figure 8-10. Notice how the subtle coloring of the texture map has already begun to help make the surface look more believable as a metal.

FIGURE 8-10

STEP 17: Let's add one more thing to this color channel of our surface. Every spacecraft had some kinds of markings on it. To add the decals to this ship we will be taking advantage of the multiple texture feature. While you are still in the Color Texture Panel, select Add New Texture at the top of the panel. This takes us into another layer of the color channel where we can add more surface information. After Automatic Sizing this texture, fill out the panel as follows:

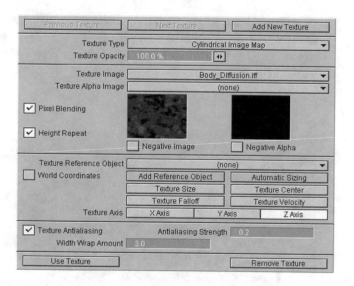

You will notice two new things about this surface. We are using the Texture Alpha Channel to define the area in which the surface will be applied. In this case the decal image map will be applied only in the light areas of the alpha image, which is the letters themselves. This allows the decals to be applied without affecting the other parts of the surface's color map. The second thing to note is that the Texture Opacity has been dropped to 60%. This means that at maximum opacity the texture will only blend 60% with the previous color map. To see how this looks, Render (F9) a frame. It should look like Figure 8-11.

FIGURE 8-11

STEP 18: Next we move down to Diffuse Level and click on the T Button on its level. Follow the same procedure as Step 15 to fill out the Diffuse Texture Panel as shown:

Previous Texture	Next Texture	Add New Texture

Texture Type	Cylindrical Image Map ▼
Texture Opacity	60.0 % ◄►

Texture Image	Decals.IFF ▼
Texture Alpha Image	Decals.IFF ▼

☑ Pixel Blending

☑ Height Repeat

☐ Negative Image   ☐ Negative Alpha

Texture Reference Object	(none) ▼
☐ World Coordinates	Add Reference Object	Automatic Sizing
	Texture Size	Texture Center
	Texture Falloff	Texture Velocity
Texture Axis	X Axis	Y Axis	Z Axis

☑ Texture Antialiasing   Antialiasing Strength 0.5

Width Wrap Amount 1.0

Use Texture	Remove Texture

Note: Another thing to note is that we are Width Wrapping these images 3 times around the body. Since we know that no one can look at the whole object at once, we can save image sizes and memory by wrapping the same image several times. This will work successfully, however, only if you make the image maps seamless.

If you Render (F9) a frame at this point it should look like Figure 8-12. Notice how the addition of the diffusion map has added a worn feeling to the surface. Our capsule now looks like it has seen a little action, which is what we are going for.

FIGURE 8-12

STEP 19: To complete the aging process let's put some detail to the way the object reacts to light. One major thing that will happen during the tremendous heat that the capsule will endure upon reentry is the loss of a shiny outer coating. We will simulate this by altering the Specular Level with a texture map. Click on the T Button on the Specular Level line and enter in the following values:

Previous Texture	Next Texture	Add New Texture

Texture Type	Cylindrical Image Map ▼
Texture Opacity	100.0 % ◄►

Texture Image	Body_Specular.iff ▼
Texture Alpha Image	(none) ▼

☑ Pixel Blending

☑ Height Repeat

☐ Negative Image   ☐ Negative Alpha

Texture Reference Object	(none) ▼

☐ World Coordinates

Add Reference Object	Automatic Sizing
Texture Size	Texture Center
Texture Falloff	Texture Velocity

Texture Axis	X Axis	Y Axis	Z Axis

☑ Texture Antialiasing   Antialiasing Strength 0.1

Width Wrap Amount 3.0

Use Texture	Remove Texture

If all went as planned your capsule should now Render (F9) out like Figure 8-13.

FIGURE 8-13

Notice how all the different layers play off each other to make the surface appear more real. We started with a black shiny object, and in a few short surfacing steps we've added the wear and tear of space travel to it. Also, when you get a chance take a look at the images in your favorite viewer. I have learned most of what I know about surfacing by inspecting the work of people I respect and admire.

STEP 20: To finish out we need to add the panel ridges that can be found on the real capsule. We'll do this with a bump map I created just for this purpose called **Slats.iff**. To add this let's go down to the bottom of the Surfaces Panel and select the T Button next to Bump Map.

As with the other surfaces we will be applying **Slats.iff** as a Cylindrical Image Map and using Automatic Sizing to stretch it to the size of the object. There are, however, a few new things to worry about since this is a Bump Map. The first of these is the Texture Amplitude. What this allows you to do is to define just how deep your grooves will appear to sink into a given surface.

Note: Be wary of setting these values too high as render errors have a tendency to appear in surfaces with overcranked Bump Maps. You can achieve some great results and indeed sometimes it is necessary to make the Texture Amplitude greater than 100%, but be cautious about doing it.

In our case 50% will be deep enough. The second change is the Width Wrap Amount. All of the other surfaces (with the exception of **Decals.iff**) we have wrapped 3 times around the capsule to help with image map detail. For this surface, however, we are going to wrap it 24 times about the body because we want to put the grooves evenly on each flat panel. Before we move on make sure your panel is filled out as follows:

Previous Texture	Next Texture	Add New Texture

Texture Type	Cylindrical Image Map ▼
Texture Opacity	100.0 % ◄►

Texture Image	Slats.iff ▼
Texture Alpha Image	(none) ▼

☑ Pixel Blending

☑ Height Repeat

☐ Negative Image   ☐ Negative Alpha

Texture Reference Object	(none) ▼

☐ World Coordinates

Add Reference Object	Automatic Sizing
Texture Size	Texture Center
Texture Falloff	Texture Velocity

Texture Axis	X Axis	Y Axis	Z Axis

☑ Texture Antialiasing   Antialiasing Strength   0.2

Texture Amplitude	50.0 % ◄►
Width Wrap Amount	24.0

Use Texture	Remove Texture

Render (F9) a frame and it should look like Figure 8-14. Notice how the grooves follow the tapering of the body and fill out each panel evenly. Also notice how the lettering seems to have gotten lost on the surface.

FIGURE 8-14

STEP 21: We can fix this by returning to Diffuse Level and clicking on its T Button. At the top of the Diffuse Texture Panel click on Add New Texture to open up another texture channel. We will be applying the **Decals.iff** image to this channel to boost the diffusion level for the lettering only. To do this click on Automatic Sizing and fill the rest of the panel out as follows:

Previous Texture	Next Texture	Add New Texture

Texture Type	Cylindrical Image Map ▼
Texture Opacity	50.0 % ◄►

Texture Image	Decals.IFF ▼
Texture Alpha Image	Decals.IFF ▼

☑ Pixel Blending

☑ Height Repeat

☐ Negative Image   ☐ Negative Alpha

Texture Reference Object	(none) ▼
☐ World Coordinates

Add Reference Object	Automatic Sizing
Texture Size	Texture Center
Texture Falloff	Texture Velocity

Texture Axis	X Axis	Y Axis	Z Axis

☐ Texture Antialiasing   Antialiasing Strength 1.0

Width Wrap Amount 1.0

Use Texture	Remove Texture

Let's take a look at how this changed things by Rendering (F9) a frame. It should look like Figure 8-15.

FIGURE 8-15

With the body taken care of we can turn our attention to making a simple texture on the top of the capsule. All we really need to do is add a color variation to the top. But first let's rotate the ship into a position so we can see the top.

STEP 22: Rotate the capsule to (H: 10, P: −140, B: −69).

STEP 23: Open the Surfaces Panel and change the current surface to Mercury_Silver. Click on the T Button next to Surface Color. We ultimately want to change the surface Texture Type to Fractal Noise, but we can use the Automatic Sizing Button in Planer Image Map to give us a good guess for how big the area is we will be texturing into. Once you have clicked on Automatic Sizing change the Texture Type to Fractal Noise. Now we can add some wear to the ring. First let's change the Texture Size as shown:

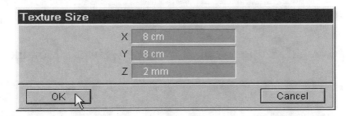

Note: These values are about one tenth the original size of the texture. Normally this is a good place to start from when adding noise, but for us, it's gonna be the end as well.

After changing those values make the following changes to the main Color Texture panel:

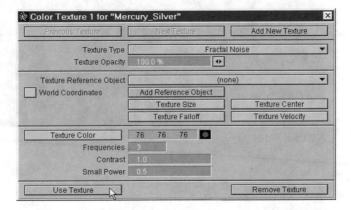

After making the changes, click Use Texture to save the changes to the surface. Last, check to see that your main texture values for the Mercury_Silver surface are as follows:

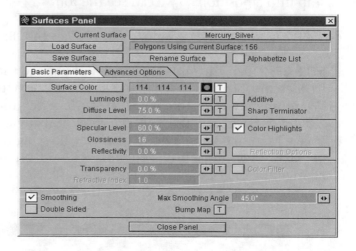

If you Render (F9) a frame it should look like Figure 8-16.

FIGURE 8-16

That's it! We won't be making any changes to the heatshield since we won't be seeing it in the shot. Make sure you save your object at this point to save all the changes we just made. Your object is now ready for the pre–splashdown shot. In the next tutorial we will be making the parachute, and after that we will move on to the shot itself.

TUTORIAL
9

The Parachute

Scott Wheeler

OVERVIEW

After having launched our rocket into orbit we must turn our attention to getting the astronauts back home in one piece. Since parading around the country with a live undamaged hero is preferable to displaying the crushed remains, we'll build a parachute to gently place our capsule down.

In this tutorial you will use:

- Modeler

What you will need:

- Time and patience

What you will learn:

- Intermediate modeling techniques
- The ancient art of spline patching

STEP 1: Start a fresh copy of Modeler on Layer 1. Activate the Ball Tool (Shift-o) and then Numeric Input (n). We will be using one quarter of this circle to construct a series of spline patches. So we need to lay down some points to make a spline path, and the easiest way to do that is to make a disk. With that in mind enter the following values:

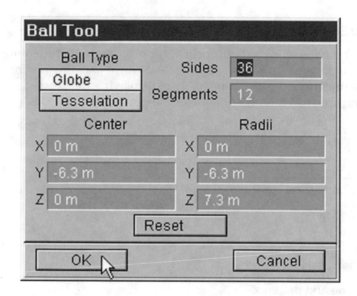

Click OK and Make (Return) the ball. Size the view to Fit All (a). Your screen should look like Figure 9-1.

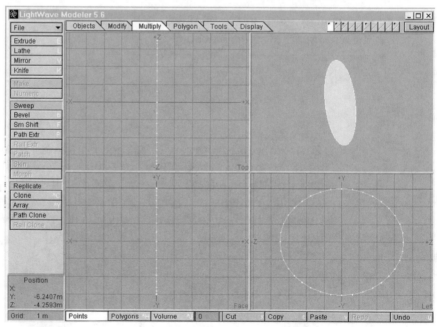

FIGURE 9-1

STEP 2: Since all we really want from this disk is the points, let's activate Points Mode (Ctrl-g) and Kill (k) the polygon. In the Left View we need to Lasso Select (Right Mouse Button) the points along the first quarter edge of the circle (Figure 9-2).

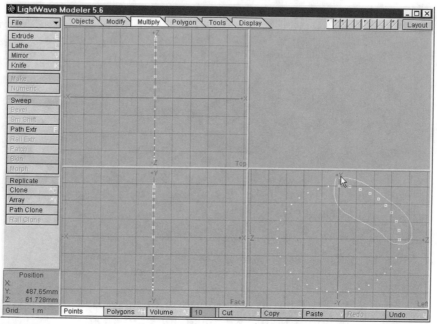

FIGURE 9-2

STEP 3: To get rid of the remaining points we do not want, Switch (Shift-") the selection and Cut (x) the other points out of the layer. Now if we enlarge the Left View our screen should look like Figure 9-3.

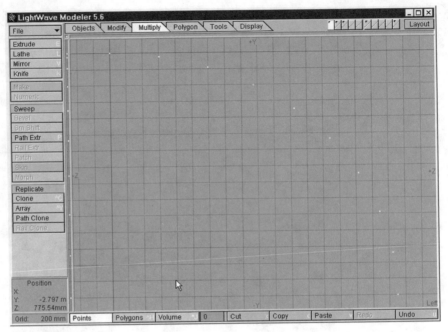

FIGURE 9-3

There is one more bit of business we need to perform on the points before we make our spline. Parachutes have a small hole in the top of them. Instead of making a complete parachute and then tunneling a hole in it we're going to make our chute with the hole already there. This saves us a step to completion and makes for a better model.

STEP 4: Activate Drag Mode (Ctrl-t) and place the cursor at (Y: 0.0 m, Z: 0.0 m). Click and drag the point at (Y: 0.0 m, Z: 0.0 m) to a value of (Y: 0.0 m, Z: 210 mm). Your screen should now look like Figure 9-4.

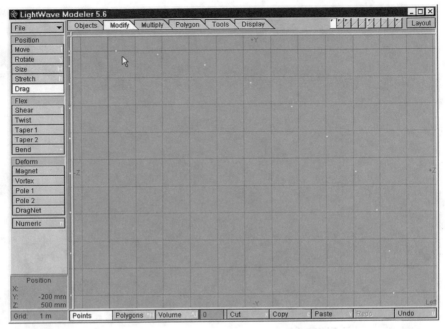

FIGURE 9-4

STEP 5: Now that we have our points in the right places we can connect them to build the spline curve. First deactivate the active tool (Space Bar) to return to Points Mode.

Note: Normally the space bar is used to switch between Selection Modes. But, as an extra bonus, when you have a tool active you can use the Space Bar to drop you out of that tools mode. A tool can also be deactivated by simply activating it again like a toggle. So (Ctrl-t) activates the Drag Tool and another (Ctrl-t) will deactivate it. As you can see, hitting the space bar is a far faster way to model.

In the Left View select the points in order from top to bottom following the direction indicated in Figure 9-5. With all points selected Make an Open Curve (Ctrl-p). If you switch to Polygon Selection Mode (Ctrl-h), your screen should look like Figure 9-6.

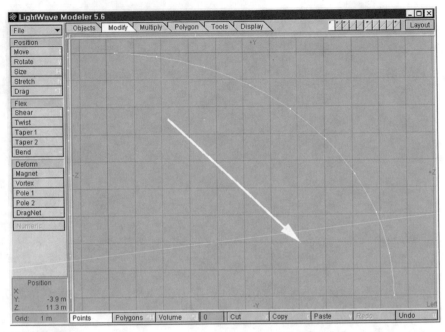

FIGURE 9-5

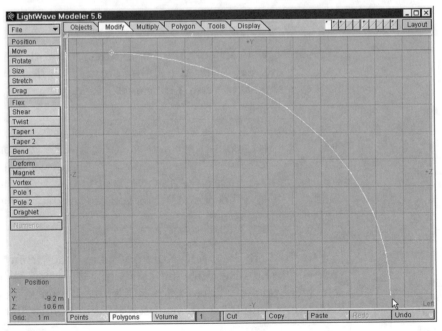

FIGURE 9-6

What we have just created is one of the rib lines we will be using to patch a section of parachute. We need now to make the other side of this section and bridge the gap between the two. The Parachute we are making is two-toned orange and white, both colors being represented 36 times across the chute. Simple mathematics thus tells us that if we have a circular object, like a parachute, which is made up of 360 degrees and you have two 36-stripe colors making it a total of 72 stripes, then you have 5 degrees per stripe.

STEP 6: Switching over to the top view Size the View (a) to fit our curve and make a Copy (c) of the active curve. Now that we have a copy of our original curve on hand we can Rotate (y) our curve 5 degrees about the Y axis.

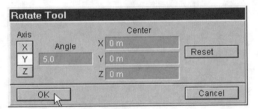

STEP 7: After rotation Paste (v) the original curve back into the active layer. Your screen should now look like Figure 9-7. Still not the most exciting model, but bear with me, it gets better.

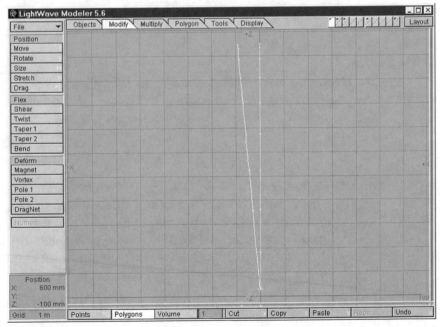

FIGURE 9-7

STEP 8: Switch back over to Point Selection Mode (Ctrl-g) and Lasso Select (Right Mouse Button) the 2 points nearest the center of the parachute, as illustrated in Figure 9-8.

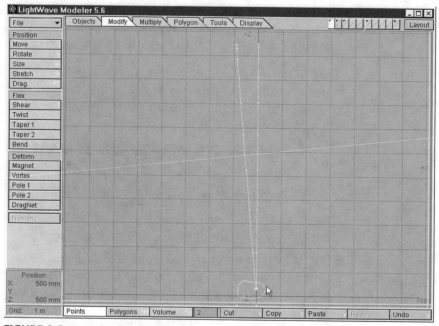

FIGURE 9-8

Note: To make patches you need to have at least 3 connected curves. It has been my experience, though, that 3 curves tend to yield poor results in the corners of the patch. Therefore whenever possible I make patches out of 4 point cages.

STEP 9: Create a Closed Curve (Ctrl-p) between those points. Now we need to close off the other side of our section. Lasso Select (Right Mouse Button) the area defined in Figure 9-9 and Create A Closed Curve (Ctrl-p). Switch to Polygon Selection Mode (Ctrl-h) and Zoom in on the Selected (Shift-a) curve for some added work.

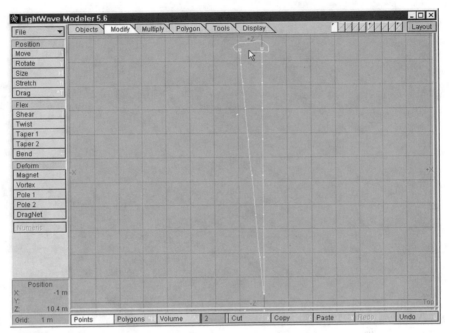

FIGURE 9-9

While it is true that we have now completed all the processes needed to make a patch, there is one more thing we need to do to make the parachute look like it is filled with air, to add a billow to the sides of the chute.

This brings us to the whole reason we chose to make our parachute section out of a spline patch. If you understand how Modeler will patch a section, you can get it to add all sorts of Free detail to your model. In this case if we add a rounded end to the bottom of the parachute and a flat end to top of the chute, the patch will start out rounded and transform to flat by the end. Since this is what parachutes do in the real world this is a good thing. Now let's make the billowing end.

STEP 10: To do this we need to Add a Point to the center of the spline. You will find Add Points in the Polygon Tab under the Revise Section, as seen in Figure 9-10. Add your point in approximately the same location as on Figure 9-11 by clicking on the spline at that point. We can now use this point as a control to bow out the spline to the desired arc.

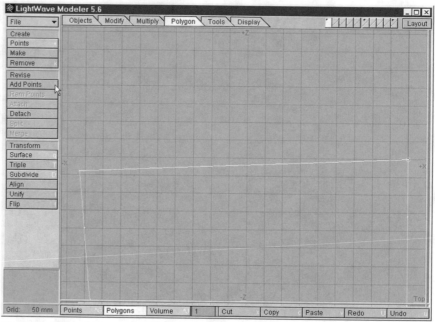

FIGURE 9-10

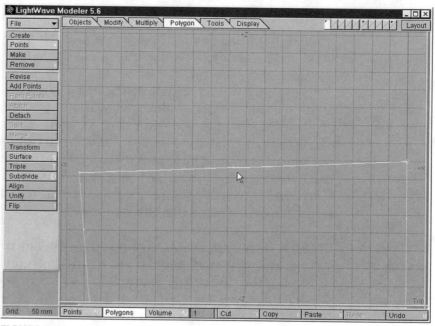

FIGURE 9-11

STEP 11: Activate the Drag Tool (Ctrl-t) and drag the control point out until it matches up with Figure 9-12.

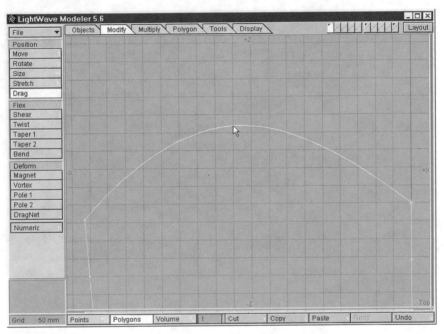

FIGURE 9-12

STEP 12: Return Modeler back to the Quad View and Fit (a) the entire object into each view. Select All Connected Curves (]) and your screen should look like Figure 9-13. With all the curves selected, we are ready to Make Spline Patch (Ctrl-f) with the following values:

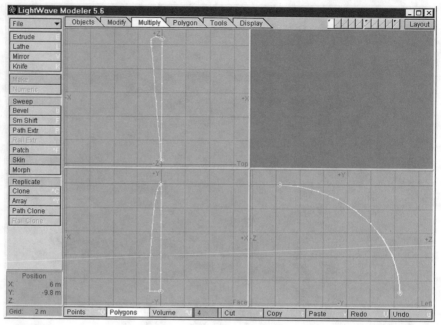

FIGURE 9-13

We should now have an Inner patch of polygons that starts bowed out at the bottom and flattens at the top. If all has gone as planned, your image should look like Figure 9-14. Since we want to make our chute out of the polygons only, and not the curves, we need to separate the two from each other. We can do this by Inverting the Selection (Shift-') and Cutting (c) the polys out of this layer. Move to Layer 2 (2) and Paste (v) the polys down.

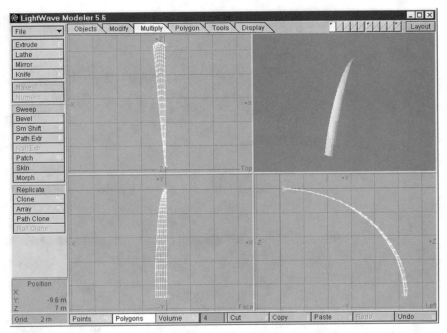

FIGURE 9-14

Another characteristic of the *Mercury* parachute was that it had small slits cut in the panels to allow air through. We will create this by cutting a few diamond-shaped holes in the sections. But before we can make those cuts, we need to align the parachute section along the Z axis so that the cuts are symmetrical.

STEP 13: This is a simple task of Rotating (y) the section back half the angle that it defines. Since we know we rotated one of our spline 5 degrees around the Y axis we know that the second section is a 5-degree sweep. Therefore the distance we need to rotate it to align it along the Z axis is −2.5 degrees, or half its total sweep. In the Numeric Requestor (n) for rotate enter the following values:

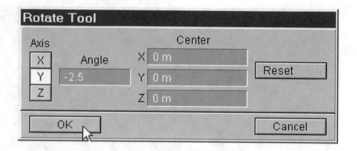

The results of the rotation should look like Figure 9-15.

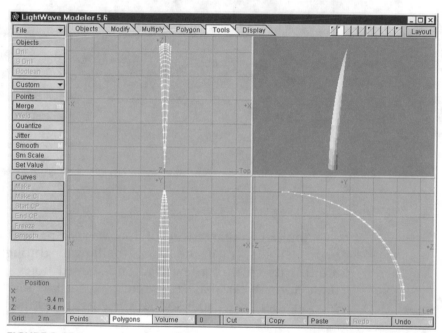

FIGURE 9-15

STEP 14: Move to Layer 3 (3) and put layer 2 in the Background (Alt-2) so we can use it as a guide for making the objects we will use to cut into it. In Point Selection Mode (Ctrl-g) shift to the Face

View and activate Create Points (+). Make (Right Mouse Button) 4 points in a diamond shape similar to Figure 9-16. It is not necessary to be exactly precise in the placement of these points since a little variation helps to make things less mechanical.

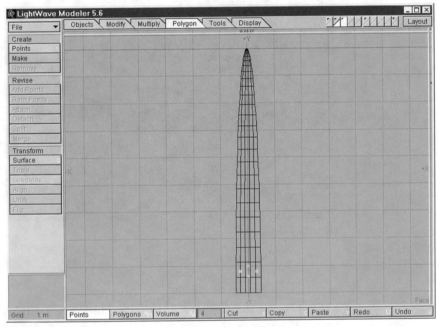

FIGURE 9-16

STEP 15: When your points are in place, Make a Polygon (p) out of them.

STEP 16: Repeat these steps and make 4 more diamonds up the side of the parachute section. Place them on every other horizontal slice and make them proportionally smaller to match the sections narrowing. Use Figure 9-17 as your guide for placement and size.

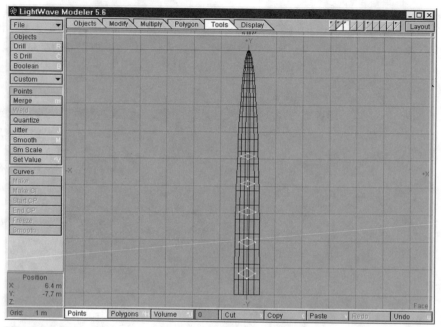

FIGURE 9-17

STEP 17: With our vent holes in place we can Switch Layers (')
making Layer 2 the foreground and Layer 3 the background. We
are now going to remove the diamond shapes from the parachute
section by using Template Drill (Shift-r) in the Tunnel configuration.

What Tunnel will do is to take the flat diamond shapes from the background layer and use them as a cookie cutter on the foreground layer along whatever axis you define. So in this case the diamonds from layer 3 project through the parachute section on layer 2, leaving holes in their wake.

Note: It is important to note that this is a cut operation only. Meaning that it will cut through any surface it comes in contact with, but will not add any interior geometry to a solid.

STEP 18: Since we know that we will be adding a displacement to our chute to make it look like billows of air are pushing it around, it is vitally important that the object be Tripled (Shift-t).

Note: By their very nature triangles are planar. Since any 3 points in space, no matter their orientation, can become a triangle, this makes tripling a model that you will be displacing important. No matter how heavily (within reason) you displace a tripled object, no nonplanar holes will appear in its surface.

Two areas of canvas, a large area of chute and a circular area on top, define the parachute, with a gap between the two areas. To create this circular area we need to eliminate a row of polygons near the top of the chute.

STEP 19: In the Top View switch to Polygon Selection Mode (Ctrl-h) and Lasso Select (Right Mouse Button) the polygons shown in Figure 9-18. With the polys selected Cut (x) them from the layer.

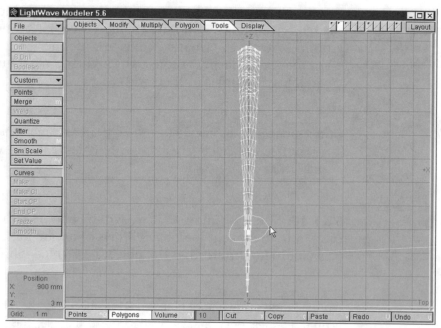

FIGURE 9-18

Now we have the two sections we need to make our parachute. To maintain realism we should connect them with a section of line that would be found on the real parachute.

STEP 20: Zoom In (.) until the gap we just created fills the Top View. In Points Selection Mode (Ctrl-g) select one point from each section of the parachute on the right-hand side as shown in Figure 9-19 by Dragging (Left Mouse Button) over both of the points. With both points selected, Make a Polygon (p) out of them and switch to Polygon Selection Mode (Ctrl-h). Open up the Change Surface (q) panel and enter the following values:

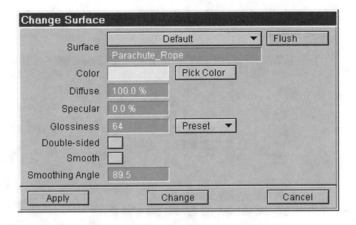

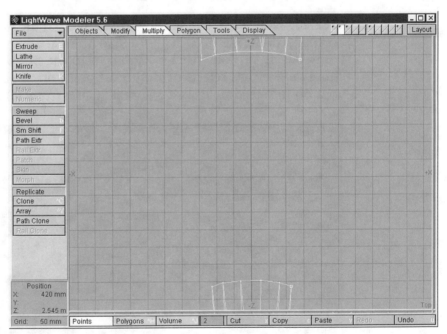

FIGURE 9-19

Before you select Apply, make the following color change to the surface color:

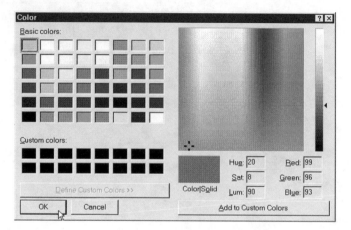

STEP 21: Now we need the ropes that attach to the *Mercury* capsule. To make these we need to switch to the Face View and activate Point Selection Mode (Ctrl-g). Zoom in to the bottom of the parachute section and select the rightmost point on the bottom. Check your point selection against Figure 9-20 and Copy (c) that point.

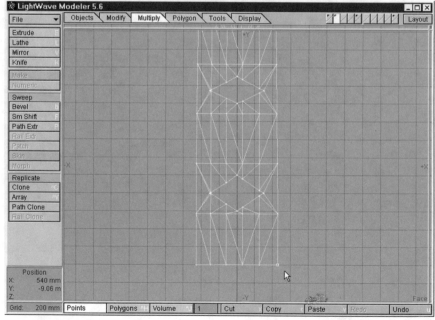

FIGURE 9-20

STEP 22: Moving to Layer 4 (4), Paste (v) the point back down. To move the point into the position we want we need to Select (Left Mouse Button) the point and get its Point Info (i). Enter the following values:

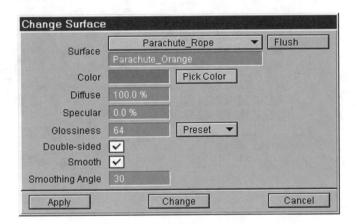

STEP 23: With the bottom point in place, let's Paste (v) another copy of our point into this layer and Size To Fit (a) both points. With the bottom point already selected, Add to Selection (Shift-Left Mouse Button) and drag over the top point until it is highlighted also. In Polygon Selection Mode (Ctrl-h), make (p) these points into a 2-point polygon and Change Surface Name (q) to Parachute_Rope. To finish off the ropes, Copy (v) the rope polygon, switch to Layer 2 (2), and Paste (v) it down. Since we do not want to have 2 points in the same place at the bottom of our chute and we need to have all points connected for displacement, we need to Merge Points (m) on this layer. If all went as planned, a total of 1 point should have been merged.

STEP 24: To set the color of our parachute section we need to open the Statistics Panel (w) and to select all the polys with the surface name Default. We do this by pressing the + key next to With Surface as shown in Figure 9-21. With all the surfaces in the fabric portion of the section active, open the Change Surface (q) panel and enter the following values:

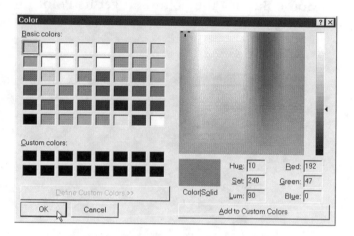

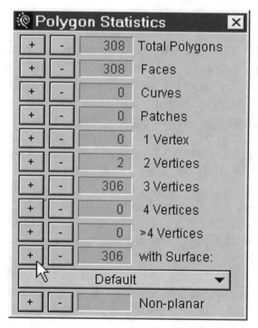

FIGURE 9-21

Again, before you select Apply, make the following color change to the surface color:

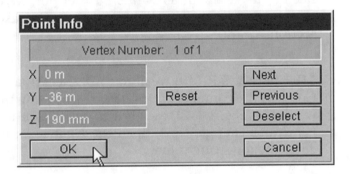

If you change your view to the Quad View and Fit to Selected (Shift-a), your screen should look like Figure 9-22.

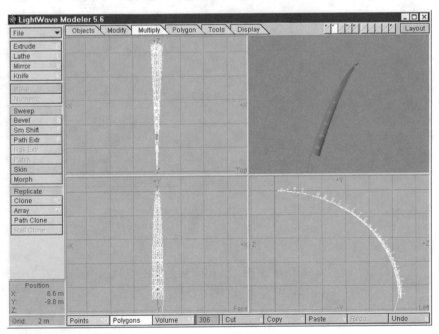

FIGURE 9-22

As we mentioned, the parachute we are making is made of two colors of fabric. We have just made one color orange, so now we need to make the other white. But fret not, we have done all the hard work, and now it will be quite easy to make another colored section.

STEP 25: To start with we need to Deselect (/) all the polygons and Copy (c) the contents of this layer. Now, using the same process as we did in Figure 9-21 we need to select all the polygons named Parachute_Orange. Next, open the Change Surface Panel (q) and enter the following values:

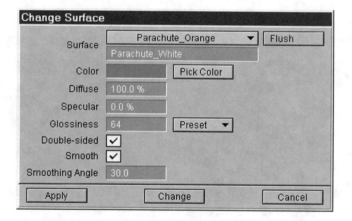

A last time, before you select Apply, make the following color change to the surface color:

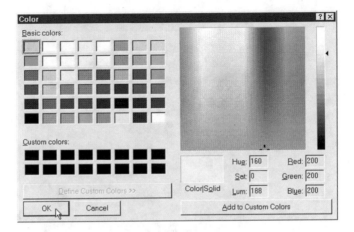

We have now created a white section.

STEP 26: To get them to line up when we paste the orange section back down we need to rotate this section 5 degrees. To accomplish this we need to Deselect (/) all the polygons then Rotate (y) the section with the following Numeric (n) values:

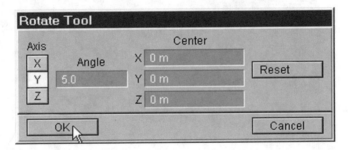

We can now Paste (v) the orange section back into this layer. Your screen should now look like Figure 9-23. Now that we have the two 5-degree pieces together we can Clone (Ctrl-c) the rest of the parachute from them with the following settings:

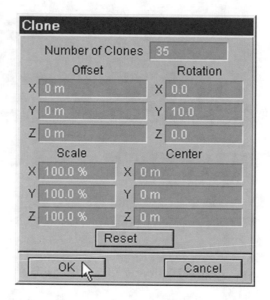

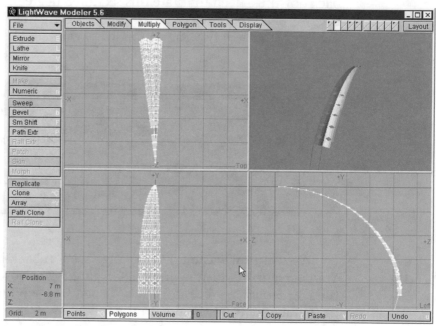

FIGURE 9-23

When cloning is complete, Merge Points (m). Save (Shift-s) this object as **Parachute.lwo**.

Congratulations! You have just created an effective system for returning our hero home to Mother Earth. In the next tutorial we will be covering how to add realistic wind displacement as part of the final water landing.

If you missed anything or you just want to review the pieces used to make the parachute I provided them for you on the CD. All the individual parts are in a layered object named **Paraparts_Mod .lwo**. The _Mod portion of the filename is my reminder to myself that this object cannot be loaded into LightWave.

10

Landing at Sea

Scott Wheeler

OVERVIEW

Now that we have our parachute and our capsule completed we can move on to the real fun of putting them in a shot. What we will be doing in this chapter is to create an environment for our objects and then, by using some camera and simple object tricks, to make a believable shot with them.

The main driving force behind the setup of this shot is that the only way to get a high angle-per-splashdown shot of the *Mercury* capsule would be to take a camera up in a chase plane or helicopter. Therefore when making any camera moves it should be considered how hard it would be to track an object through the door of a helicopter in flight.

In this tutorial you will use:

- Your imagination

What you will need:

- Time and patience
- Images from the CD
- *Mercury* capsule (built earlier)
- Parachute (built earlier)
- Objects from CD

What you will learn:

- Advanced camera techniques
- Displacement mapping
- Intermediate lighting
- Advanced motion techniques

STEP 1: Let's start by entering LightWave. Open the Objects Panel and click on Add Null Object near the top right of the panel. To set up this scene we will be parenting our camera as well as our parachute and capsule to null for movement. Since this will be in essence the master object for the scene, let's call it that. Click on Save Object and enter the following:

There are several important things to note about this step. First, you do not actually save out a Null Object. The Save Object button serves a double purpose and allows us to rename the null to whatever we like. The second thing is the naming convention. Since you do not want every null in your scene to be called "null" we need to assign null objects a better name. Last, as a matter of course I put a "_(NO)" after each null object so that I can tell at a glance in the object list where the nulls are.

STEP 2: Click on Load Object and load in the **Parachute.lwo** object.

STEP 3: Let's make some minor changes to the 3 surfaces on the parachute. First is the white striping of the chute itself. The main change we will make here that we could not do in Modeler is to add some transparency. At the distance we will be seeing the parachute for this shot any extra texture mapping would be lost. If we were going to be zeroing in closer on the chute I would want to add a weave texture to make it look more like cloth. But, for our purposes we can get away with just a slight transparency. Open the Surfaces panel and select Parachute_White as the Current

Surface. Double-check your values with those on the following panel:

STEP 4: Change the Current Surface to Parachute_Orange and again check your values with these:

STEP 5: The last surface of the parachute is Parachute_Rope, so we need to make that the Current Surface. We should talk a little about 2-point polygons since that is what our ropes are. Two-point polys can be a help and a pain at the same time. Placing a large amount of lines on an object can save poly count over using extruded boxes or other multi-polygon methods. The downside is that, unlike their cousin the single-point polygon, they have no structure and as such they do not get smaller or larger with distance. This can make it hard to use them for something like, say, parachute cables. What I have found helps tremendously with the look of these types of polygons is to use the transparency channel to regulate their size. So here we will be setting the transparency fairly high to get the look we desire.

Tip: Once we have set the shot up, it would be a good learning experience to go back and change the transparency settings to different values to see how they affect the overall look.

Set your other values to match the following panel:

Before we move on, let's go back to the Objects Panel and save our parachute to keep the changes we have made.

STEP 6: Next we should load in the **MercuryCapsule.lwo** object. After it has loaded in, close the Objects Panel (p) and go to the side view. Change the active view to the Side (ZY) View and click on Center to make the **MercuryCapsule.lwo** the center of the viewport. Your screen should look something like Figure 10-1. While this is an interesting configuration it will not look particularly real if we render it this way. So, let's move the capsule down to the bottom of the shoot lines and rotate it into position.

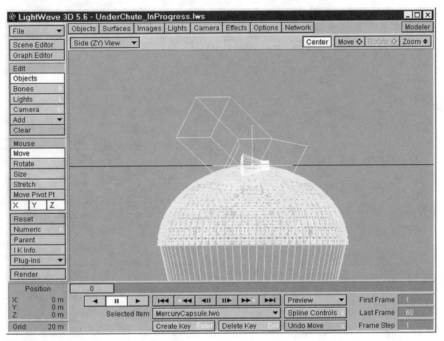

FIGURE 10-1

STEP 7: Before we move or rotate the capsule, we need to Parent it to the parachute. We do this by clicking on the Parent button on the lower left-hand side of the layout screen, as shown in Figure 10-2. In the Parent Object Panel set the capsules parent to **Parachute.lwo** as shown:

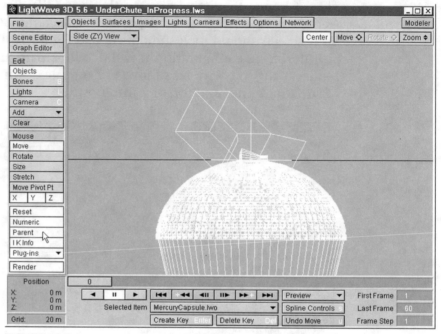

FIGURE 10-2

Tip: Since neither the parachute nor the capsule has been moved we could have placed the capsule in position prior to parenting it to the parachute. However, it's a good habit to parent and then place your objects. This will save you the pain of spending time placing an object only to have it jump to a new position when parented.

STEP 8: With the object parented select Rotate from the Mouse Section on the middle left side of the layout window and shown in Figure 10-3. Pull up Numeric Input (n) for Rotate and input the following:

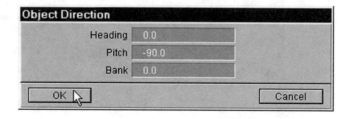

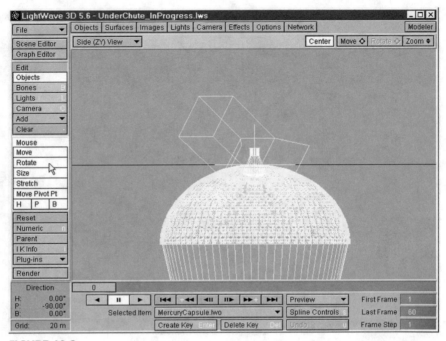

FIGURE 10-3

We can finish the capsule orientation by moving it down to the bottom of the parachute lines. Directly above Rotate is Move. Select Move, pull up Numeric Input (n), and fill in the Object Position requester as follows:

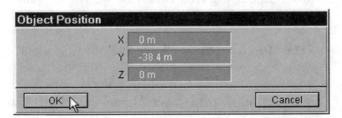

Your display should now look like Figure 10-4, with the capsule at the end of the parachute lines, where it belongs.

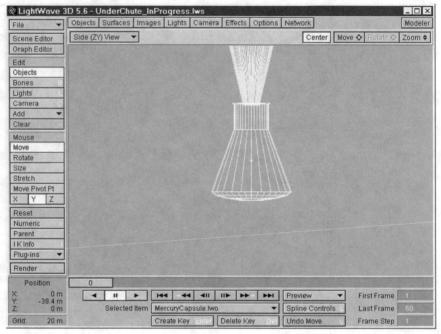

FIGURE 10-4

STEP 9: Earlier I had mentioned that we would be parenting everything to the Master_(NO) null object. So, to make that come to pass we need to change the active object to **Parachute.lwo** and follow the parenting steps we went through in Step 7. The only difference being that this time we will be parenting our parachute to Master_(NO).

STEP 10: Now that we have the objects in place and parented, let's set the camera in position. The first part of this process is to add another null object to our scene. So, open the Objects Panel and click on Add Null Object. Name this object CameraTrack_(NO) by clicking on Save Object and filling in the Null Object Name requester as follows:

As I am sure you have probably guessed, we will be using this null as a parent object for the camera.

Tip: Until LightWave has separate motion channels, the use of null objects is a good way to work around separating out certain types of motion.

With the CameraTrack_(NO) object we will be able to move and rotate the camera at different times, allowing for greater flexibility in our motion. But before we can move it around we need to again follow the process outlined in Step 7 and parent CameraTrack_(NO) to Master_(NO).

With our CameraTrack_(NO) in its place in the hierarchy we should add one more null object to the mix. Since our camera is mounted on a fictitious helicopter, we should take into account that the pounding of the blades would add some extra motion to the camera. This is a prime example of why using nulls is great for separating channels. The object we create now will have a small repeating cycle that will continue for the life of the animation. If we made this motion with the camera alone we would be locked into that cycle and the camera would be next to impossible to adjust with a keyframe at every frame.

STEP 11: In the Objects Panel click on Add Null Object to add another null to our scene. Rename the null Thumper_(NO) since it will be used to simulate the pounding of the blades.

STEP 12: Next we need to parent Thumper_(NO) to Camera-Track_(NO). To do this we are going to use a slightly different process for parenting that is far easier if you are sorting multiple objects or several differing item types. Open the Scene Editor Panel and highlight the Thumper_(NO) as shown:

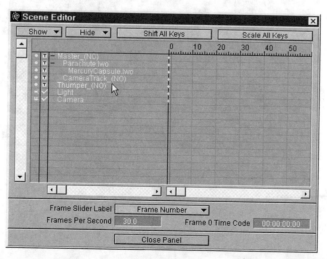

Parent Thumper_(NO) to CameraTrack_(NO) as in Step 7 and the Scene Editor should now look like the following:

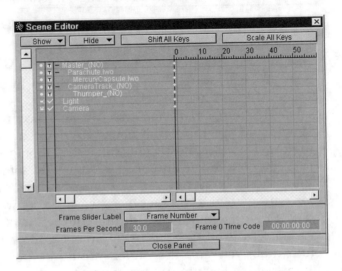

STEP 13: With Thumper_(NO) in place, it is time to move the Camera to its spot. Highlight the Camera and Parent the Camera to CameraTrack_(NO) as in Step 7. The Scene Editor Panel should now look like the following panel:

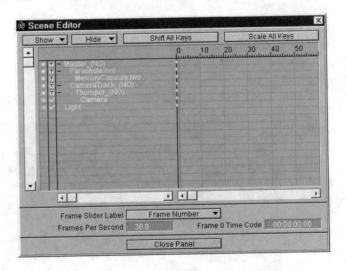

One more thing we need to do to the camera before we go on is to Reset its position so that it is centered on Thumper_(NO). We do this by clicking on Reset while in Move Mode with the Camera highlighted in the Scene Editor. If everything went as planned the Side (XY) View (3) should look like Figure 10-5 with the camera sitting at the origin.

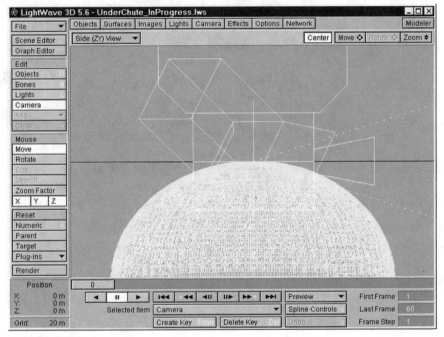

FIGURE 10-5

STEP 14: Let's start to introduce some motion to our scene. The easiest motion and therefore the one we shall tackle first is the repetitive motion caused by the chopper blades. Make Thumper_(NO) your active object and pull up the Motion Graph Editor (m). Once inside the Motion Graph Editor change the edit channel to Pitch Angle as shown:

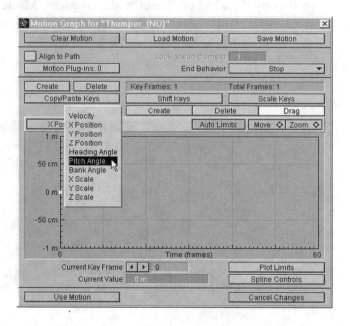

Create 3 keyframes for Pitch Angle with the following values:

Frame	Angle
0	−0.0
1	0.015
2	−0.006
3	0.01
4	−0.01

After entering in those values, set the End Behavior to Repeat so the thumping goes through the whole animation. If you click on Auto Limits to size the view your Motion Graph should look like the following:

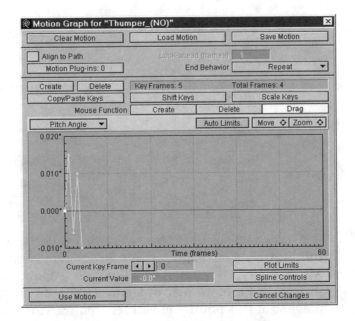

Click on Use Motion to save our changes. Don't worry about seeing any changes in the layout view for now. The subtlety of the motion will not become apparent until later in the process.

STEP 15: Let's now focus on the flight path our helicopter will be taking. Since we want the parachute to appear to be dropping away, we don't want the flight path of the camera to remain at that same altitude relative to the parachute and capsule throughout the animation. We also do not want to make the motion too static as the helicopter would most likely not be just hovering but orbiting the capsule.

Type in the following values for the CameraTrack_(NO) motion:

Frame 0				
Heading	−13		**X**	52 m
Pitch	27		**Y**	142 m
Bank	0		**Z**	−230 m

Frame 60		X	−33 m
Heading	7	Y	158 m
Pitch	31	Z	−228 m
Bank	.2		

Frame 120		X	−120 m
Heading	25	Y	174 m
Pitch	31	Z	−226 m
Bank	−0.1		

After you set those frames up it would be a good time to set the Preview Last Frame in the lower right corner of the Layout window to 120 frames as shown in Figure 10-6. Your display should also look similar to Figure 10-6 at frame 0. If you play the preview at this point you will see that the camera is making a slow pass by the capsule. You can also begin to make out the effects of the Thumper_(NO) object on the camera motion.

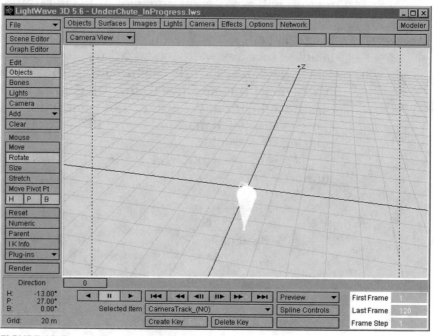

FIGURE 10-6

STEP 16: Now it's time to add a little more life to the camera and make it look like someone is actually trying to get this picture. The first part of this process is the use of the Camera Zoom Factor Envelope. Since our hapless cameraman (or woman) would most likely need to adjust the focal length of the camera we'll add that touch by zooming the camera in at the beginning of the shot and then pulling back for the final framing. In the Camera Panel click on the E Button on the Zoom Factor level as indicated:

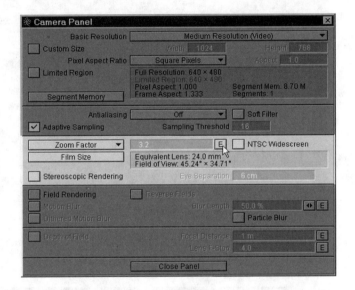

Once inside the Zoom Factor Envelope enter the following values:

Frame	Zoom Factor	Tension
0	5.84	0
17	31.7	1.0
26	31.3	1.0
46	19.6	0
73	12.9	0
121	14.8	0

With all those values entered your Zoom Envelope should look like:

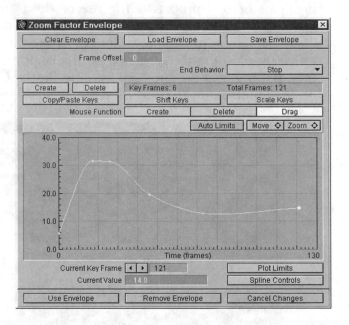

If all is well click Use Envelope to save the changes and return to the Camera Panel. In the Camera Panel change your values to match the following:

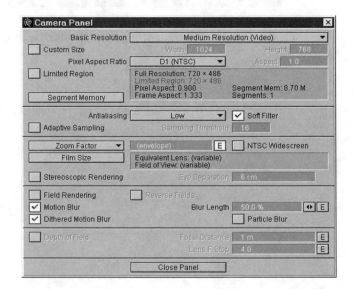

If you play the preview at this point you will notice that the camera totally zooms off the target and never really shows us a good picture.

STEP 17: Let's fix that by adding some motion to the camera. Enter the following values in for the camera:

Frame 0	
Heading	−1
Pitch	0.2
Bank	0

Frame 14	
Heading	−1.42
Pitch	4
Bank	0

Frame 37	
Heading	−0.4
Pitch	5.9
Bank	0

Frame 49	
Heading	0.1
Pitch	5.5
Bank	0

Frame 60	
Heading	1.1
Pitch	6.2
Bank	0

Frame 73	
Heading	1.7
Pitch	7.3
Bank	0

Frame 85	
Heading	1.3
Pitch	7.9
Bank	0

Frame 97	
Heading	0.5
Pitch	8.3
Bank	0

Frame 107	
Heading	0.2
Pitch	6.8
Bank	0

Frame 117	
Heading	−1
Pitch	6.2
Bank	0

Frame 120	
Heading	−1
Pitch	7.3
Bank	0

If you play the preview now you will see how all the motions added together give a feeling of randomness and natural flow that would be hard to achieve without using multiple objects for more control over the channels.

STEP 18: With the camera motion under control we can turn our attention to adding some realism to the parachute and capsule. The first step is to add a little swing to the capsule under the parachute. To do this enter the following values in for the **Parachute.lwo** object:

Frame 0		Frame 60		Frame 120	
Heading	0	Heading	0	Heading	0
Pitch	0	Pitch	0	Pitch	0
Bank	−5	Bank	5	Bank	−5

The capsule will sway back and forth throughout the animation. Although this is not readily apparent when watching a preview it really helps the overall effect. Sometimes it is the subtle things as much as the obvious ones that sell a shot.

STEP 19: The next step is to move the capsule up to a good altitude and add some downward motion. Since we parented everything to the Master_(NO) object this should be a simple task. Set 2 keyframes for Master_(NO) as follows:

Frame 0		Frame 120	
X	0 m	X	0 m
Y	2.9 km (OK)	Y	2.85 km
Z	0 m	Z	35 m

Why, you might ask, are we moving the whole structure so far up? I suppose there is no real reason to be up this high except that I want to texture the ocean object with roughly real-size waves and detail, and actually being this high lends to that. You could fake out the height, but I decided to do it this way. Hopefully nobody is afraid of heights.

STEP 20: Okay, we're falling and we're swinging. The last part is to add some billowing. Make **Parachute.lwo** your active object and open the Objects Panel (p). We are going to add the billowing motion by applying a Displacement Map to the parachute. Click on the T Button next to Displacement Map as seen:

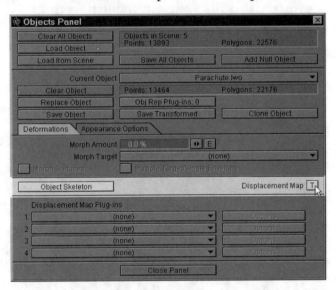

The Texture Type we want is Fractal Bumps. Since the Parachute is a large object and we do not want to add too many small ripples through the fabric, set the Texture Size as shown below:

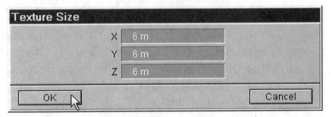

Fill out the rest of the Displacement Panel as follows:

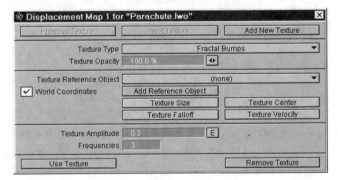

Now, those of you who have been a little curious and have rendered out a frame or two as we have been going may have been dismayed to find our astronaut hovering in a void of blackness. Let's fix that, shall we?

STEP 21: Open the Effects Panel and select the Backdrop and Fog Tab. Set your tab to match the panel below:

Notice that I did not give the fog any distance. It starts and ends at the same amount 1 meter from the camera because we are using the fog as a color wash over the image and because the object does not move far enough away in the animation to justify it receding into any heavier fog. Before we leave the Effects Panel, let's go to the Image Processing Tab and change the Dither Intensity to 4 × Normal and turn on Animated Dither. This will help give the image a grainier look. Also, since we are simulating a shot from the 1960s, drop the Color Saturation down to 75%.

Note: If you have a film grain plugin either from NewTek, Blevins, or some other vendor, you will have far more control over the grain look. But for those of you who don't, this is a decent substitute.

Now if you Render (F9) frame 63 it should look like Figure 10-7. Granted a blue void is not a lot better than a black one, but at least it's closer to the correct one.

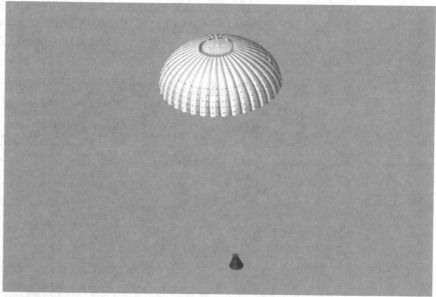

FIGURE 10-7

STEP 22: With the beginnings of our environment taking shape let's continue by adding a few lights. In the Lights Panel set the Ambient Values as shown:

This may seem a little high and for most purposes it is. But for this case we are trying to get a hazy bluish wash over the image, and a high ambient level achieves this. Change the default light to the following values:

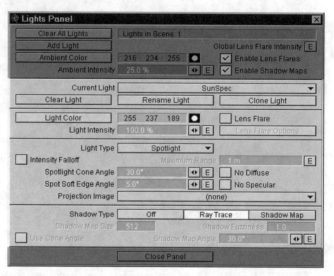

We will be adding two types of light for the sun in our shot. Each of these will perform a different task. The first one we will add will act as our specular highlight of the ocean surface. Since we want to have a sharp hit area for this light, a spot is preferable to a distant light, which will bathe the whole ocean in specularity. Next we will add a light for diffusion only:

The thing to notice about this light is that it is not generating any specular values. We will be using this to lighten the scene, but we don't want the ocean we will be adding to get anymore specular. Trust me, it will be bright enough with just one light. We will be adding one more light to our scene, but we'll do that later. For now let's move the lights we have into position.

It is important to note that most CGI and real life, for that matter, looks best when backlit or raking side lit. Watch your favorite movie or TV show (provided it's not a sitcom or a soap opera) and notice how the lighting is staged. More often than not, the main light is coming from either the side or the back with accent lights added for fill. This is how we will be setting up this scene. Both of our sun lights will be placed so that the object sits between them and the camera. The third light we will add later will be an accent or "kick" light to add a highlight and definition to the model. Set the following values for our lights:

SunDif			
H	141	**X**	0 m
P	56	**Y**	0 m
B	0	**Z**	0 m

Since SunDif is a distant light, it need not be moved from the center. It will cast its rays in the direction it is pointed only. SunSpec on the other hand is a spotlight, so its location *is* important.

SunSpec			
H	183	**X**	163 km
P	42	**Y**	606 km
B	0	**Z**	1 Mm

After the lights are in place and keyframed at 0, a Rendered (F9) frame at 63 should look like Figure 10-8.

FIGURE 10-8

STEP 23: Let's add an ocean down below. Since earlier chapters have covered in great detail the creation of an ocean surface, it would be repetitive to cover that same topic here. Therefore I have provided an object on the companion CD that we will load for our ocean object.

Note: There are some differences in how this object is surfaced, so it would be good practice to review the surfacing.

Open the Objects Panel and load in **OceanPlate.lwo** from the CD. Once it is loaded, go to the Appearance Options Tab and set it as follows:

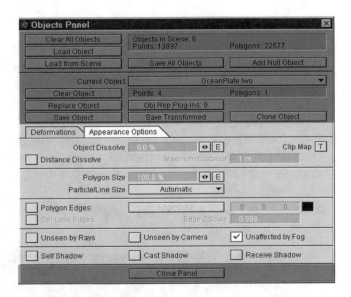

By habit I turn off the shadow casting options on objects I know will not be getting shadows. Even though we will not be tracing any shadows for this scene, it bears mentioning since it can dramatically decrease render times in scenes where you are tracing shadows.

If we Render (F9) our trusty frame 63 at this point your image should look like Figure 10-9.

FIGURE 10-9

Note: At this point the render speed should drop off considerably. The worst thing you can possibly do to hurt render times is to fill the screen with a heavily bump-mapped object. But, since we need this to get our final result, we'll just bite the bullet and move on.

As you can see, having the ocean down there really helps. However, there are two problems with the image so far: (1) the overall picture, especially the parachute, is too defined, and (2) the capsule is a solid black color with no depth.

STEP 24: Let's tackle the capsule problem first by adding another light with the following values:

You will notice that the color values are the same as our Sun-Spec light. We want to make it look like the sun is creating this edge highlight, so we need to make the colors match. This is the only light that we want to move with the capsule, so follow the process in Step 7 parent Capsule Kick to Master_(NO). After you have parented it, enter the following keyframe info:

Frame 0, 30		Frame 90, 120	
X	14 m	X	−23 m
Y	−35 m	Y	−35 m
Z	5 m	Z	5 m

Keep in mind that for the most part I am not a huge fan of the Target Button, but in some cases it can be useful. In this case we want CapsuleKick to point at the capsule at all times. The best way to do this is by selecting **MercuryCapsule.lwo** as the Target Object.

If you study the motion of the light from the Camera View (6) and move through the animation, you will notice that it makes a sweep around the capsule to simulate the changing angle of the sun. If you Render (F9) frame 23 you will see the effects of the kick on the side of the capsule, as shown in Figure 10-10.

FIGURE 10-10

STEP 25: The second problem of things being too crisp can be remedied by adding a plate of fractal noise to simulate a mist in the air. To get this mist plate go to the Objects Panel and load in **Clouds.lwo.** After it has loaded, set its values as follows:

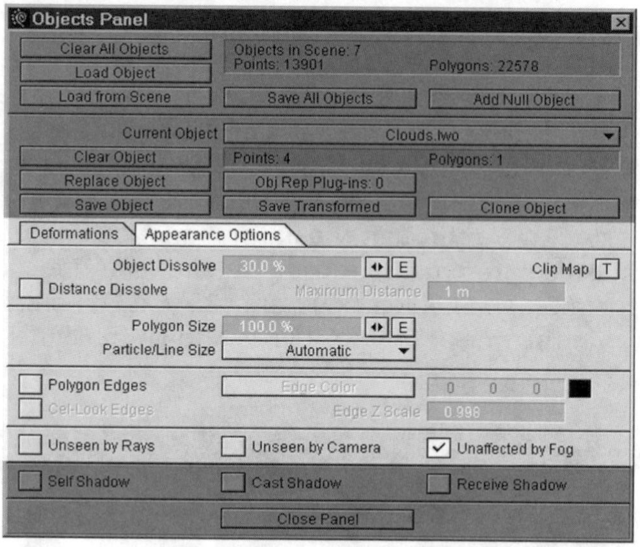

Next Move **Clouds.lwo** to the following coordinates:

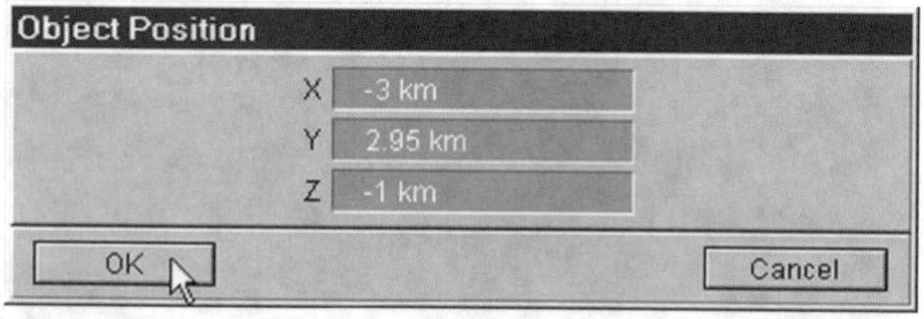

If you Render (F9) frame 23 with **Clouds.lwo** in between the camera and the capsule, you can see how they add a nice haze to the shot, as shown in Figure 10-11.

FIGURE 10-11

STEP 26: One last thing we need to do is to add that final touch to sell the shot. Since we are shooting this from a helicopter, there is one thing that shows up in almost every shot, the blades. On the CD I have provided a simple disc object with radial sections removed called **CopterBlades.lwo**. To make sure that the blades stay with the Camera as it moves, Parent them to CameraTrack_(NO). Once they have been parented enter the following values:

Frame 0		Frame 0	
H	0	X	0 cm
P	16.9	Y	1.1 m
B	0	Z	10 cm

Frame 120			Frame 120	
H	−3000		X	0 cm
P	16.9		Y	1.1 m
B	0		Z	10 cm

You will notice that if you step through the animation there are times where no blades appear at all. This is fine to a certain extent since that is what happens on film. If a frame gets exposed at just the right instant there is no blade in view. The gap however in this case is too large. We can fix this by making a Clone of CopterBlades_(NO) and applying the following value to the clone:

Frame 0			Frame 0	
H	0		X	0 cm
P	16.9		Y	1.1 m
B	0		Z	10 cm

Frame 120			Frame 120	
H	4000		X	0 m
P	16.9		Y	1.1 m
B	0		Z	10 cm

The second set of blades is counterrotating at a slightly different cycle than the first. This difference ensures that some portion of the blade is on screen at all times.

To take a look at how this has all come together, Render (F9) frame 115. It should look like Figure 10-12. All that is left for you now is to render out an animation and enjoy. Feel free to tinker with any or all of the values to see how they interrelate. After all, doing is the fastest way of learning.

FIGURE 10-12

11

Breaking into Hollywood

Joe Tracy

OVERVIEW

The dream job for most aspiring animators is to create Hollywood film and TV visual effects. The path to getting there may seem long and steep, but it is not impossible. If becoming a Hollywood animator is what you really want, then this chapter will guide you in the right direction. By following the advice in this chapter, you'll dramatically improve your chances of getting noticed by a visual effects company. Ultimately, however, this chapter solely can't get you hired. Most important will be your skills, artistry, attitude, and how you apply the information you will learn here.

The key to breaking into Hollywood can be best described as:

Hard work.
Originality.
Likeable team spirit.
Learning from experts.
Your exposure plan.
Willingness to accept creative criticism.
Objective goal setting.
Outstanding demo reel.
Desire to get hired.

HARD WORK

As mentioned, the path to getting hired as a Hollywood animator is long and steep. Yet, as most animators will tell you, hard work will get you there much quicker. So what is involved in this process?

1. *A deadline-oriented attitude.* Hollywood effects work is very deadline-oriented. Procrastination is unacceptable within the industry. If an effects company becomes known for not delivering products on time, visual effects supervisors will stop using that company. No matter how talented you are, if you can't train yourself to deliver projects and shots on time, then your value to the industry is greatly decreased.

2. *Love of animation.* If you want to make animation your career, first make sure it is something you love to do. Hard work comes naturally as a direct result of loving what you do. If you don't love doing animation, then you shouldn't be considering Hollywood animation effects as a career.

593

3. *Patience.* Hard work without patience can sometimes lead to disastrous results. For example, let's say that you saw the movie *Mask of Zorro* and now want to create a fencing animation. Your urges may say, "Okay, let's start creating right this second." However, the proper thing to do is to prepare, as analyzed in the next section, by studying fencing techniques. Such studies can take weeks and months, but will make your animation much more realistic. Furthermore, studying techniques to use in your animation takes just as much dedication and hard work as animating the final sequence. But it also takes patience not to rush yourself to the end process too soon. Even William Shakespeare said, "To climb steep hills requires a slow pace at first." Without the patience it takes to make a realistic and complete animation, your work will look weak and animated. Animated? Yes. The best special effect sequences in a film are those that are so realistic that no one even considers the possibility that they were animated.

4. *Going the extra mile.* One of the reasons the movie *Titanic* was such a great success was because director James Cameron demanded perfection of every shot, angle, prop, and effects shot. If he didn't like something, it was redone until perfected. The Digital Domain LightWave 3D team that worked on some *Titanic* shots earned a lot of respect because they went the extra mile and worked long hours to ensure that every shot was perfect. There's a difference between getting a job done and getting a job done *right*. You want to get it done right, even if it cuts into some of your personal time.

ORIGINALITY

When applying for a Hollywood visual effects job, one thing that will be analyzed is your *originality*. What makes your work and you different from the 1,200 other animators that applied at a specific company last year? Consider that fewer than 120 out of 1,200 applicants are ever given *even the slightest* interest and you can begin to see that you have to set yourself apart from the rest of the field.

Let's say, for example, that your strength is character animation. You produce a sample of a human walking and add it to your videotape showing that you can produce a solid and realistic walk cycle. That would be fine if it weren't for the fact that half of your competitors are showing the same thing! So you need to go a step further. Instead of a walk cycle, put your character in the middle of a Karate tournament doing all sorts of killer moves and you will definitely get noticed!

When thinking about originality, consider what is simple to create and what is extremely difficult to create. Master the difficult and spend an extra few months perfecting such a scene and your chances of getting your tape recognized will be dramatically improved.

One way to get into a solid mind frame is simply to role-play. Act as if you have already been hired by a visual effects company and have been given a special effects shot for a very popular TV show. Now create that killer alien attack scene for *Star Trek: Voyager* with your own original ships and pack it with solid action sequences that show off all of your abilities. "But wait," you may say. "I didn't think visual effects companies wanted ships on demo reels!" This is a *myth* and is addressed further in the section on creating an outstanding demo reel.

Being original also means avoiding public domain objects and effects, or plugins that easily create such effects. While such content works great for small video production houses and animation facilities, as a serious animator you need to be the one that creates such objects and effects to demonstrate your abilities. A visual effects company considering you wants to know what you can create, not what the plugin you're using can create. These companies can spot use of public domain items and easily created plugin material a mile away because they see it *every day* on demo tapes sent to them. Part of being original is *to push yourself to the limit of your abilities*. Only then will you be able to capture the eye of the person who makes the hiring decisions.

So what are some things you can do to increase your originality?

1. *Study life.* A lot of the movements in Disney animation like *The Lion King* are extremely realistic because the artists spent hours at the zoo studying wildlife. If you want to create a character in a Karate tournament, then you need to attend some tournaments with pad, paper, and a video camera to study the movements and methods used by those participating. If you are

going to animate a race car, then go to the races and study every aspect of the event. As important as studying the realism of the scene is to study the lighting of the scene. The importance of lighting should never be underestimated. You want to recreate a realistic action sequence that will set you apart from everyone else, and studying such sequences for weeks or even months is the first key step to creating your masterpiece.

2. *Forget the software.* Originality is developed by shutting your mind to "the way it is done" and creating it "the way it should be done." Studios hire a person not based on how well he or she knows LightWave 3D. More times than not, it is based on how good of an overall artist that person is. Can you see past the present? Consider taking a vacation away from LightWave 3D for a few months to work on some of your other artistic skills that in the end will make you much more valuable.

3. *Understand why you are creating something.* Another way to increase your originality is to understand why you are doing a particular project. This tool is often used by screenwriters who will develop a very elaborate back story to a movie that the audience will never see. Know and understand all aspects of your creation, even those that don't appear on screen, so that you can make it more believable and original.

4. *Develop a high standard through your own artistry.* Developing a high standard through your own artistry can be defined as "remembering the little guys." One thing that made Walt Disney so successful is that he cared for the little things in life. Almost daily he would spend time in Disneyland, walking the park, interacting with the guests, and even sweeping the streets! His goal was to keep the park very clean and appealing, even down to a small piece of paper in the corner. This kind of dedication is also what your animation needs. Perhaps you are learning character animation. Where is all your time spent? Is it spent trying to synch the lips to the speech? Perhaps you need to spend some time creating a character without a face so that you can gain strength in all other aspects of animating a character. Build perfection in every aspect of your work that will create a highly respectable artistic standard within your soul.

5. *Ask why.* The "why" helps shape your thinking and makes you see things in a different light, which in turn adds to your ability to be more original with your approach to certain projects. Perhaps something Bernard Baruch said can best sum up this example: "Millions saw the apple fall, but Newton was the one that asked why." But there's even another twist to the why question, as stated by George Bernard Shaw: "You see things that are and say 'Why?' But I dream things that never were and say 'Why not?'"

LIKEABLE TEAM SPIRIT

A likeable team spirit cannot be underestimated within the Hollywood visual effects industry. In fact, some companies put more hiring emphasis on an animator's attitude than they do on his or her abilities! This is because no matter how good you are, if you are not a team player, then you will only bring a company down versus enhancing it.

You may find the following idea silly, but it does work. If you are having problems interacting with other people and producing a likeable team spirit, then pick up a book similar to *How to Win Friends and Influence People* and read it! After you read it, apply the techniques you read to your everyday life and within 21 days a lot of those applications will become habit. You may be surprised at the results and if it can help you develop a more personable spirit, then why not try it?

Positive thinking is one of the most important aspects of having a likeable team spirit. People are defined by their attitudes. Your attitude also shapes how happy you are with life, which in turn shapes other people's opinions of you. Even Abraham Lincoln commented on this subject when he said, "Most folks are about as happy as they make up their minds to be." Positive thinking leads not only to a more likeable team spirit, but also to a more lively personality with a sense of purpose for your life. As Aristotle said, "We are what we repeatedly do. Excellence is therefore not an act but a habit."

LEARNING FROM EXPERTS

If your ultimate goal is to get hired as a professional Hollywood animator, then learning the tools of the trade from current Hollywood animators should be a priority! The fact that you bought this book is a good sign of your desire to learn from top industry professionals.

If you want to become a Hollywood animator, then one of your best keys to success is to learn tips, tricks, techniques, and tutorials from those already in the field. This is one reason that *NewTekniques* magazine quite frequently hires Hollywood animators to write tutorials, columns, and opinions, and to share techniques.

Learning from experts isn't just about techniques, but also about lifestyle. The lifestyle of one particular person has always amazed me—*Walt Disney*. Here is a man who always made his dreams a reality no matter what the odds. Even more important, however, he achieved success by being a genuine, sincere, and happy person. Instead of thinking money, he thought about quality, ethics, people, and originality. Success for Disney came naturally and was never forced. There are many biographies on Disney available at bookstores that are worth reading. Reading about how people have achieved ultimate success can become a valuable tool in shaping your quest. A great resource for reading about successful LightWave 3D animators is the *NewTekniques* TekMasters column. It gives you great insight into the success of people like Ron Thornton, who won a "LightWave Lifetime Achievement" award at NewTek Expo 1997.

Another excellent way to learn from the experts is to volunteer as an intern at a visual effects house. That's right. Some special effect houses offer internships, and such a position can sometimes lead to permanent employment. Even if it doesn't, you have gained the value of learning expert techniques plus the ability to list the internship on your résumé!

A perfect place to interact with experts is at the annual NewTek Expo event, where tons of Hollywood animators are in attendance and interacting through courses, panels, LightWave Theater, and the Job Fair. Whether in person or through an article, soak up the valuable advice these experts give away. Consider making a file where you put copies of articles and information valuable to your quest of making it to Hollywood. But don't let the file just collect dust! Periodically go back through it and read the information again to make sure you are on course.

YOUR EXPOSURE PLAN

An exposure plan is the way you market yourself so that your name becomes widely known within the industry. It is the ability to put yourself in a position so that when a reviewer picks up your videotape and reads your name, there will be instant name recognition. Here are some examples of people who have made their names known in the industry and whose names will be recognized by most reviewers at LightWave 3D visual effects houses:

1. *Dave Jerrard.* Here is a person who, until becoming involved with *NewTekniques,* was mostly known for his helpful nature on the LightWave Mailing List. The first article Dave Jerrard ever submitted to me for consideration was "LightWave by Candlelight" and appeared in the February/March 1998 issue of *NewTekniques* magazine. His article impressed not only me, but also the Senior LightWave Technical Editor of *NewTekniques,* John Gross. In no time at all, Jerrard was signed on to be the lead tutorial writer in *NewTekniques* with guaranteed space in every single issue. Three issues later I paid a visit to a visual effects company and took some new issues with me. Instantly two to three of the artists turned to the tutorial section to see what Jerrard's latest tutorial was about. In less than a year nearly every single LightWave 3D animator knew the name Dave Jerrard. And if you didn't know the name before you purchased this book, you sure do now! Jerrard is very detailed in his step-by-step approach to teaching people Light-Wave, and there is no doubt in my mind that when he is ready to make the big move to Hollywood, it will happen.

2. *Taron.* All it took was a simple display of Taron's work on the *NewTekniques* Web site for him to catch the eye of Station X Studios, where he is now employed full-time!

3. *Ken Brilliant.* Every issue of *NewTekniques* magazine carries four specially selected images for the Renders column out of over 40 submissions. While it is hard to get an image accepted

for publishing, it is definitely worth the effort. As of the Fall of 1998, Ken Brilliant had at different times submitted three images for Renders. All three were accepted and published in different issues. One of the images by Brilliant resulted in a LightWave newsgroup discussion on how a particular effect was achieved. His name is becoming more known with every image accepted.

These are just a few examples. Create your own exposure plan to get your work into high exposure areas. Take your best Light-Wave 3D work and enter it into contests and respectable galleries. If you have good techniques, share those techniques with the public! The more your name is associated with positive things, the better chance a good strong look will be given to your Hollywood quest. It also makes great résumé material.

WILLINGNESS TO ACCEPT CREATIVE CRITICISM

At the 1997 NewTek Expo, about a dozen professional Hollywood animators were brought in to review demo videos of Expo attendees. The feedback given to those who participated in the program was priceless, particularly for those who chose to act upon the creative criticism they obtained.

Creative criticism is when someone finds a weak area in your artwork and offers advice that can improve it to bring your work to its full potential. What you decide to do with such suggestions will determine how far your work will go. If the suggestion is a good one and you decide not to use it, then you have just closed the door on progress. Always keep an open mind, learn to listen, and learn to apply valuable suggestions. It will improve all aspects of your life.

My wife and I invented a term that we call *revisioneering.* The art of revisioneering is the ability to take something you've done in the past, create a new vision of how it can be improved, then reengineer it to reflect those positive changes. It can also be applied to the work of other people. For example, sometimes my wife and I will watch a movie that had a lot of potential, but blew it. We'll then discuss our vision of how the movie should have been and then restructure it on paper to reflect those changes.

When it comes to your work, feedback from those whose work and opinion you admire is of vital importance to making your artwork all that it can be. Creative criticism and revisioneering of your work by other people can go a long way to improve your style and the way you improve your projects.

As editor in chief of *NewTekniques,* the most important part of my job is to listen to readers to find out how they think the magazine can be improved. But even more important than listening is to take action to reflect those improvements. If I was to ignore every suggestion I received, then the magazine would never improve. Yet when I receive E-mails from people that say, "How does the magazine keep topping itself?," I am encouraged that the process of listening to readers and applying changes accordingly works so well! That is one reason why I make my E-mail address and direct phone number so widely available—so that readers can give me constructive criticism and feedback.

Learn to make constructive criticism a part of the growth cycle in your everyday life and you'll find your work reaching new levels you never thought possible. Keep in mind the Danish proverb that says "Advice to a fool goes in one ear and out the other." Even so, it is always valuable to also keep in mind the Yiddish proverb that says "Ask advice from everyone, but act with your own mind." Ultimately, taking the best advice from others and mixing it with your own revisioneering is what will boost your work to the next level and make you much more successful.

OBJECTIVE GOAL SETTING

Aristotle once said that "the only way to achieve true success is to express yourself completely in service to society. First, have a definite, clear, practical ideal—a goal, an objective. Second, have the necessary means to achieve your ends—wisdom, money, material and methods. Third, adjust all your means to that end."

Not only is objective goal setting important to you as an artist, it should be an important aspect of your entire life. Greg Anderson has stated in his *The 22 Non-Negotiable Laws of Wellness* book, "When we are motivated by goals that have deep meaning, by dreams that need completion, by pure love that needs expressing, then we truly live life."

What are your objectives? Is your objective to be an animator in Hollywood? Is it to produce excellent animation work? Perhaps your objective is to own your own animation business. Set small goals to reach one big objective and work on accomplishing those goals on a daily basis. Post the end objective in a place that you will see it every day and do at least one thing daily to get closer to that objective. This will not only lead to success, but also will give you a great feeling every step of the way because you will know you are accomplishing important tasks.

So what is one specific goal you would set with the objective of becoming a Hollywood artist? An example would be to *create an outstanding demo reel*.

OUTSTANDING DEMO REEL

The biggest initial impression you will make to a visual effects company is through your demo reel. Most visual effects companies receive between 45 and 100 demo reels a month, and over 90% of those are considered a waste of time. This means that there wasn't even the *slightest urge* to consider the artist behind the tape. Those tapes are either filed to collect dust or thrown away without any further thought. Sometimes a tape is considered so bad that it is stopped after only a few seconds or minutes, ejected, and immediately thrown away or filed.

As an animator, the artistry and skills you display in your demo tape must be superb. Your tape must immediately appeal to the viewer, or it will end up at the local dump, wasting both your time and the viewer's. So how do you know if your work is good enough? Jeff Scheetz, the human resource director for Foundation Imaging, states that he looks for work that is just as good as the work that Foundation Imaging puts out. Visual effects companies are not training centers. If your work is not as good as that of the artists already working there, then polish your skills before submitting a tape.

Here are some steps to follow when creating a demo tape that will help you be part of the elite 10% that gets farther than the closest garbage can:

1. *Do not use canned objects or effects.* Spotting public domain objects or effects is very easy for a reviewer and is the quickest way not only to get your tape thrown away, but also to have a negative typecast associated with your name. "It tells us a lot about the artist that is not good," says Scheetz. The work on your tape should be original.

2. *Claim credit only for your work.* Visual effects companies are interested only in your work. If you did a 5-second animated shot for a TV commercial, do not put the entire 30-second commercial on the tape. The only interest the reviewer has is in your 5 seconds of work. If some of the work on your tape belongs to someone else, you must state so in the video log that accompanies your demo video. Selling yourself on false assumptions is an easy way to quickly be left without a job.

3. *Put your best work upfront.* It is vitally important that your best work open up the video because the first shot is going to make a much larger impression than the last shot. If your first shot is very impressive, it also guarantees that your entire tape will be viewed. One of my favorite quotes is "You never get a second chance to make a good first impression."

4. *Don't repeat sequences.* Reviewers do not want to see your same shot over and over. Even if you think the shot is the coolest in the world, refrain from looping or repeating it.

5. *Edit the tape.* Editing your footage into a nice presentation is very important. You can make some big impressions by editing your tape. Keep in mind that some companies will mute the volume when watching your tape, so make sure that you are just as strong visually as you are audibly!

Here is a list of bonus *super selling techniques* to help your demo tape get higher marks:

1. *Tailor your work.* One way to make big impressions with your demo reel is to tailor your reel to a specific company. Study the type of work that particular visual effects company does, then make sure the tape you send is specifically tailored to the needs of that company.

2. *Create an audible feast.* At least one human resources director I talked to stated that audio can be used as a "cheat" in getting your tape noticed. While some companies will mute audio, others don't and therefore you can enhance the mood of your presentation by adding a strong musical score and proper sound effects.

3. *Use broadcast VHS tapes in SP mode.* The demo tapes you send out should be on VHS. But there are many different qualities of VHS tape that directly affect picture and sound quality. At the top of the list is a tape you can't find in local stores called *Broadcast VHS.* You will have to special-order this tape from a tape manufacturer or large reseller. If you create killer animation work, you will want the clarity of the audio and video to be as crisp as possible. Broadcast VHS tapes will deliver this type of quality. If your animation work is not top-notch, then you shouldn't be submitting a demo tape! When you edit and record your finished tape, be sure to record in SP mode. If your tape recorder is set to EP or SLP record mode, there will be a noticeable quality loss. So preserve your quality by using Broadcast VHS and recording your work in SP mode.

Here are two *frustration savers* that will help you make sure your tape is in top viewing condition.

1. *Watch your tape before sending it out.* If a company receives a tape that is full of glitches or even blank (as some have), then you have vastly improved your chances of that tape ending up in the trash. Before sending a tape to a visual effects company, be sure to view it to make sure there are no problems!

2. *Remove the record tab when done.* On the spline of your cassette tape, in the lower left-hand corner, you will find a little tab. When you finish your demo tape and are ready to send it out, remove this tab. This will keep you or anyone else from accidentally recording over the tape!

The more time you put into your demo tape, the better your chance of getting it into the elite 10% of tapes that get noticed. Be sure to read the Desire to Get Hired section for important tips on packaging your demo reel.

DEMO TAPE MYTHS AND TRUTHS

Myth—I should not have any spaceships on my demo reel.

Fact—Companies like Foundation Imaging and Digital Muse do a lot of effects work that involves spaceships. Therefore, it is important for these companies to see how good you are at modeling, texturing, lighting, and animating spaceships. As long as your work is good and original, most effects houses will want to see it.

Myth—I should include some of my animated logos on my demo reel.

Fact—You are trying to get a job in the special effects industry, not in the local TV commercial logo industry. Therefore, leave animated logos off your tape.

Myth—A demo tape must last a minimum of 3 minutes.

Fact—The saying that a demo reel must be a minimum of 3 minutes is only a suggestion, not a rule. Your demo reel can be as little as 30 seconds and still get you hired if the artistry and talents displayed in your 30 seconds of footage are superb. Don't feel that you have to cram extra work you are not fully impressed with into your tape to make the demo 3 minutes in length. If 30 seconds is all you have of your best stuff, then go with it.

Myth—Loose is better than tight.

Fact—You need to edit your demo reel as tightly as possible so that it moves at a strong pace without boring the reviewer. Keep in mind that the reviewer watches hundreds of tapes a year, so the stronger pace that yours moves at or the more creative, yet professional, way you present the material can help it stand out.

Myth—I should provide a Web site address on the demo tape that contains my résumé instead of sending a hard copy.

Fact—Very few demo tape reviewers are interested in looking at your Web site, and most of them would be extremely irritated if you provided a Web site in place of a hard copy of your résumé. Send the hard copy with the tape.

DESIRE TO GET HIRED

A burning desire to get hired will help motivate you to do a job above and beyond what others do to get noticed. When you love what you do, the end results will reflect that love and desire. So if you have a sincere desire to work in Hollywood, you will go the extra mile to make sure your submission is one of the 10% that get recognized. What are some of the things you should consider doing?

The most important thing is to *put together a killer demo package*. A demo package is not just your demo reel. It is also your résumé, tape case, VHS label, cover art, concept art, and drawings. The time you put into creating your package will be reflective of how serious you are about getting hired:

1. *Résumé.* You must include a résumé with your demo reel. It does not matter if you have prior 3D effects experience or not. After all, John Gross, co-founder of Digital Muse, was a swimming pool salesman before getting into Hollywood! Keep in mind that *a résumé often gets separated from video tapes.* This is where the tape case comes in.

2. *Tape case.* The tape case you purchase for your VHS tape is very important. You want to purchase a case that allows you to slip a special information card in the back. *The information card will become your résumé and should never be separated from your tape!* This method, highly recommended by Sheetz at Foundation Imaging, will make it much easier for a reviewer to find information on you if they like your tape.

3. *VHS label.* The VHS label must contain your name, address, and phone number. You may also include a title of the demo reel and how long it is, if desired. *Do not hand print the label!* Make sure the label is nicely laser printed, well designed, and easy to read. Do not use any fancy fonts on the label.

4. *Cover art.* Not many people use cover art, and it is an excellent way to get your tape recognized. Cover art is a color-printed collage of what is on your video. It should show the best aspects of your work. You will apply this art to the cover of the tape case. Besides being attractive, it reminds reviewers of what is on your tape. Reviewers may have a scene in their mind of something they really liked, but may not remember the tape it was on. By triggering that memory with cover art, you have saved that reviewer a lot of time fishing through tapes trying to remember which one contained the element

he or she is now interested in. Make sure the final color print is of excellent photolike quality. If your work is good, the extra effort will pay off.

5. *Concept art.* If you created any concept drawings to go along with the 3D animation in your demo reel, be sure to submit copies of those drawings! Many visual effect companies will be very interested in seeing how you came about creating your 3D masterpiece.

6. *Drawings.* This one might surprise you. A lot of companies like to receive samples of drawings you have made on paper because companies are looking not just for people who can do computer animation, but also for overall artists. Therefore, if you have some excellent sketches and artwork, be sure to have professional color copies made of them as part of your demo package. Remember to send only high-quality copies of your original artwork. You will keep the actual original drawings.

MAILING LIST

Okay, you now have your demo package all ready to go and have followed all of the tips in this chapter. The only problem left is to search for all the addresses of LightWave 3D visual effects companies to send your demo package to. You'll be glad to know that I've done all the legwork for you! Here is a list of the majority of LightWave 3D Visual Effect Companies and addresses to send your demo package to:

Digital Muse
Att.: Recruiting
1337 Third Street, Third Floor
Santa Monica, CA 90401

Digital Domain
Att.: Recruiting Manager
300 Rose Avenue
Venice, CA 90291

Netter Digital
Att.: Recruiting Department
5125 Lankershim Boulevard
North Hollywood, CA 91601

Computer Café
Att.: Jeff Barnes
3130 Skyway Drive, Suite 603
Santa Maria, CA 93455

Station X Studios
Att.: Recruiting Department
1717 Stewart Street
Santa Monica, CA 90404

OCS/Freeze Frame/Pixel Magic
Att.: Recruiting Department
10635 Riverside Drive
Toluca Lake, CA 91602

Autumn Light Entertainment
Att.: Recruiting Department
1405 Narcisco, NE
Albuquerque, NM 87112

Foundation Imaging
Att.: Jeff Scheetz
24933 West Avenue Stanford
Valencia, CA 91355

Will Vinton Studios
Att.: Recruiting Department
1400 N.W. 22nd Avenue
Portland, OR 97210

Vision Scape Imaging, Inc.
Att.: Human Resources Department
5125 Convoy Street, Suite 212
San Diego, CA 92111

Rhythm and Hughes Studios/LIVE
Att.: The Box (John-Mark Austin)
5404 Jandy Place
Los Angeles, CA 90066

Available Light, Ltd.
Att.: Tony Benezil
1125 South Flower Street
Burbank, CA 91502

Flat Earth Productions
4405 Riverside Drive, Suite 205
Burbank, CA 91505

The Walt Disney Co.
Att.: Gary Kleinman
2411 W. Olive Avenue
Burbank, CA 91505

Lemonade Visual Effects Co.
Att.: Recruiting Department
3112 Los Feliz Boulevard
Los Angeles, CA 90039

The Magic Camera Company
Att.: Gary Coulter
Shepperton Film Studios
Studios Road
Shepperton
Middlesex TW17 OQD
England, UK

Best of luck with your venture into Hollywood! When you get hired, be sure to drop me an E-mail (**jtracy@animationartist.com**) and let me know where you end up! Be sure to check out the on-line LightWave 3D Applied section for some more valuable material! You can access it at **http://www.advanstarbooks.com/ lightwave/**.

The ultimate success will come from achieving your goals while improving your lifestyle. As Albert Einstein once said, "Try not to become a man of success, but rather try to become a man of value."

Index

610

ANNUAL EDITIONS

Comparative Politics 09/10

Twenty-Seventh Edition

EDITOR

O. Fiona Yap
University of Kansas

O. Fiona Yap is an Associate Professor of Political Science and the Director of Undergraduate Studies and the International Studies co-major at the University of Kansas. Her research work is available through journals such as the *British Journal of Political Science,* the *Journal of East Asian Studies, Japanese Journal of Political Science* and the *Journal of Theoretical Politics* as well as chapter contributions in edited volumes. Her book, *Citizen Power, Politics, and the 'Asian Miracle'* (2005) has been widely reviewed. Prior to assuming the editorship, she served as an Academic Advisory Board member for *Annual Editions: Comparative Politics.* She is also a reviewer for numerous journals, including *Journal of Politics, Comparative Politics, International Studies Quarterly, International Studies Perspective, Social Science Quarterly, Governance,* and *Asian Survey.*

Higher Education

Boston   Burr Ridge, IL   Dubuque, IA   New York   San Francisco   St. Louis
Bangkok   Bogotá   Caracas   Kuala Lumpur   Lisbon   London   Madrid   Mexico City
Milan   Montreal   New Delhi   Santiago   Seoul   Singapore   Sydney   Taipei   Toronto

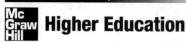

ANNUAL EDITIONS: COMPARATIVE POLITICS, TWENTY-SEVENTH EDITION

Published by McGraw-Hill, a business unit of The McGraw-Hill Companies, Inc., 1221 Avenue of the Americas, New York, NY 10020.

1 2 3 4 5 6 7 8 9 0 QPD/QPD 0 9

ISBN 978–0–07–812766–3
MHID 0–07–812766–1
ISSN 0741–7233

Managing Editor: *Larry Loeppke*
Senior Managing Editor: *Faye Schilling*
Developmental Editor: *Debra Henricks*
Editorial Coordinator: *Mary Foust*
Editorial Assistant: *Nancy Meissner*
Production Service Assistant: *Rita Hingtgen*
Permissions Coordinator: *Lenny J. Behnke*
Senior Marketing Manager: *Julie Keck*
Marketing Communications Specialist: *Mary Klein*
Marketing Coordinator: *Alice Link*
Project Manager: *Sandy Wille*
Design Specialist: *Tara McDermott*
Senior Production Supervisor: *Laura Fuller*
Cover Graphics: *Kristine Jubeck*

Compositor: Laserwords Private Limited
Cover Images: © Getty Images/RF (inset capital and flags), © PunchStock/RF (inset oil rig); U.S. Air Force/Dave Ahlschwede (background)

Library in Congress Cataloging-in-Publication Data
Main entry under title: Annual Editions: Comparative Politics. 2009/2010.
  1. Comparative Politics—Periodicals. I. Yap, O. Fiona, *comp.* II. Title: Comparative Politics.
658'.05

www.mhhe.com

Editors/Advisory Board

Members of the Advisory Board are instrumental in the final selection of articles for each edition of ANNUAL EDITIONS. Their review of articles for content, level, currentness, and appropriateness provides critical direction to the editor and staff. We think that you will find their careful consideration well reflected in this volume.

Preface

Comparative politics focuses on the empirical study of political behaviors, institutions, and rules to facilitate explanations, predictions, and theory-building. This book sets as its task the presentation of information based on systematic study of such behaviors, institutions, and rules.

To complete this task, the volume has been reorganized to emphasize political behaviors, institutions, and rules from a comparative perspective. Current comparative politics texts make similar arguments regarding the need for such a focus and probably support it. However, few are able to depart from a presentation that is country specific.

This book makes that departure. Instead of providing information on a country basis, each unit presents information about how people and governments behave and interact politically, given the rules and institutions that are in place, across a range of countries and political systems. The point I emphasize is this: systematic generalizations that address the questions of "why, what, and how" regarding political behaviors and institutions apply across countries and political systems.

As noted in unit 1, for those new to comparative politics, it is probably intriguing that people and governments across different countries and systems aim for political balance over the same issues—stability, change, security, and freedom—and try to achieve them the same way. I do not dispute that country-relevant information contextualizes behavior and interactions. Rather, I consider it necessary to clarify the generalizations that provide baseline knowledge regarding "why, what, and how" of political behaviors and institutions. With this baseline in place, particularities that are observed become even more interesting or unusual.

Each unit begins with an overview that introduces students to the systematic questions of "why, what, and how" regarding political behaviors and institutions. Often, the first readings in the units introduce students to debates and discussions regarding these systematic questions in the discipline. Subsequent readings provide the empirical "flesh," drawn from the news or the public press, to show that answers to the questions generalize across different countries. This structure ensures that students do not see the discipline as divorced from the real world.

Unit 1 introduces comparative politics as a vigorous and important subfield in political science, and compares how other disciplines study governments and politics in order to showcase the significance of the comparative political science approach. To all those who see that the comparison across disciplines provides the analogy of why, how, and what we compare, we say "Bravo!" Unit 1 also describes citizen participation and its effects on the stability and change of institutions, processes, and political systems of nations. The unit surveys citizen participation in Western industrialized countries, Africa, and the Middle-East to show that citizen participation underlies the procedures that realize democracy.

Unit 2 builds upon the discussion of citizen participation in unit 1 to address systematically why and how citizen participation is organized, and in what forms. The emphasis in unit 2 is on the relevance of interest groups and political parties as outlets of political behavior that, if repressed or ignored, may lead people to find "less democratic ways" to participate.

Units 3 through 5 consider the institutions of government to address questions regarding the roles they play in the political process, how they affect political behaviors, and, perhaps most importantly, how their successes or failures are evaluated. Unit 3 looks at the executive, noting that accountability and responsiveness to the public is the performance bar for the position. Unit 4 looks at the legislature in Japan, America, Argentina, and Lebanon to show that legislatures embody representation. This foreshadows the discussion and debate over the lack of minority and women representation in government, and how electoral systems influence that representativeness. Unit 5 examines the bureaucracy and the judiciary—the unelected policymakers—to consider the bases of popular resentment against these unelected officials.

Unit 6 focuses on public policy, that is, the outcome of the foregoing discussions of comparative behaviors and institutions. It begins with a reading on how successful policies are achieved: through a coalition of politicians and citizen-groups. This must come as no surprise; however the fact that such coalitions are not more frequent to assure successful policies is indeed surprising. The reason why they are not predominant is because of the debate over what is public versus what is private, which snags almost all discussions over the "right" policies to put in place. As the unit overview states, this debate means that there are few easy answers related to policy-making. It makes clear the importance of the roles of citizens and interest groups in clarifying their policy preferences and mobilizing for their causes. It also underscores the need for executive accountability and responsiveness, and the legislature's representation to ensure that policy-making captures the willingness of the citizenry to make the necessary trade-offs.

Unit 7 completes the volume by considering how institutional changes occur. The relationship between institutions and political behaviors is clearly reciprocal, so the question of how institutional changes occur is timely and important. The readings describe three trends—democratization, globalization, and supra-national governments—to show that domestic demand and new pressures initiate institutional changes. The readings also note that culture, which is frequently cited as an explanation for institutional change, is not a useful explanation because it lacks specificity for systematic evaluation. Those aspiring to be comparativists may take heart in that knowledge: it means that there are no "cultures" that are beyond accountability, responsiveness, representation, and civic participation.

There are several individuals to thank for this current volume. Professor Christian Søe deserves an acknowledgement for his long and hard work on previous annual editions, without which this present volume could not have been conceived. Thanks also to the editorial staff at McGraw-Hill, particularly Debra Henricks, Developmental Editor, for her immense patience with my countless questions, possibilities, and suggestions. I am grateful to Larry Loeppke, Managing Editor for the *McGraw-Hill Contemporary Learning Series,* for his encouragement and generosity in support of the current volume. My research

aide, Andrew Hodgson, provided outstanding research and editing assistance through the highs and lows of this project. There is no doubt that he spent many weekends beyond the call of duty to help with its completion, and it will be hard to fill his shoes. I also thank my colleagues at the University of Kansas, particularly Gary Reich, Hannah Britton, Mark Joslyn, Donald Haider-Markel, and Dorothy Daley, whose support, advice, and critiques helped with the construction and completion of this volume. The responses of the advisory board members are instrumental for the direction of this edition, and I thank them. Finally, thanks to the readers, whose comments helped with the selection of readings. I hope that you will continue to help improve future editions by keeping me informed of your reactions and suggestions for change. Please complete and return the article rating form in the back of the book.

O. Fiona Yap
Editor

Contents

UNIT 1
Citizen Participation: The Foundation of Political Stability and Impetus for Change

The concepts in bold italics are developed in the article. For further expansion, please refer to the Topic Guide.

the democratic label without incurring the political risks that a free society entails. The author asks, "How should such regimes be dealt with?" She notes that promoting democracy in such regimes does not begin or end with removing the leaders.

26

30

33

UNIT 2
Political Parties and Interest Groups: From Preferences to Policies

Unit Overview

36

39

45

48

The concepts in bold italics are developed in the article. For further expansion, please refer to the Topic Guide.

UNIT 3
The Executive: Instituting Accountability and Responsiveness

The concepts in bold italics are developed in the article. For further expansion, please refer to the Topic Guide.

produce the economic and social reforms demanded by the citizenry. However, unpopular decisions remain to be made, and how she pursues and achieves these reforms will be the measure of her success.

UNIT 4
The Legislature: Representation and the Effects of Electoral Systems

The concepts in bold italics are developed in the article. For further expansion, please refer to the Topic Guide.

UNIT 5
The Bureaucracy and Judiciary: Unelected Policy Thugs or Expert Policymakers?

Unit Overview   **116**

The concepts in bold italics are developed in the article. For further expansion, please refer to the Topic Guide.

UNIT 6
Public Policy: Defining Public, Effects and Trade-Offs

The concepts in bold italics are developed in the article. For further expansion, please refer to the Topic Guide.

UNIT 7
Trends and Challenges: Institutional Change through Democratization, Globalization, or Supra-National Government?

The concepts in bold italics are developed in the article. For further expansion, please refer to the Topic Guide.

The concepts in bold italics are developed in the article. For further expansion, please refer to the Topic Guide.

Correlation Guide

The *Annual Editions* series provides students with convenient, inexpensive access to current, carefully selected articles from the public press. **Annual Editions: Comparative Politics 09/10** is an easy-to-use reader that presents articles on important topics such as *citizen participation, the economy, social change,* and many more. For more information on *Annual Editions* and other *McGraw-Hill Contemporary Learning Series* titles, visit www.mhcls.com.

This convenient guide matches the units in **Annual Editions: Comparative Politics 09/10** with the corresponding chapters in one of our best-selling McGraw-Hill Political Science textbooks by Sodaro.

Annual Editions: Comparative Politics 09/10	Comparative Politics: A Global Introduction, 3/e by Sodaro
Unit 1: Citizen Participation: The Foundation of Political Stability and Impetus for Change	**Chapter 7:** Democracy: What Is It? **Chapter 8:** Democracy: How Does It Work? State Institutions and Electoral Systems **Chapter 9:** Democracy: What Does It Take? Ten Conditions **Chapter 10:** Conditions for Democracy in Afghanistan and Iraq **Chapter 11:** People and Politics: Participation in Democracies and Nondemocracies **Chapter 23:** Nigeria and South Africa
Unit 2: Political Parties and Interest Groups: From Preferences to Policies	**Chapter 8:** Democracy: How Does It Work? State Institutions and Electoral Systems **Chapter 11:** People and Politics: Participation in Democracies and Nondemocracies **Chapter 16:** The United Kingdom of Great Britain and Northern Ireland **Chapter 18:** Germany **Chapter 19:** Japan
Unit 3: The Executive: Instituting Accountability and Responsiveness	**Chapter 4:** Power **Chapter 5:** The State and Its Institutions **Chapter 16:** The United Kingdom of Great Britain and Northern Ireland **Chapter 18:** Germany **Chapter 20:** Russia **Chapter 21:** China **Chapter 22:** Mexico and Brazil
Unit 4: The Legislature: Representation and the Effects of Electoral Systems	**Chapter 5:** The State and Its Institutions **Chapter 16:** The United Kingdom of Great Britain and Northern Ireland **Chapter 17:** France **Chapter 18:** Germany **Chapter 19:** Japan
Unit 5: The Bureaucracy and Judiciary: Unelected Policy Thugs or Expert Policymakers?	**Chapter 4:** Power **Chapter 5:** The State and Its Institutions
Unit 6: Public Policy: Defining Public, Effects and Tradeoffs	**Chapter 3:** Critical Thinking About Politics: Analytical Techniques of Political Science—The Logic of Hypothesis Testing **Chapter 14:** Political Economy: Laissez-Faire—Central Planning—Mixed Economies—Welfare States **Chapter 15:** The Politics of Development
Unit 7: Trends and Challenges: Institutional Change through Democratization, Globalization, or Supra-National Government?	**Chapter 2:** Major Topics of Comparative Politics **Chapter 4:** Power **Chapter 6:** States and Nations: Nationalism-Nation Building-Supranationalism **Chapter 12:** Political Culture **Chapter 14:** Political Economy: Laissez-Faire—Central Planning—Mixed Economies—Welfare States **Chapter 15:** The Politics of Development

Topic Guide

This topic guide suggests how the selections in this book relate to the subjects covered in your course. You may want to use the topics listed on these pages to search the Web more easily.

On the following pages a number of Web sites have been gathered specifically for this book. They are arranged to reflect the units of this Annual Editions reader. You can link to these sites by going to *http://www.mhcls.com*.

All the articles that relate to each topic are listed below the bold-faced term.

African society and politics
5. Facing the Challenge of Semi-Authoritarian States
6. People Power

America in comparative perspective
3. Advanced Democracies and the New Politics
8. What Political Institutions Does Large-Scale Democracy Require?
9. Interest Groups: Ex Uno, Plures
10. Political Parties: Empty Vessels?
21. The Case for a Multi-Party U.S. Parliament?
26. Judicial Review: The Gavel and the Robe
36. Job Security, Too, May Have a Happy Medium

Asian politics and society
11. Police Clash with Monks in Myanmar
19. In Quake, Apotheosis of Premier 'Grandpa'
20. Japan's Upper House Censures Prime Minister
33. China: The Quiet Revolution
34. A Confident New Country
35. Japanese Spirit, Western Things
36. Job Security, Too, May Have a Happy Medium
37. Beijing Censors Taken to Task in Party Circles

Citizen participation and mobilization
2. Public Opinion: Is There a Crisis?
3. Advanced Democracies and the New Politics
4. Referendums: The People's Voice
7. Bin Laden, the Arab "Street," and the Middle East's Democracy Deficit
9. Interest Groups: Ex Uno, Plures
11. Police Clash with Monks in Myanmar
12. Concerns Grow About Role of Interest Groups in Elections
13. Venezuela Hands Narrow Defeat to Chávez Plan
22. An Embattled Cristina Fernández de Kirchner
31. The Formation of State Actor-Social Movement Coalitions and Favorable Policy Outcomes

The economy and economics
20. Japan's Upper House Censures Prime Minister
22. An Embattled Cristina Fernández de Kirchner
32. Capitalism and Democracy
33. China: The Quiet Revolution
34. A Confident New Country
35. Japanese Spirit, Western Things
36. Job Security, Too, May Have a Happy Medium

Elections and regime types
1. What Democracy Is . . . and Is Not
5. Facing the Challenge of Semi-Authoritarian States
8. What Political Institutions Does Large-Scale Democracy Require?
12. Concerns Grow About Role of Interest Groups in Elections
15. Russia's Transition to Autocracy
18. How Did We Get Here?
25. Equity in Representation for Women and Minorities

The executive or legislature in less-democratic systems
5. Facing the Challenge of Semi-Authoritarian States
15. Russia's Transition to Autocracy
17. Iran's Conservative Revival
19. In Quake, Apotheosis of Premier 'Grandpa'
23. Iran's Tool Fights America's Stooge

The executive or legislature in mixed systems
6. People Power
8. What Political Institutions Does Large-Scale Democracy Require?
15. Russia's Transition to Autocracy
16. Angela Merkel's Germany

The executive or legislature in parliamentary systems
6. People Power
8. What Political Institutions Does Large-Scale Democracy Require?
14. The Historic Legacy of Tony Blair
20. Japan's Upper House Censures Prime Minister
34. A Confident New Country

The executive or legislature in presidential systems
6. People Power
8. What Political Institutions Does Large-Scale Democracy Require?
18. How Did We Get Here?
21. The Case for a Multi-Party U.S. Parliament?
22. An Embattled Cristina Fernández de Kirchner

Governments in Latin America
5. Facing the Challenge of Semi-Authoritarian States
13. Venezuela Hands Narrow Defeat to Chávez Plan
18. How Did We Get Here?
22. An Embattled Cristina Fernández de Kirchner

Middle East politics
5. Facing the Challenge of Semi-Authoritarian States
7. Bin Laden, the Arab "Street," and the Middle East's Democracy Deficit
17. Iran's Conservative Revival
23. Iran's Tool Fights America's Stooge

Modern communications and politics
4. Referendums: The People's Voice
6. People Power
7. Bin Laden, The Arab "Street," and the Middle East's Democracy Deficit
11. Police Clash with Monks in Myanmar

Internet References

The following Internet sites have been selected to support the articles found in this reader. These sites were available at the time of publication. However, because Web sites often change their structure and content, the information listed may no longer be available. We invite you to visit *http://www.mhcls.com* for easy access to these sites.

Annual Editions: Comparative Politics 09/10

General Sources

Central Intelligence Agency
http://www.odci.gov

Use this official home page to get connections to *The CIA Factbook,* which provides extensive statistical and political information about every country in the world.

National Geographic Society
http://www.nationalgeographic.com

This site provides links to National Geographic's archive of maps, articles, and documents. There is a great deal of material related to political cultures around the world.

U.S. Information Agency
http://usinfo.state.gov/

This USIA page provides definitions, related documentation, and discussion of topics on global issues. Many Web links are provided.

UNIT 1: Citizen Participation: The Foundation of Political Stability and Impetus for Change

Africa News Online
http://allafrica.com/

Open this site for extensive, up-to-date information on all of Africa, with reports from Africa's leading newspapers, magazines, and news agencies. Coverage is country-by-country and regional. Background documents and Internet links are among the resource pages.

ArabNet
http://www.arab.net

This home page of ArabNet, the online resource for the Arab world in the Middle East and North Africa, presents links to 22 Arab countries. Each country Web page classifies information using a standardized system of categories.

Inter-American Dialogue (IAD)
http://www.iadialog.org

This is the Web site for IAD, a premier U.S. center for policy analysis, communication, and exchange in Western Hemisphere affairs. The 100-member organization has helped to shape the agenda of issues and choices in hemispheric relations.

The North American Institute (NAMI)
http://www.northamericaninstitute.org

NAMI, a trinational public-affairs organization concerned with the emerging "regional space" of Canada, the United States, and Mexico, provides links for study of trade, the environment, and institutional developments.

The United Nations
http://un.org/members/

This United Nations webpage provides brief profiles of member-countries and links to the individual countries. The country links include websites to news agencies and sources.

UNIT 2: Political Parties and Interest Groups: From Preferences to Policies

Human Rights Watch
http://www.hrw.org/

This official website of Human Rights Watch describes its beginnings in 1978 as Helsinki Watch. It is the largest human rights organization based in the United States that investigates human rights abuses in all regions of the world and publishes those findings in dozens of books and reports to draw attention to them.

National Geographic Society
http://www.nationalgeographic.com

This site provides links to National Geographic's archive of maps, articles, and documents. There is a great deal of material related to political cultures around the world.

Research and Reference (Library of Congress)
http://www.loc.gov/rr/

This massive research and reference site of the Library of Congress will lead you to invaluable information on the former Soviet Union and other countries attempting the transition to democracy. It provides links to numerous publications, bibliographies, and guides in area studies.

Sun SITE Singapore
http://sunsite.nus.edu.sg/noframe.html

These South East Asia Information pages provide information and point to other online resources about the region's 10 countries, including Vietnam, Indonesia, and Brunei.

UN Interactive Database
http://cyberschoolbus.un.org/infonation/index.asp

This is a United Nations interactive database, InfoNation, to provide official and up-to-date information and statistics regarding UN member countries.

UNIT 3: The Executive: Instituting Accountability and Responsiveness

Germany Chancellor's Website
http://www.bundesregierung.de/Webs/Breg/EN/Homepage/home.html

This official website of the German Chancellor provides links to executive offices and furnishes up-to-date policy and news releases from the office of the executive.

Inside China Today
http://www.einnews.com/china/

Part of the European Internet Network, this site leads to information on China, including recent news, government, and related sites pertaining to mainland China, Hong Kong, Macao, and Taiwan.

Internet References

Prime Minister's Office of Great Britain

http://www.number10.gov.uk

The official prime minister website for Great Britain that furnishes recent policy statements and press releases and provides newsletters and email messages to those signed up for direct contact with the executive.

Russian and East European Network Information Center, University of Texas at Austin

http://reenic.utexas.edu

This is the website for information on Russia and the former Soviet Union.

US White House and Cabinet

http://www.whitehouse.gov/government/cabinet.html

The official White House website for the United States government with links to each of the cabinet members as well as cabinet-ranked members that also provides statements on the executive's stance regarding topical domestic and foreign policies.

UNIT 4: The Legislature: Representation and the Effects of Electoral Systems

Inter-Parliamentary Union

http://www.ipu.org/wmn-e/world.htm

This website of the IPU comprises data for women representatives in national parliaments and some regional assemblies. The IPU is the international organization of Parliaments of sovereign States (Article 1 of the Statutes of the Inter-Parliamentary Union), established in 1889.

Japan Ministry of Foreign Affairs

http://www.mofa.go.jp

Visit this official site for Japanese foreign policy statements and discussions of regional and global relations.

Latin American Network Information Center, University of Texas at Austin

http://lanic.utexas.edu/la/region/government/

The Latin American Network Information Center (LANIC) provides Internet-based information on Latin America and includes source-links to other websites that provide information on Latin American countries.

U.S. Information Agency

http://www.america.gov/

This USIA page provides definitions, related documentation, and discussion of topics on global issues. Many Web links are provided.

World Bank

http://www.worldbank.org

News (press releases, summaries of new projects, speeches) and coverage of numerous topics regarding development, countries, and regions are provided at this site.

UNIT 5: The Bureaucracy and Judiciary: Unelected Policy Thugs or Expert Policymakers?

Central Intelligence Agency

www.cia.gov

Use this official home page to get connections to *The CIA Factbook,* which provides extensive statistical and political information about every country in the world.

Research and Reference (Library of Congress)

http://www.loc.gov/rr/

This massive research and reference site of the Library of Congress will lead you to invaluable information on the former Soviet Union and other countries attempting the transition to democracy. It provides links to numerous publications, bibliographies, and guides in area studies.

United States Executive offices

http://www.usa.gov/Agencies/Federal/Executive.shtml#vgn-executive-office-of-the-president-vgn

The website lists 15 executive departments with links to each of the departments that, in turn, lists the key bureaucratic agencies that report to the respective departments.

U.S. Information Agency

http://www.america.gov/

This USIA page provides definitions, related documentation, and discussion of topics on global issues. Many Web links are provided.

World Wide Web Virtual Library: International Affairs Resources

http://www.etown.edu/vl/

Surf this site and its extensive links to learn about specific countries and regions, to research international organizations, and to study such vital topics as international law, development, the international economy, and human rights.

UNIT 6: Public Policy: Defining Public, Effects and Trade-offs

Asian Development Bank

http://www.adb.org/Countries/

The website provides up-to-date information on 44 developing member countries in Asia regarding social and economic policies to reduce poverty and improve the quality of life of the people.

Carnegie Endowment for International Peace

http://www.ceip.org

This organization's goal is to stimulate discussion and learning among both experts and the public at large on a wide range of international issues. The site provides links to the well-respected journal *Foreign Policy,* to the Moscow Center, to descriptions of various programs, and much more.

IISDnet

http://www.iisd.org/default.asp

This site of the International Institute for Sustainable Development, a Canadian organization, presents information through links on business and sustainable development, developing ideas, and Hot Topics. Linkages is its multimedia resource for environment and development policy makers.

Organization for Economic Cooperation and Development

http://www.oecd.org/home/

Explore development, governance, and world trade and investment issues on this OECD site. It provides links to many related topics and addresses global economic issues on a country-by-country basis.

World Bank

http://www.worldbank.org

News (press releases, summaries of new projects, speeches) and coverage of numerous topics regarding development, countries, and regions are provided at this site.

Internet References

UNIT 7: Trends and Challenges: Institutional Change through Democratization, Globalization, or Supra-National Government?

Commission on Global Governance

http://www.sovereignty.net/p/gov/gganalysis.htm

This site provides access to *The Report of the Commission on Global Governance,* produced by an international group of leaders who want to find ways in which the global community can better manage its affairs.

Europa: European Union

http://europa.eu.int

This server site of the European Union will lead you to the history of the EU; descriptions of EU policies, institutions, and goals; discussion of monetary union; and documentation of treaties and other materials.

ISN International Relations and Security Network

http://www.isn.ethz.ch

This site, maintained by the Center for Security Studies and Conflict Research, is a clearinghouse for extensive information on international relations and security policy. Topics are listed by category (Traditional Dimensions of Security, New Dimensions of Security) and by major world regions.

NATO Integrated Data Service (NIDS)

http://www.nato.int/structur/nids/nids.htm

NIDS was created to bring information on security-related matters to the widest possible audience. Check out this website to review North Atlantic Treaty Organization documentation of all kinds, to read *NATO Review,* and to explore key issues in the field of European security.

United Nations Environment Program

http://www.unep.ch/

Consult this home page of UNEP for links to critical topics about global issues, including decertification and the impact of trade on the environment. The site leads to useful databases and global resource information.*http://www.amenetwork.org/*

World Map

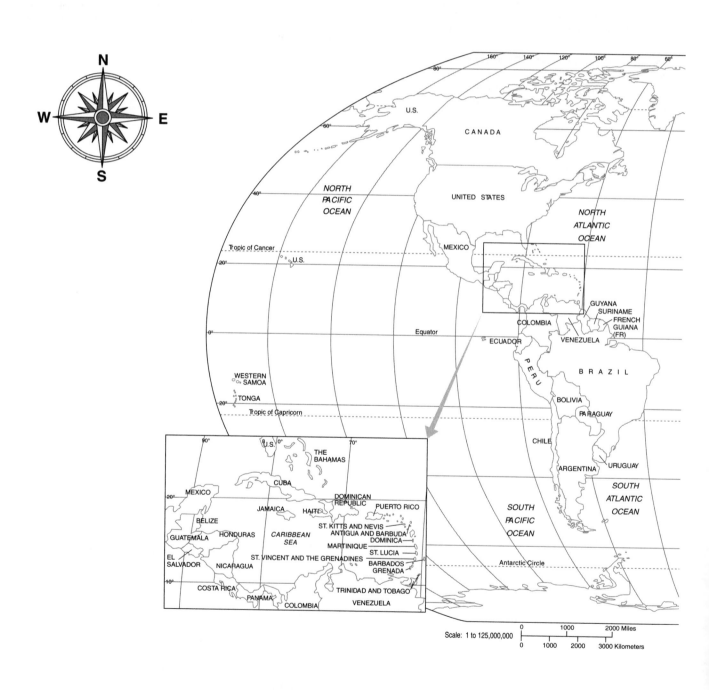

Scale: 1 to 125,000,000

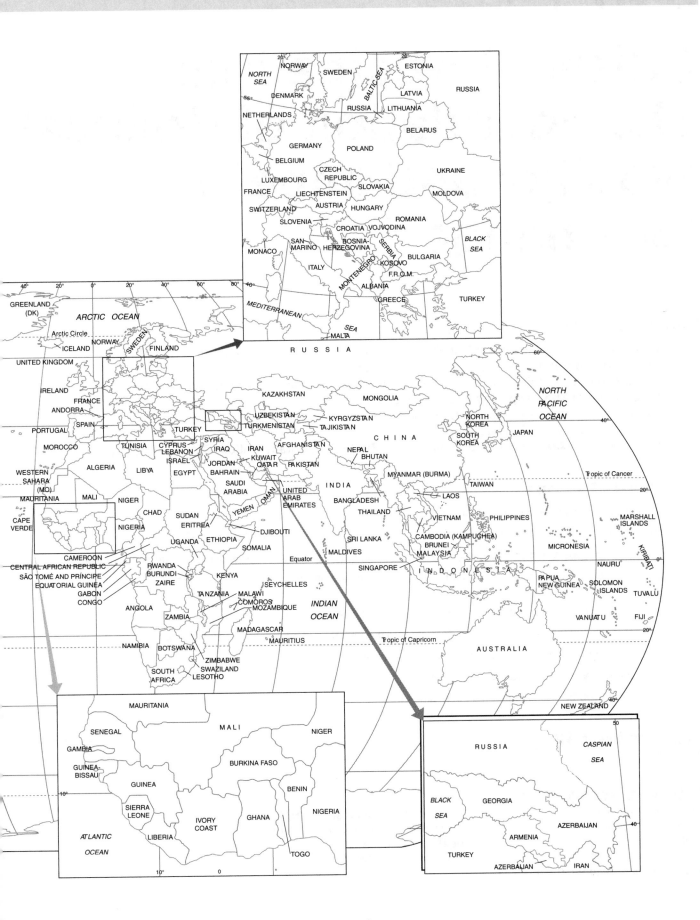

UNIT 1

Citizen Participation: The Foundation of Political Stability and Impetus for Change

Unit Selections

Key Points to Consider

- How does citizen participation buttress democracy?

- What does it mean that western democracies focus on how to "help" other countries "catch-up?"

- Is democracy in the western countries in jeopardy? What evidence suggests that? What evidence suggests otherwise?

- Is a liberal democracy always more efficient and productive than an authoritarian society? Is a liberal democracy always more affluent and harmonious than an authoritarian one?

- What are the concerns regarding citizen participation through the referendum?

- What does it mean that western democracies fear the "most democratic of devices" (the referendum)?

- What lessons do western democracies have to offer other countries?

- What lessons do western democracies have to learn?

- Why do political hybrids, or semi-authoritarian regimes exist?

Student Web Site

www.mhcls.com

Internet References

Africa News Online
http://allafrica.com/
ArabNet
http://www.arab.net
Inter-American Dialogue (IAD)
http://www.iadialog.org

The North American Institute (NAMI)
http://www.northamericaninstitute.org
The United Nations
http://un.org/members/

© Digital Vision

What is comparative politics? What do we compare? How do we compare? Why do we compare?

Comparative Politics refers to the study of governments. That seems clear. Yet, popular dictionaries such as the Merriam-Webster's Dictionary contain no less than five and as many as ten different ways of conceiving the word "government." They include[1]:

1. The exercise of authority over a state, district, or territory;
2. A system of ruling, controlling, or administering;
3. The executive branch of a government;
4. All the people and institutions that exercise control over the affairs of a nation or state;
5. The study of such systems, people, and institutions.

These definitions emphasize several concepts integral to comparative politics. They are: authority, system, people and institutions, and state, district, or territory.

What do we compare? In the broadest sense, comparative politics involves the systematic comparison of authority, systems, people and institutions across states, districts, or other territories. Its focus is on what Joseph La Palombara once called *Politics Within Nations.*[2] In other words, comparative politics focuses on the patterns of politics within a domestic territory, where political parties, interest groups, civil servants, public and published opinion are among the many participants in the political process.

How do we compare? Comparative politics emphasizes careful empirical study as the way to gain knowledge about how people and governments behave and interact politically, given rules and institutions that are in place. It is important to note that other disciplines also study how people and governments behave; however, their goals or ends for such study are different. Figure 1 lists six disciplines that study governments and describes what they are, the focus, method, strengths, appeal, and weaknesses of each of these disciplines. For example, the history discipline may also study governments; however, the focus of such study is directed at fact-finding and gathering to enhance interpretation and accuracy. This means that country or area expertise does not necessarily distinguish one as a comparative political scholar.

1

Discipline	History	Sociology	Area Studies	Political Science	Economics	Journalism
What it does	Describes, interprets, or explains individual events or time-related series of events.	Understands what connects the person (personal) to the group (social).	Provides country or region-specific information, particularly on language, customs, religion, or culture.	Identifies systematic patterns over time.	Deduces reasoning from mathematical models.	"Spot" analysis/ description of individual events or policy.
Focus	Past events	Groups, relations	City, region, country, area	Institutions, behaviors	Mathematical models	Current events, policies
Method	Akin to fitting a jigsaw—are all the pieces there? The end picture is available.	Solving mystery—what group identities lead people to behave the way they do?	Akin to fitting a jigsaw—are all the pieces there? The end picture is sometimes available.	Solving mystery—what do people do in order to keep/ protect what they have?	Solving mystery—how do different incentives lead people to behave differently? (Behaviors are known.)	Uncovering information—through investigation, expert testimony, debate, inference.
Strengths	Uncovers situations, information, motivations, personalities, of the past.	Clarifies racial, ethnic, area and women's studies. (Probabilistic predictions.)	Rich, detailed knowledge of predispositions.	Prediction, generalization (Probabilistic predictions.)	Prediction, generalization (Probabilistic predictions.)	Details (information, motivations) from spot analysis of situation, event.
Appeal	Intelligence & information to enhance interpretation and accuracy. Story-telling, puzzle-solving approach allows students to improve insights and affirm expectations.	Provide connections between student and larger society. Allows student to investigate personally significant behaviors in larger context.	Intelligence & information to enhance interpretation and accuracy. Story-telling and puzzle-solving approach allows students to improve insights and affirm expectations.	Explains why and how institutions/ processes are developed, evolved, changed. Supported by evidence that is methodically culled.	Mathematical modeling, allows for study and theorizing of human behaviors that is not otherwise possible.	Story-telling, expose, investigation, debate. Spot analysis provides information, specifics, and may reduce uncertainty surrounding situation/ event/ policy.
Weaknesses	Focus on interpretation and insights, not predictions. Therefore, theories not always generalizable.	Individual motivations entirely developed from the group.	Focus on interpretation and insights, not predictions. Therefore, theories not always generalizable.	Individual events are low on totem pole of study.	Empiricism not always important.	Not theoretically driven—therefore, cannot explain change or predict (conjecture).

Figure 1 Disciplinary differences in the study of governments

2

Why do we compare? Two reasons are particularly noteworthy: First, as depicted in the figure and reiterated in the previous paragraph, we compare in order to clarify, explain, derive predictions, and enhance theory-building. Thus, for the political practitioner, analyst, or scholar, comparative politics is applied toward understanding, in order to generate explanations or predictions about changes or stability. Second, it provides a way to systematically consider how people and institutions across different countries, districts, or systems balance the competing goals of stability, change, security, freedom, growth, accountability and responsiveness.[3]

Here's another way to think about it: The UN recognizes 192 countries; that does not include several that are not UN members.[4] The U.S. government recognizes 194 autonomous countries in the world.[5] The list easily expands beyond 250 if we include nations that are self-governing as well as those that are not. A nation is defined as "a group of people whose members share a common identity on the basis of distinguishing characteristics and claim to a territorial homeland" (Sodaro 2007).[6] Each of these nations or countries has long histories that may bear on the government's behaviors or the responses of their people and also influence what institutions and rules are considered and adopted. Clearly, learning about the particularities of even one country requires considerable time and effort, let alone the more than 100 formally recognized ones.

Comparative politics provides systematic generalizations regarding political behaviors, processes, and institutions to promote learning with greater efficiency. This is not to say that the particularities are not important. Rather, it emphasizes that, at a minimum, generalizations are necessary to provide baseline knowledge from which particularities are observed, described, explained, and predicted. And, for those new to comparative politics, it is probably intriguing that different countries and systems, nevertheless, share fundamental behaviors, processes, and institutions to achieve the balance between stability, change, security, freedom, growth, accountability and responsiveness.

Each of the units in this book introduces some of these generalizations and shows how even nations, institutions, or behaviors that are conventionally presented as particularistic or peculiar, are actually consistent with such generalizations. This first unit describes citizen participation and its effects on the stability and change of institutions, processes, political systems, or nations. Citizen participation refers to acts of political involvement. Its most common and basic form is the electoral vote, but it includes more complex forms, such as direct policy-making through the referendum.

Citizen participation is fundamental to democracy. What is interesting, of course, is that most advocates of democracy discuss and debate democracy in normative terms without clarifying how citizen participation relates to democracy. The first article, "What Democracy Is . . . and Is Not," returns the discussion back to its roots—citizen participation—and outlines clearly how citizen participation underpins democracy. The set of guidelines on procedural democracy shows that there is "no single set of actual institutions, practices, or values embodying democracy."

The articles in the unit show that no country or nation can lay claim to encompassing the ideal of democracy. Thus, the next set of three articles show that even as the Western industrialized democracies are quick to "help" other countries achieve democracy, their citizens are expressing dissatisfaction and loss of confidence in political leaders and institutions and, in fact, jockeying for greater participation in policy-making in their respective countries. One may think that this is a welcome development among democracy advocates in these countries. Yet, the article, "Referendums: The People's Voice" shows that there are significant concerns with the use of this "most democratic of devices." Does this seem hypocritical? If it does, it underscores the problem of considering democracy from a moral or normative standpoint.

The alternative, offered in comparative politics, is to consider democracy from the perspective of empirical study. From this viewpoint, democracy is an evolution of practices and procedures that fundamentally encapsulates citizens' preferences as expressed through their participation.

What is to be gained from this perspective? At a minimum, it highlights the importance of increasing citizen participation. Increasing citizen participation allows practices and procedures to evolve and, hence, promotes stability; reducing or dismissing citizen participation leads to potentially dangerous forms of participation to push for change. How dangerous? The article on the African subcontinent highlights how the failure to increase participation led citizens in Zimbabwe to mobilize and challenge Mugabe's regimes. The article on Bin Laden also shows how citizens are responding to limitations on participation by involvement in extremist activities. And, the article on political hybrids explains how semi-authoritarian regimes that have opened up the participation processes have achieved a level of stability that allows the governments there to remain semi-authoritarian.

There is no question of our responses to the three situations: we are infinitely more impressed by the efforts and determination of the opposition movement in Zimbabwe; unambiguously more disturbed by Bin Laden's appeal; and appalled at the political stasis in the semi-authoritarian states. What we learn from a systematic perspective is that all three situations underscore the same argument: citizen participation underpins stability, so that the failure to provide for that participation leads potentially to perilous forms of participation to push for change.

Comparative politics, then, shows the problems of letting our own biases dictate who gets to participate, and how or when. In the process, we also learn a fundamental and important lesson about participation: if we provide for citizen participation, then the available venues free any potentially bottled up responses that may otherwise find relief through dangerous or extremist appeals.

Notes

1. *Merriam-Webster's Online Dictionary.*
   http://www.merriam-webster.com/dictionary/government.
   <accessed August 7, 2008>

2. Joseph La Palombara. 1974. *Politics within Nations.* Englewood Cliffs, N.J. : Prentice Hall.

3. See also Gabriel Almond, G. Bingham Powell, Russell Dalton, and Kaare Strom. 2007. *Comparative Politics Today: A World View.* New York: Pearson Longman Publishers, 9th edition.

4. The United Nations.
   http://un.org/News/Press/docs//2007/org1479.doc.htm
   <accessed August 7, 2008> http://www.countryreports.org/

5. US Department of State.
   http://www.state.gov/s/inr/rls/4250.htm <accessed August 7, 2008>

6. Michael Sodaro. 2007. *Comparative Politics: A Global Introduction.* 3rd edition. New York: McGraw Hill.

What Democracy Is . . . and Is Not

Philippe C. Schmitter and Terry Lynn Karl

For some time, the word democracy has been circulating as a debased currency in the political marketplace. Politicians with a wide range of convictions and practices strove to appropriate the label and attach it to their actions. Scholars, conversely, hesitated to use it—without adding qualifying adjectives—because of the ambiguity that surrounds it. The distinguished American political theorist Robert Dahl even tried to introduce a new term, "polyarchy," in its stead in the (vain) hope of gaining a greater measure of conceptual precision. But for better or worse, we are "stuck" with democracy as the catchword of contemporary political discourse. It is the word that resonates in people's minds and springs from their lips as they struggle for freedom and a better way of life; it is the word whose meaning we must discern if it is to be of any use in guiding political analysis and practice.

The wave of transitions away from autocratic rule that began with Portugal's "Revolution of the Carnations" in 1974 and seems to have crested with the collapse of communist regimes across Eastern Europe in 1989 has produced a welcome convergence toward [a] common definition of democracy.[1] Everywhere there has been a silent abandonment of dubious adjectives like "popular," "guided," "bourgeois," and "formal" to modify "democracy." At the same time, a remarkable consensus has emerged concerning the minimal conditions that polities must meet in order to merit the prestigious appellation of "democratic." Moreover, a number of international organizations now monitor how well these standards are met; indeed, some countries even consider them when formulating foreign policy.[2]

What Democracy Is

Let us begin by broadly defining democracy and the generic *concepts* that distinguish it as a unique system for organizing relations between rulers and the ruled. We will then briefly review *procedures*, the rules and arrangements that are needed if democracy is to endure. Finally, we will discuss two operative *principles* that make democracy work. They are not expressly included among the generic concepts or formal procedures, but the prospect for democracy is grim if their underlying conditioning effects are not present.

One of the major themes of this essay is that democracy does not consist of a single unique set of institutions. There are many types of democracy, and their diverse practices produce a similarly varied set of effects. The specific form democracy takes is contingent upon a country's socioeconomic conditions as well as its entrenched state structures and policy practices.

Modern political democracy is a system of governance in which rulers are held accountable for their actions in the public realm by citizens, acting indirectly through the competition and cooperation of their elected representatives.[3]

A *regime or system of governance* is an ensemble of patterns that determines the methods of access to the principal public offices; the characteristics of the actors admitted to or excluded from such access; the strategies that actors may use to gain access; and the rules that are followed in the making of publicly binding decisions. To work properly, the ensemble must be institutionalized—that is to say, the various patterns must be habitually known, practiced, and accepted by most, if not all, actors. Increasingly, the preferred mechanism of institutionalization is a written body of laws undergirded by a written constitution, though many enduring political norms can have an informal, prudential, or traditional basis.[4]

For the sake of economy and comparison, these forms, characteristics, and rules are usually bundled together and given a generic label. Democratic is one; others are autocratic, authoritarian, despotic, dictatorial, tyrannical, totalitarian, absolutist, traditional, monarchic, obligarchic, plutocratic, aristocratic, and sultanistic.[5] Each of these regime forms may in turn be broken down into subtypes.

Like all regimes, democracies depend upon the presence of *rulers*, persons who occupy specialized authority roles and can give legitimate commands to others. What distinguishes democratic rulers from nondemocratic ones are the norms that condition how the former come to power and the practices that hold them accountable for their actions.

> "However central to democracy, elections occur intermittently and only allow citizens to choose between the highly aggregated alternatives offered by political parties . . . "

The *public realm* encompasses the making of collective norms and choices that are binding on the society and backed by state coercion. Its content can vary a great deal across democracies, depending upon preexisting distinctions between the public and the private, state and society, legitimate coercion and voluntary exchange, and collective needs and individual preferences. The liberal conception of democracy advocates circumscribing the public realm as narrowly as possible, while the socialist or social-democratic approach would extend that realm through regulation, subsidization, and, in some cases, collective ownership of property. Neither is intrinsically more democratic than the other—just *differently* democratic. This implies that measures aimed at "developing the private sector" are no more democratic than those aimed at "developing the public sector." Both, if carried to extremes, could undermine the practice of democracy, the former by destroying the basis for satisfying collective needs and exercising legitimate authority; the latter by destroying the basis for satisfying individual preferences and controlling illegitimate government actions. Differences of opinion over the optimal mix of the two provide much of the substantive content of political conflict within established democracies.

Citizens are the most distinctive element in democracies. All regimes have rulers and a public realm, but only to the extent that they are democratic do they have citizens. Historically, severe restrictions on citizenship were imposed in most emerging or partial democracies according to criteria of age, gender, class, race, literacy, property ownership, tax-paying status, and so on. Only a small part of the total population was eligible to vote or run for office. Only restricted social categories were allowed to form, join, or support political associations. After protracted struggle—in some cases involving violent domestic upheaval or international war—most of these restrictions were lifted. Today, the criteria for inclusion are fairly standard. All native-born adults are eligible, although somewhat higher age limits may still be imposed upon candidates for certain offices. Unlike the early American and European democracies of the nineteenth century, none of the recent democracies in southern Europe, Latin America, Asia, or Eastern Europe has even attempted to impose formal restrictions on the franchise or eligibility to office. When it comes to informal restrictions on the effective exercise of citizenship rights, however, the story can be quite different. This explains the central importance (discussed below) of procedures.

Competition has not always been considered an essential defining condition of democracy. "Classic" democracies presumed decision making based on direct participation leading to consensus. The assembled citizenry was expected to agree on a common course of action after listening to the alternatives and weighing their respective merits and demerits. A tradition of hostility to "faction," and "particular interests" persists in democratic thought, but at least since *The Federalist Papers* it has become widely accepted that competition among factions is a necessary evil in democracies that operate on a more-than-local scale. Since, as James Madison argued, "the latent causes of faction are sown into the nature of man," and the possible remedies for "the mischief of faction" are worse than the disease, the best course is to recognize them and to attempt to control their effects.[6] Yet while democrats may agree on the inevitability of factions, they tend to disagree about the best forms and rules for governing factional competition. Indeed,

differences over the preferred modes and boundaries of competition contribute most to distinguishing one subtype of democracy from another.

The most popular definition of democracy equates it with regular *elections*, fairly conducted and honestly counted. Some even consider the mere fact of elections—even ones from which specific parties or candidates are excluded, or in which substantial portions of the population cannot freely participate—as a sufficient condition for the existence of democracy. This fallacy has been called "electoralism" or "the faith that merely holding elections will channel political action into peaceful contests among elites and accord public legitimacy to the winners"—no matter how they are conducted or what else constrains those who win them.[7] However central to democracy, elections occur intermittently and only allow citizens to choose between the highly aggregated alternatives offered by political parties, which can, especially in the early stages of a democratic transition, proliferate in a bewildering variety. During the intervals between elections, citizens can seek to influence public policy through a wide variety of other intermediaries: interest associations, social movements, locality groupings, clientelistic arrangements, and so forth. *Modern democracy, in other words, offers a variety of competitive processes and channels for the expression of interests and values—associational as well as partisan, functional as well as territorial, collective as well as individual. All are integral to its practice.*

Another commonly accepted image of democracy identifies it with *majority rule*. Any governing body that makes decisions by combining the votes of more than half of those eligible and present is said to be democratic, whether that majority emerges within an electorate, a parliament, a committee, a city council, or a party caucus. For exceptional purposes (e.g., amending the constitution or expelling a member), "qualified majorities" of more than 50 percent may be required, but few would deny that democracy must involve some means of aggregating the equal preferences of individuals.

A problem arises, however, when *numbers* meet *intensities*. What happens when a properly assembled majority (especially a stable, self-perpetuating one) regularly makes decisions that harm some minority (especially a threatened cultural or ethnic group)? In these circumstances, successful democracies tend to qualify the central principle of majority rule in order to protect minority rights. Such qualifications can take the form of constitutional provisions that place certain matters beyond the reach of majorities (bills of rights); requirements for concurrent majorities in several different constituencies (confederalism); guarantees securing the autonomy of local or regional governments against the demands of the central authority (federalism); grand coalition governments that incorporate all parties (consociationalism); or the negotiation of social pacts between major social groups like business and labor (neocorporatism). The most common and effective way of protecting minorities, however, lies in the everyday operation of interest associations and social movements. These reflect (some would say, amplify) the different intensities of preference that exist in the population and bring them to bear on democratically elected decision makers. Another way of putting this intrinsic tension between numbers and intensities would be to say that "in modern democracies, votes may be counted, but influences alone are weighted."

Cooperation has always been a central feature of democracy. Actors must voluntarily make collective decisions binding on the polity as a whole. They must cooperate in order to compete. They must be capable of acting collectively through parties, associations, and movements in order to select candidates, articulate preferences, petition authorities, and influence policies.

But democracy's freedoms should also encourage citizens to deliberate among themselves, to discover their common needs, and to resolve their differences without relying on some supreme central authority. Classical democracy emphasized these qualities, and they are by no means extinct, despite repeated efforts by contemporary theorists to stress the analogy with behavior in the economic marketplace and to reduce all of democracy's operations to competitive interest maximization. Alexis de Tocqueville best described the importance of independent groups for democracy in his *Democracy in America*, a work which remains a major source of inspiration for all those who persist in viewing democracy as something more than a struggle for election and re-election among competing candidates.[8]

In contemporary political discourse, this phenomenon of cooperation and deliberation via autonomous group activity goes under the rubric of "civil society." The diverse units of social identity and interest, by remaining independent of the state (and perhaps even of parties), not only can restrain the arbitrary actions of rulers, but can also contribute to forming better citizens who are more aware of the preferences of others, more self-confident in their actions, and more civic-minded in their willingness to sacrifice for the common good. At its best, civil society provides an intermediate layer of governance between the individual and the state that is capable of resolving conflicts and controlling the behavior of members without public coercion. Rather than overloading decision makers with increased demands and making the system ungovernable,[9] a viable civil society can mitigate conflicts and improve the quality of citizenship—without relying exclusively on the privatism of the marketplace.

Representatives—whether directly or indirectly elected—do most of the real work in modern democracies. Most are professional politicians who orient their careers around the desire to fill key offices. It is doubtful that any democracy could survive without such people. The central question, therefore, is not whether or not there will be a political elite or even a professional political class, but how these representatives are chosen and then held accountable for their actions.

As noted above, there are many channels of representation in modern democracy. The electoral one, based on territorial constituencies, is the most visible and public. It culminates in a parliament or a presidency that is periodically accountable to the citizenry as a whole. Yet the sheer growth of government (in large part as a byproduct of popular demand) has increased the number, variety, and power of agencies charged with making public decisions and not subject to elections. Around these agencies there has developed a vast apparatus of specialized representation based largely on functional interests, not territorial constituencies. These interest associations, and not political parties, have become the primary expression of civil society in most stable democracies, supplemented by the more sporadic interventions of social movements.

The new and fragile democracies that have sprung up since 1974 must live in "compressed time." They will not resemble the European democracies of the nineteenth and early twentieth centuries, and they cannot expect to acquire the multiple channels of representation in gradual historical progression as did most of their predecessors. A bewildering array of parties, interests, and movements will all simultaneously seek political influence in them, creating challenges to the polity that did not exist in earlier processes of democratization.

Procedures That Make Democracy Possible

The defining components of democracy are necessarily abstract, and may give rise to a considerable variety of institutions and subtypes of democracy. For democracy to thrive, however, specific procedural norms must be followed and civic rights must be respected. Any polity that fails to impose such restrictions upon itself, that fails to follow the "rule of law" with regard to its own procedures, should not be considered democratic. These procedures alone do not define democracy, but their presence is indispensable to its persistence. In essence, they are necessary but not sufficient conditions for its existence.

Robert Dahl has offered the most generally accepted listing of what he terms the "procedural minimal" conditions that must be present for modern political democracy (or as he puts it, "polyarchy") to exist:

1. Control over government decisions about policy is constitutionally vested in elected officials.
2. Elected officials are chosen in frequent and fairly conducted elections in which coercion is comparatively uncommon.
3. Practically all adults have the right to vote in the election of officials.
4. Practically all adults have the right to run for elective offices.
5. Citizens have a right to express themselves without the danger of severe punishment on political matters broadly defined. . . .
6. Citizens have a right to seek out alternative sources of information. Moreover, alternative sources of information exist and are protected by law.
7. . . . Citizens also have the right to form relatively independent associations or organizations, including independent political parties and interest groups.[10]

These seven conditions seem to capture the essence of procedural democracy for many theorists, but we propose to add two others. The first might be thought of as a further refinement of item (1), while the second might be called an implicit prior condition to all seven of the above.

1. Popularly elected officials must be able to exercise their constitutional powers without being subjected to overriding (albeit informal) opposition from unelected officials. Democracy is in jeopardy if military officers, entrenched civil servants, or state managers retain the capacity to act independently of elected civilians or even veto decisions made by the people's representatives. Without this additional caveat, the militarized polities of contemporary Central America, where civilian control over the military does not exist, might be classified by many scholars as democracies, just as they have been (with the exception of Sandinista Nicaragua) by U.S. policy makers. The caveat thus guards against what we earlier called "electoralism"—the tendency to focus on the holding of elections while ignoring other political realities.

2. The polity must be self-governing; it must be able to act independently of constraints imposed by some other overarching political system. Dahl and other contemporary democratic theorists probably took this condition for granted since they referred to formally sovereign nation-states. However, with the development of blocs, alliances, spheres of influence, and a variety of "neocolonial" arrangements, the question of autonomy has been a salient one. Is a system really democratic if its elected officials are unable to make binding decisions without the approval of actors outside their territorial domain? This is significant even if the outsiders are relatively free to alter or even end the encompassing arrangement (as in Puerto Rico), but it becomes especially critical if neither condition obtains (as in the Baltic states).

Principles That Make Democracy Feasible

Lists of component processes and procedural norms help us to specify what democracy is, but they do not tell us much about how it actually functions. The simplest answer is "by the consent of the people"; the more complex one is "by the contingent consent of politicians acting under conditions of bounded uncertainty."

In a democracy, representatives must at least informally agree that those who win greater electoral support or influence over policy will not use their temporary superiority to bar the losers from taking office or exerting influence in the future, and that in exchange for this opportunity to keep competing for power and place, momentary losers will respect the winners' right to make binding decisions. Citizens are expected to obey the decisions ensuing from such a process of competition, provided its outcome remains contingent upon their collective preferences as expressed through fair and regular elections or open and repeated negotiations.

The challenge is not so much to find a set of goals that command widespread consensus as to find a set of rules that embody contingent consent. The precise shape of this "democratic bargain," to use Dahl's expression,[11] can vary a good deal from society to society. It depends on social cleavages and such subjective factors as mutual trust, the standard of fairness, and the willingness to compromise. It may even be compatible with a great deal of dissensus on substantive policy issues.

All democracies involve a degree of uncertainty about who will be elected and what policies they will pursue. Even in those polities where one party persists in winning elections or one policy is consistently implemented, the possibility of change through independent collective action still exists, as in Italy, Japan, and the Scandinavian social democracies. If it does not, the system is not democratic, as in Mexico, Senegal, or Indonesia.

But the uncertainty embedded in the core of all democracies is bounded. Not just any actor can get into the competition and raise any issue he or she pleases—there are previously established rules that must be respected. Not just any policy can be adopted—there are conditions that must be met. Democracy institutionalizes "normal," limited political uncertainty. These boundaries vary from country to country. Constitutional guarantees of property, privacy, expression, and other rights are a part of this, but the most effective boundaries are generated by competition among interest groups and cooperation within civil society. Whatever the rhetoric (and some polities appear to offer their citizens more dramatic alternatives than others), once the rules of contingent consent have been agreed upon, the actual variation is likely to stay within a predictable and generally accepted range.

This emphasis on operative guidelines contrasts with a highly persistent, but misleading theme in recent literature on democracy—namely, the emphasis upon "civic culture." The principles we have suggested here rest on rules of prudence, not on deeply ingrained habits of tolerance, moderation, mutual respect, fair play, readiness to compromise, or trust in public authorities. Waiting for such habits to sink deep and lasting roots implies a very slow process of regime consolidation—one that takes generations—and it would probably condemn most contemporary experiences *ex hypothesi* to failure. Our assertion is that contingent consent and bounded uncertainty can emerge from the interaction between antagonistic and mutually suspicious actors and that the far more benevolent and ingrained norms of a civic culture are better thought of as a *product* and not a producer of democracy.

How Democracies Differ

Several concepts have been deliberately excluded from our generic definition of democracy, despite the fact that they have been frequently associated with it in both everyday practice and scholarly work. They are, nevertheless, especially important when it comes to distinguishing subtypes of democracy. Since no single set of actual institutions, practices, or values embodies democracy, polities moving away from authoritarian rule can mix different components to produce different democracies. It is important to recognize that these do not define points along a single continuum of improving performance, but a matrix of potential combinations that are *differently* democratic.

1. *Consensus*: All citizens may not agree on the substantive goals of political action or on the role of the state (although if they did, it would certainly make governing democracies much easier).

2. *Participation*: All citizens may not take an active and equal part in politics, although it must be legally possible for them to do so.

3. *Access*: Rulers may not weigh equally the preferences of all who come before them, although citizenship implies that individuals and groups should have an equal opportunity to express their preferences if they choose to do so.

4. *Responsiveness*: Rulers may not always follow the course of action preferred by the citizenry. But when they deviate from such a policy, say on grounds of "reason of state" or "overriding national interest," they must ultimately be held accountable for their actions through regular and fair processes.

5. *Majority rule*: Positions may not be allocated or rules may not be decided solely on the basis of assembling the most votes, although deviations from this principle usually must be explicitly defended and previously approved.

6. *Parliamentary sovereignty*: The legislature may not be the only body that can make rules or even the one with final authority in deciding which laws are binding, although where executive, judicial, or other public bodies make that ultimate choice, they too must be accountable for their actions.

7. *Party government*: Rulers may not be nominated, promoted, and disciplined in their activities by well-organized and programmatically coherent political parties, although where they are not, it may prove more difficult to form an effective government.

8. *Pluralism*: The political process may not be based on a multiplicity of overlapping, voluntaristic, and autonomous private groups. However, where there are monopolies of representation, hierarchies of association, and obligatory memberships, it is likely that the interests involved will be more closely linked to the state and the separation between the public and private spheres of action will be much less distinct.

9. *Federalism*: The territorial division of authority may not involve multiple levels and local autonomies, least of all ones enshrined in a constitutional document, although some dispersal of power across territorial and/or functional units is characteristic of all democracies.

10. *Presidentialism*: The chief executive officer may not be a single person and he or she may not be directly elected by the citizenry as a whole, although some concentration of authority is present in all democracies, even if it is exercised collectively and only held indirectly accountable to the electorate.

11. *Checks and Balances*: It is not necessary that the different branches of government be systematically pitted against one another, although governments by assembly, by executive concentrations, by judicial command, or even by dictatorial fiat (as in time of war) must be ultimately accountable to the citizenry as a whole.

While each of the above has been named as an essential component of democracy, they should instead be seen either as indicators of this or that type of democracy, or else as useful standards for evaluating the performance of particular regimes. To include them as part of the generic definition of democracy itself would be to mistake the American polity for the universal model of democratic governance. Indeed, the parliamentary, consociational, unitary, corporatist, and concentrated arrangements of continental Europe may have some unique virtues for guiding polities through the uncertain transition from autocratic to democratic rule.[12]

What Democracy Is Not

We have attempted to convey the general meaning of modern democracy without identifying it with some particular set of rules and institutions or restricting it to some specific culture or level of development. We have also argued that it cannot be reduced to the regular holding of elections or equated with a particular notion of the role of the state, but we have not said much more about what democracy is not or about what democracy may not be capable of producing.

There is an understandable temptation to load too many expectations on this concept and to imagine that by attaining democracy, a society will have resolved all of its political, social, economic, administrative, and cultural problems. Unfortunately, "all good things do not necessarily go together."

First, democracies are not necessarily more efficient economically than other forms of government. Their rates of aggregate growth, savings, and investment may be no better than those of nondemocracies. This is especially likely during the transition, when propertied groups and administrative elites may respond to real or imagined threats to the "rights" they enjoyed under authoritarian rule by initiating capital flight, disinvestment, or sabotage. In time, depending upon the type of democracy, benevolent long-term effects upon income distribution, aggregate demand, education, productivity, and creativity may eventually combine to improve economic and social performance, but it is certainly too much to expect that these improvements will occur immediately—much less that they will be defining characteristics of democratization.

Second, democracies are not necessarily more efficient administratively. Their capacity to make decisions may even be slower than that of the regimes they replace, if only because more actors must be consulted. The costs of getting things done may be higher, if only because "payoffs" have to be made to a wider and more resourceful set of clients (although one should never underestimate the degree of corruption to be found within autocracies). Popular satisfaction with the new democratic government's performance may not even seem greater, if only because necessary compromises often please no one completely, and because the losers are free to complain.

Third, democracies are not likely to appear more orderly, consensual, stable, or governable than the autocracies they replace. This is partly a byproduct of democratic freedom of expression, but it is also a reflection of the likelihood of continuing disagreement over new rules and institutions. These products of imposition or compromise are often initially quite ambiguous in nature and uncertain in effect until actors have learned how to use them. What is more, they come in the aftermath of serious struggles motivated by high ideals. Groups and individuals with recently acquired autonomy will test certain rules, protest against the actions of certain institutions, and insist on renegotiating their part of the bargain. Thus the presence of antisystem parties should be neither surprising nor seen as a failure of democratic consolidation. What counts is whether such parties are willing, however reluctantly, to play by the general rules of bounded uncertainty and contingent consent.

Governability is a challenge for all regimes, not just democratic ones. Given the political exhaustion and loss of legitimacy that have befallen autocracies from sultanistic Paraguay to totalitarian Albania, it may seem that only democracies can now be expected to govern effectively and legitimately. Experience has shown, however, that democracies too can lose the ability to govern. Mass publics can become disenchanted with their performance. Even more threatening is the temptation for leaders to fiddle with procedures and ultimately undermine the principles of contingent consent and bounded uncertainty. Perhaps the most critical moment comes once the politicians begin to settle into the more predictable roles and relations of a consolidated democracy. Many will find their expectations frustrated; some will discover that the new rules of competition put them at a disadvantage; a few may even feel that their vital interests are threatened by popular majorities.

Finally, democracies will have more open societies and polities than the autocracies they replace, but not necessarily more open economies. Many of today's most successful and well-established democracies have historically resorted to protectionism and closed borders, and have relied extensively upon public institutions to promote economic development. While the long-term compatibility between democracy and capitalism does not seem to be in doubt, despite their continuous tension, it is not clear whether the promotion of such liberal economic goals as the right of individuals to own property and retain profits, the clearing function of markets, the private settlement of disputes, the freedom to produce without government regulation, or the privatization of state-owned enterprises necessarily furthers the consolidation of democracy. After all, democracies do need to levy taxes and regulate certain transactions, especially where private monopolies and oligopolies exist. Citizens or their representatives may decide that it is desirable to protect the rights of collectivities from encroachment by individuals, especially propertied ones, and

they may choose to set aside certain forms of property for public or cooperative ownership. In short, notions of economic liberty that are currently put forward in neoliberal economic models are not synonymous with political freedom—and may even impede it.

Democratization will not necessarily bring in its wake economic growth, social peace, administrative efficiency, political harmony, free markets, or "the end of ideology." Least of all will it bring about "the end of history." No doubt some of these qualities could make the consolidation of democracy easier, but they are neither prerequisites for it nor immediate products of it. Instead, what we should be hoping for is the emergence of political institutions that can peacefully compete to form governments and influence public policy, that can channel social and economic conflicts through regular procedures, and that have sufficient linkages to civil society to represent their constituencies and commit them to collective courses of action. Some types of democracies, especially in developing countries, have been unable to fulfill this promise, perhaps due to the circumstances of their transition from authoritarian rule.[13] The democratic wager is that such a regime, once established, will not only persist by reproducing itself within its initial confining conditions, but will eventually expand beyond them.[14] Unlike authoritarian regimes, democracies have the capacity to modify their rules and institutions consensually in response to changing circumstances. They may not immediately produce all the goods mentioned above, but they stand a better chance of eventually doing so than do autocracies.

Notes

1. For a comparative analysis of the recent regime changes in southern Europe and Latin America, see Guillermo O'Donnell, Philippe C. Schmitter, and Laurence Whitehead, eds., *Transitions from Authoritarian Rule*, 4 vols. (Baltimore: Johns Hopkins University Press, 1986). For another compilation that adopts a more structural approach see Larry Diamond, Juan Linz, and Seymour Martin Lipset, eds., *Democracy in Developing Countries*, vols. 2, 3, and 4 (Boulder, Colo.: Lynne Rienner, 1989).

2. Numerous attempts have been made to codify and quantify the existence of democracy across political systems. The best known is probably Freedom House's *Freedom in the World: Political Rights and Civil Liberties*, published since 1973 by Greenwood Press and since 1988 by University Press of America. Also see Charles Humana, *World Human Rights Guide* (New York: Facts on File, 1986).

3. The definition most commonly used by American social scientists is that of Joseph Schumpeter: "that institutional arrangement for arriving at political decisions in which individuals acquire the power to decide by means of a competitive struggle for the people's vote." *Capitalism, Socialism, and Democracy* (London: George Allen and Unwin, 1943), 269. We accept certain aspects of the classical procedural approach to modern democracy, but differ primarily in our emphasis on the accountability of rulers to citizens and the relevance of mechanisms of competition other than elections.

4. Not only do some countries practice a stable form of democracy without a formal constitution (e.g., Great Britain and Israel), but even more countries have constitutions and legal codes that offer no guarantee of reliable practice. On paper, Stalin's 1936 constitution for the USSR was a virtual model of democratic rights and entitlements.

5. For the most valiant attempt to make some sense out of this thicket of distinctions, see Juan Linz, "Totalitarian and Authoritarian Regimes" in *Handbook of Political Science*, eds. Fred I. Greenstein and Nelson W. Polsby (Reading Mass.: Addison Wesley, 1975), 175–411.

6. "Publius" (Alexander Hamilton, John Jay, and James Madison), *The Federalist Papers* (New York: Anchor Books, 1961). The quote is from Number 10.

7. See Terry Karl, "Imposing Consent? Electoralism versus Democratization in El Salvador," in *Elections and Democratization in Latin America, 1980–1985*, eds. Paul Drake and Eduardo Silva (San Diego: Center for Iberian and Latin American Studies, Center for US/Mexican Studies, University of California, San Diego, 1986), 9–36.

8. Alexis de Tocqueville, *Democracy in America*, 2 vols. (New York: Vintage Books, 1945).

9. This fear of overloaded government and the imminent collapse of democracy is well reflected in the work of Samuel P. Huntington during the 1970s. See especially Michel Crozier, Samuel P. Huntington, and Joji Watanuki, *The Crisis of Democracy* (New York: New York University Press, 1975).

For Huntington's (revised) thoughts about the prospects for democracy, see his "Will More Countries Become Democratic?," *Political Science Quarterly* 99 (Summer 1984): 193–218.

10. Robert Dahl, *Dilemmas of Pluralist Democracy* (New Haven: Yale University Press, 1982), 11.

11. Robert Dahl, *After the Revolution: Authority in a Good Society* (New Haven: Yale University Press, 1970).

12. See Juan Linz, "The Perils of Presidentialism," *Journal of Democracy* 1 (Winter 1990): 51–69, and the ensuing discussion by Donald Horowitz, Seymour Martin Lipset, and Juan Linz in *Journal of Democracy* 1 (Fall 1990): 73–91.

13. Terry Lynn Karl, "Dilemmas of Democratization in Latin America" *Comparative Politics* 23 (October 1990): 1–23.

14. Otto Kirchheimer, "Confining Conditions and Revolutionary Breakthroughs," *American Political Science Review* 59 (1965): 964–974.

Philippe C. Schmitter is professor of political science and director of the Center for European Studies at Stanford University. **Terry Lynn Karl** is associate professor of political science and director of the Center for Latin American Studies at the same institution. The original, longer version of this essay was written at the request of the United States Agency for International Development, which is not responsible for its content.

Public Opinion: Is There a Crisis?

After the collapse of communism, the world saw a surge in the number of new democracies. But why are the citizens of the mature democracies meanwhile losing confidence in their political institutions? This is the first in a series of articles on democracy in transition.

Everyone remembers that Winston Churchill once called democracy the worst form of government—except for all the others. The end of the cold war seemed to prove him right. All but a handful of countries now claim to embrace democratic ideals. Insofar as there is

a debate about democracy, much of it now centers on how to help the "emerging" democracies of Asia, Africa, Latin America and Eastern Europe catch up with the established democratic countries of the West and Japan. The new democracies are used to having well-meaning observers from the

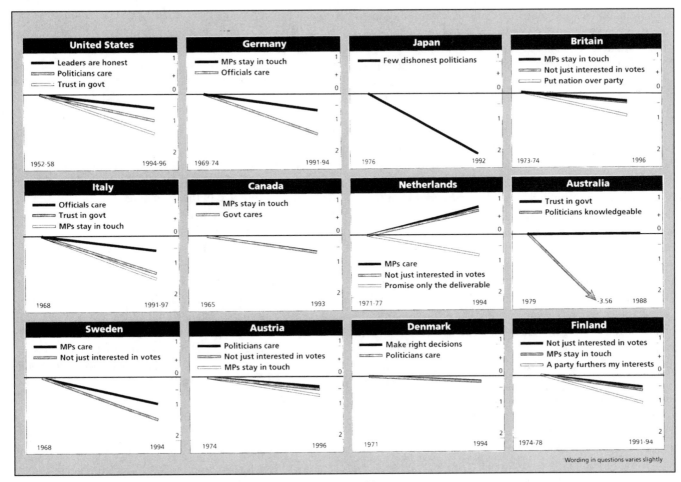

Figure 1   Our Elected Rascals.   Political Confidence, annual % Change.

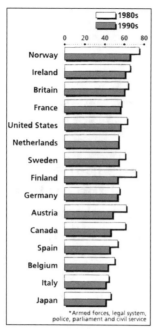

Figure 2   Losing Faith.   Confidence in Political Institutions*, %.

Sources: R. Dalton; World Values Surveys

mature democracies descend on them at election time to ensure that the voting is free and fair. But is political life in these mature democracies as healthy as it should be?

If opinion research is any guide, the mature democracies have troubles of their own. In the United States in particular, the high opinion which people had of their government has declined steadily over the past four decades. Regular opinion surveys carried out as part of a series of national election studies in America show that the slump set in during the 1960s. The civil-rights conflict and the Vietnam War made this an especially turbulent decade for the United States. But public confidence in politicians and government continued to decline over the next quarter-century. Nor (remember the student unrest in Paris and elsewhere in 1968) was this confined to the United States.

It is hard to compare attitudes toward democracy over time, and across many different countries. Most opinion surveys are carried out nation-by-nation: they are conducted at different times and researchers often ask different sorts of questions. But some generalizations can be made. In their introduction to a forthcoming book "What is Troubling the Trilateral Democracies?", Princeton University Press, 2000) three academics—Robert Putnam, Susan Pharr, and Russell Dalton—have done their best to analyze the results of surveys conducted in most of the rich countries.

Figure 1 summarises some of these findings. The downward slopes show how public confidence in politicians seems to be falling, measured by changes in the answers voters give to questions such as "Do you think that politicians are trustworthy?"; "Do members of parliament (MPs) care about voters like you?"; and "How much do you trust governments of

any party to place the needs of the nation above their own political party?" In most of the mature democracies, the results show a pattern of disillusionment with politicians. Only in the Netherlands is there clear evidence of rising confidence.

Nor is it only politicians who are losing the public's trust. Surveys suggest that confidence in political institutions is in decline as well. In 11 out of 14 countries, for example, confidence in parliament has declined, with especially sharp falls in Canada, Germany, Britain, Sweden and the United States. World-wide polls conducted in 1981 and 1990 measured confidence in five institutions: parliament, the armed services, the judiciary, the police and the civil service. Some institutions gained public trust, but on average confidence in them decreased by 6% over the decade (see figure 2). The only countries to score small increases in confidence were Iceland and Denmark.

Other findings summarised by Mr Putnam and his colleagues make uncomfortable reading:

- In the late 1950s and early 1960s **Americans** had a touching faith in government. When asked "How many times can you trust the government in Washington to do what is right?", three out of four answered "most of the time" or "just about always". By 1998, fewer than four out of ten trusted the government to do what was right. In 1964 only 29% of the American electorate agreed that "the government is pretty much run by a few big interests looking after themselves". By 1984, that figure had risen to 55%, and by 1998 to 63%. In the 1960s, two-thirds of Americans rejected the statement "most elected officials don't care what people like me think". In 1998, nearly two-thirds agreed with it. The proportion of Americans who expressed "a great deal of" confidence in the executive branch fell from 42% in 1966 to 12% in 1997; and trust in Congress fell from 42% to 11%.

- **Canadians** have also been losing faith in their politicians. The proportion of Canadians who felt that "the government doesn't care what people like me think" rose from 45% in 1968 to 67% in 1993. The proportion expressing "a great deal of" confidence in political parties fell from 30% in 1979 to 11% in 1999. Confidence in the House of Commons fell from 49% in 1974 to 21% in 1996. By 1992 only 34% of Canadians were satisfied with their system of government, down from 51% in 1986.

- Less information is available about attitudes in **Japan**. But the findings of the few surveys that have been carried out there match the global pattern. Confidence in political institutions rose in the decades following the smashing of the country's old politics in the second world war. Happily for democracy, the proportion of Japanese voters who agree that "in order

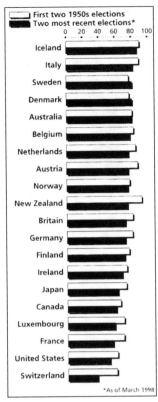

First two 1950s elections
Two most recent elections*

0 20 40 60 80 100

Iceland
Italy
Sweden
Denmark
Australia
Belgium
Netherlands
Austria
Norway
New Zealand
Britain
Germany
Finland
Ireland
Japan
Canada
Luxembourg
France
United States
Switzerland

*As of March 1998

Figure 3   Staying Home.   Voter Turnout, %.

Source: Martin P. Wattenberg, University of California, Irvine

to make Japan better, it is best to rely on talented politicians, rather than to let the citizens argue among themselves" has been falling for 40 years. However, the proportion who feel that they exert at least "some influence" on national politics through elections or demonstrations also fell steadily between 1973 and 1993.

- Although it is harder to generalize about **Western Europe**, confidence in political institutions is in decline in most countries. In 1985 48% of Britons expressed quite a lot of confidence in the House of Commons. This number had halved by 1995. The proportion of Swedes disagreeing with the statement that "parties are only interested in people's votes, not in their opinions" slumped from 51% in 1968 to 28% in 1994. In 1985 51% expressed confidence in the Rikstad (parliament); by 1996 only 19% did. In Germany, the percentage of people who said they trusted their Bundestag deputy to represent their interests rose from 25% in 1951 to 55% in 1978, but had fallen again to 34% by 1992. The percentage of Italians who say that politicians "don't care what people like me think" increased from 68% in 1968 to 84% in 1997.

Such findings are alarming if you take them at face value. But they should be interpreted with care. Democracy may just be a victim of its own success. It could just be that people nowadays expect more from governments, impose

new demands on the state, and are therefore more likely to be disappointed. After all, the idea that governments ought to do such things as protect or improve the environment, maintain high employment, arbitrate between moral issues, or ensure the equal treatment of women or minorities, is a relatively modern and still controversial one. Or perhaps the disillusionment is a healthy product of rising educational standards and the scepticism that goes with it. Or maybe it is caused by the media's search-light highlighting failures of government that were previously kept in the dark. Whatever the causes, the popularity of governments or politicians ought not to be the only test of democracy's health.

Moreover, there is encouraging evidence to put beside the discouraging findings. However much confidence in government may be declining, this does not seem to have diminished popular support for democratic principles. On average, surveys show, more than three out of four people in rich countries believe that democracy is the best form of government. Even in countries where the performance of particular governments has been so disappointing as to break up the party system itself (such as Japan and Italy in 1993–95), this has brought no serious threat to fundamental democratic principle. It may seem paradoxical for people to express strong support for democracy even while their confidence in politicians and political institutions crumbles. But it hardly amounts to the "crisis of democracy" which political scientists tend to proclaim from time to time.

Nor, though, is it a ringing endorsement, especially given that the evidence of opinion surveys is reinforced by other trends. These include a decline both in the membership of political parties and in the proportion of people who turn out to vote. Numbers compiled by Martin Wattenberg, also at the University of California, show that in 18 out of 20 of the rich established democracies the proportion of the electorate voting has been lower than it was in the early 1950s (see figure 3), with the median change being a decline of 10%. More controversially, some political scientists see the growth of protest movements since the 1960s as a sign of declining faith in the traditional institutions of representative democracy, and an attempt to bypass them. Others reckon that the most serious threat comes from the increasingly professional pressure groups and lobbying organisations that work behind the scenes to influence government policy and defend special interests, often at the expense of the electorate as a whole.

What is to be done? Those who believe that government has over-reached itself call on governments to become smaller and to promise less. Thus, it is hoped, people will come to do more for themselves. But whatever the appropriate size and reach of governments, there is also scope for making the machinery of democracy work better.

Indeed, some commentators see the public's declining confidence in political institutions as an opportunity for

13

democratic renewal. Pippa Norris, at Harvard University's Kennedy School of Government, hails the advent of a new breed of "critical citizens" (in a book of that name, Oxford University Press, 1999) who see that existing channels of participation fall short of democratic ideals and want to reform them.

There are some signs of this. Countries as different as Italy, Japan, Britain and New Zealand have lately considered or introduced changes in their electoral systems. Countries around the world are making growing use of referendums and other forms of direct democracy. Many are reducing the power of parliaments by giving judges new powers to review the decisions that elected politicians make. And governments everywhere are introducing new rules on the financing of politicians and political parties. The rest of the articles in this series will look at some of these changes and the forces shaping them.

Advanced Democracies and the New Politics

Russell J. Dalton, Susan E. Scarrow, and Bruce E. Cain

Over the past quarter-century in advanced industrial democracies, citizens, public interest groups, and political elites have shown decreasing confidence in the institutions and processes of representative government. In most of these nations, electoral turnout and party membership have declined, and citizens are increasingly skeptical of politicians and political institutions.[1]

Along with these trends often go louder demands to expand citizen and interest-group access to politics, and to restructure democratic decision-making processes. Fewer people may be voting, but more are signing petitions, joining lobby groups, and engaging in unconventional forms of political action.[2] Referenda and ballot initiatives are growing in popularity; there is growing interest in processes of deliberative or consultative democracy;[3] and there are regular calls for more reliance on citizen advisory committees for policy formation and administration—especially at the local level, where direct involvement is most feasible. Contemporary democracies are facing popular pressures to grant more access, increase the transparency of governance, and make government more accountable.

Amplifying these trends, a chorus of political experts has been calling for democracies to reform and adapt. Mark Warren writes, "Democracy, once again in favor, is in need of conceptual renewal. While the traditional concerns of democratic theory with state-centered institutions remain importantly crucial and ethically central, they are increasingly subject to the limitations we should expect when nineteenth-century concepts meet twenty-first century realities."[4] U.S. political analyst Dick Morris similarly observes, "The fundamental paradigm that dominates our politics is the shift from representative to direct democracy. Voters want to run the show directly and are impatient with all forms of intermediaries between their opinions and public policy."[5] As Ralf Dahrendorf recently summarized the mood of the times, "Representative government is no longer as compelling a proposition as it once was. Instead, a search for new institutional forms to express conflicts of interest has begun."[6]

Many government officials have echoed these sentiments, and the OECD has examined how its member states could reform their governments to create new connections to their publics.[7] Its report testifies:

> New forms of representation and public participation are emerging in all of our countries. These developments have expanded the avenues for citizens to participate more fully in public policy making, within the overall framework of representative democracy in which parliaments continue to play a central role. Citizens are increasingly demanding more transparency and accountability from their governments, and want greater public participation in shaping policies that affect their lives. Educated and well-informed citizens expect governments to take their views and knowledge into account when making decisions on their behalf. Engaging citizens in policy making allows governments to respond to these expectations and, at the same time, design better policies and improve their implementation.[8]

If the pressures for political reform are having real effects, these should show up in changes to the institutional structures of democratic politics. The most avid proponents of such reforms conclude that we may be experiencing the most fundamental democratic transformation since the beginnings of mass democracy in the early twentieth century. Yet cycles of reform are a recurring theme in democratic history, and pressures for change in one direction often wane as new problems and possibilities come to the fore. What is the general track record for democratic institutional reforms in the advanced industrial democracies over the latter half of the twentieth century? And what are the implications of this record for the future of democracy?

Three Modes of Democracy

In a sense, there is nothing new about the call to inject "more democracy" into the institutions of representative government. The history of modern democracies is punctuated by repeated waves of debate about the nature of the democratic process, some of which have produced major institutional reforms. In the early twentieth century, for example, the populist movement in the United States prompted extensive electoral and governing-process reforms, as well as the introduction of new forms of direct democracy.[9] Parallel institutional changes occurred in Europe. By the end of this democratic-reform period in the late 1920s, most Western democracies had become much more "democratic" in the sense of providing citizens with access to the political process and making governments more accountable.

A new wave of democratic rhetoric and debate emerged in the last third of the twentieth century. The stimulus for this first appeared mainly among university students and young professionals contesting the boundaries of conventional representative democracy. Although their dramatic protests subsequently waned, they stimulated new challenges that affect advanced industrial democracies to this day. Citizen interest groups and other public lobbying organizations, which have proliferated since the 1960s, press for more access to government; expanding mass media delve more deeply into the workings of government; and people demand more from government while trusting it less.

The institutional impact of the reform wave of the late twentieth century can be understood in terms of three different modes of democratic politics. One aims at improving the process of *representative democracy* in which citizens elect elites. Much like the populism of the early twentieth century, reforms of this mode seek to improve electoral processes. Second, there are calls for new types of *direct democracy* that bypass (or complement) the processes of representative democracy. A third mode seeks to expand the means of political participation through a new style of *advocacy democracy,* in which citizens participate in policy deliberation and formation—either directly or through surrogates, such as public interest groups—although the final decisions are still made by elites.

1) Representative democracy.

A major example of reform in representative democracy can be seen in changes to processes of electing the U.S. president. In a 30-year span, these elections underwent a dramatic transformation, in which citizen influence grew via the spread of state-level primary elections as a means of nominating candidates. In 1968, the Democratic Party had just 17 presidential primaries while the Republicans had only 16; in 2000 there were Democratic primaries in 40 states and Republican primaries in 43. As well, both parties-first the Democrats, then the Republicans—instituted reforms intended to ensure that convention delegates are more representative of the public at large, such as rules on the representation of women. Meanwhile, legislators introduced and expanded public funding for presidential elections in an effort to limit the influence of money and so promote citizen equality. If the 1948 Republican and Democratic candidates, Thomas E. Dewey and Harry S. Truman, were brought back to observe the modern presidential election process, they would hardly recognize the system as the same that nominated them. More recently, reformers have championed such causes as term limits and campaign-finance reform as remedies for restricting the influence of special interests. In Europe, populist electoral reform has been relatively restrained by institutionalized systems of party government, but even so, there are

parallels to what has occurred in the United States in many European countries. On a limited basis, for example, some European political parties have experimented with, or even adopted, closed primaries to select parliamentary candidates.[10]

In recent decades, changes in both attitudes and formal rules have brought about a greater general reliance on mechanisms of direct democracy within the advanced industrial democracies.

Generally, the mechanisms of representative democracy have maintained, and in places slightly increased, citizen access and influence. It is true that, compared with four decades ago, electoral turnout is generally down by about 10 percent in the established democracies.[11] This partially signifies a decrease in political access (or in citizens' use of elections as a means of political access). But at the same time, the "amount of electing" is up to an equal or greater extent. There has been a pattern of reform increasing the number of electoral choices available to voters by changing appointed positions into elected ones.[12] In Europe, citizens now elect members of Parliament for the European Union; regionalization has increased the number of elected subnational governments; directly elected mayors and directly elected local officials are becoming more common; and suffrage now includes younger voters, aged 18 to 20. Moreover, the number of political parties has increased, while parties have largely become more accountable—and the decisions of party elites more transparent—to their supporters. With the general expansion in electoral choices, citizens are traveling to the polls more often and making more electoral decisions.

2) Direct democracy.

Initiatives and referenda are the most common means of direct democracy. These allow citizens to decide government policy without relying on the mediating influence of representation. Ballot initiatives in particular allow nongovernmental actors to control the framing of issues and even the timing of policy debates, further empowering the citizens and groups that take up this mode of action. In recent decades, changes in both attitudes and formal rules have brought about a greater general reliance on mechanisms of direct democracy within the advanced industrial democracies. The Initiative and Referendum Institute calculates, for example, that there were 118 statewide referenda in the United States during the 1950s but 378 such referenda during the 1990s. And a number of other nations have amended laws and constitutions to provide greater opportunities for direct democracy at the national and local levels.[13] Britain had its first national referendum in 1975; Sweden introduced the referendum in a constitutional reform of 1980; and Finland adopted the referendum in 1987. In these and other cases, the referendum won new legitimacy as a basis for national decision making, a norm that runs strongly counter to the ethos of representative democracy. There has also been mounting interest in expanding direct democracy through the innovation of new institutional forms, such as methods of deliberative democracy and citizen juries to advise policy makers.[14]

How fundamental are these changes? On the one hand, the political impact of a given referendum is limited, since only a single policy is being decided, so the channels of direct democracy normally provide less access than do the traditional channels of representative democracy. On the other hand, the increasing use of referenda has influenced political discourse—and the principles of political legitimacy in particular—beyond the policy at stake in any single referendum. With Britain's first referendum on European Community membership in 1975, for instance, parliamentary sovereignty was now no longer absolute, and the concept of popular sovereignty was concomitantly legitimized. Accordingly, the legitimacy of subsequent decisions on devolution required additional referenda, and today contentious issues, such as acceptance of the euro, are pervasively considered as matters that "the public should decide." So even though recourse to direct democracy remains relatively limited in Britain, the expansion of this mode of access represents a significant institutional change—and one that we see occurring across most advanced industrial democracies.

3) Advocacy democracy. In this third mode, citizens or public interest groups interact directly with governments and even participate directly in the policy-formation process, although actual decisions remain in the official hands. One might consider this as a form of traditional lobbying, but it is not. Advocacy democracy involves neither traditional interest groups nor standard channels of informal interest-group persuasion. Rather, it empowers individual citizens, citizen groups, or nongovernmental organizations to participate in advisory hearings; attend open government meetings ("government in the sunshine"); consult ombudsmen to redress grievances; demand information from government agencies; and challenge government actions through the courts.

Evidence for the growth of advocacy democracy is less direct and more difficult to quantify than is evidence for other kinds of institutional change. But the overall expansion of advocacy democracy is undeniable. Administrative reforms, decentralization, the growing political influence of courts, and other factors have created new opportunities for access and influence. During the latter 1960s in the United States, "maximum feasible participation" became a watchword for the social-service reforms of President Lyndon Johnson's "Great Society" programs. Following this model, citizen consultations and public hearings have since been embedded in an extensive range of legislation, giving citizens new points of access to policy formation and administration. Congressional hearings and state-government meetings have become public events, and legislation such as the 1972 Federal Advisory Committee Act even extended open-meeting requirements to advisory committees. While only a handful of nations had freedom-of-information laws in 1970, such laws are now almost universal in OECD countries. And there has been a general diffusion of the ombudsman model across advanced industrial democracies.[15] "Sunshine" provisions reflect a fundamental shift in understanding as to the role that elected representatives

should play-one which would make Edmund Burke turn in his grave, and which we might characterize as a move away from the *trustee* toward the *delegate* model.

Reforms in this category also include new legal rights augmenting the influence of individuals and citizen groups. A pattern of judicialization in the policy process throughout most Western democracies, for instance, has enabled citizen groups to launch class-action suits on behalf of the environment, women's rights, or other public interests.[16] Now virtually every public interest can be translated into a rights-based appeal, which provides new avenues for action through the courts. Moreover, especially in European democracies, where direct citizen action was initially quite rare, the expansion of public interest groups, *Bürgerinitiativen,* and other kinds of citizen groups has substantially enlarged the public's repertoire for political action. It is worth noting that "unconventional" forms of political action, such as protests and demonstrations, have also grown substantially over this time span.

Citizens and the Democratic State

If the institutional structure of democracy is changing, how does this affect the democratic process? The answer is far from simple and not always positive, for democratic gains in some areas can be offset by losses in others, as when increased access produces new problems of democratic governability. In the following pages, we limit our attention to how these institutional changes affect the relationship between citizens and the state.

Robert A. Dahl's writings are a touchstone in this matter.[17] Like many democratic theorists, Dahl tends to equate democracy with the institutions and processes of representative democracy, paying much less attention to other forms of citizen participation that may actually represent more important means of citizen influence over political elites. Thus, while we draw from Dahl's *On Democracy* to define the essential criteria for a democratic process, we broaden the framework to include not only representative democracy but direct democracy and advocacy democracy also. Dahl suggests five criteria for a genuinely democratic system:[18]

1. **Inclusion:** With minimal exceptions, all permanent adult residents must have full rights of citizenship.
2. **Political equality:** When decisions about policy are made, every citizen must have an equal and effective opportunity to participate.
3. **Enlightened understanding:** Within reasonable limits, citizens must have equal and effective opportunities to learn about relevant policy alternatives and their likely consequences.
4. **Control of the agenda:** Citizens must have the opportunity to decide which matters are placed on the public agenda, and how.
5. **Effective participation:** Before a policy is adopted, all the citizens must have equal and effective opportunities for making their views known to other citizens.

Robert A. Dahl's Democratic Criteria

Democratic Criteria	Representative Democracy	Direct Democracy	Advocacy Democracy
Inclusion	**Universal suffrage provides inclusion**	**Universal suffrage provides inclusion**	Equal citizen access *(Problems of access to nonelectoral arenas)*
Political Equality	**One person, one vote with high turnout maximizes equality.** *(Problems of low turnout, inequality due to campaign finance issues, etc.)*	**One person, one vote with high turnout maximizes equality** *(Problems of equality with low turnout)*	Equal opportunity *(Problems of very unequal use)*
Enlightened Understanding	*(Problems of information access, voter decision processes)*	*(Problems of greater information and higher decision-making costs)*	**Increased public access to information** *(Problems of even greater information and decision-making demands on citizens)*
Control of the Agenda	*(Problems of control of campaign debate, selecting candidates, etc.)* **Control through responsible parties**	**Citizen initiation provides control of agenda** *(Problems of influence by interest groups)*	**Citizens and groups control the locus and focus of activity**
Effective Participation	*(Principal-agent problems: fair elections, responsible party government, etc.)*	**Direct policy impact ensures effective participation**	**Direct access avoids mediated participation**

Note. Criteria that are well addressed are presented in **bold**, criteria that are at issue are presented in *italics* in the shaded cells.

The first column of the Table lists Dahl's five democratic criteria. The second column summarizes the prevailing view on how well representative democracy fulfills these criteria. For example, advanced industrial democracies have met the *inclusion* criterion by expanding the franchise to all adult citizens (by way of a long and at times painful series of reforms). General success in this regard is illustrated by the bold highlighting of "universal suffrage" in the first cell of this column.

Nearly all advanced industrial democracies now meet the *political equality* criterion by having enacted the principle of "one person, one vote" for elections, which we have highlighted in the second cell. In most nations today, a majority of citizens participate in voting, while labor unions, political parties, and other organizations mobilize participation to achieve high levels of engagement. Indeed, that noted democrat, the late Mayor Richard Daley of Chicago, used to say that electoral politics was the only instrument through which a working-class citizen could ever exercise equal influence with the socially advantaged. At the same time, certain problems of equality remain, as contemporary debates about campaign financing and voter registration illustrate, and full equality in political practice is probably unattainable. We note these problems in the shaded area of the second cell. Nevertheless, overall the principle of

equality is now a consensual value for the electoral processes of representative democracy.

At first glance, it may seem that expanding the number of elections amounts to extending these principles. But increasing the number of times that voters go to the polls and the number of items on ballots actually tends to depress turnout. And when voter turnout is less than 50 percent, as it tends to be in, say, EU parliamentary elections-or less than 25 percent, as it tends to be in local mayoral or school-board elections in the United States-then one must question whether the gap between "equality of access" and "equality of usage" has become so wide that it undermines the basic principle of *political equality*. Moreover, second-order elections tend to mobilize a smaller and more ideological electorate than the public at large, and so more second-order elections tend to mean more distortions in the representativeness of the electoral process.

The tension between Dahl's democratic criteria and democratic practice becomes even more obvious when we turn to the criterion of *enlightened understanding*. Although we are fairly sanguine about voters' abilities to make informed choices when it comes to high-visibility (for instance, presidential or parliamentary) elections, we are less so when it comes to lower-visibility elections. How does a typical resident of Houston,

Texas, make enlightened choices regarding the dozens of judgeship candidates whose names appeared on the November 2002 ballot, to say nothing of other local office seekers and referenda? In such second- and third-order elections, the means of information that voters can use in first-order elections may be insufficient or even altogether lacking. So the expansion of the electoral marketplace may empower the public in a sense, but in another sense may make it hard for voters to exercise meaningful political judgment.

Another criterion is citizen *control of the political agenda.* Recent reforms in representative democracy have gone some way toward broadening access to the political agenda. Increasing the number of elected offices gives citizens more input and presumably more avenues for raising issues, while reforming political finance to equalize campaign access and party support has made for greater openness in political deliberations. More problematic, though, is performance on the *effectiveness of participation* criterion. Do citizens get what they vote for? Often, this principal-agent problem is solved through the mechanism of party government: Voters select a party, and the party ensures the compliance of individual members of parliament and the translation of electoral mandates into policy outcomes.[19] But the impact of recent reforms on the *effectiveness of participation* is complex. On the one hand, more openness and choice in elections should enable people to express their political preferences more extensively and in more policy areas. On the other hand, as the number of office-holders proliferates, it may become more difficult for voters to assign responsibility for policy outcomes. Fragmented decision making, divided government, and the sheer profusion of elected officials may diminish the political responsiveness of each actor.

How much better do the mechanisms of direct democracy fare when measured against Dahl's five criteria (see column 3 of the Table)? Because referenda and initiatives are effectively mass elections, they seek to ensure inclusion and political equality in much the same way as representative elections do. Most referenda and initiatives use universal suffrage to ensure inclusion and the "one person, one vote" rule to ensure political equality. However, whereas turnout in direct-democracy elections is often lower than in comparable elections for public officials, the question of democratic inclusion becomes more complicated than a simple assessment of equal access. For instance, when Proposition 98—which favored altering the California state constitution to mandate that a specific part of the state budget be directed to primary and secondary education—appeared on the 1996 general election ballot, barely half of all voting-age Californians turned out, and only 51 percent voted for the proposition. But as a consequence, the state's constitution was altered, reshaping state spending and public financing in California. Such votes raise questions about the fairness of elections in which a minority of registered voters can make crucial decisions affecting the public welfare. Equality of opportunity clearly does not mean equality of participation.

Moreover, referenda and initiatives place even greater demands for information and understanding on voters. Many of the heuristics that they can use in party elections or candidate elections are less effective in referenda, and the issues themselves are often more complex than what citizens are typically called upon to consider in electing office-holders. For instance, did the average voter have enough information to make enlightened choices in Italy's multi-referendum ballot of 1997? This ballot asked voters to make choices concerning television-ownership rules, television-broadcasting policy, the hours during which stores could remain open, the commercial activities which municipalities could pursue, labor-union reform proposals, regulations for administrative elections, and residency rules for mafia members. In referenda, voters can still rely on group heuristics and other cues that they use in electing public officials,[20] but obviously the proliferation of policy choices and especially the introduction of less-salient local issues raise questions about the overall effectiveness of such cue-taking.

The real strengths of direct democracy are highlighted by Dahl's fourth and fifth criteria. Referenda and initiatives shift the focus of agenda-setting from elites toward the public, or at least toward public interest groups. Indeed, processes of direct democracy can bring into the political arena issues that elites tend not to want to address: for example, tax reform or term limits in the United States, abortion-law reform in Italy, or the terms of EU membership in Europe generally. Even when referenda fail to reach the ballot or fail to win a majority, they can nevertheless prompt elites to be more sensitive to public interests. By definition, moreover, direct democracy should solve the problem of effective participation that exists with all methods of representative democracy. Direct democracy is unmediated, and so it ensures that participation is effective. Voters make policy choices with their ballot-to enact a new law, to repeal an existing law, or to reform a constitution. Even in instances where the mechanisms of direct democracy require an elite response in passing a law or a revoting in a later election, the link to policy action is more direct than is the case with the channels of representative democracy. Accordingly, direct democracy seems to fulfill Dahl's democratic criteria of agenda control and effective participation.

But direct democracy raises questions in these areas as well. Interest groups may find it easier to manipulate processes of direct democracy than those of representative democracy.[21] The discretion to place a policy initiative on the ballot can be appealing to interest groups, which then have unmediated access to voters during the subsequent referendum campaign. In addition, decisions made by way of direct democracy are less susceptible to bargaining or the checks and balances that occur within the normal legislative process. Some recent referenda in California may illustrate this style of direct democracy: Wealthy backers pay a consulting firm to collect signatures so as to get a proposal on the ballot, and then bankroll a campaign to support their desired legislation. This is not grassroots democracy at work; it is the representation of wealthy interests by other means.

The expansion of direct democracy has the potential to complement traditional forms of representative democracy. It can expand the democratic process by allowing citizens and public interest groups new access to politics, and new control over political agendas and policy outcomes. But direct democracy also raises new questions about equality of actual influence, if not formal access, and the ability of the public to make fair and reasoned judgments about issues. Perhaps the most important question about direct democracy is not whether it is expanding, but *how* it is expanding: Are there ways to increase access and influence without sacrificing inclusion and equality? We return to this question below.

Formal Access and Actual Use

The final column in our Table considers how new forms of advocacy democracy fulfill Dahl's democratic criteria. These new forms of action provide citizens with significant access to politics, but it is also clear that this access is very unevenly used. Nearly everyone can vote, and most do. But very few citizens file lawsuits, file papers under a freedom-of-information act, attend environmental-impact review hearings, or attend local planning meetings. There is no clear equivalent to "one person, one vote" for advocacy democracy. Accordingly, it raises the question of how to address Dahl's criteria of inclusion, political equality, and enlightened understanding.

"Equality of access" is not adequate if "equality of usage" is grossly uneven. For instance, when Europeans were asked in the 1989 European Election Survey whether they voted in the election immediately preceding the survey, differences in participation according to levels of education were very slight (see the Figure, Social-Status Inequality in Participations). A full 73 percent of those in the "low education" category said they had voted in the previous EU parliamentary election (even though it is a second-order election), and an identical percentage of those in the "high education" category claimed to have voted. Differences in campaign activity according to educational levels are somewhat greater, but still modest in overall terms.

A distinctly larger inequality gap emerges when it comes to participation through forms of direct or advocacy democracy. For instance, only 13 percent of those in the "low education" category had participated in a citizen action group, while nearly three times the percentage of those in the "high education" category had participated. Similarly, there are large inequalities when it comes to such activities as signing a petition or participating in a lawful demonstration.

With respect to the criterion of *enlightened understanding,* advocacy democracy has mixed results. On the one hand, it can enhance citizen understanding and make for greater inclusion. Citizens and public interest groups can increase the amount of information that they have about government activities, especially by taking advantage of freedom-of-information laws, attending administrative hearings, and participating in government policy making. And with the assistance of the press in disseminating this information, citizens and public interest groups can better influence political outcomes. By ensuring that the public receives information in a timely fashion, advocacy democracy allows citizens to make informed judgments and hold governments more accountable. And by eliminating the filtering that governments would otherwise apply, advocacy democracy can help citizens to get more accurate pictures of the influences affecting policy decisions, with fewer cover-ups and self-serving distortions. On the other hand, advocacy democracy makes greater cognitive and resource demands on citizens, and thus may generate some of the same inequalities in participation noted above. It requires much more of the citizen to participate in a public hearing or to petition an official than it does simply to cast a vote. The most insightful evidence on this point comes from Jane Mansbridge's study of collective decision making in New England town meetings.[22] She finds that many participants were unprepared or overwhelmed by the deliberative decision-making processes.

Advocacy democracy fares better when it comes to the remaining two criteria. It gives citizens greater control of the political agenda, in part by increasing their opportunity to press their interests outside of the institutionalized time and format constraints of fixed election cycles. By means of advocacy democracy, citizens can often choose when and where to challenge a government directive or pressure policy makers. Similarly, even though advocacy democracy typically leaves final political decisions in the hands of elites, it nevertheless provides direct access to government. Property owners can participate in a local planning hearing; a public interest group can petition government for information on past policies; and dissatisfied citizens can attend a school board session. Such unmediated participation brings citizens into the decision-making process-which ultimately might not be as effective as the efforts of a skilled representative, but greater direct involvement in the democratic process should improve its accountability and transparency (see the bold entries in these last two cells of the Table).

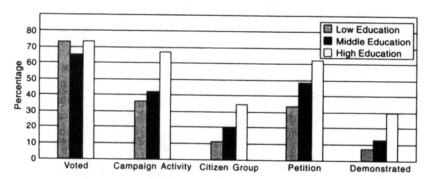

Social-Status Inequality in Participation

Source: Eurobarometers 31 and 31A conducted in connection with the 1989 European Parliament election. Results combine the 12 nations weighted to represent the total EU population.

All in all, advocacy democracy increases the potential for citizen access in important ways. It can give citizens and public interest groups new influence over the agenda-setting process, and it can give them unmediated involvement in the policy-formation process. These are significant extensions of democratic participation. At the same time, advocacy democracy may exacerbate political inequality on account of inequalities in usage. New access points created through advisory panels, consultative hearings, and other institutional reforms empower some citizens to become more involved. But other citizens, relatively lacking in the skills or resources to compete in these new domains, may be left behind. In other words, advocacy democracy may in some ways respond to the strength of the claimants, rather than to the strength of their claims. It can even alter the locus of political expertise. While advocacy democracy values know-how and expertise in the citizenry, it devalues those same characteristics among policy makers.

Environmental policy provides a good illustration of this problem. Here, citizens and public interest groups have gained new rights and new access to the policy process. But these are disproportionately used by relatively affluent and skilled citizens, who are already participating in conventional forms of representative democracy, while the poor, the unskilled, and the otherwise disadvantaged tend to get left behind. So while environmentalism is an example of citizen empowerment, it is also a source of increasing inequality.

No form of democratic action is ideal, each having its advantages and limitations. As democratic practice shifts from a predominant reliance on representation toward a mixed repertoire—including greater use of direct and advocacy democracy—a new balance must be struck among democratic goals. It is possible that new institutional arrangements will maximize the benefits of these new modes while limiting their disadvantages—as, for example, the institutions of representative democracy depend on parties and interest groups. But thus far, the advanced industrialized democracies have not fully recognized the problems generated by the new mixed repertoire of democratic action, and so have yet to find institutional or structural means of addressing them. Democratic reforms create opportunities, but they also create challenges. Our goal should be to ensure that progress on some democratic criteria is not unduly sacrificed for progress on others.

Notes

1. Martin P. Wattenberg, *Where Have All the Voters Gone?* (Cambridge: Harvard University Press, 2002); Susan E. Scarrow, "From Social Integration to Electoral Contestation," in Russell J. Dalton and Martin P. Wattenberg, eds., *Parties Without Partisans: Political Change in Advanced Industrial Democracies* (New York: Oxford University Press, 2000); Russell J. Dalton, *Democratic Challenges, Democratic Choices: The Decline in Political Support in Advanced Industrial Democracies* (Oxford: Oxford University Press, 2004); Susan J. Pharr and Robert D. Putnam, eds., *Disaffected Democracies: What's Troubling the Trilateral Countries?* (Princeton: Princeton University Press, 2000).

2. Russell J. Dalton, *Citizen Politics: Public Opinion and Political Parties in Advanced Industrial Democracies* (New York: Chatham House, 2002), ch. 4; Ronald Inglehart, *Modernization and Postmodernization: Cultural, Economic, and Political Change in 43 Societies* (Princeton: Princeton University Press, 1997); Sidney Verba, Kay Schlozman, and Henry Brady, *Voice and Equality: Civic Volunteerism in American Politics* (Cambridge: Harvard University Press, 1995), 72.

3. James S. Fishkin, *The Voice of the People: Public Opinion and Democracy* (New Haven: Yale University Press, 1995); John Elster, *Deliberative Democracy* (New York: Cambridge University Press, 1998).

4. Mark Warren, *Democracy and Association* (Princeton: Princeton University Press, 2001), 226.

5. Dick Morris, *The New Prince: Machiavelli Updated for the Twenty-First Century* (New York: Renaissance Books, 2000).

6. Ralf Dahrendorf, "Afterword," in Susan J. Pharr and Robert D. Putnam, eds., *Disaffected Democracies: What's Troubling the Trilateral Countries?* 311.

7. OECD, *Government of the Future: Getting from Here to There* (Paris: Organization for Economic Co-operation and Development, 2000).

8. OECD, *Citizens as Partners: OECD Handbook on Information, Consultation and Public Participation in Policy-Making* (Paris: Organization of Economic Cooperation and Development, 2001), 9.

9. Lawrence Goodwyn, *Democratic Promise: The Populist Movement in America* (New York: Oxford University Press, 1976).

10. Susan E. Scarrow, Paul Webb, and David M. Farrell, "From Social Integration to Electoral Contestation," in Russell J. Dalton and Martin P. Wattenberg, eds., *Parties without Partisans: Political Change in Advanced Industrial Democracies;* Jonathan Hopkin, "Bringing the Members Back in: Democratizing Candidate Selection in Britain and Spain," *Party Politics* 7 (May 2001): 343–61.

11. Martin P. Wattenberg, *Where Have All the Voters Gone?*

12. Russell J. Dalton and Mark Gray, "Expanding the Electoral Marketplace," in Bruce E. Cain, Russell J. Dalton, and Susan E. Scarrow, eds., *Democracy Transformed? Expanding Political Opportunities in Advanced Industrial Democracies* (Oxford: Oxford University Press, 2003).

13. Susan E. Scarrow, "Direct Democracy and Institutional Design: A Comparative Investigation," in *Comparative Political Studies* 34 (August 2001): 651–65; also see David Butler and Austin Ranney, eds., *Referenda Around the World* (Washington, D.C.: American Enterprise Institute, 1994); Michael Gallagher and Pier Vincenzo Uleri, eds., *The Referendum Experience in Europe* (Basingstoke: Macmillan, 1996).

14. James S. Fishkin, *The Voice of the People: Public Opinion and Democracy;* Forest David Matthews, *Politics for People: Finding a Responsive Voice,* 2nd ed. (Urbana: University of Illinois Press, 1999).

15. Roy Gregory and Philip Giddings, eds., *Righting Wrongs: The Ombudsman in Six Continents* (Amsterdam: IOS Press, 2000); see also Christopher Ansell and Jane Gingrich, "Reforming the Administrative State," in Bruce E. Cain, Russell J. Dalton, and

Susan E. Scarrow, eds., *Democracy Transformed? Expanding Political Opportunities in Advanced Industrial Democracies.*

16. Alec Stone Sweet, *Governing with Judges: Constitutional Politics in Europe* (New York: Oxford University Press, 2000).

17. Robert A Dahl, *Polyarchy: Participation and Opposition* (New Haven: Yale University Press, 1971); *Democracy and Its Critics* (New Haven: Yale University Press, 1991); *On Democracy* (New Haven: Yale University Press, 1998).

18. Robert A. Dahl, *On Democracy,* 37–38.

19. 1Hans-Dieter Klingemann et al., *Parties, Policies, and Democracy* (Boulder: Westview, 1994).

20. Arthur Lupia, "Shortcuts versus Encyclopedias," *American Political Science Review* 88 (March 1994): 63–76.

21. Elisabeth Gerber, *The Populist Paradox: Interest Group Influence and the Promise of Direct Legislation* (Princeton: Princeton University Press, 1999); see also David S. Broder, *Democracy Derailed: Initiative Campaigns and the Power of Money*

22. Jane Mansbridge, *Beyond Adversary Democracy* (New York: Basic Books, 1980).

RUSSELL J. DALTON is director of the Center for the Study of Democracy at the University of California, Irvine. **SUSAN E. SCARROW** is associate professor of political science at the University of Houston. **BRUCE E. CAIN** is Robson Professor of Political Science at the University of California, Berkeley, and director of the Institute of Governmental Studies. This essay is adapted from their edited volume, *Democracy Transformed? Expanding Political Opportunities in Advanced Industrial Democracies* (2003).

Referendums: The People's Voice

Is the growing use of referendums a threat to democracy or its salvation? The fifth article in our series on changes in mature democracies examines the experience so far, and the arguments for and against letting voters decide political questions directly.

When Winston Churchill proposed a referendum to Clement Attlee in 1945 on whether Britain's wartime coalition should be extended, Attlee growled that the idea was an "instrument of Nazism and fascism". The use by Hitler and Mussolini of bogus referendums to consolidate their power had confirmed the worst fears of sceptics. The most democratic of devices seemed also to be the most dangerous to democracy itself.

Dictators of all stripes have continued to use phony referendums to justify their hold on power. And yet this fact has not stopped a steady growth in the use of genuine referendums, held under free and fair conditions, by both established and aspiring democracies. Referendums have been instrumental in the dismantling of communism and the transition to democracy in countries throughout the former soviet empire. They have also successfully eased democratic transitions in Spain, Greece, South Africa, Brazil and Chile, among other countries.

In most established democracies, direct appeals to voters are now part of the machinery for constitutional change. Their use to resolve the most intractable or divisive public issues has also grown. In the 17 major democracies of Western Europe, only three—Belgium, the Netherlands and Norway—make no provision for referendums in their constitution. Only six major democracies—the Netherlands, the United States, Japan, India, Israel and the Federal Republic of Germany—have never held a nationwide referendum.

The Volatile Voter

Frustrated voters in Italy and New Zealand have in recent years used referendums to force radical changes to voting systems and other political institutions on a reluctant political elite. Referendums have also been used regularly in Australia, where voters go to the polls this November to decide whether to cut their country's formal link with the British crown. In Switzerland and several American states, referendums are a central feature of the political system, rivalling legislatures in significance.

Outside the United States and Switzerland, referendums are most often called by governments only when they are certain of victory, and to win endorsement of a policy they intend to implement in any case. This is how they are currently being used in Britain by Tony Blair's government.

But voters do not always behave as predicted, and they have delivered some notable rebuffs. Charles de Gaulle skillfully used referendums to establish the legitimacy of France's Fifth Republic and to expand his own powers as president, but then felt compelled to resign in 1969 after an unexpected referendum defeat.

Francois Mitterrand's decision to call a referendum on the Maastricht treaty in 1992 brought the European Union to the brink of breakdown when only 51% of those voting backed the treaty. Denmark's voters rejected the same treaty, despite the fact that it was supported by four out of five members of the Danish parliament. The Danish government was able to sign the treaty only after renegotiating its terms and narrowly winning a second referendum. That same year, Canada's government was not so lucky. Canadian voters unexpectedly rejected a painstakingly negotiated constitutional accord designed to placate Quebec.

Referendums come in many different forms. **Advisory referendums** test public opinion on an important issue. Governments or legislators then translate their results into new laws or policies as they see fit. Although advisory referendums can carry great weight in the right circumstances, they are sometimes ignored by politicians. In a 1955 Swedish referendum, 85% of those voting said they wanted to continue driving on the left side of the road. Only 12 years later the government went ahead and made the switch to driving on the right without a second referendum, or much protest.

By contrast, **mandatory referendums** are part of a law-making process or, more commonly, one of the procedures for constitutional amendment.

Both advisory and mandatory referendums can usually be called only by those in office—sometimes by the president, sometimes by parliamentarians, most often by the government of the day. But in a few countries, petitions by voters themselves can put a referendum on the ballot. These are known as **initiatives**. Sometimes these can only repeal an already existing law—so-called "abrogative" initiatives such as those in Italy. Elsewhere, initiatives can also be used to propose and pass new legislation, as in Switzerland and many American states. In this form they can be powerful and unpredictable political tools.

The rules for conducting and winning referendums also vary greatly from country to country. Regulations on the drafting of ballot papers and the financing of Yes and No campaigns are different everywhere, and these exert a great influence over how referendums are used, and how often.

The hurdle required for victory can be a critical feature. A simple majority of those voting is the usual rule. But a low turn-out can make such victories seem illegitimate. So a percentage of eligible voters, as well as a majority of those voting, is some-times required to approve a proposal.

Such hurdles, of course, also make failure more likely. In 1978 Britain's government was forced to abandon plans to set up a Scottish parliament when a referendum victory in Scotland failed to clear a 40% hurdle of eligible voters. Referendums have also failed in Denmark and Italy (most recently in April) because of similar voter-turnout requirements. To ensure a wide geographic consensus, Switzerland and Australia require a "double majority", of individual voters and of cantons or states, for constitutional amendments.

The use of referendums reflects the history and traditions of individual countries. Thus generalising about them is difficult. In some countries referendums have played a central, though peripatetic, role. In others they have been marginal or even irrel-evant, despite provisions for their use.

Hot Potatoes

Although referendums (outside Switzerland and the United States) have been most often used to legitimise constitutional change or the redrawing of boundaries, elected politicians have also found them useful for referring to voters those issues they find too hot to handle or which cut across party lines. Often these concern moral or lifestyle choices, such as alcohol prohi-bition, divorce or abortion. The outcome on such emotive topics can be difficult to predict. In divorce and abortion referendums, for example, Italians have shown themselves more liberal, and the Irish more conservative, than expected.

One of the best single books on referendums—"Referendums Around the World" edited by David Butler and Austin Ranney, published by Macmillan—argues that many assumptions about them are mistaken. They are not usually habit-forming, as those opposed to them claim. Many countries have used them to settle a specific issue, or even engaged in a series of them, and then turned away from referendums for long periods. But this is mostly because politicians decide whether referendums will be held. Where groups of voters can also put initiatives on the bal-lot, as in Switzerland and the United States, they have become addictive and their use has grown in recent years.

Messrs Butler and Ranney also point out that referen-dums are not usually vehicles for radical change, as is widely believed. Although they were used in this way in Italy and New Zealand, referendums have more often been used to support the status quo or to endorse changes already agreed by politi-cal parties. Most referendums, even those initiated by voters, fail. In Australia, 34 of 42 proposals to amend the constitu-tion have been rejected by voters. According to an analysis by David Magleby, a professor at Brigham Young University in Utah, 62% of the 1,732 initiatives which reached the ballot in American states between 1898 and 1992 were rejected.

Arguments for and against referendums go to the heart of what is meant by democracy. Proponents of referendums main-tain that consulting citizens directly is the only truly democratic way to determine policy. If popular sovereignty is really to mean anything, voters must have the right to set the agenda, discuss the issues and then themselves directly make the final decisions. Delegating these tasks to elected politicians, who have interests of their own, inevitably distorts the wishes of voters.

Referendums, their advocates say, can discipline representa-tives, and put the stamp of legitimacy on the most important political questions of the day. They also encourage participation by citizens in the governing of their own societies, and political participation is the source of most other civic virtues.

The Case Against

Those sceptical of referendums agree that popular sovereignty, majority rule and consulting voters are the basic building blocks of democracy, but believe that representative democracy achieves these goals much better than referendums. Genuine direct democracy, they say, is feasible only for political groups so small that all citizens can meet face-to-face—a small town perhaps. In large, modern societies, the full participation of every citizen is impossible.

Referendum opponents maintain that representatives, as full-time decision-makers, can weigh conflicting priorities, negotiate compromises among different groups and make well-informed decisions. Citizens voting in single-issue referendums have difficulty in doing any of these things. And as the bluntest of majoritarian devices, referendums encourage voters to brush aside the concerns of minority groups. Finally, the frequent use of referendums can actually undermine democracy by encour-aging elected legislators to sidestep difficult issues, thus dam-aging the prestige and authority of representative institutions, which must continue to perform most of the business of govern-ment even if referendums are used frequently.

Testing any of these claims or counter-claims is difficult. Most countries do not, in fact, use referendums regularly enough to bear out either the hopes of proponents or the fears of oppo-nents. The two exceptions are Switzerland and some American states, where citizen initiatives are frequent enough to draw tentative conclusions on some of these points, although both examples fall far short of full-fledged direct democracy.

Voters in both countries seem to believe that referendums do, in fact, lend legitimacy to important decisions. The Swiss are unlikely now to make a big national decision without a referendum. Swiss voters have rejected both UN membership and links with the EU in referendums, against the advice of their political leaders. Similarly, American polls show healthy majorities favouring referendums and believing that they are more likely to produce policies that most people want. Polls also show support for the introduction of referendums on the national level.

The claim that referendums increase citizen participation is more problematic. Some referendum campaigns ignite enormous public interest and media attention. Initiatives also give political outsiders a way to influence the public agenda. But in the United States, much of the activity involved in getting initiatives on the ballot, such as collecting signatures, has been taken over by professional firms, and many referendum campaigns have become slick, expensive affairs far removed from the grassroots (so far, this is much less true in Switzerland). Even more surprising, voter participation in American referendums is well below that of candidate elections, even when these are held at the same time. The average turnout for Swiss referendums has fallen by a third in the past 50 years to about 40%. On big issues, however, turnout can still soar.

Many of the fears of those opposed to referendums have not been realised in either country. Initiatives have not usually been used to oppress minorities. A proposal to limit the number of foreigners allowed to live in Switzerland was rejected by two-thirds of voters in 1988. In 1992 Colorado's voters did approve an initiative overturning local ordinances protecting gays from discrimination, but more extreme anti-gay initiatives in Colorado and California have been defeated by large majorities. Since 1990 voters have consistently upheld certain abortion rights in initiative ballots. Minorities and immigrants have been the targets of initiatives in some states, but voters have generally rejected extreme measures and have often proven themselves no more illiberal than legislators. Most initiatives are, in fact, about tax and economic questions, not civil liberties or social issues, although the latter often gain more attention.

While the frequent use of initiatives has not destroyed representative government, as some feared, it has changed it. Party loyalty among Swiss voters is strong at general elections, but evaporates when it comes to referendum voting. Initiatives, and the threat of mounting one, have become an integral part of the legislative process in Switzerland, as they have in California, Oregon and the other American states where they are most used. Referendums now often set the political agenda in both countries. In the United States they are frequently seen, rightly or wrongly, as a barometer of the national mood. And they can occasionally spark a political revolution. California's Proposition 13, for example, a 1978 initiative lowering local property taxes, set off a tax revolt across America. Elected officials themselves are often active in launching initiatives, and relatively successful in getting their proposals approved, which hardly indicates that voters have lost all faith in their politicians. Initiatives have made legislating more complicated, but also more responsive to the public's concerns.

There is some evidence that American voters, at least, are sometimes overwhelmed by the volume of information coming their way, and cast their vote in ignorance, as critics contend. Mr Magleby cites studies showing that on several ballots, 10–20% of the electorate mistakenly cast their vote the wrong way. Ballot material dropping through the letterboxes of residents in California is now often more than 200 pages long. According to one poll, only one in five Californians believes that the average voter understands most of the propositions put before him. Quite rationally, this has also bred caution. Californians approve only one-third of initiatives.

Hybrid Democracy?

The Swiss and American experience suggests that in the future there is unlikely to be a headlong rush away from representative to direct democracy anywhere, but that, even so, the use of referendums is likely to grow. The Internet and other technological advances have not yet had much impact on referendums, but they should eventually make it easier to hold them, and to inform voters of the issues they are being asked to decide upon.

Representative institutions are likely to survive because of the sheer volume of legislation in modern societies, and the need for full-time officials to run the extensive machinery of government. Nevertheless in an age of mass communication and information, confining the powers of citizens to voting in elections every few years seems a crude approach, a throwback to an earlier era. In a political system based on popular sovereignty, it will become increasingly difficult to justify a failure to consult the voters directly on a wider range of issues.

Facing the Challenge of Semi-Authoritarian States

MARINA OTTAWAY

The last decade of the 20th century saw the rise of a great number of regimes that cannot be easily classified as either authoritarian or democratic but display some characteristics of both—in short, they are *semi-authoritarian.* They are ambiguous systems that combine rhetorical acceptance of liberal democracy, the existence of some formal democratic institutions, and respect for a limited sphere of civil and political liberties with essentially illiberal or even authoritarian traits. That ambiguous Character, furthermore, is deliberate. Semi-authoritarian systems are not imperfect democracies struggling toward improvement and consolidation but regimes determined to maintain the appearance of democracy without exposing themselves to the political risks that free competition entails.

Political hybrids, semi-authoritarian regimes allow little real competition for power, thus reducing government accountability. However, they leave enough political space for political parties and organizations of civil society to form, for an independent press to function to some extent, and for some political debate to take place. Such regimes abound in the Soviet successor states: In countries like Kazakhstan and Azerbaijan, for example, former Communist Party bosses have transformed themselves into elected presidents, but in reality remain strongmen whose power is barely checked by weak democratic institutions.

Semi-authoritarian regimes are also numerous in sub-Saharan Africa, where most of the multiparty elections of the 1990s failed to produce working parliaments or other institutions capable of holding the executive even remotely accountable. In the Arab world, tentative political openings in Algeria, Morocco, and Yemen appear to be leading to the modernization of semi-authoritarianism rather than to democracy, in keeping with a pattern first established by Egypt. In the Balkans, the Communist regimes have disappeared, but despite much international support most governments are semi-authoritarian, with only Slovenia and—more recently and tentatively—Croatia moving toward democracy.

Even more worrisome is the case of Latin America, where economic crises and sharply unequal distribution of income create the risk of popular disenchantment with incumbent democratic governments, and even with democratic institutions.

Already in two countries, first Peru and then Venezuela, steady progress toward democracy has been interrupted by the emergence of semi-authoritarian regimes. In Asia, formal democratic processes are accompanied by strong authoritarian features in countries such as Pakistan, Singapore, and Malaysia, putting them in the realm of semi-authoritarianism.

Semi-authoritarianism is not a new phenomenon—many past regimes have paid lip service to democracy while frequently violating its basic tenets. But the number of such regimes was limited because until the end of the cold war many governments, often supported by their countries' leading intellectuals, rejected liberal democracy outright. They did so in the name of people's democracy (that is, socialism), or in the name of communal cultural traditions that precluded the egoistic individualism on which, they claimed, liberal democracy is based. Since the end of the cold war, few governments and even fewer intellectuals are willing to mount an ideological defense of nondemocratic systems of government; most feel they have to at least pretend adherence to the concept of democracy. On the other hand, the number of governments willing to accept the strict limitations on the extent and duration of their power imposed by democratic rule remains small. As a result, semi-authoritarian regimes have become more numerous.

The number of such regimes is likely to increase even further. In many countries that have experienced a political transition since the early 1990s, unfavorable conditions—including weak democratic institutions and political organizations, persistent authoritarian traditions, major socioeconomic problems, and ethnic and religious conflicts—create formidable obstacles to the establishment and, above all, the consolidation of democracy. Nevertheless, citizens everywhere have shown their disillusionment with authoritarian regimes, and a widespread return to the unabashedly top-down forms of government so common in the past is improbable. These conditions, unfavorable to both genuine democracy and overt authoritarianism, further enhance the prospects for the spread of semi-authoritarianism.

With their combination of positive and negative traits, semi-authoritarian regimes pose a considerable challenge to U.S. policy makers. Such regimes often represent a significant improvement over their predecessors or appear to provide a measure of stability that is welcome in troubled regions. But that superficial stability usually masks a host of severe problems and unsatisfied demands that need to be dealt with lest they lead to crises in the future. Despite their growing importance, however, semi-authoritarian regimes have not received systematic attention.

It is tempting to dismiss the problems created by the proliferation of semi-authoritarian regimes with the argument that, all things considered, they are not that bad and should be accepted as yet-imperfect democracies that will eventually mature into the real thing. For instance, compared to the old Communist Yugoslavia, or to a deeply divided Bosnia suffering from the aftermath of civil war and ethnic cleansing, or to a Serbia in a state of economic collapse but still defiant, Croatia under Franjo Tudjman did not appear too badly off; nor did it create insurmountable problems for the international community. Similarly, the semi-authoritarianism of President Heydar Aliyev in oil-rich Azerbaijan poses fewer immediate problems for policy makers and for oil companies than would a protracted power struggle with uncertain outcome. The widespread discontent in at least some semi-authoritarian states, however, suggests that further change is inevitable and that it is not in the interest of the United States to ignore the problem until crises erupt.

Promoting the democratization of semi-authoritarian regimes is a frustrating undertaking, since they are resistant to the arsenal of reform programs on which the United States and other donor countries usually rely. Semi-authoritarian regimes already do much of what the most widely used democratization projects encourage: They hold regular multiparty elections, allow parliaments to function, and recognize, within limits, the rights of citizens to form associations and of an independent press to operate. Indeed, many countries with semi-authoritarian regimes are beehives of civil-society activity, with hundreds of nongovernmental organizations, or NGO's, operating with foreign support. Many have a very outspoken, even outrageously libelous, independent press. Nevertheless, incumbent governments and parties are in no danger of losing their hold on power, not because they are popular but because they know how to play the democracy game and still retain control. Imposing sanctions on these regimes is usually ineffective, and the political and economic costs it entails, both for those who impose the measures and for the citizens of the targeted country, do not appear justified under the circumstances.

If sticks are in short supply for donors seeking to address the problem of semi-authoritarian regimes, carrots are even scarcer: There is little the international community can offer to a stable regime to entice it to risk losing power. The deepening of democracy is in the long-run interest of these countries, but it is definitely not in the short-term interest of the leaders who stand to lose power if their country becomes more democratic. Going down in history as an enlightened leader appears to be less attractive to most politicians than maintaining their power intact.

Such regimes challenge the assumption, dominant since the end of the cold war, that the failure of the socialist regimes means the triumph of democracy. This "end of history" argument, encapsulated in a book by Francis Fukuyama, of the Johns Hopkins University, puts too much emphasis on the importance of ideologies. It accurately notes that socialism, viewed for the best part of the 20th century as the ideological alternative to democracy, lost its appeal with the collapse of the Communist regimes of the Soviet Union anti Eastern Europe. As a result, the particular type of naked, institutionalized authoritarianism associated with socialism, with its massive single party and complex ideological apparatus, has become exceedingly rare. But relatively few governments, propelled by the genuine pluralism of their society and by an economic system capable of supporting such pluralism, have embraced democracy. Many have devised less heavy-handed, more nimble, and in a sense more imaginative systems that combine authoritarian and liberal traits.

The deliberate character of semi-authoritarian regimes also forces a reconsideration of the visually appealing image of countries that fail to democratize because they are caught in a "reverse wave." This idea, set forth and popularized by Samuel Huntington, of Harvard University, is that in a particular period many countries embrace democracy—figuratively, a wave propels them forward. Some of these countries safely ride the wave to dry land and prosper as democracies. Others are sucked back into the nondemocratic sea as the wave recedes, hopefully to be pushed back toward land by the next wave some decades in the future. It is an enticing idea, but it is not entirely accurate. It assumes that the leaders of all the countries supposedly being caught in a reverse wave intended to reach the shore, but in many cases they did not, and probably neither did many of these countries' citizens. Most countries that fail to reach the shore are not failed democracies caught in the wave's reflux; on the contrary, many are successful semi-authoritarian states that rode the wave as far as they wanted and managed to stop.

Another widespread idea challenged by the proliferation of semi-authoritarian regimes is that liberalization is a step toward democracy because it unleashes the democratic forces of a country. Liberalization undoubtedly allows all types of previously repressed ideas and political forces to bubble up. What actually surfaces depends on what was there. If a strong substratum of democratic ideas and, above all, of democratic organizations existed in the country, then liberalization indeed leads to greater democracy. But it can also lead to an outburst of ethnic nationalism, as in Yugoslavia, or of religious fundamentalism, as in Egypt.

How should such regimes be dealt with? Should the United States try to force democratization programs on Egypt, an important U.S. ally in the Middle East, although the Egyptian government would resist and the programs might even prove destabilizing? How should the international community react to Heydar Aliyev's plan to anoint his son as his successor as president of Azerbaijan, as if the country were a monarchy rather than a republic? What action is warranted when Venezuela starts slipping back from democracy to a semi-authoritarian populism? How can donors facilitate Croatia's second transition, the one from semi-authoritarianism?

But there is another layer of issues raised by semi-authoritarian regimes, which may appear abstract when first formulated but are actually very important to the outcome of democracy-promotion policies. Generally, these issues can be organized under the question, Why do semi-authoritarian regimes come into existence? Is it because of bad leaders (support efforts to vote them out of office), weak institutions (set up a capacity-building program), or a disorganized civil society incapable of holding the government accountable (finance and train nongovernmental organizations)? Or is it because there are underlying conditions that seriously undermine the prospects for democracy (and what can be done about underlying conditions)? Even more fundamentally, does the proliferation of semi-authoritarian regimes indicate that the assumptions about democratic transitions that undergird assistance programs need rethinking?

Democracy-assistance programs are based a lot on theory and relatively little on concrete evidence. That's not strange. Democratization is a complicated and little-understood process. In part, that is because the number of well-established democracies is relatively small, making it difficult to detect regular patterns. In part, it is because studies of democratization vary widely in their approaches and methodologies, yielding noncomparable conclusions. As a result, we understand much better how democratic systems function than why and how they emerged in the first place.

In the course of more than a decade of democracy-promotion efforts, policy makers in the United States and other countries have developed their own model of democratic transitions. That model is based in part on a highly selective reading of the literature on democratization and in part on the operational requirements of agencies that need to show results within a fairly short time frame—in the world of democracy promotion, 10 years already qualifies as long-term, although many studies of democratization highlight processes unfolding over many decades and even centuries. Inevitably, historical studies of democratization that point to the long process of socioeconomic transformation underlying the emergence of democracy have been ignored. There is little policy guidance to be derived from learning that the social capital that made democratic development possible in Northern Italy after World War II started to be built up in the 15th century, or that the rise of the gentry in the 17th century contributed to the democratic evolution of Britain. As a result, the studies with the greatest impact on democracy promotion have been those that looked narrowly at the final phase of democratic transitions, without asking too many questions about what had happened earlier or what kind of conditions had made the democratic outcome possible.

Furthermore, sophisticated studies are often given simplistic interpretations when they become a tool to justify policy choices. For example, among the most influential works often cited by democracy promoters are the studies of transitions from authoritarian rule in Latin America and Southern Europe carried out in the 1980s by a team of investigators, with Philippe Schmitter, now an emeritus professor at Stanford, and Guillermo O'Donnell, of the University of Notre Dame, drawing the overall conclusions. These conclusions were highly preliminary, as Schmitter and O'Donnell made clear with the final volume's subtitle: *Tentative Conclusions about Uncertain Democracies.* As is often the case with successful works, these highly qualified conclusions took on a life of their own, losing their nuances and turning into outright policy prescriptions. In the midst of the transition from apartheid in South Africa in the early 1990s, I heard many political commentators invoke O'Donnell and Schmitter in support of their favorite policies, ignoring the two authors' careful qualifications of their conclusions. A similar fate has befallen Robert Putnam, of Harvard, whose concept of social capital has been transformed to denote not a culture of trust and cooperation developed over centuries, but something that could be quickly created by financing NGO's and training them in the techniques of lobbying the government, administering funds, and reporting to donors.

Through this process of distilling the complex lessons of history into policy prescriptions capable of implementation, donors have developed a simple model of democratization as a three-phase process: liberalization, lasting at most a few years, but preferably much less; the transition proper, accomplished through the holding of a multiparty election; and consolidation, a protracted process of strengthening institutions and deepening a democratic culture. The tools used to facilitate this project are also fairly simple: in the liberalization phase, support for civil society and the independent press; during the transition, support for elections, including voter education, training of NGO's for observing elections, and, more rarely, training of all political parties in the techniques of organizing and campaigning; and in the consolidation phase, new programs to build democratic institutions and the rule of law, as well as the continuation of activities to further strengthen civil society and the media, educate citizens, or train parties.

Semi-authoritarian regimes call into question the model's validity. First, these regimes show that liberalization and transitional elections can constitute the end of the process rather than its initial phases, creating governments determined to prevent further change rather than imperfect but still-evolving democracies. Furthermore, this outcome is not necessarily a failure of democratization, but the result of a deliberate decision to prevent democratization on the part of the elites controlling the process.

Second, an analysis of the workings of semi-authoritarian regimes shows that all sorts of conditions—for example, stagnant economies or ethnic polarization—matter, and matter a great deal at that. The semi-authoritarian outcome is not always something imposed by autocratic leaders on a population that wanted something quite different, but is often accepted and even desired by the population. In many countries—Venezuela, for example—people willingly, even enthusiastically, reject democracy at least for a time. The problem cannot be explained away by arguing that what people reject in such cases was not true democracy to begin with. The reality is more complicated. Conditions affect citizens' priorities and the way they perceive democracy.

Third, semi-authoritarian regimes also challenge the view that democracy can be promoted by an elite of true believers.

Democracy promoters extol in theory the virtue and necessity of broad citizen participation beyond the vote, and innumerable projects target the strengthening of civil society. But civil society as defined by donors is much more part of the elite than of the society at large. Donors favor professional-advocacy NGO's, which speak the language of democracy and easily relate to the international community. For understandable reasons, donors are leery of mass movements, which can easily slip into radical postures and can get out of hand politically. But a problem strikingly common to all countries with semi-authoritarian regimes is that the political elite, whether in the government, opposition parties, or even civil-society organizations, has great difficulty reaching the rest of the society. In the end, that situation plays into the hands of semi-authoritarian regimes.

Dealing with semi-authoritarian regimes thus requires going beyond blaming leaders for nondemocratic outcomes of once-promising democratization processes, no matter how tempting that is. To be sure, leaders with authoritarian tendencies are a real obstacle to democratic transformation. It was pointless to hope for real democratization in Serbia as long as Slobodan Milosevic was in power, and Azerbaijan will likely never be a democratic country under the leadership of Heydar Aliyev. Hugo Chavez is not the man who will restore and revitalize Venezuela's now-shaky democracy. But the problem goes well beyond personalities. Countries do not necessarily deserve the leaders they get, but they do get the leaders whose rise conditions facilitate. If the leader is removed, the conditions remain. For democracy promoters that is an unpleasant thought, because it is easier to demonize individuals and even to oust them from power than to alter the conditions that propel those leaders to the fore.

MARINA OTTAWAY is senior associate in the Democracy and Rule of Law Project at the Carnegie Endowment for International Peace. This is an excerpt from her new book, *Democracy Challenged: The Rise of Semi-Authoritarianism* (Carnegie Endowment).

People Power

In Africa, Democracy Gains Amid Turmoil

SARAH CHILDRESS

In late March, Noel Kututwa's colleagues fanned out across Zimbabwe to monitor the country's presidential elections. The democracy advocates quickly published their tally, projecting President Robert Mugabe had lost his first election since taking power in 1980.

"We expected to be arrested immediately," he says in an interview, but "we wanted to make sure our election was legitimate."

Mr. Kututwa's work in Zimbabwe is part of a shift obscured by his country's bloody election season: Democracy is making gradual gains in sub-Saharan Africa. The trend is driven by a cadre of activists, armed with little more than determination and cheap cellphones, who are outmaneuvering Africa's ruling strongmen.

African democracy has faced jarring setbacks recently. In Kenya, tribal violence killed more than 1,000 people and threatened to tear the nation apart after contested elections earlier this year. In Nigeria, the ruling party blatantly stuffed ballot boxes in national polls last year, according to international observers.

In Zimbabwe today, the opposition party and human-rights groups report near-daily acts of intimidation carried out by Mugabe supporters. Since the election, the opposition Movement for Democratic Change says at least 60 members have been killed, including four who had their eyes and tongues cut out. The government denies participation in the violence. Morgan Tsvangirai, the opposition leader, has been detained by police five times.

Mr. Mugabe raised the stakes this week, promising "war" if Mr. Tsvangirai triumphs in the hotly contested run-off scheduled for June 27, and accused the opposition of fomenting the violence. On Monday, Mr. Mugabe vowed to hold on to power even if he loses. If he acts on that threat, Africa's democratic march will have suffered a significant blow.

But in many ways, the unrest stirring Zimbabwe and other nations is coming because democracy has chalked up modest advances. Mr. Mugabe's ruling party lost its stranglehold on Parliament in the March 29 vote. And the president, whom international observers and the opposition accuse of rigging previous elections, was forced into an embarrassing run-off.

Mr. Kututwa and the Zimbabwe Election Support Network—the nonpartisan coalition of local nonprofit groups he heads—played a crucial role in that defeat. Field workers at far-flung polling stations called in, faxed or text-messaged results to organizers in the capital of Harare.

Working out of a command center at the capital's Holiday Inn, the group crunched the numbers and came up with Mr. Tsvangirai as the projected winner. Faced with an independent count, most of the international community accepted those numbers, making manipulation harder.

These days, "it is very difficult for any dictator or any incumbent to falsify the results of an election and just get away with it," says Mo Ibrahim, a Sudanese telecom tycoon who has become a democracy advocate.

The democratic gains across sub-Saharan Africa come amid the fastest economic growth the region has seen in three decades. Foreign investment is flooding in on the back of soaring prices for the oil, metals and minerals that are plentiful across the continent. The boom, coupled with the region's democratic progress, offers some hope that after a period of post-colonial turmoil, sub-Saharan Africa may be slowly emerging into a more peaceful and prosperous era.

In many countries, democracy is already robust. Ghana, sub-Saharan Africa's first independent nation, is now a thriving democracy and one of Africa's most stable countries. Tanzania, Mauritius, Senegal and Mozambique also have burgeoning, multiparty systems.

Late last year, South Africa's two-term President Thabo Mbeki was voted out of the ruling party's top seat. In April, Botswana's president handed over power to an interim leader ahead of elections next year.

The number of "free" countries among the 48 nations of sub-Saharan Africa—those with multiparty governance, civil rights and a free press—has risen to 11 in 2008 from just three in 1977, according Freedom House, a U.S.-based group that tracks freedom around the world. The number of nations ranked as not free at all has fallen to 14 from 25.

Some of the recent democratic setbacks may come to look less like catastrophic defeats than stress tests. Challengers sued over the disputed results of the 2007 elections in Nigeria, and the courts eventually threw out the results for seven governors, the senate president and several other lawmakers. In Kenya, the incumbent president was forced to share power with his opponent after results were contested.

In a growing number of countries, including Zimbabwe, grass-roots democracy groups are working to keep their leaders in check. The Africa Progress Panel, an international assessment body chaired by former United Nations chief Kofi Annan, released a report this week crediting nongovernmental organizations and other civil-society groups with increasingly holding governments accountable.

"Democratic change is coming to the forefront faster than institutional change," said Tendai Biti, the Zimbabwe opposition party's secretary-general, at a recent panel on African governance in Cape Town, South Africa.

Last week, Mr. Biti was jailed upon his return to Zimbabwe and charged with treason. The opposition party says he is innocent. Tuesday night, the High Court rejected the opposition's bid to have him released. He remains in jail.

Despite the tense situation in Zimbabwe, Mr. Kututwa says his Zimbabwe Election Support Network plans to mobilize again in next week's run-off.

Government spokesman Bright Matonga says the network is biased toward the opposition. But "they were open and honest with the way they put the results together," he says, adding that the government plans to accredit them again. The network says it is nonpartisan.

Mr. Kututwa's network had long sent observers to monitor Zimbabwean voting, typically issuing reports documenting government interference. A long-time human-rights worker in Zimbabwe, Mr. Kututwa took over as ZESN's chairman in 2002. He watched from afar as democracy advocates used cellphones to transmit local results during elections in Sierra Leone in 2007. The results, which affirmed President Ernest Bai Koroma's narrow victory, calmed tensions in the post-war environment.

Mr. Kututwa resolved to do the same during Zimbabwe's 2008 presidential election. "We wanted to take our observation to the next level," he says.

In March 2007, Mr. Tsvangirai was arrested and beaten in police custody. The government said he had attacked police. Images of his gashed and swollen face brought international outrage, and neighboring nations demanded talks between the government and the opposition over how to ensure a fair vote. The talks fell apart, but they produced one key change in election rules: The government agreed that results from each polling station would be posted locally before they were sent to election headquarters to be tallied by the country's election commission.

It seemed a small concession at the time. Mr. Mugabe was confident of a win. His policies have turned the region's onetime bread basket into an economic basket case. The International Monetary Fund says Zimbabwe is in hyperinflation, and can't even make meaningful projections about the rate anymore.

But Mr. Mugabe is revered, at home and across Africa, as the father of an independent Zimbabwe, having liberated the country from white rule in 1980. His freedom-fighter credentials had long bolstered his popularity in the countryside, and he had cracked down hard on dissenters. He had never lost an election, although he had been accused by international observers and the opposition of rigging the 2002 presidential vote and 2005 parliamentary elections.

Posting the local results, Mr. Kututwa knew, would allow monitors to make their own count before any alleged rigging began in Harare.

The network team settled on a technique known as "parallel-vote tabulation." The idea: Volunteers record local results from a sample of polling stations, and send them to a central database. Organizers then calculate a statistical projection of the total vote.

The method is simple enough to work in places with poor infrastructure, and it avoids the pitfalls of exit polling in oppressive regimes. The method isn't meant to replace an official count, but rather to serve as a barometer of the official tally's accuracy.

The counting method bolstered allegations of fraud in the Philippines' 1986 election. The vote, which had reinstated President Ferdinand Marcos, was later nullified after demonstrations that sent Mr. Marcos into exile. The method was also used later in elections in Malawi and Zambia.

By election day this March in Zimbabwe, 8,900 network volunteers had received official accreditation by the government to observe the voting. They spread out through Zimbabwe's bush to observe at 435 polling stations—about 5% of the total in a country slightly larger than the state of Montana.

The stations selected came from all of Zimbabwe's 10 electoral provinces, and were based on population density. Voters had camped out at polling places as early as 1 A.M. on the eve of the vote. When they began casting ballots six hours later, ZESN's command center at the Holiday Inn started buzzing.

Organizers' cellphones lighted up with received text-messages, and fax machines creaked to life. The polls closed that evening. ZESN's teams reported final local vote counts to Harare by text message, satellite phones and fax. Some drove in their findings.

Shortly after the polls closed, Mr. Kututwa and his team had their projection. The group decided to wait for the official count. In the past, the country's electoral commission—whose members are appointed by Mr. Mugabe's government—announced official results around midnight. But that night the commission stayed silent.

The following day, Sunday, came and went with no word from the commission. The opposition, which had conducted its own polling, claimed victory. Riot police patrolled the capital streets.

By late Monday, March 31, Mr. Kututwa decided his group couldn't wait any longer and called a news conference for 8 that evening.

The group's projections showed Mr. Tsvangirai winning 49.8%, just shy of the majority he needed to avoid a run-off. Mr. Mugabe captured 41.3%. A third independent candidate won 8%. The group determined the margin of error at a little over 2%.

Journalists, human-rights groups and governments around the world seized on the numbers. Rumors swirled that Mr. Mugabe was considering stepping down.

But the regime slowly regrouped. Four weeks after the ZESN news conference, armed Zimbabwean police raided the group's Harare office. Carrying a warrant to search for "subversive material," they carted away documents. A member of ZESN was beaten and his home burned, the group says.

The police also detained another member, questioning him for six hours. When he heard police were looking for him, Mr. Kututwa fled the country, though he returned days later.

On May 2, five weeks after Mr. Kututwa's news conference, the electoral commission announced its own results. They jibed with ZESN's figures—up to a point. Mr. Mugabe received 43.2%, the highest number statistically consistent with ZESN's projection and margin of error, according to Mr. Kututwa. Mr. Tsvangirai received 47.9%, the lowest possible figure.

"Statistically, it's unusual," Mr. Kututwa says, but he felt validated anyway. "We still don't agree with the final results, but it's not [altered] as much as it could have been," he says.

The group hopes to conduct another projection for the June 27 run-off.

Mr. Kututwa's project has inspired others. Ghana is respected as a model of democracy in Africa. President John Kufuor, after serving two elected terms, will step aside this year as two new candidates vie for his seat. Most observers predict a fair contest.

But E. Gyimah-Boadi, executive director of the Ghana Center for Democratic Development, and other advocacy groups plan to compute their own statistical projection for the December elections. The vote could be close, and the winner will likely emerge with only a slight majority.

"There will be a lot of room for dispute," Mr. Gyimah-Boadi says. "Which means, we'd better get it right."

Bin Laden, the Arab "Street," and the Middle East's Democracy Deficit

"Bin Laden speaks in the vivid language of popular Islamic preachers, and builds on a deep and widespread resentment against the West and local ruling elites identified with it. The lack of formal outlets to express opinion on public concerns has created [a] democracy deficit in much of the Arab world, and this makes it easier for terrorists such as bin Laden, asserting that they act in the name of religion, to hijack the Arab street."

DALE F. EICKELMAN

In the years ahead, the role of public diplomacy and open communications will play an increasingly significant role in countering the image that the Al Qaeda terrorist network and Osama bin Laden assert for themselves as guardians of Islamic values. In the fight against terrorism for which bin Laden is the photogenic icon, the first step is to recognize that he is as thoroughly a part of the modern world as was Cambodia's French-educated Pol Pot. Bin Laden's videotaped presentation of self intends to convey a traditional Islamic warrior brought up-to-date, but this sense of the past is a completely invented one. The language and content of his videotaped appeals convey more of his participation in the modern world than his camouflage jacket, Kalashnikov, and Timex watch.

Take the two-hour Al Qaeda recruitment videotape in Arabic that has made its way to many Middle Eastern video shops and Western news media.[1] It is a skillful production, as fast paced and gripping as any Hindu fundamentalist video justifying the destruction in 1992 of the Ayodhya mosque in India, or the political attack videos so heavily used in American presidential campaigning. The 1988 "Willie Horton" campaign video of Republican presidential candidate George H. W. Bush—in which an off-screen announcer portrayed Democratic presidential candidate Michael Dukakis as "soft" on crime while showing a mug shot of a convicted African-American rapist who had committed a second rape during a weekend furlough from a Massachusetts prison—was a propaganda masterpiece that combined an explicit although conventional message with a menacing, underlying one intended to motivate undecided voters. The Al Qaeda video, directed at a different audience—presumably alienated Arab youth, unemployed and often living in desperate conditions—shows an equal mastery of modern propaganda.

The Al Qaeda producers could have graduated from one of the best film schools in the United States or Europe. The fast-moving recruitment video begins with the bombing of the USS *Cole* in Yemen, but then shows a montage implying a seemingly coordinated worldwide aggression against Muslims in Palestine, Jerusalem, Lebanon, Chechnya, Kashmir, and Indonesia (but not Muslim violence against Christians and Chinese in the last). It also shows United States generals received by Saudi princes, intimating the collusion of local regimes with the West and challenging the legitimacy of many regimes, including Saudi Arabia. The sufferings of the Iraqi people are attributed to American brutality against Muslims, but Saddam Hussein is assimilated to the category of infidel ruler.

Osama bin Laden . . . is thoroughly imbued with the values of the modern world, even if only to reject them.

Many of the images are taken from the daily staple of Western video news—the BBC and CNN logos add to the videos' authenticity, just as Qatar's al-Jazeera satellite television logo rebroadcast by CNN and the BBC has added authenticity to Western coverage of Osama bin Laden.

Alternating with these scenes of devastation and oppression of Muslims are images of Osama bin Laden: posing in front of bookshelves or seated on the ground like a religious scholar, holding the Koran in his hand. Bin Laden radiates charismatic authority and control as he narrates the Prophet Mohammed's flight from Mecca to Medina, when the early Islamic movement was threatened by the idolaters, but returning to conquer them. Bin Laden also stresses the need for jihad, or struggle for the cause of Islam, against the "crusaders" and "Zionists." Later images show military training in Afghanistan (including target practice at a poster of Bill Clinton), and a final sequence—the word "solution" flashes across the screen—captures an Israeli soldier in full riot gear retreating from a Palestinian boy throwing stones, and a reading of the Koran.

The Thoroughly Modern Islamist

Osama bin Laden, like many of his associates, is imbued with the values of the modern world, even if only to reject them. A 1971 photograph shows him on family holiday in Oxford at the age of 14, posing with two of his half-brothers and Spanish girls their own age. English was their common language of communication. Bin Laden studied English at a private school in Jidda, and English was also useful for his civil engineering courses at Jidda's King Abdul Aziz University. Unlike many of his estranged half-brothers, educated in Saudi Arabia, Europe, and the United States, Osama's education was only in Saudi Arabia, but he was also familiar with Arab and European society.

The organizational skills he learned in Saudi Arabia came in to play when he joined the mujahideen (guerrilla) struggle against the 1979 Soviet invasion of Afghanistan. He may not have directly met United States intelligence officers in the field, but they, like their Saudi and Pakistani counterparts, were delighted to have him participate in their fight against Soviet troops and recruit willing Arab fighters. Likewise, his many business enterprises flourished under highly adverse conditions. Bin Laden skillfully sustained a flexible multinational organization in the face of enemies, especially state authorities, moving cash, people, and supplies almost undetected across international frontiers.

The organizational skills of bin Laden and his associates were never underestimated. Neither should be their skills in conveying a message that appeals to some Muslims. Bin Laden lacks the credentials of an established Islamic scholar, but this does not diminish his appeal. As Sudan's Sorbonne-educated Hasan al-Turabi, the leader of his country's Muslim Brotherhood and its former attorney general and speaker of parliament, explained two decades ago, "Because all knowledge is divine and religious, a chemist, an engineer, an economist, or a jurist" are all men of learning.[2] Civil engineer bin Laden exemplifies Turabi's point. His audience judges him not by his ability to cite authoritative texts, but by his apparent skill in applying generally accepted religious tenets to current political and social issues.

The Message on the Arab "Street"

Bin Laden's lectures circulate in book form in the Arab world, but video is the main vehicle of communication. The use of CNN-like "zippers"—the ribbons of words that stream beneath the images in many newscasts and documentaries—shows that Al Qaeda takes the Arab world's rising levels of education for granted. Increasingly, this audience is also saturated with both conventional media and new media, such as the Internet.[3] The Middle East has entered an era of mass education and this also implies an Arabic lingua franca. In Morocco in the early 1970s, rural people sometimes asked me to "translate" newscasts from the standard transnational Arabic of the state radio into colloquial Arabic. Today this is no longer required. Mass education and new communications technologies enable large numbers of Arabs to hear—and see—Al Qaeda's message directly.

Bin Laden's message does not depend on religious themes alone. Like the Ayatollah Ruhollah Khomeini, his message contains many secular elements. Khomeini often alluded to the "wretched of the earth." At least for a time, his language appealed equally to Iran's religiously minded and to the secular left. For bin Laden, the equivalent themes are the oppression and corruption of many Arab governments, and he lays the blame for the violence and oppression in Palestine, Kashmir, Chechnya, and elsewhere at the door of the West. One need not be religious to rally to some of these themes. A poll taken in Morocco in late September 2001 showed that a majority of Moroccans condemned the September 11 bombings, but 41 percent sympathized with bin Laden's message. A British poll taken at about the same time showed similar results.

Osama bin Laden and the Al Qaeda terrorist movement are thus reaching at least part of the Arab "street." Earlier this year, before the September terrorist attacks, United States policymakers considered this "street" a "new phenomenon of public accountability, which we have seldom had to factor into our projections of Arab behavior in the past. The information revolution, and particularly the daily dose of uncensored television coming out of local TV stations like al-Jazeera and international coverage by CNN and others, is shaping public opinion, which, in turn, is pushing Arab governments to respond. We don't know, and the leaders themselves don't know, how that pressure will impact on Arab policy in the future."[4]

Director of Central Intelligence George J. Tenet was even more cautionary on the nature of the "Arab street." In testimony before the Senate Select Committee on Intelligence in February 2001, he explained that the "right catalyst—such as the outbreak of Israeli-Palestinian violence—can move people to act. Through access to the Internet and other means of communication, a restive public is increasingly capable of taking action without any identifiable leadership or organizational structure."

Because many governments in the Middle East are deeply suspicious of an open press, nongovernmental organizations, and open expression, it is no surprise that the "restive" public, increasingly educated and influenced by hard-to-censor new media, can take action "without any identifiable leadership or organized structure." The Middle East in general has a democracy deficit, in which "unauthorized" leaders or critics, such as Egyptian academic Saad Eddin Ibrahim—founder and director of the Ibn Khaldun Center for Development Studies, a nongovernmental organization that promotes democracy in Egypt—suffer harassment or prison terms.

One consequence of this democracy deficit is to magnify the power of the street in the Arab world. Bin Laden speaks in the vivid language of popular Islamic preachers, and builds on a deep and widespread resentment against the West and local ruling elites identified with it. The lack of formal outlets to express opinion on public concerns has created the democracy deficit in much of the Arab world, and this makes it easier for terrorists such as bin Ladin, asserting that they act in the name of religion, to hijack the Arab street.

The immediate response is to learn to speak directly to this street. This task has already begun. Obscure to all except specialists until September 11, Qatar's al-Jazeera satellite television is a premier source in the Arab world for uncensored news and opinion. It is more, however, than the Arab equivalent of CNN. Uncensored news and opinions increasingly shape "public opinion"—a term without the pejorative overtones of "the street"—even in places like Damascus and Algiers. This public opinion in turn pushes Arab governments to be more responsive to their citizens, or at least to say that they are.

Rather than seek to censor al-Jazeera or limit Al Qaeda's access to the Western media—an unfortunate first response of the United States government after the September terror attacks—we should avoid censorship. Al Qaeda statements should be treated with the same caution as any other news source. Replacing Sinn Fein leader Gerry Adams' voice and image in the British media in the 1980s with an Irish-accented actor appearing in silhouette only highlighted what he had to say, and it is unlikely that the British public would tolerate the same restrictions on the media today.

Ironically, at almost the same time that national security adviser Condoleezza Rice asked the American television networks not to air Al Qaeda videos unedited, a former senior CIA officer, Graham Fuller, was explaining in Arabic on al-Jazeera how United States policymaking works. His appearance on al-Jazeera made a significant impact, as did Secretary of State Colin Powell's presence on a later al-Jazeera program and former United States Ambassador Christopher Ross, who speaks fluent Arabic. Likewise, the timing and content of British Prime Minister Tony Blair's response to an earlier bin Laden tape suggests how to take the emerging Arab public seriously. The day after al-Jazeera broadcast the bin Laden tape, Blair asked for and received an opportunity to respond. In his reply, Blair—in a first for a Western leader—directly addressed the Arab public through the Arab media, explaining coalition goals in attacking Al Qaeda and the Taliban and challenging bin Laden's claim to speak in the name of Islam.

Putting Public Diplomacy to Work

Such appearances enhance the West's ability to communicate a primary message: that the war against terrorism is not that of one civilization against another, but against terrorism and fanaticism in all societies. Western policies and actions are subject to public scrutiny and will often be misunderstood. Public diplomacy can significantly diminish this misapprehension. It may, however, involve some uncomfortable policy decisions. For instance, America may be forced to exert more diplomatic pressure on Israel to alter its methods of dealing with Palestinians.

Western public diplomacy in the Middle East also involves uncharted waters. As Oxford University social linguist Clive Holes has noted, the linguistic genius who thought up the first name for the campaign to oust the Taliban, "Operation Infinite Justice," did a major disservice to the Western goal. The

expression was literally and accurately translated into Arabic as *adala ghayr mutanahiya,* implying that an earthly power arrogated to itself the task of divine retribution. Likewise, President George W. Bush's inadvertent and unscripted use of the word "crusade" gave Al Qaeda spokesmen an opportunity to attack Bush and Western intentions.

Mistakes will be made, but information and arguments that reach the Arab street, including on al-Jazeera, will eventually have an impact. Some Westerners might condemn al-Jazeera as biased, and it may well be in terms of making assumptions about its audience. However, it has broken a taboo by regularly inviting official Israeli spokespersons to comment live on current issues. Muslim religious scholars, both in the Middle East and in the West, have already spoken out against Al Qaeda's claim to act in the name of Islam. Other courageous voices, such as Egyptian playwright Ali Salem, have even employed humor for the same purpose.[5]

We must recognize that the best way to mitigate the continuing threat of terrorism is to encourage Middle Eastern states to be more responsive to participatory demands, and to aid local nongovernmental organizations working toward this goal. As with the case of Egypt's Saad Eddin Ibrahim, some countries may see such activities as subversive. Whether Arab states like it or not, increasing levels of education, greater ease of travel, and the rise of new communications media are turning the Arab street into a public sphere in which greater numbers of people, and not just a political and economic elite, will have a say in governance and public issues.

Notes

1. It is now available on-line with explanatory notes in English. See <http://www.ciaonet.org/cbr/cbr00/video/excerpts_index.html>.

2. Hasan al-Turabi, "The Islamic State," in *Voices of Resurgent Islam,* John L. Esposito, ed. (New York: Oxford University Press, 1983), p. 245.

3. On the importance of rising levels of education and the new media, see Dale F. Eickelman, "The Coming Transformation in the Muslim World," *Current History,* January 2000.

4. Edward S. Walker, "The New US Administration's Middle East Policy Speech," *Middle East Economic Survey,* vol. 44, no. 26 (June 25, 2001). Available at <http://www.mees.com/news/a44n26d01.htm>.

5. See his article in Arabic, "I Want to Start a Kindergarten for Extremism," *Al-Hayat* (London), November 5, 2001. This is translated into English by the Middle East Media Research Institute as Special Dispatch no. 298, Jihad and Terrorism Studies, November 8, 2001, at <http://www.memri.org>.

DALE F. EICKELMAN is Ralph and Richard Lazarus Professor of Anthropology and Human Relations at Dartmouth College. His most recent book is *The Middle East and Central Asia: An Anthropological Approach,* 4th ed. (Englewood Cliffs, N. J.: Prentice Hall, 2002). An earlier version of this article appeared as "The West Should Speak to the Arab in the Street," *Daily Telegraph* (London), October 27, 2001.

From *Current History,* January 2002, pp. 36–39. Copyright © 2002 by Current History, Inc. Reprinted by permission.

UNIT 2

Political Parties and Interest Groups: From Preferences to Policies

Unit Selections

8. **What Political Institutions Does Large-Scale Democracy Require?**, Robert A. Dahl
9. **Interest Groups: Ex Uno, Plures,** *The Economist*
10. **Political Parties: Empty Vessels?,** *The Economist*
11. **Police Clash with Monks in Myanmar,** Seth Mydans
12. **Concerns Grow About Role of Interest Groups in Elections,** Glen Justice
13. **Venezuela Hands Narrow Defeat to Chávez Plan,** Simon Romero

Key Points to Consider

- Why would you join a group?

- When is an interest group considered successful?

- When is an interest group considered to have failed?

- What are the roles of interest groups and political parties in a political system?

- When are political parties considered successful?

- What characterizes political parties as failures?

- How has the availability of and improvement in communications helped interest groups?

- How has the availability of and improvement in communications helped political parties?

Student Web Site

www.mhcls.com

Internet References

Human Rights Watch
http://www.hrw.org/
National Geographic Society
http://www.nationalgeographic.com
Research and Reference (Library of Congress)
http://www.loc.gov/rr/
Sun SITE Singapore
http://sunsite.nus.edu.sg/noframe.html
UN Interactive Database
http://cyberschoolbus.un.org/infonation/index.asp

Unit 2 builds upon the discussion of citizen participation in Unit 1 to address systematically why and how citizen participation is organized, and what forms it takes. The unit begins with Robert Dahl's article, "What Political Institutions Does Large-Scale Democracy Require?", which points out two obvious advantages to organizing citizens. First, it improves efficiency and effectiveness of participation. In particular, aggregating the interests and preferences of citizens is invaluable as the size of the citizenry increases, and as more people are dispersed over larger geographic areas. Second, organized citizen groups provide the counterbalance to coercive governments who may not be willing to tolerate or accommodate interests that depart from the government's goals. As the author points out, "the degree of coercion" required to suppress larger associations is generally considered objectionable. Consequently, groups are able to exist and express themselves where individual citizens are unable to. The article, "Interest Groups: Ex Uno, Plures," adds two additional considerations. One, interest groups keep

political parties and the politicians affiliated therewith, honest and accountable for their actions in between elections. Two, interest groups provide expertise and advice; after all, they have to be well versed in the area of their interest in order to put forth their arguments.

How are interests organized? Mancur Olson's *Logic of Collective Action,* which is discussed in the article "Interest Groups: Ex Uno, Plures," argues that citizens are not persuaded to join groups easily. Instead, there is a temptation to "free-ride," that is, to not participate in groups but, nevertheless, enjoy the fruits of policies that interest groups pressure their governments to implement. However, other scholars find numerous reasons beyond personal gain that motivate individual citizens to join interests groups. They include altruism, personal values, shared values, and self-expression.

The articles regarding Myanmar and Venezuela in 2007 certainly support the latter view. The article on Myanmar reports that protestors, led by monks, stayed true to the spirit of the demonstrations notwithstanding "troop deployments and initial bursts of violence" from the government. The report on Venezuela likewise points out that former supporters of Hugo Chávez were responsible for the defeat of the referenda to change the constitution in order to increase the political strength of the executive. In both cases, it is evident that citizens mobilized and participated as groups to express values beyond personal gain.

The articles on Myanmar and Venezuela also reveal the effects of such group activity in that they bring recognition to the groups or movement. This may be domestic, as in Venezuela, where organized farm and student groups inflamed the opposition and the military to stand up against an increasingly willful President Chávez. Or it may be international, as in Myanmar, where international organizations such as the UN and foreign governments such as the U.S. and Great Britain were moved to adopt sanctions and consider other forms of pressure to aid the protest groups and their cause.

However, the effects of interest groups are not all good. For instance, the article, "Concerns Grow About Role of Interest Groups in Elections" describes the success of 527 committees in raising campaign funds that are subsequently used to influence election outcomes. In this case, it seems that the interests of a few, may dominate over the interests of the many. Likewise, the article, "Interest Groups: Ex Uno, Plures," points out that governments may make decisions that are in favor of interest groups but go against the interest of the wider public, given the disparities in fervor between the two in pursuing policies that affect them. The abilities of interest groups to exercise influence disproportionate to their numbers is one reason for considering the need to control such influence, and how to do so.

What other existing forms of organized participation provide a potentially countervailing influence to interest groups? One form is the political party. Political parties are like interest groups, only with more depth and broader scope. Indeed, Dahl's article points out that political parties are often morphed from interest groups. The transformation occurs when the interest groups or factions in legislature find themselves thwarted in pursuing policy ideas, or find that merely checking the policies of the existing government does not lead to the policies they desire.

Political parties of the past enjoyed more successes. These days, political parties appear to be caught in the web of growing public dissatisfaction. Thus, membership in political parties is declining. Also, ideological differences between political parties, which in part explain party appeal and loyalties, have narrowed. In fact, it may make more sense to speak of the Center-Left and Center-Right, rather than the traditional left-right distinction, because of this political convergence.[1] Even the traditional job of parties—communicating with members—has been replaced by the media.

Yet, notwithstanding evidence of party decline, political parties remain vital: they still control nomination for office and, in fact, independent candidates are rarely successful. Membership may be down but the parties continue to be able to organize and bring in funding. And, while membership is falling, political parties can count on increasing alliances with groups. Most importantly, parties continue to be able to exercise power in office. This power and the persistence of political parties is relevant: it serves as a countervailing force to any growing might of interest groups. Notably, even at their most effective, the impact of interest groups on policy-making and implementation are far from certain.

It is safe to say that political parties and interest groups are not likely to disappear from the political landscape. While we may be concerned about their effects from time to time, they allow for voices to be heard and act as relief valves that release pressures within the political system. As a result, the way to control undue influence from political parties or interest groups may not be to restrict them but, rather, to pluralize them.

Note

1. **The Right** is usually far more ready to accept as "normal" or "inevitable" the existence of social or economic inequalities, and normally favors lower taxes and the promotion of market forces—with some very important exceptions intended to protect the nation as a whole (national defense and internal security) as well as certain favored values and interest groups (clienteles). In general, the Right sees the state as an instrument that should provide security, order, and protection for an established way of life. **The Left,** by contrast, traditionally emphasizes that government has an important task in opening greater opportunities or "life chances" for everyone, delivering affordable public services, and generally reducing social inequality.

What Political Institutions Does Large-Scale Democracy Require?

Robert A. Dahl

What does it mean to say that a country is governed democratically? Here, we will focus on the political institutions of *democracy on a large scale*, that is, the political institutions necessary for a *democratic country*. We are not concerned here, then, with what democracy in a very small group might require, as in a committee. We also need to keep in mind that every actual democracy has always fallen short of democratic criteria. Finally, we should be aware that in ordinary language, we use the word *democracy* to refer both to a goal or ideal and to an actuality that is only a partial attainment of the goal. For the time being, therefore, I'll count on the reader to make the necessary distinctions when I use the words *democracy, democratically, democratic government, democratic country*, and so on.[1]

How Can We Know?

How can we reasonably determine what political institutions are necessary for large-scale democracy? We might examine the history of countries that have changed their political institutions in response, at least in part, to demands for broader popular inclusion and effective participation in government and political life. Although in earlier times those who sought to gain inclusion and participation were not necessarily inspired by democratic ideas,

from about the eighteenth century onward they tended to justify their demands by appealing to democratic and republican ideas. What political institutions did they seek, and what were actually adopted in these countries?

Alternatively, we could examine countries where the government is generally referred to as democratic by most of the people in that country, by many persons in other countries, and by scholars, journalists, and the like. In other words, in ordinary speech and scholarly discussion the country is called a democracy.

Third, we could reflect on a specific country or group of countries, or perhaps even a hypothetical country, in order to imagine, as realistically as possible, what political institutions would be required in order to achieve democratic goals to a substantial degree. We would undertake a mental experiment, so to speak, in which we would reflect carefully on human experiences, tendencies, possibilities, and limitations and design a set of political institutions that would be necessary for large-scale democracy to exist and yet feasible and attainable within the limits of human capacities.

Fortunately, all three methods converge on the same set of democratic political institutions. These, then, are minimal requirements for a democratic country (Figure 1).

The Political Institutions of Modern Representative Democracy

Briefly, the political institutions of modern representative democratic government are

- *Elected officials.* Control over government decisions about policy is constitutionally vested in officials elected by citizens. Thus modern, large-scale democratic governments are *representative*.
- *Free, fair and frequent elections.* Elected officials are chosen in frequent and fairly conducted elections in which coercion is comparatively uncommon.

What Political Institutions Does Large-Scale Democracy Require?

Large-scale democracy requires:

1. Elected officials
2. Free, fair, and frequent elections
3. Freedom of expression
4. Alternative sources of information
5. Associational autonomy
6. Inclusive citizenship

Figure 1

- *Freedom of expression.* Citizens have a right to express themselves without danger of severe punishment on political matters broadly defined, including criticism of officials, the government, the regime, the socioeconomic order, and the prevailing ideology.
- *Access to alternative sources of information.* Citizens have a right to seek out alternative and independent sources of information from other citizens, experts, newspapers, magazines, books, telecommunications, and the like. Moreover, alternative sources of information actually exist that are not under the control of the government or any other single political group attempting to influence public political beliefs and attitudes, and these alternative sources are effectively protected by law.
- *Associational autonomy.* To achieve their various rights, including those required for the effective operation of democratic political institutions, citizens also have a right to form relatively independent associations or organizations, including independent political parties and interest groups.
- *Inclusive citizenship.* No adult permanently residing in the country and subject to its laws can be denied the rights that are available to others and are necessary to the five political institutions just listed. These include the right to vote in the election of officials in free and fair elections; to run for elective office; to free expression; to form and participate in independent political organizations; to have access to independent sources of information; and rights to other liberties and opportunities that may be necessary to the effective operation of the political institutions of large-scale democracy.

The Political Institutions in Perspective

Ordinarily these institutions do not arrive in a country all at once; the last two are distinctly latecomers. Until the twentieth century, universal suffrage was denied in both the theory and practice of democratic and republican government. More than any other single feature, universal suffrage distinguishes modern representative democracy from earlier forms of democracy.

The time of arrival and the sequence in which the institutions have been introduced have varied tremendously. In countries where the full set of democratic institutions arrived earliest and have endured to the present day, the "older" democracies, elements of a common pattern emerge. Elections to a legislature arrived early on—in Britain as early as the thirteenth century, in the United States during its colonial period in the seventeenth and eighteenth centuries. The practice of electing higher lawmaking officials was followed by a gradual expansion of the rights of citizens to express themselves on political matters and to seek out and exchange information. The right to form associations with explicit political goals tended to follow

still later. Political "factions" and partisan organization were generally viewed as dangerous, divisive, subversive of political order and stability, and injurious to the public good. Yet because political associations could not be suppressed without a degree of coercion that an increasingly large and influential number of citizens regarded as intolerable, they were often able to exist as more or less clandestine associations until they emerged from the shadows into the full light of day. In the legislative bodies, what once were "factions" became political parties. The "ins" who served in the government of the day were opposed by the "outs," or what in Britain came to be officially styled His (or Her) Majesty's Loyal Opposition. In eighteenth-century Britain, the faction supporting the monarch and the opposing faction supported by much of the gentry in the "country" were gradually transformed into Tories and Whigs. During that same century in Sweden, partisan adversaries in Parliament somewhat facetiously called themselves the Hats and the Caps.[2]

During the final years of the eighteenth century in the newly formed republic of the United States, Thomas Jefferson, the vice president, and James Madison, leader of the House of Representatives, organized their followers in Congress to oppose the policies of the Federalist president, John Adams, and his secretary of the treasury, Alexander Hamilton. To succeed in their opposition, they soon realized that they would have to do more than oppose the Federalists in the Congress and the cabinet: they would need to remove their opponents from office. To do that, they had to win national elections, and to win national elections they had to organize their followers throughout the country. In less than a decade, Jefferson, Madison, and others sympathetic with their views created a political party that was organized all the way down to the smallest voting precincts, districts, and municipalities, an organization that would reinforce the loyalty of their followers between and during election campaigns and make sure they came to the polls. Their Republican Party (soon renamed Democratic Republican and, a generation later, Democratic) became the first popularly based *electoral* party in the world. As a result, one of the most fundamental and distinctive political institutions of modern democracy, the political party, had burst beyond its confines in parliaments and legislatures in order to organize the citizens themselves and mobilize party supporters in national elections.

By the time the young French aristocrat Alexis de Tocqueville visited the United States in the 1830s, the first five democratic political institutions described above had already arrived in America. The institutions seemed to him so deeply planted and pervasive that he had no hesitation in referring to the United States as a democracy. In that country, he said, the people were sovereign, "society governs itself for itself," and the power of the majority was unlimited.[3] He was astounded by the multiplicity of associations into which Americans organized themselves, for every purpose, it seemed. And towering among these associations were the two major political parties. In the United States, it appeared to Tocqueville, democracy was about as complete as one could imagine it ever becoming.

During the century that followed, all five of the basic democratic institutions Tocqueville observed during his visit to America were consolidated in more than a dozen other countries. Many observers in Europe and the United States concluded that any country that aspired to be civilized and progressive would necessarily have to adopt a democratic form of government.

Yet everywhere, the sixth fundamental institution—inclusive citizenship—was missing. Although Tocqueville affirmed that "the state of Maryland, which had been founded by men of rank, was the first to proclaim universal suffrage," like almost all other men (and many women) of his time he tacitly assumed that "universal" did not include women.[4] Nor, indeed, some men. Maryland's "universal suffrage," it so happened, also excluded most African Americans. Elsewhere, in countries that were otherwise more or less democratic, as in America, a full half of all adults were completely excluded from national political life simply because they were women; in addition, large numbers of men were denied suffrage because they could not meet literacy or property requirements, an exclusion supported by many people who considered themselves advocates of democratic or republican government. Although New Zealand extended suffrage to women in national elections in 1893 and Australia in 1902, in countries otherwise democratic, women did not gain suffrage in national elections until about 1920; in Belgium, France, and Switzerland, countries that most people would have called highly democratic, women could not vote until after World War II.

Because it is difficult for many today to grasp what "democracy" meant to our predecessors, let me reemphasize the difference: in all democracies and republics throughout twenty-five centuries, the rights to engage fully in political life were restricted to a minority of adults. "Democratic" government was government by males only—and not all of them. It was not until the twentieth century that in both theory and practice democracy came to require that the rights to engage fully in political life must be extended, with very few if any exceptions, to the entire population of adults permanently residing in a country.

Taken in their entirety, then, these six political institutions constitute not only a new type of political system but a new kind of popular government, a type of "democracy" that had never existed throughout the twenty-five centuries of experience since the inauguration of "democracy" in Athens and a "republic" in Rome. Because the institutions of modern representative democratic government, taken in their entirety, are historically unique, it is convenient to give them their own name. This modern type of large-scale democratic government is sometimes called *polyarchal* democracy.

Although other factors were often at work, the six political institutions of polyarchal democracy came about, in part at least, in response to demands for inclusion and participation in political life. In countries that are widely referred to as democracies today, all six exist. Yet you might well ask: Are some of these institutions no more than past products of historical struggles? Are they no longer necessary for democratic government? And if they are still necessary today, why?[5]

The Factor of Size

Before answering these questions, I need to call attention to an important qualification. We are considering institutions necessary for the government of a democratic country. Why "country"? *Because all the institutions necessary for a democratic country would not always be required for a unit much smaller than a country.*

Consider a democratically governed committee, or a club, or a very small town. Although equality in voting would seem to be necessary, small units like these might manage without many elected officials: perhaps a moderator to preside over meetings, a secretary-treasurer to keep minutes and accounts. The participants themselves could decide just about everything directly during their meetings, leaving details to the secretary-treasurer. Governments of small organizations would not have to be full-fledged *representative* governments in which citizens elect representatives charged with enacting laws and policies. Yet these governments could be democratic, perhaps highly democratic. So, too, even though they lacked political parties or other independent political associations, they might be highly democratic. In fact, we might concur with the classical democratic and republican view that in small associations, organized "factions" are not only unnecessary but downright harmful. Instead of conflicts exacerbated by factionalism, caucuses, political parties, and so on, we might prefer unity, consensus, agreement achieved by discussion and mutual respect.

The political institutions strictly required for democratic government depend, then, on the size of the unit. The six institutions listed above developed because they are necessary for governing *countries*, not smaller units. Polyarchal democracy is democratic government on the large scale of the nation-state or country.

To return to our questions: Are the political institutions of polyarchal democracy actually necessary for democracy on the large scale of a country? If so, why? To answer these twin questions, let us recall what a democratic process requires (Figure 2).

Why (and When) Does Democracy Require Elected Representatives?

As the focus of democratic government shifted to large-scale units like nations or countries, the question arose: How can citizens *participate effectively* when the number of citizens becomes too numerous or too widely dispersed geographically (or both, as in the case of a country) for them to participate conveniently in making laws by assembling in one place? And how can they make sure that matters with which they are most concerned are adequately considered by officials—that is, how can citizens *control the agenda of* government decisions?

How best to meet these democratic requirements in a political unit as large as a country is, of course, enormously difficult, indeed to some extent unachievable. Yet just as with

Why the Institutions Are Necessary

In a unit as large as a country, these political institutions of polyarchal democracy. . .	are necessary to satisfy the following democratic criteria:
1. Elected representatives. . .	Effective participation
	Control of the agenda
2. Free, fair and frequent elections. . .	Voting equality
	Control of the agenda
3. Freedom of expression. . .	Effective participation
	Enlightened understanding
	Control of the agenda
4. Alternative information. . .	Effective participation
	Enlightened understanding
	Control of the agenda
5. Associational autonomy. . .	Effective participation
	Enlightened understanding
	Control of the agenda
6. Inclusive citizenship. . .	Full inclusion

Figure 2

the other highly demanding democratic criteria, this, too, can serve as a standard for evaluating alternative possibilities and solutions. Clearly the requirements could not be met if the top officials of the government could set the agenda and adopt policies independently of the wishes of citizens. The only feasible solution, though it is highly imperfect, is for citizens to elect their top officials and hold them more or less accountable through elections by dismissing them, so to speak, in subsequent elections.

To us that solution seems obvious. But what may appear self-evident to us was not at all obvious to our predecessors.

Until fairly recently the possibility that citizens could, by means of elections, choose and reject representatives with the authority to make laws remained largely foreign to both the theory and practice of democracy. The election of representatives mainly developed during the Middle Ages, when monarchs realized that in order to impose taxes, raise armies, and make laws, they needed to win the consent of the nobility, the higher clergy, and a few not-so-common commoners in the larger towns and cities.

Until the eighteenth century, then, the standard view was that democratic or republican government meant rule by the people, and if the people were to rule, they had to assemble in one place and vote on decrees, laws, or policies. Democracy would have to be town meeting democracy; representative democracy was a contradiction in terms. By implication, whether explicit or implicit, a republic or a democracy could actually exist only in a small unit, like a town or city. Writers who held this view, such as Montesquieu and Jean-Jacques Rousseau, were perfectly

aware of the disadvantages of a small state, particularly when it confronted the military superiority of a much larger state, and were therefore extremely pessimistic about the future prospects for genuine democracy.

Yet the standard view was swiftly overpowered and swept aside by the onrushing force of the national state. Rousseau himself clearly understood that for a government of a country as large as Poland (for which he proposed a constitution), representation would be necessary. And shortly thereafter, the standard view was driven off the stage of history by the arrival of democracy in America.

As late as 1787, when the Constitutional Convention met in Philadelphia to design a constitution appropriate for a large country with an ever-increasing population, the delegates were acutely aware of the historical tradition. Could a republic possibly exist on the huge scale the United States had already attained, not to mention the even grander scale the delegates foresaw?[6] Yet no one questioned that if a republic were to exist in America, it would have to take the form of a *representative* republic. Because of the lengthy experience with representation in colonial and state legislatures and in the Continental Congress, the feasibility of representative government was practically beyond debate.

By the middle of the nineteenth century, the traditional view was ignored, forgotten, or, if remembered at all, treated as irrelevant. "It is evident," John Stuart Mill wrote in 1861

that the only government which can fully satisfy all the exigencies of the social state is one in which the whole people participate; that any participation, even in the smallest public function, is useful; that the participation should everywhere be as great as the general degree of improvement of the community will allow; and that nothing less can be ultimately desirable than the admission of all to share in the sovereign power of the state. But since all cannot, in a community exceeding a single small town, participate personally in any but some very minor portions of the public business, it follows that the ideal type of a perfect government must be representative.[7]

Why Does Democracy Require Free, Fair, and Frequent Elections?

As we have seen, if we accept the desirability of political equality, then every citizen must have an *equal and effective opportunity to vote, and all votes must be counted as equal.* If equality in voting is to be implemented, then clearly, elections must be free and fair. To be free means that citizens can go to the polls without fear of reprisal; and if they are to be fair, then all votes must be counted as equal. Yet free and fair elections are not enough. Imagine electing representatives for a term of, say, twenty years! If citizens are to retain *final control over the agenda*, then elections must also be frequent.

How best to implement free and fair elections is not obvious. In the late nineteenth century, the secret ballot began to replace a public show of hands. Although open voting still has a few defenders, secrecy has become the general standard; a country in which it is widely violated would be judged as lacking free and fair elections. But debate continues as to the kind of voting system that best meets standards of fairness. Is a system of proportional representation (PR), like that employed in most democratic countries, fairer than the first-past-the-post system used in Great Britain and the United States? Reasonable arguments can be made for both. In discussions about different voting systems, however, the need for a fair system is assumed; how best to achieve fairness and other reasonable objectives is simply a technical question.

How frequent should elections be? Judging from twentieth-century practices in democratic countries, a rough answer might be that annual elections for legislative representatives would be a bit too frequent and anything more than five years would be too long. Obviously, however, democrats can reasonably disagree about the specific interval and how it might vary with different offices and different traditional practices. The point is that without frequent elections, citizens would lose a substantial degree of control over their elected officials.

Why Does Democracy Require Free Expression?

To begin with, freedom of expression is required in order for citizens to *participate* effectively in political life. How can citizens make their views known and persuade their fellow citizens and representatives to adopt them unless they can express themselves freely about all matters bearing on the conduct of the government? And if they are to take the views of others into account,

they must be able to hear what others have to say. Free expression means not just that you have a right to be heard. It also means that you have a right to hear what others have to say.

To acquire an *enlightened understanding* of possible government actions and policies also requires freedom of expression. To acquire civic competence, citizens need opportunities to express their own views; learn from one another; engage in discussion and deliberation; read, hear, and question experts, political candidates, and persons whose judgments they trust; and learn in other ways that depend on freedom of expression.

Finally, without freedom of expression, citizens would soon lose their capacity to influence *the agenda* of government decisions. Silent citizens may be perfect subjects for an authoritarian ruler; they would be a disaster for a democracy.

Why Does Democracy Require the Availability of Alternative and Independent Sources of Information?

Like freedom of expression, the availability of alternative and relatively independent sources of information is required by several of the basic democratic criteria. Consider the need for *enlightened understanding.* How can citizens acquire the information they need in order to understand the issue if the government controls all the important sources of information? Or, for that matter, if any single group enjoys a monopoly in providing information? Citizens must have access, then, to alternative sources of information that are not under the control of the government or dominated by any other group or point of view.

Or think about *effective participation* and influencing the *public agenda.* How could citizens participate effectively in political life if all the information they could acquire were provided by a single source, say the government, or, for that matter, a single party, faction, or interest?

Why Does Democracy Require Independent Associations?

It took a radical turnabout in ways of thinking to accept the need for political associations—interest groups, lobbying organizations, political parties. Yet if a large republic requires that representatives be elected, then how are elections to be contested? Forming an organization, such as a political party, gives a group an obvious electoral advantage. And if one group seeks to gain that advantage, will not others who disagree with their policies? And why should political activity cease between elections? Legislators can be influenced; causes can be advanced, policies promoted, appointments sought. So, unlike a small city or town, the large scale of democracy in a country makes political associations both necessary and desirable. In any case, how can they be prevented without impairing the fundamental right of citizens to participate effectively in governing? In a large republic, then, they are not only necessary and desirable but inevitable. Independent associations are also a source of *civic education and enlightenment.* They provide citizens not only with information but also with opportunities for discussion, deliberation, and the acquisition of political skills.

Why Does Democracy Require Inclusive Citizenship?

We can view the political institutions summarized in Figure 1 in several ways. For a country that lacks one or more of the institutions, and is to that extent not yet sufficiently democratized, knowledge of the basic political institutions can help us to design a strategy for making a full *transition* to modern representative democracy. For a country that has only recently made the transition, that knowledge can help inform us about the crucial institutions that need to be *strengthened, deepened, and consolidated*. Because they are all necessary for modern representative democracy (polyarchal democracy), we can also view them as establishing a *minimum level for democratization*.

Those of us who live in the older democracies, where the transition to democracy occurred some generations ago and the political institutions listed in Figure 1 are by now solidly established, face a different and equally difficult challenge. For even if the institutions are necessary to democratization, they are definitely not *sufficient* for achieving fully the democratic criteria listed in Figure 1. Are we not then at liberty, and indeed obligated, to appraise our democratic institutions against these criteria? It seems obvious to me, as to many others, that judged against democratic criteria, our existing political institutions display many shortcomings.

Consequently, just as we need strategies for bringing about a transition to democracy in nondemocratic countries and for consolidating democratic institutions in newly democratized countries, so in the older democratic countries, we need to consider whether and how to move beyond our existing level of democracy.

Let me put it this way. In many countries, the task is to achieve democratization up to the level of polyarchal democracy. But the challenge to citizens in the older democracies is to discover how they might achieve a level of democratization *beyond* polyarchal democracy.

Notes

1. Political *arrangements* sound as if they might be rather provisional, which they could well be in a country that has just moved away from nondemocratic rule. We tend to think of *practices* as more habitual and therefore more durable. We usually think of *institutions* as having settled in for the long haul, passed on from one generation to the next. As a country moves from a nondemocratic to a democratic government, the early democratic *arrangements* gradually become *practices*, which in due time turn into settled *institutions*. Helpful though these distinction may be, however, for our purposes it will be more convenient if we put them aside and settle for *institutions*.

2. "The Hats assumed their name for being like the dashing fellows in the tricorne of the day. . . . The Caps were nicknamed because of the charge that they were like timid old ladies in nightcaps." Franklin D. Scott, *Sweden: The Nation's History* (Minneapolis: University of Minnesota Press, 1977), 243.

3. Alexis de Tocqueville, *Democracy in America*, vol. 1 (New York: Schocken Books, 1961), 51.

4. Tocqueville, *Democracy in America*, 50.

5. Polyarchy is derived from Greek words meaning "many" and "rule," thus "rule by the many," as distinguished from rule by the one, or monarchy, and rule by the few, oligarchy or aristocracy. Although the term had been rarely used, a colleague and I introduced it in 1953 as a handy way of referring to a modern representative democracy with universal suffrage. Hereafter I shall use it in that sense. More precisely, a polyarchal democracy is a political system with the six democratic institutions listed above. Polyarchal democracy, then, is different from representative democracy with restricted suffrage, as in the nineteenth century. It is also different from older democracies and republics that not only had a restricted suffrage but lacked many of the other crucial characteristics of polyarchal democracy, such as political parties, rights to form political organizations to influence or oppose the existing government, organized interest groups, and so on. It is different, too, from the democratic practices in units so small that members can assemble directly and make (or recommend) policies or laws.

6. A few delegates daringly forecast that the United States might ultimately have as many as one hundred million inhabitants. This number was reached in 1915.

7. John Stuart Mill, *Considerations on Representative Government* [1861] (New York: Liberal Arts Press, 1958), 55.

ROBERT A. DAHL is Sterling Professor Emeritus of Political Science, Yale University. He has published many books on democratic theory and practice, including *A Preface to Democratic Theory* (1956) and *Democracy and Its Critics* (1989). This article was adapted from his recent book, *On Democracy,* Yale University Press.

Interest Groups: Ex Uno, Plures

The last article in our series on the mature democracies asks whether they are in danger of being strangled by lobbyists and single-issue pressure groups.

Previous briefs in this series have looked at the imperfections in democracy as it is currently practised in the rich countries, and at some of the efforts that different countries are making to overcome them. Evidence that all is not well includes declining public confidence in politicians, falling membership of political parties and smaller turnouts for elections. Ideas for improvement range from making greater use of referendums and other forms of direct democracy, to giving more power to courts to check the power of politicians. This article asks a different question: far from being too powerful, are elected politicians in modern democracies too weak?

When Alexis de Tocqueville visited the United States in the 19th century, he was impressed by the enthusiasm of Americans for joining associations. This, he felt, spread power away from the centre and fostered the emergence of democratic habits and a civil society. Until quite recently, most political scientists shared De Tocqueville's view. Lately, however, and especially in America, doubts have set in. At a certain point, say the doubters, the cumulative power of pressure groups, each promoting its own special interests, can grow so strong that it prevents elected politicians from adopting policies that are in the interest of the electorate as a whole.

A Hitchhiker's Guide

A key text for such critics was a short book published in 1965 by Mancur Olson, an American economist. Called "The Logic of Collective Action", this took issue with the traditional idea that the health of democracy was served by vigorous competition between pressure groups, with governments acting as a sort of referee, able to choose the best policy once the debate between the contending groups was over. The traditional view, Olson argued, wrongly assumed that pressure groups were more or less equal. In fact, for a reason known to economists as the free-rider problem, they weren't.

Why? Take the example of five car firms, which form a lobbying group in the hope of raising the price of cars. If they succeed, each stands to reap a fifth of the gains. This makes forming the group and working for its success well worth each firm's investment of time and money. If the car makers succeed, of course, motorists will suffer. But organising millions of individual motorists to fight their corner is a great deal harder because it involves co-ordinating millions of people and because the potential gain for each motorist will be relatively small. Individual motorists will be tempted to reason that, with millions of other people involved, they do not need to do anything themselves, but can instead hitch a "free ride" on the efforts of everyone else.

This simple insight has powerful implications. Indeed, in a later book Olson went on to argue that his theory helped to explain why some nations flourish and others decline. As pressure groups multiply over time, they tend to choke a nation's vitality by impairing the government's ability to act in the wider interest. That, he argued, is why countries such as Germany and Japan—whose interest groups had been cleared away by a traumatic defeat—had fared better after the second world war than Britain, whose institutions had survived intact. With its long record of stability, said Olson, "British society has acquired so many strong organisations and collusions that it suffers from an institutional sclerosis that slows its adaptation to changing circumstances and changing technologies."

Olson's ideas have not gone unchallenged. But they have had a big impact on contemporary thinking about what ails American democracy. In "Demosclerosis" (Times Books, 1994), Jonathan Rauch, a populariser of Olson's work, says that America is afflicted by "hyperpluralism". With at least seven out of ten Americans belonging to at least one such association, the whole society, not just "special" parts of it, is now involved in influence peddling.

The result is that elected politicians find it almost impossible to act solely in the wider public interest. Bill Clinton wants to reform the health system? The health-insurance industry blocks him. China's membership in the World Trade Organisation would benefit America's consumers? America's producers of textiles and steel stand in the way. Jimmy Carter complained when he left the presidency that Americans were increasingly drawn to single-issue groups to ensure that, whatever else happened, their own private interest would be protected. The trouble is, "the national interest is not always the sum of all our single or special interests".

Pressure groups are especially visible in the United States. As Oxford University's Jeremy Richardson puts it ("Pressure Groups", Oxford University Press, 1993), "pressure groups take account of (and exploit) the multiplicity of access points which is so characteristic of the American system of government—the presidency, the bureaucracy, both houses of Congress, the powerful congressional committees, the judiciary and state and local government."

Nevertheless pressure groups often wield just as much influence in other countries. In those where parliaments exercise tighter control of the executive—Canada, Britain or Germany, say—the government controls the parliamentary timetable and the powers of committees are much weaker. This means that pressure groups adopt different tactics. They have more chance of influencing policy behind closed doors, by bargaining with the executive branch and its civil servants before legislation comes before parliament. In this way pressure groups can sometimes exert more influence than their counterparts in America.

Political Tribes

Many European countries have also buttressed the influence of pressure groups by giving them a semi-official status. In Germany, for example, the executive branch is obliged by law to consult the various big "interest organisations" before drafting legislation. In some German states, leading interest groups (along with political parties) have seats on the supervisory boards of broadcasting firms.

French pressure groups are also powerful, despite the conventional image of a strong French state dominating a relatively weak civil society. It is true that a lot of France's interest groups depend on the state for both money and membership of a network of formal consultative bodies. But a tradition of direct protest compensates for some of this institutional weakness. In France, mass demonstrations, strikes, the blocking of roads and the disruption of public services are seen as a part of normal democratic politics.

In Japan, powerful pressure groups such as the Zenchu (Central Union of Agricultural Co-operatives) have turned large areas of public policy into virtual no-go areas. With more than 9m members (and an electoral system that gives farming communities up to three times the voting weight of urban voters), farmers can usually obstruct any policy that damages their interests. The teachers' union has similarly blocked all attempts at education reform. And almost every sector of Japanese society has its *zoku giin* (political tribes), consisting of Diet members who have made themselves knowledgeable about one industry or another, which pays for their secretaries and provides campaign funds. A Diet member belonging to the transport tribe will work hand-in-glove with senior bureaucrats in the transport ministry and the trucking industry to form what the Japanese call an "iron triangle" consisting of politicians, bureaucrats and big business.

Pressure groups are also increasingly active at a transnational level. Like any bureaucracy, the European Union has spawned a rich network of interest groups. In 1992 the European Commission reckoned that at least 3,000 special-interest groups employing some 10,000 people acted as lobbyists. These range from big operations, such as the EU committee of the American Chamber of Commerce, to small firms and individual lobbyists-for-hire. Businesses were the first to spot the advantages of influencing the EU's law making. But trade unions swiftly followed, often achieving in Brussels breakthroughs (such as regulations on working conditions) that they could not achieve at home.

The Case for the Defense

So pressure groups are ubiquitous. But are they so bad? Although it has been influential, the Olson thesis has not swept all before it. Many political scientists argue that the traditional view that pressure groups create a healthy democratic pluralism is nearer the mark than Olson's thesis.

The case in favour of pressure groups begins with some of the flaws of representative democracy. Elections are infrequent and, as a previous brief in this series noted, political parties can be vague about their governing intentions. Pressure groups help people to take part in politics between elections, and to influence a government's policy in areas that they care and know about. Pressure groups also check excessive central power and give governments expert advice. Although some groups may flourish at the expense of the common weal, this danger can be guarded against if there are many groups and if all have the same freedom to organise and to put their case to government.

Critics of Olson's ideas also point out that, contrary to his prediction, many broad-based groups have in fact managed to flourish in circumstances where individual members stand to make little personal gain and should therefore fall foul of his "free-rider" problem. Clearly, some people join pressure groups for apparently altruistic reasons—perhaps simply to express their values or to be part of an organisation in which they meet like-minded people. Some consumer and environmental movements have flourished in rich countries, even though Olson's theory suggests that firms and polluters should have a strong organisational advantage over consumers and inhalers of dirty air.

Moreover, despite "demosclerosis", well-organised pressure groups can sometimes ease the task of government, not just throw sand into its wheels. The common European practice of giving pressure groups a formal status, and often a legal right to be consulted, minimises conflict by ensuring that powerful groups put their case to governments before laws are introduced. Mr Richardson argues in a forthcoming book ("Developments in the European Union", Macmillan, 1999) that even the pressure groups clustering around the institutions of the EU perform a valuable function. The European Commission, concerned with the detail of regulation, is an eager consumer of their specialist knowledge. As the powers of the European Parliament have grown, it too has attracted a growing band of lobbyists. The parliament has created scores of "intergroups" whose members gain expertise in specific sectors, such as pharmaceuticals, from industry and consumer lobbies.

Governments can learn from pressure groups, and can work through them to gain consent for their policies. At some point, however, the relationship becomes excessively cosy. If pressure groups grow too strong, they can deter governments from pursuing policies which are in the wider public interest. The temptation of governments to support protectionist trade policies at the behest of producer lobbies and at the expense of consumers is a classic example supporting Olson's theories. But problems also arise when it is governments that are relatively strong, and so able to confer special status on some pressure groups and withhold it from others. This puts less-favoured groups at a disadvantage, which they often seek to redress by finding new and sometimes less democratic ways of making their voices heard.

In Germany, for example, disenchantment with what had come to be seen as an excessively cosy system of bargaining between elite groups helped to spark an explosion of protest movements in the 1980s. In many other countries, too, there is a sense that politics has mutated since the 1960s from an activity organised largely around parties to one organised around specialised interest groups on the one hand (such as America's gun lobby) and broader protest and social movements on the other (such as the women's movement, environmentalism and consumerism). One reason for the change is clearly the growth in the size and scope of government. Now that it touches virtually every aspect of people's lives, a bewildering array of groups has sprung up around it.

Many of Olson's disciples blame pressure groups for making government grow. As each special group wins new favours from the state, it makes the state bigger and clumsier, undermining the authority of elected parties, loading excessive demands on government in general, and preventing any particular government from acting in the interest of the relatively disorganised majority of people. By encouraging governments to do too much, say critics on the right, pressure groups prevent governments from doing anything well. Their solution is for governments to do less. Critics on the left are more inclined to complain that pressure groups exaggerate inequalities by giving those better-organised (ie, the rich and powerful) an influence out of all proportion to their actual numbers.

So what is to be done? A lot could be, but little is likely to be. There is precious little evidence from recent elections to suggest that the citizens of the rich countries want to see a radical cut in the size or scope of the state. As for political inequality, even this has its defenders. John Mueller, of America's University of Rochester, argues that democracy has had a good, if imperfect, record of dealing with minority issues, particularly when compared with other forms of government. But he claims that this is less because democratic majorities are tolerant of minorities and more because democracy gives minorities the opportunity

to increase their effective political weight—to become more equal, more important, than their arithmetical size would imply—on issues that concern them. This holds even for groups held in contempt by the majority, like homosexuals. Moreover, the fact that most people most of the time pay little attention to politics—the phenomenon of political apathy—helps interested minorities to protect their rights and to assert their interests.

Adaptability

This series of briefs has highlighted some of the defects in the practice of democracy, and some of the changes that the mature democracies are making in order to improve matters. But the defects need to be kept in perspective.

One famous critic of democracy claimed that for most people it did nothing more than allow them "once every few years, to decide which particular representatives of the oppressing class should be in parliament to represent and oppress them". When Marx wrote those words in the 19th century, they contained an element of truth. Tragically, Lenin treated this view as an eternal verity, with calamitous results for millions of people. What they both ignored was democracy's ability to evolve, which is perhaps its key virtue. Every mature democracy continues to evolve today. As a result, violent revolution in those countries where democracy has taken deepest root looks less attractive, and more remote, than ever.

Political Parties: Empty Vessels?

Alexis de Tocqueville called political parties an evil inherent in free governments. The second of our briefs on the mature democracies in transition asks whether parties are in decline.

What would democracy look like if there were no political parties? It is almost impossible to imagine. In every democracy worth the name, the contest to win the allegiance of the electorate and form a government takes place through political parties. Without them, voters would be hard put to work out what individual candidates stood for or intended to do once elected. If parties did not "aggregate" people's interests, politics might degenerate into a fight between tiny factions, each promoting its narrow self-interest. But for the past 30 years, political scientists have been asking whether parties are "in decline". Are they? And if so, does it matter?

Generalising about political parties is difficult. Their shape depends on a country's history, constitution and much else. For example, America's federal structure and separation of powers make Republicans and Democrats amorphous groupings whose main purpose is to put their man in the White House. British parties behave quite differently because members of Parliament must toe the party line to keep their man in Downing Street. An American president is safe once elected, so congressmen behave like local representatives rather than members of a national organisation bearing collective responsibility for government. Countries which, unlike Britain and America, hold elections under proportional representation are different again: they tend to produce multi-party systems and coalition governments.

Despite these differences, some trends common to almost all advanced democracies appear to be changing the nature of parties and, on one view, making them less influential. Those who buy this thesis of decline point to the following changes:

People's behaviour is becoming more **private**. Why join a political party when you can go fly fishing or surf the web? Back in the 1950s, clubs affiliated to the Labour Party were places for Britain's working people to meet, play and study. The Conservative Party was, among other things, a marriage bureau for the better-off. Today, belonging to a British political party is more like being a supporter of some charity: you may pay a membership fee, but will not necessarily attend meetings or help to turn out the vote at election time.

Running Out of Ideas

Politics is becoming more **secular**. Before the 1960s, political struggles had an almost religious intensity: in much of Western Europe this took the form of communists versus Catholics, or workers versus bosses. But ideological differences were narrowing by the 1960s and became smaller still after the collapse of Soviet communism. Nowadays, politics seems to be more often about policies than values, about the competence of leaders rather than the beliefs of the led. As education grows and class distinctions blur, voters discard old loyalties. In America in 1960, two out of five voters saw themselves as "strong" Democrats or "strong" Republicans. By 1996 less than one in three saw themselves that way. The proportion of British voters expressing a "very strong" affinity with one party slumped from 44% to 16% between 1964 and 1997. This process of **"partisan de-alignment"** has been witnessed in most mature democracies.

The erosion of loyalty is said to have pushed parties towards the **ideological centre**. The political extremes have not gone away. But mainstream parties which used to offer a straight choice between socialists and conservatives are no longer so easy to label. In the late 1950s Germany's Social Democrats (SPD) snipped off their Marxist roots in order to recast themselves is a *Volkspartei* appealing to all the people. "New" Labour no longer portrays itself as the political arm of the British working class or trade-union movement. Bill Clinton, before he became president, helped to shift the Democratic Party towards an appreciation of business and free trade. Neat ideological labels have become harder to pin on parties since they have had to contend with the emergence of what some commentators call **post-material issues** (such as the environment, personal morality and consumer rights) which do not slot elegantly into the old left-right framework.

The **mass media** have taken over many of the information functions that parties once performed for themselves. "Just as radio and television have largely killed off the door-to-door salesman," says Anthony King, of Britain's Essex University, "so they have largely killed off the old-fashioned party worker." In 1878 the German SPD had nearly 50 of its own newspapers. Today the mass media enable politicians to communicate directly with voters without owning printing presses or needing party workers to knock on doors. In many other ways, the business of winning elections has become more capital-intensive and less labour-intensive, making political donors matter more and political activists less.

Another apparent threat to the parties is the growth of **interest and pressure groups**. Why should voters care about the broad sweep of policy promoted during elections by a party when other organisations will lobby all year round for their special interest, whether this is protection of the environment, opposition to abortion, or the defence of some subsidy? Some academics also claim that parties are playing a smaller role, and **think tanks** a bigger one, in making policy. Although parties continue to draw up election manifestos, they are wary of being too specific. Some hate leaving policymaking to party activists, who may be more extreme than voters at large and so put them off. Better to keep the message vague. Or why not let the tough choices be taken by **referendums**, as so often in Switzerland?

Academics have found these trends easier to describe than to evaluate. Most agree that the age of the "mass party" has passed and that its place is being taken by the "electoral-professional" or "catch-all" party. Although still staffed by politicians holding genuine beliefs and values, these modern parties are inclined to see their main objective as winning elections rather than forming large membership organisations or social movements, as was once the case.

Is this a bad thing? Perhaps, if it reduces participation in politics. One of the traditional roles of political parties has been to get out the vote, and in 18 out of 20 rich countries, recent turnout figures have been lower than they were in the 1950s. Although it is hard to pin down the reasons, Martin Wattenberg, of the University of California at Irvine, points out that turnout has fallen most sharply in countries where parties are weak: Switzerland (thanks to those referendums), America and France (where presidential elections have become increasingly candidate- rather than party-centred), and Japan (where political loyalties revolve around ties to internal factions rather than the party itself). In Scandinavia, by contrast, where class-based parties are still relatively strong, turnout has held up much better since the 1950s.

Running Out of Members

It is not only voters who are turned off. Party membership is falling too, and even the most strenuous attempts to reverse the decline have faltered. Germany is a case in point. The Social Democrats there increased membership rapidly in the 1960s and 1970s, and the Christian Democrats responded by doubling their own membership numbers. But since the end of the 1980s membership has been falling, especially among the young. In 1964 Britain's Labour Party had about 830,000 members and the Conservatives about 2m. By 1997 they had 420,000 and 400,000 respectively. The fall is sharper in some countries than others, but research by Susan Scarrow of the University of Houston suggests that the trend is common to most democracies (see figure 1). With their membership falling, ideological differences blurring, and fewer people turning out to vote, the decline thesis looks hard to refute.

Or does it? The case for party decline has some big holes in it. For a start, some academics question whether political parties ever really enjoyed the golden age which other academics hark back to. Essex University's Mr King points out that a lot of the evidence for decline is drawn from a handful of parties—Britain's two main ones, the German SPD, the French and Italian Communists—which did indeed once promote clear ideologies, enjoy mass memberships, and organise local branches and social activities. But neither of America's parties, nor Canada's, nor many of the bourgeois parties of Western Europe, were ever mass parties of that sort. Moreover, in spite of their supposed decline, parties continue to keep an iron grip on many aspects of politics.

In most places, for example, parties still control **nomination for public office**. In almost all of the mature democracies, it is rare for independent candidates to be elected to federal or state legislatures, and even in local government the proportion of independents has declined sharply since the early 1970s. When state and local parties select candidates, they usually favour people who have worked hard within the party. German parties, for example, are often conduits to jobs in the public sector, with a say over appointments to top jobs in the civil service and to the boards of publicly owned utilities or media organisations. Even in America, where independent candidates are more common in local elections, the parties still run city, county and state "machines" in which most politicians start their careers.

Naturally, there are some exceptions. In 1994 Silvio Berlusconi, a media tycoon, was able to make himself prime minister at the head of Forza Italia, a right-wing movement drawing heavily on his personal fortune and the resources of his television empire. Ross Perot, a wealthy third-party candidate, won a respectable 19% vote in his 1992 bid for the American presidency. The party declinists claim these examples as evidence for their case. But it is notable that in the end Mr Perot could not compete against the two formidable campaigning and money-raising machines ranged against him.

This suggests that a decline in the membership of parties need not make them weaker in **money and organisation**. In fact, many have enriched themselves simply by passing laws that give them public money. In Germany, campaign subsidies to the federal parties more than trebled between 1970 and 1990, and parties now receive between 20% and 40% of their income from public funds. In America, the paid professionals who have taken over from party activists tend to do their job more efficiently. Moreover, other kinds of political activity—such as donating money to a party or interest group, or attending meetings and rallies—have become more common in America. Groups campaigning for particular causes or candidates (the pro-Republican Christian Coalition, say, or the pro-Democrat National Education Association) may not be formally affiliated with the major party organisations, but are frequently allied with them.

The role of the mass media deserves a closer look as well. It is true that they have weakened the parties' traditional methods of communicating with members. But parties have invested heavily in managing relations with journalists, and making use of new media to reach both members and wider audiences. In Britain, the dwindling of local activists has gone hand-in-hand with a more professional approach to communications. Margaret Thatcher caused a stir by using an advertising firm, Saatchi & Saatchi, to push the Tory cause in the 1979 election. By the

time of Britain's 1997 election, the New Labour media operation run from Millbank Tower in London was even slicker.

Another way to gauge the influence of parties is by their **reach**—that is, their power, once in office, to take control of the governmental apparatus. This is a power they have retained. Most governments tend to be unambiguously under the control of people who represent a party, and who would not be in government if they did not belong to such organisations. The French presidential system may appear ideal for independent candidates, but except—arguably—for Charles de Gaulle, who claimed to rise above party, none has ever been elected without party support.

The Fire Next Time

Given the cautions that must be applied to other parts of the case for party decline, what can be said about one of the declinists' key exhibits, the erosion of ideological differences? At first sight, this is borne out by the recent movement to the centre of left-leaning parties such as America's Democrats, New Labour in Britain, and the SPD under Gerhard Schröder. In America, Newt Gingrich stoked up some fire amongst Republicans in 1994, but it has flickered out. The most popular Republican presidential hopefuls, and especially George W. Bush, the front-runner, are once again stressing the gentler side of their conservatism.

Still, the claim of ideological convergence can be exaggerated. It is not much more than a decade since Ronald Reagan and Mrs Thatcher ran successful parties with strong ideologies. And the anecdotal assumption that parties are growing less distinct is challenged by longer-term academic studies. A look at the experience of ten western democracies since 1945 ("Parties, Policies and Democracy", Westview Press, 1994) concluded that the leading left and right parties continued to keep their distance and maintain their identity, rather than clustering around the median voter in the centre. Paul Webb of Britain's Brunel University concludes in a forthcoming book ("Political Parties in Advanced Industrial Democracies", Oxford University Press) that although partisan sentiment is weaker than it was, and voters more cynical, parties have in general adapted well to changing circumstances.

Besides, even if party differences are narrowing at present, why expect that trend to continue? In Western Europe, the ending of the cold war has snuffed out one source of ideological conflict, but new sparks might catch fire. Battered right-wing parties may try to revive their fortunes by pushing the nationalist cause against the encroachments of the European Union. In some places where ideas are dividing parties less, geography is dividing them more.

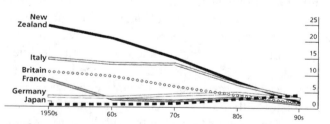

Figure 1 The Few Not the Many. Party members as % of electorate

Source: Susan E. Scarrow, Centre for German and European Studies Working Paper 2.59, University of California, Berkeley

Politics in Germany and Britain has acquired an increasingly regional flavour: Labour and the Social Democrats respectively dominate the north, Conservatives and Christian Democrats the south. Disaffected *Ossis* are flocking to the Party of Democratic Socialism in eastern Germany. Britain, Italy, Canada and Spain have strong separatist parties.

So there is life in the party system yet. But the declinists are on to something. The Germans have a word for it. One reason given for the rise of Germany's Greens in the 1980s and America's Mr Perot in 1992 was *Parteienverdrossenheit*—disillusionment with mainstream parties that seemed to have abandoned their core beliefs and no longer offered meaningful choices. A "new politics" of citizens' protests appeared to be displacing conventional politics.

In the end, far from undermining the domination of the parties, the German Greens ended up by turning themselves into one and joining the government in an uneasy coalition with the SPD. The balance of evidence from around the world is that despite all the things that are changing them, parties continue to dominate democratic politics.

Indeed, there are grounds for wondering whether their continuing survival is more of a worry than their supposed decline. Is it so very comforting that parties can lose members, worry less about ideas, become detached from broader social movements, attract fewer voters and still retain an iron grip on politics? If they are so unanchored, will they not fall prey to special-interest groups? If they rely on state funding instead of member contributions, will they not turn into creatures of the state? The role of money in politics will be the subject of another brief.

Police Clash with Monks in Myanmar

Seth Mydans

The government of Myanmar began a violent crackdown today after tolerating more than a month of ever-larger protests in cities around the country, clubbing and tear-gassing protesters, firing shots into the air and arresting hundreds of the monks who are at the heart of the demonstrations.

A government announcement said security forces fired at demonstrators who failed to disperse, killing one man. Foreign news agencies and exile groups reported a higher death toll, ranging from two to seven people.

Despite threats and warnings by the authorities and despite the beginnings of a violent response, tens of thousands of chanting, cheering protesters flooded the streets, witnesses reported. Monks were in the lead, "like religious storm troopers," as one foreign diplomat described the scene.

In response to today's violence, the United Nations Security Council called a special meeting for 3 P.M. today to discuss the crisis.

Though the crowds were large and energetic, they were smaller than on previous days, apparently in part because of the deployment of armed soldiers to prevent monks from leaving some of the main temples.

But it appeared that an attempt by the military to halt the protests through warnings, troop deployments and initial bursts of violence had not succeeded. Analysts said that the next steps in the crackdown might be yet more aggressive and widespread.

The foreign diplomat described "an amazing scene" today as a column of 8,000 to 10,000 people flooded past his embassy following a group of about 800 monks.

They were trailed by four truckloads of military men, watching but not taking action. The diplomat, in keeping with embassy policy, spoke on condition of anonymity.

According to news reports and telephone interviews from Myanmar, which is sealed off to foreign reporters, the day began with a confrontation at the giant, gold-spired Shwedagon Pagoda, which has been one focus of the demonstrations.

In the first reported violence in nine days of demonstrations by monks in the country's main city, Yangon, police officers with riot shields dispersed up to 100 monks who were trying to enter the temple, firing tear gas and warning shots and knocking some monks to the ground. As many as 200 monks were reported to have been arrested at the pagoda.

Several hundred monks then walked through the city downtown to the Sule Pagoda, another focus of the demonstrations, where truckloads of soldiers had been seen arriving Tuesday.

Another violent confrontation was reported here, with more shots fired and a number of arrests.

On a broad avenue near the temple, hundreds of people sat facing a row of soldiers, calling out to them: "The people's armed forces, our armed forces!" and, "The armed forces should not kill their own people!"

Tens of thousands of people were reported to be demonstrating in the streets of Mandalay, the country's second-largest city.

The demonstrations have grown from several hundred people protesting a fuel price rise in mid-August to as many as 100,000 Sunday, led by tens of thousands of monks in the largest and most sustained antigovernment protests since 1988.

That earlier peaceful uprising was crushed by the military, which shot into crowds, killing an estimated 3,000 people. It was during the turmoil a decade ago that the current military junta took power in Myanmar, and it has maintained its grip by arresting dissidents, quashing political opposition and using force and intimidation to control the population.

Now, emboldened by the presence of the monks, huge crowds have joined the demonstrations in protests that reflect years of discontent over economic hardship and political repression.

At first, the government held back as the protests grew. It issued its first warning Monday night, when the religious affairs minister said the government was prepared to take action against the protesting monks.

On Tuesday night, the government announced a dawn-to-dusk curfew, banned gatherings of more than five people and placed the cities of Yangon and Mandalay under what amounts to martial law. Troops began taking up positions at strategic locations around Yangon and tried to seal off five of the largest and most active monasteries.

As the protests grew, public figures began to come forward, and on Tuesday the government arrested the first of them, a popular comedian, Zarganar, who had urged people to join the demonstrations. He had irritated the government in the past with his veiled political gibes.

The crackdown today came in the face of warnings and pleas from around the world to refrain from the kind of violence that has made the country's ruling generals international pariahs.

A spokesman for President Bush, who was in New York City for the United Nations General Assembly, today denounced the crackdown and urged restraint. A day before, Mr. Bush had announced a largely symbolic tightening of American sanctions against Myanmar's government, and White House officials had hoped that the announcement of the sanctions, which would affect the military government's leaders directly, would intensify pressure on the government not to use violence.

"The United States is very troubled by the action of the junta against the Burmese people," the spokesman, Gordon D. Johndroe, said, referring to the country's former name. "We call on them to show restraint and to move to a peaceful transition to democracy."

The European Union has also threatened to tighten its own sanctions if violence was used. Today, the British prime minister, Gordon Brown, said the first step after any meeting of the United Nations Security Council should be to send a United Nations envoy to Myanmar.

The Dalai Lama and Desmond Tutu, the former South African archbishop and anti-apartheid campaigner, have spoken out in support of their fellow Nobel Peace Prize laureate, Daw Aung San Suu Kyi, Myanmar's pro-democracy leader, who has been held under house arrest for 12 of the last 18 years.

The junta was also hearing the message directly from diplomats based in Yangon. The British ambassador, Mark Canning, said he met with a government official Tuesday to urge restraint.

"You need to look very carefully at the underlying political and economic hardships," he said he told the official. "The government must also understand what this is about—not fuel prices, but decades of dissatisfaction."

Concerns Grow About Role of Interest Groups in Elections

GLEN JUSTICE

It was just two weeks before Election Day in Colorado's tight Senate race last year when a television advertisement attacking the Republican candidate, Peter H. Coors, began running hundreds of times.

The commercial ripped into Mr. Coors, chairman of the beer company that bears his family's name, for statements he made about lowering the drinking age. It depicted a series of mangled automobiles as an announcer said, "As far as Pete Coors is concerned, it doesn't matter if it's bad for kids as long as it's really good for business."

The advertisement was the work of Citizens for a Strong Senate, a group that attracted little attention as it raised almost $11 million and unleashed more than 7,000 commercials to help Democrats in six states, including Colorado, where Mr. Coors was defeated. And it could offer a glimpse of the future.

Other free-spending "527 committees" like Swift Vets and P.O.W.'s for Truth and the MoveOn.org Voter Fund spent millions of dollars to influence the presidential election last year, and some say such groups will have a far greater impact on Congressional races next year unless Congress moves to restrain them.

"We not only have to look at the 527's' impact on the presidential campaign but on other campaigns," Senator John McCain, Republican of Arizona, said on Tuesday at a Congressional hearing on the issue. "I think they can have tremendous impact—far more than they did on the presidential campaign."

Mr. McCain and others who support tighter campaign finance laws have introduced a bill to regulate the 527 groups, including contribution caps that would stop them from raising unlimited soft money. How the legislation fares could determine how campaigns are financed in 2006 and beyond.

The bill has attracted an unusual coalition of support. Senator Trent Lott, a Mississippi Republican who opposed the 2002 McCain-Feingold campaign finance legislation, has signed on. So has Senator Charles E. Schumer, a New York Democrat in charge of Senate fund-raising for his party. President Bush also supports regulating 527 groups, which are named for the section of the tax code that applies to them.

Supporters say lawmakers fear the type of attacks that Mr. Bush and Senator John Kerry endured during the presidential race. They contend that the money raised by 527 groups—more than $400 million in the 2004 election—could

be even more effective in Congressional races, where spending is much lower.

"Some billionaire decides he or she doesn't like you in office, and they decide to form a 527 and contribute $10 million or $20 million and dive-bomb into your state or district," Mr. McCain said, describing the theory last month. "That should alarm every federally elected member of Congress."

Citizens for a Strong Senate, one of only a few 527 committees that focused on Congressional races last year, bears some resemblance to that chain of events.

Three quarters of its money came from Herbert and Marion Sandler, large Democratic donors who run a financial services company in California and contributed more than $8.5 million to the group.

The organization is run by Jonathan Prince, a deputy campaign manager to Senator John Edwards during his presidential candidacy, who used the money to run thousands of biting television advertisements in states including Alaska, Colorado, Kentucky, North Carolina, Oklahoma and South Carolina.

One commercial attacking Senator Richard M. Burr, Republican of North Carolina, showed only a man's back. "This is Richard Burr's back," an announcer said. "We know it's annoying to look at for 30 seconds, but the truth is, he's turned his back on North Carolina."

Though the 527 bill has gained early support, it also has many opponents, including a group of nonprofit organizations—charities, social welfare groups, trade associations and labor unions operating under section 501(c) of the tax code—that say the legislation will quash free speech rights and lead to more restrictions on their organizations.

Some opponents also say that if 527 committees are restricted, the money will simply be funneled to 501(c) groups, which generally do not have to disclose their donors the way most 527 groups do.

One example is Americans for Job Security, a business trade association that ran more than 5,000 television advertisements in at least five states last year, all without having to disclose the source of its money. The group, which has strong ties to Republicans, has been criticized by Democrats and public interest groups.

"They completely operate under the radar screen," said Frank Clemente, director of Public Citizen's Congress Watch.

Michael Dubke, president of Americans for Job Security, said the group had about 500 members and spent about $8 million in last year's election cycle. The group was better off not disclosing its donors, Mr. Dubke said, adding: "If we take a knock, fine. But it won't distract from our issues."

Campaign finance and tax laws limit what 501(c) groups can do in politics. But Mr. Dubke said his organization had adjusted.

When restrictions in the McCain-Feingold law prevented it from advertising on television, the group turned to mail and billboards.

During the 2002 election, the group hired a plane to tow a banner with a message attacking a Minnesota Senate candidate.

"We try to find creative ways to get our message out," Mr. Dubke said, "even with the restrictions."

Venezuela Hands Narrow Defeat to Chávez Plan

Simon Romero

Voters in this country narrowly defeated a proposed overhaul to the constitution in a contentious referendum over granting President Hugo Chávez sweeping new powers, the Election Commission announced early Monday.

It was the first major electoral defeat in the nine years of his presidency. Voters rejected the 69 proposed amendments 51 to 49 percent.

The political opposition erupted into celebration, shooting fireworks into the air and honking car horns, when electoral officials announced the results at 1:20 A.M. The nation had remained on edge since polls closed Sunday afternoon and the wait for results began.

The outcome is a stunning development in a country where Mr. Chávez and his supporters control nearly all of the levers of power. Almost immediately after the results were broadcast on state television, Mr. Chávez conceded defeat, describing the results as a "photo finish."

"I congratulate my adversaries for this victory," he said. "For now, we could not do it."

Opposition leaders were ecstatic. "Tonight, Venezuela has won," said Manuel Rosales, governor of Zulia State and the opposition's candidate in presidential elections last year.

In recent weeks, members of previously splintered opposition movements joined disillusioned Chávez supporters in an attempt to defeat the referendum on constitutional changes. The plan would abolish term limits, allow Mr. Chávez to declare states of emergency for unlimited periods and increase the state's role in the economy, among other measures.

The defeat slows Mr. Chávez's socialist-inspired transformation of the country. Venezuela, once a staunch ally of the United States, has become a leading opponent of the Bush administration's policies in the developing world. It has also taken the most profound leftward turn of any large Latin American nation in decades.

The referendum followed several weeks of street protests and frenetic campaigning over the amendments to the Constitution proposed by Mr. Chávez and his supporters. It caps a year of bold moves by the president, who forged a single Socialist party among his followers, forced a television network critical of the government off the public airwaves, and nationalized oil, telephone and electricity companies.

In Caracas on Sunday, turnout in poorer neighborhoods, where support for Mr. Chávez is strong, indicated that the referendum was drawing a mixed response. Lines were long in some areas and nonexistent in others.

"The whole proposal is marvelous," said Francis Veracierta, 52, a treasurer at a communal council here, one of thousands of local governing entities loyal to Mr. Chávez that he created this year. After awakening to predawn fireworks, she said she joined a line at 6 A.M. to vote at a school in Petare, an area of sprawling hillside slums here.

"The power is for us in the community," said Ms. Veracierta, wearing a red shirt, red cap and belt with Che Guevara's face on it. She said she credited Mr. Chávez's government for giving her a $3,800 loan to start a small clothing business.

Some of Mr. Chávez's populist proposals, including an increase in social security benefits for some workers, have been praised even by his critics.

Turnout in some poor districts was unexpectedly low, indicating that even the president's backers were willing to follow him only so far. Some Chávez supporters expressed concern that if they voted against the measures they might be retaliated against. Turnout of registed voters was just 56 percent.

There was no line in front of the voting center at the Cecilio Acosta school in Petare on Sunday morning, as a few dozen people who had already voted milled about the street. Some volunteers working the voting machines sat idle, waiting for more voters to arrive. Other voting centers in Petare had lines outside, but they were less than half a block long.

"I'm impressed by the lack of voters," said Ninoska González, 37, who sells cigarettes on the street. "This was full last year." She described herself as a "Chavista" who voted for the president in last year's presidential elections, but said she voted against his proposed changes on Sunday.

"I don't agree with some articles," Ms. González said. Asked about the measure to pay social security benefits to workers in the informal economy like her, she said, "That's a lie."

Confusion persisted Sunday over the amendments, with a major complaint among the president's supporters and critics that they had too little time to study the proposals.

Unlike in past votes here, this time the government did not invite observers from the Organization of American States or the European Union, opening itself to potential claims of fraud.

The voting seemed to unfold largely without irregularities, though there were isolated reports of fraud and violence in parts of the country. Recounts are allowed under Venezuelan law, but would have to be approved by the Supreme Court, which is controlled by Mr. Chávez's supporters.

In recent weeks, Mr. Chávez has adopted an increasingly confrontational tone with critics abroad, who have been multiplying even in friendly countries with moderate leftist governments like Brazil and Chile.

In the days before the referendum, Mr. Chávez recalled his ambassador from Colombia and threatened to nationalize the Venezuelan operations of Spanish banks after Spain's king told him to shut up during a meeting. Mr. Chávez said he would cut off oil exports to the United States in the event of American interference in the vote.

The United States remains the largest buyer of Venezuela's oil, despite deteriorating political ties, but that long commercial relationship is starting to change as Mr. Chávez increases exports of oil to China and other countries while gradually selling off the oil refineries owned by Venezuela's government in the United States.

Venezuela's political opposition, normally divided among several small political parties, found common cause in calling on its members to vote against the amendments. An increasingly defiant student movement also protested here and in other large interior cities against the proposed charter.

In a move that alarmed the opposition, electoral officials over the weekend revoked the observer credentials of Jorge Quiroga, a former president of Bolivia and an outspoken critic of Mr. Chávez. Mr. Quiroga accused security forces here of following him after his arrival in Caracas. "They've taken my credential but not my tongue," Mr. Quiroga said.

Mr. Chávez, whose followers already control many powerful institutions—the National Assembly, the federal bureaucracy, the national oil company, the Supreme Court and all but a handful of state governments—relied on an unrivaled political machine to gather support for the measures.

Uncertainty over Mr. Chávez's reforms, meanwhile, has led to accelerating capital flight as rich Venezuelans and private companies rush to buy assets abroad denominated in dollars or euros. The currency, the bolívar, currently trades at about 6,100 to the dollar in street trading, compared with an official rate of 2,150.

Venezuela's state-controlled oil industry is also showing signs of strain, grappling with a purge of opposition management by Mr. Chávez and a retooling of the state oil company to focus on social welfare projects while aging oil fields need maintenance.

Petróleos de Venezuela, the state oil company, says it produces 3.3 million barrels a day, but OPEC places its output at just 2.4 million barrels. And private economists estimate that a third of oil production goes to meet domestic consumption, which is surging because of a subsidy that keeps gasoline prices at about seven cents a gallon.

Still, Mr. Chávez already has unprecedented discretionary control over Venezuela's oil revenues, valued at more than $60 billion a year. "Because of its oil, Venezuela has global reach in OPEC and the rest of Latin America," said Kenneth R. Maxwell, a professor of Latin American history at Harvard University.

UNIT 3

The Executive: Instituting Accountability and Responsiveness

Unit Selections

Key Points to Consider

- What are the roles of the executive?

- What are the constraints on the executive?

- How do we measure executive success?

- How and why do executives who are not popularly elected, demonstrate accountability or responsiveness?

- Does a strong executive act without restraint?

- What factors are necessary for successful executive leadership?

Student Web Site
www.mhcls.com

Internet References

Germany Chancellor's Website
   http://www.bundesregierung.de/Webs/Breg/EN/Homepage/home.html
Inside China Today
   http://www.einnews.com/china/
Prime Minister's Office of Great Britain
   http://www.number10.gov.uk
Russian and East European Network Information Center, University of Texas at Austin
   http://reenic.utexas.edu
US White House and Cabinet
   http://www.whitehouse.gov/government/cabinet.html

The previous units focused on citizens and groups and their impact on government and policy-making. The next three units address the questions: how do governments govern and how is the performance evaluated? That is, we consider the institutions of governments and their roles in policy-making, specifically, the executive, the legislature, and the bureaucracy and judiciary. Unit 3 addresses the systematic questions (why, what, and how) regarding executives and their roles.

Why executives? The explanation may be found in political theories of government, as envisioned by John Locke, John Stuart Mill, Jean-Jacques Rousseau, or the framers of the U.S. Constitution. It is this: notwithstanding society's ambivalence, we use representative government to achieve efficient and efficacious policy-making that embraces and promotes "social diversity" rather than chokes it (Sedgwick 1988: 5).[1] That is, the reason for representative government is the recognition that even if a community is small enough to allow everyone to partake in policy-making and implementation, it is inefficient to do so. Think about a community the size of a country and it

becomes clear that it is prohibitive to have everyone partake in policy-making. Thus, citizens choose a representative government to make those policies on their behalf.

Of course, the paradox is that the more diverse the society, the larger and more diverse the representative government becomes and that progressively impacts on efficient policy-making. This is why we need executives in political systems: executives remove that potential spiral into inefficiency by bringing the "power," "tyranny," and "arbitrariness" of a single decisionmaker into policy-making without the objectionable aspects of those qualities (Sedgwick 1988: 5). Or, to put it more kindly, they rise above the fray of legislative bickering or indecision to ensure that policies are formulated, approved, and executed.

What are the roles of the executive? As the articles in this unit point out, there are many, from the lofty to the petty, including: originating policies, executing policies, acting as the point person for the day-to-day operations of government, meeting and negotiating with foreign governments, meeting and negotiating with local governments, meeting and negotiating with corporations, interest groups and other key groups, presenting agreements for public support, brokering, budgeting, and so on. Thus, the article on the accomplishments of former Prime Minister of Great Britain, Tony Blair, focuses on some of the larger or grander tasks of the executive, including reforming the economy, pushing forward constitutional changes, and serving as commander-in-chief of wars. The piece on Angela Merkel, the Chancellor of Germany, describes her accomplishments in terms of the success of day-to-day government operations, which relies on her ability to navigate policies through a coalition-government that comprises a major party that is ideologically opposed to her own. Mexican President Calderon's duties included defusing the tension from a bitterly contested presidential election. Then, there are the articles on Vladimir Putin, the former president and current premier of Russia, and President Mahmoud Ahmadinejad of Iran that describe their roles in reversing democratic development in their respective countries, partly by adopting aggressive foreign postures that play up nationalism but that may also subvert civil and political rights.

All these duties may be condensed to providing leadership.[2] That is, the executive's performance is ultimately based on his or her ability to lead. As an aside, it is no coincidence that one of the key questions that faced the U.S. presidential candidates in the 2008 elections was their ability to lead.

How does the executive achieve such leadership? Institutionally, the executive is structured in one of three ways: as president in a presidential system; as prime minister and cabinet in a parliamentary system; as president and prime minister in a presidential-parliamentary hybrid system. In a presidential system, the executive—the president—is independently elected by the people to the office. In the parliamentary system, the executive—generally a reference to the Prime Minster, but more accurately applied to the entire cabinet—is chosen by the elected legislature or parliament. In parliamentary systems, there is no independent election for the executive. In a hybrid system, also known as the semi-presidential system or mixed system, the President is elected independently, while the Prime Minister and cabinet are chosen by the legislature. The mixed system is increasingly the political system of choice in emerging democracies: at last count in 2002, there were 25 nations with mixed systems, up from only three in 1946 (Cheibub and Cherynkh, 2008).[3] Why is that? Michael Sodaro suggests that it is because the mixed systems maximize efficiency in policy-making while maintaining stability in the executive authority. In short, it ensures the executive's performance.

This leads us to the question of how to assess executive performance. Some of the readings in this unit suggest that it is captured through policy success. Thus, Tony Blair's performance was reflected in his successful implementation of economic and political reforms, while Angela Merkel's performance on foreign policy is considered excellent. Some of the readings suggest that it is popularity. Hence, notwithstanding our own discomfort with these leaders, Putin in Russia and Wen Jiabao in China are considered successful executives.

However, there is a higher bar of executive performance: the executive's responsiveness and accountability. This responsiveness and accountability bring us full-circle to why executives are needed: to bring the power and tyranny of a single decision-maker into policy-making without their objectionable aspects. The executive's responsiveness and accountability—pursuing policies for or in response to the people and being accountable for policy mistakes and mishaps is the higher bar of executive leadership that some executives fail to reach. Thus, Tony Blair's legacy may be tainted as a result of his failure to connect to the people over the Iraq war. Likewise, Angela Merkel's leadership is judged less by her foreign policy success than by her ability to implement the difficult, but necessary reforms favored by the Germans. Conversely, even though there were protests against Calderon's presidency, his ability to respond and demonstrate accountability since the 2006 elections is more important for assessing his performance than the conditions under which he took office.

It is this higher bar of executive performance that underlies predictions that some of these executives—such as Putin and Wen Jiabao—will fall, notwithstanding their current popularity. Popularity may be manipulated, especially in the face of unexpected events. It is the executives who lead—who respond to and for their people, and accept responsibility for policy mistakes or mishaps—that withstand assessments over time.

Notes

1. See Jeffrey Sedgwick, "James Madison and the Problem of Executive Character," *Polity* vol 21 no 1 (1988): pp. 5–23.

2. See Michael Sodaro, *Comparative Politics: A Global Introduction* (3rd edition). New York: Macgraw-Hill (2007).

3. See José Antonio Cheibub and Svitlana Chernykh. 2008 (forthcoming). "Constitutions and Democratic Performance in Semi-Presidential Democracy." *Japanese Journal of Political Science* vol. 9 no 3.

The Historic Legacy of Tony Blair

"The public service and constitutional reforms undertaken by the prime minister represent historic achievements, but in recent years these have been overshadowed by the Iraq War. . . . "

VERNON BOGDANOR

Every hero, Emerson once said, becomes a bore at last. The Blair era, an era of unparalleled success for the Labor Party that began so triumphantly in 1997, is now moving, inexorably, toward its close. Electorally, Prime Minister Tony Blair has been by far the most successful leader that Labor has ever had, the only one to have won three consecutive elections, two of them with landslide majorities. In fact, he has had a longer continuous run in office than any prime minister since the Napoleonic wars, with the sole exception of Margaret Thatcher.

Moreover, Blair has led the most successful left-of-center government in Europe. Of the three leaders who shared the new dawn of social democracy in the late 1990s, only he survives; both Lionel Jospin, the former French prime minister, and Gerhard Schröder, the former German chancellor, have departed in ignominy, almost forgotten figures. Yet, despite all this, Blair's current reputation is low, and recent allegations that honors have been given in return for party contributions have not helped. Indeed, survey evidence suggests he is now the most unpopular prime minister since opinion polls began.

This is unlikely to prove the final verdict of history. The twilight of a prime ministership, or of a presidency for that matter, is not the best vantage point from which to analyze its significance. In the United States, for example, the reputations of Harry Truman and Gerald Ford were low when those men left office, but have risen steadily since. Ultimately, Blair's tenure of leadership will be remembered for three things: for his reforms of British public services; for a wide-ranging set of constitutional reforms, most of which occurred between 1997 and 2001; and, finally, for the war in Iraq.

The Third Way Taken

Constitutional reform occupied much of Blair's first term. The second term, which ran from 2001 to 2005, was dominated by public service reform and by the war in Iraq. Both of these involved bold if unpopular decisions. Both alienated Blair from his party. Public service reform, however, is likely to be accepted both by the British people and by the Labor Party—in contrast with the Iraq War, which is in the process of being repudiated by both.

Before coming to office, Blair modernized the Labor Party, much as Bill Clinton did America's Democrats. Blair transformed Old Labor into New Labor, removing the commitment in the party's constitution to the nationalization of the means of production, distribution, and exchange. Indeed, the 1997 general election was the first since Labor became a national party in which nationalization was not an issue. In the place of traditional Labor bromides, Blair touted a "Third Way" between old-fashioned socialism and unfettered capitalism. Tony Giddens, a leading theorist of the Third Way, has argued that Blair was successful because he understood that changes in society, such as the decline of the working class, globalization, and the growth of a knowledge-based economy, had rendered old-style social democracy irrelevant.

Until Blair, Labor had been imprisoned in an old pattern of mind according to which the public sector was inherently good and the private inherently bad. New Labor seeks to escape this crude dichotomy. The essence of New Labor is that public services, if they are to improve, need to use the techniques of private business and the market to increase efficiency. Injections of new money into government programs, therefore, should be dependent on reform.

Moreover, the state should no longer be expected to be the sole provider of public services. Thus, while public schooling and health care under the National Health Service remain free, the business sector is being encouraged to finance new schools—City Academies—for the state sector, particularly in blighted inner cities; and Foundation Hospitals are being allowed, and indeed encouraged, to establish contracts with private bodies to improve their services.

These changes are likely to prove permanent. They go with the grain of British opinion. Most voters are nonideological. They care little whether schools or hospitals are financed privately or publicly so long as their children learn to read and write and medical operations are carried out speedily and effectively.

Thus, while it is possible that the balance between public and private provision will alter with time, no future government of the left is likely to abandon City Academies or Foundation Hospitals. Here, too, there are perhaps parallels with the reforms in America by Clinton and others who sought to modernize the Democratic Party.

Public service issues are, for most British voters, the most important issues, the ones on which they judge the government of the day. The chances of success for the next prime minister, therefore, largely depend on the skill with which he continues public service reforms. But continued reform will be difficult, since public finances will have to be operated on a more stringent basis than has hitherto been the case, because the rate of economic growth is slowing. Moreover, Blair's likely successor, Chancellor of the Exchequer Gordon Brown, is widely thought to be less sympathetic to major public service reform than Blair. (The prime minister has expressed regret with himself for not pressing for more radical change.)

In addition, Brown will face a rejuvenated Conservative Party, under its new leader, David Cameron, who argues that the Conservatives are better equipped to continue the process of reforming public services than is a party of the left that has to struggle to persuade trade unions to accept a role for the private sector. The question of which party is better placed to manage public services will be the key issue of British politics in the post-Blair era.

The New Constitution

Britain now has a new constitution, the result of some very radical reforms implemented since Labor came to power in 1997—and this represents a second enduring achievement of Blair. The reforms include a series of referendums and measures devolving more political authority to Scotland, Wales, and Northern Ireland, in effect putting the non-English parts of the United Kingdom into a quasi-federal relationship with Westminster. Scotland and Wales now have directly elected legislatures. Northern Ireland has one as well, though it is currently in abeyance. Proportional representation in elections has been introduced for these devolved bodies, for a new London authority, and for elections to the European Parliament.

London, for the first time in British history, has a directly elected mayor, following a referendum. Other local authorities have been required to adopt cabinet systems of government, while a few have directly elected mayors following referendums. Today, 5 percent of registered voters can *require* a local authority to hold a referendum on the mayor option. The ballot initiative is a political instrument familiar in the United States, but this is the first statutory provision for its use in Britain.

The Human Rights Act of 1998 requires public bodies to comply with the provisions of the European Convention on Human Rights, allowing judges to declare a British statute incompatible with the Convention and providing a fast-track procedure for Parliament to amend or repeal such a statute. This comes near to providing Britain with a bill of rights. In addition, the Freedom of Information Act of 2000 provides, for the first time in British history, a statutory right to freedom of information, subject to certain important exemptions.

The Political Parties, Elections, and Referendums Act of 2000 requires the registration of parties and places controls on political donations and national campaign expenditures. It also provides for the establishment of an Electoral Commission to oversee elections and to advise on improvements in electoral procedures. This act brings political parties, for the first time, within the framework of British law. Previously, they had been treated, for the purposes of the law, as voluntary organizations, like golf or tennis clubs.

The House of Lords Act of 1999 has removed all but 92 of the hereditary peers from the House of Lords, as the first phase of a wider reform of that body. The Constitutional Reform Act of 2005 has restructured the historic office of Lord Chancellor, establishing a new Supreme Court and removing its judges from the House of Lords. The head of the judiciary will now be the Lord Chief Justice, not the Lord Chancellor, and the Lord Chancellor will no longer be the Speaker of the House of Lords. Instead, the House of Lords chooses its own Lord Speaker. All this goes toward creating a system of separation of powers in Britain. Before this act, the role of the Lord Chancellor was a standing contradiction to the separation of powers, since he was, at the same time, head of the judiciary, Speaker of the Lords, and a cabinet minister. Now the first two of these positions have been devolved to others.

Blair revived a liberal imperialism that owed more to William Gladstone than to traditional Labor doctrine.

Some of the constitutional changes of the past decade (including the Bank of England's new independence in the setting of monetary policy) make the British system of government more like the American—though, of course, they remain fundamentally different, since Britain is still a parliamentary system while the United States has a presidential system. Almost any one of these reforms, taken singly, would constitute a radical change. Taken together, they allow us to label the years since 1997 a historic era of constitutional reform. Indeed, these years bear comparison with two previous periods of constitutional revision in Britain: (1) the 1830s, the era of the Great Reform Act; and (2) the years immediately preceding the First World War, which saw the passage of the Parliament Act of 1911, restricting the powers of the House of Lords; and the abortive Government of Ireland Act of 1914, providing home rule to Ireland; as well as agitation by suffragettes to extend the vote to women, who finally gained the franchise in 1918.

The recent changes, radical though they are, by no means complete the process of constitutional reform. The Blair government is currently holding discussions on reforms of party finance and on further reform of the House of Lords, perhaps including the introduction of an elected element. Moreover, Brown, the likely prime minister-to-be, gives an even higher priority than Blair has done to constitutional reform. Brown is eager to see an elected House of Lords, and has made speeches suggesting that Britain should follow nearly every other democracy in the world and produce a codified constitution.

Since Blair came to office, Britain has been engaged in a process quite unique in the democratic world, that of converting an uncodified constitution into a codified one, but by piecemeal means. There is today neither the political will to do more, nor any consensus on what the final resting-place should be. The British, a member of a public ethics panel recently declared, seem to "like to live in a series of halfway houses." It is beginning to look as if they will need to accustom themselves to living in such halfway houses for rather a long time, at least until the foundations of the new constitution have been fully tested by experience.

Constitutional reform, in short, is an ongoing story in British politics. It is unlikely to come to an end with Blair's resignation. What is already clear, however, is that the constitutional reforms of the Blair government are far-reaching in their implications and almost certainly permanent. They will be remembered long after most current political squabbles are forgotten.

Gladstone Redux

The public service and constitutional reforms undertaken by the prime minister represent historic achievements, but in recent years these have been overshadowed by the Iraq War, a war for which many will never forgive him. Before the invasion of Iraq, more than 40 percent of voters had a favorable opinion of Blair. That figure fell, immediately after the war began, to around 30 percent, and it has hardly risen since. Only 33 percent now think that the invasion was justified, while around two-thirds of those polled believe that Blair either exaggerated the threat from Iraq to justify the war or deliberately deceived the public.

In Iraq, however, survey evidence at the beginning of 2006 indicated that a large majority of Iraqis approved of the ouster of Saddam Hussein. Oddly enough, Blair may have more supporters in Baghdad than in Birmingham, where he is seen as anti-Muslim, even though he might argue that he has liberated more Muslims—in Afghanistan, Kosovo, and Iraq—than any previous British prime minister.

In Britain, it is often suggested that Blair has been George W. Bush's poodle, tamely following the American president. Yet Blair's conception of foreign policy was unveiled well before Bush came to the White House. Speaking in April 1999 in Chicago, Blair said, "We need to enter a new millennium where dictators know that they cannot get away with ethnic cleansing or repress their people with impunity." His next sentence defined his foreign policy. "We are fighting," he said of the war in Kosovo, "not for territory but for values."

The constitutional reforms of the Blair government are far-reaching in their implications and almost certainly permanent.

Blair called for "a new doctrine of international community" that would qualify the principle of noninterference and explicitly recognize the facts of interdependence. Britain, together with other countries that sought to uphold international morality, had a right if not a duty to intervene where necessary to prevent genocide, to deal with "massive flows of refugees" that become "threats to international peace and security," and to combat rogue states. Blair revived a liberal imperialism that owes more to William Gladstone than to traditional Labor doctrine, just as Bush's foreign policy may owe more to Woodrow Wilson than it does to the neoconservatives.

In the past, British foreign policy had been based for the most part on a cool and pragmatic calculation of the national interest. The British had, it was suggested, permanent interests but no permanent allies. The main concern of British foreign policy had been to preserve the balance of power in Europe, whether against Louis XIV, Napoleon, the Kaiser, or Hitler. Moreover, British governments, whether Labor, Conservative, or Liberal, had sought stability and a reduction in international tensions—appeasement in the best sense of that much-abused term.

In the early days of the Labor Party, at the beginning of the twentieth century, there had been much talk of an alternative approach, a "socialist foreign policy," but it was never clear precisely what this meant. In its first election manifesto in 1906, Labor devoted just one half-sentence to foreign policy: "Wars are fought to make the rich richer. . . . " The sentence concluded: " . . . and school children are still neglected." Keir Hardie, Labor's first leader, felt that foreign policy issues were perfectly straightforward. Indeed, a Labor foreign policy was unnecessary, since the working class in all countries would rise up to prevent the ruling classes from making war. Thus, the coming to power of socialist governments would enable foreign ministries everywhere to shut up shop. Had not Karl Marx insisted that the working class had no country? This illusion died, of course, in 1914.

In 1937, Labor leader Clement Attlee, in his book *The Labor Party in Perspective,* had to confess that his party had "no real constructive foreign policy, but shared the views which were traditional in radical circles." The foreign policy of the first two, minority, Labor governments had not in practice been very different from that of its Liberal predecessors. After World War II, under the foreign secretaryship of Ernest Bevin, from 1945 to 1951, Labor became committed to collective security, and the postwar Labor government played a major role in the setting up of NATO.

All the while, however, there had been an alternative principle of foreign policy on the left, the policy of humanitarian intervention. Gladstone had been its greatest practitioner. He had certainly not equated liberalism with appeasement or nonintervention. When he denounced the Bulgarian Horrors in 1876, he was not suggesting that Britain should disinterest herself in the Balkans. On the contrary, his complaint was that Britain was intervening on the wrong side, supporting the oppressor, Turkey, rather than the victim, Bulgaria. Indeed, wherever there was injustice, Gladstone sometimes seemed inclined to imply, Britain should make her voice felt even if this led to armed conflict. For "However deplorable wars may be," he insisted in one of his Midlothian speeches in 1879, "they are among the necessities of our condition; and there are times when justice, when faith, when the failure of mankind, require a man not to shrink from the responsibility of undertaking them."

So it was that, in 1882, Gladstone inaugurated a humanitarian but "temporary" occupation of Egypt, an occupation that lasted more than 70 years. The one occasion on which President Gamal Abdel Nasser of Egypt met then-Foreign Secretary Anthony Eden, in 1954, was when British troops were at last being removed from Egypt. Nasser was invited to dinner at the British Embassy in Cairo, and said that he would be glad to enter the building from which Egypt had been governed for so long. "Not governed, perhaps," Eden replied, "advised, rather." Perhaps the Americans are saying something similar in Iraq.

It is this Gladstonian foreign policy that Blair has revived. He is perhaps the most Gladstonian prime minister to have occupied 10 Downing Street since the Grand Old Man himself.

The Moral Imperative

The impact of Labor's new foreign policy was first felt in the Balkans. Prime Minister John Major's Conservative government had resisted involvement in the former Yugoslavia, arguing that what happened in the Balkans did not affect British interests. The policy was one of appeasement. Appeasement, however, works best in a community unified by broadly shared values and with some sense of mutual obligations and interests. It had as little to offer in the world of Slobodan Milosevic, Al Qaeda, and Saddam Hussein—the world of ethnic cleansing and the suicide bomber—as it had in the Europe of the 1930s, the Europe of Hitler and Mussolini. In the Balkans, as in Iraq, governments felt little sense of obligation toward their peoples, and there was not even a semblance of community or shared values.

In March 1999, the Blair government committed troops to Kosovo to counter what it regarded as a Serbian threat of genocide against the Albanian Muslim population. Intervention was, Blair believed, a moral duty. The same was true, he believed, in Afghanistan and Iraq. Of course, ministers also insisted that Afghan terrorism and Iraqi weapons of mass destruction constituted a genuine danger to Britain. Indeed, after the attacks of September 11, 2001, on the United States, the definition of British security widened. The war on terror meant that security involved more than mere territorial defense. It meant tackling terrorist networks and financing, and perhaps also removing regimes that promoted or allowed terrorist activity.

Still, this broader definition of security came to be intertwined with humanitarian arguments against the horrible regimes in Kabul and Baghdad. Part at least of the impetus for Blair's foreign policy derives from its moral fervor, not from any careful calculation of British interests. The British went to war in Kosovo, and to some extent in Afghanistan and Iraq also, partly on humanitarian grounds. It would certainly be difficult to pretend that what happened in Kosovo affected British national interests.

And the Blair approach diverged from more than the traditional British focus on narrow national interest. In the past, British foreign policy had also on the whole ignored the internal nature of different regimes. Where it was in Britain's interest to form an alliance with a regime whose internal politics

were repugnant to her, as with the Soviet Union in 1941, she would unhesitatingly do so. The twentieth century, however, had seemed to show that the internal nature of a regime could not be divorced from its foreign policy, and that how a country treated its own people might well prove a good indicator of how it would behave in international affairs.

Blair's interventionist foreign policy offended the instincts of many if not most Labor members of Parliament, as it did the social democratic parties of Western Europe. These parties, while being committed to collective security, have been much more hesitant than Blair when it comes to the use of force. Labor was in fact the only social democratic party in Western Europe to support the Iraq War. It is by no means clear, therefore, whether the Blair reorientation of British foreign policy will survive into a new prime ministership.

A Good European?

Blair's foreign policy aligned Britain with the United States rather than with France and Germany, hitherto the leading powers in the European Union. This is at first sight surprising. For whatever President Bush is, he is not a man of the left. He has defined himself as conservative, or perhaps a neoconservative. Classical American conservatism, however, derives from John Quincy Adams's dictum of 1821, according to which America "goes not abroad in search of monsters to destroy." Conservatives in the United States have generally adhered to a "realist" foreign policy, exemplified by former Secretary of State Henry Kissinger, an approach based on hardheaded calculations of the American national interest. It was, by contrast, Woodrow Wilson, a liberal, who had asked a very nonconservative question— How can the world be made safe for democracy?—a question that seemed to gain more relevance after 9-11. And Bush's foreign policy has more in common with that of Wilson than with that of Kissinger. Bush is a Wilsonian, not a conservative, just as Blair is a Gladstonian. Gladstone, after all, would have had far more in common with Wilson than with Kissinger's realism or the principle of *raison d'etat,* another form of realism, which animates Gaullist France.

All the same, Blair's foreign policy alignment with the United States seems paradoxical, since from the time he came to power he had sought to improve relations with the European Union and show himself to be a good European. In the Saint Malo Declaration of 1998, for example, Blair stressed the need for a European defense force. On receiving the Charlemagne prize in May 1999, he insisted that "full use" be made of "the potential Europe has to be a global force for good." His government seemed the first to display a constructive attitude toward Europe since Edward Heath's administration more than 30 years ago.

Blair was successful because he understood that changes in society had rendered old-style social democracy irrelevant.

The paradox, however, is more apparent than real. Blair's ethical foreign policy is incompatible with being a good European only if being a good European is defined in Gaullist terms. In the Iraq crisis, President Jacques Chirac simply proceeded to label the French position "European" and rebuked as *non-communautaire* anyone who could not accept it. Yet Gaullism is not necessarily the same as Europeanism. Indeed, Gaullism may be regarded as but a high-sounding name for the pursuit of the French national interest, a pursuit that has dominated French foreign policy under governments of both left and right since the inauguration of the Fifth Republic in 1958. This is not the same as a European foreign policy.

Gaullism rests on a limited conception of Europe in which Germany remains subordinate while Britain keeps to the sidelines. Enlargement, however, is already causing a diplomatic revolution in Europe. The ex-communist states, as the Iraq crisis shows, are far more likely to accept the Anglo-American position in foreign policy than the Gaullist. (When these states announced that they supported Bush and Blair, President Chirac accused them of being *mal élevé*—badly brought up.) Moreover, the ex-communist states are far more likely to accept the British conception of a loosely organized Europe than the more federalist conceptions of the Germans. Having struggled hard to win the right of national self-determination from Moscow, they are hardly eager to surrender their sovereignty to a supranational organization. The negative outcome of the French referendum on the EU constitution in May 2005 shows that President Chirac's conception of Europe is not shared even by a majority of voters in France, let alone the continent as a whole.

From the time of Charles de Gaulle's veto, in 1963, of Britain's first application to enter the European Community, as it was then called, until the European Union's enlargement during the 1990s, France was the dominant power in Europe, and a Franco-German motor drove the continent. France and Germany set the agenda; Britain was cast in the role of spoiler on the sidelines, the bad boy of Europe. Today, as Prime Minister Blair prepares to leave office, Britain is in a much stronger position in foreign affairs, able to influence both the United States and Europe, as both continents find themselves groping toward a new conception of collective security in a world facing new kinds of threats.

The "International Community"

Of course, the doctrine of humanitarian intervention raises as many questions as it answers, and both Bush and Blair have been struggling to grapple with them. Who is to decide when such intervention is justified? Is humanitarian intervention not in danger of leading to universal war for the sake of universal peace? Where is the "new doctrine of international community" of which Blair spoke at Chicago? One obvious, if flawed, answer to the question of who decides the conditions under which intervention is justified, is that it should be the United Nations. That,

indeed, was the answer given by critics of the war in Iraq, as it had been by critics of the Suez War in 1956.

Woodrow Wilson's conception of the League of Nations had been that of a Parliament of Man. The United Nations, however, is hardly that and perhaps can never be that, since not all of the member states represented there derive legitimacy from the consent of those whom they govern. Perhaps it can be realized only on a more limited basis by those countries whose governments do owe their legitimacy to the citizens whom they govern—that is, the democracies. Perhaps there is a need for the democracies to get together, to form a caucus, a new organization to help secure their interests in an increasingly dangerous international environment.

Blair at least pointed in this direction, as he searched for a middle way between Gaullism and unilateralism. The Gaullists had sought to unite Europe on the basis of an anti-American foreign policy. But such a policy, as the Iraq crisis showed, serves only to divide Europe. It could never unite it. Some in the Bush administration, by contrast, have sought a unilateral approach to problems of international terrorism and rogue states. This, too, has caused a rift in the Atlantic alliance, and it could never form the basis for a stable international order. The "new doctrine of international community" must, therefore, be genuinely multilateralist. Working out precisely what this new doctrine should be constitutes the most important challenge facing Blair's successor as British foreign policy finds itself struggling to adapt the concept of collective security to the conditions of the post–9-11 era.

Is There Anything Left?

The central question raised by Blair's long premiership—and it is highly relevant to the American left as well—is whether there is anything left of social democracy as an ideology. Blair's public service reforms are, in practice, a continuation of those championed by Major, his Conservative predecessor. Blair's constitutional reforms undermine the social democratic principle that benefits and burdens should depend on need and not on geography. For Scotland and Wales are now following principles of state welfare divergent from those of Westminster. In foreign policy, humanitarian interventionism has few roots in Labor's past.

In 1894, a Liberal Chancellor of the Exchequer, Sir William Harcourt, declared, "We are all socialists now." What he meant was that all believed in state intervention. The twentieth century was to be, for much of its duration, the century of state intervention. However, under Margaret Thatcher, the Conservative prime minister from 1979 to 1990, the state began to withdraw from society and the economy. Blair did nothing to reverse this process. Indeed, he could persuade British voters to support Labor only by, in effect, assuring them that "We are none of us socialists now." It is a strange legacy for a prime minister of the left.

Vernon Bogdanor is a professor of government at Oxford University. His latest book, *The New British Constitution*, will be published by Allen Lane/Penguin next year.

From *Current History*, March 2007, pp. 99–105. Copyright © 2007 by Current History, Inc. Reprinted by permission.

Russia's Transition to Autocracy

Pierre Hassner

It was with great trepidation that I accepted the invitation to deliver this distinguished lecture, together with the suggestion that my remarks should focus on Russia. Although my lifelong preoccupation with international politics—and in particular with the struggle between freedom and tyranny—has led me to follow closely developments in Russia (and, of course, the Soviet Union), I must confess at the outset that I am not an "old Russia hand." I do not speak Russian, and I have never spent more than two consecutive weeks in Russia.

Why, then, did I agree to speak on this subject? In the first place, as an analyst of international relations I have a strong interest in the political role of human passions, and I think that understanding wounded pride, repressed guilt, resentment, and the manipulation of fear is central for interpreting Russia today. But I was also attracted by the idea of paying tribute to the memory of Seymour Martin Lipset. I met him and his wife Sydnee only once, toward the end of his life, at a celebration of the fiftieth anniversary of the Congress for Cultural Freedom. To my knowledge, Lipset did not write much on Russia or on communism, but he did write extensively on the connection between economic development, the rise of a middle class, and democracy, as well as on the impact of political culture and traditions. As I expected, in preparing this lecture, I found a good deal of inspiration in Lipset's intellectual approach.

Today, analysts of Russia are threatened by three temptations: economic determinism, cultural determinism, and political determinism. For instance, the excellent Russian author Dmitri Trenin is optimistic about Russia's future because, although not democratic, it is capitalist; hence he argues that it will give birth to a middle class that will want the rule of law.[1] Other authors believe that Russia will never become democratic, because its culture is basically authoritarian. A third group, composed largely of Americans, believes in politics as a *deus ex machina:* Because all people want democracy and the market, no matter what their culture or their state of economic development is, these can be installed virtually overnight. For avoiding these simplifications and for grasping the complicated interrelationship between politics, economics, and culture, I think there is no better guide than the work of Seymour Martin Lipset.

For my part, I shall concentrate on the role of politics and especially of a single person—Vladimir Putin. Although he is neither the beginning nor the end of the story of democracy and capitalism in Russia, he does play a crucial role.

The Seymour Martin Lipset Lecture on Democracy in the World

Pierre Hassner delivered the fourth annual Seymour Martin Lipset Lecture on Democracy in the World on 15 November 2007 at the Canadian Embassy in Washington, D.C., and on November 22 at the Munk Centre for International Studies at the University of Toronto. The Lipset Lecture is cosponsored by the National Endowment for Democracy and the Munk Centre, with financial support this year from the Canadian Donner Foundation, the Canadian Embassy in Washington, the American Federation of Teachers, the Albert Shanker Institute, William Schneider, and other donors.

Seymour Martin Lipset, who passed away at the end of 2006, was one of the most influential social scientists and scholars of democracy of the past half-century. A frequent contributor to the *Journal of Democracy* and a founding member of its Editorial Board, Lipset taught at Columbia, the University of California at Berkeley, Harvard, Stanford, and George Mason University. He was the author of numerous important books including *Political Man, The First New Nation, The Politics of Unreason,* and *American Exceptionalism: A Double-Edged Sword.* He was the only person ever to have served as president of both the American Political Science Association (1979–80) and the American Sociological Association (1992–93).

Lipset's work covered a wide range of topics: the social conditions of democracy, including economic development and political culture; the origins of socialism, fascism, revolution, protest, prejudice, and extremism; class conflict, structure, and mobility; social cleavages, party systems, and voter alignments; and public opinion and public confidence in institutions. Lipset was a pioneer in the study of comparative politics, and no comparison featured as prominently in his work as that between the two great democracies of North America. Thanks to his insightful analysis of Canada in comparison with the United States, most fully elaborated in *Continental Divide,* he has been dubbed the "Tocqueville of Canada."

I came here, however, neither to praise Putin nor to bury him. I did not come to praise him because I agree with Sergei Kovalev that "Putin is the most sinister figure in contemporary Russia history."[2] He has led Russia into a harsh brand of authoritarianism with some fascist features, and he remains under strong suspicion of having inspired a number of criminal acts, including the fires that served as a pretext for launching the second war in Chechnya, and the assassination of political opponents such as Anna Politovskaya.

On the other hand, I did not come to bury him. His rule is full of contradictions and, while it has some extremely ominous aspects, he cannot be said to have burned all his bridges or to have made it impossible for Russia to evolve in a more positive direction once circumstances change. Whatever our final judgment, we must not close our minds to the case made by his defenders, who stress his popular support among the Russian people, the improvements that he has achieved in certain areas (as compared to the catastrophic situation he found when coming to power), and the fact that his undoubtedly authoritarian rule has stopped well short of totalitarian terror.

Many Russians and some Westerners assert that, no matter how dubious public opinion polls or how rigged elections are in Russia, a majority of the people still support Putin. In their eyes, that is sufficient to make the regime a democracy of sorts, and one more in line with Russian traditions than is the pluralistic Western model. According to Putin's defenders, he is not hostile to pluralism as such but merely claims the right to choose a different model, equally imperfect but more suitable to Russia's present circumstances. For precedents, they cite not only Peter the Great and Alexander Nevsky but also Franklin Roosevelt, who also fought the oligarchs of his time and, in addition, ran for a third (and fourth) term.

Another comparison, implicit in some sympathetic French commentaries, invokes the precedent of Charles de Gaulle. One of the most shocking features of Putin's policies is his attempt to claim continuity with both the Czarist and the Soviet pasts. In a way, de Gaulle followed a similar approach in a France that traditionally had been divided between the heirs of the French Revolution and those of the *ancien régime*. De Gaulle belonged to the Bonapartist tradition, which wanted to unify French history and to promote a nationalism that embraced *all* of France's past. Moreover, although France was no longer a great power, de Gaulle's great game was to pretend that she still was and to get her to punch above her military or economic weight in the Great Powers League. As we shall see, Putin has been trying to do something similar with Russia.

Unfortunately, however, there is also much else in Putin's dossier, and the overall verdict has to be much harsher. True, the case made by defenders of Putin's foreign policy, largely backed even by many liberal Russians who are critical of Putin's authoritarianism, should not be dismissed out of hand: After all the shocks that Russia has suffered—the loss of Eastern Europe, the dissolution of the Soviet Union, the great economic crisis of 1998, the huge increase in economic inequality through the enrichment of some and the impoverishment of most, the

enlargement of NATO, the presence of U.S troops in Central Asia, and the talk of Ukraine and Georgia joining NATO—it is only normal that there should be a reaction of resentment and a wish for reassertion now that conditions permit. But, his liberal defenders add, with time a more balanced attitude will emerge. The problem with this argument is that the evolution of Putin's policies is heading in the wrong direction. Rather than being a preparation for democracy or for a more realistic and constructive role in world affairs, it looks much more like a tendency toward greater authoritarianism at home and trouble-making abroad.

The first question I would like to consider concerns the link between the evolution of the Russian regime and changes in its attitude toward the outside world. Recent years have witnessed a spectacular hardening against the domestic opposition, the freedom of the press, and any democratic life inside Russia, as well as against Russia's former satellites and the West. There has also been an encouragement of nationalism, which initially took on a primarily ethnic character (directed particularly against people from the Caucasus), but has increasingly targeted the West. The most dangerous aspect of all this is the growing hostility toward Russia's neighbors—Estonia, Georgia, and other former members of the Soviet Union and even of the Warsaw Pact (such as Poland). This is especially worrying because, paradoxically, it is in dealing with its neighbors that Moscow's policy has been the least successful and has met the greatest resistance—much more than from either the Russian population or the West.

From Anarchy to Autocracy?

Russia's progress toward democracy began going off the rails even before Putin came to power. Lilia Shevtsova dates the trouble from 1993, when Yeltsin ordered troops to fire on a rebellious parliament.[3] The crisis of democracy under Yeltsin culminated with his reelection in 1996 , which was manipulated by the oligarchs to give him a victory in spite of his disastrous standing in the opinion polls. This was an essential first step for Putin's subsequent ascension to power. Under Yeltsin, of course, some important elements of democracy existed that have vanished under Putin—above all, freedom of the media and wide-ranging public debate. But there was no equality and no real rule of law; privatization amounted to a seizure of public wealth by the oligarchs; the power and corruption of the Yeltsin family turned the pretense of democracy into a farce; and Moscow (though it had the power to start a war in Chechnya) was unable to collect taxes from many regions.

Early in Putin's presidency, there emerged some open signs of a further slide toward autocracy in the name of restoring the authority of the state (indicated by such slogans as "the dictatorship of the law"). But the predominant strategy sought to maintain the appearance of democracy while progressively emptying democratic institutions of their content. This kind of deception is an old art in Russia, whose most famous example is the Potemkin villages of the eighteenth century; various contemporary authors have coined new terms for the phenomenon more appropriate to the Putin era, speaking of "virtual" or "imitation" democracy. While under Gorbachev and Yeltsin a real attempt had been made to emulate Western democracy and to follow Western models and advice, under Putin the attempt at deception became ever more apparent.

A residual desire for respectability in the eyes of the West and the world is evident, however, in Putin's decision not to modify the constitution in order to run for a third term. Instead he has chosen to designate a virtual president for a virtual democracy, while keeping real power himself. Throughout his second term, one could observe an increasingly self-assured and provocative claim that Russia had come up with its own brand of "sovereign democracy," which was probably superior to Western-style liberal democracy and certainly more appropriate for Russian conditions. One can debate whether this term merely implies a rejection of Western interference and lecturing, or whether "sovereign" also means that this kind of democracy is based on the authority of the leader and the unity of the nation, to the exclusion of any real pluralism.

What is certain, however, is that key aspects of the new dispensation are strongly reminiscent of fascism. These include not only the elimination of any rival centers of power (whether economic, political, legal, or cultural), but also phenomena such as the "personality cult" of Putin, the appeals to proclaim him "leader of the nation," and the creation of youth organizations devoted to bullying the opposition and ethnic minorities and to helping the police. These trends seem increasingly to be influencing the Russian population at large. Two indications of this are the rise in xenophobia to a level comparable to that found among Germans in the years preceding Nazism,[4] and the growing public admiration for Stalin, whose ranking as a leader is second only to that of Putin himself and contrasts sharply with the popular contempt toward Gorbachev and Yeltsin. Yet, according to the polls, while an increasing proportion of Russians (2 percent) believe that Russia should follow its own path in terms of government, a plurality (42 percent) are still in favor of liberal democracy.

From Joining the West to Blasting It

Since Putin came to power, Russia has continually been moving away from democracy, and of late at an accelerating pace. By contrast, Moscow's foreign policies and Russian attitudes toward the outside world, in particular toward the West, have made a number of spectacular U-turns. After the collapse of the Soviet Union, attraction to the West, the urge to imitate it, and the hope of being welcomed and helped by it were predominant, as reflected in the stance of Yeltsin's foreign minister, Andrei Kozyrev. Toward the end of the Yeltsin period, however, Russian dissatisfaction with the West started to show, and Kozyrev was replaced by Yevgeny Primakov, who favored a policy oriented toward "multi-polarity" and a greater emphasis on Asia. Another sign of the shift was Yeltsin's unhappiness with the NATO intervention in Kosovo. This led him into an intemperate outburst mentioning Russia's nuclear might, but ultimately did not prevent him from contributing to peace by pressuring Serbian dictator Slobodan Milošević to give in.

During the early years of Putin's presidency, Russian policies toward the United States were remarkably conciliatory. Putin's passive reaction to U.S. abandonment of the Anti-Ballistic-Missile Treaty, his immediate offer of support for the United States after 9/11, his cooperation against terrorism, and his acceptance (apparently against the objections of the Russian elite) of a U.S. military presence in Central Asia all contributed to what seemed to be a very positive relationship. This was the period when President George W. Bush looked into Putin's soul and famously declared that he could trust him.

After 2003, however, the relationship changed radically. Putin started to hurl the wildest accusations and insults against the West, charging that the Beslan atrocity had been engineered by those who always wanted to isolate Russia and to put it down, calling Western powers neocolonialists, and comparing the United States to Nazi Germany. Putin began to take the most intransigent diplomatic positions against U.S. initiatives on almost every subject (ranging from Kosovo to anti-missile systems in Eastern Europe), threatening escalation and retaliation.

What caused this shift? First of all, there was a change in what the Soviets used to call "the correlation of forces." This is best summed up by a formulation often used nowadays by Russian interlocutors: "Russia up, America down, and Europe out." Russia is up because of the price of oil, America down due to the consequences of its Iraq adventure, and Europe out because of the defeat of the EU Constitution, the failure to get its act together on energy matters, and the influence of new member states (like Poland and the Baltic republics) that Russia considers both hostile and contemptible.

Second, by warning against external dangers and enemies, Putin helps to inspire a "fortress" mentality in Russia, and gives himself a pretext for branding any domestic opposition as treason and for calling upon everyone to rally behind the leader. But while the first reason explains what made the change possible and the second what makes it useful for the transition to autocracy, Russia's foreign policy cannot be fully understood without taking into account the postimperial humiliation and resentment of the Russian people and the neoimperial ambition of its leaders.

Imperialism, Nationalism, and Autocracy

Two quotations seem to me to sum up the role of these sentiments. The first was stated by Andrei Kozyrev, Russia's most pro-Western foreign minister, in 1995: "Two things will kill the democratic experiment here—a major economic catastrophe and NATO enlargement."[5] Both, of course, came to pass. So it was very easy to convince the Russian public that *both* were engineered by the West, that the advice of Western economic experts, like the admission of former Soviet allies into NATO, was part of a great conspiracy against Russia.

The second statement was made by Vladimir Putin himself a number of times, most conspicuously, if in condensed form, in May 2005 in Germany. The complete text, as quoted by the British historian Geoffrey Hosking, is as follows: "He who does not regret the break-up of the Soviet Union has no heart; he who wants to revive it in its previous form has no head."[6]

Together these two statements point to the twin problems of resentment and revanchism on the part of postimperial powers, and to the effects of these passions upon the prospects for democracy. Zbigniew Brzezinski has suggested that it was in Russia's interest to lose Ukraine, because Russia can either be an empire or a democracy, but it cannot be both.[7] With Ukraine, Russia is an empire; without Ukraine it is not an empire and thus can become a democracy. This may well be true in the long run, but in the short term losing an empire is not the most promising prelude to the task of building democracy. The Weimar syndrome inevitably comes to mind.

If you have lost an empire and not found a role, as Dean Acheson once said about Britain, what can you do? One solution, adopted in various ways by Germany, France, Britain, Austria, and Turkey, is to try to adapt to the new situation. You may do this by abandoning imperial ambitions, or by trying to transfer them to a larger whole like Europe, or by becoming the junior partner of a bigger power, as Britain has done with the United States. On the other hand, one can try to recover one's past imperial position, a process that members of the permanent Russian elite such as Sergei Karaganov think is well under way. Dmitri Rogozin, a well-known nationalist leader and Russia's new ambassador to NATO, calls upon his fellow radical nationalists to join the government in helping Russia to "recover its status as a great power."[8]

Virtual democracy and virtual empire go together. Just as Russia's leaders pretend that they are ruling over a democracy, they also pretend that they are ruling over an empire.

A third possibility is simply to *pretend* that you still are (or again have become) a superpower. Here, virtual democracy and virtual empire go together. Just as Russia's leaders pretend that they are ruling over a democracy, they also pretend that they are ruling over an empire.

Gorbachev, Yeltsin, and the whole Russian elite had been entertaining a somewhat analogous hope ever since the collapse of the Soviet Union. They thought that Russia's conversion to democracy would automatically earn it a kind of duopoly—the co-leadership of the West with the United States, and the co-leadership of Europe with the European Union (with a special sphere of influence over the former Soviet satellites). As Dmitri Trenin puts it, "What Russia craves is respect. It does not want to be a junior partner—it wants to be an equal."[9]

To some extent, Western leaders understood this craving and tried to satisfy it by such steps as inviting Russia to join the G-7 and creating the NATO-Russia Council. But Russians soon concluded that the West, instead of giving them the "instant accession to co-leadership" to which they felt entitled, was "trading symbolism for substance."[10] This gave rise to feelings of disappointment, suspicion, and resentment, which were exacerbated by the Russians' view that the United States and Europe, adding insult to injury, were adopting former Russian satellites and penetrating former Russian territory.

Today, thanks to his country's improved economic and strategic bargaining position, Putin has found a rather skillful way to make Russia's virtual empire seem more credible. It is to demonstrate that Russia (to borrow Madeleine Albright's expression about the United States) is "the indispensable nation," that it is a great power at least in a negative sense, inasmuch as it can block any Western strategy or diplomatic initiative with which it does not agree or on which it was not consulted. Sometimes opposing the West—or at least not following its lead—may be based on strategic considerations, such as competition for clients. But obstructionism seems to be a priority even when Moscow shares Western goals, such as avoiding an Iranian nuclear capacity. Indeed, in some cases thwarting the West appears to become a goal in itself, as recent Russian policy toward Kosovo illustrates.

The same mindset is applied even more strongly to the weaker states surrounding Russia. Putin may not be able to reintegrate them into the Russian empire, but, as a second-best alternative, he can punish them for wanting to be independent. Above all, he seeks to prevent them from becoming models of democracy and prosperity that might be compared favorably to Russia. Ivan Krastev may exaggerate in stating that the 2004 Orange Revolution in Ukraine had the same effect on Russia as 9/11 had on the United States,[11] but it does seem that it really was a shock. Putin's highest priority is to oppose "color revolutions"—to keep them from succeeding where they have occurred, and to prevent one from coming to Russia.

The Russians and the World

Two questions crucial to our subject remain to be answered: What has been the reaction of Russian society to Putin's policies, and what has been their global or international impact?

As regards the first question, the evidence seems to show that, while most Russians are aware of and condemn the regime's human rights violations, and in principle favor liberal democracy, they are also grateful to Putin for restoring Russia's international power and authority. As a researcher at the Levada Analytical Center, Russia's leading institute for the study of public opinion, writes: "Today, all categories of the population care about Russia recovering its power. As soon as a young man becomes conscious of his citizenship, the following idea emerges: The country is in bad shape, its authority in the world needs to be enhanced."[12] Indeed, in 2006, among those who regret the collapse of the USSR, 55 percent (as opposed to only 29 percent in 1990) cite as their main reason: "People no longer feel they belong to a great power." And those who regret the passing of the Soviet Union are not a small minority. In answer to the question, "Would you like the Soviet Union and the socialist system to be reestablished," 12 percent answer, "Yes, and I think it quite realistic"; 48 percent say, "Yes, but I think now it is unrealistic"; and only 31 percent say, "No, I would not."[13]

Russian sociologist Emil Pain speaks of a "revival of the imperialist syndrome." While, in principle, imperial sentiment should be an antidote to ethnic nationalism directed against non-Russian peoples from the former Soviet Union, Pain points out that the two are currently blended in a generalized xenophobia.[14] Gorbachev, in trying to save the Soviet system, opened the way to forces that overwhelmed it; is it possible that Putin, by encouraging radical nationalists, may similarly unleash forces that will go well beyond his intention and his capacity to control them? There are signs, albeit disputed ones, that he may already be more and more isolated, that he has to arbitrate a severe fight between competing "clans," and that he may experience "the impotence of omnipotence"[15] and be sidelined by his own appointees. While we cannot exclude the hypothesis that Russia (or China) will become a stable authoritarian or illiberal capitalist regime, it does seem more likely that in the long run both these countries will have to evolve either toward new forms of nationalistic fascism or toward some form of democracy.

Internationally, Putin is playing a skillful and (for the time being) successful game. He has effected a turn toward Asia in Russian foreign policy (not out of any Eurasian ideology, although he does play upon this strand of Russian public opinion). His motive is, first, to play the China card as a way of balancing the United States (as Nixon and Kissinger did to balance the Soviet Union). Putin knows full well that in the long run China constitutes a bigger danger to Russia than does the United States, but this approach offers him a way to invoke the virtual multipolar world to which China also pays lip service and to buttress Russia's credentials as a virtual Asian power. More important, Russia and China jointly are able to use their indifference to human rights to block Western attempts to sanction rogue states, from Uzbekistan and Burma to Sudan and Zimbabwe, and instead to deal with these countries in purely economic and strategic terms.

In this, Russia and China are at one with almost all the countries of the global South, including India, for whom national sovereignty and noninterference in internal affairs trump democracy promotion and the defense of human rights. Russia and China thus put themselves in the position of balancers, mediators, or arbiters in a potential conflict between the North and the South, or between the United States and countries like Iran or North Korea.

One should not see this new situation as a universal confrontation between the democratic West and a coalition of totalitarians that includes everyone from Putin to Ahmadinejad and Bin Laden. It comes closer to the triangular configuration that prevailed between the two World Wars, though it is even more complicated. But one result is clear and obvious: The international struggle for democracy and human rights is made much more difficult by the existence of countries that are, at the same time, indispensable partners for the West (as Russia is for nuclear and energy matters), but also competitors and adversaries. If one adds to this the non-Western world's quasi-universal distrust of the West, it is hard not to be pessimistic about the international prospects for democracy, at least in the near term.

But lack of optimism for the short run should not mean lack of commitment and faith. The French philosopher Henri Bergson put forward a thesis that seems to me as true as it is shocking: Liberal democracy is the least natural regime on earth.[16] What is natural is the rule of the strongest. Democracy can come into being only through an uphill struggle that requires courage and perseverance and that aims at a profound change in attitudes and institutions. That is why I would like to dedicate this lecture to those who, in the most difficult situations, fight against the tide—in the first place, to the late Anna Politovskaya, but also to all those who, in Russia and countries with similar regimes, continue to write freely and truthfully about democracy and about autocracy.

Notes

1. Dmitri V. Trenin, *Getting Russia Right* (Washington, D.C.: Carnegie Endowment for International Peace, 2007), 101–15.

2. Sergei Kovalev, "Why Putin Wins," *New York Review of Books,* 22 November 2007.

3. Lilia Shevtsova, *Russia—Lost in Transition* (Washington, D.C.: Carnegie Endowment for International Peace, 2007), ch. 2.

4. Paul Goble, citing Sergei Arutyunov, head of the Caucasus section of the Institute of Ethnology at the Russian Academy of Sciences, in "Window on Eurasia: Russia Ever More Like Pre-Nazi Germany, Moscow Scholar Says," 12 October 2007, http://windowoneurasia.blogspot.com.

5. Quoted by Zoltan Barany, *Democratic Breakdown and the Decline of the Russian Military* (Princeton: Princeton University Press, 2007), 184.

6. Quoted by Geoffrey Hosking, *Rulers and Victims: The Russian in the Soviet Union* (Cambridge: Belknap Press of Harvard University Press, 200), 409.

7. See Zbigniew Brzezinski, *The Grand Chessboard* (New York: Basic Books, 1997), 92, 104, 122; and Zbigniew Brzezinski, "The Premature Partnership," *Foreign Affairs* 73 (March–April 1994): 80.

8. Paul Goble, "Window on Eurasia: Putin's New Man at NATO Urges Russian Nationalists to Infiltrate Moscow Regime," 13 January 2007, http://windowoneurasia .blogspot.com.

9. "Last Tango in Tehran," *Economist,* 20 October 2007.

10. A. Horelick and T. Graham, *U.S.-Russian Relations at the Turn of the Century* (Washington, D.C.: Carnegie Endowment for International Peace, 2000).

11. Ivan Krastev, "Russia vs. Europe: The Sovereignty Wars" *Open Democracy,* 5 December 2007. See also his "Ukraine

and Europe: A Fatal Attraction," *Open Democracy,*
16 December 2004.

12. Alexei Levinson cited by Leonid Sedov, "Les Russes
    et les valeurs démocratiques," *Futuribles* (September 2006),
    n322.

13. Levada Analytical Center, *Russian Public Opinion 2006*
    (Moscow, 2007), 183.

14. Emil Pain, "On the Revival of the Imperialist Syndrome," in
    After Empire (Moscow: Liberal Mission Foundation Press,
    2007), 115.

15. Shevtsova, *Russia—Lost in Transition,* 324.

16. Henri Bergson, *Les deux sources de la morale et de la religion,*
    Remarques finales, Société naturelle et démocratie (Paris: Presses
    Universitaires de France, 1932), 299, in Quadrige Series, 1990.

PIERRE HASSNER, research director emeritus at the Centre d'Etudes
et de Recherches Internationales (CERI) in Paris, delivered the 2007
Seymour Martin Lipset Lecture on Democracy in the World. For many
years he was a professor of international relations at the Institut d'Etudes
Politiques in Paris and a senior visiting lecturer at the European Center
of Johns Hopkins University in Bologna. He is the author of *La terreur
et l'empire* (2003) and *La violence et la paix: De la bombe atomique au
nettoyage ethnique* (1995, with an English translation in 1997).

From *Journal of Democracy,* April 2008, pp. 5–15. Copyright © 2008 by National Endowment for Democracy and The Johns Hopkins University Press. Reprinted with permission of The Johns Hopkins University Press.

Angela Merkel's Germany

"In part because of deadlock within the government on domestic policy, the chancellor has turned to foreign policy as her main stage."

JACKSON JANES AND STEPHEN SZABO

Angela Merkel, whom *The Economist* has called a "world star," is the most prominent of a new generation of leaders emerging in Europe. She is in charge of Europe's pivotal country at a time of great challenges to the EU as it seeks to come out of its constitutional and enlargement crises. Germany has the presidency of the EU and of the Group of Eight industrial nations in 2007, but Merkel and her country will be central to Europe's evolution long beyond this spring.

With Tony Blair in Britain and Jacques Chirac in France serving as lame ducks, and with many other European countries locked in political stalemates, much of Europe today is experiencing a vacuum of leadership. Thus, both George W. Bush and his successor as US president will look to the German chancellor as America's most important partner in Europe for years to come. Understanding Merkel and the political and economic context in which she operates is, consequently, important for anticipating what to expect from her chancellorship—in its impact both on Germany and on the future direction of the continent.

The Pragmatist

A number of Merkel's personal characteristics influence her approach to leadership and policy making. First, as a natural scientist, having studied and practiced physics, she is a highly rational person, without a strong ideological bent or approach. A problem solver and an incrementalist, Merkel favors a trial-and-error approach to policy and is able to make quick adjustments when they are needed. As she put it, "Many will say, 'This government takes a lot of small steps but not one decisive one.' And I reply, 'Yes. That is precisely what we are doing. Because this is the modern way to do things.'" Merkel lacks a big, unifying vision, and in this respect resembles her predecessor as chancellor, Gerhard Schröder. Unlike Schröder, however, she avoids personalizing political relationships and prefers a businesslike and interest-based approach in policy making.

Second, Merkel is a political latecomer and an outsider to German politics. An East German, she did not become active in politics until after the fall of the Berlin Wall, when she was well into her 30s. She is, consequently, not anchored in her party,

the Christian Democratic Union (CDU), and has not been able to take advantage of an extensive political network—a problem aggravated by her gender in a male-dominated party. She has begun to change this by creating her own network, both within and outside the party, but she still faces many rivals and lacks a deep regional base, something that is normally essential in German politics.

Third, her East German upbringing has made her a very private person who reveals very little about herself or what she is thinking. She is not a social animal or backslapper and is always in control of her emotions.

Finally, Merkel is not among the so-called '68ers, the generation of Schröder and his Green foreign minister, Joschka Fischer, who cut their political teeth in the late 1960s partly in resistance to the American role in the world. Merkel, born in 1954 and raised in East Germany, is the first of a new generation of leaders who were never among the 1960s rebels nor among the Atlanticist generation of her mentor, Helmut Kohl. Although she came of age during the end of the cold war, her political career was shaped in the post–Berlin Wall era of a unified Germany.

Merkel will be joined in power soon by others of her generation in France and the United Kingdom—people like Ségolène Royal or Nicolas Sarkozy in France, and David Cameron or Gordon Brown in Britain—as well as José Manuel Barroso in the EU. This group is pragmatic regarding both Europe, which is no longer seen as the great peace project of the Kohl-Mitterrand era, and the United States, which is neither the model it was for the postwar leaders who shaped Europe nor the anti-model it was for many of the '68ers.

Squabbling in the Ranks

Merkel was sworn in as chancellor on November 22, 2005. The first year of her tenure was marked by uncertainty over whether her political coalition (the "grand coalition"), which includes both Merkel's CDU and the Social Democratic Party (SPD), would have the stamina to hold together for another three years. The SPD holds almost as many seats in the Bundestag (parliament) as does Merkel's own CDU—making the coalition far more challenging to manage than was Schröder's coalition, which consisted of the SPD and the smaller, ideologically kindred Green party.

The German people's skepticism regarding domestic reforms is compounded by a policy making system that discourages strong leadership.

Despite current tensions between the parties in Merkel's coalition, however, there is at present no real alternative to this political equation in Germany. Speculation about the need for new elections remains exactly that, primarily because the voters would lose even more confidence in the political leadership if it declared bankruptcy so soon after taking over. Neither the Greens nor the Free Democrats can offer a viable alternative by themselves. And the idea of creating a red, green, and yellow mixture (SPD, Greens, and Free Democrats) or a black, green, and yellow coalition (CDU, Greens, and Free Democrats) is not in the cards. There is still a great deal of political baggage left over from the September 2005 elections that will prevent any such reconfiguring from happening very soon.

Merkel enjoys a solid level of personal popularity among Germans, but confidence in the two large political partners, the CDU and SPD—which between them have close to three-quarters of the Bundestag under their control—has waned. After all, voters ask, if there is no viable opposition to stop them, why can they not get more done in the way of reforms instead of making so much noise about why they cannot agree on such reforms? Even the CDU and its conservative Bavarian partner, the Christian Social Union, are increasingly bickering over the issue of health care reform.

All this wrangling comes during a continuing slide in membership in the SPD and the CDU. The Social Democrats have lost over 40 percent of their members from a high of more than 1 million in 1980, while the Christian Democrats in the same period have lost 14 percent of their members. Currently, the two parties are virtually tied in membership, at around 600,000 each. The smaller parties have lost ground in the past eight years as well, and the number of citizens choosing not to vote has been increasing steadily.

This frustration is causing a backlash that has allowed a right-wing party, the National Party of Germany (NPD), to squeeze into two state parliaments in eastern Germany. Many of the NPD votes have come from Germans under 30 years old who are beleaguered by high unemployment rates and see dim prospects for their future.

Still, the general loss of confidence among voters and the cross-party bickering that has contributed to it should come as no surprise. Domestic political battles were destined to throw sand into the machine of the CDU-SPD coalition. After all, the domestic policy realm is where the full forces of particular interests meet in battle. Health care reform legislation is the best, or worst,

example, and not only in Germany. It remains a dangerous area for the coalition's future. Indeed, one can also see the wreckage of health care reform efforts in the United States going back many years, not to speak of social security reform efforts more recently. These are the deadly third rails for all politicians.

Pressures for Reform

Merkel has been able to push through important reforms that have toughened up policies dealing with pensions. And corporate tax rates are set to come down significantly. As Germany's export machine continues to hum along at record levels, the economy in 2007 looks to be as strong as it was last year.

In general, though, reform efforts so far have produced a mix of some change but also continued stalemate. Germans are struggling to finance the social systems they have built up over the past five decades, and are trying to redistribute the load. This is not unique to Germany—Sweden, Denmark, and the Netherlands have been struggling with these problems as well. Yet Germany seems to be uncertain about the scope and pace of change. A question being newly framed amid today's global competition is how much of the acclaimed "social market economy" that was developed after World War II should be accounted for by "market" and how much by "social."

The very fact that the 2005 elections resulted in a so-called grand coalition of the two major political blocs was a reflection of the voters' uncertainty in the face of rising pressures to reform social and labor protections. The challenge any government faces is proposing realistic goals and then maintaining support for reaching them, even when changes pinch people where it hurts. It is precisely then when a government must be persuasive in explaining to the public why the goal is worth the pain and the adjustments needed to reach the goal.

On EU enlargement, Germany has moved from being the great promoter to being a skeptic.

This has proved difficult in Germany. For example, the government's decision in November 2006 to raise the statutory retirement age from 65 to 67 was vital to maintaining the viability of the social security system, but it requires a major adjustment in the national psyche. Likewise, reducing unemployment insurance is crucial in encouraging people to search for new jobs, but it violates long-entrenched expectations of the unemployed.

The German people's skepticism regarding domestic reforms is compounded by a policy-making system that is designed for consensus politics and discourages strong leadership. Suspicion of strong leaders is a legacy of Hitler's Third Reich, with its concentration of power at the top. In contrast to Japan, for example, contemporary Germany has a weak state and a strong civil society. This makes unpopular reforms very difficult to achieve.

On top of this, Germany's parliament is one of the largest in the world, with 614 representatives. And Germany has a federal system with powerful state governments. Wrestling with serious problems that involve so many actors, in a 24-7 media environment no less, is not a formula for smooth decision-making.

Berlin's coalition partners are stuck with each other for the moment, whether they like it or not. But they should not be stuck in political mud when it comes to implementing their agenda. Bringing down the national debt and encouraging job growth by deregulating the labor market can generate some confidence in the future. Yet Germany also faces formidable structural problems in the business and banking sectors, and it continues to pay a high cost for the reintegration of (less affluent) eastern Germany. The coalition partners need to look like they are focused on confronting the country's problems, rather than themselves, if they are to bring the voters along with them. This seems to work better with foreign policy than it does at home.

Balancing with Bush

In part because of deadlock within the government on domestic policy, the chancellor has turned to foreign policy as her main stage. Schröder had centralized policy making in the chancellery and marginalized the role of the foreign office and the parliament—since his Social Democrats were in a coalition with the small Green party, this was relatively easy to accomplish. Merkel, on the other hand, is in a much more challenging coalition. In contrast to Fischer, who was Schröder's foreign minister, Merkel must contend with a Social Democrat, Frank Walter Steinmeier, as foreign minister. This means there are far greater checks on Merkel's power than on any chancellor over the past three decades.

This has not stopped her from forming an effective foreign policy team. Merkel generally values analytical thinkers over party politicians in the chancellery. As her chief of staff, Thomas De Mazière, told the German weekly *Die Zeit,* "A clear head can learn about compromises and contacts better than a political tactician can learn clear thinking." Thus, Merkel has tended to hire technocrats or specialists in foreign policy positions. A good example is her key foreign policy adviser, Christoph Heusgen, a thorough Europeanist who served six years in Brussels working for the EU foreign policy chief, Javier Solana.

Merkel entered office believing that the Schröder foreign policy had lost the traditional German balance between France and the United States. She has made the US relationship her primary responsibility and priority, with the goal of reestablishing a constructive and balanced relationship with Washington after the *Sturm und Drang* of the Schröder years. Her East German experience left her with a very positive image of America, which she associates not only with freedom but also with innovation and flexibility.

Nevertheless, Merkel is a politician who understands the deep suspicion toward George W. Bush among the German public and media. This reflects in part the new sense of sovereignty and status of a unified Germany that is no longer as dependent on the United States as it was during the cold war. Merkel understands that she needs to be regarded as a reliable partner in Washington while not being seen as Bush's dachshund back home.

Ever the realist, the German chancellor understands that it is in the national interest to have a good working relationship with the world's dominant power, and that trying to use Europe as a counterweight to America only ends up splitting Europe and isolating Germany. On the other hand, drawing too close to Bush and to America carries its own dangers, as the case of Britain's Blair demonstrates. Thus, the Merkel approach toward the United States combines a close personal relationship between Merkel and Bush with a continuing, critical distance from unilateral aspects of Bush's foreign policy. In many ways she is rebuilding some bridges while waiting for the next American administration, which she hopes will be more user-friendly for Europe.

This approach is apparent in a number of policy areas. On NATO, the Merkel government has emphasized a NATO-first approach, giving the alliance priority in the security realm over the European Union's Security and Defense Policy. The new German Defense White Book, issued in November 2006, underlines a shift in German defense strategy away from the old territorial-defense focus of the cold war to a crisis-intervention rationale with light, mobile forces. Merkel intends to maintain the important German contribution to NATO peacekeeping forces in Afghanistan, without widening its mandate or increasing that commitment. She has also deployed German peacekeepers to Congo and Lebanon, and a German commander now heads the EU force in Bosnia. Along with France and Britain, Germany is working closely with the us administration to forge a unified approach toward thwarting Iran's nuclear ambitions.

In foreign economic policy, the chancellor is interested in maintaining some momentum in trade liberalization despite the likely failure of the Doha round of global trade negotiations. In particular, she has put forward new proposals for a transatlantic free trade area. Merkel has also moved to reduce the German fiscal deficit by raising the value-added tax, thus restoring Germany's reputation for fiscal responsibility in hopes of serving as an example to other EU deficit states. The German leadership remains concerned about the impact that US trade and fiscal deficits will have on the international financial system. As the world's largest exporter, German business worries about the impact of a falling dollar on its foreign markets.

Enlargement Fatigue

Merkel is now on center stage in Europe. Germany will hold the EU presidency during the first half of 2007. In this capacity, Merkel will have a chance to help restore some momentum to the European project, which has been staggering since the rejection of the EU constitutional treaty by French and Dutch voters in 2006. Because of the current leadership vacuum in Europe and the impending French presidential election this spring, the German role is likely to be limited to finding some ground for action in the future regarding the constitutional treaty. So no dramatic breakthroughs should be expected during the German term.

On the other important dimension of the European project, EU enlargement, Germany has moved from being the great promoter to being a skeptic. Past German governments supported the "big bang" enlargement of 2004, which brought in 10 member states, mostly from East-Central Europe. The Merkel government reluctantly went along with the entry of Bulgaria and Romania on January 1, 2007, but seems to have reached its limit regarding future enlargement. The Schröder government supported the entry of Turkey, but the Christian Democrats are opposed, and the governing coalition remains deeply divided on this key issue.

Germany's enlargement fatigue results in part from a fear of immigration and the cheap labor that it brings. Although immigration into Germany has been curtailed by legislation, the foreign population of the country stands at 7.3 million, or about 9 percent of the population. This is a larger proportion of the population than is the case in the United States. Of this group, 1.8 million have Turkish origins, with about one-third having been born in Germany. Another half-million of Turkish origin have been naturalized and are now German citizens. Germans are struggling to deal with the issue of how to define citizenship, which has traditionally been based on German heritage. Although citizenship laws have been liberalized somewhat, Germany is still a long way from becoming a multicultural society, and demands for German language competence for new immigrants have been increasing.

Germany's growing skepticism about enlargement is also the result of strained federal budgets, themselves a consequence of years of slow economic growth and high unemployment. Berlin in the past financed the union's enlargement through its contributions to the EU budget. But Germany is no longer willing or able to serve as Europe's pay-master. This marks an important shift in German foreign policy and implies that the EU is probably approaching its final borders.

Realism on Russia

The German-Russian relationship is once again a central issue in the European political equation. During the cold war, when Germany was divided, it depended on American security guarantees for its territorial integrity. This situation, and the Soviet occupation of East Germany and East-Central Europe, limited Germany's options and flexibility in dealing with the Soviet Union, although the German policy of détente (known as *Ostpolitik)* did develop an independent German approach toward the East.

She needs to be regarded as a reliable partner in Washington while not being seen as Bush's dachshund back home.

After the cold war, the German-Russian relationship regained dynamism. Chancellor Kohl ensured that Russian interests were taken into account during NATO's enlargement to the east. But Schröder took the relationship to a new level by siding with Russia and France against the Bush administration during the lead-up to the Iraq War. He forged an unusually close personal relationship with Russian President Vladimir Putin. He signed the important Baltic Sea gas pipeline agreement with Russia just before leaving office and then, after leaving office, joined the board of Russia's state-controlled energy giant Gazprom.

Merkel came into office resolved to change the tenor of this relationship. She has depersonalized the relationship with Putin, and in her first visit to Moscow as chancellor openly showed her support for human rights groups. Her suspicion of Russian power has been deepened by Russia's use of its energy resources as a foreign policy tool in its relations with Ukraine, Belarus, and Georgia. She is also aware of the suspicions that the close Schröder-Putin relationship raised in the Baltic states and Central Europe, especially in Poland, and wants to repair Germany's relationships with these states.

Merkel has made a priority of improving the Polish-German relationship, but has met resistance from the Polish government, led by the Kaczynski brothers. The German government's decision to establish a Center for Refugees and Expellees, possibly in Berlin, has raised concerns in Poland about potential German property claims for land taken from Germans who lived in Poland before the end of World War II. More generally, the Law and Justice Party of the twins is suspicious of Europe and of Germany in particular. A deeply parochial and nationalist grouping, it has questioned attempts by Poles to reconcile with Germany and is deeply suspicious of Germany's close relationship with Russia.

Yet Merkel the realist has continued to talk about a "strategic partnership" with Russia. Whatever this might mean, it implies that energy dependence and the close economic ties between the two countries remain paramount in German policy. Russia is Germany's largest natural-gas provider, currently providing 40 percent of Germany's natural gas, and this dependence is due to rise above 60 percent once the Baltic pipeline is completed. While Merkel would like to find alternative sources of energy, and is looking at a combination of liquefied natural gas, Central Asian gas, and nuclear power, her options are severely limited. She and her successors are faced with no real alternatives to substantial dependence on Russian natural gas during the coming decades. Moreover, although Russia has used energy as a lever against its former republics, it has never done so with Germany. For its part, Russia has no real alternatives to the EU market for its gas in the medium term. Half of Russia's energy trade is with the EU.

Germany is likely to remain Russia's most important advocate in the EU. The Merkel government continues to resist a common EU energy policy, and thus has made it easier for Russia to play off one EU state against another. In addition, Merkel's foreign minister was a key architect of the close German-Russian relationship when he was Schröder's chief of staff. His presence in the Merkel government is seen as a guarantee of continuity in this policy area.

A New Role in the World

A key change in German foreign policy since the end of the cold war is its increasingly global perspective. While the transatlantic and European relationships remain central to Berlin's view of the world, the Middle East and Asia have increased in importance. This reflects the end of a Western-centric world order and the need for Germany to adapt to the rise of new economic and military powers as well as to its vulnerabilities in the Middle East.

China and India have emerged both as important economic partners and as competitors for scarce sources of energy and raw materials. Germany's role in negotiations with Iran over its nuclear program, its participation in a peacekeeping force in Lebanon, and its efforts to engage Syria in a constructive relationship with the West are further indications of an expanding sense of German interests and responsibilities. As Germany's role in the world expands, it sees itself as deserving more international recognition. This includes a desire to have a seat as a permanent member of the UN Security Council. While Merkel has been less vocal in her pursuit of this goal than was her predecessor, it remains a key objective.

The agenda for the European Union is going to be a difficult one for Merkel to steer. Apart from the uncertain outcome of leadership changes in Great Britain and France, achieving consensus on anything among the union's now-27 members is a challenge at any time and on any issue one picks. Merkel has sent a clear signal that she intends to exercise leadership this year in shaping the still-fragile framework of the EU foreign policy agenda. But merely pushing forward the next phase of the EU constitutional process will give her a full plate, and keeping her fellow member states in line on everything from the Balkans to the Middle East will be a tall order.

The longer-term issues of further EU expansion, particularly with regard to Turkey, will consume Merkel's energies well after this leadership year for Berlin. Here there is a clear division between the views of the chancellor and her party and those of her coalition partners, the Social Democrats. The CDU is opposed to Turkish membership in the EU, favoring a "privileged partnership" instead, while the SPD continues to strongly advocate Turkish membership.

Since becoming chancellor, Merkel has felt confident in the international arena. As with many politicians facing domestic troubles—her coalition with the SPD continues to be a noisy and uncomfortable one—the opportunity to shine as a world leader offers advantages. Despite low poll numbers on domestic issues during the past year, both Merkel and her foreign minister, Steinmeier, top the popularity scales among the German public. The year ahead therefore offers unique opportunities to make progress on the foreign policy front.

Of course, the opportunities will be shadowed by risks. Keeping political squabbles from affecting the foreign policy agenda will not be easy, either at home or within the EU. Still, Merkel has the baton now in Berlin and in Brussels. We will have to wait to see how well the orchestras can perform.

JACKSON JANES is executive director of the American Institute for Contemporary German Studies at Johns Hopkins University. STEPHEN SZABO is research director at the institute and a professor of European Studies at Johns Hopkins's School of Advanced International Studies.

From *Current History*, March 2007, pp. 106–111. Copyright © 2007 by Current History, Inc. Reprinted by permission.

Iran's Conservative Revival

"No one has benefited more from American blunders in the Middle East than the conservatives in Iran who now control all the power centers. . . . "

BAHMAN BAKTIARI

The rise to the Iranian presidency of ultra-conservative Mahmoud Ahmadinejad reflects how much Iran has changed in recent years. Today it is Ahmadinejad, in the eyes of the world, who embodies Iran's increasing hard-line assertiveness. In light of this, how should we assess Ahmadinejad's impact on Iranian politics? And how have recent developments in Iraq and elsewhere in the region affected Iran?

Iranian officials remember the 2002 speech by President George W. Bush in which he labeled the Islamic Republic of Iran part of an "axis of evil." Coming at a time when Iran's own politics was characterized by rivalry between reformists and conservatives, and hot on the heels of the American invasion of Iran's neighbor Afghanistan, that speech was interpreted by many Iranians as a signal that the United States intended to topple the ruling theocracy. This conviction hardened after America's seemingly effortless dislodging of another neighboring ruler, Saddam Hussein.

Indeed, during the us invasion of Iraq, Iran put out feelers to explore the possibility of détente. Iranians wrote a letter in April 2003 to their American counterparts offering to discuss the mutual interests of the two countries, including the suspension of uranium enrichment, accepting a two-state solution for Palestinians and Israelis, and helping the United States to secure post-Hussein Iraq. The Americans, high on their "mission accomplished" in Iraq, chose to ignore the letter.

Much has changed since then. Just as the United States felt strong enough then to spurn Iran's overture, the Iranians have now rejected incentives that the Americans and others proffered in the summer of 2006 to tempt the Iranian regime to give up its ambition to make the country an industrial producer of nuclear fuel. Now it is the Iranian government's turn to enjoy the Americans' failure, which the regime vicariously considers its own success. If history is any guide, the Iranian government will overplay its hand, and the absurd hostility between the United States and Iran will continue beyond 2007.

With Iran's regional position stronger than ever and its coffers bulging with oil receipts, hubris alone might seem to threaten the country's good fortunes. Inside the country, however, economic mismanagement, human rights abuses, and popular resentment are as prevalent as ever. Ahmadinejad's administration has launched crackdowns on independent journalists and human rights activists since he became president. In September 2006, he urged conservative, pro-regime students to push for a purge of liberal and secular teachers from universities, a reflection of his determination to create an Islamic revival in the country.

But for most of Iran's defeated reformers, it is Bush's policies, not the clergy's inspired leadership, that have put the Iranian regime in its present strong position. No one has benefited more from American blunders in the Middle East than the conservatives in Iran who now control all the power centers: the presidency, the parliament, the judiciary, the security forces, and the office of the supreme leader.

Ahmadinejad's Ascent

Iranian politics is a complicated affair, involving such institutions as the Expediency Council (which mediates between the parliament and an unelected high chamber called the Council of Guardians), and the Assembly of Experts (an 86-member body whose job is to select the country's supreme leader). The Islamic Republic has always followed a limited system of electoral politics; both the parliament and the president are elected, though candidates who stand for office must be approved by the conservatives. This system has helped the Islamic Republic to survive, but it also prevents the national political discourse from moving forward.

Ahmadinejad came to power in 2005 on a platform of piety, honesty, and the redistribution of wealth, a set of principles reminiscent of the 1979 Islamic revolution that displaced the shah and brought to power Ayatollah Ruhollah Khomeini. Ahmadinejad was born the son of a blacksmith in 1956 in Garmsar, near Tehran. He earned a Ph.D. in traffic and transportation from Tehran's University of Science and Technology and served for four years as the governor of the northwestern towns of Maku and Khoy. In 1993, he was appointed the cultural adviser for Ali Larijani—then Minister of Islamic Culture and Guidance and currently the head of the Supreme National Security

Council and the country's chief nuclear negotiator. A few months later, Ahmadinejad was appointed governor of the newly created Ardebil province. In 2003, the Tehran Municipal Council, which is controlled by conservatives, appointed him mayor of Tehran. When he announced his candidacy for president, he received barely any attention from either reformist or conservative news outlets.

After the first round of voting for president, support for the reformist and conservative camps appeared evenly split. The independent centrist Hashemi Rafsanjani led the voting with over 6 million votes. Ahmadinejad came in second with something under 6 million. An additional 6 million votes were split between conservatives Mohammad Baqer Qalibaf and Larijani—which meant that conservative candidates received about 12 million votes combined. Approximately 11 million votes were won by reformists, including third-place finisher Mehdi Karroubi, a cleric who received more than 5 million votes, along with Mostafa Moin and Mohsen Mehr-alizadeh. If at that point reformist voters had united behind Rafsanjani, the centrist would have coasted to victory with about 17 million votes.

But reformists did not unite behind Rafsanjani because they did not approve of his record. When he had served as president from 1989 to 1997, his administration, though it practiced some socioeconomic liberalization early on, failed to reform Iran's bureaucracy and attract foreign investment. Rafsanjani had also failed to engage the Clinton administration when it made quiet overtures to restore diplomatic ties. When Rafsanjani left the presidency, all member states of the European Union had recalled their ambassadors from Iran because Iranian agents had allegedly assassinated dissidents abroad.

Because Rafsanjani could not easily run on his record, he organized his campaign around the policies that he would pursue if elected again. He also cast himself as a veteran of government who could draw on his long experience in Iran's factional politics to re-energize the economy, bring Iran's nuclear dispute with foreign powers to a close, and normalize diplomatic relations with the United States. In the end, however, Ahmadinejad in a runoff trounced Rafsanjani, by 17.3 million votes to 10 million, a far bigger margin than anyone had predicted.

Ahmadinejad's election resulted partly from his manipulation of the electoral process, partly from his personal drive and determination, and partly from the deficiencies of the other candidates. He managed to qualify for the runoff election to begin with, after the first round in which five of seven candidates were eliminated, partly because of illegal canvassing on his behalf by a nationwide militia of religious vigilantes known as *basijis*. And according to the Interior Ministry, which was then controlled by the reformist government of President Muhammad Khatami, the runoff election itself was tarnished by "unprecedented irregularities."

A Surprising Alliance

In analyzing the reasons why a populist like Ahmadinejad won election in 2005, Iranian intellectuals draw parallels with the period before the revolution of 1979, a time characterized, like today, by oil riches, high inflation, and social upheaval. Between 2004 and 2005, Iran's imports increased by 26 percent, and the wealthy areas of its cities were full of Western items that most Iranians could not afford. Meanwhile, one-third of Iranians in their 20s were unemployed, and the country's infrastructure could not accommodate the huge demographic group that was reaching adulthood. Some 1.4 million young people took the university entrance exams in the summer of 2005, competing for just 200,000 spots.

Conservative Iranians, including the pious poor, were attracted to Ahmadinejad's apparent honesty and his modest lifestyle, along with the insular vision of the world that he projected. He drew on popular resentment against Iran's elite classes, which are widely viewed as enriching themselves through corruption. Rafsanjani, who was seen as the face of that elite, argued that the way forward for Iran should include better relations with the United States and increased foreign investment in Iran. Ahmadinejad saw no need for improved relations with "the Great Satan."

After the election it appeared to many that Rafsanjani's political career was finished. Yet, a year and a half later, Rafsanjani remained a potent force, vying for the speakership of the Assembly of Experts in elections slated for December of 2006, and aspiring ultimately to become supreme leader when the current holder of that position, Ayatollah Ali Khamenei, leaves office. Rafsanjani's bid for power sets him up against Ayatollah Mohammed Taghi Mesbah-Yazdi, an archconservative and a mentor of Ahmadinejad. Mesbah-Yazdi is believed to want the supreme leader's job for himself, and he lined up support among hard-line clerics for his own candidacy for the speakership of the Assembly of Experts.

This dynamic has produced a surprising new alliance between the reformists and Rafsanjani. The same bloc that once treated the former president with scorn is now supporting him for fear that the alternative would be worse. The reformists, comprised mainly of educated urbanites who recoil from the populism of Ahmadinejad, are alarmed by Mesbah-Yazdi's support for violent measures against political opponents and his connections to intelligence personnel, who have in the past been involved in the killing of dissidents. Reformists were strongly put off by language in a May 2006 magazine published by Mesbah-Yazdi that characterized Rafsanjani, along with the reformist former president Khatami and the former chief nuclear negotiator Hassan Rowhani, as "traitors to Islam and Iran" who should not be allowed to hold office.

Ayatollah Khamenei is now firmly in the camp of the hardliners, welcoming the election of Ahmadinejad after apparently having tried to dissuade Rafsanjani from running at all.

The Sputtering Economy

"Serving the Iranian people," Ahmadinejad says, "is more worthy than lording it over the world." But despite the conservative president's rhetoric about improving living conditions for the impoverished and making the country even more Islamic, Ahmadinejad so far has not brought much change to Iran, a country facing serious demographic and economic challenges.

Iran has 70 million inhabitants, of whom one-third are under 14 and another one-third under 35. The country registered 6 percent gdp growth in 2005, but that was not enough to meet the growing population's need for jobs. Unemployment has been running above 15 percent, and the real rate may be higher than reported in official figures. Inflation is about 17 percent, outstripping wage increases. Although the government heavily subsidizes staple foods among other items, the urban poor live in a discouraging economic environment.

In 2006, Iran's per capita income was projected to rise to $3,465, which would be $700 higher than in the previous year. Yet the Iranian Social Security Organization reports that 30 percent of Iranians live in poverty. Meanwhile, the wealthiest 20 percent of Iran's citizens account for 50 percent of national income and 80 percent of total wealth. Ahmadinejad came into office pledging to address this situation, saying he would deliver "oil revenues to people's dinner tables," and that he would not ignore poverty as his predecessors had done. "My whole family voted for Ahmadinejad because he promised to improve our lives," said a 67-year-old pensioner quoted in the *Asia Times.* "He said oil money belonged to the people. I haven't seen any of the oil money in my house yet, but I have to deal with the ever-increasing prices anyway."

Under Ahmadinejad, conservative forces are determined to make the Islamic Republic more Islamic than republican.

Iran's economic problems are numerous. The country has suffered a large decline in the value of its stock market, and low interest rates have left some banks on the verge of bankruptcy. The government's budget deficit amounts to about $8 billion a year. Highly subsidized and highly dependent on oil revenues, the Iranian economy now faces inflation and stagnation simultaneously. Although it is OPEC's second-largest producer of oil, Iran actually faces a shortage of refining capacity and has had to consider rationing gasoline.

High oil revenues have helped the public sector grow—in February 2006, for instance, the government increased the budget of the state broadcasting monopoly by 46 percent and that of the Institute for Islamic Propagation by 96 percent. The private sector on the other hand is falling behind, and the government has aggravated the situation by granting large contracts to military entities without going through tendering processes. Over the past few months, the Islamic Revolutionary Guards Corps has received government contracts amounting to $8 billion.

Ahmadinejad has been president for more than a year, yet Iran's economy is as inefficient as it was when Khatami was president. It also depends as much as ever on oil revenues. Indeed, the key parts of Ahmadinejad's program for populist uplift, including the government's increased control over the economy, seem less intended to stoke economic activity than to fix in place the state of affairs that existed before attempts were made at reform. Already, the government's populist economic policies have provoked criticism from some former allies of Ahmadinejad, including Ahmad Tavakkoli and Mahmoud Khoshchehreh, both hard-line members of parliament.

For these reasons and others, Ahmadinejad's grip on power must be seen as somewhat tenuous. Some reckon that only about 15 percent of Iranians strongly support Ahmadinejad's fundamentalism and the political factions that back it. His official powers are subject to constitutional and other constraints. And, despite ongoing efforts to make the country yet more Islamic, Iranian society continues to become more secularized in the cities. At some point, political upheaval could result from the dismal outcomes of the high expectations that the new government has created. Most Iranians identify their primary problems as economic ones, and Ahmadinejad has failed so far to improve the people's economic lot.

International Isolation

Compounding Ahmadinejad's political problems is his tendency to anger many in the international community with his verbal attacks against the West and particularly Israel, including his expressions of doubt that the Holocaust occurred. In October 2005, at a conference for students organized by the government and called "World Without Zionism," Ahmadinejad alarmed many by suggesting that Israel should be "wiped off the map." In July 2006, while Israel and Lebanon were engaged in conflict, he likened Israel's offensive to Adolf Hitler's aggression. In August, he said that "the main solution" to tensions in the Middle East would be "the elimination of the Zionist regime."

Opposition to Israel is written into Iran's constitution, but the country's approach to the Israeli-Palestinian issue has never been as cut-and-dried as might be inferred from listening to the public comments of Iranian officials. In the 1980s, for example, although Iran's Revolutionary Guards were providing assistance to Syria in setting up the Hezbollah militia in Lebanon, the Iranian government was buying American arms through Israel for its war against Iraq. Khatami, the reformist president, gave indications during his term that he would not rule out a two-state solution for the Israelis and Palestinians—and Khatami has since criticized Ahmadinejad's anti-Israel remarks.

At times, when state control over media content and intellectual discourse has been reduced, discussions have taken place as to whether Israel has a right to exist. Although Israel certainly views Iran's nuclear program as a threat to its existence, the threat is probably not imminent or severe. The CIA believes that Iran is still five to ten years away from being able to manufacture nuclear weapons. And Iran's nuclear ambitions may be driven more by the regime's desire to ensure its own survival than by any desire to destroy Israel. Indeed, any attack against Israel might invite a massive response that could very well cause the end of the Islamic Republic.

Still, Ahmadinejad's comments on the Holocaust and Israel have not benefited Iran. They have only served to increase tensions, and have also made it easier for Israel and the United States to portray Iran as a threat that must be confronted.

Nuclear Nationalism

Western nations have suspected for a number of years that Iran has been attempting to develop nuclear weapons. Iran has only made the suspicions stronger with its tough negotiating tactics and its willingness to lie about its nuclear programs. Although Ahmadinejad's election heralded a further assertiveness in Iran's positions regarding the nuclear programs, the president himself does not determine his country's foreign or nuclear policies. These remain the province of the supreme leader, Ayatollah Khamenei, and Larijani of the Supreme National Security Council.

That said, Ahmadinejad has done all he can to become the face of Iran's nuclear programs and ambitions. This is because, as both a populist and a politician whose fate ultimately rests in the hands of voters, he benefits from fomenting nationalist fervor. This may be why he chose to announce personally that Iran had succeeded in enriching small amounts of uranium, and to later state publicly that "Iran is a nuclear country. It has the full gamut of nuclear technology at its disposal."

Ahmadinejad has been able to project such assertiveness in part because of high oil prices, which paradoxically enough have stayed at high levels in part because of world oil markets' concerns about Iran. Oil revenues in Iran for the year ending in March 2006 came in at about $50 billion, almost double the amount from two years before. Moreover, as long as oil prices stay high, Iranian leaders know that they face little danger of an international oil embargo, because such an action would cause oil prices to go still higher.

Officials in Iran are thus able to cultivate the idea that international actions cannot hurt them. They assert that no embargo will take place, and that sanctions short of an embargo would have no tangible effect. They also suggest that any interruption in the flow of imports from Europe could be circumvented by increasing imports from China and other Asian countries, many of which are perfectly willing to continue doing business with Iran.

Although the nuclear powers China and Russia would prefer not to see Iran join the nuclear club, in part because this might prompt other Middle Eastern countries such as Turkey and Saudi Arabia to develop nuclear weapons of their own, both powers are wrapped up in Iran's energy sector. China is aggressively pinning down future sources of energy around the world, and Russia is assisting Iran in its construction of a civilian nuclear reactor in Bushehr. Therefore, it seems unlikely that China or Russia, both permanent members of the United Nations Security Council, would support meaningful sanctions against Iran. This in turn allows Iran more maneuvering room as it faces down the United States and the European Union.

The Iranian public's views on the nuclear program are generally positive, even if many Iranians doubt the official claim that the program's purposes are peaceful. In fact, according to public opinion research conducted by the InterMedia Survey Institute, 41 percent of Iranians strongly support the development of nuclear weapons. Among those who support the development of these weapons, 84 percent would be willing to face UN sanctions, and 75 percent would risk hostilities with the United States in order to develop them.

Iranians tend to support the nuclear program as a matter of national pride, something that is not likely to change as long as they do not believe the program threatens their security or impinges on their standard of living. Approval of the program is also stoked by anger over what Iranians see as a double standard in international attitudes toward other countries that have joined the nuclear club—Pakistan and Israel, for example.

Through the state media, Iran's leadership has popularized the idea that the nation's nuclear program is about much more than nuclear weapons. Government propaganda about nuclear activities is intended to reinforce the public's pride, and the nuclear program is cast as a way to force Western countries to recognize the Iranian revolution as legitimate. The program is also portrayed as a remedy to Iranians' historical dissatisfactions and as a source of hope for the future.

Iran's leaders suggest the nuclear problem will be solved when the United States and countries in the EU realize that they will have to deal with Iran as an equal. Thus, the conservatives in Iran's government are successfully using the nuclear issue as a means to cement their own power through nationalist fervor. In this, they have been unwittingly assisted by President Bush.

In this sensitive political environment, nothing is more counterproductive than talking of a military strike against Iran. Israeli Prime Minister Ehud Olmert has said that Iran must not have nuclear weapons "under any circumstances." The head of the Israeli air force, asked how far he would go to stop the development of nuclear weapons in Iran, joked "two thousand kilometers." In fact, any air strikes against Iran's nuclear facilities would be extremely risky, prompting Iran to retaliate through terrorist activities in Israel, Iraq, and Afghanistan. Moreover, air strikes in all likelihood would only slow Iran's program, not stop it, since nuclear facilities are probably spread throughout the country.

If history is any guide, the Iranian government will overplay its hand, and the absurd hostility between the United States and Iran will continue beyond 2007.

Hedging on Iraq

The Middle East has been undergoing great change since the US invasion of Iraq, and one of the effects, not intended by the United States, is Iran's growing power in the region. When Tehran was presented with Hussein's removal and the resulting power vacuum, it could not pass up the chance to pursue its desire for greater regional influence. For years Iranian leaders had promoted Islamic interests ahead of national interests; since the Iraq invasion they have gone back to the nationalist approach employed 30 years ago by Mohammad Reza Shah.

The US removal of Hussein eliminated Iran's main regional rival. Elections in Iraq have given power to that country's Shiite majority, among whom Shiite Iran retains influence. Weakened by violent chaos, Iraq has now come to see Iran as the more powerful player in the two countries' relationship. Iran's top interest in Iraq is to ensure that Iraq cannot emerge again as a military, political, or ideological threat.

Potential threats to Iran could be posed by Iraq's success—that is, if the country manages to succeed as a democracy or as a workable state arranged on religious lines different from Iran's. Threats might also be posed by Iraq's failure—that is, if Iraq falls into all-out civil war, or if it allows an independent Kurdistan to come into being (which Iran does not wish to see because of its own Kurdish minority).

Iran does not wish to see Iraq partitioned. It does not want full-scale instability or civil war. Rather, it would like to see a friendly Shiite government rule Iraq, and would also like for the United States to remain preoccupied with that country so that it cannot turn its attention to Iran. To achieve these aims, Tehran has pursued a three-part strategy. First, it has encouraged democracy as a way to achieve Shiite rule. Second, it has worked to promote disorder, while taking care to ensure that such disorder does not spin out of control entirely. Third, it has backed a wide variety of protagonists in Iraq to make sure that it has a working relationship with whatever faction finally gains control of the country.

Worried that the United States intends to bring Iran's nuclear ambitions to a halt through the use of force, Tehran has sought to build large networks of pro-Iranian actors within Iraq. These include special-forces units called the Quds Brigade, which could carry out attacks against US troops in Iraq in the event of American military action against Iran. Such elements in Iraq, combined with the threat that Iran poses to Israel through Hezbollah in Lebanon, provide leverage for Iran against possible US hostile action.

The worsening violence in Iraq, however, is causing strategy to change in Tehran as much as it is in Washington. The Iranian leadership was initially gleeful about Hussein's removal. But now this joy has been overwhelmed by the realization that if Iraq tears apart completely along ethnic and religious lines, and if the United States retreats hastily as a result, Iranian interests in the region would be gravely threatened. These threats would include the possibility of chaos leaping the border into Iran and provoking unrest among Iran's minorities. Therefore, Iran is working vigorously to prevent utter collapse from taking place.

Any end to US involvement in Iraq will have to include cooperation from Iran, the most powerful player in the area because of its links to Iraq's majority Shiites, to power centers in the Iraqi government, and to militias. In exchange for its cooperation, Iran will want a guarantee of its own security—incidentally, the same thing it wants in exchange for ending the conflict over its nuclear programs. Iran would also like to see the end of trade restrictions against it, and progress toward diplomatic normalization with the United States. The Americans in turn would expect Iran to exercise maximum possible restraint with its allies within Iraq.

Prospects for Change

Under Ahmadinejad, conservative forces are determined to make the Islamic Republic more Islamic than republican. Whether they will succeed is another matter. Power in Iran is a complicated matter, and various factions exist even among conservatives, who run the gamut from hard-liners to pragmatists. Some among Iran's leadership would accept accommodation with the West in exchange for economic and strategic concessions, while others are content to accept isolation from the West. Others favor a "Chinese model," which in Iran would mean opening the economy to international investment while maintaining the clergy's dominance. It is these complex internal forces that will decide the future of Iranian politics.

For now, not much optimism can be attached to the notion that sanctions and similar measures will cause regime change in Tehran. Nor is military action, short of full-scale invasion, likely to bring about regime change, since a limited attack by either the United States or Israel would only cause Iranians to throw more support behind the government.

BAHMAN BAKTIARI is the director of research and academic programming at the University of Maine's William S. Cohen Center for International Policy and Commerce.

From *Current History,* January 2007, pp. 11–16. Copyright © 2007 by Current History, Inc. Reprinted by permission.

How Did We Get Here?
Mexican Democracy after the 2006 Elections

Chappell Lawson

1. Introduction

On July 2, 2006, Mexican voters elected National Action Party (PAN) candidate Felipe Calderón as the next president of Mexico. Calderón's victory was extremely narrow; he won under 36% of the total vote and less that 0.6% more than his leftist rival, Andrés Manuel López Obrador. This potentially problematic situation was aggravated by López Obrador's decision to challenge Calderón's victory, both in the courts and in the streets. López Obrador's protest campaign culminated on September 16, when tens of thousands of his followers gathered in downtown Mexico City to acclaim him "legitimate president" of Mexico. Meanwhile, in the legislature, leaders of López Obrador's Party of the Democratic Revolution (PRD) oscillated between hints that they would collaborate with Calderón's administration and signs that they would adopt a posture of untrammeled hostility.

Post-electoral controversies raised the specter of a Left that had abandoned parliamentary tactics and returned to mass mobilization as its principal political strategy. At worst, they presaged the sort of political upheaval that could threaten Mexico's young democratic institutions. There was certainly no missing the symbolism involved in López Obrador's choice of the date on which he would take the oath of office—November 20, the anniversary of the Mexican Revolution—nor could students of Mexican history fail to recall that a contested election had sparked that decade-long conflagration.

How did Mexico find itself in the middle of such a crisis? Why had the country's vaunted electoral regime, generally regarded as a model for other democracies, failed to produce an outcome that all parties considered legitimate? Were Mexican political institutions so shaky that the actions of a single man could threaten their collapse? And, given the answers to these questions, what does the future hold for Mexico's political system?

Over the last decade, research on Mexican politics has focused on (1) institutional reform, especially in the electoral sphere, and (2) mass behavior, especially voting. Both areas of research are, of course, essential to understanding Mexico's transition from a one-party-dominant regime to a multiparty democracy.

However, scholarly attention to them has tended to understate the importance of political leadership and informal arrangements among elites, topics which were so central to earlier work on democratization (see O'Donnell and Schmitter 1986).

This article argues that the way these elites interact plays a pivotal role in the current situation. It first summarizes Mexico's transition to democracy over the last 15 years. It then addresses the simmering tensions between the PRD and the PAN during the administration of Vicente Fox that boiled over in the 2006 elections. The third section suggests that Mexico's current climate of polarization is a function of elite attitudes and interactions, rather than those of the mass public. The fourth section shows how these same interactions exercise a far greater influence on Mexican politics than do those institutions most often implicated in poor governance. The route out of Mexico's political impasse thus runs through pacting and compromise among members of Mexico's current political class, rather than further institutional tinkering.

2. Incomplete Transition

For close to seven decades, a single party (known today as the Institutional Revolutionary Party, or PRI) won all elections for significant posts. Over time, however, modernization weakened the corporatist and clientelist apparatuses through which the "official" party and the state had ensured social control. The collapse of Mexico's economy in the 1980s further undermined autocratic institutions and provoked mass disaffection with the old regime.

In the face of mounting social unrest, representatives of Mexico's political establishment negotiated a series of reforms with the leaders of the main opposition parties during the 1990s. These elite pacts, most notably the 1996 "Reform of the State," ultimately leveled the electoral playing field. In 1997, the PRI lost control of the Chamber of Deputies, and in 2000 PAN candidate Vicente Fox captured the presidency.

Data from standard measures of democracy nicely capture both the scope and the limitations of Mexico's political transition during the 1990s. In 1991, Mexico scored a zero on the combined Polity IV index; by 2001, it scored an eight.[1] Freedom House scores show a similar trend, with Mexico's score falling from eight in 1991 to four 10 years later.[2] By either measure, this transition left Mexico in the same league as many other new democracies at the beginning of the twenty-first century, such as Argentina, Brazil, Mongolia, South Korea, Taiwan, or Romania. In the prevailing scholarly discourse, Mexico had undergone a gradual transition from a moderately authoritarian regime to an "electoral democracy," but it had not yet become a "liberal democracy" (Diamond 1999).

A closer view of Mexico's political transition reveals the unevenness of democratization across different institutions and spheres of governance. For instance, Mexico's electoral regime and party system were quite well developed (see Todd Eisenstadt's essay in this symposium). As in the old regime, the military and the security services remained small and firmly under civilian control. Finally, despite the domination of broadcast television by two relentlessly commercial networks, Mexico's mass media had become quite open by the time of Fox's election in 2000 (Lawson 2003). By contrast, progress toward reforming the police, the judiciary, the prosecutorial apparatus, and other parts of the bureaucracy remained painfully slow. The PRI remained the country's largest party (until 2006); businessmen with longstanding ties to conservative factions of the regime continued to monopolize most sectors of the economy; and corrupt bosses affiliated with the PRI controlled most labor unions.

As president, Fox presided over modest democratic deepening. Civic groups and opposition parties successfully challenged the PRI's remaining strongholds at the state and local level; independent newspapers sprouted throughout the country; state-level electoral authorities became more independent and professional; prominent PRI figures and organizations began to defect to the opposition; and the passage of a federal Transparency Law exposed government operations to public scrutiny. Although corruption remained a serious problem, especially in the criminal justice system, the administration itself managed to avoid major scandals.

For most Mexicans, the PRI's defeat in 2000 represented the culmination of a long process of democratic transition and the beginning of an equally arduous process of democratic deepening. For the Left, however, alternation in power between the old ruling party and the conservative PAN constituted only partial or cosmetic change. Three episodes during Fox's tenure seemed to confirm their fears.

In 2003, the PAN and the PRI joined forces to name the new leaders of the Federal Electoral Institute (IFE) over the objections of the PRD. In contrast to the previous set of "Citizen Councilors," who included a number of distinguished academics and activists, the new cohort included a number of political unknowns and party hacks. Their selection signaled the breakdown of the partisan consensus that had characterized the political accords of 1996–1997.

Two years later, PAN and PRI legislators voted to impeach López Obrador, then mayor of Mexico City, on the grounds that he had violated a court injunction in a zoning dispute. Had the legal proceedings continued, they would have prevented López

Obrador from seeking the presidency. The Fox administration backed down in the face of widespread public opposition, international pressure, and massive demonstrations in Mexico City organized by López Obrador. Most Mexicans saw the affair as an attempt to trump up charges against a popular rival.

A third insult came in the midst of the 2006 presidential race, with the passage of the new broadcasting law (the "Ley Televisa") that was notoriously favorable to Mexico's two main television networks. During the second half of the race, television coverage of Calderón became more favorable, while reporting on López Obrador turned rather sour. In the leftist narrative, all of these events signaled a conspiracy between the government, the PAN, the old ruling party, leading businessmen, and a now-perverted electoral authority to deprive their candidate of victory.

Panistas (PAN partisans), of course, saw matters in an entirely different light. Their party stood for the same Christian Democratic principles that it had represented steadfastly since the late 1930s; by contrast, the PRD represented both the radicalism of the Marxist left and the corruption of the old PRI (from which many of the PRD's founders had come). It was the PRD that had rejected Fox's offer to form something like a government of national unity in 2000, and it was PRD obstructionism that had prevented partisan consensus in the selection of a new set of IFE Councilors.

Despite López Obrador's moderate position on many policy issues, his administration as mayor of Mexico City struck opponents as eerily reminiscent of PRI rule. For instance, López Obrador incorporated whole hog into the PRD apparatus almost two dozen PRI organizations, several with decidedly unsavory reputations. Episodes of corruption among his top aides, some captured on videotape, raised serious questions about financial probity, as did López Obrador's refusal to endorse a local transparency law modeled after the federal statute.

For his opponents, post-electoral controversies only confirmed their instincts: López Obrador was simply unwilling to accept the results of an election that the IFE, the Federal Electoral Court, and most international observers considered free and fair (see Eisenstadt's article). His ad-libbed responses to critics in speeches after the elections—e.g., "to hell with your institutions"—betrayed a casual attitude toward the rule of law that would have imperiled democracy had he won. This perspective contrasted starkly with Calderón's pledges to respect the autonomy of regulatory institutions, insulate the office of the public prosecutor from direct control by the executive, reform the judicial system, and further devolve authority to state and local governments—precisely the steps Mexico needed to overcome its autocratic legacy.

Since 2003, the tactics adopted by Mexican political elites in their partisan disputes have proven more tendentious and incendiary than analysts predicted. For instance, few political observers in 2001 would have anticipated PRI and PAN attempts to prevent López Obrador from contesting the 2006 elections through an act of legal legerdemain. Even fewer would have guessed how far López Obrador was willing to escalate his tactics after July 2, 2006.

3. Elites or Masses?

Do trends at the elite level reflect increasing polarization among ordinary Mexicans? Over the last five decades, support for the PRI in the mass public has declined at a rate of about 3% per election cycle. The weakness of the PRI's presidential candidate in 2006, Roberto Madrazo, only accelerated this process by hastening defections from the old ruling party (see Langston's contribution to this symposium). Because the PRI was ideologically and socially amorphous, its unraveling should theoretically have divided Mexico along lines of class and ideology. Left-Right differences should also become more salient as the issue of democratization faded from the agenda, forcing people to choose between very different political alternatives rather than simply selecting the one that was most likely to defeat the regime.

Nevertheless, the way in which voters have attached themselves to the PRD and the PAN has not seem to followed such a clear logic. Most Mexicans do not base their electoral choices on the policy positions adopted by parties and candidates (see Moreno's and Bruhn and Greene's articles in this collection). Still less do Mexicans vote along class lines (see Moreno). Although indicators of social status—such as living standards, education, skin color, and occupation—influence voting behavior at the margin, for ordinary Mexicans, region is a far more important predictor.[3] Consider, for instance, the "classic" PRD voter in May 2006: a brown-skinned, low-income man with a modest education who never attends church. A person with this demographic profile living in the north of the country had a 20% chance of favoring López Obrador—far lower than his probability of favoring Calderón. If his home was in the center of the country, however, his probability of supporting López Obrador rose to 34%. If he lived in the south, it was 44%, and if he resided in the Mexico City metropolitan area, it was 72%. Even this regional cleavage is muddled by the continued strength of the PRI in many areas of the country (see Klesner's essay in this symposium). In other words, divisions between the PRD and the PAN at the mass level are not simply less pronounced than those at the elite level, the fundamental axis of cleavage is different.

The episodes so central to polarization at the elite level have played out very differently in the electorate. For instance, polling data indicate that there is little support for continued protests by López Obrador; even many of those who voted for him express ambivalence about his tactics.[4] This situation echoes public sentiment during the impeachment of López Obrador: not only did an overwhelming majority of Mexicans oppose attempts to prevent him from running in the 2006 election, so did a majority of *panistas*.[5] These facts lend credence to arguments advanced by Bermeo (2003) and others that political crises are typically the product of elite machinations, rather than of mass preferences.

Acknowledging the truth of this argument, however, tells us little about why elite conflict has become so pronounced. The principal answer to this question lies in the patterns of party-building in Mexico. During the period of one-party rule, the PRI's eclectic nature gave rise to a fragmented opposition. Because opposition politics promised few tangible rewards, it tended to draw more extreme or ideologically purist members of society, on both the Right and the Left (Greene, forthcoming). Today, PAN and PRD activists come from strikingly different backgrounds. PAN candidates to Congress in 2006 were generally introduced to politics through their ties to the private sector and the Church; PRD candidates came up through labor unions and popular social movements (see the Mexico 2006 Candidate and Party Leader Survey, described in Bruhn and Greene's contribution to this collection). Although many leaders in both parties have attended public school, PAN politicians are far more likely to have attended private or parochial institutions. As a result of these patterns of political recruitment, party elites share relatively few cultural reference points.

Despite steps toward internal democracy in both parties, old guard elements still exercise substantial influence. The PAN remains a "club" party, in the sense that membership is not automatically open to anyone. Rather, those who wish to join must first be accepted as junior members (*miembros adherentes*); after a minimum trial period of six months and participation in various party activities, they may then apply to become full, dues-paying members (*miembros activos*). Both types of members could vote in the 2006 presidential primary, but only full members can vote for candidates for other offices or for party leaders. Not surprisingly, the party's current leadership remains far more conservative than party voters, not to mention ordinary citizens. In the case of the PRD, presidents have exercised rather wide discretion in whom they appoint to the National Executive Committee. Many of the current members were placed there by López Obrador. This fact may help to explain why, despite the steady influx of pragmatic PRI defectors into the PRD, its leadership supported López Obrador's post-electoral protest movement. These party elites are, in turn, the principal source of political polarization in Mexico.

4. Elites or Institutions?

For those political scientists who emphasize the role of institutions, the roots of Mexico's current political predicament lie in a cluster of familiar constitutional rules. First, Mexico's electoral system contains a large component of proportional representation, which in turn encourages multipartism. A multiparty system is not inherently problematic, but it becomes so when paired with a second institution: presidentialism. The combination of these two institutions virtually guarantees divided government. The adverse effects of these arrangements are compounded by the lack of run-off elections for president, which permits the election of non-Condorcet winners, and by the length of the presidential term (six years). Finally, to make matters worse, the prohibition on consecutive reelection renders politicians less accountable.

Dysfunctional institutions, however, cannot account for the most salient features of Mexico's current political topography. Most obviously, they cannot explain why one of the best-designed electoral systems in the world failed to produce a result that party leaders on the losing side would accept. If institutions are the main issue, governance problems should be the product of gridlock, rather than political polarization. Today, the reverse is true: as a result of likely collaboration between the PAN and elements of the PRI, legislative gridlock is now relatively unlikely; on the other hand, alleged electoral irregularities provoked a crisis.

Choice and leadership have more to do with today's situation than do formal institutions. In the case of post-electoral protests, for instance, other men in the same situation would have made different decisions than did López Obrador. In 1988, PRD candidate Cuauhtémoc Cárdenas proved less vigorous in protesting the official results of the election than López Obrador is today, even though the Left had much stronger grounds to do so then. Likewise, had Calderón lost the election, there is no doubt that he would have accepted the result or challenged it through strictly constitutional channels. The problem, then, lies less in how Mexico's president was elected than in how elites reacted to his election.

The simple fact that institutions have played a role in permitting the overrepresentation of extremists at the top of Mexico's main parties does not consign Mexico to crisis. Even fairly doctrinaire politicians can compromise, as the 1996–1997 inter-party negotiations showed. Nothing in the current context compels the PRD's leadership in Congress to adopt a relentlessly obstructionist stance, and the electoral benefits of doing so are at best unclear. Nor do present circumstances prevent Mexico's president-elect from reaching out to the Left.

There is not necessarily anything wrong with further institutional reform in Mexico, of course. But such reform is important as a symptom of agreement among the main political parties, not as its cause. In the end, it is the way particular leaders interact that will propel events toward compromise, or toward crisis.

References

Bermeo, Nancy. 2003. *Ordinary People in Extraordinary Times: The Citizenry and the Breakdown of Democracy.* Princeton: Princeton University Press.

Bruhn, Kathleen, and Kenneth F. Greene. 2007. "Elite Polarization Meets Mass Moderation in Mexico's 2006 Elections." *PS: Political Science and Politics* 40 (January): 33–38.

Diamond, Larry. 1999. *Developing Democracy: Toward Consolidation.* Baltimore: Johns Hopkins University Press.

Eisenstadt, Todd A. 2007. "The Origins and Rationality of the 'Legal versus Legitimate' False Dichotomy Invoked in Mexico's 2006 Post-Electoral Conflict." *PS: Political Science and Politics* 40 (January): 39–43.

Greene, Kenneth F. Forthcoming. *Defeating Dominance: Party Politics and Mexico's Democratization in Comparative Perspective.* Cambridge: Cambridge University Press.

Klesner, Joseph. 2007. "The 2006 Mexican Elections: Manifestation of a Divided Society?" *PS: Political Science and Politics* 40 (January): 27–32.

Langston, Joy. 2007. "The PRI's 2006 Electoral Debacle." *PS: Political Science and Politics* 40 (January): 21–25.

Lawson, Chappell. 2003. *Building the Fourth Estate: Democratization and the Rise of a Free Press in Mexico.* Berkeley: University of California Press.

———. 2006. "Preliminary Findings from the Mexico 2006 Panel Study: Blue States and Yellow States." Unpublished manuscript available at http://web.mit.edu/polisci/research/mexico06/Pres.htm.

Mainwaring, Scott. 1993. "Presidentialism, Multipartism, and Democracy: The Difficult Combination." *Comparative Political Studies* 26 (2): 198–228.

Moreno, Alejandro. 2007. "The 2006 Mexican Presidential Election: The Economy, Oil Revenues, and Ideology." *PS: Political Science and Politics* 40 (January): 15–19.

O'Donnell, Guillermo, and Philippe C. Schmitter. 1986. *Transitions from Authoritarian Rule: Tentative Conclusions about Uncertain Democracies.* Baltimore: Johns Hopkins University Press.

Notes

1. The combined Polity IV score ranges from –10 (utter autocracy) to 10 (full democracy). A score of zero indicates that autocratic features of the regime evenly balance.

2. Freedom House scores range from 2–14; higher scores indicate *less* freedom.

3. Results are based on simulations from a multinomial logit model of vote choice, in which the dependent variable took on one of four values (Calderón, López Obrador, Madrazo, or none/undecided). Independent variables included: age, gender, living standards (as measured by an index of material possessions, education, church attendance, region, political engagement, skin color, and urban or rural residence). Data are taken from the Mexico 2006 Panel Study, Wave 2. For full results, see Lawson 2006, available at: http://web.mit.edu/polisci/research/mexico06/Pres.htm.

4. Mexico 2006 Panel Study, Wave 3 and accompanying cross-section; Consulta Mitovsky, National Household Survey, August 2006.

5. Parametría, "El desafuero de López Obrador," National Household Survey, August 2004; Consulta Mitovsky, Household Survey in the Federal District, September 2004; Consulta Mitovsky, National Household Survey, January 2005; Consulta Mitovsky, National Telephone Survey and National Household Survey, April 2005; Consulta Mitovsky, Household Survey in the Federal District, February 2005.

In Quake, Apotheosis of Premier 'Grandpa'

Andrew Jacobs

He is widely known as "the crying prime minister," although he prefers to be called "Grandpa Wen." Over the past week, as Wen Jiabao toured earthquake-shattered towns and cities across northern Sichuan, he has hollered out words of encouragement to those trapped beneath fallen buildings and shared tearful moments with newly orphaned children.

If a story widely circulated on the Internet is to be believed, Prime Minister Wen has been barking orders to army generals and dispatching paratroopers to remote towns hit hard in the quake, even though as China's head of government operations he has no power over the military.

Since ascending to the post in 2003, Mr. Wen, 65, has cultivated an image as a man of the people, a rarity in the pantheon of Chinese leaders, who are often seen as placing stability and the authority of the Communist Party above the wants of individuals. The state news media have long labored to spread the notion that Mr. Wen cares for ordinary folks, broadcasting his visits with coal miners and migrant workers, and showing him eagerly shaking the hands of drug addicts and people with AIDS.

Now, as the nation grapples with its greatest natural disaster in three decades, Mr. Wen's persona as an empathetic, benevolent official has been cemented in popular lore. He has become the public and inescapable face of a nation's grief since he jumped on a government jet bound for Sichuan Province less than two hours after the earthquake struck.

His high-profile humanitarian gestures, played again and again on television, have stood in stark contrast to the response of the rulers of Myanmar, who have been widely denounced for inaction toward the victims of a devastating cyclone. But Mr. Wen also appears to have forged a new, media-savvy mold for Chinese leaders, who have long delegated propaganda work to lower-ranking officials and the state-run press.

"He really loves the common people, and we can see this is not an act," said Wang Liangen, 72, a retired math teacher from the devastated city of Dujiangyan, who watched last week as the prime minister climbed over the wreckage of a school where hundreds of children were buried. "He has brought the people closer together, and brought the people closer to the government."

Some analysts say Mr. Wen's unusually public role may signal at least a modest shift in the way the Communist Party interacts with the Chinese citizenry. In a country where many millions live in poverty and thousands perish each year in mine accidents, for example, Mr. Wen ordered shortly after the quake that lives must be saved "at any cost." And while Mr. Wen is not known to have supported any substantive political change during his first five-year term as prime minister, his frequent calls for more democratic-style consultation with ordinary people and for greater economic parity have resonated with the poor.

"Wen's efforts will absolutely leave a long-lasting influence on government work in the future," said Fang Ning, a political scientist at the China Academy of Social Science in Beijing. "His quick response and immediate appearance will set a precedent for other officials."

It is difficult to know if the rescue effort Mr. Wen has led will ultimately be judged a success. And it is unlikely that the unusually vigorous press coverage of the quake and of Mr. Wen's hands-on role in managing the rescue effort signal a shift away from strict censorship.

But Mr. Wen and his boss, President Hu Jintao, do seem inclined to show the world a kindler, gentler side of official China in advance of the Olympic Games. After the international backlash over China's crackdown on ethnic Tibetans, the leaders have used the earthquake in an effort to show that their authoritarian government can be responsive, even populist, at crucial moments.

"I think the earthquake really has the potential to change things," said Cheng Li, a senior fellow of the Brookings Institution, who argues that Mr. Wen—whose second appointed term expires in 2012—is one of China's brightest and most pragmatic modern leaders. Even before his actions in Sichuan, he said, Mr. Wen was a muscular champion for China's have-nots, an advocate of broadening the use of legal norms to help govern the country, and a bulwark against party conservatives. "A lot of Chinese have been overwhelmed by Wen and his sincerity, honesty and humanity," Dr. Li said. "Not many leaders have his qualities."

Mr. Wen often talks about democracy but is not a proponent of Western-style democratic reforms. He remains an unwavering advocate of single-party rule, and he has taken a hard line on Tibet, accusing the Dalai Lama of instigating the ethnic Tibetan unrest in March. In public statements, he has said China is unafraid to use its military might to prevent Taiwan from declaring independence from the mainland.

Despite Mr. Wen's well-tended image as an apolitical pragmatist, cynics note that he did not earn his lofty post by playing nice. "It takes a considerable amount of political skill and cunning to become premier of China," said Fred Teiwes, a professor of Chinese politics at the University of Sydney in Australia.

Mr. Wen is nothing if not the consummate survivor. A lifelong technocrat, he made his way to the top of the heap by pleasing his superiors, hewing to the party line and making few enemies. A trained geologist who comes from a family of teachers, he is sometimes ridiculed for indecisiveness and for long-winded speeches flecked with quotations from Descartes and classical Chinese poetry. In the 1980s he served as a top aide to successive party bosses, Hu Yaobang and Zhao Ziyang; both leaders were purged after opposing harsh crackdowns on liberal forces in society, but Mr. Wen went on to serve in senior posts under their more conservative successors.

As with most Chinese leaders, much about him remains a mystery. But he presents himself as self-effacing and penurious. For more than a decade, he wore the same dull green overcoat. Unlike most of his fellow cadres, he refuses to tint his graying hair with gobs of black dye.

In contrast to Mr. Hu, an opaque and aloof statesman, Mr. Wen favors a colloquial speaking style, even if his comments always hew closely to the party script. Unlike his predecessor, Zhu Rongji, who was known for his jocular manner and snap decisions, Mr. Wen, when faced with tough economic policy choices, will often spend days ruminating and consulting before deferring to fellow members of the ruling Politburo Standing Committee for a collective decision, party officials have said.

"He may not be a good leader," said Dr. Li, of Brookings, "but the perception out there is that he's a good person."

That has been the overwhelming impression since a somber-looking Mr. Wen announced news of the earthquake on May 12 as he flew from Beijing to Sichuan. In the days that followed, he was frequently shown hugging quake victims and promising government aid. According to people who saw him in those first few days, he cried more than once.

In recent days, a pro-government newspaper in Hong Kong and a Guangzhou-based Web site wrote that Mr. Wen had tripped and fallen as he walked on earthquake rubble and had refused medical treatment for a bloody arm.

A more intriguing account described his fury when he learned that rescuers from the People's Liberation Army had yet to reach Wenchuan, a city of 100,000 at the quake's epicenter. Even if concocted by Mr. Wen's admirers, the report reveals a shift away from the prime minister's persona as a vacillating, avuncular bureaucrat.

According to the account—which has been ricocheting by text message for days—Mr. Wen screamed on the phone to a general, who, under Beijing's pecking order, does not answer to the prime minister. "I don't care what you do," Mr. Wen reportedly yelled, his face drenched in rain. "I just want 100,000 people saved. This is my order."

Then, according to the story, he slammed the phone down.

UNIT 4

The Legislature: Representation and the Effects of Electoral Systems

Unit Selections

Key Points to Consider

- What are the roles of the legislature?

- Why is it important to elect minority groups to the legislature?

- What are the impediments to successful election of minority groups in the legislature?

- When is a legislature successful?

- What are the different types of electoral systems?

- How does a single-member plurality election work?

- How does proportional representation work?

- What is a divided government?

Student Web Site

www.mhcls.com

Internet References

Inter-Parliamentary Union
http://www.ipu.org/wmn-e/world.htm

Japan Ministry of Foreign Affairs
http://www.mofa.go.jp

Latin American Network Information Center, University of Texas at Austin
http://lanic.utexas.edu/la/region/government/

U.S. Information Agency
http://www.america.gov/

World Bank
http://www.worldbank.org

Unit 4 focuses on the legislature's roles in government, the significance of its roles, and how its performance is evaluated; in short, the systematic questions of "why, what, and how" regarding the legislature. The question, "Why do we need legislatures?", coincides with the previous unit regarding the executive: legislatures demonstrate and capture representation of their constituents in government. Whereas the executive imposes the "discipline" of a single policymaker in lawmaking, the legislature aims at representing the range of citizens' responses and needs in policy and legislation making. Indeed, the ideal legislature may be the perfect replica of the citizenry in all its diversity in a smaller version.

What are the roles that legislatures perform? The primary role is representing the range of citizens' needs and responses in making policies. It is important, however, to distinguish between making policies and initiating policies. Legislatures do not have to initiate policies in order to make them. What legislatures must do to demonstrate representation in policy-making is to approve them, which entails the essential tasks of discussing, examining, and debating the policies introduced. At the various points of discussing, examining, and debating the proposed legislation, the individual legislator gets to perform her/his role of representing his/her constituency's responses and needs. Thus, in principle, the aggregation of all legislators' input ensures that proposed legislation captures or is amended in the end product to contain the diversity of citizens' responses and needs, or it is rejected.

The essential legislative role of approving policies is described in all the articles in this unit. Thus, the article on the Japanese Upper House refers to its ability to "block or delay" legislation introduced by the Prime Minister, rather than its ability to initiate or write legislation. Likewise, the article on the possibility of the U.S. parliament, talks about the significance of "congressional voting" along partisan lines that delays the process of lawmaking. The article on Argentina President Kirchner's difficulties is most explicit in outlining the role of the legislature in approving legislation: the export tax on farm grains was a policy initiated by President Kirchner that was accepted by the Lower House but ultimately failed because of the rejection by the Senate. In Lebanon, part of the difficulty in governance is obtaining approvals from the legislature. While legislative approval is required to pass a proposed bill into law, legislative rejection does not necessarily mean that a bill is dead or that the executives' hands are tied. Indeed, executives are usually granted the power to override such rejection. Nevertheless, this rarely occurs because, to the extent that legislatures are considered to represent the people's preferences, such overrides may be

© Library of Congress, Prints & Photographs Division (LC-USZ62-107702)

construed as dismissing the people's preferred outcome and generally occurs at considerable political costs.

In its role of making legislation, the legislature may find itself pitted against the executive. Some of the articles suggest that this may be the result of divided government, a situation where competing political parties control different branches of government. For instance, the articles on the possibility of a U.S. parliament and the Japanese Upper House point out that opposition dominance of one or more of the legislative branches of government intensifies such challenges against the executive. However, the articles on Argentina and Lebanon point out that the tension does not derive from opposing parties in control of different branches of government. Rather, they derive from the different constituencies that support or elect the members of each branch of government. In particular, Argentina President Kirchner's export tax on grains failed not because of opposition control of the legislature (It is useful to note here that her party enjoyed a majority in both branches of the government at the time of the proposed tax.), but because her party members in the legislature responded to their farm and rural constituencies to reject the tax.

Given the significance of the legislature as a representative institution, how is this representativeness ensured? In principle, it is achieved through elections that give offices to candidates with popular appeal. That is, candidates who are able or promise to deliver on policies to and for their constituencies, are expected to be the ones who will enjoy the most support and, hence, be chosen as the legislative representative. However, in practice, elections and electoral systems may skew, rather than ensure, representativeness. Two readings on women and minority representation describe how this occurs. Specifically, elections and electoral systems may not achieve representation because of the costs of campaigning, the benefits of incumbency that penalizes new candidates, the advantage of political families that daunts minorities and newcomers, and electoral rules that favor candidates with the largest popular appeal—generally the majority group—and leads to overrepresentation of the majority and underrepresentation of minorities.

Many of the potential barriers to such representation from electoral systems are easily remedied. For instance, transparent campaign finance laws have helped address the disadvantages faced by minority or women candidates. Likewise, a change from an electoral system of first-past-the-post, or single-member districts, to proportional or at-large systems removes any financial or majority advantage to balance representation. Is such minority representation or women's representation important? In both readings, the authors note that such representation in legislatures reduces political alienation and, consequently, the tensions and conflicts from such alienation. Thus, increasing the representativeness of legislature is not merely a political principle but another means of assuring political stability.

Japan's Upper House Censures Prime Minister

Norimitsu Onishi

The opposition-controlled upper house of Parliament passed a nonbinding censure motion against Prime Minister Yasuo Fukuda on Wednesday, the first against a prime minister in postwar Japan.

But the motion was largely symbolic because Mr. Fukuda's governing Liberal Democratic Party enjoys an overwhelming majority in the more powerful lower house of Parliament, and Mr. Fukuda immediately said he would neither resign nor call an early general election.

On Thursday, the lower house passed a vote of confidence in Mr. Fukuda to counter the censure motion.

The opposition introduced the censure because it said that the Fukuda administration had lost the public's confidence over its handling of several issues, especially an unpopular plan that would require Japanese 75 years and older to pay more for health care.

Anger over the plan has helped lower Mr. Fukuda's approval ratings to about 20 percent.

The opposition, led by the Democratic Party, wanted to use the censure motion to press Mr. Fukuda to call a general election by forcing him to dissolve the lower house, which selects the prime minister.

The motion further embarrassed Mr. Fukuda, who is scheduled to host a Group of 8 summit meeting of major economic powers in Hokkaido next month.

"The only way to resolve this is to seek the people's judgment in a general election," Ichiro Ozawa, the leader of the Democratic Party, said at a news conference.

Mr. Fukuda, who does not have to call a general election until September 2009, said he would take the censure seriously. But asked whether he would dissolve the lower house, he told reporters, "I'm not thinking of that right now."

The opposition took over the upper house for the first time last summer, weakening the Liberal Democrats' half-century grip on power, and has used its new powers to block or delay legislation pushed by Mr. Fukuda. But the governing party has been able to override opposition on key legislation by using its two-thirds majority in the lower house.

It inherited that majority from the popular former prime minister, Junichiro Koizumi, who won a landslide election in 2005, the last time that Japanese have voted in a general election.

The opposition has argued that the upper house has a greater popular mandate. But polls show that voters, used to one-party rule, have misgivings about handing the prime minister's office to the opposition, especially one led by Mr. Ozawa, who is known for his erratic behavior.

More recently, Mr. Fukuda's approval ratings have fallen so steeply that rivals inside his own party, like Taro Aso, the hawkish former foreign minister, have begun criticizing him openly in their bid to succeed him as party leader.

The Case for a Multi-Party U.S. Parliament?
American Politics in Comparative Perspective

This article supports the inclusion of American political institutions within the study of comparative politics. This is a brief on behalf of a multi-party parliamentary system for the United States that can be read as a "what if" experiment in institutional transplantation. It underscores the basic insight that institutions are not neutral but have consequences for the political process itself and encourages American students to think more broadly about the possibilities of reforming the American political system.

CHRISTOPHER S. ALLEN

Introduction

Americans revere the constitution but at the same time also sharply and frequently criticize the government. (Dionne 1991) Yet since the constitution is responsible for the current form of the American government, why not change the constitution to produce better government? After all, the founders of the United States did create the amendment process and we have seen 27 of them in 220 years.

Several recent events prompt a critical look at this reverence for the constitution: unusual developments regarding the institution of the Presidency, including the Clinton impeachment spectacle of 1998–1999; the historic and bizarre 2000 Presidential election that required a Supreme Court decision to resolve; the apparent mandate for fundamental change that President Bush inferred from this exceedingly narrow election; and the increasingly numerous constitutional questions concerning Presidential powers and the conduct of the "war on terror." In the early 21st century, American politics confronted at least three other seemingly intractable problems: significant erosion in political accountability; out of control costs of running for public office; and shamefully low voter turnout. More seriously, none of these four problems is of recent origin, as all four have eroded the functioning of the American government for a period of between 25 and 50 years! The core features of these four problems are:

- Confusion of the roles of head of state and head of government, of which the impeachment issue—from Watergate through Clinton's impeachment and beyond—is merely symptomatic of a much larger problem.
- Eroding political accountability, taking the form of either long periods of divided government, dating back to the "Do Nothing" 80th congress elected in 1946, to the recent "gerrymandering industry" producing a

dearth of competitive elections. The result is millions of "wasted votes" and an inability for voters to assign credit or blame for legislative action.
- Costly and perennial campaigns for all offices producing "the best politicians that money can buy." This problem had its origins with the breakdown of the party caucus system and the growth of primary elections in the 1960s; and
- The world's lowest voter turnout among all of the leading OECD countries, a phenomenon that began in the 1960s and has steadily intensified.

When various American scholars acknowledge these shortcomings, however, there is the occasional, offhand comparison to parliamentary systems which have avoided many of these pathologies. The unstated message is that we don't—or perhaps should never, ever want to—have that here.

Why not? What exactly is the problem with a parliamentary system? In the US, durable trust in government, sense of efficacy, and approval ratings for branches in government have all declined in recent decades. Such phenomena contribute to declining voter turnout and highlight what is arguably a more significant trend toward a crisis in confidence among Americans concerning their governing institutions. So why is institutional redesign off the table?

This article examines these four institutional blockages of the American majoritarian/Presidential system and suggests certain features of parliamentary or consensus systems might overcome these persistent shortcomings of American politics.

Less normatively, the article is framed by three concepts central to understanding and shaping public policy in advanced industrialized states with democratic constitutional structures.

First, is the issue of comparability and 'American Exceptionalism' (Lipset 1996). The article's goal is to initiate a long-delayed dialogue on comparative constitutional structures with scholars of American politics. Second, the article hopes to participate in the active discussion among comparativists on the respective strengths and weaknesses of majoritarian and consensus systems. (Birchfield and Crepaz 1998) Third, scandals surrounding money and politics in a number of democratic states (Barker 1994) should prompt a comparison of parties and party systems and the context within which they function.

This article does not underestimate the quite significant problems associated with "institutional transplantation" (Jacoby 2000) from one country to another. The more modest and realistic goal is to engage American and Comparative scholars in a fruitful debate about political institutions and constitutional design that (finally) includes American politics in a Comparative orbit.

This article is organized in 5 sections that address: 1) the cumbersome tool of impeachment; 2) eroding political accountability due to divided government and safe seats; 3) the costly, never-ending campaign process; 4) the continued deterioration of voter turnout; and 5) the quite formidable obstacles that initiating a parliamentary remedy to these problems would clearly face.

1. Impeachment: Head of State vs Head of Government

The tool of impeachment is merely a symptom of a larger problem. Its more fundamental flaw is that it highlights the constitutional confusion between the two functions of the US presidency: head of state and head of government.

Americanists have delved deeply into the minutiae of the impeachment process during the past thirty years but comparativists would ask a different question. How would other democracies handle similar crises affecting their political leaders? More than two years transpired from the Watergate break-in to Nixon's resignation (1972–74), the Iran-Contra scandal (1986–87) produced no impeachment hearings; and an entire year (1998–99) transpired from the onset of the Clinton-Lewinsky saga to the completion of the impeachment process. Finally, the revelations from 2005–2007 concerning the Bush Administration's clandestine spying on American citizens by the National Security Agency have once again caused some Democrats to mention preliminary impeachment inquiries. Comparativists and citizens of other democratic polities find this astounding, since in a parliamentary system a fundamental challenge to the executive would take the form of a vote of no confidence, (Lijphart 1994) and the issue would be politically resolved within weeks. The executive would either survive and continue or resign.

The portrayal of the Clinton impeachment and trial is characterized as historic. For only the second time in American politics, an American president has been impeached in the House and put on trial in the Senate. Yet, the idea of using impeachment has been much less rare, having been raised three times in the past thirty years; and has only a very slim possibility of being seriously considered in the early 21st century. Basically, impeachment is an extremely blunt tool that has not "worked" at all. It is either not brought to fruition (Watergate), not used when it should have been (Iran-Contra), or completely trivial-ized (Clinton-Lewinsky) when another path was clearly needed. But impeachment itself isn't the real problem; a larger constitutional design flaw is.

The United States has a constitutional structure based on a separation of powers, while most parliamentary systems have a "fusion" of powers in that the Prime Minister is also the leader of the major party in parliament. However, within the American executive itself, there is a "fusion" of functions, which is the exact opposite of Parliamentary regimes.

The US is the only developed democracy where head of state and head of government are fused in one person. The President is the Head of State and, effectively, the Head of Government. In Parliamentary systems these two functions are performed by two different people. (Linz 1993) Thus impeachment of one person removes two functions in one and likely explained the dichotomy of popular desire for Clinton's retention on the one hand, but also for some form of political censure on the other.

Beyond the impeachment issue, when American presidents undertake some action as head of government for which they are criticized, they then become invariably more remote and inaccessible. For example, Presidents Johnson (Vietnam), Nixon (Watergate), Reagan (Iran/Contra), Clinton (the Lewinsky Affair) and G.W. Bush (Iraq) all reduced their appearances at press conferences as criticism of their policies mounted. In short, when criticized for actions taken in their head of government capacity, they all retreated to the Rose Garden or other "safe" locations and sometimes created the impression that criticizing the President—now wearing the head of state hat (or perhaps, crown)—was somehow unpatriotic. This was especially the case with George W. Bush, who in the post 9/11 and Iraq war periods, has tried to emphasize the commander in chief aspect of the presidency rather than his role as steward of the economy and domestic politics.

Toward a Politically Accountable Prime Minister and a Ceremonial President

A parliamentary system with a separate head of state and head of government would produce two "executive" offices instead of just one. It's odd that the US is so fearful of centralized power yet allows the executive to perform functions that no other leader of an OECD country (France excepted) performs alone. The US Vice President serves many of the functions of heads of state in other countries. But the United States has a comparatively odd way of dividing executive constitutional functions. One office, the Presidency, does everything while the other, the Vice Presidency, does virtually nothing and simply waits until the president can no longer serve (although Vice President Cheney sees this role differently). An American parliamentary system would redefine these 2 offices so that one person (the head of state) would serve as a national symbol and preside over ceremonial functions. The second person (the head of government) would function much like a prime minister does in a parliamentary system, namely as the head of government who could be criticized, censured and held accountable for specific political actions without creating a constitutional crisis.

Thus were it necessary to censure or otherwise take action against the head of government (i.e. prime minister), the solution would be a relatively quick vote of no confidence that would solve the problem and move on and let the country address its political business. (Huber 1996) And unlike impeachment which is the political equivalent of the death penalty, a vote of no confidence does not preclude a politician's making a comeback and returning to lead a party or coalition. Impeachment and removal from office, on the other hand, is much more final.

Prime Ministers, unlike US presidents, are seen much more as active politicians and not remote inaccessible figures. In a parliament, the prime minister as the head of government is required to engage—and be criticized—in the rough-and-tumble world of daily politics. In short, the head of government must be accountable. The British prime minister, for example, is required to participate in a weekly "question time" in which often blunt and direct interrogatories are pressed by the opposition. (Rundquist 1991) There is no equivalent forum for the American president to be formally questioned as a normal part of the political process.

But could such a power be used in a cavalier fashion, perhaps removing the head of government easily after a debilitating scandal? This is unlikely in a well-designed parliamentary system because such cynicism would likely produce a backlash that would constrain partisanship. In fact, the Germans have institutionalized such constraints in the "constructive vote of no confidence" requiring any removal of the head of government to be a simultaneous election of a new one. The context of such a parliamentary system lowers the incentives to engage in the politics of destruction. The political impact of destroying any particular individual in a collective body such as a cabinet or governing party or coalition is much less significant than removing a directly elected president.

A parliamentary head of state is above the kind of criticism generated from no confidence votes and simply serves as an apolitical symbol of national pride. In nation states that have disposed of their monarchies, ceremonial presidents perform many of the same roles as constitutional monarchs such as Queen Elizabeth do, but much less expensively. In fact, many of these ceremonial roles are performed by the American vice president (attending state dinners/funerals, cutting ribbons, presiding over the Senate, etc.) The problem is that the Vice President is often a political afterthought, chosen more for ticket-balancing functions and/or for inoffensive characteristics than for any expected major political contributions. On the other hand, the type of individual usually chosen as a ceremonial president in a parliamentary system is a retired politician from the moderate wing of one of the major parties who has a high degree of stature and can serve as a figure of national unity. In effect, the office of ceremonial president is often a reward or honor for decades of distinguished national service, hardly the characteristics of most American vice presidents.

In retrospect, one might say that President Clinton was impeached not for abusing head of government functions, but for undermining the decorum and respect associated with heads of state. The separation of head of state and head of government would have a salutary effect on this specific point. Scan-dals destroying heads of state would have little real political significance since the head of state would not wield real political power. Similarly, scandals destroying heads of government would have significantly less impact than in the current American system. The head of government role, once separated from the head of state role, would no longer attract monolithic press and public attention or be subject to extraordinarily unrealistic behavioral expectations.

2. Political Accountability: Divided Government & "Safe Seats"

From the "do nothing" 80th Congress elected in 1946 to the 110th elected in 2006, a total of thirty-one Congresses, the United States has experienced divided government for more than two-thirds of this period. In only ten of those thirty-one Congresses has the president's party enjoyed majorities in both houses of Congress. (Fiorina 1992; Center for Voting and Democracy 2007) Some might observe this divided government phenomenon and praise the bipartisan nature of the American system. (Mayhew 1991) But to justify such a conclusion, defenders of bipartisanship would have to demonstrate high public approval of governmental performance, particularly when government was divided. Based on over four decades of declining trust in government, such an argument is increasingly hard to justify.

One explanation for the American preference for divided government is the fear of concentrated political power. (Jacobson 1990) Yet in a search for passivity, the result often turns out to be simply inefficiency.

While the fear of concentrated government power is understandable for historical and ideological reasons, many of the same people who praise divided government also express concern regarding government efficiency. (Thurber 1991) Yet divided government quite likely contributes to the very inefficiencies that voters rightfully lament. Under divided government, when all is well, each of the two parties claims responsibility for the outcome; when economic or political policies turn sour, however, each party blames the other. This condition leads to a fundamental lack of political accountability and the self-fulfilling prophesy that government is inherently inefficient.

Rather than being an accidental occurrence, divided government is much more likely to result due to the American constitutional design. For it is constitutional provisions that are at the heart of divided government; 2 year terms for Congress, 4 year terms for the Presidency, and 6 year terms for the Senate invariably produce divided government.

Were it only for these "accidental" outcomes of divided government, political accountability might be less deleterious. Exacerbating the problem, however, is the decline of parties as institutions. This has caused individuals to have weaker partisan attachments—despite the increased partisan rhetoric of many elected officials since the 1980s—and has thereby intensified the fragmentation of government. (Franklin and Hirczy de Mino 1998) Clearly, divided government is more problematic when partisan conflict between the two parties is greater as the sharper ideological conflict and the increased party line congressional

Table 1 Trust in the Federal Government 1964–2004

	None of the Time	Some of the Time	Most of the Time	Just about Always	Don't Know
1964	0	22	62	14	1
1966	2	28	48	17	4
1968	0	36	54	7	2
1970	0	44	47	6	2
1972	1	44	48	5	2
1974	1	61	34	2	2
1976	1	62	30	13	3
1978	4	64	27	2	3
1980	4	69	23	2	2
1982	3	62	31	2	3
1984	1	53	40	4	2
1986	2	57	35	3	2
1988	2	56	36	4	1
1990	2	69	25	3	1
1992	2	68	26	3	1
1994	1	74	19	2	1
1996	1	66	30	3	0
1998	1	58	36	4	1
2000	1	55	40	4	1
2002	0	44	51	5	0
2004	1	52	43	4	0

Percentage within study year

Source: The National Election Studies (http://www.electionstudies.org/nesguide/toptable/tab5a_1.htm)

Question Text:

"How much of the time do you think you can trust the government in Washington to do what is right—just about always, most of the time or only some of the time?"

Source: The National Election Studies, University of Michigan, 2005

Table 2 The Persistence of Divided Government

Year	President	House	Senate	Divided/ Unified Government
1946	D – Truman	Rep	Rep	D
1948	D – Truman	Dem	Rep	D
1950	D – Truman	Rep	Rep	D
1952	R – Eisenhower	Rep	Rep	U
1954	R – Eisenhower	Dem	Dem	D
1956	R – Eisenhower	Dem	Dem	D
1958	R – Eisenhower	Dem	Dem	D
1960	D – Kennedy	Dem	Dem	U
1962	D – Kennedy	Dem	Dem	U
1964	D – Johnson	Dem	Dem	U
1966	D – Johnson	Dem	Dem	U
1968	R – Nixon	Dem	Dem	D
1970	R – Nixon	Dem	Dem	D
1972	R – Nixon	Dem	Dem	D
1974	R – Ford	Dem	Dem	D
1976	D – Carter	Dem	Dem	U
1978	D – Carter	Dem	Dem	U
1980	R – Reagan	Dem	Rep	D
1982	R – Reagan	Dem	Rep	D
1984	R – Reagan	Dem	Rep	D
1986	R – Reagan	Dem	Dem	D
1988	R – Bush	Dem	Dem	D
1990	R – Bush	Dem	Dem	D
1992	D – Clinton	Dem	Dem	U
1994	D – Clinton	Rep	Rep	D
1996	D – Clinton	Rep	Rep	D
1998	D – Clinton	Rep	Rep	D
2000	R – Bush	Rep	Dem*	D
2002	R – Bush	Rep	Rep	U
2004	R – Bush	Rep	Rep	U
2006	R – Bush	Dem	Dem	D

*After a 50-50 split (with Vice President Cheney as the tiebreaker), Senator Jeffords (I-VT) switched from the Republican Party shortly after the 2000 Election, thereby swinging the Senate to the Democrats.

voting since the mid-1990s would suggest. Under these circumstances, divided government seems to be more problematic, since two highly partisan parties within the American political system seem potentially dangerous. Persistent divided government over time will likely produce a fundamental change in the relationship between Presidents and the Congress. Presidents are unable to bargain effectively with a hostile congress—witness the 1995 government shutdown—leading the former to make appeals over the heads of Congress directly and, hence undermine the legitimacy of the legislative branch. (Kernell 1997) This argument parallels the one made in recent comparative scholarship (Linz 1993) regarding the serious problem of dual legitimacy in presidential systems.

A second component of the political accountability problem is the increasing non-competitiveness of American elections. Accounts of the 2000 Presidential election stressed its historic closeness, settled by only 540,000 popular votes (notwithstanding the Electoral College anomaly). And the narrow Republican majorities in the House and Senate apparently indicated that every congressional or senate seat could be up for grabs each election. The reality is something different. (Center for Voting and Democracy 2007) Out of 435 House seats, only 60 (13.8%)

were competitive, the outcome of most Senate races is known well in advance, and the 2000 and 2004 Presidential races were only competitive in 15 of 50 states. In the remaining 35, the state winners (Bush or Gore; or Bush or Kerry, respectively) were confident enough of the outcome to forgo television advertising in many of them. In essence, voters for candidates who did not win these hundreds of "safe seats" were effectively disenfranchised and unable to hold their representatives politically accountable.

For those who lament the irresponsibility—or perhaps irrelevance—of the two major parties, an institutional design that would force responsibility should be praised. Quite simply, those who praise divided government because it "limits the damage" or see nothing amiss when there are hundreds of safe seats are faced with a dilemma. They can not simultaneously complain about the resulting governmental inefficiency and political cynicism that ultimately follows when accountability is regularly clouded.

Political Accountability and the Fusion of Government

A number of scholars have addressed the deficiencies of divided government, but they suggest that the problem is that the electoral cycle, with its "midterm" elections, intensifies the likelihood of divided government in non-presidential election years. Such advocates propose as a solution the alteration of the electoral cycle so that all congressional elections are on four year terms, concurrent with presidential terms, likely producing a clear majority. (Cutler 1989) Yet this contains a fatal flaw. Because there is no guarantee that this proposal would alleviate the residual tension between competing branches of government, it merely sidesteps the accountability factor strongly discouraging party unity across the executive and legislative branches of government.

This suggestion could also produce the opposite effect from divided government, namely exaggerated majorities common to parliamentary regimes with majoritarian electoral systems such as the UK. The "safe seats" phenomenon would be the culprit just as in the UK. The most familiar examples of this phenomenon were the "stop-go" policies of post-World War II British governments, as each succeeding government tried to overturn the previous election. While creating governing majorities is important for political accountability, the absence of proportional representation creates a different set of problems.

Under a fusion of power system, in which the current presidency would be redefined, the resulting parliamentary system would make the head of the legislative branch the executive, thus eliminating the current separation of powers. Yet if a government should lose its majority between scheduled elections due to defection of its party members or coalition partners, the head of state then would ask the opposition to form a new government and, failing that, call for new elections. This avoids the constitutional crises that the clamor for impeachment seems to engender in the American system.

But what if coalition members try to spread the blame for poor performance to their partners? In theory, the greater the flexibility available in shifting from one governing coalition to another (with a different composition), the greater is the potential for this kind of musical cabinet chairs. The potential for such an outcome is far less than in the American system, however. A century of experience in other parliamentary regimes (Laver and Shepsle 1996) shows that members of such a party

capriciously playing games with governing are usually brought to heel at the subsequent election.

In other words, the major advantage to such a parliamentary system is that it heightens the capacity for voters and citizens to evaluate government performance. Of course, many individuals might object to the resulting concentration of power. However, if voters are to judge the accomplishments of elected officials, the latter need time to succeed or fail, and then the voters can make a judgment on their tenure. The most likely outcome would be a governing party or coalition of parties that would have to stay together to accomplish anything, thereby increasing party salience. (Richter 2002) Phrased differently, such an arrangement would likely lead to an increase in responsible government.

Many Americans might react unfavorably at the mention of the word coalition due to its supposed instability. Here we need to make the distinction between transparent and opaque coalitions. Some argue that coalition governments in parliamentary systems have the reputation of increased instability. That, or course, depends on the substance of the coalition agreement and the willingness of parties to produce a stable majority. (Strom et al. 1994) But in most parliamentary systems, these party coalitions are formed transparently before an election so the voters can evaluate and then pass judgment on the possible coalition prior to Election Day. It's not as if there are no coalitions in the US Congress. There they take the opaque form of ad-hoc groups of individual members of Congress on an issue-by-issue basis. The high information costs to American voters in understanding the substance of such layered bargains hardly are an example of political transparency.

Finally, for those concerned that the "fusion" of the executive and legislative branches—on the British majoritarian model—would upset the concept of checks and balances, a multi-party consensus parliamentary system produces them slightly differently. (Lijphart 1984) Majoritarianism concentrates power and makes "checking" difficult, while consensus democracies institutionalize the process in a different and more accountable form. A multi-party parliamentary system would also provide greater minority representation, fewer safe seats, and protection by reducing majoritarianism's excessive concentration of power. A consensus parliamentary system would also address the "tyranny of the majority" problem and allow checking and balancing by the voters in the ballot box since the multiple parties would not likely allow a single party to dominate. Consensus systems thus represent a compromise between the current U.S. system and the sharp concentration of British Westminster systems. Americans who simultaneously favor checks and balances but decry inefficient government need to clarify what they actually want their government to do.

Table 3 Comparative Coalitions

American	Parliamentary
Opaque	Transparent
Issue-by-Issue	Programmatic
Back Room	Open Discussion
Unaccountable	Election Ratifies
Unstable	Generally Stable

3. Permanent and Expensive Campaigns

The cost to run for political office in the United States dwarfs that spent in any other advanced industrialized democracy. The twin problems are time and money; more specifically a never-ending campaign "season" and the structure of political advertising that depend so heavily on TV money. (Gans 1993) In listening to the debates about "reforming" the American campaign finance system, students of other democratic electoral systems find these discussions bizarre. More than $2 billion was raised and spent (Corrado 1997) by parties, candidates and interest groups in the 1996 campaign, and for 2000 it went up to $3 billion. Finally, the Center for Responsive Politics estimated the total cost for 2004 Presidential and Congressional elections was $3.9 billion (Weiss 2004) and the preliminary estimates for the 2006 mid-term elections—in which there was no presidential race—were approximately $3 billion.

The two year congressional cycle forces members of the House of Representatives to literally campaign permanently. The amount of money required to run for a Congressional seat has quadrupled since 1990. Presidential campaigns are several orders of magnitude beyond the House of Representatives or the Senate. By themselves they are more than two years long, frequently longer. Unless a presidential candidate is independently wealthy or willing and able to raise upfront $30–$50 million it is simply impossible to run seriously for this office.

Many of the problems stem from the post-Watergate "reforms" that tried to limit the amount of spending on campaigns which then produced a backlash in the form of a 1976 Supreme Court decision (Buckley vs Valeo) that undermined this reform attempt. In essence, Buckley vs Valeo held that "paid speech" (i.e. campaign spending) has an equivalent legal status as "free speech". (Grant 1998) Consequently, since then all "reform" efforts have been tepid measures that have not been able to get at the root of the problem. As long as "paid speech" retains its protected status, any changes are dead in the water.

At its essence this issue is a fissure between "citizens" and "consumers". What Buckley vs Valeo has done is to equate the citizenship function (campaigning, voting, civic education) with a market-based consumer function (buying and selling consumer goods as commodities). (Brubaker 1998) Unlike the United States, most other OECD democracies consider citizenship a public good and provide funding for parties, candidates and the electoral process as a matter of course. The Buckley vs Valeo decision conflates the concepts of citizen and consumer, the logical extension of which is there are weak limits on campaign funding and no limits on the use of a candidate's own money. We are all equal citizens, yet we are not all equal consumers. Bringing consumer metaphors into the electoral process debases the very concept of citizenship and guarantees that the American political system produces the best politicians money can buy.

Free Television Time and the Return of Political Party Dues

Any broadcaster wishing to transmit to the public is required to obtain a broadcast license because the airways have the legal status of public property. To have access to such property, the government must license these networks, cable channels, and stations to serve the public interest. In return, broadcasters are able to sell airtime to sponsors of various programs. Unfortunately for those concerned with campaign costs, candidates for public office fall into the same category as consumer goods in the eyes of the broadcasters. (Weinberg 1993) What has always seemed odd to observers of other democratic states is that there is no Quid Pro Quo requiring the provision of free public airtime for candidates when running for election.

Any serious reform of campaign finance would require a concession from all broadcasters to provide free time for all representative candidates and parties as a cost of using the public airways. Since the largest share of campaign money is TV money, this reform would solve the problem at its source. Restricting the "window" when these free debates would take place to the last two months before a general election would thus address the time dimension as well. Such practices are standard procedure in all developed parliamentary systems. Very simply, as long as "reform" efforts try to regulate the supply of campaign finance, it will fail. A much more achievable target would be the regulation of demand.

The United States could solve another money problem by borrowing a page from parliamentary systems: changing the political party contribution structure from individual voluntary contributions (almost always from the upper middle class and the wealthy) to a more broad-based dues structure common to parties other developed democracies. This more egalitarian party dues structure would perform the additional salutary task of rebuilding parties as functioning institutions. (Allen 1999) Rather than continuing in their current status as empty shells for independently wealthy candidates, American political parties could become the kind of dynamic membership organizations they were at the turn of the 20th century when they did have a dues structure.

4. Low Voter Turnout?

The leading OECD countries have voter turnout ranging from 70% to 90% of their adult population while the US lags woefully behind.

Among the most commonly raised explanations for the US deficiency are: registration requirements, the role of television, voter discouragement, and voter contentment (although the latter two are clearly mutually exclusive). None are particularly convincing nor do they offer concrete suggestions as to how it might be overcome.

The two party system and the electoral method that produces it: the single member district, first past the post, or winner take all system with its attendant "safe seats" often escapes criticism. The rise of such new organizations as the Libertarian, and Green parties potentially could threaten the hegemony of the Democrats and Republicans. Yet the problem of a third (or fourth) party gaining a sufficient number of votes to actually win seats and challenge the two party system is formidable. The electoral arithmetic would require any third party to win some 25% of the vote on a nationwide basis—or develop a highly-concentrated regional presence—before it would actually gain more than a token number of seats. And failing to actually win seats produces a "wasted

Table 4 Voter Turnout and Type of Electoral System Major Developed Democracies–1945–2005

Country	% Voter Turnout	Type of Electoral System
Italy	91.9	PR
Belgium	84.9	PR
Netherlands	84.8	PR
Australia	84.4	Mixed Member
Denmark	83.6	PR
Sweden	83.3	PR
Germany	80.0	Mixed-PR
Israel	80.0	PR
Norway	79.2	PR
Finland	79.0	PR
Spain	76.4	PR
Ireland	74.9	SMD
UK	73.0	SMD
Japan	68.3	SMD/Mixed
France	67.3	SMD + runoff
Canada	66.9	SMD
USA – Presidential	55.1	SMD
USA – Congress (Midterm)	40.6	SMD

Source: Voter Turnout: A Global Survey (Stockholm: International IDEA, 2005)

Table 5 The Advantages of Proportional Representation

Higher Voter Turnout
No "Wasted" Votes
Few Safe, Uncontested Seats
More Parties
Greater Minority Representation
Greater Gender Diversity in Congress
Greater Ideological Clarity
Parties Rebuilt as Institutions
6% Threshold Assumed
No More Gerrymandered Redistricting

vote" syndrome among party supporters which is devastating for such a party. (Rosenstone et al. 1996) Most voters who become disillusioned with the electoral process refer to the "lesser of two evils" choices they face. In such a circumstance, declining voter turnout is not surprising.

The US is a diverse country with many regional, religious, racial, and class divisions. So why should we expect that two "catch all" parties will do a particularly good job in appealing to the interests of diverse constituencies? The solution to lower voter turnout is a greater number of choices for voters and a different electoral system.

Proportional Representation

Under electoral systems using proportional representation, the percentage of a party's vote is equivalent to the percentage of seats allocated to the party in parliament. Comparative analysis shows that those countries with proportional representation—and the multiple parties that PR systems produce—invariably have higher voter turnout. (Grofman and Lijphart 1986) In other words, PR voting systems provide a wider variety of political choices and a wider variety of political representation.

Eliminating majoritarian single member districts (SMDs) in favor of PR voting would have several immediate effects. First, it would increase the range of choices for voters, since parties would have to develop ideological and programmatic distinctions to make themselves attractive to voters. As examples in other countries have shown, it would lead to formation of several new parties representing long underserved interests.

Such a change would force rebuilding of parties as institutions, since candidates would have to run as members of parties and not as independent entrepreneurs. The so-called Progressive "reforms" at the turn of the 20th century and the 1960s introduction of primaries—plus TV advertising—plus the widespread use of referenda have all had powerful effects in undermining parties as coherent political organizations. (Dwyre et al. 1994) In trying to force market-based individual "consumer choice" in the form of high-priced candidates, the collective institutions that are political parties have been hollowed out and undermined.

There are, of course, a wide range of standard objections to PR voting systems by those favoring retention of majoritarian SMD systems.

The first of these, coalitional instability, was addressed briefly above, but it needs to be restated here. The US has unstable coalitions in the Congress right now, namely issue-by-issue ones, usually formed in the House cloakroom with the "assistance" of lobbyists. Few average voters know with certainty how "their" member of Congress will vote on a given issue. (Gibson 1995) With ideologically coherent parties, they would.

An American parliament with several parties could very effectively produce self-discipline. Clearly there would have to be a coalition government since it is unlikely that any one party would capture 50% of the seats. The practice in almost all other coalition governments in parliamentary systems is that voters prefer a predictable set of political outcomes. Such an arrangement forces parties to both define their programs clearly and transparently, once entering into a coalition, and to do everything possible to keep the coalition together during the course of the legislative term.

The second standard objection to PR is the "too many parties" issue. PR voting has been practiced in parliaments for almost 100 years in many different democratic regimes. There is a long history of practices that work well and practices that don't. (Norris 1997) Two countries are invariably chosen as bad examples of PR, namely Israel and Italy. There is an easy solution to this problem of an unwieldy number of parties, namely an electoral threshold requiring any party to receive a certain minimal percentage to gain seats in the parliament. The significant question is what should this minimal threshold be? The Swedes have a 4% threshold and have 7 parties in their parliament, the Germans have a 5% threshold and have 5 parties represented in the Bundestag.

The third standard objection to PR voting is "who's my representative?" In a society so attuned to individualism, most Americans want a representative from their district. This argument presumes that all Americans have a member of Congress that represents their views. However, a liberal democrat who lived in former House Speaker Tom Delay's district in Texas might genuinely wonder in what way he represented that liberal's interests. By the same token, conservative Republicans living in Vermont had for almost twenty years the independent socialist, Bernard Sanders as the state's lone member of Congress representing "their" interests.

Yet if Americans reformers are still insistent on having individual representatives (Guinier 1994) the phenomenon of "Instant Runoff Voting" (Hill 2003) where voters rank order their preferences could produce proportionality among parties yet retain individual single member districts. It also could be used in Presidential elections and avoid accusations of "spoiler" candidates such as Ralph Nader in 2000.

If there were PR voting in an American parliament, what would the threshold be? The US threshold probably should be at least 6%. The goal is to devise a figure that represents all significant interests yet does not produce instability. The "shake out" of parties would likely produce some strategic "mergers" of weak parties which, as single parties, might not attain the 6% threshold. For example, a separate Latino party and an African-American party might insure always attaining a 6% threshold by forming a so-called "rainbow" party. Similarly the Reform Party and the Libertarian Party might find it electorally safer to merge into one free market party.

There are four primary arguments in favor of PR.

The first is simplicity; the percentage of the votes equals the percentage of the seats. To accomplish this, the more individualistic US could borrow the German hybrid system of "personalized" proportional representation. This system requires citizens to cast two votes on each ballot: the first for an individual candidate; and the second for a list of national/regional candidates grouped by party affiliation. (Allen 2001) This system has the effect of personalizing list voting because voters have their own representative but also can choose among several parties. Yet allocation of seats by party in the Bundestag corresponds strongly with the party's percentage of the popular vote.

The second advantage to PR is diversity. The experience of PR voting in other countries is that it changes the makeup of the legislature by increasing both gender and racial diversity. Obviously, parties representing minority interests who find it difficult to win representation in 2 person races, will more easily be able to win seats under PR. (Rule and Zimmerman 1992) Since candidates would not have to run as individuals—or raise millions of dollars—the parties would be more easily able to include individuals on the party's list of candidates who more accurately represent the demographics of average Americans. What a multi-party list system would do would provide a greater range of interests being represented and broaden the concept of "representation" to go beyond narrow geography to include representation of such things as ideas and positions on

policy issues that would be understandable to voters. Moreover, as for geographic representation on a list system, it would be in the self interest of the parties to insure that there was not only gender balance—if this is what the party wanted—on their list, but also other forms of balance including geography, ideology, and ethnicity, among others.

The third advantage is government representativeness. Not only is a consensus-based parliamentary system based on proportional representation more representative of the voting public, it also produces more representative governments. (Birchfield and Crepaz 1998) This study finds that consensus-based, PR systems also produce a high degree of "popular cabinet support," namely the percentage of voters supporting the majority party or coalition.

The fourth advantage to a PR system in the US is that it would eliminate the redistricting circus. Until recently, the decennial census occasioned the excruciating task of micro-managing the drawing of congressional districts. Yet, since the 2002 elections, Republicans in Texas and Georgia have redistricted a second time, creating even "safer" seats by manipulating district lines to their advantage. (Veith et al. 2003) Under PR however, districts would be eliminated. Candidate lists would be organized statewide, in highly populated states, or regionally in the case of smaller states like those in New England. To insure geographical representation, all parties would find it in their own self-interest that the candidate list included geographical diversity starting at the top of the list.

Getting from Here to There: From Academic Debates to Constitutional Reform?

Clearly, none of these four structural reforms will take place soon. But if reformers wanted to start, what would be the initial steps? Of the four proposals, two of them could be accomplished by simple statute: campaign reform and the electoral system. The other two would require constitutional change: head of state/government and divided government. Given the above caveats, it would be easiest to effect campaign reform (the Supreme Court willing) and to alter the electoral system.

The largest obstacles to such a radical change in the American constitutional system are cultural and structural. Culturally, the ethos of American individualism would have difficulty giving up features such as a single all-powerful executive and one's own individual member of congress, no matter how powerful the arguments raised in support of alternatives. Ideology and cultural practice change very slowly. A more serious obstacle would be the existing interests privileged by the current system. All would fight tenaciously to oppose this suggested change.

Finally, specialists in American politics may dismiss this argument as the farfetched "poaching" of a comparativist on a terrain that only Americanists can write about with knowledge and expertise. However, the durability of all four of the above-mentioned problems, stretching back anywhere from 25 to 50 years, suggests that Americanists have no monopoly of wisdom on overcoming these pathologies. More seriously, what this comparativist perceives is a fundamental failure of imagination based largely on the "N of 1" problem that all comparativists struggle to avoid. If a single observed phenomenon—in this case, the American political system—is not examined comparatively, one never knows whether prevailing practice is optimal or suboptimal. In essence, those who do not look at these issues comparatively suffer a failure of imagination because they are unable to examine the full range of electoral and constitutional options.

References

Allen, Christopher S. 1999. *Transformation of the German Political Party System: Institutional Crisis or Democratic Renewal?* New York: Berghahn Books.

———. 2001. "Proportional Representation." In *Oxford Companion to Politics of the World,* ed. J. Krieger. Oxford: Oxford University Press.

Barker, A. 1994. "The Upturned Stone: Political Scandals and their Investigation Processes in 20 Democracies." *Crime Law and Social Change* 24 (1):337–73.

Birchfield, Vicki, and Markus M. L. Crepaz. 1998. "The Impact of Constitutional Structures and Collective and Competitive Veto Points on Income Inequality in Industrialized Democracies." *European Journal of Political Research* 34 (2):175–200.

Brubaker, Stanley C. 1998. "The Limits of U.S. Campaign Spending Limits." *Public Interest* 133:33–54.

Center for Voting and Democracy. *Dubious Democracy 2007,* September 3 2007 [cited. Available from http://www.fairvote.org/?page=1917.

Corrado, Anthony. 1997. *Campaign Finance Reform: A Sourcebook.* Washington, D.C.: Brookings Institution.

Cutler, Lloyd. 1989. "Some Reflections About Divided Government." *Presidential Studies Quarterly* 17:485–92.

Dionne, E. J., Jr. 1991. *Why Americans Hate Politics.* New York: Simon and Schuster.

Dwyre, D., M. O'Gorman, and J. Stonecash. 1994. "Disorganized Politics and the Have-Notes: Politics and Taxes in New York and California." *Polity* 27 (1):25–48.

Fiorina, Morris. 1992. *Divided Government.* New York: Macmillan.

Franklin, Mark N., and Wolfgang P. Hirczy de Mino. 1998. "Separated Powers, Divided Government, and Turnout in U.S. Presidential Elections." *American Journal of Political Science* 42 (1):316–26.

Gans, Curtis. 1993. "Television: Political Participation's Enemy #1." *Spectrum: the Journal of State Government* 66 (2):26–31.

Gibson, Martha L. 1995. "Issues, Coalitions, and Divided Government." *Congress & the Presidency* 22 (2):155–66.

Grant, Alan. 1998. "The Politics of American Campaign Finance." *Parliamentary Affairs* 51 (2):223–40.

Grofman, Bernard, and Arend Lijphart. 1986. *Electoral Laws and Their Consequences.* New York: Agathon Press.

Guinier, Lani. 1994. *The Tyranny of the Majority: Fundamental Fairness in Representative Democracy.* New York: The Free Press.

Hill, Steven. 2003. *Fixing Elections: The Failure of America's Winner Take All Politics.* New York: Routledge.

Huber, John D. 1996. "The Vote of Confidence in Parliamentary Democracies." *American Political Science Review* 90 (2): 269–82.

Jacobson, Gary C. 1990. *The Electoral Origins of Divided Government: Competition in U.S. House Elections, 1946–1988.* Boulder, CO: Westview.

Jacoby, Wade. 2000. *Imitation and Politics: Redesigning Germany.* Ithaca: Cornell University Press.

Kernell, Samuel. 1997. *Going Public: New Strategies of Presidential Leadership.* 3rd ed. Washington, D.C.: CQ Press.

Laver, Michael, and Kenneth A. Shepsle. 1996. *Making and Breaking Governments: Cabinets and Legislatures in Parliamentary Democracies.* New York: Cambridge University Press.

Lijphart, Arend. 1984. *Democracies: Patterns of Majoritarian and Consensus Government in Twenty-One Countries.* New Haven: Yale University Press.

———. 1994. "Democracies: Forms, Performance, and Constitutional Engineering." *European Journal of Political Research* 25 (1):1–17.

Linz, Juan. 1993. "The Perils of Presidentialism." In *The Global Resurgence of Democracy,* ed. L. Diamond and M. Plattner. Baltimore: Johns Hopkins University Press.

Lipset, Seymour Martin. 1996. *American Exceptionalism: A Double-Edged Sword.* New York: Norton.

Mayhew, David. 1991. *Divided We Govern: Party Control, Lawmaking, and Investigations, 1946–1990.* New Haven: Yale University Press.

Norris, Pippa. 1997. "Choosing Electoral Systems: Proportional, Majoritarian and Mixed Systems." *International Political Science Review* 18 (3):297–312.

Richter, Michaela. 2002. "Continuity or Politikwechsel? The First Federal Red-Green Coalition." *German Politics & Society* 20 (1):1–48.

Rosenstone, Steven J. , Roy L. Behr, and Edward H. Lazarus. 1996. *Third Parties in America: Citizen Response to Major Party Failure.* Princeton: Princeton University Press.

Rule, Wilma, and Joseph F. Zimmerman, eds. 1992. *United States Electoral Systems: Their Impact on Women and Minorities.* New York: Praeger.

Rundquist, Paul S. 1991. *The House of Representatives and the House of Commons: A Brief Comparison of American and British Parliamentary Practice.* Washington, DC: Congressional Research Service, Library of Congress.

Strom, Kaare, Ian Budge, and Michael J. Laver. 1994. "Constraints on Cabinet formation in Parliamentary Democracies." *American Journal of Political Science* 38 (2):303–35.

Thurber, James A. 1991. "Representation, Accountability, and Efficiency in Divided Party Control of Government." *PS* 24:653–7.

Veith, Richard, Norma Jean Veith, and Susan Fuery. 2003. "Oral Argument." In *U.S. Supreme Court.* Washington, DC.

Weinberg, Jonathan. 1993. "Broadcasting and Speech." *California Law Review* 81 (5):1101–206.

Weiss, Stephen. 2004. "'04 Elections Expected to Cost Nearly $4 Billion." In *opensecrets.org—Center for Responsive Politics:* http://www.opensecrets.org/pressreleases/2004/04spending.asp.

An Embattled Cristina Fernández de Kirchner

Can She Restore Her Popularity and Aid in Argentina's Recovery?

EMILY DUNN

To the outrage of President Cristina Fernández de Kirchner, Vice President Julio Cobos cast the decisive vote on July 17 against her plan to increase the export tax on grains being shipped abroad, effectively putting a full stop to a very tense domestic situation. As a result, Argentina today is considerably more tranquil now that the hostile demonstrations and strikes by Argentine farmers, which led to chaos in the domestic and overseas food markets, have ended. The crisis averted, average Argentines can now breathe a sigh of relief knowing that the nation's most unsettling issue, a crushing annual inflation rate of almost 30 percent, can be addressed.

During last year's electoral campaign, Cristina was consistently 20 to 30 percentage points ahead of the other presidential candidates in the polls. Her victory was expected as her husband, Nestor Kirchner, had just ended his own presidential term with high popularity ratings, and the country looked forward to the continuity of his economic success paired with Cristina's less heavy-handed style of governance. But President Fernández's unwillingness to reduce the agricultural export tax and her obdurate approach to the dispute—perceived by many to be haughty and authoritarian—severely damaged her popularity. Even some of her most fervent supporters became disappointed by her uncompromising attitude. In addition, many complain that Nestor holds too much sway over Cristina and has had a negative influence on her dealings with the rural sector.

For months, the farming conflict paralyzed the Fernández de Kirchner government, with a poll by *Giacobbe & Asociados* showing that her approval rating dropped to 19.2 percent in July, in contrast to a poll by *Poliarquia Consultores* which showed her approval rating at 57 percent when she took office last December. High inflation and a slow growth rate, along with her confrontational attitude and inability to extinguish the corruption she had inherited from her predecessors, have caused this plunge in national approval. There is no question then that the new leader, who perhaps was prematurely labeled as Argentina's new "Evita," has severely disappointed her people and must now work single-mindedly to gain back their esteem.

The Rejection

In early July, after four months of protests by the rural farming sector and urban sympathizers, Argentina's lower house approved the plan that Fernández had put into effect on March 11 to increase export taxes on grains and oilseeds. Passing by a vote of 128 to 122, the measure then moved on to the Senate for approval before becoming law. On July 17, after sixteen hours of debate, the Senate caused political chaos to erupt by rejecting the sliding-scale tax reform proposal, which had been identified by the president as critical in the fight against poverty. The Kirchners, certain that the Senate would approve the rural tax reform measure, were stunned when Vice President Cobos cast the deciding vote against it. "A law that does not solve the conflict is no use," said an embattled Cobos, defending his position. "May history judge me. Forgive me if I am mistaken, but my vote is not in favor, it's against."

Indeed many have called Cobos' move treacherous, and Cristina herself alluded to it as an act of "betrayal." Disparagers say that it is very much like the Kirchners to blame someone else for their problems rather than accept responsibility for failure, and this has only intensified their already fading popularity. But the setback could be seen as more than just a political defeat for Cristina. It is also an unanticipated opportunity for Argentina to reorient its political profile. As noted political analyst Fernando Laborda explains, "It is unheard of in the history of Argentina that a vice-president, in his role as Senate speaker, [should] vote against the government. It means that Congress has shown itself to be independent in the face of the executive power, and our institutions have come out stronger than before." Cobos has unexpectedly become a national hero for resolving the four-month conflict once and for all, and is being promoted as a unifying figure and a potential political force for the future.

Despite the Senate vote, the taxes could not be rescinded without further presidential action. After a tense silence during which many were unsure what move Cristina and Nestor would make, the economic minister, Carlos Fernández, announced on July 18 that the government would officially be discarding the proposed tax reforms that had caused four months of revolts and food shortages.

The Current State of Change

In order for Cristina to restore her credibility, the government's image needs to be radically recast. Her administration must deal with the hard facts of the country's economic situation, particularly the growing inflation rate. The president has announced an increase of 27 percent in the minimum wage, and it is hypothesized that she will increase benefits for families entrapped in near poverty as well. Additionally, there is a growing consensus that a dramatic change of faces in Cristina's cabinet would be for the best. If the government can implement these social programs effectively and efficiently, confidence in it could recover.

On July 21, President Cristina Fernández de Kirchner announced the re-nationalization of Aerolineas Argentinas and its sister carrier, Austral. This was a well-timed move for Cristina, as there was widespread support for the airline buyback. The action will certainly increase the favorable image of the government after its humiliating defeat in the Senate last week and the plummeting indices of its popularity.

Moreover, the president has already begun to shake up the top level of her administration, in wake of the political chaos caused by the endemic opposition to her tax plans, so that she might begin a new chapter in her still young presidency. Agriculture secretary Javier De Urquiza stepped down on July 22 and will be replaced by Carlos Cheppi, the president of the National Institute of Agricultural Technology. Urquiza is not the only casualty of the fiasco in the Senate; Cabinet Chief Alberto Fernández resigned the following day, with Cristina announcing that the former head of the social security agency, Sergio Massa, will take office as her new top aide. Alberto Fernández was also Nestor Kirchner's chief of cabinet and provides living evidence of Nestor's presiding influence over Cristina's presidency. Many are glad to see the senior aide go. Latin News postulates, however, that, "Most Argentines want more ministers to be sacked . . . So his lone departure is unlikely to re-invigorate Fernández's presidency."

From Here on Out

Most Argentines seem to hope that Cristina Fernández de Kirchner will now rule from a position of consensus rather than from a contemptuous and domineering stance. While the popularity of Vice President Cobos is surely increasing as a result of halting the crisis by double-crossing President Fernandez, it remains uncertain whether Cristina and Nestor will regain favor anytime soon. If so, it will certainly be a very difficult and delicate process, which will have to be done sooner rather than later, so that Argentina will not suffer a protracted ordeal.

Iran's Tool Fights America's Stooge

A delicate balance between Christians, Druze, Sunnis and Shias has broken down. Reassembly will be hard.

It looked disturbingly like a sequel to Lebanon's bloody civil war of 1975–90: gun battles in city streets, kidnappings, execution-style slayings and tearful vows of vengeance. With at least 81 people killed so far, the violence of past days represents the most serious internal strife since those years. And it is unclear who can stop it.

The most striking scene was the invasion of the capital, Beirut, mounted by opponents of the government. This was not exactly a conquest of the city, but rather the takeover of one part, Sunni-dominated West Beirut, by another, the dense, gritty and largely Shia-populated southern suburbs. This act quickly rippled across the mountainous country's sectarian patchwork, setting off clashes to the north and south. Because of Lebanon's position as a cockpit for regional power struggles, it also reverberated further afield, from Washington to the Iranian capital, Tehran.

It was natural that this latest turmoil should carry echoes of the civil war. That contest was only fudgingly resolved, and the country has struggled to recover. Small triumphs have been notched up here and there. One was the physical revival of Beirut from a bomb-scarred wreck to a gleaming magnet for tourism; another the brave popular uprising of 2005, which forced neighbouring Syria to pull out its long-overstayed "peacekeeping" troops. For many Lebanese, too, the hounding of Israel by the guerrillas of Hizbullah, the Shia party-cum-militia, leading to the Israeli army's withdrawal in 2000 after 22 years occupying the southern borderlands, and its humiliation in the 33-day war of 2006, were epic victories.

Syria's Role

Yet none of those achievements was solidly shared by all. Reconstruction generated corruption and a giant pile of debt. Syria's removal alienated its many allies inside Lebanon and prompted it to sponsor what looks like a campaign of sabotage, including assassinations. The Sunni-led, anti-Syrian factions that gained power through the 2005 uprising failed to accommodate dangerous rivals, and suffered by close association with America.

Meanwhile, Hizbullah's lock-step allegiance to Shia Iran frightened not just Lebanese nationalists, but also the predominantly Sunni Arab world and Western powers. The UN Security Council resolved in 2004 that all Lebanon's militias must be disarmed, but Hizbullah insisted its noble cause was resistance to Israel, despite the Jewish state's abandonment of all but a tiny corner of Lebanon. The party continued to receive a supply of heavy weapons from Syria and Iran. In the end, the fight with Israel that Hizbullah provoked in 2006 brought massive and needless ruin.

Such strains would have tested any country, let alone a small one with a violent history, a population made up of 18 jealous religious minorities and a weak central state built on power-sharing between them. The wonder may be that Lebanon has held together at all, and even maintained a veneer of democracy. But this veneer has grown steadily thinner since the end of the 2006 war, which, aside from leaving 1,200 Lebanese dead and 100,000 homeless, also widened the central fissure in Lebanese politics.

This division is often defined, for simplicity's sake, as a split between Hizbullah, backed by Syria and Iran in the interest of confronting Israel and blocking American influence, against the Western-backed, democratically elected government of Fuad Siniora, the Sunni prime minister. The reality is more complicated.

Mr Siniora's coalition of Sunni Muslims, right-wing Christian parties, liberals, and the main Druze faction led by Walid Jumblatt, did indeed win 72 of the Lebanese parliament's 128 seats in the spring of 2005, riding on sympathy generated by the assassination of Mr Siniora's patron Rafik Hariri, a billionaire and five-term prime minister. But the election was run under rules drafted during Syrian control, before Mr Hariri's fatal falling-out with the Syrian regime. Many Lebanese Christians, who had been the core of opposition to Syria, felt these rules diluted their influence.

Moreover, the winning coalition, which adopted the name of "March 14th" after the date of a large anti-Syrian rally, secured some districts through an electoral alliance with Hizbullah. The Shia party was rewarded with seats in Mr Siniora's cabinet, but also believed there was tacit agreement to provide political cover for its massive rocket arsenal—perhaps, at some distant point, by incorporating its guerrilla force into the Lebanese army.

This alliance quickly unravelled, as Mr Siniora's Western backers pushed him to contain what they regarded as a terrorist group, and Hizbullah responded by forging a growing opposition coalition. This came to include not only its rival Shia party Amal, but also some pro-Syrian Christian, Sunni and Druze factions that had flourished, many with vigorous armed wings, under Syrian tutelage. Surprisingly, it was also joined by the Free Patriotic Movement (FPM), the Christian party of Michel Aoun, a maverick former general who had led a rising against Syria at the close of the civil war.

Mr Aoun bore several grudges against March 14th. As a battle-hardened foe of Syria, he felt entitled to a leading role after Syria's hasty withdrawal. He wanted to replace Emile Lahoud, the garishly pro-Syrian president whose term was due to expire in November 2007. (By custom, Lebanon's president must be a Maronite Christian, its prime minister a Sunni Muslim, and the speaker of parliament a Shia.) The FPM far outpolled the Christian parties inside Mr Siniora's coalition, reflecting wide distrust of the older, right-wing Christian parties who had gained a reputation for thuggery during the civil war.

In Hizbullah's Embrace

Mr Aoun's abrasiveness, and March 14th's unwillingness to give him the presidency, ensured that the FPM remained in opposition. It was widely assumed that with his anti-Syrian credentials and largely pro-Western Christian constituency, the general would avoid Hizbullah, yet the two parties made an alliance in

The Jigsaw Puzzle
Lebanese Factions

March 14th Alliance*	Religious Groups	Leader
Future Movement	Mostly Sunni	Saad Harini
Progressive Socialist Party	Druze	Walid Jumblatt
Lebanese Forces	Maronite Christian	Samir Geagea
Kataeb Party	Maronite Christian	Amin Gemayel

ALSO: smaller anti-Syrian parties, liberals, independents, dissident Shias.

Opposition Alliance	Religious Groups	Leader
Hizbullah	Shia	Hassan Nasrallah
Amal	Shia	Nabih Berri
Free Patriotic Movement	Mostly Christian	Michel Aoun
Syrian Social Nationalist Party	Mostly Orthodox Christian	Ali Qansuh

ALSO: pro-Syrian parties, dissident Sunnis, most Armenians, most Alawites.

Source: *The Economist.*   *Government loyalists.

February 2006. Mr Aoun lost some Christian support over this, but then came the war with Israel.

Most Christians blamed Hizbullah for the fighting. Yet many also credited the FPM, which mobilised aid for thousands of Shias displaced by the war, with healing a historic rift between the traditionally dominant but dwindling Christians and the long-disenfranchised but now formidable Shias. In Hizbullah's view, the alliance with Mr Aoun allowed it to clothe its Iranian-tinted Islamist militancy in Lebanese nationalist colours.

Hizbullah emerged from the war with its prestige enhanced, and speedily boosted it further with a big and efficient Iranian-financed reconstruction programme. By contrast, Mr Siniora's government, reduced during the war to issuing vain pleas to its Western friends to fend off the Israeli onslaught, looked vulnerable. It was given little credit for helping secure the eventual ceasefire, and even less for winning massive pledges of aid from Sunni Gulf countries. Privately, supporters of March 14th believed Hizbullah had recklessly exposed Lebanon to disaster. Yet the trauma of the war, and the sight of Israel, for the first time, being mauled by an Arab force, kept them quiet.

Soon after the war's end, in November 2006, the opposition moved to cash in their political gains by demanding a national unity government, in which their members would have enough cabinet seats to block its decisions. Mr Siniora refused, suspecting a Syrian-inspired plot. The opposition responded by withdrawing the cabinet's six Shia members. This, they said, rendered the government illegal, since it was constitutionally required to represent all the main sects. The Shia speaker of parliament, Nabih Berri, leader of Hizbullah's sister party Amal, refused to convene the legislature. Over subsequent months the opposition increased its demands, including a revision of electoral laws to address Mr Aoun's concerns that Christians were being cheated.

As the lame-duck presidency of Mr Lahoud came to an end in November last year, the opposition stalled talks over the successor to be elected by parliament. Agreeing at last on Michel Suleiman, who commands the non-sectarian army, it insisted that its other conditions be fulfilled before Mr Berri summoned parliament.

So, to the frustration of ordinary Lebanese, the factions have produced an 18-month stalemate. Hizbullah and its allies call the government an American stooge; March 14th blasts the opposition as a tool of Iran and a cat's-paw for Syria. Mediators, including Amr Moussa, chief of the Arab League, have come and despaired.

The Galvanising Moment

March 14th has naturally tried to drive a wedge between Hizbullah and its Christian allies. Earlier this month, citing alleged evidence of suspicious traffic monitoring at Beirut airport, it reassigned the pro-Hizbullah head of airport security. It also declared illegal the party's communications network. If this was intended to highlight to Christians and Western powers Hizbullah's rogue status, it backfired. On May 8th Hizbullah's carefully-spoken leader, Hassan Nasrallah, described the government's moves as "treachery", and said the time had come to defend the arms of the "resistance".

Within minutes, a combined force of Hizbullah, Amal and allied fighters blasted their way into Beirut's Sunni quarter, eventually surrounding the residences of Mr Hariri's son and political heir, Saad, and of his Druze ally Mr Jumblatt. By May 10th fighting moved to outlying areas, affecting Mr Jumblatt's stronghold in the Chouf mountains south-east of Beirut and the Sunni-dominated north, as Mr Hariri's allies exacted revenge on pockets of opposition fighters. In other tit-for-tat action, Hizbullah blocked access to Beirut airport, while Sunni militiamen sealed the road to Syria's capital, Damascus.

The opposition stopped short of overthrowing the government, though it probably could have done so. It also promptly handed over control of most areas it invaded to the Lebanese army, ushering in a nervous calm after five days of fighting. But the 70,000-man army, which is wary of being infected itself by sectarianism, is scarcely a match for Hizbollah's trained and hardened guerrillas.

Government leaders have declared they will not be cowed by force of arms. Yet they have already backed down on the immediate issues that angered Hizbullah. Other concessions are likely to follow, if the Arab League, which has sent in a hurried diplomatic mission, can find a face-saving formula. This might include swift passage of electoral reform, the installation of Mr Suleiman as president and the formation of a "technocratic" transitional government before fresh elections.

This may all prove a tall order, however. The sense of injury among non-Shias is powerful, as is the urge for March 14th to exploit for political advantage Hizbullah's breaking of a long-standing pledge never to use its arms in internal squabbles. Should the government refuse to bend, the chances are that its opponents will push back even harder. Such a result, tipping Lebanon back into full-scale conflict, would suit no one.

Let Women Rule

Missing Out

SWANEE HUNT

W omen have made significant strides in most societies over the last century, but the trend line has not
been straight. In recent interviews with hundreds of
female leaders in over 30 countries, I have discovered that where
women have taken leadership roles, it has been as social reformers and entrepreneurs, not as politicians or government officials.
This is unfortunate, because the world needs women's perspectives and particular talents in top positions. In 1998, Francis
Fukuyama wrote in Foreign Affairs that women's political leadership would bring about a more cooperative and less conflict-
prone world ("Women and the Evolution of World Politics,"
September/October 1998). That promise has yet to be fulfilled.

Granted, a few women are breaking through traditional barriers and becoming presidents, prime ministers, cabinet members, and legislators. But even as the media spotlight falls on
the 11 female heads of government around the world, another
significant fact goes unreported: most of the best and the brightest women eschew politics. Women are much more likely to
wield influence from a nongovernmental organization (NGO)
than from public office.

Women are still severely underrepresented in governments
worldwide. A recent World Economic Forum report covering
115 countries notes that women have closed over 90 percent of
the gender gap in education and in health but only 15 percent of
it when it comes to political empowerment at the highest levels.
Although 97 countries have some sort of gender quota system
for government positions, according to the Inter-Parliamentary
Union, an organization that fosters exchange among parliaments, women fill only 17 percent of parliamentary seats worldwide and 14 percent of ministerial-level positions—and most of
those are related to family, youth, the disabled, and the elderly.
At NGOs, the story is very different: women are consistently
overrepresented at the top levels.

This pattern also holds for the United States, where 16 of 100
members of the Senate and 71 of 435 members of the House of
Representatives are women. The United States ranks 68 out of
189 countries, behind a dozen in Latin America, in terms of the
number of women in the legislature. Those low numbers are
consistent with Capitol Hill's historic antipathy toward females.
Women were denied the vote for 133 years, refused an equal
rights amendment, and shut out of government-funded health
research for decades. At the same time, American women have
gravitated en masse toward NGOs, where they have found fewer
barriers to leadership. The 230 NGOs in the National Council of Women's Organizations represent ten million American
women, and women lead many of the country's largest phil-
anthropic organizations, including the Bill and Melinda Gates
Foundation and the Ford Foundation. As for academia, Harvard,
MIT, and Princeton currently have women at the helm.

Most other countries follow a similar pattern. The number of
NGOs in the former Soviet republics grew exponentially after
the fall of the Iron Curtain, and women formed the backbone of
this new civil society, but the percentage of women in eastern
European parliaments plummeted. In Lithuania, that percentage
declined from approximately 33 percent during the communist
era to 17.5 percent in 1997 and 10.6 percent in 2004. According
to a group of journalists in Kyrgyzstan, women head 90 percent of
NGOs but hold not a single seat in parliament, even though they
made up 33 percent of the legislature at the end of the Soviet era. In
China, the Communist Party-controlled All-China Women's Federation functions much as an NGO does, engaging women across
the country on community issues, but despite the government's
claims of equality, Chinese women have rarely held positions of
political power. Likewise, in South Korea, women run some 80
percent of the country's NGOs but occupy less than 14 percent
of the seats in the National Assembly. The story is the same in
Africa. According to Robert Rotberg, director of the Program on
Intrastate Conflict and Conflict Resolution at Harvard's Kennedy
School of Government, "African women, who traditionally do the
hard work of cultivation and all of the family rearing, also nurture
NGOs and motivate civic initiatives. But they are widely expected
to leave politics—and corruption and conflict—to men."

Women may thrive in NGOs. The world, however, needs
them to take that experience into the political sphere. As the
Sierra Leonean activist and former presidential candidate Zai-
nab Bangura points out, "The real power isn't in civil society;
it's in policymaking."

A Woman's View

Greater female political participation would bring significant
rewards. Research sponsored by the World Bank has shown that
countries with a high number of *women* in parliament enjoy
lower levels of corruption. Another World Bank-sponsored

study concludes that *women* are less likely to be involved in bribery and that corruption is less severe where *women* make up a large share of senior government officials as well as the labor force. A survey of research by Rachel Croson, of the Wharton School, and Uri Gneezy, of the University of California, San Diego, similarly concluded that *women* are more trustworthy than men. Consider Nigeria. The watchdog group Transparency International ranked it as the most corrupt country in the world in 2003. But that year, Ngozi Okonjo-Iweala left her job as a vice president at the World Bank to become the country's finance minister, and by 2005 Transparency International was hailing Nigeria as one of 21 most improved states. Change came thanks to the indictment of corrupt officials, as well as to reform in banking, insurance, the foreign exchange market, pensions, and income taxation. Similarly, in Liberia, international policymakers have been heartened to see President Ellen Johnson-Sirleaf prioritize the eradication of corruption. Knowing that foreign investment would flow only after a crackdown on the plundering culture of her predecessors, Johnson-Sirleaf fired the entire Finance Ministry staff and brought in *women* for the positions of finance minister, chief of police, commerce minister, and justice minister, among others.

Electing and appointing women to positions of political leadership turns out to be good for the broader economy as well. There is a correlation between women holding political office and the overall economic competitiveness of a nation. Augusto Lopez-Claros, chief economist and director of the World Economic Forum's Global Competitiveness Network, argues that "the Nordic countries seem to have understood the economic incentive behind empowering women: countries that do not fully capitalize on one-half of their human resources are clearly undermining their competitive potential. "The high percentage of women in parliament in countries such as Rwanda (almost 49 percent of members in the lower house), Costa Rica (40 percent), and Mozambique (35 percent) suggests that it is not simply a nation's affluence that causes more women to assume leadership positions. If that were the case, the relatively prosperous United States should be in the top ranks of countries sending women to Congress instead of lagging behind countries such as El Salvador, Nepal, and Tajikistan.

In 2000, an Inter-Parliamentary Union poll of 187 female politicians in 65 countries found that 80 percent of the respondents believed that increased representation of women renews public trust in government, which in turn helps economic welfare. The politicians cited examples from countries as varied as El Salvador, Ethiopia, New Zealand, and Russia in which political activism by women led to "tangible improvements" in social services, the environment, the safety of women and children, and gender equality.

Worldwide, female legislators as a group tend to concentrate on helping marginalized citizens. In the United States, for example, Democratic and moderate Republican congresswomen are more likely than men to focus on socially conscious legislation. Perhaps female politicians take such concerns to heart because they have often honed their skills in the NGO arena. Chilean President Michelle Bachelet, for instance, returned from exile in 1979 to work with children of people who were tortured or who disappeared during the dictatorship of Augusto Pinochet. South Korean Prime Minister Han Myeong Sook was a social activist (and political prisoner) during her country's military dictatorship.

The lessons women learn while leading civil society may also explain why they have "higher moral or ethical standards than their male counterparts," according to the International NGO Training and Research Center. Hannah Riley Bowles, professor of public policy at Harvard's Kennedy School of Government, found that when negotiating for jobs, American women asked for 15 percent less than men did, but when negotiating on behalf of others, women's demands increased substantially. (No such difference was found among male negotiators.) Carrying that tendency into the political sphere, "women may hold back when promoting their own candidacy or securing the resources they need to rise to the fore," argues Bowles. But they can be "fabulous advocates for their constituents."

Given these qualities, it is no surprise that women's involvement in political negotiations tends to solidify conflict resolution. "If we put women in leadership, they have a degree of tolerance, an understanding that allows them to persist even when things seem to be very bad," notes Pumla Gobodo-Madikizela, a South African clinical psychologist who worked in grass-roots NGOs during apartheid and helped establish the Truth and Reconciliation Commission. Unlike men, she continues, "women have the power and emotional inclination to hold onto hope when it comes to negotiating with former enemies." As documented by the Initiative for Inclusive Security, in numerous settings, women have joined forces across party lines to shape peace agreements, sponsor legislation, and influence the drafting of constitutions.

They also come to the table with a different perspective on conflict resolution. Women are more likely to adopt a broad definition of security that includes key social and economic issues that would otherwise be ignored, such as safe food and clean water and protection from gender-based violence. This sentiment was expressed to me by South Korea's Song Young Sun, the National Assembly's military watchdog. Most of the men she serves with define security as protecting South Korea's territory against North Korea, she said; she believes that security considerations should also include "everything from economics to culture, environment, health, and food."

A Man's World

If having women wield political power is so beneficial, why are there not more female leaders? A fundamental reason is that women themselves are not eager or willing to stand for political office. Women view politics as a dirty game, and their loftier standards may keep them away from the grit and grind of it. More than 200 public officials and NGO leaders throughout Kyrgyzstan responded to a 2004 United Nations Development Program poll by saying women would bring transparency, "a strong sense of responsibility," and "fair attitudes" to politics. But Nurgul Djanaeva, who heads a coalition of 88 Kyrgyz women's groups, bemoaned the situation: "The only way for me to feed my family, while working in government, is to be corrupt, so I'd rather work for an NGO and have a living wage."

It does not help that politics has traditionally been a man's world, and that many men—and some women—want to keep it that way. A woman may be considered "too soft" for political leadership—or "unfeminine" if she runs. Often, however, it is women themselves who doubt their own leadership abilities. According to the 2000 World Values Survey, women comprised 21 percent of respondents in Chile and 45 percent of respondents in Mexico who agreed strongly with the statement that men make better political leaders than women do. This distinct lack of self-assurance persists across cultures. According to research by the political scientists Richard Lawless and Jennifer Fox, authors of It Takes a Candidate: Why Women Don't Run for Office, American women were twice as likely as men to describe themselves as "not at all qualified to run for office," even when their credentials were equivalent. Only 25 percent of the women saw themselves as likely or very likely winners, compared with 37 percent of the men.

The traditional role society expects women to play does not spur them on to political leadership either. Reconciling political life with family commitments was the primary concern of the female politicians surveyed in 2000 by the Inter-Parliamentary Union. Women usually believe that their obligations to family members—including parents and in-laws—as the primary caregiver are incompatible with holding public office. Rebeca Grynspan, former vice president of Costa Rica, voices the dilemma: "Society doesn't provide conditions under which we can do our jobs with tranquility and leave our children home with peace of mind, even if we can count on stable, supportive partners." The pressures for women to stay home and tend to their families are compounded by conservative religious doctrines. A fundamentalist interpretation of Islam threatens women's nascent political hopes in countries such as Kuwait, where women gained the right to vote and run for office in the 2006 elections but did not win any parliamentary seats. Similarly, Afghanistan and Iraq, where new constitutions reserve a quarter of parliamentary seats for women, are in danger of backsliding into a collision with resurgent extremism. In the West, the Catholic Church in such countries as Croatia urges women to focus on family rather than public life. Likewise, most women in U.S. politics find their views incompatible with the religious right: in 2004, only two of the 14 female senators, compared with 48 of the 86 male senators, voted consistently with the Christian Coalition.

Even when women want to run for political office, they encounter roadblocks. In most countries, male political party gatekeepers determine candidate lists, and the ordering of candidates on the lists is a fundamental factor in determining who goes to parliament. It takes more than affirmative-action measures, such as quotas or reserved seats, to ensure women's places on those lists; it takes parties' will. According to the Harvard political scientist Pippa Norris, who analyzed the 1997 British elections, the Labour Party showed rare resolve in setting aside for women half of the seats from which members of parliament were retiring and half of those considered "most winnable." That move doubled the total percentage of women in parliament from 9.2 to 18.2 percent of all seats. More typical, however, is the complaint of a Bosnian politician who told me wryly that her place on her party's candidate list dropped precipitously, thanks to backroom hacks and men muscling their way to the top.

Money constitutes another barrier for women. Coming up with fees to file as a candidate or run a campaign can be daunting. Few countries have emulated the creation of organizations such as EMILY's List ("EMILY" stands for "Early Money Is Like Yeast"), which raises contributions across the United States for Democratic pro-choice women.

The financial squeeze can be further compounded by the threat of physical harm. According to Phoebe Asiyo, a prominent Kenyan member of parliament for more than a quarter century, the greatest expense for women running for parliament in Kenya is around-the-clock security, which is necessary because of the danger of rape, a common intimidation tactic. Mary Okumu, a Stanford-educated Kenyan public health expert, was beaten up when she stood for election in 2002. Okumu says that she and other candidates routinely carried concealed knives and wore two sets of tights under their dresses in order to buy more time to scream during an attempted rape. Male opponents were also at risk of physical attack, but Okumu says that "for women political aspirants the violence also includes foul verbal abuse, beatings, abduction, and death threats."

Given prevailing social norms and the numerous barriers to entry to the political arena, as well as women's own perception of politics as a dirty game, it is unsurprising that many women turn away from elected office, believing that they have a better chance of achieving results in the NGO realm. In 1991, as a child, Ala Noori Talabani fled on foot from Saddam Hussein's army. Fourteen years later, she was elected to the interim Iraqi National Assembly. She seemed a model legislator—a well-educated, articulate former diplomat equally comfortable among villagers in Kirkuk, politicians in Baghdad, and policy analysts in Washington. Yet in 2006, she left politics in frustration to work with an NGO so that she could focus on the problems she cares about most: honor killings, domestic violence, and rape.

What is to Be Done?

The forces excluding women from political leadership are so strong that only a serious and comprehensive effort can bring about change. Fortunately, governments, foreign-aid organizations, think tanks, and academic institutions can stimulate both the supply of and the demand for women in the political arena.

At the most basic level, national governments should implement "family-friendly" policies, including straightforward measures such as easier access to daycare, flexible office hours, and limits to evening meetings. But in some countries, to be effective, policies will have to be designed according to more progressive interpretations of religious doctrine regarding gender roles. In 2004, Moroccan King Muhammad VI personally backed a new version of family law that was compatible with sharia and that gave women equal rights. His support of gender-sensitive legislation also increased women's political representation (from two in 2001 to 35 in 2002 of the 325 seats in parliament's lower house) and made Morocco one of the most socially progressive countries in the Muslim world. In May 2006, thanks to another of the king's initiatives, the first class of 50 female imams graduated from an academy in Rabat. They are expected to do everything male imams do except lead Friday prayers in a mosque.

NGOs and governments have an important role to play in equipping women with the confidence and skills necessary to run for office. Grass-roots programs could help recruit and train women across the political spectrum. The Cambodian organization Women for Prosperity, for instance, has prepared more than 5,500 female candidates for elections in Cambodia. Embassies abroad could encourage established female officials to mentor new candidates, learning from the Forum of Rwandan Women Parliamentarians. In 2006, Rwanda's female parliamentarians returned to their districts to rally women to run for local office, increasing the proportion of female mayors and deputy mayors in the country from 24 to 44 percent in one election. Outsiders ought to boost the profile of Liberia's Johnson-Sirleaf, the only elected African female head of state, who recently urged female officeholders, "Don't stop with parliament. Join me. I'm lonely." The Initiative for Inclusive Security, which has brokered relationships between hundreds of female leaders in conflict regions and thousands of policymakers, is a creative and strong model of an external player working to encourage women's political participation. And governments should look to replicate innovative political party reforms that ensure gender equality, such as those promoted by Michal Yudin's group in Israel—WE (Women's Electoral) Power—which has pressured Knesset members to increase funding for parties that exceed the quota for women's participation.

Supporting transparent and equitable campaign-finance *rules* would also help women in the political arena. Women told me that when they have to choose between their children's school fees or their own campaign, their children win. Government campaign subsidies spread across political parties help level the field. Governments should go further by rewarding parties that boost the representation of women on their candidate lists and penalizing those that do not.

Female politicians also need to be protected. In Afghanistan, where women running for parliament in 2005 were attacked, local and international organizations asked governors, chiefs of police, tribal elders, and other community leaders to provide security details. At least one candidate who reported threats had police protection 24 hours a day. Security measures reassured women that state and community leaders backed their right to engage in politics.

Finally, and most important, governments ought to support quotas for women at all levels of government. In systems with proportional representation, "zippering," requiring that a woman be in every second or third slot on a ballot, has helped raise women's numbers; still, women rarely appear in the top two ballot slots. Although quotas may initially result in female members of parliament being taken less seriously, the upside far outweighs the downside, since quotas propel women into politics. Sixteen of the 19 countries—including Cuba, Iceland, South Africa, Spain, and Sweden—that have parliaments in which at least 30 percent of the members are women have implemented either legislative or party quotas.

Less Swagger, More Sway

Women's community-based wisdom, fresh ideas, and commitment to the social good may be the best news in domestic policy today. They have much to contribute to decisions regarding the environment, security, health care, finance, and education. In foreign policy as well, the world could use more sway and less swagger.

A critical mass of female leaders will change norms; that may be why President Bachelet appointed ten women alongside the ten men in her cabinet. Of course, there are exceptions, but generally speaking, stereotypical "feminine" qualities (such as the tendency to nurture, compromise, and collaborate) have been confirmed by social science research. The world needs those traits. With so many intractable conflicts, conventional strategies—economic sanctions, boycotts, or military intervention—have clearly proved inadequate. Women's voices would provide a call/row arms.

None of these benefits to domestic and foreign policy, however, will be realized if just a few women reach positions of leadership. The few women who now make it to the top of a predominantly male hierarchy, and who do not come out of a women's movement, usually have attributes more similar to those of most men. Indira Gandhi, Margaret Thatcher, and Golda Meir had more "masculine" qualities than many of the men they bested, and they pushed little of the social agenda commonly of interest to women in politics. General wisdom about critical mass would predict that approximately 30 percent of officeholders have to be female for a significant effect to be felt on policy. As Anita Gradin remarked to me about her experience as a member of Sweden's parliament, the same group of women who were once in a small minority in the legislature talked, acted, and voted differently when their proportion increased significantly.

The more women shift from civil society into government, the more political culture will change for the better, and the more other women will follow. Advocates of women's leadership need to stop their handwringing over whether gender differences exist and appreciate the advantages women have over men's brawny style of governance, whether because of biology, social roles, or a cascading combination of the two. In the meantime, however, they will have to put up with some paternalistic responses, such as the one I received from a colonel at the Pentagon shortly after the United States' "shock and awe" attack on Iraq in 2003. When I urged him to broaden his search for the future leaders of Iraq, which had yielded hundreds of men and only seven women, he responded, "Ambassador Hunt, we'll address women's issues after we get the place secure." I wondered what "women's issues" he meant. I was talking about security.

SWANEE HUNT is Director of the Women and Public Policy Program at Harvard University's Kennedy School of Government and Chair of the Initiative for Inclusive Security. She was U.S. Ambassador to Austria from 1993 to 1997 and is the author of *This Was Not Our War: Bosnian Women Reclaiming the Peace*.

Equity in Representation for Women and Minorities

JOSEPH ZIMMERMAN

The approach of the twenty-first century finds women and most minority groups grossly underrepresented in elective offices throughout the world because of cultural, legal, and political barriers. The token representation of women and minorities in elective offices that exists in many nations is little more than symbolic.

This underrepresentation has three major undesirable consequences. First, the lack of women and members of minority groups on governing bodies may mean that important issues receive little or no consideration during the policy-making process. Second, minorities may become alienated from the political system and display less respect for laws enacted without their direct input by legislative bodies they view as illegitimate.

Third, the electoral system in nations with several large minority groups can promote national unity or can encourage the splintering of a nation. If a sizeable minority group is able to elect only a few or no members to public offices, pressure for secession and establishment of a new nation may increase. One electoral system, proportional representation (PR), can guarantee a minority group direct representation in proportion to its voting strength, thereby helping to prevent the disintegration of a nation.

This chapter (1) identifies barriers to the election of women and members of minority groups to public offices, (2) describes the significance of cultural and socioeconomic factors in terms of their influence on election results, (3) offers alternatives among electoral systems to increase the number of women and minorities in elective offices based upon experience in various nations, and (4) presents criteria for determining the fairness of representation produced by various electoral systems.

Barriers to Election

Authors of chapters in this volume identify the following barriers to the election of women and members of minority groups to public offices: the dominant political culture, unequal education and employment opportunities, unfavorable electoral system, incumbents' advantages in seeking reelection to office, inadequate campaign funds for women and minority candidates, and election laws making it difficult for potential candidates or new parties to have their names included on the ballot. Each barrier may affect women or a specific minority group in a different manner, and two or more barriers may be interrelated in a particular nation.

Political Culture and Change

Every society over time develops dominant cultural norms governing the proper roles of individuals and groups. Failure of an individual or a group to follow assigned roles can cause society-at-large to discriminate against the offending individual or group.

Cultural norms are affected by changing economic and other societal conditions. The new or modified norms may be reflected in law, as in the United States, where the national Voting Rights Act offers protection to blacks and foreign-language minorities. On the other hand, it may be nearly impossible for a group such as the untouchables in India to have cultural practices changed other than very slowly, even though the law prohibits discrimination.

Cultural norms currently affect adversely the prospect for the election of women to public office in every nation. As'ad AbuKhalil describes the historical association between the Middle Eastern culture and the social and political oppression of women. However, changing political conditions have resulted in women's attaining voting rights in several Arab countries in recent years. Michelle A. Saint-Germain explains that the *machismo* culture emphasizes humility, passivity, and submissiveness as the proper behavior for women, thereby erecting major barriers to women interested in seeking election to public office. Similarly, traditional German culture delimited the roles of women as *kinder, kuche,* and *kirche* (children, kitchen, and church) and made it exceptionally difficult for a woman to be elected to public office. Traditional culture in both countries has been weakened in recent decades. Similarly, Avraham Brichta and Yael Brichta report that in Israel orthodox Jews reject women's participation in the political process and that Arabs also have a traditional negative attitude toward women's political activism.

Studies reveal that when women are first elected to parliament they are typically members of families long active in electoral politics. Fanny Tabak points out that Brazilian wives and daughters of deceased or retired public officials often replaced them. Today, many Brazilian women members of parliament (MPs) are professionals with personal prestige. Joan Rydon relates a similar pattern on Australian MPs. She also notes that older women years beyond their roles as wives and mothers were first elected, but currently young women also are being recruited as candidates.

The Nordic culture generally has been favorable to women's involvement in electoral politics. Jill M. Bystydzienski reports that Norway in 1986 became the first nation to have a government headed by a woman prime minister and a cabinet that was 44 percent women. She attributes women's electoral success in part to the Nordic values of equality and social justice.

Socioeconomic Opportunities

Socioeconomic conditions influence the opportunities for women and members of minority groups to become successful candidates for elective offices. If a nation has an educational system that is open to all young persons and prepares many students for professional careers, opportunities for election of women and minorities to public office will be enhanced.

Michelle A. Saint-Germain points out that the college graduation rate for women in Costa Rica is twice as high as the rate in Nicaragua and hence women in the latter nation do not have as many opportunities to become professionals, which would have improved prospects for women being elected to serve in the national legislature. Beate Hoecker, however, reports that many Germans harbor a strong prejudice against professionally and politically active women.

Feldblum and Lawson explain that changes in political attitudes and participation between first-generation and second-generation Franco-North Africans in France are attributable to the latter generation's education, which produced many professionals. Particularly striking is the sharp increase in the number of female Franco-North African candidates for election.

Opportunities for women to participate in local and national organizations can enhance their prospects for becoming elected public representatives. Jill Bystydzienski notes that in Norway men frequently were absent from fishing villages for long periods of time and women in these villages often organized various types of campaigns and also sought to promote the election of women to public office. Furthermore, Norwegians have a tradition of joining local and national organizations, and women's experiences in such organizations promote their opportunities to win elective offices.

Women in the former Soviet Union had open access to educational facilities, and many became professionals. Quotas were used to select approximately one-half of the members of the Supreme Soviet and women constituted one-third of its members. Constitutional changes in 1988–89 included replacement of the Supreme Soviet by the Congress of People's Deputies and the abandonment of quotas. Although democratic features were added to the single-member district system, it operates against the election of women, whose representation in the Congress declined to 15.7 percent in the 1989 election. Similarly, the single-member district system is a major barrier to the election of women to public office in the United States.

The Electoral System

Political scientists in recent years have studied the impact of different voting systems upon the election prospects of women and various minority groups. Experience with the single-member district system (known as the first-past-the-post system in the United Kingdom) reveals that it generally favors the election of candidates of the majority group in each district, with the exception of women. Argentina during the 1950s was an exception to the general finding that women are disadvantaged by the single-member district system.

As Enid Lakeman explains, the majority group in a district in the United Kingdom is a political party that cannot afford to offer voters a choice between a male and a female candidate or a black and a white candidate for fear of splitting the party's vote and defeating both candidates. She also explains that in local elections additional women candidates are nominated by parties in multimember districts and that voters are more apt to cast a ballot for a woman candidate when more than one candidate is to be elected.

Municipal reformers in the United States early in the 20th century launched a campaign to replace the single-member district system with an at-large system to elect a city council, on the grounds that the former system perpetuated boss control of the council.[1] By mid-century, the reformers had achieved success in changing the electoral system to at-large in numerous local governments. But by the 1960s several political scientists and black activists commenced to criticize the system by alleging it produced an overrepresentation of white middle-class values.[2]

Several cities incorporated a provision for a modified at-large system in the city charter to ensure neighborhood representation. The modified system employs district residency requirements for council members. If the two highest vote-getters in an election reside in the same district, only the top vote-getter is elected to the council. This system facilitates the election of a minority candidate if his or her group is concentrated in a district, but it does not guarantee the election of the candidate. Other United States cities have adopted a combination of the single-member and at-large electoral systems.

Limited voting is employed in a number of local governments to elect governing bodies. Each voter may cast a ballot for more than one candidate, but for fewer candidates than there are seats to be filled. This system, which can be employed on an at-large or multimember district basis, guarantees direct representation for members of the largest minority party or group.[3] As each voter gives the same support to the candidate least favored as to the candidate most favored, the voter may contribute to the defeat of his or her favorite candidate. Hence, this system encourages casting a ballot for only one candidate. Furthermore, limited voting does not ensure that each group or party will be represented in proportion to its voting strength. In addition, the system may allow a minority to elect a majority of council members if several strong slates of candidates divide the votes.

Cumulative voting has the same goal as limited voting, that is, enabling the largest minority group or party to elect one or more of its members to a governing body. Each elector has the same number of votes as there are seats to be filled on a governing body or in a multimember district. The elector may cast all votes for one candidate or apportion the votes among several candidates in accordance with the intensity of the elector's preferences. This system was employed to elect members of the Illinois House of Representatives in the period 1870 to 1980 and has been employed since 1988 in Alamogordo, New Mexico, and in Chilton County and three towns in Alabama.[4] In Norway, voters in several local governments may give a second vote to a candidate.

To ensure direct representation for minority parties, PR has been adopted by several nations for national and local elections. There are two types of PR, the list system and the single-transferable-vote system (STV). The former is more common and is designed to reward parties with seats on a governing body in accordance with their respective share of the total vote. Interestingly, the party-list PR system was employed in the United Nations—supervised election that marked the peaceful transition of Namibia from a colony of the Republic of South Africa to an independent nation and allocated seats in close approximation to the votes received by each party.

There are two variants of the list system. Under the fixed or rigid system, each party determines the order in which the names of its candidates appear on its list and the voter may cast a ballot only for that list of candidates. The other variant allows the voters to determine the place of each candidate on a party list. The list system can be combined with another system, such as the single-member district system, to elect members of a parliamentary body. A minimum vote threshold, such as 5 percent, also may be adopted for allocation of seats to political parties.

STV is employed in the Republic of Ireland to elect members of Dáil Eireann (the lower house of parliament) and members of local governing bodies. The system is used in the United States to elect the city council and school committee in Cambridge, Massachusetts, and thirty-two community school boards in New York City.[5]

STV is a type of preferential voting in a district that elects more than one representative. Each elector places a number next to the name of each candidate, with a number "1" indicating the first preference, number "2" second preference, and so on. Winning candidates are determined by a quota—the total number of valid ballots cast divided by the number of seats to be filled plus 1, with 1 added to the product of the division. If 100,000 valid ballots were cast to elect a nine-member governing body, the quota would be

$$\frac{100,000}{9+1} + 1 = 10,001$$

This formula always produces the smallest number of votes that ensures a candidate's election regardless of how the votes are distributed among the candidates.

The next step in the STV election involves sorting the ballots by first choices. Candidates receiving a total of number "1" votes equal to or exceeding the quota are declared elected. Ballots exceeding the quota are transferred to the other candidates according to the second choices indicated. Following this step, the candidate with the fewest number "1" votes is declared defeated and his or her votes are transferred to the remaining candidates according to the next choices marked on them. If a second choice already has been elected or defeated, the ballot is distributed to the third choice. A new count is conducted, and candidates are declared elected if they have a total of number "1" and transferred ballots exceeding the quota. Elected candidates' surplus ballots are transferred to the remaining candidates. The process of declaring defeated the lowest candidate and transferring his or her ballots to the other candidates as indicated by the next choice continues until the full governing body is elected. Most ballots, either on first choice or by transfer, help to elect a candidate.

Surplus ballots can be distributed by one of two methods. Under the first method, candidates are not allowed to exceed the quota. On reaching the quota, surplus ballots immediately are transferred to the next choices indicated. Under the second method, the ballots of a candidate receiving a surplus of number "1" votes are reexamined to determine the distribution of number "2" votes. The surplus ballots are distributed proportionally according to second choices. If candidate X received 12,000 number "1" votes and the quota is 10,000, the candidate has a surplus of 2,000 ballots. Assuming that candidate Y was the number "2" choice on 6,000 of candidate X's number "1" ballots, candidate Y would be given one-half of the surplus or 1,000 ballots.

In contrast to the single-member district system, STV allows a geographically dispersed minority to elect a candidate, as the constituency is based on interest and not on residence. In addition, the strength of a minority group is not dissipated whether the group gives most of its number "1" votes to one of its candidates or scatters its votes among several of its candidates. Furthermore, a minority group cannot elect a majority of the members of a governing body in the event of a split among opposition groups, as can occur under limited voting or cumulative voting. Joan Rydon notes that the adoption of STV with five members chosen in each district markedly increased the election of women candidates to the Australian Senate.

Direct representation of women and minorities on governing bodies can be increased without changing the voting system. The election law in Taiwan provides for reserved seats, thereby encouraging women to seek election and guaranteeing that a specific number of women will be elected. Similarly, political parties in several nations have decided to establish a quota of women candidates for public offices.

Incumbency

A major barrier to the election of women and minorities to public office is the incumbent advantage in seeking reelection. Unless an incumbent has been involved in a scandal or his or her party is blamed by the voters for an unpopular occurrence, an incumbent officeholder has many more political resources than a challenger in an election campaign, including name recognition because of media attention.

In the United States, incumbent state legislators in several states and members of the national Congress employ relatively large staffs that may devote part of their time and efforts to promoting legislators' reelection. Elected officials also communicate with constituents through newsletters prepared and posted at public expense and may make public-service announcements that generate or reinforce their name recognition. Although a number of state constitutions and city charters limit the number of terms a governor or a mayor may serve, no such restrictions were placed upon state legislators until 1990, when voters in California, Colorado, and Oklahoma approved constitutional amendments limiting the number of terms that state legislators may serve. Such limitations should facilitate the election of women to state legislatures.

Campaign Finance

That incumbents have a decided advantage over challengers in terms of campaign fund raising has been documented in many studies in the United States. If the term of office is only two years, as in the House of Representatives, incumbents may engage in fund-raising activities throughout the term of office and may not completely separate their fund-raising activities from their official activities.

In contrast to the United States, funds are raised in many nations primarily by the political parties and/or government. These funds help finance the reelection campaigns of incumbent public officers and party candidates. Women

and minorities in other countries usually have little access to campaign funds, which limits their opportunities for election to public offices.

Complex Election Rules

The election playing field for incumbents and challengers also may be uneven because of election regulations. In 1988, the New York State Commission on Government Integrity reported that complex requirements in the state's election law often necessitate that candidates who collect more than the required number of signatures must "participate in expensive, time-consuming litigation in order to defend their right to run for office."[6]

Technical failure to comply with all provisions of election laws may prevent women and minority candidates from qualifying to have their names on the ballot. In addition, the complex legal obstacles to ballot access may discourage other competent individuals from seeking election to public office.

The "threshold" rule in certain proportional representation counties—which may require, for example, 5 percent of the popular vote for a seat parliament—also discourages new parties from forming. Complex regulations in many states in the United States make it difficult for third parties to elect candidates, thereby limiting the election opportunity of women and minorities.

Six Criteria for Fair Representation

In a polity where no legal or other impediments prevent adult citizens from registering and voting in elections, the following six canons of a good electoral system can be employed to assess the equity of representation produced by various electoral systems. The canons, or criteria, are interrelated and overlapping rather than discrete.

Effectiveness of Ballots Cast

The effectiveness canon measures the potency of each ballot cast by a registered voter. A nondiscriminatory electoral system does not cancel or dilute invidiously the effectiveness of ballots cast by any citizen or group of citizens. In the eyes of a minority group, the election must be more than a type of periodic consultation ritual that is meaningless to the group because their ballots are rendered ineffective by the design of the electoral system. If a minority group perceives that the electoral system makes the group powerless, group participation in the political process will be low and the public interest will suffer accordingly.

Maximization of Participation

A fair electoral system encourages the registration of eligible voters because they can visualize that their exercise of the franchise will be effective in helping to determine one or more winners in an election contest. Logically, voter participation by members of a group in an election will be in direct relation to the possible influence that the group can exert. Low voter registration and turnout on election day may be the product of alienation—a sense of powerlessness—rather than apathy.

Representation of Competing Interests

An electoral system that guarantees direct representation on a legislative body for members of a minority group and women will facilitate the necessary political accommodation. Such a system will help to ensure responsiveness by the legislators to the special needs of the minority groups and women.

Maximization of Access to Decision Makers

A proper system of voting will result in the selection of legislators who are willing to listen to and to seek out the views of all groups in the polity. Consultation with constituents must be genuine and not pro forma, or alienation and cynicism will be promoted.

Equity in Group Members' Representation

Fairness in representation is the hallmark of a democratic political system. If members of a group are underrepresented grossly in terms of their population strength in a legislature or other elected offices, the election system should be changed to guarantee that they will be able to elect more members of their group to bring their direct representation closer to parity.

Legitimization of the Legislative Body

An important function of an electoral system is to legitimize the legislative body in the eyes of the citizenry, thereby facilitating the implementation of policy decision. The effectiveness of a government's policies depends in many instances on the active cooperation and support of citizens. A widespread view that the electoral system is designed deliberately to favor one group over another and that the legislators fail to represent citizens adequately will weaken seriously the perceived legitimacy of the policy-makers and their policies.

Summary and Conclusions

A review of elected legislative bodies in various nations reveals that women and members of minority groups tend to be grossly underrepresented. To increase the number of women and minority legislators, important barriers to their election will have to be removed or lowered. Changing a political culture that rejects women's participation in the political process will be a difficult task and may require

generations. The barriers created by the lack of socioeconomic opportunities for women and minorities potentially can be lessened in a much shorter period of time, but lack of resources may slow the pace of increasing educational opportunities.

The barrier created by use of the single-member district electoral system could be removed immediately with adoption of a proportional or semiproportional electoral system. There is, however, strong opposition in many nations to the abandonment of the single-member district system. In the United States, the system has been promoted by the national government to increase the number of blacks elected to public office, although proportional representation would achieve the same goal more effectively without the disadvantages associated with the single-member district system.

The advantages typically possessed by incumbent officials seeking reelection reduce the opportunities for women and minorities to be elected. In the United States, a growing anti-incumbent movement has resulted in voters in several states ratifying constitutional amendments placing limits on the number of terms members of the state legislature may serve. Non-incumbents' relative disadvantage in campaign funds can be offset by public financing of campaigns. Similarly, complex election laws and regulations that discourage non-incumbents from seeking office and forming new political parties could be repealed or simplified.

Direct representation for minorities and women, in approximate accordance with their respective proportions in the general population, should be a deliberate goal of the electoral system and not a product of happenstance. Such a system will ensure the election of public representatives who have a special sensitivity to the needs of minority groups and women and will also ensure that all citizens are treated fairly in the process of accommodating competing interests.

The major argument advanced by PR advocates is its ability to provide direct representation for minority parties or groups voting as blocs. It should be noted that PR also can provide the majority party or group with more seats than it would gain under the single-member district system if the party or group members are concentrated in only a few districts.

Notes

1. Richard S. Childs, *The First 50 Years of the Council-Manager Plan of Government* (New York: National Municipal League, 1965), p. 37.

2. See in particular Edward C. Banfield and James Q. Wilson, *City Politics* (Cambridge: Harvard University Press and M.I.T. Press, 1963), pp. 139–42.

3. See Edward Still, "Cumulative Voting and Limited Voting in Alabama," in Wilma Rule and Joseph F. Zimmerman, eds., *United*

States Electoral Systems: Their Impact on Women and Minorities (Westport, Conn.: Greenwood Press, 1992), pp. 183–96.

4. For details, see George S. Blair, *Cumulative Voting: An Effective Electoral Device in Illinois Politics* (Urbana: University of Illinois Press, 1960); and Edward Still, "Cumulative Voting and Limited Voting in Alabama."

5. Leon Weaver and Judith Baum, "Proportional Representation on New York City Community School Boards," in Rule and Zimmerman, eds., *United States Electoral Systems,* pp. 197–205.

6. *Access of the Ballot in Primary Elections: The Need for Fundamental Reform* (New York: New York State Commission on Government Integrity, 1988), p. 1.

UNIT 5

The Bureaucracy and Judiciary: Unelected Policy Thugs or Expert Policymakers?

Unit Selections

Key Points to Consider

- What is administrative or bureaucratic oversight? What does it achieve?

- What is the problem of "many masters?" Why is this a problem?

- Should the judiciary be elected?

- What is the danger of granting intelligence agencies more authority for surveillance?

- What measures prevent unelected officials from gaining too much influence on policies or lawmaking?

- If there are alternatives to improving intelligence operations, should intelligence authority be increased? Why or why not?

Student Web Site
www.mhcls.com

Internet References

Central Intelligence Agency
   www.cia.gov
Research and Reference (Library of Congress)
   http://www.loc.gov/rr/
United States Executive offices
   http://www.usa.gov/Agencies/Federal/Executive.shtml#vgn-executive-office-of-the-president-vgn
U.S. Information Agency
   http://www.america.gov/
World Wide Web Virtual Library: International Affairs Resources
   http://www.etown.edu/vl/

© Stockbyte/Getty Images

Unit 5 describes the workings of two unelected branches of the government—the judiciary and the bureaucracy—to show their impact on policy-making. The articles in the unit are quick to note the popular ambivalence regarding these two branches. Even though they are unelected, these officials are able to exert considerable influence as administrators or interpreters of if and how laws are carried out, as well as their effects. Given this ambivalence, why not remove the ability? Why continue the practice and possibility for unelected branches of government to challenge or even reverse the laws made by elected representatives?

The readings in this unit point out that there are at least three reasons why the unelected branches of government continue to have such policy-making influence. First, they fill in for government "failures" in representation. Thus, the article on judicial review reports that in countries where governments may not govern effectively, the judiciary has kept the state "up and running" by stepping in to provide the necessary laws and interpretation of laws, such

as in Israel or India. It also points out that the judiciary often steps in to give voice to those unrepresented or poorly represented, such as following the Civil War in the U.S. and during the rise of facism in Europe. The article on the Turkish judiciary shows how this "filling in" for government failures is carried out in practice: the judiciary puts the government "on notice" for pursuing policies that jeopardizes the secular state, but gives it the grudging nod to stay in office so that politics and social stability are maintained.

Second, they have the expertise to evaluate, reveal, or remedy policy failures from an apolitical perspective. This assures that their influence does not derive from a political stake but, rather, is administratively motivated or justice-centered. Thus, the article on bureaucratic oversight points out that bureaucrats have a level of expertise on the policy issues greater than the legislature and the executive that compensates for overlooked or unconsidered aspects of policy-making. Likewise, the article on U.S. intelligence points out that few challenge the paradox

117

that intelligence and covert action essentially supplement the protection of U.S. constitutionalism. And, the article on judicial review points out that while judicial decisions are political, they are not "party political."

Third, their influence on legislation largely relies on the support or, at least, the lack of challenge from other branches of the government. Thus, the article on judicial review emphasizes that the judiciary is "the least dangerous branch of government" because it has no independent resource to enforce its ruling. To the contrary, its decisions may be overturned or simply ignored. Likewise, the article on bureaucratic oversight points out that there are multiple sources of challenge to the influence of the bureaucracy, including the executive, legislature, courts, and interest groups. Given the "many masters," the ability of the bureaucracy to exercise independent influence is severely limited. Indeed, both articles suggest that the influence of these unelected officials may be over-rated.

Yet, the article on the KGB shows that bureaucratic influence and even the abuse of power is very real. And the consequences of such abuse are considerable: in Russia, the abuse by the KGB's successor, the Federal Security Service (FSB) has deprived citizens of their businesses and even their lives, as in the case of Anna Politkovskaya, a renowned journalist, and Litvinenko, a former KGB officer. It is, thus, important that constraints are put in place to preempt and prevent such abuse.

How are unelected officials constrained? The articles on the bureaucratic influence, the U.S. intelligence, and the KGB point out that executive or legislative oversight of bureaucracies that carries penalties or rewards significantly constrain bureaucratic abuse or misuse. The penalties or rewards that are highly successful in conjunction with oversight—budget and reorganization—fundamentally affect how bureaucrats function. When this is contrasted with less effective techniques, such as congressional hearings or even executive or legislative vetoes, they suggest that the effectiveness stems from the possible penalties—akin to "carrying a big stick"—that bureaucrats may face if they overstep their roles. The article on the KGB corroborates the significance of budget or resources: it predicts that businesses seized by the FSB will not be run successfully and that this will turn out to be its undoing. Likewise, the articles on the judiciary show that the judiciary is constrained by the equivalent of the budget, that is, the lack of independent resources.

An important corollary to constraining unelected officials: it is better to put them in place and tie their hands than respond to the abuses from the lack of restraints. Thus, the articles on U.S. intelligence and the KGB draw attention to the fact that constraints may be reviewed and loosened, if necessary, to ensure smooth and efficient operations. However, imposing constraints in response to abuses, such as in the U.S. in the 1970s and Russia in the 1990s, may focus on the effects of such abuses but fail to address their sources. This failure to get at the source is fundamental to our ambivalence of the unelected officials: their potential as policy thugs.

Judicial Review: The Gavel and the Robe

Established and emerging democracies display a puzzling taste in common: both have handed increasing amounts of power to unelected judges. Th[is] article examines the remarkable growth and many different forms of judicial review.

To some they are unaccountable elitists, old men (and the rare women) in robes who meddle in politics where they do not belong, thwarting the will of the people. To others they are bulwarks of liberty, champions of the individual against abuses of power by scheming politicians, arrogant bureaucrats and the emotional excesses of transient majorities.

Judges who sit on supreme courts must get used to the vilification as well as the praise. They often deal with the most contentious cases, involving issues which divide the electorate or concern the very rules by which their countries are governed. With so much at stake, losers are bound to question not only judges' particular decisions, but their right to decide at all. This is especially true when judges knock down as unconstitutional a law passed by a democratically elected legislature. How dare they?

Despite continued attacks on the legitimacy of judicial review, it has flourished in the past 50 years. All established democracies now have it in some form, and the standing of constitutional courts has grown almost everywhere. In an age when all political authority is supposed to derive from voters, and every passing mood of the electorate is measured by pollsters, the growing power of judges is a startling development.

The trend in western democracies has been followed by the new democracies of Eastern Europe with enthusiasm. Hungary's constitutional court may be the most active and powerful in the world. There have been failures. After a promising start, Russia's constitutional court was crushed in the conflict between Boris Yeltsin and his parliament. But in some countries where governments have long been riven by ideological divisions or crippled by corruption, such as Israel and India, constitutional courts have filled a political vacuum, coming to embody the legitimacy of the state.

In western democracies the growing role of constitutional review, in which judges rule on the constitutionality of laws and regulations, has been accompanied by a similar growth in what is known as administrative review, in which judges rule on the legality of government actions, usually those of the executive branch. This second type of review has also dragged judges into the political arena, frequently pitting them against elected politicians in controversial cases. But it is less problematic for democratic theorists than constitutional review for a number of reasons.

Democracy's Referees

The expansion of the modern state has seemed to make administrative review inevitable. The reach of government, for good or ill, now extends into every nook and cranny of life. As a result, individuals, groups and businesses all have more reason than ever before to challenge the legality of government decisions or the interpretation of laws. Such challenges naturally end up before the courts.

In France, Germany, Italy and most other European countries, special administrative tribunals, with their own hierarchies of appeal courts, have been established to handle such cases. In the United States, Britain, Canada and Australia, the ordinary courts, which handle criminal cases and private lawsuits, also deal with administrative law cases.

The growth of administrative review can be explained as a reaction to the growth of state power. But the parallel expansion of constitutional review is all the more remarkable in a democratic age because it was resisted for so long in the very name of democracy.

The idea was pioneered by the United States, the first modern democracy with a written constitution. In fact, the American constitution nowhere explicitly gives the Supreme Court the power to rule laws invalid because of their unconstitutionality. The court's right to do this was first asserted in *Marbury v Madison*, an 1803 case, and then quickly became accepted as proper. One reason for such ready acceptance may have been that a Supreme Court veto fitted so well with the whole design and spirit of the constitution itself, whose purpose was as much to control the excesses of popular majorities as to give the people a voice in government decision-making.

In Europe this was the reason why the American precedent was not followed. As the voting franchise was expanded, the will of the voting majority became ever more sacrosanct, at least in theory. Parliamentary sovereignty reigned supreme. European democrats viewed the American experiment with constitutionalism as an unwarranted restraint on the popular will.

Even in the United States, judicial review was of little importance until the late 19th century, when the Supreme Court became more active, first nullifying laws passed after the civil war to give former slaves equal rights and then overturning laws regulating economic activity in the name of contractual and property rights.

After a showdown with Franklin Roosevelt over the New Deal, which the court lost, it abandoned its defence of laissez-faire economics. In the 1950s under Chief Justice Earl Warren it embarked on the active protection and expansion of civil rights. Controversially, this plunged the court into the mainstream of American politics, a position it retains today despite a retreat from Warren-style activism over the past two decades.

Attitudes towards judicial review also changed in Europe. The rise of fascism in the 1920s and 1930s, and then the destruction wrought by the second world war, made many European democrats reconsider the usefulness of judges. Elections alone no longer seemed a reliable obstacle to the rise of dangerously authoritarian governments. Fascist dictators had seized power by manipulating representative institutions.

The violence and oppression of the pre-war and war years also convinced many that individual rights and civil liberties needed special protection. The tyranny of the executive branch of government, acting in the name of the majority, became a real concern. (Britain remained an exception to this trend, sticking exclusively to the doctrine of parliamentary sovereignty. It is only now taking its first tentative steps towards establishing a constitutional court.)

While the goals of constitutional judicial review are similar almost everywhere, its form varies from country to country, reflecting national traditions. Some of the key differences:

• **Appointments.** The most famous method of appointment is that of the United States, largely because of a handful of televised and acrimonious confirmation hearings. The president appoints a Supreme Court judge, subject to Senate approval, whenever one of the court's nine seats falls vacant. Political horsetrading, and conflict, are part of the system. Judges are appointed for life, though very few cling to office to the end.

Other countries may appoint their constitutional judges with more decorum, but politics always plays some part in the process. France is the most explicitly political. The directly elected president and the heads of the Senate and the National Assembly each appoint three of the judges of the Constitutional Council, who serve non-renewable nine-year terms, one-third of them retiring every three years. Former presidents are awarded life membership on the council, although none has yet chosen to take his seat.

Half of the 16 members of Germany's Federal Constitutional Tribunal are chosen by the Bundestag, the lower house of parliament, and half by the Bundesrat, the upper house. Appointments are usually brokered between the two major parties. The procedure is similar in Italy, where one-third of the 15-strong Constitutional Court is chosen by the head of state, one-third by the two houses of parliament and one-third by the professional judiciary.

Senior politicians—both before and after serving in other government posts—have sat on all three constitutional courts, sometimes with unhappy results. In March Roland Dumas, the president of France's Constitutional Council, was forced to step down temporarily because of allegations of corruption during his earlier tenure as foreign minister. The trend in all three countries is towards the appointment of professional judges and legal scholars rather than politicians.

• **Powers.** Most constitutional courts have the power to nullify laws as unconstitutional, but how they do this, and receive cases, varies. Once again, the most anomalous is France's Constitutional Council which rules on the constitutionality of laws only before they go into effect and not, like all other courts, after.

The 1958 constitution of France's Fifth Republic allowed only four authorities to refer cases to the council: the president, the prime minister, and the heads of the two houses of parliament. In 1974, a constitutional amendment authorised 60 deputies or senators to lodge appeals with the council as well. Since then, the council has become more active, and most appeals now come from groups of legislators. Individuals have no right to appeal to the council.

French jurists argue that judicial review before a law goes into effect is simpler and faster than review after a law's promulgation. But it is also more explicitly political, and leaves no room for making a judgment in the light of a law's sometimes unanticipated effect.

No other major country has adopted prior review exclusively, but it is an option in Germany and Italy as well, usually at the request of the national or one of the regional governments. However, most of the work of the constitutional courts in both countries comes from genuine legal disputes, which are referred to them by other courts when a constitutional question is raised.

The Supreme Courts of the United States, Canada and Australia, by contrast, are the final courts of appeal for all cases, not just those dealing with constitutional issues. The United States Supreme Court does not give advisory or abstract opinions about the constitutionality of laws, but only deals with cases involving specific disputes. Moreover, lower courts in the United States can also rule on constitutional issues, although most important cases are appealed eventually to the Supreme Court.

Canada's Supreme Court can be barred from ruling a law unconstitutional if either the national or a provincial legislature has passed it with a special clause declaring that it should survive judicial review "notwithstanding" any breach of the country's Charter of Rights. If passed in this way, the law must be renewed every five years. In practice, this device has rarely been used.

• **Judgments.** The French and Italian constitutional courts deliver their judgments unanimously, without dissents. Germany abandoned this method in 1971, adopting the more transparent approach of the common-law supreme courts, which allow a tally of votes cast and dissenting opinions to be published alongside the court's judgment. Advocates of unanimity argue that it reinforces the court's authority and gives finality to the law. Opponents deride it as artificial, and claim that publishing dissents improves the technical quality of judgments, keeps the public better informed, and makes it easier for the law to evolve in the light of changing circumstances.

Also noteworthy is the growth in Europe of supra-national judicial review. The European Court of Justice in Luxembourg is the ultimate legal authority for the European Union. The court's primary task is to interpret the treaties upon which the EU is founded. Because EU law now takes precedence over national law in the 15 member states, the court's influence has grown considerably in recent years. The European Court of Human Rights in Strasbourg, the judicial arm of the 41-member Council of Europe, has, in effect, become the final court of appeal on human-rights issues for most of Europe. The judgments of both European courts carry great weight and have forced many countries to change their laws.

Despite the rapid growth of judicial review in recent decades, it still has plenty of critics. Like all institutions, supreme courts make mistakes, and their decisions are a proper topic of political debate. But some criticisms aimed at them are misconceived.

Unelected Legislators?

To criticise constitutional courts as political meddlers is to misunderstand their role, which is both judicial and political. If constitutions are to play any part in limiting government, then someone must decide when they have been breached and how they should be applied, especially when the relative powers of various branches or levels of government—a frequent issue in federal systems—are in question. When a court interprets a constitution, its decisions are political by definition—though they should not be party political.

Supreme courts also are not unaccountable, as some of their critics claim. Judges can be overruled by constitutional amendment, although this is rare. They must also justify their rulings to the public in written opinions. These are pored over by the media, lawyers, legal scholars and other judges. If unpersuasive, judgments are sometimes evaded by lower courts or legislatures, and the issue eventually returns to the constitutional court to be considered again.

Moreover, the appointment of judges is a political process, and the complexions of courts change as their membership changes, although appointees are sometimes unpredictable once on the bench. Nevertheless, new appointments can result in the reversal of earlier decisions which failed to win public support.

Constitutional courts have no direct power of their own. This is why Alexander Hamilton, who helped write America's constitution, called the judiciary "the least dangerous branch of government." Courts have no vast bureaucracy, revenue-raising ability, army or police force at their command—no way, in fact, to enforce their rulings. If other branches of government ignore them, they can do nothing. Their power and legitimacy, especially when they oppose the executive or legislature, depend largely on their moral authority and credibility.

Senior judges are acutely aware of their courts' limitations. Most tread warily, preferring to mould the law through interpretation of statutes rather than employing the crude instrument of complete nullification. Even the American Supreme Court, among the world's most activist, has ruled only sections of some 135 federal laws unconstitutional in 210 years, although it has struck down many more state laws.

Finally, it is worth remembering that judges are not the only public officials who exercise large amounts of power but do not answer directly to voters. Full-time officials and appointees actually perform most government business, and many of them have enormous discretion about how they do this. Even elected legislators and prime ministers are not perfect transmitters of the popular will, but enjoy great latitude when making decisions on any particular issue. Constitutional courts exist to ensure that everyone stays within the rules. Judges have the delicate, sometimes impossible, task of checking others' power without seeming to claim too much for themselves.

Political Influence on the Bureaucracy: The Bureaucracy Speaks

SCOTT R. FURLONG

Introduction

Scholars of political science and public policy have studied the bureaucracy and its relative power vis-a-vis other political institutions in the United States. The extent of Congress's delegation of authority to executive agencies has made the issue of bureaucratic power and discretion more topical. Some have argued that the power of the bureaucracy is too great and violates constitutional principles (Lowi 1979), while others see delegation as a necessity in modern American government (Bryner 1987).

Two veins of thought dominate the recent literature on this topic. The first, bureaucratic autonomy, emanates from the early history of the dichotomy between politics and administration (Wilson 1887; Goodnow 1900). This literature states that bureaucratic agencies have autonomy in policymaking due to factors such as expertise on issues, the agency's mission (Rourke 1984), and constituent support (Rourke 1984; M.A. Eisner and Meier 1990). These factors give agencies a great amount of discretion when they make policy. The second vein of thought, political influence, states that institutions in our system, beyond the bureaucracy, can significantly influence the bureaucracy and its policies. The influence literature focuses on constitutional issues regarding shared authority by Congress and the president over agencies, the role of the judiciary in such a system, and interest group influence on these agencies. Principal-agent theory (Mitnick 1980 and 1991) and oversight research (Gormley 1989; West 1995) also may be included with this vein by providing an understanding of the interaction between different institutions within our government system.

This study examines the political influence model from a different perspective. While most researchers have examined the mechanisms used by various institutions to influence bureaucratic behavior, very few have examined whether or not the bureaucrats themselves perceive this influence and respond to this pressure (see Waterman, Wright, and Rouse 1994). This exploratory study examines the bureaucratic agent's perception of influence from five other institutions in our system: Congress, the president, courts, interest groups, and the general public. How do agency officials perceive influence by these institutions? What mechanisms used by Congress, the president, and interest groups are used most often and which are seen as most effective? These questions were asked in a survey of bureaucratic managers. The instrument focused on the managers' perceptions of influence by these institutions and the different mechanisms used by Congress, the president, and interest groups. The study sheds additional light on political influence theory from the perspective of the executive agency personnel.

Literature Review

Research on influence, or control over bureaucratic agencies, has examined the ability of one or more institutions to participate and influence bureaucratic policy (Moe 1985; Kaufman 1981; Mitnick 1991; Krause 1994 and 1996). Kaufman's *The Administrative Behavior of Federal Bureau Chiefs* (1981) recognizes both the multiplicity of the external forces on an agency and the complexity of the relationship between bureaus and other institutions. According to Kaufman, "The relations were intricate, involving negotiations, exchanges of favors, accommodations, and endlessly shifting alliances and lines of conflict among the participants. Kaufman states that the congressional set, including committees, individuals, and offices, occupied the "center of the pattern of relationships for all the chiefs" and the external force to which the bureau chiefs were most sensitive. Within the executive branch set, Kaufman recognizes the partial independence of a bureau vis-a-vis the larger department or the presidency. Therefore, these "superiors" also qualify as external groups trying to influence the bureau. The nongovernmental set, typically interest groups, also represents important external actors to the bureau chief from substantive as well as political perspectives. Kaufman also discusses the role of other governmental actors, the general public, and the media and their relationship with the bureau. The courts are not given a major role in the bureau chief's environment. In general, Kaufman examines many of the external actors that may affect agency policymaking and provides information as to how the chiefs within the agencies perceive the influence on the agency.

Mitnick (1991), in his discussion of principal-agent theory, also recognizes the existence of multiple actors attempting to influence administrative agencies. His study addresses five components that are crucial to the regulatory environment: industry, public interest groups, legislators, chief executive, and the courts. These actors, along with the regulatory agency, interact under an incentive systems framework in order to achieve desired goals. The study attempts to model the relationships between the actors. Many of the actors discussed by Mitnick are included in this study as well. The following sections discuss other studies of external influence on the bureaucracy by different institutions.

Congress and the Bureaucracy

Political scientists have studied the relationship between Congress and the bureaucracy for many years. Since oversight of the bureaucracy is considered a major component of Congress's job, it is no wonder that researchers have explored the ability to engage in both oversight and the effects of that oversight (Ogul 1976; Foreman 1988; Aberbach 1990).

Many of these studies argue that Congress can influence bureaucratic policy through a variety of ex post controls including the use of the appropriation process, oversight hearings, and statutory changes (Weingast and Moran 1983; Bendor and Moe 1985; Aberbach 1990; Scholz and Wei 1986). Others argue that ex ante techniques—such as procedural requirements, agency structure, and requiring reports are also quite effective ways to influence bureaucratic policymaking (McCubbins 1985; McCubbins, Noll, and Weingast 1987; Calvert, McCubbins and Weingast 1989). Studies of oversight suggest that both ex post and ex ante techniques have some impact on bureaucratic policymaking.

Gormley (1989) classifies congressional oversight mechanisms as either prayers or muscles. Prayers are coercive controls such as legislative vetoes and legislative hammer provisions. A legislative hammer is a provision placed into a law that takes effect if the agency fails to meet the schedule. Muscles are catalytic controls that force the bureaucracy to perform a function but do not force a particular decision. An example might be the requirement to conduct an environmental impact statement. Based on this categorization, one might hypothesize that bureaucrats may perceive these techniques differently. For example, muscle strategies, due to their more forceful nature, may be perceived as more often used and more effective in influencing bureaucratic policy.

Congressional oversight also can be categorized in terms of formal versus informal methods of oversight (Ogul 1976; West 1995). Formal techniques include items such as committee hearings or changes in the enabling statutes, whereas informal methods include private meetings and telephone contacts. Once again, bureaucrats may perceive the frequency and effectiveness of these two forms of oversight differently. Information is available concerning who is testifying in front of a congressional committee, but most people do not know about phone calls and conversations that occur off the record.

President and the Bureaucracy

Increasingly, political scientists have explored the president's relationship to the bureaucracy. One would expect that the president, the constitutional head of the executive branch, would have influence over administrative policymaking. The president has mechanisms to influence bureaucratic policymaking, and research has begun to examine these as well. For example, the president has budgetary power (Bendor and Moe 1985), reorganization power (Wood 1988), and appointment power (Moe 1982; 1985; Ringquist 1995). All of these have been shown to have an impact on agency policymaking. Research has focused more specifically on the president's use of executive orders, the Office of Management and Budget (OMB), and other presidential offices to monitor and influence regulatory policy and rule making in the agencies (Cooper and West 1988; Durant 1992; Kerwin 1994; Furlong 1995). Executive Order 12291, instituted by President Reagan, provided the OMB with a mechanism to review agency regulations. The Council on Competitiveness, established by President Bush, provided yet another level of presidential review of agency actions. President Bush also instituted his regulatory moratorium as a way to limit agency actions. President Clinton continues to use executive orders and the OMB as a way to monitor and influence agency policies. Scholars have argued that all of these presidential mechanisms give the president significant influence over the bureaucracy.

The distinction between muscle and prayer techniques also may be relevant in presidential influence (Gormley 1989), and their perceived use and effectiveness may affect bureaucratic policymaking. In the case of presidential influence, muscle techniques may include reorganization, certain executive orders, or the strong use of OMB in policy review. On the other hand, prayers may include personnel appointments or the conducting of a cost-benefit analysis. Again, the more dominant muscle strategies seem to be more likely to get the attention of bureaucrats and potentially influence their decisions.

West's (1995) distinction in presidential influence is between what he deems personnel actions, such as appointment and removal power, and centralized management techniques such as reorganization, budgetary powers, executive orders, and the use of OMB as policy reviewers. In this case, the sheer number of techniques categorized under centralized management would seem to assure that bureaucrats would perceive them to be used more often and perhaps more effectively.

Courts and the Bureaucracy

Research has shown that courts have the ability to influence agency actions. The court systems have tremendous influence on executive agencies through their role of judicial review. The courts can make procedural rulings that may affect agency decision-making ability, or they can make substantive rulings that interpret statutory intent; both of these can influence the bureaucracy. In addition, the setting of judicial deadlines for issuing regulations often will set or change the priorities of an executive agency. Studies by Moe (1985) and Wood and Waterman (1993) conclude that courts play an active role in decision making within the bureaucracy. Likewise, in their study of EPA regional personnel, Waterman, Wright, and Rouse (1994) find that the judiciary has considerable influence over EPA enforcement activities.

Other studies have found the courts to have influence on agency policymaking. Melnick (1983) found that court decisions had major impacts on EPA rule-making programs. Likewise, O'Leary (1993) found that court actions influence EPA decisions. According to O'Leary, EPA often wins its cases in courts, but the simple action of filing the lawsuit appears to change EPA policy. As Kerwin states: "Our judges are full and active players in the rulemaking process and, in some instances, exert a degree of control that exceeds the reach and grasp of either the Congress or the president" (1994, 266).

Interest Groups and the Bureaucracy

Theories that discuss interest group influence on the bureaucracy mostly have centered around two not necessarily incompatible ideas. The first, capture theory (Bernstein 1955; Stigler 1971), posits that the agency is beholden to a certain industry that it is supposed to regulate. Capture theory has been associated primarily with economic regulation; it has been mostly dismissed because of its limitations in trying to explain interest group influence on current regulatory activity, particularly in the social regulatory arena.

The second idea revolves around the various theories associated with policy subsystems (Thurber 1991), issue networks (Heclo 1978), and advocacy coalitions (Sabatier and Jenkins-Smith 1993; Meier and Garman 1995). In all of these theories, interest groups from multiple perspectives of an issue participate in the decision-making process and attempt to influence the executive agencies through direct and indirect communication. While this study does not specifically explore these theories, it does examine the techniques used by interest groups attempting to influence agency decisions. Providing comments to proposed rule makings, participating in regulatory negotiations, and having informal contact with agency personnel can all help an interest group influence agency policy. While some have examined the indirect impact of interest groups (Bendor and Moe 1985), little research has examined the direct impact that these interest groups may have on agency policymaking (Golden 1995; Kerwin 1994; Furlong 1997; Hoefer 1994). One must assume that interest groups would not spend the resources to participate in this process without some perceived benefits.

Interest group participation in the bureaucratic process, as Gormley (1989) states, are limited to catalytic controls (prayers). This is because interest group techniques, in almost all cases of influence, are limited to providing information to the bureaucracy. Only rarely can an interest group actually force an action—a citizen suit may be one example. Interest group information may move a bureaucrat one way or another, but it does not predetermine the decision.

This study does not make a distinction between different types of interest groups (e.g., economic vs. noneconomic groups). While research suggests that influence by different group types may vary (Schattschneider 1960; Schlozman and Tierney 1986; Wright 1996), this study concerns itself with interest group influence compared to other institutions, not from a comparative interest group perspective. Saying this, one must recognize that the agencies surveyed in this study are influenced by different types of interest groups. Therefore they may perceive differing levels of influence depending on the particular interest groups involved with that agency. . . .

Discussion and Conclusions

The study . . . examines relative influence that a variety of institutions can have on agency policy . . . [I]t also examines the different methods used by these institutions in their pursuit of influence. Finally, the article explores the differences perceived by respondents who work in executive agencies and independent regulatory commissions.

The results of this study support much of the political influence research previously conducted by scholars using top-down approaches. That is, in general, the respondents of the survey perceive that Congress and the president have the greatest influence on agency policy. Yet, these results do support the general conclusions of the Waterman, Wright, and Rouse (1994) study in terms of the perceived importance of political principals in the making of agency policy. In addition, results of this study provide no significant proof that either branch of government dominates the bureaucracy. Rather, as the framers of the Constitution likely wanted, both Congress and the president share the ability and responsibility to make and influence policy, including agency policy. The issue is not one of congressional dominance or presidential control, but rather of shared authority and the ability to influence policy in one direction or another.

These results also suggest that further research dealing with political influence on the bureaucracy must include interest groups as a factor that can have an impact on executive policy. While little research has specifically compared the influence of interest groups with the influence of Congress on executive policymaking, interest groups' ability to access and shape policy both directly and indirectly is evident and must not be overlooked by researchers. Too often research that examines the role of Congress and the president in bureaucratic policymaking does not consider other important elements that may shape policy, such as interest groups. Interest group participation and influence can and do have relevance in agency policymaking and should not be overlooked.

Finally, the perceived effectiveness of the techniques used by the institutions provides supporting evidence, albeit from a different perspective, of much of the literature that examines executive agency relations with other institutions. Respondents from the agencies perceive certain congressional, presidential, and interest group techniques used to influence executive policy as particularly effective. Scholars have highlighted these techniques (e.g., budget changes, appointments, and participation on advisory committees) in their studies of the political influence on the executive branch as well. From the presidential perspective, it appears that bureaucratic managers are more aware of presidential management techniques, especially those associated with coercive controls (muscle), and consider them more effective. On the congressional side, formal congressional oversight mechanisms, again particularly those leaning toward muscle strategies, appear to be used more often and are more effective in influencing policy. The implication is that bureaucracies do respond to outside pressures, especially to those that speak loudly and carry a big stick.

The role of agencies and agency officials in policymaking is clear. Delegation of power has provided these agencies with the ability not only to implement policy but in many cases to develop policy as well. What is in question, though, is the amount of discretion these agencies have in policymaking. The debate between bureaucratic autonomy and political influence continues, but most scholars acknowledge that outside institutions have the ability to influence bureaucratic policy. Literature on bureaucratic influence mostly has examined these institutions and how they act upon the bureaucracy. This study has examined the perceptions of those within the bureaucracy so as to determine if they perceive pressure and make policy changes accordingly. Studies that examine this relationship from the top-down are important and necessary, but those within the agencies must first realize that this pressure exists and then react to it. This study provides some preliminary results suggesting that agency officials do perceive this pressure and react to it in much the same way as previous top-down studies conclude. The broader implications from a policy standpoint are that the bureaucracy serves many masters. Balancing the many and conflicting demands of these masters is a difficult task, made more problematic if they are unwilling to compromise. These many perspectives will continue to challenge the bureaucratic manager's ability to find an acceptable alternative and will frustrate the bureaucracy's development and implementation of policy.

References

Aberbach, Joel D. 1990. *Keeping a Watchful Eye: The Politics of Congressional Oversight.* Washington, D.C.: Brookings.

Bendor, Jonathan, and Moe, Terry M. 1985 "An Adaptive Model of Bureaucratic Politics." *American Political Science Review* 79:755–74.

Bernstein, Marver H. 1955. *Regulating Business by Independent Commission.* Princeton, N.J.: Princeton University Press.

Berry, Jeffrey M. 1977. *Lobbying for the People: The Political Behavior of Public Interest Groups.* Princeton, N.J.: Princeton University Press.

Brownson, Ann L. 1995. *Federal Staff Directory/l.* Staff Directories, LTD. Mount Vernon, Virginia.

Bryner, Gary C. 1987. *Bureaucratic Discretion: Law and Policy in Federal Regulatory Agencies.* New York: Pergamon.

Calvert, Randall; McCubbins, Matthew; and Weingast, Barry. 1989 "A Theory of Political Control of Agency Discretion." *American Journal of Political Science* 33:588–610.

Calvert, Randall; Moran, Mark J.; and Weingast, Barry. 1987 "Congressional Influence over Policymaking: The Case of the FTC." In Matthew D. McCubbins and Terry Sullivan, eds. *Congress: Structure and Policy.* New York: Cambridge University Press.

Coglianese, Cary. 1994 *Challenging the Rules: Litigation and Bargaining in the Administrative Process.* Ph.D. diss., University of Michigan.

Cooper, Joseph, and West, William F. 1988 "Presidential Power and Republican Government: The Theory and Practice of OMB Review of Agency Rules." *Journal of Politics* 50:864–95.

Durant, Robert F. 1992. *The Administrative Presidency Revisited: Public Lands, the BLM, and the Reagan Revolution.* Albany: State University of New York Press.

Eisner, Marc Allen, and Meier, Kenneth J. 1990 "Presidential Control versus Bureaucratic Power: Explaining the Reagan Revolution in Antitrust." *American Journal of Political Science* 34:269–87.

Eisner, Neil. 1989 "Agency Delay in Informal Rulemaking." *Administrative Law Journal* 3:7–52.

Fiorina, Morris. 1977. *Congress: Keystone of the Washington Establishment.* New Haven, Conn.: Yale University Press.

Foreman, Christopher H. 1988. *Signals from the Hill: Congressional Oversight and the Challenges of Social Regulation.* New Haven, Conn.: Yale University Press.

Furlong, Scott R. 1995 "The 1992 Regulatory Moratorium: Did it Make a Difference?" *Public Administration Review* 55:254–62.

_____. 1997 "Interest Group Influence on Rule Making." *Administration and Society* 29:213–35.

Golden, Marissa Martino. 1995. "Interest Groups in the Rulemaking Process: Who Participates? Whose Voices Get Heard?" Paper presented at the third national Public Management Research Conference, Lawrence, Kansas, October 5–7.

Gormley, William T. 1989. *Taming the Bureaucracy. Muscles, Prayers and Other Strategies.* Princeton, N.J.: Princeton University Press.

Goodnow, Frank J. 1900. *Politics and Administration.* New York: Macmillan.

Harter, Phillip. 1982 "Regulatory Negotiation: A Cure for the Malaise." *Georgetown Law Review* 71:1–113.

Heclo, Hugh. 1978. "Issue Networks and the Executive Establishment." In Anthony King, ed. *The New American Political System.* Washington, D.C.: American Enterprise Institute.

Hoefer, Richard. 1994 "Social Welfare Interest Groups' Advocacy Efforts on the Executive Branch." Paper presented at the annual meeting of the American Political Science Association, New York, Sept.

Kaufman, Herbert. 1981. *The Administrative Behavior of Federal Bureau Chiefs.* Washington, D.C.: Brookings.

Kerwin, Cornelius M. 1994. *Rulemaking: How Government Agencies Write Law and Make Policy.* Washington, D.C.: Congressional Quarterly.

Kerwin, Cornelius M., and Furlong, Scott R. 1992 "Time and Rulemaking: An Empirical Test of Theory." *Journal of Public Administration Research and Theory* 2:113–38.

Krause, George A. 1994 "Political Control, Bureaucratic Autonomy, or Somewhere in Between?: A Dynamic Systems Theory of Administrative Politics." Paper presented at the annual meeting of the Midwest Political Science Association, Chicago, April.

_____. 1996 "The Institutional Dynamics of Policy Administration: Bureaucratic Influence Over Securities Regulation." *American Journal of Political Science* 40:1083–1121.

Lowi, Theodore. 1979. *The End of Liberalism,* 2d ed. New York: Norton.

McCubbins, Matthew D. 1985 "The Legislative Design of Regulatory Structure." *American Journal of Political Science* 29:721–48.

McCubbins, Matthew D., and Schwartz, Thomas. 1984 "Congressional Oversight Overlooked: Police Patrols versus Fire Alarms." *American Journal of Political Science* 28:165–79.

McCubbins, Matthew D.; Noll, Roger G.; and Weingast, Barry R. 1987 "Administrative Procedures as Instruments of Political Control." *Journal of Law, Economics and Organization* 3:243–77.

_____. 1989 "Structure as Process as Solutions to the Politicians Principal-Agency Problems." *Virginia Law Review* 74:431–82.

Meier, Kenneth J. 1993. *Politics and the Bureaucracy: Policymaking in the Fourth Branch of Government.* Pacific Grove, Calif: Brooks/Cole.

Meier, Kenneth J., and Garman, E. Thomas. 1995. *Regulation and Consumer Protection.* Houston: Dame.

Melnick, R. Shep. 1983 *Regulation and the Courts.* Washington, D.C.: Brookings.

Mitnick, Barry M. 1980. *The Political Economy of Regulation.* New York: Columbia University Press.

_____. 1991 "An Incentive Systems Model of the Regulatory Environment." In Melvin J. Dubnick and Alan Gitelson, eds. *Public Policy and Economic Institutions,* volume 10 in Public Policy Studies: A Multi-Volume Treatise, Stuart S. Nagel, ed. Greenwich, Conn.: JAI.

Moe, Terry M. 1982 "Regulatory Performance and Presidential Administration." *American Journal of Political Science* 26:197–224.

_____. 1985 "Control and Feedback in Economic Regulation: The Case of the NLRB." *American Political Science Review* 79:1094–1116.

Ogul, Morris S. 1976. *Congress Oversees the Bureaucracy.* Pittsburgh: University of Pittsburgh Press.

O'Leary, Rosemary. 1993. *Environmental Change: Federal Courts and EPA.* Philadelphia: Temple University Press.

Reagan, Michael D. 1987. *Regulation: The Politics of Policy.* Boston: Little, Brown.

Ringquist, Evan J. 1995 "Political Control and Policy Impact in EPA's Office of Water Quality." *American Journal of Political Science* 39:336-63.

Rourke, Francis E. 1984. *Bureaucracy, Politics, and Public Policy.* Boston: Little, Brown.

Sabatier, Paul, and Jenkins-Smith, Hank. 1993. *Policy Change and Learning: An Advocacy Coalition Approach.* Boulder, Colo.: Westview.

Schattschneider, E.E. 1960. *The Semi-Sovereign People.* New York: Holt, Rinehart and Winston.

Schlozman, Kay L., and Tierey, John T. 1986. *Organized Interests and American Democracy.* New York: HarperCollins.

Scholz, John T., and Wei, Feng Heng. 1986 "Regulatory Enforcement in a Federalist System." *American Political Science Review* 80:1247–70.

Stigler, George J. 1971 "The Theory of Economic Regulation." *Bell Journal of Economics and Management Science* 2:3-21.

Thurber, James A. 1991 "Dynamics of Policy Subsystems in American Politics." In Alan Cigler and Burdette Loomis, eds. *Interest Group Politics,* 3d ed. Washington, D.C.: Congressional Quarterly.

Waterman, Richard W.; Wright, Robert; and Rouse, Amanda. 1994 "The Other Side of Political Control of the Bureaucracy: Agents' Perceptions of Influence and Control." Paper presented at the annual meeting of the American Political Science Association, New York, Sept.

Weingast, Barry R., and Moran, Mark J. 1983 "Bureaucratic Discretion or Congressional Control: Regulatory Policymaking by the Federal Trade Commission." *Journal of Political Economy* 91:765–80.

West, William F. 1995. *Controlling the Bureaucracy. Institutional Constraints in Theory and Practice.* Armonk, N.Y.: Sharpe.

Wilson, Woodrow. 1887 "The Study of Administration." *Political Science Quarterly* 2:197–222.

Wood, B. Dan. 1988 "Principals, Bureaucrats, and Responsiveness in Clean Air Enforcement." *American Political Science Review* 82:213–34.

Wood, B. Dan, and Waterman, Richard. 1991 "The Dynamics of Political Control of the Bureaucracy." *American Political Science Review* 85:801–28.

_____. 1993. "The Dynamics of PoliticalBureaucratic Adaptation." *American Journal of Political Science* 37:497–528.

Wright, John R. 1996. *Interest Groups and Congress: Lobbying, Contributions, and Influence.* Boston: Allyn and Bacon.

Wilson, James Q. 1989. *Bureaucracy: What Government Agencies Do and Why They Do It.* New York: Basic Books.

From *Journal of Public Administration Research and Theory: vol. 8, no. 1,* January 1998, pp. 39–65. Copyright © 1998 by Oxford University Press. Reprinted by permission.

Turkish Court Calls Ruling Party Constitutional

SABRINA TAVERNISE AND SEBNEM ARSU

Turkey's governing party narrowly missed being banned in a court ruling on Wednesday that relieved months of pressure in the country and handed a victory to the party's leader, a former Islamist.

The party, Justice and Development, or AKP, as it is known in Turkish, was kept alive by just one vote—six members of Turkey's Constitutional Court voted to close it for violating the country's secular principles, but seven were required. A ban would have brought down the government, forcing elections for the second time in a year and pitching Turkey into political chaos.

"A great uncertainty blocking Turkey's future has been lifted," said Prime Minister Recep Tayyip Erdogan, the leader of the party, speaking in Ankara, the capital.

The court case was the culmination of an epic battle between the country's secular establishment—a powerful coterie of judges and generals that has deposed elected governments four times in Turkish history—and Mr. Erdogan, a broadly popular politician whose supporters say that his past as a political Islamist is firmly behind him.

And while the ruling was widely viewed as a victory for Mr. Erdogan, and in turn for Turkish democracy, the court reined the party in, imposing a strong but not fatal sanction to cut its public financing in half and issuing a "serious warning" that it was steering the country in too Islamic a direction. Legislation pressed by the party that would have allowed women in head scarves to attend universities, for example, raised suspicions about its agenda.

"AKP is on probation," said Soli Ozel, a professor of international relations at Bilgi University in Istanbul. "The court clearly said it sees the party as a focal institution for Islamizing the country."

Still, by overcoming the case, which accused the party of trying to bring Islamic rule to Turkey, the party and its supporters have prevailed against the country's staunchly secular old guard, which has steered the country from behind the scenes since Turkey's founding by Ataturk in 1923.

The ruling releases the political deadlock that had paralyzed politics in Turkey since March, when the case was filed, and seems to have softened the sharp polarization that had formed between parts of Turkish society—those who want a more openly religious society and those who fear that too much space for Islam will end up curbing secular lifestyles. In a live news conference interrupted by jubilant supporters, Mr. Erdogan said his party had "never been the focus of antisecular activities," and pledged that it would "continue to protect the fundamental principles of our republic also in the future."

Turkey is overwhelmingly Muslim, but its system of government is secular. While the case against the AKP was broadly criticized as weak, secular Turks still worry that the party, with its control of Parliament, the presidency and the government, has too much leeway to impose policies that appeal to its socially conservative base.

But the ruling seemed to have something for everyone, clearing the air politically and allowing even Turkey's most adamant secularists to claim it as a victory.

"AKP can no longer continue with its previous line in politics," said Onur Oymen, the deputy chairman of the secular opposition Republican People's Party. "They have been granted a chance. In order to make the best of it, they need to go through some serious self-critique."

There appear to be no practical implications for the party aside from the cut in financing, which is expected to be made up from other sources in the party's vast middle- and upper-class network of supporters. The ruling opens a new opportunity for Mr. Erdogan to reach out to liberal Turks, who oppose the secular elite but resented his legislation on the head scarves. They felt that he had abandoned other liberal issues like freedom of speech.

"They can no longer afford to act single-handedly," said Ersin Kalaycioglu, political science professor of Sabanci University in Istanbul, who compared the party to a soccer player "with a yellow card to be expelled from the game after one more mistake."

The ruling was an "elegant solution," said Soner Cagaptay, a senior fellow at the Washington Institute for Near East Policy, who used a metaphor to describe its effect: "If the AKP was a river that has overflown its banks, the court has set up embankments, forcing it back into its bed. It has not put a dam in front of it."

The ruling came at a time of great tension in the country. A bomb attack had killed 17 people in Istanbul just three days before, and a ban of the party and its senior members would have brought great instability. On Wednesday, the Istanbul police detained nine people in connection with the blast, Turkey's state-run Anatolian News Agency reported.

"The judges must have judged that the consequences of closure would have been intolerable for the country," Mr. Ozel said.

A government official, who spoke on condition of anonymity, said the party had taken the ruling to heart. "A new period is ahead," the official said. "The self-critique following the verdict," he said, "will be seen in our actions, not in words."

Turkey is trying to gain membership in the European Union, and its chances could have been dented if the party was closed.

"There is a great sense of relief among the Europeans," said Joost Lagendijk, a member of the European Parliament who works on matters regarding Turkey.

The case has paralleled another sensational legal proceeding—the prosecution of 86 people, including writers, members of civic organizations and former military officers who are charged with plotting to overthrow the government—and many in Turkey saw the effects of that case in the ruling on Wednesday.

The case, referred to as Ergenekon, the name of the ultra-nationalist organization the people belong to, is one of the first public accountings of the darker side of Turkey's deep state.

Baskin Oran, a professor of international relations at Ankara University, said the ruling was a sign that Turkey's judiciary, long believed to be well in the sphere of the secular establishment, seemed to have broken ranks.

"Everybody is very happy with this decision," he said. "Otherwise it would have created a hell of a situation for Turkey."

SABRINA TAVERNISE reported from Baghdad, and **SEBNEM ARSU** from Istanbul.

The Making of a Neo-KGB State

Political power in Russia now lies with the FSB, the KGB's successor.

On the evening of August 22nd 1991—16 years ago this week—Alexei Kondaurov, a KGB general, stood by the darkened window of his Moscow office and watched a jubilant crowd moving towards the KGB headquarters in Lubyanka Square. A coup against Mikhail Gorbachev had just been defeated. The head of the KGB who had helped to orchestrate it had been arrested, and Mr Kondaurov was now one of the most senior officers left in the fast-emptying building. For a moment the thronged masses seemed to be heading straight towards him.

Then their anger was diverted to the statue of Felix Dzerzhinsky, the KGB's founding father. A couple of men climbed up and slipped a rope round his neck. Then he was yanked up by a crane. Watching "Iron Felix" sway in mid-air, Mr Kondaurov, who had served in the KGB since 1972, felt betrayed "by Gorbachev, by Yeltsin, by the impotent coup leaders". He remembers thinking, "I will prove to you that your victory will be short-lived."

Those feelings of betrayal and humiliation were shared by 500,000 KGB operatives across Russia and beyond, including Vladimir Putin, whose resignation as a lieutenant-colonel in the service had been accepted only the day before. Eight years later, though, the KGB men seemed poised for revenge. Just before he became president, Mr Putin told his ex-colleagues at the Federal Security Service (FSB), the KGB's successor, "A group of FSB operatives, dispatched under cover to work in the government of the Russian federation, is successfully fulfilling its task." He was only half joking.

Over the two terms of Mr Putin's presidency, that "group of FSB operatives" has consolidated its political power and built a new sort of corporate state in the process. Men from the FSB and its sister organisations control the Kremlin, the government, the media and large parts of the economy—as well as the military and security forces. According to research by Olga Kryshtanovskaya, a sociologist at the Russian Academy of Sciences, a quarter of the country's senior bureaucrats are *siloviki*—a Russian word meaning, roughly, "power guys", which includes members of the armed forces and other security services, not just the FSB. The proportion rises to three-quarters if people simply affiliated to the security services are included. These people represent a psychologically homogeneous group, loyal to roots that go back to the Bolsheviks' first political police, the Cheka. As Mr Putin says repeatedly, "There is no such thing as a former Chekist."

By many indicators, today's security bosses enjoy a combination of power and money without precedent in Russia's history. The Soviet KGB and its pre-revolutionary ancestors did not care much about money; power was what mattered. Influential though it was, the KGB was a "combat division" of the Communist Party, and subordinate to it. As an outfit that was part intelligence organisation, part security agency and part secret political police, it was often better informed, but it could not act on its own authority; it could only make "recommendations". In the 1970s and 1980s it was not even allowed to spy on the party bosses and had to act within Soviet laws, however inhuman.

The KGB provided a crucial service of surveillance and suppression; it was a state within a state. Now, however, it has become the state itself. Apart from Mr Putin, "There is nobody today who can say no to the FSB," says Mr Kondaurov.

All important decisions in Russia, says Ms Kryshtanovskaya, are now taken by a tiny group of men who served alongside Mr Putin in the KGB and who come from his home town of St Petersburg. In the next few months this coterie may well decide the outcome of next year's presidential election. But whoever succeeds Mr Putin, real power is likely to remain in the organisation. Of all the Soviet institutions, the KGB withstood Russia's transformation to capitalism best and emerged strongest. "Communist ideology has gone, but the methods and psychology of its secret police have remained," says Mr Kondaurov, who is now a member of parliament.

Scotched, Not Killed

Mr Putin's ascent to the presidency of Russia was the result of a chain of events that started at least a quarter of a century earlier, when Yuri Andropov, a former head of the KGB, succeeded Leonid Brezhnev as general secretary of the Communist Party. Andropov's attempts to reform the stagnating Soviet economy in order to preserve the Soviet Union and its political system have served as a model for Mr Putin. Early in his presidency Mr Putin unveiled a plaque at the Lubyanka headquarters that paid tribute to Andropov as an "outstanding political figure".

Staffed by highly educated, pragmatic men recruited in the 1960s and 1970s, the KGB was well aware of the dire state of the Soviet economy and the antique state of the party bosses. It was therefore one of the main forces behind *perestroika*, the loose policy of restructuring started by Mr Gorbachev in the

1980s. *Perestroika*'s reforms were meant to give the Soviet Union a new lease of life. When they threatened its existence, the KGB mounted a coup against Mr Gorbachev. Ironically, this precipitated the Soviet collapse.

The defeat of the coup gave Russia an historic chance to liquidate the organisation. "If either Gorbachev or Yeltsin had been bold enough to dismantle the KGB during the autumn of 1991, he would have met little resistance," wrote Yevgenia Albats, a journalist who has courageously covered the grimmest chapters in the KGB's history. Instead, both Mr Gorbachev and Yeltsin tried to reform it.

The "blue blood" of the KGB—the First Chief Directorate, in charge of espionage—was spun off into a separate intelligence service. The rest of the agency was broken into several parts. Then, after a few short months of talk about openness, the doors of the agency slammed shut again and the man charged with trying to reform it, Vadim Bakatin, was ejected. His glum conclusion, delivered at a conference in 1993, was that although the myth about the KGB's invincibility had collapsed, the agency itself was very much alive.

Indeed it was. The newly named Ministry of Security continued to "delegate" the officers of the "active reserve" into state institutions and commercial firms. Soon KGB officers were staffing the tax police and customs services. As Boris Yeltsin himself admitted by the end of 1993, all attempts to reorganise the KGB were "superficial and cosmetic"; in fact, it could not be reformed. "The system of political police has been preserved," he said, "and could be resurrected."

Yet Mr Yeltsin, though he let the agency survive, did not use it as his power base. In fact, the KGB was cut off from the post-Soviet redistribution of assets. Worse still, it was upstaged and outwitted by a tiny group of opportunists, many of them Jews (not a people beloved by the KGB), who became known as the oligarchs. Between them, they grabbed most of the country's natural resources and other privatised assets. KGB officers watched the oligarchs get super-rich while they stayed cash-strapped and sometimes even unpaid.

Some officers did well enough, but only by offering their services to the oligarchs. To protect themselves from rampant crime and racketeering, the oligarchs tried to privatise parts of the KGB. Their large and costly security departments were staffed and run by ex-KGB officers. They also hired senior agency men as "consultants". Fillip Bobkov, the head of the Fifth Directorate (which dealt with dissidents), worked for a media magnate, Vladimir Gusinsky. Mr Kondaurov, a former spokesman for the KGB, worked for Mikhail Khodorkovsky, who ran and largely owned Yukos. "People who stayed in the FSB were B-list," says Mark Galeotti, a British analyst of the Russian special services.

Lower-ranking staff worked as bodyguards to Russia's rich. (Andrei Lugovoi, the chief suspect in the murder in London last year of Alexander Litvinenko, once guarded Boris Berezovsky, an oligarch who, facing arrest in Russia, now lives in Britain.) Hundreds of private security firms staffed by KGB veterans sprang up around the country and most of them, though not all, kept their ties to their *alma mater*. According to Igor Goloshchapov, a former KGB special-forces commando who is now a spokesman for almost 800,000 private security men,

In the 1990s we had one objective: to survive and preserve our skills. We did not consider ourselves to be separate from those who stayed in the FSB. We shared everything with them and we saw our work as just another form of serving the interests of the state. We knew that there would come a moment when we would be called upon.

That moment came on New Year's Eve 1999, when Mr Yeltsin resigned and, despite his views about the KGB, handed over the reins of power to Mr Putin, the man he had put in charge of the FSB in 1998 and made prime minister a year later.

The Inner Circle

As the new president saw things, his first task was to restore the management of the country, consolidate political power and neutralise alternative sources of influence: oligarchs, regional governors, the media, parliament, opposition parties and non-governmental organisations. His KGB buddies helped him with the task.

The most politically active oligarchs, Mr Berezovsky, who had helped Mr Putin come to power, and Mr Gusinsky, were pushed out of the country, and their television channels were taken back into state hands. Mr Khodorkovsky, Russia's richest man, was more stubborn. Despite several warnings, he continued to support opposition parties and NGOs and refused to leave Russia. In 2003 the FSB arrested him and, after a show trial, helped put him in jail.

To deal with unruly regional governors, Mr Putin appointed special envoys with powers of supervision and control. Most of them were KGB veterans. The governors lost their budgets and their seats in the upper house of the Russian parliament. Later the voters lost their right to elect them.

All the strategic decisions, according to Ms Kryshtanovskaya, were and still are made by the small group of people who have formed Mr Putin's informal politburo. They include two deputy heads of the presidential administration: Igor Sechin, who officially controls the flow of documents but also oversees economic matters, and Viktor Ivanov, responsible for personnel in the Kremlin and beyond. Then come Nikolai Patrushev, the head of the FSB, and Sergei Ivanov, a former defence minister and now the first deputy prime minister. All are from St Petersburg, and all served in intelligence or counter-intelligence. Mr Sechin is the only one who does not advertise his background.

That two of the most influential men, Mr Sechin and Viktor Ivanov, hold only fairly modest posts (each is a deputy head) and seldom appear in public is misleading. It was, after all, common Soviet practice to have a deputy, often linked to the KGB, who carried more weight than his notional boss. "These people feel more comfortable when they are in the shadows," explains Ms Kryshtanovskaya.

In any event, each of these KGB veterans has a plethora of followers in other state institutions. One of Mr Patrushev's former deputies, also from the KGB, is the minister of the interior, in charge of the police. Sergei Ivanov still commands authority within the army's headquarters. Mr Sechin has close family ties to the minister of justice. The prosecution service, which in Soviet times at least nominally controlled the KGB's work, has now become its instrument, along with the tax police.

The political clout of these *siloviki* is backed by (or has resulted in) state companies with enormous financial resources. Mr Sechin, for example, is the chairman of Rosneft, Russia's largest state-run oil company. Viktor Ivanov heads the board of directors of Almaz-Antei, the country's main producer of air-defence rockets, and of Aeroflot, the national airline. Sergei Ivanov oversees the military-industrial complex and is in charge of the newly created aircraft-industry monopoly.

But the *siloviki* reach farther, into all areas of Russian life. They can be found not just in the law-enforcement agencies but in the ministries of economy, transport, natural resources, telecoms and culture. Several KGB veterans occupy senior management posts in Gazprom, Russia's biggest company, and its pocket bank, Gazprombank (whose vice-president is the 26-year-old son of Sergei Ivanov).

Alexei Gromov, Mr Putin's trusted press secretary, sits on the board of Channel One, Russia's main television channel. The railway monopoly is headed by Vladimir Yakunin, a former diplomat who served his country at the United Nations in New York and is believed to have held a high rank in the KGB. Sergei Chemezov, Mr Putin's old KGB friend from his days in Dresden (where the president worked from 1985 to 1990), is in charge of Rosoboronexport, a state arms agency that has grown on his watch into a vast conglomerate. The list goes on.

Many officers of the active reserve have been seconded to Russia's big companies, both private and state-controlled, where they draw a salary while also remaining on the FSB payroll. "We must make sure that companies don't make decisions that are not in the interest of the state," one current FSB colonel explains. Being an active-reserve officer in a firm is, says another KGB veteran, a dream job: "You get a huge salary and you get to keep your FSB card." One such active-reserve officer is the 26-year-old son of Mr Patrushev who was last year seconded from the FSB to Rosneft, where he is now advising Mr Sechin. (After seven months at Rosneft, Mr Putin awarded Andrei Patrushev the Order of Honour, citing his professional successes and "many years of conscientious work".) Rosneft was the main recipient of Yukos's assets after the firm was destroyed.

The attack on Yukos, which entered its decisive stage just as Mr Sechin was appointed to Rosneft, was the first and most blatant example of property redistribution towards the *siloviki,* but not the only one. Mikhail Gutseriev, the owner of Russneft, a fast-growing oil company, was this month forced to give up his business after being accused of illegal activities. For a time, he had refused; but, as he explained, "they tightened the screws" and one state agency after another—the general prosecutor's office, the tax police, the interior ministry—began conducting checks on him.

From Oligarchy to Spookocracy

The transfer of financial wealth from the oligarchs to the *siloviki* was perhaps inevitable. It certainly met with no objection from most Russians, who have little sympathy for "robber barons".

It even earned the *siloviki* a certain popularity. But whether they will make a success of managing their newly acquired assets is doubtful. "They know how to break up a company or to confiscate something. But they don't know how to manage a business. They use force simply because they don't know any other method," says an ex-KGB spook who now works in business.

Curiously, the concentration of such power and economic resources in the hands of a small group of *siloviki,* who identify themselves with the state, has not alienated people in the lower ranks of the security services. There is trickle-down of a sort: the salary of an average FSB operative has gone up several times over the past decade, and a bit of freelancing is tolerated. Besides, many Russians inside and outside the ranks believe that the transfer of assets from private hands to the *siloviki* is in the interests of the state. "They are getting their own back and they have the right to do so," says Mr Goloshchapov.

The rights of the *siloviki,* however, have nothing to do with the formal kind that are spelled out in laws or in the constitution. What they are claiming is a special mission to restore the power of the state, save Russia from disintegration and frustrate the enemies that might weaken it. Such idealistic sentiments, says Mr Kondaurov, coexist with an opportunistic and cynical eagerness to seize the situation for personal or institutional gain.

The security servicemen present themselves as a tight brotherhood entitled to break any laws for the sake of their mission. Their high language is laced with profanity, and their nationalism is often combined with contempt for ordinary people. They are, however, loyal to each other.

Competition to enter the service is intense. The KGB picked its recruits carefully. Drawn from various institutes and universities, they then went to special KGB schools. Today the FSB Academy in Moscow attracts the children of senior *siloviki;* a vast new building will double its size. The point, says Mr Galeotti, the British analyst, "is not just what you learn, but who you meet there".

Graduates of the FSB Academy may well agree. "A Chekist is a breed," says a former FSB general. A good KGB heritage— a father or grandfather, say, who worked for the service—is highly valued by today's *siloviki.* Marriages between *siloviki* clans are also encouraged.

Viktor Cherkesov, the head of Russia's drug-control agency, who was still hunting dissidents in the late 1980s, has summed up the FSB psychology in an article that has become the manifesto of the *siloviki* and a call for consolidation.

We [*siloviki*] must understand that we are one whole. History ruled that the weight of supporting the Russian state should fall on our shoulders. I believe in our ability, when we feel danger, to put aside everything petty and to remain faithful to our oath.

As well as invoking secular patriotism, Russia's security bosses can readily find allies among the priesthood. Next to the FSB building in Lubyanka Square stands the 17th-century church of the Holy Wisdom, "restored in August 2001 with zealous help from the FSB," says a plaque. Inside, freshly painted icons gleam with gold. "Thank God there is the FSB. All power is from God and so is theirs," says Father Alexander, who leads the service. A former KGB general agrees: "They really believe that they were chosen and are guided by God and that even the high oil prices they have benefited from are God's will."

Sergei Grigoryants, who has often been interrogated and twice imprisoned (for anti-Soviet propaganda) by the KGB, says the security chiefs believe "that they are the only ones who have the real picture and understanding of the world." At the centre of this picture is an exaggerated sense of the enemy, which justifies their very existence: without enemies, what are they for? "They believe they can see enemies where ordinary people can't," says Ms Kryshtanovskaya.

"A few years ago, we succumbed to the illusion that we don't have enemies and we have paid dearly for that," Mr Putin told the FSB in 1999. It is a view shared by most KGB veterans and their successors. The greatest danger comes from the West, whose aim is supposedly to weaken Russia and create disorder. "They want to make Russia dependent on their technologies," says a current FSB staffer. "They have flooded our market with their goods. Thank God we still have nuclear arms." The siege mentality of the *siloviki* and their anti-Westernism have played well with the Russian public. Mr Goloshchapov, the private agents' spokesman, expresses the mood this way: "In Gorbachev's time Russia was liked by the West and what did we get for it? We have surrendered everything: eastern Europe, Ukraine, Georgia. NATO has moved to our borders."

From this perspective, anyone who plays into the West's hands at home is the internal enemy. In this category are the last free-thinking journalists, the last NGOs sponsored by the West and the few liberal politicians who still share Western values.

To sense the depth of these feelings, consider the response of one FSB officer to the killing of Anna Politkovskaya, a journalist whose books criticising Mr Putin and his brutal war in Chechnya are better known outside than inside Russia. "I don't know who killed her, but her articles were beneficial to the Western press. She deserved what she got." And so, by this token, did Litvinenko, the ex-KGB officer poisoned by polonium in London last year.

In such a climate, the idea that Russia's security services are entitled to deal ruthlessly with enemies of the state, wherever they may be, has gained wide acceptance and is supported by a new set of laws. One, aimed at "extremism", gives the FSB and other agencies ample scope to pursue anyone who acts or speaks against the Kremlin. It has already been invoked against independent analysts and journalists. A lawyer who complained to the Constitutional Court about the FSB's illegal tapping of his client's telephone has been accused of disclosing state secrets. Several scientists who collaborated with foreign firms are in jail for treason.

Despite their loyalty to old Soviet roots, today's security bosses differ from their predecessors. They do not want a return to communist ideology or an end to capitalism, whose fruits they enjoy. They have none of the asceticism of their forebears. Nor do they relish mass repression: in a country where fear runs deep, attacking selected individuals does the job. But the concentration of such power and money in the hands of the security services does not bode well for Russia.

And Not Very Good at Their Job

The creation of enemies may smooth over clan disagreements and fuel nationalism, but it does not make the country more secure or prosperous. While the FSB reports on the ever-rising numbers of foreign spies, accuses scientists of treason and hails its "brotherhood", Russia remains one of the most criminalised, corrupt and bureaucratic countries in the world.

During the crisis at a school in Beslan in 2004, the FSB was good at harassing journalists trying to find out the truth. But it could not even cordon off the school in which the hostages were held. Under the governorship of an ex-FSB colleague of Mr Putin, Ingushetia, the republic that borders Chechnya, has descended into a new theatre of war. The army is plagued by crime and bullying. Private businessmen are regularly hassled by law-enforcement agencies. Russia's foreign policy has turned out to be self-fulfilling: by perpetually denouncing enemies on every front, it has helped to turn many countries from potential friends into nervous adversaries.

The rise to power of the KGB veterans should not have been surprising. In many ways, argues Inna Solovyova, a Russian cultural historian, it had to do with the qualities that Russians find appealing in their rulers: firmness, reserve, authority and a degree of mystery. "The KGB fitted this description, or at least knew how to seem to fit it."

But are they doing the country any good? "People who come from the KGB are tacticians. We have never been taught to solve strategic tasks," says Mr Kondaurov. The biggest problem of all, he and a few others say, is the agency's loss of professionalism. He blushes when he talks about the polonium capers in London. "We never sank to this level," he sighs. "What a blow to the country's reputation!"

From *The Economist*, August 25, 2007, pp. 25–28. Copyright © 2007 by The Economist Newspaper Ltd. Reprinted by permission via Copyright Clearance Center.

Why Can't Uncle Sam Spy?

The problem is red tape, turf battles and no spies on the ground, say experts.

ANTHONY YORK

What's wrong with American intelligence? Not surprisingly, it's a question that is being asked everywhere in the wake of last Tuesday's horrific terrorist attacks. There is no simple answer, say former law enforcement officials and experts in intelligence. But they point to three things: excessive bureaucratic oversight, which ties intelligence agencies' hands and prevents them from responding quickly; an over-reliance on high-tech surveillance and a corresponding failure to develop on-the-ground operations; and poor coordination, both between the FBI and the CIA and between those agencies and their foreign counterparts.

Efforts to address the first problem—cutting through the bureaucracy that tangles intelligence operations—have already begun. Law enforcement officials, led by Attorney General John Ashcroft and FBI Director Robert Mueller, are asking Congress to give the intelligence community more leeway in both international and domestic surveillance.

But the call to give more authority to intelligence operations has alarmed civil libertarians, who fear that America's latest crisis will, like so many crises before it, erode liberties guaranteed by the Fourth Amendment, which prohibits "unreasonable" search and seizure.

"Terror, by its very nature, is intended not only to kill and destroy," says Anthony Romero, executive director of the ACLU. "Terror is also designed to intimidate a people and force them to take actions that may not be in their long-term best interests. If we allow our freedoms to be undermined, the terrorists will have won."

There is an inherent tension between a constitutional system that strives to protect civil liberties, and one that also must work clandestinely to protect its citizens. But American intelligence agencies exacerbated this tension, and brought many of their current problems on themselves, by illegally spying on American citizens.

These activities were first revealed in December 1974, when New York Times reporter Seymour Hersh reported how the CIA violated its own charter by spying on antiwar protesters and others on the left during the Johnson and Nixon administrations. Similar revelations about the COINTELPRO operation at the FBI under J. Edgar Hoover led to even widespread mistrust of our intelligence agencies.

Within days of Hersh's story, President Gerald Ford appointed a commission headed by Vice President Nelson Rockefeller to look into the allegations. That was soon followed by two congressional committees, one headed by Idaho Democrat Frank Church, the other by Rep. Otis Pike, D-N.Y. In the months that followed, the Pike and Church committees shone the spotlight on an intelligence operation run amok with nobody to keep it in check.

Until the Church and Pike committees called for reform, there was no congressional oversight of American intelligence agencies. Pike and Church's investigations led to a series of reforms and legislative checks on those agencies, including the creation of the House and Senate intelligence committees.

Even ex-spooks acknowledge that America's intelligence agencies were out of control. "These were by and large problems of our own making," says Daniel Coulson, a former FBI commander who founded the bureau's counter-terrorism squad. "We did some things that were absolutely ridiculous, and because of that a tremendous cloud of suspicion grew over the FBI. Even now, I think that's part of the problem. People are concerned with how much authority you should give to the bureau."

But Coulson and others in the intelligence community say the reforms spawned by Church and Pike, while well-intentioned, were clumsy, bureaucratic and overly restrictive. And they say that Congress doesn't give intelligence agencies enough credit for how much they have changed since the mid-1970s.

"The bureau has changed the way they do business, in part because there is tremendous oversight," he says. "But I think that Congress doesn't fully appreciate the fact that the bureau did change."

One of the big changes to come out of the investigations of the mid-'70s was instituting a Department of Justice review of the legality of any FBI request to conduct surveillance. That, Coulson said, has created a labyrinth of bureaucracy, and has left the agency unable to keep up with terrorists and criminal organizations.

"You don't want to take the Constitution out of the process, but you can take the administrative burden out of the process," Coulson says. "Just take the B.S. out of it. You have a head of the bureau who is appointed by the president, and confirmed by the Senate. Then you emasculate him by putting a level of bureaucracy in with the Department of Justice. I'm not saying the FBI should divorce itself from the Department of Justice. But if you have a presidential appointee making these requests, I don't think you should subject his judgment to scrutiny from a low- or mid-level DOJ attorney who doesn't understand intelligence. Agents need to be cut loose to do their thing."

In fact, the bureaucratic shackles on intelligence agencies were significantly loosened just a few years ago. After the bombing of the federal building in Oklahoma City in 1995, Congress quickly approved a measure known as the Omnibus Counterterrorism Act of 1995. That bill addressed many of the same concerns the FBI and CIA are raising now. It granted much broader wiretapping authority for law enforcement with less judicial oversight and access to personal and financial records without a warrant. The bill also gave the president more leeway to designate groups as official terrorist organizations, in effect enabling the government to seize the assets of those groups and their supporters.

But Coulson and other critics think there's still too much structural bureaucracy.

In a press conference Monday, Attorney General Ashcroft called for further latitude, asking for even more wiretap authority and stiffer penalties for nations that harbor terrorists. "We need these tools to fight the terrorism threat which exists in the United States and we must meet that growing threat," he said.

Craig Eisendrath, a senior fellow at CIP and editor of the book "National Insecurity: U.S. Intelligence After the Cold War," doesn't buy the argument that reforms have hampered the CIA and the FBI. The '70s reforms "have not inhibited the intelligence community one whit," he says.

"If we're going to increase the CIA and FBI's ability to spy," he adds, "we also should take another look at the legal procedures by which Americans can protect themselves against unauthorized restrictions of free speech and movement."

Robert White, president of the Center for International Policy and former ambassador to El Salvador under President Carter, agrees with Coulson that intelligence efforts have been bogged down by red tape. "It has become a huge, layered bureaucracy. It's much worse than any other civilian agency," he says. "It's impossible to get a fast response or fast action out of that of bureaucracy."

That, he says, should be a justification to reassess and perhaps even cut intelligence budgets, rather than just throw more money at an agency in need of structural reform.

"It seems to me that what you need is a small agency with a few highly skilled people that can go and get the assets that they need. I have just seen time and again the failures of our efforts. I was in Afghanistan in the late '80s; I talked to our chargé there. We didn't have any assets there."

But bureaucracy isn't the only problem facing U.S. intelligence. Eisendrath puts the blame for the poor quality of U.S. intelligence in recent years on the spies themselves.

"What needs to be improved is the quality of the personnel," he says. "A lot of people don't have adequate area skills. Our human intelligence is not working well. We're not giving our people the kind of training they need to do good jobs."

One of the places where the agencies are weakest is in infiltration of terrorist organizations. Neither the CIA nor the FBI has shown the ability to put operatives in the field to do this slow, dirty and dangerous work. A sign of just how dire the situation is came Monday, when Mueller publicly stumped for new FBI recruits, saying the agency needs people with a "professional level in Arabic and Farsi."

Coulson says much of the blame for poor intelligence gathering can be laid at the feet of the Carter administration, which focused on technology as a substitute for agents on the ground. "This really started with Stansfield Turner," Coulson says of Carter's CIA chief. "He bounced and went almost exclusively with NSA intercepts and satellite photos. We knew it was a mistake then. It's been a mistake forever. It's absolute insanity. But, a guy gets appointed as the head of the CIA with a huge ego and not a lot of experience, and that's what happens.

"That totally changed the face of the CIA," Coulson says of the focus on technology. "Years of building up contacts and goodwill and rapport were just flushed down the drain. That takes decades to recover from."

Organization and turf are other significant problems, experts agree. Coulson says there must be a diminution of the interagency rivalry between the FBI and CIA, and more multi-lateral cooperation. "I think there has to be more cooperation. Maybe we have to offer other countries some incentives to cooperate with us. They are natives and native speakers. We need them to get good information. We're not going to solve this through technology. We're going to solve it by people telling us what happened, and where these people are hiding."

While White agrees, he says now would be an ideal time to overhaul the entire structure of our domestic and international intelligence networks. "The CIA has failed to adjust to the post-Cold War era," he says. "We have an oversupply in CIA officials mucking around in Latin America and Western Europe and Africa and Australia, and nobody concentrating on the hard targets."

Some of the concerns expressed by Coulter will be addressed on Thursday, when Sen. Bob Graham, D-Fla., chairman of the Senate's Select Committee on Intelligence, is expected to introduce a package of intelligence reforms. One of the aims of the new measures will be to centralize all intelligence information under a single intelligence coordinator, to be based in the White House. Currently, eight of the 13 agencies that gather intelligence report directly to the secretary of defense, instead of the director of the CIA.

As America's intelligence agencies take center stage in the battle to ensure national security, Coulson says civil libertarians must moderate their shrill demands for privacy—demands which he says often fly in the face of reason.

"It's a built-in resistance to giving the FBI more authority, that comes from private interest groups or civil libertarians who don't understand it," Coulson says. He points to certain policy changes that would enable law enforcement agencies to keep up with modern technology—such as the rise of digital and cellular phones—without compromising civil rights.

For example, he says, the way the rules work now, agents must receive a new warrant every time they want to tap a given phone line. But with the rise in cellular phones, criminals can change numbers often. In their effort to keep up, Coulson says, law enforcement wastes precious time requesting new warrants, a problem that could be solved if they were given permission to listen in on individuals rather than one specific phone number.

"Congress thinks we're asking for increased authority to go out and tap everybody's phone. That's not it at all. You'd still have to get a warrant and all that. We just want the technical ability to keep up. This should have been done 5–6 years ago."

UNIT 6

Public Policy: Defining Public, Effects and Trade-offs

Unit Selections

Key Points to Consider

- What are the criteria of a good policy?

- What factors facilitate the successful pursuit of policies?

- What are the trade-offs between economic growth and job security?

- Is it acceptable that some are made worse off if others are made better off?

- How does economic success affect institutional transformation in China, India, and Japan?

- How does economic success affect cultural transformation in China, India, and Japan?

Student Web Site

www.mhcls.com

Internet References

Asian Development Bank
   http://www.adb.org/Countries/
Carnegie Endowment for International Peace
   http://www.ceip.org
IISDnet
   http://www.iisd.org/default.asp
Organization for Economic Cooperation and Development
   http://www.oecd.org/home/
World Bank
   http://www.worldbank.org

The previous three units focused on how institutions in government affect political behavior and responses. This unit discusses the systematic treatment of the outcomes from government institutions, specifically, public policy. That is, the articles address the "why, what, and how" questions regarding public policy.

We begin with, "What is public policy?". Public policy refers to the government decisions and actions taken in response to social problems. Christopher Wlezien (2004) identifies nine public policy spending areas: environment, health, education, city-development, social welfare, defense, space, foreign aid, and crime.[1] Francis and Weber (1980) describe 20 policy areas that include finance and economics, taxation, labor, business, civil rights, highways, and elections.[2] The lists are not exhaustive; this suggests that many social issues may fall within the scope of public concerns. Consequently, it means that few issues are beyond the purview of government response.

This raises a major debate in public policy: what is public and what private? That is, a major consideration regarding what is public policy lies with clarifying what are the limits to the public sphere and how to limit government authority so that it does not intrude into individual privacy. Few policy areas are free from this debate; even in the realm of economic development, there is the argument that public policy is interfering with the decisions of private capital. In fact, businesses argue that government should minimize its policy presence to allow the free market, or the "invisible-hand," to work the economy. However, as the article on job security argues, this presumes that the free market is the only way to economic development. The successes of Japan, and European nations such as Germany and Denmark, suggest otherwise: that there may be room to incorporate some security. If the dispute about what is private and what is public in economics seems tense, consider areas such as reproductive rights, or the right to die.

The tensions over the debate of what constitutes public policy may lead to the temptation to circumvent the debate by limiting the government's role. Why pursue public policy and open that can of worms? We need public policy because many of the social issues that are of public concern—such as foreign aid, defense, health, and the environment—are not confined to a community. In these instances, government response provides the efficient and authoritative resolution. Thus, the article on state actor-social movement coalitions reveals that the turnaround in Japan's environment lies in the local government's enactment of anti-pollution policies in response to citizens' demands that calcified into national laws and the institutionalization of the Environment Agency in 1971. Likewise, the articles on China and India show how government policies, such as the encouragement of foreign investment, helped develop their respective economies that were once deemed as having "little prospect."

Yet, public policy involves trade-offs; indeed, it is probably realistic to consider that social issues are sometimes unsolvable

© Royalty-Free/CORBIS

within or between communities because there are trade-offs that require the weight and enforcement of government authority. Where there are clear winners and losers, disputes perpetuate over what is public policy or how it is pursued in order to overturn the existing stance. Thus, the article on state actor-social movement coalitions shows that prior to the environmental turnaround in Japan, the citizens were on the losing side of the government's refusal to enact anti-pollution laws, while businesses benefited from the government's stance. More than a decade of mobilization passed before the hard-earned environmentally friendly laws were enacted, only to suffer from a backlash following Japan's economic slowdown in the 1970s. The article on China points out that the economic reforms to encourage foreign investment also ended "lifetime employment" for workers. Lifetime employment in China is the equivalent of social security in the U.S., that is, it is the workers' source of social and economic stability toward the end of life. Hence, the article reports that workers are using the language of labor contracts to sue for compensation in efforts to redress that loss. And the article on India's surging economy shows that many are left behind and some are even worse-off economically, and their situation is all the more stark given the wealth in the country. In this situation, not only are there winner and losers, but it seems that some losers may not be in any position to improve their lot.

Given the trade-offs, how is public policy evaluated? Largely, the evaluation of public policy may be boiled down to different values associated therewith: Is it about economic growth or security? Is it about wealth or inequality? Is it about equal opportunities or equal outcomes? Is it acceptable that public policy leaves some behind, or worse off, if others are better off? Such value-debates show that it is not often obvious that there is an overall "positive" to be gained from public policy. Thus, the article "Capitalism and Democracy" points out that there is no clear relationship between capitalism and democracy to support advocating capitalism. Indeed, the article on China supports that argument: China is shown as a success for developing economically by using some, but not all, aspects of capitalism. And the article on Japan hits the argument home: Japan is touted as the model for other Asian countries of a successful economy that does not succumb to western pressures of economic accountability or reciprocity to the West. The value-conflicts afflict the industrialized economies as much as the industrializing ones. The article on job security shows that industrialized countries continue to grapple with the trade-offs between job security and economic growth. More recently, in the U.S., legislators and economists questioned how the $700 billion bailout of financial institutions in 2008 might be better spent. The alternatives are numerous, including: giving $3,704 to every adult over 18; creating an education fund of $9333 for every person younger than 18; spending $14,894 to fund health care for every American who currently lacks health insurance; starting an emergency relief and job retraining program for the 9.4 million unemployed workers.[3]

The foregoing suggests that there are few easy answers related to policy-making. This emphasizes the importance of the roles of citizens and interest groups in clarifying their policy preferences and mobilizing for their causes. It also underscores the need for executive accountability and responsiveness and the legislature's representation to ensure that policy-making captures the willingness of the citizenry to make the necessary trade-offs.

Notes

1. Christopher Wlezien. 2004. "Patterns of Representation: Dynamics of Public Preferences and Policy," *Journal of Politics,* Vol. 66, No. 1 (Feb., 2004), pp. 1–24.

2. Wayne L. Francis and Ronald E. Weber. 1980. "Legislative Issues in the 50 States: Managing Complexity through Classification." *Legislative Studies Quarterly,* Vol. 5, No. 3 (Aug., 1980), pp. 407–421.

3. I thank my colleague, Gary Reich, who gathered the information from census data.

The Formation of State Actor-Social Movement Coalitions and Favorable Policy Outcomes

LINDA BREWSTER STEARNS AND PAUL D. ALMEIDA

This study examines the role of loosely-coupled state actor-social movement coalitions in creating positive policy outcomes. It specifies the organizational locations within the state most conducive to state actor-social movement ties. Using the case of Japanese anti-pollution politics between 1956 and 1976, we demonstrate that favorable policy outcomes were the result of multiple coalitions between anti-pollution movements and state agencies, opposition political parties, local governments, and the courts.

In the 1960s Japan was internationally recognized with the notorious distinction of being the most polluted country in the advanced capitalist world. Literally, hundreds of people died (and thousands more chronically sickened) as a direct result of industrial pollution (Methyl Mercury poisoning, Cadmium poisoning, PCB poisoning, SMON disease, and various airborne pollutants). By the early 1970s, the Japanese state had made a rapid U-turn and implemented a series of environmental reforms viewed as a model for the industrialized world. This article aims to explain this dramatic shift in state policy-making priorities via the formation of multiple state-movement coalitions.

For social activists state policy reform happens too infrequently. Yet when it does, it can usually be accredited to two groups: 1) the actors external to the state that have made reform a political issue—social movement organizations, the mass media, and public opinion; and 2) the actors internal to the state that have ushered the reform through the state apparatus—politicians and state managers. Much has been written about social movements and the conditions that facilitate or hamper their success (Amenta and Young 1999b; Burstein, Einwohner, and Hollander 1995; Cress and Snow 2000; Gamson 1990; Giugni 1998; Piven and Cloward 1979). Less scholarly attention has focused on the relationship between social movements and state actors (Goldstone 2003; Wolfson 2001), specifically the organizational structures that give rise to the loosely-coupled

coalitions that form between these two groups and lead to favorable policy outcomes. In this article, we focus on this partnership between state actors and a social movement, rather than on the social movement itself.

Modern states are typically composed of nested and segmented administrative units that house many competing actors. Given this structural patterning, social movements can take advantage of the complex and decentralized nature of most democratic states to create state actor-social movement coalitions that represent potential venues for action. We define a state actor-social movement coalition broadly. A state-movement coalition comes into existence when state actors agree to apply their organizational resources and influence in ways that further the general aims of a social movement.

State actors participate in state-movement coalitions for a variety of reasons. Some state-movement coalitions involve institutional activists (i.e., "social movement participants who occupy formal statuses within the government and who pursue social movement goals through conventional bureaucratic channels" [Santoro and McGuire 1997:503]). These institutional activists are committed to the social movement's objectives and motivated by intrinsic rewards (Ganz 2000). While such coalitions have the potential to be ongoing, most state-movement coalitions are loosely coupled and temporary, consisting of state actors with shifting interests. Some state actors enter a state-movement coalition because they are ideologically predisposed to the movement's objectives. Other state actors participate in coalitions as a means of promoting their own agendas (Skocpol 1985). They enter state-movement coalitions primarily to pursue their own extrinsic rewards (i.e., further their careers and/or increase their status). Still other state actors, because of the location and function of their unit, take up the claims of a social movement to increase their unit's vitality and legitimacy within the state apparatus. State-movement coalitions, regardless of the state actors' motivations, increase the probability of producing positive outcomes for social movements. With the creation of state-movement coalitions, social movements are granted a level of legitimacy, and perhaps more important, indirect access to the state's decision-making structures.

In this article we examine the coalitions created between the Japanese environmental movement and four groups of state actors: 1) weak state agencies; 2) opposition political parties; 3) local governments; and 4) the courts. Initially, all five groups—the environmental movement and the four categories of state actors—had little influence in state policy-making and faced three powerful adversaries: 1) the industrial business establishment; 2) the entrenched Liberal Democratic Party (LDP); and 3) the more powerful state bureaucracies (in particular the most influential—the Ministry of International Trade and Industry [MITI] with its close relations to the business establishment). Building on recent developments in political sociology, we identify the institutional structures conducive to the formation of the state-movement coalitions that shaped policy reform. We also examine the policy impact of each state-movement coalition and show that the unprecedented change in state environmental policy that occurred in Japan depended on the creation of multiple state actor-movement coalitions.

Political Institutions and State Actor-Movement Coalitions

Once a social movement forms and is relatively unified, a state's reaction to a social movement might range from ignoring or repressing it, to addressing its demands either symbolically or with real change (Tilly 1978). The first choice of a democratic government is often to ignore a social movement with the expectation that it will defuse and disappear. In such a situation, a movement is likely to attempt to engage the state by influencing public opinion, employing disruptive actions, and creating electoral uncertainty (Almeida and Stearns 1998; Burstein 1979; Piven and Cloward 1979). Disruptive actions work to raise public awareness and increase the pressure on the state to address the issue. Changing public opinion catches the attention of state actors by increasing electoral uncertainty and raising the possibility that the distribution of status and power within the state will change. Because social movements threaten the status quo or the "rules of the game," few state actors have the incentive and/or the opportunity to enter into a state-movement coalition (Kriesi et al. 1995:54).

We argue that the political institutional structure of the state plays a key role in determining which state actors benefit or are receptive to forming state-movement coalitions. Specifically we discuss how the level of bureaucratic development, the electoral system, and the degree of fragmentation of authority within the state (Amenta 1998; McCarthy and Wolfson 1992) affect the prospects that a state-movement coalition will form with the following state actors: 1) state agencies; 2) oppositional political parties; 3) local governments; and 4) courts.

State Agencies

When a social movement grows in size and public opinion support to where the state must acknowledge it as a political actor, the probability increases that the movement will form a coalition with an "in-house" state agency. State agencies in their roles as policy advocates and regulators have the potential to grant social movements important access into the state's policy-making apparatus.

A social movement introducing a new issue may find there is no agency to address its demands. Moreover, state-oriented social movements are often in conflict with agencies involved in promoting business confidence and supporting capital accumulation (Block 1987). Such agencies are often the larger, better-funded, and more politically influential members of the polity. Their agendas reflect the strong lobbying efforts of large corporations, and their staffs frequently come from the very groups the social movement opposes (Domhoff 2002). Hence, these agencies are not usually candidates for a state-movement coalition.

The more highly developed the democratic state bureaucracy (i.e., in terms of size and differentiation), however, the more likely there resides within it an agency favorable to the social movement's objectives (Amenta and Young 1999a). In most cases the agency is tied to the state's legitimation function and handles citizens' rights and quality of life programs (Faber and O'Connor 1989). Historically, such agencies are under-funded and politically weak. As a result, an agency might be receptive to forming a state-movement coalition if the movement's issue falls within the agency's policy domain, promotes its agenda, advances its status, and/or increases its budget.

When no appropriate agency exists, designate or otherwise, a social movement often pushes to have one established (Baumgartner and Jones 1993). If successful, the new agency in order to overcome the "liability of newness" and survive will seek internal and external support for its raison d'etre (Stinchcombe 1965). Internally, as part of its staff, the agency might appoint institutional activists or known movement supporters. Externally, as part of its constituency, the agency might foster an ongoing relationship with the social movement.

In cases where the social movement addresses an established issue, the designated agency might have been created in a past social struggle over a similar issue (Bourdieu 1998). In general, we expect such an agency to be amenable to forming a state-movement coalition. Even more so if its staff consists of insider institutional activists and, in addressing the issue, the agency stands to acquire greater resources and status (Amenta and Zylan 1991). Indeed, prior to the formation of the state-movement coalition, the agency might have attempted to realize some of the same kinds of policies as desired by the social movement but lacked the political capital to do so. Such was the situation of hazardous waste policymaking in the United States. Only in the late 1970s, with the rise of local movements against toxic waste (in particular Love Canal) and their exposure in the mass media, was the EPA strong enough to pass through Congress the Superfund in 1980 (Szasz 1994)—a nationally comprehensive hazardous waste remediation and disposal program.

The above discussion suggests that the more highly developed a democratic state's bureaucracy the greater the likelihood a social movement will form a coalition with an established or new state agency. Furthermore, this partnership most likely occurs when the agency's primary mission is the maintenance of the state's institutional credibility (e.g., healthcare, social welfare, anti-discrimination, environment, labor, housing, etc.).

Oppositional Political Parties

Looking at such things as the restrictions on political assembly, voting, and choices among leadership groups, Edwin Amenta (1998) argues, "where people count little in politics, money and access matter even more". As "people power" is the main resource of a social movement (not money or access to elite decision making) (Tarrow 1994), the level of democratic participation is key to its influence and the possibility of coalition formation. Under democratic conditions or during regime liberalization, it is often an oppositional political party that takes up the demands of a social movement (Almeida 2003; Kriesi et al. 1995).

An oppositional political party becomes a state actor when the following criteria are met: 1) the party has been granted (by the state) the legal recognition needed to run for and hold office; and 2) the party has successfully exercised that right. For it is in their role as elected officials that members of opposition parties provide social movements access to the state's policy-making apparatus.

The political party entering into a coalition will be determined in large part by the type of electoral system. One basic distinction in electoral systems is between winner-take-all and proportional representation (Amenta and Young 1999a). Proportional representation systems generally offer social movements a greater choice of parties (which translates into more ideological and policy options) from which to form a coalition (Dalton, Recchia, and Rohrschneider 2003). In addition, competition between oppositional parties increases the incentive of these parties to form a coalition with a social movement. For not only is the oppositional party competing against the dominant party for support and votes, but against other oppositional parties as well. In winner-take-all systems, on the other hand, there is less incentive for the out-of-power party to align itself with a social movement (especially one without much initial public support). Such systems also limit the social movements' options to

the ideology and policy agendas of a few (generally two) well-established parties.

In either system, all things being equal, a social movement would prefer to form a coalition with a powerful political party because such a party improves its chances of accomplishing its goals (i.e., more policy implementation capacity) (Burstein et al. 1995:289). This is often not possible, as entrenched powerful parties tend to view social movements as challengers to the status quo and routine politics (Kriesi et al. 1995). One exception might be in a perceived tight election if a political party views the social movement's sympathy pools as large enough to influence the election's outcome. Such was the case with the Social Democratic Party (SDP) in West Germany in the mid-1980s when the party took up the peace movement's cause of anti-nuclear energy and nuclear weapons deployment. Although in sharp contrast to the SDP's pro-nuclear stance of the late 1970s and early 1980s, this powerful party used the issue not only to take votes away from the increasingly successful Green Party, but also to win back their parliamentary majority by 1990 (Koopmans 1995:100–3).

Given political circumstances often the best a social movement can manage, however, is to create a coalition with a stable reform or minority party (Maguire 1995). For example, in recently democratized El Salvador, state employed medical workers and unionized physicians formed coalitions in 1999–2000 and 2002–2003 with the largest oppositional political party to prevent the privatization of the state-managed public healthcare system. Both times this oppositional party-movement coalition materialized during the months of the parliamentary election campaign and vote (Almeida 2002:179). On both occasions the movement achieved their stated goal of halting the privatization process, while the opposition party increased its number of parliamentary seats (Schuld 2003). The political and electoral weakness of opposition parties makes them more receptive to creating new coalitions and constituencies. For this reason, a social movement is more likely to form a coalition with a stable, ideologically similar, minority or reform opposition party.

Local Governments and Courts

We maintain that state-movement coalitions are more likely to develop in democratic nation states characterized by autonomous local governments and/or courts. Several studies (Amenta and Young 1999a; Andrews 2001:90; Baiocchi 2003; Kriesi and Wisler 1999) have shown that federalist political structures (e.g., Brazil, Canada, India, New Zealand, Switzerland, and the United States) delegate more power to local governments than top-down centralized governments (e.g., Austria, France, Norway, and Sweden). By increasing the number of "entree points," we expect the fragmentation of governmental authority to expand the potential for state-movement coalition formation (McCarthy and Wolfson 1992:287–92). Local governments offer social movements the potential for a more straightforward, hence quicker, path to policy channels (e.g., face-to-face interactions in publicly accessible city council meetings). Courts assist social movements by granting them a public forum for their views (with the cases themselves often eliciting important media coverage)." Courts also facilitate social movements by handing down decisions ordering changes (e.g., integrating schools). Finally courts can enjoin legislative action, rule on compensation settlements, and issue cease-and-desist orders.

That local government and court-movement coalitions can influence social policy has been effectively demonstrated in the United States in the case of the ban on same-sex marriages. During the late 1990s and early 2000s, the gay and lesbian movement took its case for equal access to marriage rights to the courts and local governments. It found support for its struggle in places such as Hawaii (courts), Vermont (courts), Massachusetts (courts), San Francisco (local government and courts), New Mexico (local government), and Oregon (local government). In 2004, San Francisco Mayor Gavin Newsom announced that the city would issue marriage licenses to same-sex couples. On four separate occasions, judges have refused to stop San Francisco from issuing marriage licenses to same-sex couples. When California Governor Schwarzenegger declared the licenses illegal, San Francisco city and county officials, with the help of such groups as Lambda Legal (a gay rights legal organization), went on the offensive and filed a lawsuit against the state. So successful has the gay and lesbian movement's tactic to change social policy at the local government and court levels been that President Bush announced his support for a Constitutional amendment to define marriage as the legal union between one man and one woman. In a February 2004 press speech, the President referred several times to "activist judges and local authorities" and stated that, "unless action is taken, we can expect more arbitrary court decisions, more litigation, more defiance of the law by local officials" (CNN.com 2004). Below, we specify the mechanisms that bring local governments and courts into coalitions with social movements.

Local Government. Municipal governments are generally more likely to enter coalitions with social movements than national governments because of the more volatile nature of local elections. At the local level, a social movement needs to mobilize fewer voters to have an electoral impact. In addition, campaign financing by more powerful lobbying groups is less common at the local level, providing a relatively more balanced playing field for reform-minded movements (Pollin and Luce 1998; Wolfson 2001:173–6).

The likelihood that a social movement will form a coalition with a local government is greatest when the social movement's cause has a widespread, direct, and negative effect on the locality, as in the case of toxic dumps and plant layoffs. The greater the consensus within the community that a problem exists, the more likely the social movement will form a state-movement coalition (Lofland 1989; McCarthy and Wolfson 1992) with an established local political party (Swarts 2003). If the established party refuses to take up its cause, a social movement will align itself with a reform party or run their own candidates. This was the strategy of the Chicano civil rights movement in south Texas in the 1960s and 1970s. Mexican Americans created their own slates of candidates and political parties (e.g., PASSO and La Raza Unida) to compete in city council and school board elections long held by white minorities (Navarro 1998).

If a local government-movement coalition is successful implementing reform (and this is never easy given the embeddedness of political and economic power and the outsider status of challenger movements), it provides a commanding example. Success imparts a template for change and a sense of efficacy—"it can be done!" Both strengthen a social movement's mobilization efforts (Klandermans 1997) and encourage further local government-movement coalitions. For example, Robert Pollin and Stephanie Luce (1998) show in the United States that campaigns for a living wage have rapidly multiplied as a result of local government-movement coalition victories. In 1999 only five years after the passage of the first local living wage ordinance in Baltimore, 22 other major cities had implemented similar statutes, including New York and Los Angeles (Martin 2001). By 2003, 112 cities, towns, and school districts had enacted such laws. Hanspeter Kriesi and Dominique Wisler (1999) also demonstrated that the movement for direct democracy laws (e.g., direct legislation and popular referendum) in Switzerland spread rapidly across cantons in the late nineteenth century once they were adopted in the canton of Zurich. The actual practice of direct democracy laws at the local level gave them "empirical credibility" for national diffusion and eventual enactment at the federal level.

Courts. Social movements often try to engage the court system. Social movement-court coalitions differ from state agency-, opposition party-, or local government-coalitions in that courts do not, nor can they, seek out or maintain an ongoing relation with a social movement. Because courts must maintain an appearance of neutrality, if a social movement-court coalition is to form, it is the social movement that must initiate and set the agenda for the relation. Nevertheless, courts are very important coalition partners for furthering the claims of social movements. This is demonstrated by the fact that mature social movements maintain their own legal organization(s) (e.g., abortion rights: National Abortion Rights Action League; environmental movement: National Resources Defense Council; etc.).

While the rationale of lifetime appointments is to guarantee impartial judicial officials, judges vary in their ability and desire to be neutral. The political intensity surrounding judicial appointments attests to this. For example, in the United States, the Republican and Democratic Parties consistently battle over the selection of judges. Furthermore, U.S.

presidents have on occasion taken control over the process to guarantee the assignment of their selected candidates. In 2004, during a congressional recess, President Bush did an end run around the "advise and consent" clause of the Constitution by appointing two conservative judges the Senate failed to confirm—Charles Pickering and William Pryor.

By initiating cases, social movements attempt to address immediate grievances, receive monetary compensation, and most importantly set legal precedent (Burstein 1991; McCammon and Kane 1997). For example, Lambda Legal litigated a case for marriage equality in Hawaii in the mid-1990s. In the first ruling of its kind, a Hawaii judge ordered that civil marriage licenses could not be restricted to heterosexual couples. Although a voter initiative later quashed the ruling, Lambda Legal (2004) went on to serve as a "friend of the court" in similar lawsuits in Vermont and Massachusetts. These actions led to civil unions for same-sex couples in Vermont and the order for the issuance of marriage licenses to applicants of the same gender by May 2004 in Massachusetts.

The acceptance by a court to address a case brought by a social movement creates the opportunity for a court-movement coalition to develop. While it is unlikely that any judge or court would openly acknowledge an ideological leaning, historical accounts (e.g., the liberal Warren court) and present day events (e.g., the Supreme Court's involvement in the 2000 Florida election decision) led social scientists to question otherwise. Once a social movement's case is accepted by a court, it can expect at minimum to have its claims given public voice, and at maximum, if successful, some action granted (Kane 2003).

In sum, the relative autonomy and greater access of court systems and local governments increase the likelihood for coalitions to form between these units and a social movement. Furthermore, the formation of a successful local government-movement coalition can lead to other local government-movement coalitions (Martin 2001).

Power in Numbers

Finally, by creating as many state-movement coalitions as possible, a social movement increases its probability of having its demands addressed. For example, recent cross-national work on environmental organizations suggests that environmental movements try to influence public opinion and to establish on-going relations with multiple state actors including state agencies, political parties, local governments, and courts. According to Russell Dalton and associates (2003:751) in a study of 248 environmental groups in 59 nations, they report: 1) 64 percent of environment groups claimed that they had made efforts to mobilize public opinion; 2) 51 percent had informal meetings with civil servants or government ministers while 39 percent had formal meetings; 3) 44 percent participated in government advisory commissions; 4) 45 percent reported contact with local government

authorities; 5) 15 percent acknowledged having contact with officials of political parties; and 6) 15 percent reported taking legal action through the courts or other judicial bodies.

We contend that there is power in numbers. First, with more than one coalition, a social movement cannot be relegated to a single "institutional home" or ineffectual state agency (Bonastia 2000). Second, the more coalitions formed across different state structures, the more entree points a social movement has to strategically apply and sustain pressure. Third, a greater number of coalitions helps to decrease the impact of a veto or unfavorable ruling by state actors in political structures where authoritative power is fragmented. Finally, multiple coalitions can have an additive effect, increasing the potential impact of each individual coalition.

Although we believe that a coordinated effort among coalitions increases their political impact, such an effort is not always possible. State-movement coalitions are not only loosely coupled within themselves but between themselves as well. Often the only common denominator among coalitions is the social movement and its goals. This is because each group of state actors enters into a coalition with its own interests and agenda.

It is also not necessary for all four types of coalitions to be present for positive national policy outcomes to occur. At minimum a state-movement coalition must exist with a national level state actor (state agency, opposition political party, or national court). The reason being, there has to be within the national state apparatus a coalition member with access to the organizational resources, legitimacy, and most important, authority required to usher through (state agency and/or opposition party) or decree (courts) national policy reforms (Burstein et al. 1995:284). Local coalition partners (government, opposition party, or court), while important as examples of change, are ultimately limited by the geographical scope of their authority.

The more entrenched the in-power party, however, the greater the need for multiple coalitions. In such cases, court and local government-movement coalitions help to chip away at the hold of the ruling party. Court-movement coalitions increase the costs (in terms of dollars, mass-media coverage, and public opinion) of government inaction; local government-movement coalitions provide a blueprint for change (in terms of electoral shifts and models of policy reform).

It should also be noted that state actors in general have more direct access to the media, and are more likely to be perceived as authorities regarding a policy conflict, than are social movement activists by themselves (Best 1989). Hence, social movements that form coalitions with state actors can expect to reach a much wider audience via the mass media, as the media is more willing to listen to sympathetic governmental authorities, especially when public policy is being debated.

In summary, we believe state agency-, oppositional party-, local government-, and court-movement coalitions all play key roles in bringing about shifts in social policy that favorably address the demands of social movements. We expect the greater the number of state-movement coalitions (i.e., state agency, oppositional party, local government, and court) present, the more likely policy change will occur. . . .

Conclusion

Even into the late 1990s and early 2000s several notable review, empirical, and theoretical articles on movement impacts and consequences concurred that the study of movement outcomes is much more underdeveloped than studies focusing on movement emergence, recruitment, tactical choices, and the mobilization process (see Amenta and Young 1999b:22; Andrews 2002:105; Burstein et al. 1995:276; Cress and Snow 2000:1063–4; Giugni 1998:373; Giugni 1999:xiv–xv; Meyer 2002:6). We believe the kinds of state actor-social movement coalitions found in this case provide a useful framework to advance the study of policy outcomes of state-oriented social movements. Political process models of social movements have long noted the importance of influential and elite allies (e.g., scientific and legal experts, mass media, other social movements, celebrities, etc.) for explaining movement outcomes. Indeed, as Edwin Amenta and Michael Young (1999b) note, "challengers are rarely alone in pressing for collective benefits for a group".

This study suggests that a focus on state-centered allies may be the most fruitful avenue for understanding the variation in the level of policy reform achieved by national social movements. The most successful movements of the past few decades (e.g., civil rights, women's rights, environmental, and anti-nuclear/peace movements) seem to have generated similar kinds of multiple state actor-social movement relations as observed in Japan in the late 1960s and early 1970s. That is, they entered into loose coalitions with the courts, local governments, state agencies, and political parties to enact policy change (Burstein 1991; Costain 1992; Meyer and Marullo 1992; Sawyers and Meyer 1999). Along these lines, scholars are increasingly examining the relationship between social movements and state actors (e.g., courts, political parties, legislatures, and institutional activists) to explain the variation in policy outcomes (see Burstein 1991; Goldstone 2003; Kane 2003; McCammon and Kane 1997; Santoro and McGuire 1997; Wolfson 2001). Not only do we concur with this recent trend of analyzing the intersection of specific state actors and social movements to understand differential levels of policy change, but also propose that the existence of multiple coalitions between state actors and social movements greatly raises the probability that favorable policy implementation occurs.

Favorable policy outcomes range from the state's acceptance of demands, placing them on the policy agenda to adopting new policies and finally implementing them (Burstein et al. 1995:283–5). The present study suggests that state actor-movement coalitions may be indispensable at each stage of the policy reform process as well as increasing the likelihood of more substantive enactment—beyond mere symbolic gestures. Courts, political parties, and sympathetic state agencies all have the capacity to place social movement policy issues on the political agenda for further political debate/deliberation. Political parties and state agencies have the bureaucratic power to get new laws passed. State agencies are the primary sources for policy implementation. At the local level, city councils and regional governments have the ability to push through all stages of the policy process within their delimited jurisdictions. Local policy enactment and implementation provide both viable models (Martin 2001) and increasing pressure for national level state actors to move in the same direction for policy reform on the issue in question (Kriesi and Wisler 1999:53–6). Courts have the ability to order changes as well as issue cease-and-desist orders, award compensation settlements, and call for legislative action. Furthermore court actions establish legal precedents.

Although the cultural context of policymaking and the strong and enduring presence of the LDP are unique to Japan, we believe our framework may be useful to help explain policy outcomes in other democratic settings. Variation among democratic state structures would obviously have important implications for the kinds of state actor-social movement coalitions likely to form, and which coalitions would be most efficacious in terms of policy change. For example, parliamentary systems with multi-party competition provide greater potential for the establishment of opposition party-movement coalitions (Kitschelt 1986; Kriesi et al. 1995), as is the case for several European and Latin American polities in the contemporary period. Furthermore, democratic states integrated into the world system of emerging global standards (e.g., environmental quality, health, human rights, and labor protections) with large bureaucracies are more likely to house state agencies that specialize in institutional credibility and legitimacy (Meyer et al. 1997). It is precisely such state agencies where reform-minded social movements may find receptive allies to push forward policy changes.

Legal systems also vary across democratic polities in terms of their autonomy and political strength. The fact that Japan's court system was relatively marginal demonstrates the potential power (symbolic and real) of courts even in states where they have historically been weak. Lastly, the power of local and regional governments depends on the level of national government centralization. We expect federalist political structures (e.g., Brazil, Canada, India, New Zealand, Switzerland, and the United States) that give more power to local governments than top-down centralized governments (e.g., Austria, France, Norway, and Sweden) would supply greater potential for social movements to form coalitions with them (Amenta and Young 1999a; Andrews 2001:90; Baiocchi 2003; Martin 2001).

Besides variations in national political structures, the pattern of state actor-movement coalitions and policy reform will also vary by the type of state-oriented social movement under consideration. Once a movement is relatively powerful with widespread mass media and public opinion support, it will more likely find sympathetic state actors that fall within its issue domain. Thus labor-based movements will more likely coalesce with ministries of labor and/or occupational health agencies, gender and ethnic-based movements will find more support within anti-discrimination offices of the modern state, while environmental movements form coalitional relations with environmental and public health agencies. Opposition political parties are also more prone to align with movements closer to their ideological platforms (Rucht 1999) (e.g., green parties with environmental movements; labor parties with labor-based movements). Courts and local governments, on the other hand, are more catholic and potentially penetrable by a variety of state-oriented social movements.

The claims made in the present analysis regarding the efficacy of state actor-movement coalitions require further study in other polities and with different kinds of state-oriented social movements. Comparative and quantitative designs may be especially informative when they include cases of both successful and failed social movements in terms of achieving policy reform (Cress and Snow 2000; Giugni 1999:xxiv). Analysts should give special attention to the kinds of state actor-movement coalitions that form (courts, local governments, political parties, and state agencies) as well as the overall number of state actor-movement coalitions for each of the compared cases in order to decipher if these variations result in differential rates of movement success. Additionally, scholars may want to expand the theoretical scope of state actor-movement coalitions to incorporate cases in which the policy conflict includes a well-organized countermovement (Meyer and Staggenborg 1996) that also forges ties to state actors. Such settings may include coalitions between economic elites and state actors that shape policy-making.

Finally, while this article has introduced the cumulative effect of multiple state actor-social movement coalitions with regards to promoting new policy reforms, the same thesis might be useful in analyzing the ability of coalitions to prevent unwanted policy retrenchments (Reese 1996) (e.g., welfare state cutbacks, pension system economizing, and public sector privatization schemes). Political conflicts involving policy retrenchments increasingly characterize the period of neo-liberal economic reform around the globe (Almeida 2002; Korpi and Palme 2003). Analyzing the kinds of defensive state actor-social movement partnerships that coalesce to prevent such "reforms" may help to explain the variation in the pace of such policy changes within and between countries in democratic polities in the late twentieth and early twenty-first centuries.

References

Almeida, Paul D. 2003. "Opportunity Organizations and Threat Induced Contention: Protest Waves in Authoritarian Settings." *American Journal of Sociology* 109:345–400.

_____. 2002. "Los Movimientos Populares contra las Politicas de Austeridad Economica en America Latina entre 1996 y 2001."

Realidad: Revista de Ciencias Sociales y Humanidades 86:177–89.

Almeida, Paul and Linda Brewster Stearns. 1998. "Political Opportunities and Local Grassroots Environmental Movements: The Case of Minamata." *Social Problems* 45:37–60.

Amenta, Edwin. 1991. "Making the Most of a Case Study: Theories of the Welfare State and the American Experience." *International Journal of Comparative Sociology* 32: 172–94.

_____. 1998. *Bold Relief: Institutional Politics and the Origins of Modern American Policy.* Princeton, NJ: Princeton University Press.

Amenta, Edwin, Kathleen Dunleavy, and Mary Bernstein. 1994. "Stolen Thunder? Huey Long's 'Share Our Wealth,' Political Mediation, and the Second New Deal." *American Sociological Review* 59:678–702.

Amenta, Edwin and Michael Young. 1999a. "Democratic States and Social Movements: Theoretical Arguments and Hypotheses." *Social Problems* 46:153–68.

_____. 1999b. "Making an Impact: Conceptual and Methodological Implications of the Collective Goods Criterion." pp. 22–41 in *How Social Movements Matter,* edited by Marco Giugni, Doug McAdam, and Charles Tilly. Minneapolis: University of Minnesota Press.

Amenta, Edwin and Yvonne Zylan. 1991. "It Happened Here: Political Opportunity, the New Institutionalism, and the Townsend Movement." *American Sociological Review* 56:250–65.

Andrews, Kenneth. 2001. "Social Movements and Policy Implementation: The Mississippi Civil Rights Movement and the War on Poverty." *American Sociological Review* 66:71–95.

_____. 2002. "Creating Social Change: Lessons from the Civil Rights Movement." pp. 105–17 in *Social Movements: Identity, Culture, and the State,* edited by David S. Meyer, Nancy Whittier, and Belinda Robnett. Oxford: Oxford University Press.

Apter, David and Nagayo Sawa. 1984. *Against the State: Politics and Social Protest in Japan.* Cambridge, MA: Harvard University Press.

Baiocchi, Gianpaolo. 2003. "Emergent Public Spheres: Talking Politics in Participatory Governance." *American Sociological Review* 68:52–74.

Barrett, Brendan and Riki Therivel. 1991. *Environmental Policy and Impact Assessment in Japan.* London: Routledge.

Baumgartner, Frank R. and Bryan D. Jones. 1993. *Agendas and Instability in American Politics.* Chicago: University of Chicago Press.

Best, Joel. 1989. "Secondary Claims-Making: Claims about Threats to Children on the Network News." *Perspectives on Social Problems* 1:259–82.

Block, Fred. 1987. *Revising State Theory.* Philadelphia: Temple University Press.

Bonastia, Chris. 2000. "Why Did Affirmative Action in Housing Fail during the Nixon Era? Exploring the 'Institutional Homes' of Social Policies." *Social Problems* 47:523–42.

Bourdieu, Pierre. 1998. *Acts of Resistance: Against the Tyranny of the Market.* New York: New Press.

Bradshaw, York and Michael Wallace. 1991. "Informing Generality and Explaining Uniqueness: The Place of Case Studies in Comparative Research." *International Journal of Comparative Sociology* 32:154–71.

Broadbent, Jeffrey. 1998. *Environmental Politics in Japan: Networks of Power and Protest.* Cambridge: Cambridge University Press.

Burstein, Paul. 1979. "Public Opinion, Demonstrations, and the Passage of Anti-Discrimination Legislation." *Public Opinion Quarterly* 43:157–72.

_____. 1991. "Legal Mobilization as a Social Movement Tactic: The Struggle for Equal Employment Opportunity." *American Journal of Sociology* 96:1202–25.

Burstein, Paul, Rachel Einwohner, and Jocelyn A. Hollander. 1995. "The Success of Political Movements: A Bargaining Perspective." pp. 275–95 in *The Politics of Social Protest: Comparative Perspectives on States and Social Movements,* edited by J. Craig Jenkins and Bert Klandermans. Minneapolis: University of Minnesota Press.

CNN.com. 2004. "Transcript of Bush Statement." CNN.com. February 24. Retrieved April 17, 2004 (http://www.cnn.com/ 2004/ALLPOLITICS/02/24/elecO4.prez.bush.transcript/).

Costain, Anne N. 1992. *Inviting Women's Rebellion: A Political Process Interpretation of the Women's Movement.* Baltimore: Johns Hopkins University Press.

Cress, Daniel and David Snow. 2000. "The Outcomes of Homeless Mobilization: The Influence of Organization, Disruption, Political Mediation, and Framing." *American Journal of Sociology* 105:1063–104.

Dalton, Russell J., Steve Recchia, and Robert Rohrschneider. 2003. "The Environmental Movement and the Modes of Political Action." *Comparative Political Studies* 36:743–71.

Diamond, Larry. 1999. *Developing Democracy: Toward Consolidation.* Baltimore, MD: Johns Hopkins University Press.

Domhoff, G. William. 2002. *Who Rules America?* 4th ed. Columbus, OH: McGraw-Hill.

Environment Agency. 1974. *Quality of the Environment in Japan.* Tokyo: Ministry of Finance.

_____. 1977. *Quality of the Environment in Japan.* Tokyo: Ministry of Finance.

_____. 1978. *Quality of the Environment in Japan.* Tokyo: Ministry of Finance.

Faber, Daniel and James O'Connor. 1989. "The Struggle for Nature: Environmental Crises and the Crisis of Environmentalism in the United States." *Capitalism Nature Socialism* 2:12–39.

Frank, David John, Ann Hironaka, and Evan Schofer. 2000. "The Nation-State and the Natural Environment over the Twentieth Century." *American Sociological Review* 65:96–116.

Gamson, William A. 1990. *Strategy of Social Protest.* 2d ed. Belmont, CA: Wadsworth Publishing.

Ganz, Marshall. 2000. "Resources and Resourcefulness: Strategic Capacity in the Unionization of California Agriculture, 1959–1966." *American Journal of Sociology* 105:1003–62.

Giugni, Marco. 1998. "Was It Worth the Effort? The Outcomes and Consequences of Social Movements." *Annual Review of Sociology* 24:371–93.

_____. 1999. "How Social Movements Matter: Past Research, Present Problems, Future Developments." pp. xiii–xxxiii in How Social Movements Matter, edited by Marco Giugni, Doug McAdam, and Charles Tilly. Minneapolis: University of Minnesota Press.

Goldstone, Jack A. 2003. "Introduction: Bridging Institutionalized and Noninstitutionalized Politics." pp. 1–24 in *States, Parties, and Social Movements,* edited by Jack Goldstone. Cambridge: Cambridge University Press.

Gresser, Julian, Koichiro Fujikara and Akio Morishima. 1981. *Environmental Law in Japan.* Cambridge, MA: MIT Press.

Huddle, Norrie and Michael Reich. 1975. *Island of Dreams: Environmental Crisis in Japan.* New York: Autumn Press.

Iijima, Nobuko. 1979. *Pollution Japan: Historical Chronology.* Tokyo: Asahi Evening News.

Kane, Melinda D. 2003. "Social Movement Policy Success: Decriminalizing State Sodomy Laws, 1969–1998." *Mobilization* 8:313–34.

Kitschelt, Herbert P. 1986. "Political Opportunity Structures and Political Protest: Anti-Nuclear Movements in Four Democracies." *British Journal of Political Science* 16:57–85.

Klandermans, Bert. 1997. *The Social Psychology of Protest.* Oxford: Blackwell Publishers.

Kondo, Shozo. 1981. "Summary Procedures for the Settlement of Pollution Cases." pp. 103–12 in *Environmental Law and Policy in the Pacific Basin Area,* edited by Ichiro Kato, Nobio Kumamoto, and William H. Mathews. Tokyo: University of Tokyo Press.

Koopmans, Ruud. 1995. *Democracy from Below: New Social Movements and the Political System in Germany.* Boulder, CO: Westview Press.

Korpi, Walter and Joakim Palme. 2003. "New Politics and Class Politics in the Context of Austerity and Globalization: Welfare State Regress in 18 Countries, 1975–1995." *American Political Science Review* 97:425–46.

Krauss, Ellis and Bradford Simcock. 1980. "Citizens' Movements: The Growth and Impact of Environmental Protest in Japan." pp. 187–227 in *Political Opposition and Local Politics in Japan,* edited by Kurt Steiner, Ellis S. Krauss, and Scott C. Flanagan. Princeton, NJ: Princeton University Press.

Kriesi, Hanspeter, Ruud Koopmans, Jan-Willem Duyvendak, and Marco G. Giugni. 1995. *The Politics of New Social Movements in Western Europe: A Comparative Analysis.* Minneapolis: University of Minnesota Press.

Kriesi, Hanspeter and Dominique Wisler. 1999. "The Impact of Social Movements on Political Institutions: A Comparison of the Introduction of Direct Legislation in Switzerland and the United States." pp. 42–65 in *How Social Movements Matter,* edited by Marco Giugni, Doug McAdam, and Charles Tilly. Minneapolis: University of Minnesota Press.

Lambda Legal Defense Fund. 2004. "Background and Pending Cases Seeking Full Equity for Gay Couples." Lambda Legal. Retrieved June 8, 2004 (http://www.lambdalegal.org/cgi-bin/iowa/ documents/record?record= 1459).

Lewis, Jack G. 1980. "Civic Protest in Mishima: Citizens' Movements and the Politics of the Environment in Contemporary Japan." pp. 274–313 in *Political Opposition and Local Politics in Japan,* edited by Kurt Steiner, Ellis S. Krauss, and Scott C. Flanagan. Princeton, NJ: Princeton University Press.

Lofland, John. 1989. "Consensus Movements: City Twinning and Derailed Dissent in the American Eighties." *Research in Social Movements, Conflict and Change* 11:163–96.

MacDougall, Terry E. 1976. "Japanese Urban Local Politics: Toward a Viable Progressive Political Opposition." pp. 31–56 in *Japan: The Paradox of Power,* edited by Lewis Austin. New Haven, CT: Yale University Press.

Maguire, Diarmuid. 1995. "Opposition Movements and Opposition Parties: Equal Partners or Dependent Relations in the Struggle for Power and Reform." pp. 199–228 in *The Politics of Social*

Protest: Comparative Perspectives on States and Social Movements, edited by J. Craig Jenkins and Bert Klandermans. Minneapolis: University of Minnesota Press.

Martin, Isaac. 2001. "Dawn of the Living Wage: The Diffusion of a Redistributive Municipal Policy." *Urban Affairs Review* 36:470–96.

Matsui, Saburo. 1992. *Industrial Pollution Control in Japan: A Historical Perspective.* Tokyo: Asian Productivity Organization.

McAdam, Doug. 1996. "Conceptual Origins, Current Problems, Future Directions." pp. 23–40 in *Comparative Perspectives on Social Movements: Political Opportunities, Mobilizing Structures, and Cultural Framings,* edited by Doug McAdam, John D. McCarthy, and Mayer N. Zald. Cambridge: Cambridge University Press.

McCammon, Holly and Melinda Kane. 1997. "Shaping Judicial Law in the Post-World War II Period: When Is Labor's Legal Mobilization Successful." *Sociological Inquiry* 67:27 5–98.

McCarthy, John D. and Mark Wolfson. 1992. "Consensus Movements, Conflict Movements, and the Cooptation of Civic and State Infrastructures." pp. 273–97 in *Frontiers in Social Movement Theory,* edited by Aldon D. Morris and Carol M. Mueller. New Haven, CT: Yale University Press.

McKean, Margaret. 1977. "Pollution and Policymaking." pp. 201–38 in *Policymaking in Contemporary Japan,* edited by T. J. Pempel. Ithaca, NY: Cornell University Press.

_____. 1981. *Environmental Protest in Japan.* Berkeley, CA: University of California Press.

Meyer, David S. 2002. "Opportunities and Identities: Bridge-Building in the Study of Social Movements." pp. 3–21 in *Social Movements: Identity, Culture, and the State,* edited by David S. Meyer, Nancy Whittier, and Belinda Robnett. Oxford: Oxford University Press.

Meyer, David S. and Suzanne Staggenborg. 1996. "Movements, Countermovements, and the Structure of Political Opportunity." *American Journal of Sociology* 101:1628–60.

Meyer, David S. and Sam Marullo. 1992. "Grassroots Mobilization and International Politics: Peace Protest and the End of the Cold War." *Research in Social Movements, Conflicts, and Change* 14:99–140.

Meyer, John W., John Boli, George M. Thomas, and Francisco O. Ramirez. 1997. "World Society and the NationState." *American Journal of Sociology* 103:144–81.

Miyamoto, Keflichi. 1991. "Japanese Environmental Policies Since World War II." *Capitalism Nature Socialism* 2:71–100.

Morishima, Akio. 1981. "Japanese Environmental Policy and Law." pp. 77–84 in *Environmental Law and Policy in the Pacific Basin Area,* edited by Ichiro Kato, Nobio Kumamoto, and W.H. Mathews. Tokyo: University of Tokyo Press.

Navarro, Armando. 1998. *The Cristal Experiment: A Chicano Struggle for Community Control.* Madison: University of Wisconsin Press.

Organization for Economic Co-operation and Development (OECD). 1977. *Environmental Policies in Japan.* Paris: OECD.

_____. 1994. *OECD Performance Reviews: Japan.* Paris: OECD.

Piven, Frances Fox and Richard A. Cloward. 1979. *Poor People's Movements: Why They Succeed, How They Fail.* New York: Vintage.

Pollin, Robert and Stephanie Luce. 1998. *The Living Wage: Building a Fair Economy.* New York: The New Press.

Reed, Steven. 1981. "Environmental Politics: Some Reflections Based on the Japanese Case." *Comparative Politics* 13:253–70.

Reese, Ellen. 1996. "Maternalism and Political Mobilization: How California's Postwar Childcare Campaign was Won." *Gender and Society* 10:566–89.

Reich, Michael. 1983. "Environmental Policy and Japanese Society: Part II, Lessons about Japan and about Policy." *International Journal of Environmental Policy* 20:199–207.

_____. 1984a. "Mobilizing for Environmental Policy in Italy and Japan." *Comparative Politics* 16:379–402.

_____. 1984b. "Crisis and Routine: Pollution Reporting by the Japanese Press." pp. 148–65 in *Institutions for Change in Japanese Society,* edited by George De Vos. Berkeley, CA: Institute for East Asian Studies.

_____. 1991. *Toxic Politics: Responding to Chemical Disasters.* Ithaca, NY: Cornell University Press.

Reischauer, Edwin O. 1988. *The Japanese Today: Change and Continuity.* Cambridge, MA: Belknap Press.

Rucht, Dieter. 1999. "The Impact of Environmental Movements in Western Societies." pp. 204–24 in *How Social Movements Matter,* edited by Marco Giugni, Doug McAdam, and Charles Tilly. Minneapolis: University of Minnesota Press.

Santoro, Wayne A. and Gail M. McGuire. 1997. "Social Movement Insiders: The Impact of Institutional Activists on Affirmative Action and Comparable Worth Policies." Social Problems 44:503–19.

Sawyers, Traci M. and David S. Meyer. 1999. "Missed Opportunities: Social Movement Abeyance and Public Policy." *Social Problems* 46:187–206.

Schuld, Leslie. 2003. "El Salvador: Who Will Save the Hospitals?" *NACLA Report on the Americas* 21:42–5.

Skocpol, Theda. 1985. "Bringing the State Back In: Strategies of Analysis in Current Research." pp. 3–37 in *Bringing the State Back In,* edited by Peter B. Evans, Dietrich Rueschemeyer, and Theda Skocpol. New York: Cambridge University Press.

Snow, David and Robert Benford. 1992. "Master Frames and Cycles of Protest." pp. 133–55 in *Frontiers in Social Movement Theory,* edited by Aldon D. Morris and Carol M. Mueller. New Haven, CT: Yale University Press.

Steiner, Kurt. 1980. "Progressive Local Administrations: Local Public Policy and Local-National Relations." pp. 317–52 in *Political Opposition and Local Politics in Japan,* edited by Kurt Steiner, Ellis S. Krauss, and Scott C. Flanagan. Princeton, NJ: Princeton University Press.

Stinchcombe, Arthur. 1965. "Social Structure and Organizations." pp. 142–93 in *Handbook of Organizations,* edited by James G. March. Chicago: Rand-McNally.

Sumisato, Arima and Imazu Hiroshi. 1977. "The Opposition Parties: Organizations and Policies." *Japan Quarterly* 24:148–84.

Swarts, Heidi J. 2003. "Setting the State's Agenda: Church-Based Community Organizations in American Urban Politics." pp. 78–106 in *States, Parties, and Social Movements, edited by Jack Goldstone.* Cambridge: Cambridge University Press.

Szasz, Andrew. 1994. *Ecopopulism: Toxic Waste and the Movement for Environmental Justice.* Minneapolis: University of Minnesota Press.

Tarrow, Sidney. 1994. *Power in Movement.* Cambridge: Cambridge University Press.

Tilly, Charles. 1978. *From Mobilization to Revolution.* Reading, MA: Addison-Wesley.

Tsuru, Shigeto. 1970. *International Symposium on Environmental Disruption in the Modern World.* Tokyo: International Social Science Council.

Tsurutani, Taketsugu. 1977. *Political Change in Japan.* New York: David McKay.

Upham, Frank. 1976. "Litigation and Moral Consciousness in Japan: An Interpretive Analysis of Four Japanese Pollution Suits." *Law and Society Review* 10:579–619.

_____. 1987. *Law and Social Change in Postwar Japan.* Cambridge, MA: Harvard University Press.

Vogel, Ezra. 1980. *Japan as Number One: Lessons for America.* New York: Harper Colophon Books.

Weidner, Helmut. 1986. "Japan: The Success and Limitations of Technocratic Environmental Policy." *Policy and Politics* 14:43–70.

Wolfson, Mark. 2001. *The Fight Against Big Tobacco: The Movement, the State, and the Public's Health.* Hawthorne, NY: Aldine de Gruyter.

Capitalism and Democracy*

GABRIEL A. ALMOND

Joseph Schumpeter, a great economist and social scientist of the last generation, whose career was almost equally divided between Central European and American universities, and who lived close to the crises of the 1930s and '40s, published a book in 1942 under the title, *Capitalism, Socialism, and Democracy*. The book has had great influence, and can be read today with profit. It was written in the aftergloom of the great depression, during the early triumphs of Fascism and Nazism in 1940 and 1941, when the future of capitalism, socialism, and democracy all were in doubt. Schumpeter projected a future of declining capitalism, and rising socialism. He thought that democracy under socialism might be no more impaired and problematic than it was under capitalism.

He wrote a concluding chapter in the second edition which appeared in 1946, and which took into account the political-economic situation at the end of the war, with the Soviet Union then astride a devastated Europe. In this last chapter he argues that we should not identify the future of socialism with that of the Soviet Union, that what we had observed and were observing in the first three decades of Soviet existence was not a necessary expression of socialism. There was a lot of Czarist Russia in the mix. If Schumpeter were writing today, I don't believe he would argue that socialism has a brighter future than capitalism. The relationship between the two has turned out to be a good deal more complex and intertwined than Schumpeter anticipated. But I am sure that he would still urge us to separate the future of socialism from that of Soviet and Eastern European Communism.

Unlike Schumpeter I do not include Socialism in my title, since its future as a distinct ideology and program of action is unclear at best. Western Marxism and the moderate socialist movements seem to have settled for social democratic solutions, for adaptations of both capitalism and democracy producing acceptable mixes of market competition, political pluralism, participation, and welfare. I deal with these modifications of capitalism, as a consequence of the impact of democracy on capitalism in the last half century.

At the time that Adam Smith wrote *The Wealth of Nations*, the world of government, politics and the state that he knew—pre-Reform Act England, the French government of Louis XV and XVI—was riddled with special privileges, monopolies, interferences with trade. With my tongue only half way in my check

I believe the discipline of economics may have been traumatized by this condition of political life at its birth. Typically, economists speak of the state and government instrumentally, as a kind of secondary service mechanism.

I do not believe that politics can be treated in this purely instrumental and reductive way without losing our analytic grip on the social and historical process. The economy and the polity are the main problem solving mechanisms of human society. They each have their distinctive means, and they each have their "goods" or ends. They necessarily interact with each other, and transform each other in the process. Democracy in particular generates goals and programs. You cannot give people the suffrage, and let them form organizations, run for office, and the like, without their developing all kinds of ideas as to how to improve things. And sometimes some of these ideas are adopted, implemented and are productive, and improve our lives, although many economists are reluctant to concede this much to the state.

My lecture deals with this interaction of politics and economics in the Western World in the course of the last couple of centuries, in the era during which capitalism and democracy emerged as the dominant problem solving institutions of modern civilization. I am going to discuss some of the theoretical and empirical literature dealing with the themes of the positive and negative interaction between capitalism and democracy. There are those who say that capitalism supports democracy, and those who say that capitalism subverts democracy. And there are those who say that democracy subverts capitalism, and those who say that it supports it.

The relation between capitalism and democracy dominates the political theory of the last two centuries. All the logically possible points of view are represented in a rich literature. It is this ambivalence and dialectic, this tension between the two major problem solving sectors of modern society—the political and the economic—that is the topic of my lecture.

Capitalism Supports Democracy

Let me begin with the argument that capitalism is positively linked with democracy, shares its values and culture, and facilitates its development. This case has been made in historical, logical, and statistical terms.

*Lecture presented at Seminar on the Market, sponsored by the Ford Foundation and the Research Institute on International Change of Columbia University, Moscow, October 29—November 2.

Albert Hirschman in his *Rival Views of Market Society* (1986) examines the values, manners and morals of capitalism, and their effects on the larger society and culture as these have been described by the philosophers of the 17th, 18th, and 19th centuries. He shows how the interpretation of the impact of capitalism has changed from the enlightenment view of Montesquieu, Condorcet, Adam Smith and others, who stressed the *douceur* of commerce, its "gentling," civilizing effect on behavior and interpersonal relations, to that of the 19th and 20th century conservative and radical writers who described the culture of capitalism as crassly materialistic, destructively competitive, corrosive of morality, and hence self-destructive. This sharp almost 180-degree shift in point of view among political theorists is partly explained by the transformation from the commerce and small-scale industry of early capitalism, to the smoke blackened industrial districts, the demonic and exploitive entrepreneurs, and exploited laboring classes of the second half of the nineteenth century. Unfortunately for our purposes, Hirschman doesn't deal explicitly with the capitalism–democracy connection, but rather with culture and with manners. His argument, however, implies an early positive connection and a later negative one.

Joseph Schumpeter in *Capitalism, Socialism, and Democracy* (1942) states flatly, "History clearly confirms . . . [that] . . . modern democracy rose along with capitalism, and in causal connection with it . . . modern democracy is a product of the capitalist process." He has a whole chapter entitled "The Civilization of Capitalism," democracy being a part of that civilization. Schumpeter also makes the point that democracy was historically supportive of capitalism. He states, ". . . the bourgeoisie reshaped, and from its own point of view rationalized, the social and political structure that preceded its ascendancy . . ." (that is to say, feudalism). "The democratic method was the political tool of that reconstruction." According to Schumpeter capitalism and democracy were mutually causal historically, mutually supportive parts of a rising modern civilization, although as we shall show below, he also recognized their antagonisms.

Barrington Moore's historical investigation (1966) with its long title, *The Social Origins of Dictatorship and Democracy; Lord and Peasant in the Making of the Modern World*, argues that there have been three historical routes to industrial modernization. The first of these followed by Britain, France, and the United States, involved the subordination and transformation of the agricultural sector by the rising commercial bourgeoisie, producing the democratic capitalism of the 19th and 20th centuries. The second route followed by Germany and Japan, where the landed aristocracy was able to contain and dominate the rising commercial classes, produced an authoritarian and fascist version of industrial modernization, a system of capitalism encased in a feudal authoritarian framework, dominated by a military aristocracy, and an authoritarian monarchy. The third route, followed in Russia where the commercial bourgeoisie was too weak to give content and direction to the modernizing process, took the form of a revolutionary process drawing on the frustration and resources of the peasantry, and created a mobilized authoritarian Communist regime along with a state-controlled industrialized economy. Successful capitalism dominating and transforming the rural agricultural sector, according

to Barrington Moore, is the creator and sustainer of the emerging democracies of the nineteenth century.

Robert A. Dahl, the leading American democratic theorist, in the new edition of his book (1990) *After the Revolution? Authority in a Good Society*, has included a new chapter entitled "Democracy and Markets." In the opening paragraph of that chapter, he says:

> It is an historical fact that modern democratic institutions . . . have existed only in countries with predominantly privately owned, market-oriented economies, or capitalism if you prefer that name. It is also a fact that all "socialist" countries with predominantly state-owned centrally directed economic orders—command economies—have not enjoyed democratic governments, but have in fact been ruled by authoritarian dictatorships. It is also an historical fact that some "capitalist" countries have also been, and are, ruled by authoritarian dictatorships.

> To put it more formally, it looks to be the case that market-oriented economies are necessary (in the logical sense) to democratic institutions, though they are certainly not sufficient. And it looks to be the case that state-owned centrally directed economic orders are strictly associated with authoritarian regimes, though authoritarianism definitely does not require them. We have something very much like an historical experiment, so it would appear, that leaves these conclusions in no great doubt. (Dahl 1990)

Peter Berger in his book *The Capitalist Revolution* (1986) presents four propositions on the relation between capitalism and democracy:

> Capitalism is a necessary but not sufficient condition of democracy under modern conditions.

> If a capitalist economy is subjected to increasing degrees of state control, a point (not precisely specifiable at this time) will be reached at which democratic governance becomes impossible.

> If a socialist economy is opened up to increasing degrees of market forces, a point (not precisely specifiable at this time) will be reached at which democratic governance becomes a possibility.

> If capitalist development is successful in generating economic growth from which a sizable proportion of the population benefits, pressures toward democracy are likely to appear.

This positive relationship between capitalism and democracy has also been sustained by statistical studies. The "Social Mobilization" theorists of the 1950s and 1960s which included Daniel Lerner (1958), Karl Deutsch (1961), S. M. Lipset (1959) among others, demonstrated a strong statistical association between GNP per capita and democratic political institutions. This is more than simple statistical association. There is a logic in the relation between level of economic development and democratic institutions. Level of economic development has been shown to be associated with education and literacy, exposure to mass media, and democratic psychological propensities such as subjective efficacy, participatory aspirations and skills. In a major investigation of the social psychology of industrialization and modernization, a research team led by the sociologist Alex Inkeles (1974) interviewed several thousand workers in the modern industrial and the traditional economic sectors of six countries of differing culture. Inkeles found empathetic, efficacious, participatory and activist propensities much more frequently among the modern industrial workers, and to a much lesser extent in the traditional sector in each one of these countries regardless of cultural differences.

The historical, the logical, and the statistical evidence for this positive relation between capitalism and democracy is quite persuasive.

Capitalism Subverts Democracy

But the opposite case is also made, that capitalism subverts or undermines democracy. Already in John Stuart Mill (1848) we encounter a view of existing systems of private property as unjust, and of the free market as destructively competitive—aesthetically and morally repugnant. The case he was making was a normative rather than a political one. He wanted a less competitive society, ultimately socialist, which would still respect individuality. He advocated limitations on the inheritance of property and the improvement of the property system so that everyone shared in its benefits, the limitation of population growth, and the improvement of the quality of the labor force through the provision of high quality education for all by the state. On the eve of the emergence of the modern democratic capitalist order John Staurt Mill wanted to control the excesses of both the market economy and the majoritarian polity, by the education of consumers and producers, citizens and politicians, in the interest of producing morally improved free market and democratic orders. But in contrast to Marx, he did not thoroughly discount the possibilities of improving the capitalist and democratic order.

Marx argued that as long as capitalism and private property existed there could be no genuine democracy, that democracy under capitalism was bourgeois democracy, which is to say not democracy at all. While it would be in the interest of the working classes to enter a coalition with the bourgeoisie in supporting this form of democracy in order to eliminate feudalism, this would be a tactical maneuver. Capitalist democracy could only result in the increasing exploitation of the working classes. Only the elimination of capitalism and private property could result in the emancipation of the working classes and the attainment of true democracy. Once socialism was attained the basic political problems of humanity would have been solved through the elimination of classes. Under socialism there would be no distinctive democratic organization, no need for institutions to resolve conflicts, since there would be no conflicts. There is not much democratic or political theory to be found in Marx's writings. The basic reality is the mode of economic production and the consequent class structure from which other institutions follow.

For the followers of Marx up to the present day there continues to be a negative tension between capitalism, however reformed, and democracy. But the integral Marxist and Leninist rejection of the possibility of an autonomous, bourgeois democratic state has been left behind for most Western Marxists. In the thinking of Poulantzas, Offe, Bobbio, Habermas and others, the bourgeois democratic state is now viewed as a class struggle state, rather than an unambiguously bourgeois state. The working class has access to it; it can struggle for its interests, and can attain partial benefits from it. The state is now viewed as autonomous, or as relatively autonomous, and it can be reformed in a progressive direction by working class and other popular movements. The bourgeois democratic state can be moved in the direction of a socialist state by political action short of violence and institutional destruction.

Schumpeter (1942) appreciated the tension between capitalism and democracy. While he saw a causal connection between competition in the economic and the political order, he points out ". . . that there are some deviations from the principle of democracy which link up with the presence of organized capitalist interests. . . . [T]he statement is true both from the standpoint of the classical and from the standpoint of our own theory of democracy. From the first standpoint, the result reads that the means at the disposal of private interests are often used in order to thwart the will of the people. From the second standpoint, the result reads that those private means are often used in order to interfere with the working of the mechanism of competitive leadership." He refers to some countries and situations in which ". . . political life all but resolved itself into a struggle of pressure groups and in many cases practices that failed to conform to the spirit of the democratic method." But he rejects the notion that there cannot be political democracy in a capitalist society. For Schumpeter full democracy in the sense of the informed participation of all adults in the selection of political leaders and consequently the making of public policy, was an impossibility because of the number and complexity of the issues confronting modern electorates. The democracy which was realistically possible was one in which people could choose among competing leaders, and consequently exercise some direction over political decisions. This kind of democracy was possible in a capitalist society, though some of its propensities impaired its performance. Writing in the early years of World War II, when the future of democracy and of capitalism were uncertain, he leaves unresolved the questions of ". . . Whether or not democracy is one of those products of capitalism which are to die out with it . . ." or ". . . how well or ill capitalist society qualifies for the task of working the democratic method it evolved."

Non-Marxist political theorists have contributed to this questioning of the reconcilability of capitalism and democracy. Robert A. Dahl, who makes the point that capitalism historically has been a necessary precondition of democracy, views contemporary democracy in the United States as seriously compromised, impaired by the inequality in resources among the citizens. But Dahl stresses the variety in distributive patterns, and in politico-economic relations among contemporary democracies. "The category of capitalist democracies" he writes, "includes an extraordinary variety . . . from nineteenth century, laissez faire, early industrial systems to twentieth century, highly regulated, social welfare, late or postindustrial systems. Even late twentieth century 'welfare state' orders vary all the way from the Scandinavian systems, which are redistributive, heavily taxed, comprehensive in their social security, and neocorporatist in their collective bargaining arrangements to the faintly redistributive, moderately taxed, limited social security, weak collective bargaining systems of the United States and Japan" (1989).

In *Democracy and Its Critics* (1989) Dahl argues that the normative growth of democracy to what he calls its "third transformation" (the first being the direct city-state democracy of classic times, and the second, the indirect, representative inegalitarian democracy of the contemporary world) will require democratization of the economic order. In other words, modern corporate capitalism needs to be transformed. Since government control and/or ownership of the economy would be destructive of the pluralism which is an essential requirement of democracy, his preferred solution to the problem of the mega-corporation is employee control of corporate industry. An economy so organized, according to Dahl, would improve the distribution of political resources without at the same time destroying the pluralism which democratic competition requires. To those who question the realism of Dahl's solution to the problem of inequality, he replies that history is full of surprises.

Charles E. Lindblom in his book, *Politics and Markets* (1977), concludes his comparative analysis of the political economy of modern capitalism and socialism, with an essentially pessimistic conclusion about contemporary market-oriented democracy. He says

> We therefore come back to the corporation. It is possible that the rise of the corporation has offset or more than offset the decline of class as an instrument of indoctrination. . . . That it creates a new core of wealth and power for a newly constructed upper class, as well as an overpowering loud voice, is also reasonably clear. The executive of the large corporation is, on many counts, the contemporary counterpart to the landed gentry of an earlier era, his voice amplified by the technology of mass communication. . . . [T]he major institutional barrier to fuller democracy may therefore be the autonomy of the private corporation.

Lindblom concludes, "The large private corporation fits oddly into democratic theory and vision. Indeed it does not fit.

There is then a widely shared agreement, from the Marxists and neo-Marxists, to Schumpeter, Dahl, Lindblom, and other liberal political theorists, that modern capitalism with the dominance of the large corporation, produces a defective or an impaired form of democracy.

Democracy Subverts Capitalism

If we change our perspective now and look at the way democracy is said to affect capitalism, one of the dominant traditions of economics from Adam Smith until the present day stresses the importance for productivity and welfare of an economy that is relatively free of intervention by the state. In this doctrine of minimal government there is still a place for a framework of rules and services essential to the productive and efficient performance of the economy. In part the government has to protect the market from itself. Left to their own devices, according to

Smith, businessmen were prone to corner the market in order to exact the highest possible price. And according to Smith businessmen were prone to bribe public officials in order to gain special privileges, and legal monopolies. For Smith good capitalism was competitive capitalism, and good government provided just those goods and services which the market needed to flourish, could not itself provide, or would not provide. A good government according to Adam Smith was a minimal government, providing for the national defense, and domestic order. Particularly important for the economy were the rules pertaining to commercial life such as the regulation of weights and measures, setting and enforcing building standards, providing for the protection of persons and property, and the like.

For Milton Friedman (1961, 1981), the leading contemporary advocate of the free market and free government, and of the interdependence of the two, the principal threat to the survival of capitalism and democracy is the assumption of the responsibility for welfare on the part of the modern democratic state. He lays down a set of functions appropriate to government in the positive interplay between economy and polity, and then enumerates many of the ways in which the modern welfare, regulatory state has deviated from these criteria.

A good Friedmanesque, democratic government would be one ". . . which maintained law and order, defended property rights, served as a means whereby we could modify property rights and other rules of the economic game, adjudicated disputes about the interpretation of the rules, enforced contracts, promoted competition, provided a monetary framework, engaged in activities to counter technical monopolies and to overcome neighborhood effects widely regarded as sufficiently important to justify government intervention, and which supplemented private charity and the private family in protecting the irresponsible, whether madman or child. . . ." Against this list of proper activities for a free government, Friedman pinpointed more than a dozen activities of contemporary democratic governments which might better be performed through the private sector, or not at all. These included setting and maintaining price supports, tariffs, import and export quotas and controls, rents, interest rates, wage rates, and the like, regulating industries and banking, radio and television, licensing professions and occupations, providing social security and medical care programs, providing public housing, national parks, guaranteeing mortgages, and much else.

Friedman concludes that this steady encroachment on the private sector has been slowly but surely converting our free government and market system into a collective monster, compromising both freedom and productivity in the outcome. The tax and expenditure revolts and regulatory rebellions of the 1980s have temporarily stemmed this trend, but the threat continues. "It is the internal threat coming from men of good intentions and good will who wish to reform us. Impatient with the slowness of persuasion and example to achieve the great social changes they envision, they are anxious to use the power of the state to achieve their ends, and confident of their own ability to do so." The threat to political and economic freedom, according to Milton Friedman and others who argue the same position, arises out of democratic politics. It may only be defeated by political action.

In the last decades a school, or rather several schools, of economists and political scientists have turned the theoretical models of economics to use in analyzing political processes. Variously called public choice theorists, rational choice theorists, or positive political theorists, and employing such models as market exchange and bargaining, rational self interest, game theory, and the like, these theorists have produced a substantial literature throwing new and often controversial light on democratic political phenomena such as elections, decisions of political party leaders, interest group behavior, legislative and committee decisions, bureaucratic, and judicial behavior, lobbying activity, and substantive public policy areas such as constitutional arrangements, health and environment policy, regulatory policy, national security and foreign policy, and the like. Hardly a field of politics and public policy has been left untouched by this inventive and productive group of scholars.

The institutions and names with which this movement is associated in the United States include Virginia State University, the University of Virginia, the George Mason University, the University of Rochester, the University of Chicago, the California Institute of Technology, the Carnegie Mellon University, among others. And the most prominent names are those of the leaders of the two principal schools: James Buchanan, the Nobel Laureate leader of the Virginia "Public Choice" school, and William Riker, the leader of the Rochester "Positive Theory" school. Other prominent scholars associated with this work are Gary Becker of the University of Chicago, Kenneth Shepsle and Morris Fiorina of Harvard, John Ferejohn of Stanford, Charles Plott of the California Institute of Technology, and many others.

One writer summarizing the ideological bent of much of this work, but by no means all of it (William Mitchell of the University of Washington), describes it as fiscally conservative, sharing a conviction that the ". . . private economy is far more robust, efficient, and perhaps, equitable than other economies, and much more successful than political processes in efficiently allocating resources. . . ." Much of what has been produced ". . . by James Buchanan and the leaders of this school can best be described as contributions to a theory of the failure of political processes." These failures of political performance are said to be inherent properties of the democratic political process. "Inequity, inefficiency, and coercion are the most general results of democratic policy formation." In a democracy the demand for publicly provided services seems to be insatiable. It ultimately turns into a special interest, "rent seeking" society. Their remedies take the form of proposed constitutional limits on spending power and checks and balances to limit legislative majorities.

One of the most visible products of this pessimistic economic analysis of democratic politics is the book by Mancur Olson, *The Rise and Decline of Nations* (1982). He makes a strong argument for the negative democracy–capitalism connection. His thesis is that the behavior of individuals and firms in stable societies inevitably leads to the formation of dense networks of collusive, cartelistic, and lobbying organizations that make economies less efficient and dynamic and polities less governable. "The longer a society goes without an upheaval, the more powerful such organizations become and the more they slow down economic expansion. Societies in which these narrow interest groups have been destroyed, by war or revolution, for example, enjoy the greatest gains in growth." His prize cases are Britain on the one hand and Germany and Japan on the other.

> The logic of the argument implies that countries that have had democratic freedom of organization without upheaval or invasion the longest will suffer the most from growth-repressing organizations and combinations. This helps explain why Great Britain, the major nation with the longest immunity from dictatorship, invasion, and revolution, has had in this century a lower rate of growth than other large, developed democracies. Britain has precisely the powerful network of special interest organization that the argument developed here would lead us to expect in a country with its record of military security and democratic stability. The number and power of its trade unions need no description. The venerability and power of its professional associations is also striking. . . . In short, with age British society has acquired so many strong organizations and collusions that it suffers from an institutional sclerosis that slows its adaptation to changing circumstances and technologies. (Olson 1982)

By contrast, post-World War II Germany and Japan started organizationally from scratch. The organizations that led them to defeat were all dissolved, and under the occupation inclusive organizations like the general trade union movement and general organizations of the industrial and commercial community were first formed. These inclusive organizations had more regard for the general national interest and exercised some discipline on the narrower interest organizations. And both countries in the post-war decades experienced "miracles" of economic growth under democratic conditions.

The Olson theory of the subversion of capitalism through the propensities of democratic societies to foster special interest groups has not gone without challenge. There can be little question that there is logic in his argument. But empirical research testing this pressure group hypothesis thus far has produced mixed findings. Olson has hopes that a public educated to the harmful consequences of special interests to economic growth, full employment, coherent government, equal opportunity, and social mobility will resist special interest behavior, and enact legislation imposing anti-trust, and anti-monopoly controls to mitigate and contain these threats. It is somewhat of an irony that the solution to this special interest disease of democracy, according to Olson, is a democratic state with sufficient regulatory authority to control the growth of special interest organizations.

Democracy Fosters Capitalism

My fourth theme, democracy as fostering and sustaining capitalism, is not as straightforward as the first three. Historically there can be little doubt that as the suffrage was extended in the last century, and as mass political parties developed, democratic development impinged significantly on capitalist institutions and practices. Since successful capitalism requires risk-taking entrepreneurs with access to investment capital, the democratic propensity for redistributive and regulative policy tends to reduce the incentives and the resources available for risk-taking and creativity. Thus it can be argued that propensities inevitably resulting from democratic politics, as Friedman, Olson and many others argue, tend to reduce productivity, and hence welfare.

But precisely the opposite argument can be made on the basis of the historical experience of literally all of the advanced capitalist democracies in existence. All of them without exception are now welfare states with some form and degree of social insurance, health and welfare nets, and regulatory frameworks designed to mitigate the harmful impacts and shortfalls of capitalism. Indeed, the welfare state is accepted all across the political spectrum. Controversy takes place around the edges. One might make the argument that had capitalism not been modified in this welfare direction, it is doubtful that it would have survived.

This history of the interplay between democracy and capitalism is clearly laid out in a major study involving European and American scholars, entitled *The Development of Welfare States in Western Europe and America* (Flora and Heidenheimer 1981). The book lays out the relationship between the development and spread of capitalist industry, democratization in the sense of an expanding suffrage and the emergence of trade unions and left-wing political parties, and the gradual introduction of the institutions and practices of the welfare state. The early adoption of the institutions of the welfare state in Bismarck Germany, Sweden, and Great Britain were all associated with the rise of trade unions and socialist parties in those countries. The decisions made by the upper and middle class leaders and political movements to introduce welfare measures such as accident, old age, and unemployment insurance, were strategic decisions. They were increasingly confronted by trade union movements with the capacity of bringing industrial production to a halt, and by political parties with growing parliamentary representation favoring fundamental modifications in, or the abolition of capitalism. As the calculations of the upper and middle class leaders led them to conclude that the costs of suppression exceeded the costs of concession, the various parts of the welfare state began to be put in place—accident, sickness, unemployment insurance, old age insurance, and the like. The problem of maintaining the loyalty of the working classes through two world wars resulted in additional concessions to working class demands: the filling out of the social security system, free public education to higher levels, family allowances, housing benefits, and the like.

Social conditions, historical factors, political processes and decisions produced different versions of the welfare state. In the United States, manhood suffrage came quite early, the later bargaining process emphasized free land and free education to the secondary level, an equality of opportunity version of the welfare state. The Disraeli bargain in Britain resulted in relatively early manhood suffrage and the full attainment of parliamentary government, while the Lloyd George bargain on the eve of World War I brought the beginnings of a welfare system to Britain. The Bismarck bargain in Germany produced an early welfare state, a postponement of electoral equality and parliamentary

government. While there were all of these differences in historical encounters with democratization and "welfarization," the important outcome was that little more than a century after the process began all of the advanced capitalist democracies had similar versions of the welfare state, smaller in scale in the case of the United States and Japan, more substantial in Britain and the continental European countries.

We can consequently make out a strong case for the argument that democracy has been supportive of capitalism in this strategic sense. Without this welfare adaptation it is doubtful that capitalism would have survived, or rather, its survival, "unwelfarized," would have required a substantial repressive apparatus. The choice then would seem to have been between democratic welfare capitalism, and repressive undemocratic capitalism. I am inclined to believe that capitalism as such thrives more with the democratic welfare adaptation than with the repressive one. It is in that sense that we can argue that there is a clear positive impact of democracy on capitalism.

We have to recognize, in conclusion, that democracy and capitalism are both positively and negatively related, that they both support and subvert each other. My colleague, Moses Abramovitz, described this dialectic more surely than most in his presidential address to the American Economic Association in 1980, on the eve of the "Reagan Revolution." Noting the decline in productivity in the American economy during the latter 1960s and '70s, and recognizing that this decline might in part be attributable to the "tax, transfer, and regulatory" tendencies of the welfare state, he observes,

> The rationale supporting the development of our mixed economy sees it as a pragmatic compromise between the competing virtues and defects of decentralized market capitalism and encompassing socialism. Its goal is to obtain a measure of distributive justice, security, and social guidance of economic life without losing too much of the allocative efficiency and dynamism of private enterprise and market organization. And it is a pragmatic compromise in another sense. It seeks to retain for most people that measure of personal protection from the state which private property and a private job market confer, while obtaining for the disadvantaged minority of people through the state that measure of support without which their lack of property or personal endowment would amount to a denial of individual freedom and capacity to function as full members of the community. (Abramovitz 1981)

Democratic welfare capitalism produces that reconciliation of opposing and complementary elements which makes possible the survival, even enhancement of both of these sets of institutions. It is not a static accommodation, but rather one which fluctuates over time, with capitalism being compromised by the tax-transfer-regulatory action of the state at one point, and then correcting in the direction of the reduction of the intervention of the state at another point, and with a learning process over time that may reduce the amplitude of the curves.

The case for this resolution of the capitalism-democracy quandary is made quite movingly by Jacob Viner who is quoted in the concluding paragraph of Abramovitz's paper, ". . . If . . . I nevertheless conclude that I believe that the welfare state, like old Siwash, is really worth fighting for and even dying for as compared to any rival system, it is because, despite its imperfection in theory and practice, in the aggregate it provides more promise of preserving and enlarging human freedoms, temporal prosperity, the extinction of mass misery, and the dignity of man and his moral improvement than any other social system which has previously prevailed, which prevails elsewhere today or which outside Utopia, the mind of man has been able to provide a blueprint for" (Abramovitz 1981).

References

Abramovitz, Moses. 1981. "Welfare Quandaries and Productivity Concerns." *American Economic Review*, March.

Berger, Peter. 1986. *The Capitalist Revolution.* New York: Basic Books.

Dahl, Robert A. 1989. *Democracy and Its Critics.* New Haven: Yale University Press.

_____. 1990. *After the Revolution: Authority in a Good Society.* New Haven: Yale University Press.

Deutsch, Karl. 1961. "Social Mobilization and Political Development." *American Political Science Review*, 55 (Sept.).

Flora, Peter, and Arnold Heidenheimer. 1981. *The Development of Welfare States in Western Europe and America.* New Brunswick, NJ: Transaction Press.

Friedman, Milton. 1981. *Capitalism and Freedom.* Chicago: University of Chicago Press.

Hirschman, Albert. 1986. *Rival Views of Market Society.* New York: Viking.

Inkeles, Alex, and David Smith. 1974. *Becoming Modern: Individual Change in Six Developing Countries.* Cambridge, MA: Harvard University Press.

Lerner, Daniel. 1958. *The Passing of Traditional Society.* New York: Free Press.

Lindblom, Charles E. 1977. *Politics and Markets.* New York: Basic Books.

Lipset, Seymour M. 1959. "Some Social Requisites of Democracy." *American Political Science Review*, 53 (September).

Mill, John Stuart. 1848, 1965. *Principles of Political Economy*, 2 vols. Toronto: University of Toronto Press.

Mitchell, William. 1988. "Virginia, Rochester, and Bloomington: Twenty-Five Years of Public Choice and Political Science." *Public Choice*, 56: 101–119.

Moore, Barrington. 1966. *The Social Origins of Dictatorship and Democracy.* New York: Beacon Press.

Olson, Mancur. 1982. *The Rise and Decline of Nations.* New Haven: Yale University Press.

Schumpeter, Joseph. 1946. *Capitalism, Socialism, and Democracy.* New York: Harper.

GABRIEL A. ALMOND, professor of political science emeritus at Stanford University, is a former president of the American Political Science Association.

From *PS: Political Science and Politics,* September 1991, pp. 467–474. Copyright © 1991 by American Political Science Association—APSA. Reprinted by permission.

China: The Quiet Revolution
The Emergence of Capitalism

DOUG GUTHRIE

When Deng Xiaoping unveiled his vision of economic reform to the Third Plenum of the 11th Central Committee of the Chinese Communist Party in December 1978, the Chinese economy was faltering. Reeling from a decade of stagnation during the Cultural Revolution and already falling short of the projections set forth in the 1976 10-year plan, China needed more than a new plan and the Soviet-style economic vision of Deng's political rival, Hua Guofeng, to improve the economy. Deng's plan was to lead the country down a road of gradual and incremental economic reform, leaving the state apparatus intact, while slowly unleashing market forces. Since that time, the most common image of China, promulgated by members of the US Congress and media, is of an unbending authoritarian regime that has grown economically but seen little substantive change.

There is often a sense that China remains an entrenched and decaying authoritarian government run by corrupt Party officials; extreme accounts depict it as an economy on the verge of collapse. However, this vision simply does not square with reality. While it is true that China remains an authoritarian one-party system, it is also the most successful case of economic reform among communist planned economy in the 20th century. Today, it is fast emerging as one of the most dynamic market economies and has grown to be the world's sixth largest. Understanding how this change has come about requires an examination of three broad changes that have come together to shape China's transition to capitalism: the state's gradual recession from control over the economy, which caused a shift in economic control without privatization; the steady growth of foreign investment; and the gradual emergence of a legal-rational system to support these economic changes.

Reform Without Privatization

During the 1980s and 1990s, economists and institutional advisors from the West advocated a rapid transition to market institutions as the necessary medicine for transforming communist societies. Scholars argued that private property provides the institutional foundation of a market economy and that, therefore, communist societies making the transition to a market economy must privatize industry and other public goods. The radical members of this school argued that rapid privatization—the so-called "shock therapy" or "big bang" approach to economic reforms—was the only way to avoid costly abuses in these transitional systems.

The Chinese path has been very different. While countries like Russia have followed Western advice, such as rapidly constructing market institutions, immediately removing the state from control over the economy, and hastily privatizing property, China has taken its time in implementing institutional change. The state has gradually receded from control over the economy, cautiously experimenting with new institutions and implementing them incrementally within existing institutional arrangements. Through this gradual process of reform, China has achieved in 20 years what many developing states have taken over 50 to accomplish.

The success of gradual reform in China can be attributed to two factors. First, the gradual reforms allowed the government to retain its role as a stabilizing force in the midst of the turbulence accompanying the transition from a planned to a market economy. Institutions such as the "dual-track" system kept large state-owned enterprises partially on the plan and gave them incentives to generate extra income by selling what they could produce above the plan in China's nascent markets. Over time, as market economic practices became more successful, the "plan" part of an enterprise's portfolio was reduced and the "market" part grew. Enterprises were thus given the stability of a continued but gradually diminishing planned economy system as well as the time to learn to set prices, compete for contracts, and produce efficiently. Second, the government has gradually promoted ownership-like control down the government administrative hierarchy to the localities. As a result, the central government was able to give economic control to local administrators without privatization. But with economic control came accountability, and local administrators became very invested in the successful economic reform of the villages, townships, and municipalities under their jurisdictions. In a sense, as Professor Andrew Walder of Stanford University has argued, pushing economic responsibilities onto local administrators created an incentive structure much like those experienced by managers of large industrial firms.

Change from Above

Even as economic reform has proceeded gradually, the cumulative changes over two decades have been nothing short of radical. These reforms have proceeded on four levels: institutional changes instigated by the highest levels of government; firm-level institutions that reflect the legal-rational system emerging at the state level; a budding legal system that allows workers institutional backing outside of the factory and is heavily influenced by relationships with foreign investors; and the emergence of new labor markets, which allow workers the freedom and mobility to find new employment when necessary. The result of these changes has been the emergence of a legal-rational regime of labor, where the economy increasingly rests upon an infrastructure of ordered laws that workers can invoke when necessary.

Under Deng Xiaoping, Zhao Ziyang brought about radical change in China by pushing the country toward constitutionality and the rule of law to create rational economic processes. These changes, set forth ideologically as a package of reforms necessary for economic development, fundamentally altered the role of politics and the Communist Party in Chinese society. The early years of reform not only gave a great deal of autonomy to enterprise managers and small-scale entrepreneurs, but also emphasized the legal reforms that would undergird this process of change. However, by creating a body of civil and economic law, such as the 1994 Labor Law and Company Law and the 1995 National Compensation Law upon which the transforming economy would be based, the Party elites held themselves to the standards of these legal changes. Thus the rationalization of the economy led to a decline in the Party's ability to rule over the working population.

In recent years, this process has been continued by global integration and the tendency to adopt the norms of the international community. While championing global integration and the Rule of Law, Zhu Rongji also brought about broader political and social change, just as Zhao Ziyang did in China's first decade of economic reform.

Zhu's strategy has been to ignore questions of political reform and concentrate instead on the need to adopt economic and legal systems that will allow the country to integrate smoothly into the international community. From rhetoric on "linking up with the international community" to laws such as the 2000 Patent Law to institutions such as the State Intellectual Property Office and the Chinese International Economic Trade and Arbitration Commission, this phase of reform has been oriented toward enforcing the standards and norms of the international investment community. Thus, Zhu's objective is to deepen all of the reforms that have been discussed above, while holding these changes to the standards of the international community.

After two decades of transition, the architects of the reforms have established about 700 new national laws and more than 2,000 new local laws. These legal changes, added regulations, and experiments with new economic institutions have driven the reform process. A number of laws and policies in the 1980s laid the groundwork for a new set of policies that would redefine labor relations in fundamental ways. For example, the policies that set in motion the emergence of labor contracts in China were first introduced in an experimental way in 1983, further codified in 1986, and eventually institutionalized with the Labor Law in 1994. While there are economic incentives behind Chinese firms' willingness to embrace labor contracts, including the end of lifetime employment, these institutional changes have gradually rationalized the labor relationship, eventually providing a guarantee of due process in the event of unfair treatment and placing workers' rights at the center of the labor relationship. Incremental changes such as these have been crucial to the evolution of individual rights in China.

The obvious and most common response to these changes is that they are symbolic rather than substantive, that a changing legal and policy framework has little meaning when an authoritarian government still sits at the helm. Yet the scholarship that has looked extensively at the impact of these legal changes largely belies this view. Workers and managers take the new institutions seriously and recognize that the institutions have had a dramatic impact on the structure of authority relations and on the conception of rights within the workplace.

Other research shows that legal and policy changes that emphasize individual civil liberties are also significant. In the most systematic and exhaustive study to date of the prison system, research shows that changes in the treatment of prisoners have indeed resulted in the wake of the Prison Reform Law. And although no scholarship has been completed on the National Compensation Law, it is noteworthy that 97,569 suits were filed under this law against the government in 1999, a proportional increase of over 12,000 percent since the beginning of the economic reforms. These institutions guarantee that, for the first time in the history of the People's Republic of China, individuals can have their day in court, even at the government's expense.

The 1994 Labor Law and the Labor Arbitration Commission (LAC), which has branches in every urban district, work hand-in-hand to guarantee workers their individual rights as laborers. Chapter 10 of the Labor Law, entitled "Labor Disputes," is specifically devoted to articulating due process, which laborers are legally guaranteed, should a dispute arise in the workplace. The law explicitly explains the rights of the worker to take disputes to outside arbitration (the district's LAC) should the resolution in the workplace be unsatisfactory to the worker. Further, many state-owned enterprises have placed all of their workers on fixed-term labor contracts, which significantly rationalize the labor relationships beyond the personalized labor relations of the past. This bundle of changes has fundamentally altered the nature of the labor relationship and the mechanisms through which authority can be challenged. For more than a decade, it has been possible for workers to file grievances against superiors and have those grievances heard at the LACs. In 1999, 52 percent of the 120,191 labor disputes settled by arbitration or mediation were decided wholly in favor of the workers filing the suits. These are official statistics from the Chinese government, and therefore should be viewed skeptically. However, even if the magnitude is incorrect, these numbers illuminate an important trend toward legal activity regarding workers' rights.

Many of these changes in labor practices were not originally adopted with workers' rights in mind, but the unintended consequence of the changes has been the construction of a regime of labor relations that emphasizes the rights of workers. For instance, extending the example of labor contracts that were being experimented with as early as 1983, these were originally intended as a form of economic protection for ailing enterprises, allowing a formal method of ending lifetime employment. However, workers began using the terms of employment codified in the contracts as the vehicle for filing grievances when contractual agreements were not honored. With the emergence of the LACs in the late 1980s and the further codification of these institutions in the Labor Law, the changes that were in progress became formalized in a set of institutions that ultimately benefited workers in the realm of rights. In a similar way, workers' representative committees were formed in the state's interest, but became an institution workers claimed as their own. These institutions, which many managers refer to as "our own little democracy," were adopted early in the reforms to co-opt the agitation for independent labor unions. These committees do not have the same power or status as independent labor unions in the West, but workers have made them much more significant in factories today than they were originally intended to be.

Foreign Investment's Impact

At the firm level, there is a process of rationalization in which firms are adopting a number of rational bureaucratic systems, such as grievance filing procedures, mediation

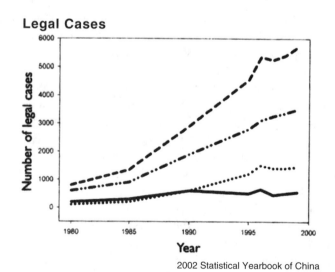

2002 Statistical Yearbook of China

Figure 1 An Age of Jurisprudence.

The above graphs depict two recent trends in China: a growing body of lawyers and an increasing number of legal cases. As the graph at left indicates, the number of lawyers in China has increased dramatically in the past 20 years, rising from fewer than 10,000 in 1980 to over 100,000 in 2000. The graph at right shows the growth in various types of legal cases over the same period. In particular, there have been significant increases in civil, economic, and first-trial cases.

committees, and formal organizational processes, that are more often found in Western organizations. In my own work on these issues, I have found that joint venture relationships encourage foreign joint ventures to push their partner organizations to adopt stable legal-rational structures and systems in their organizations. These stable, legal-rational systems are adopted to attract foreign investors, but have radical implications for the structure of authority relations and the lives of individual Chinese citizens. Chinese factories that have formal relationships with foreign, and particularly Western, firms are significantly more likely to have institutionalized formal organizational rules, 20 times more likely to have formal grievance filing procedures, five times more likely to have worker representative committee meetings, and about two times more likely to have institutionalized formal hiring procedures. They also pay about 50 percent higher wages than other factories and are more likely to adopt China's new Company Law, which binds them to abide by the norms of the international community and to respect international legal institutions such as the Chinese International Economic Arbitration and Trade Commission. Many managers openly acknowledge that the changes they have set in place have little to do with their own ideas of efficient business practices and much more to do with pressure brought on them by their foreign partners. Thus, there is strong evidence that foreign investment matters for on-the-ground change in China.

Foreign investors and Chinese firms are not interested in human rights per se, but the negotiations in the marketplace lead to transformed workplaces, which affect millions of Chinese citizens on a daily basis.

Given the common image of multinational corporations seeking weak institutional environments to capitalize on cheap labor, why would joint venture relationships with Western multinationals have a more positive impact in the Chinese case? The answer has to do with the complex reasons for foreign investment there. Corporations are rarely the leading advocates of civil liberties and labor reform, but many foreign investors in China are more interested in long-term investments that position them to capture market share than they are in cheap labor. They generally seek Chinese partners that are predictable, stable, and knowledgeable about Western-style business practices and negotiations. Chinese factories desperately want to land

these partnerships and position themselves as suitable investment partners by adopting a number of the practices that Western partners will recognize as stable and reform-minded. Among the basic reforms they adopt to show their fitness for "linking up" with the international community are labor reforms. Thus, the signaling of a commitment to stable Western-style business practices through commitments to labor reform has led to fundamental changes in Chinese workplace labor relations. Foreign investors and Chinese firms are not interested in human rights per se, but the negotiations in the marketplace lead to transformed workplaces, which affect millions of Chinese citizens on a daily basis.

However, changes at the firm level are not meaningful if they lack the legal infrastructure upon which a legal-rational system of labor is built. The construction of a legal system is a process that takes time; it requires the training of lawyers and judges, and the emergence of a culture in which individuals who are part of the legal system come to process claims. This process of change is difficult to assess because it relies on soft variables about the reform process, such as, for example, how judges think about suits and whether a legal-rational culture is emerging. But we can look at some aspects of fundamental shifts in society. All of these changes, in turn, rest upon a legal-rational system that is slowly but surely emerging in China.

Finally, beyond the legal and institutional changes that have begun to transform Chinese society fundamentally, workers are no longer tied to workplaces in the way that they once were. In the pre-reform system, there was very little mobility of labor, because workers were generally bound to their "work units" for life. The system created a great deal of stability for workers, but it also became one of the primary means through which citizens were controlled. Individuals were members of their work units, which they were dependent on for a variety of fundamental goods and services.

This manufactured dependence was one of the basic ways that the Party exercised control over the population. Writing about the social uprisings that occurred in 1989, Walder points out that the erosion of this system is what allowed citizens to protest with impunity on a scale never before observed in communist China: "[W]hat changed in these regimes in the last decade was not their economic difficulties, widespread cynicism or corruption, but that the institutional mechanisms that served to promote order in the past—despite these long-standing problems—lost their capacity to do so." It is precisely because labor markets have opened up that workers are no longer absolutely dependent upon the government for job placements; they now have much more leverage to assert the importance of their own rights in the workplace. And while the private sector was nonexistent when the economic reforms began, the country has seen this sector, which includes both private enterprises and household businesses, grow to more than 30 million individuals. With the growth of the private sector, there is much greater movement and autonomy among laborers in the economy. This change has afforded workers alternative paths to status attainment, paths that were once solely controlled by the government.

Quiet Revolution

Much like the advocates of rapid economic reform, those demanding immediate political and social reform often take for granted the learning that must occur in the face of new institutions. The assumption most often seems that, given certain institutional arrangements, individuals will naturally know how to carry out the practices of capitalism. Yet these assumptions reflect a neoclassical view of human nature in which rational man will thrive in his natural environment—free markets. Completely absent from this view are the roles of history, culture, and pre-existing institutions; it is a vision that is far too simplistic to comprehend the challenge of making rational economic and legal systems work in the absence of stable institutions and a history to which they can be linked. The transition from a command economy to a market economy can be a wrenching experience, not only at the institutional level but also at the level of individual practice. Individuals must learn the rules of the market and new institutions must be in place long enough to gain stability and legitimacy.

The PRC government's methodical experimentation with different institutional forms and the Party's gradual relinquishing of control over the economy has brought about a "quiet revolution." It is impossible to create a history of a legal-rational economic system in a dramatic moment of institutional change. The architects of China's transition to capitalism have had success in reforming the economy because they have recognized that the transition to a radically different type of economic system must occur gradually, allowing for the maximum possible institutional stability as economic actors slowly learn the rules of capitalism. Capitalism has indeed arrived in China, and it has done so via gradual institutional reform under the communist mantle.

DOUG GUTHRIE is Associate Professor of Sociology at New York University.

A Confident New Country

JO JOHNSON

In the 60 years since India won its independence, it has confounded dire predictions made for its future. Winston Churchill once famously described the country as a mere "geographical expression", a land that was "no more a united nation than the Equator".

He warned that "to abandon India to the rule of the Brahmins would be an act of cruel and wicked negligence". If the British left, he predicted, India would "fall back quite rapidly through the centuries into the barbarism and privations of the Middle Ages", a fear that the massacre of an estimated 1m refugees during the partition of the subcontinent in 1947 seemed at first to confirm.

Self-government, let alone good government, colonialists said, could never be possible in a country with such ethnic, religious, linguistic, climatic and developmental diversity. With more than 35 languages—and each one of them spoken by 1m people—and with profound cleavages along caste and communal lines, India seemed destined to fragment within a few years of the British departure. Post-independence history has been "peppered with forecasts of imminent dissolution, or of its descent into anarchy or authoritarian rule", notes Ramachandra Guha, a leading historian. That India could sustain democracy seemed in 1947 highly improbable.

Only by the late 1970s—after the country rejected Indira Gandhi's authoritarian tendencies—did fears for democracy start to recede. But doubts persisted that the country would ever attain the great power status coveted by its elites. India seemed "destined always to be 'emerging' but never actually arriving", a country fated to be forever "lodged in the second rank of international politics", as Stephen P Cohen of the Brookings Institution put it.* With its economy growing at just 3 or per cent a year until the 1980s—a pace disparagingly termed the "Hindu rate of growth"—there seemed little prospect that India would ever rise in the hierarchy of states.

Churchill claimed that India was 'no more a united nation than the Equator.'

The pessimists were wrong. Now, 60 years on, India has consolidated a vibrant and competitive form of democracy; banished famine; more than halved its absolute poverty rate; dramatically improved literacy and health conditions; achieved global competitiveness in information technology, business process outsourcing, telecommunications and pharmaceuticals; acquired de facto membership of the elite club of acknowledged nuclear powers; created more billionaires than any other country in Asia; and became one of the world's most dynamic and fastest growing economies, ranked the world's fourth largest in purchasing power parity terms.

Over the past decade, India has acquired a new geo-strategic importance. The US National Intelligence Council's "Mapping the Global Future" project argued that the emergence of China and India would transform the geopolitical landscape with an impact comparable with the rise of Germany in the 19th century and that of the US in the early 20th century. Between the two Asian powers, there is little doubt where US affinities lie. An India that can emerge as a "geopolitical counterweight" to China and buttress of the Pax Americana is a persistent private theme of administration officials. George W Bush regularly notes that New Delhi's "commitment to secular government and religious pluralism" makes India a natural partner for the US.

The most telling indication of this new stature and perceived value as an ally came in March 2005, when Condoleezza Rice, secretary of state, formally proclaimed the US's determination to support India's emergence as global power. The second Bush administration has worked tirelessly to construct a deep strategic partnership with India, from which it had been estranged during the cold war. Pivotal to this has been an agreement to resume civil nuclear co-operation, abruptly suspended following India's test of a nuclear device in 1974. The deal, now awaiting approval by the US Congress and the International Atomic Energy Agency, promises to end three decades of isolation for the Indian scientific establishment.

"India is a rising global power with a rapidly growing economy," says Nicholas Burns, US under-secretary of state for political affairs, who has led the two-year negotiations on the nuclear deal. "Within the first quarter of this century, it is likely to be included among the world's five largest economies. It will soon be the world's most populous nation and it has a demographic distribution that bequeaths it a huge, skilled and youthful workforce. India's military forces will continue to be large, capable and increasingly sophisticated." That consciousness of India's significance is echoed in the American private sector. Membership of the US India Business Council, a 32-year-old lobby group, has soared from 90 companies at the start of 2005 to more than 250.

Nothing more clearly illustrates the new confidence than the spate of cross-border takeovers involving Indian companies.

Tata Steel's $11bn acquisition of Corus, the Anglo-Dutch steel group, and Vodafone's $11bn purchase of a controlling interest in Hutchison Essar, the fourth-largest Indian mobile operator, have only smashed existing records for mergers and acquisitions involving Indian companies, both as predators and prey, but also mark what many see as a new era of India-centric corporate activity. At the heart of this trend is a reappraisal of the country's economic potential after decades of miserly growth. Over the past three years, growth in gross domestic product has expanded at an unprecedented pace. It touched 9.4 per cent last year, making India's the second-fastest growing economy in Asia.

Even though higher interest rates may trigger a slowdown this year, with Morgan Stanley predicting GDP growth will fall to 7.7 per cent, India's Planning Commission expects the economy to grow by 9 per cent during the 11th five-year plan period (2008-2012). India is now growing nearly as fast as China and globalising almost as rapidly. Whether measured in terms of trade as a share of GDP, the number of Indian companies seeking overseas listings and acquisitions, or the global ambitions of its resurgent manufacturers, India is intertwining with the world as never before.

Decades of socialist experimentation with import substitution, high tariffs and industrial licensing left India a minnow in world trade at the start of the 1990s. Today it accounts for a smaller share of global merchandise exports than in 1947 and its economy remains far less trade-intensive than China's. This is starting to change. Kamal Nath, the commerce minister, hopes the country will exports goods worth $160bn this year despite the sharp appreciation of the rupee, an increase of 28 per cent over 2006-7.

Many challenges still face even this confident new India. One of the most worrying is that its highly competitive democracy has been increasingly unable to provide voters with a means of holding governments accountable for the delivery of core public services. As incomes rise and media penetration boosts awareness of inequalities, there is mounting frustration at the state's failure to provide decent water, sanitation, power, education, policing, roads and healthcare. Progress has been made in getting more children into primary school but the education imparted remains of an abysmally low standard.

Although population growth has fallen below 2 per cent a year, many of the country's human development indicators still flash red. In some states, malnutrition rates have been rising in recent years.

In the excitement about the "new" India, it is often forgotten that it has a child malnutrition rate higher than sub-Saharan Africa—at 45.9 per cent of children aged under three, a rate that reflects "negligible improvement" over the past five years, according to Unicef, the United Nations children's agency.

Above all, India faces the challenge of making growth more inclusive. Senior Congress party leaders are worried that the United Progressive Alliance government, which has lost a series of state elections in recent months and suffered from a backlash against its promotion of special economic zones, has neglected the "aam admi" (common man) in pursuit of economic growth.

Substantial disparities persist. The World Bank notes that, in a marked departure from previous decades, the reforms of the 1990s were accompanied by a visible increase in income inequality. Although this continues to be relatively low by global standards—on the Gini index, where 0 represents perfect equality and 100 absolute inequality, India measures 32.5 and China 44.7—disparities between urban and rural areas, prosperous and lagging states, skilled and low-skilled workers are growing. Evidence of social unrest in some disadvantaged regions is alarming, with an extreme leftist revolutionary movement, known as Naxalism, now affecting more than a quarter of the country's 600 or so districts.

Slow agricultural growth—at just 2.7 per cent, it is far below the government's 4 per cent target—is perhaps the single greatest worry for policymakers concerned at the prospect of uncontrollable migration to the cities. The World Bank believes that current agricultural practices are neither economically nor environmentally sustainable. Poorly maintained irrigation systems, inadequate roads, over-regulation and lack of access to formal sources of finance are all factors that hamper farmers' access to markets.

Rural indebtedness to money-lenders has resulted in a politically explosive wave of suicides among small, marginal and tenant farmers. With yields for many agricultural commodities low and falling, India has been forced to start importing wheat and other essential foodstuffs.

While the services sector booms with promising job opportunities for skilled workers, 90 per cent of India's labour force remains trapped in low productivity informal sector jobs.

Sixty years ago, on the eve of independence, Jawaharlal Nehru, the country's first prime minister, in a famous speech to parliament, evoked India's "tryst with destiny" and called on his then 340m fellow countrymen to help him "build the noble mansion of free India where all her children may dwell. There is no resting for any one of us till we redeem our pledge in full, till we make all the people of India what destiny intended them to be".

With one in four Indians still living in absolute poverty, Nehru's promise remains unfulfilled for more than 260m people. Confronted by a population set to expand from 1.1bn to perhaps 1.5bn by the time it stabilises in the middle of the century, with more than half of this increase in five of the poorest states, there will be no rest for India's leaders for years to come.

It is forgotten that India has a child malnutrition rate higher than sub-Saharan Africa.

India: Emerging Power, STEPHEN P COHEN, Oxford University Press, 2001.

Japanese Spirit, Western Things

When America's black ships forced open Japan, nobody could have predicted that the two nations would become the world's great economic powers.

Open up. With that simple demand, Commodore Matthew Perry steamed into Japan's Edo (now Tokyo) Bay with his "black ships of evil mien" 150 years ago this week. Before the black ships arrived on July 8th 1853, the Tokugawa shoguns had run Japan for 250 years as a reclusive feudal state. Carrying a letter from America's president, Millard Fillmore, and punctuating his message with cannon fire, Commodore Perry ordered Japan's rulers to drop their barriers and open the country to trade. Over the next century and a half, Japan emerged as one of history's great economic success stories. It is now the largest creditor to the world that it previously shunned. Attempts to dissect this economic "miracle" often focus intently on the aftermath of the second world war. Japan's occupation by the Americans, who set out to rebuild the country as a pacifist liberal democracy, helped to set the stage for four decades of jaw-dropping growth. Yet the origins of the miracle—and of the continual tensions it has created inside Japan and out—stretch further back. When General Douglas MacArthur accepted Japan's surrender in 1945 aboard the battleship Missouri, the Americans made sure to hang Commodore Perry's flag from 1853 over the ship's rear turret. They had not only ended a brutal war and avenged the attack on Pearl Harbour—they had also, they thought, won an argument with Japan that was by then nearly a century old.

America's enduring frustration—in the decades after 1853, in 1945, and even today—has not been so much that Japan is closed, but that it long ago mastered the art of opening up on its own terms. Before and after those black ships steamed into Edo Bay, after all, plenty of other countries were opened to trade by western cannon. What set Japan apart—perhaps aided by America's lack of colonial ambition—was its ability to decide for itself how to make the process of opening suit its own aims.

One consequence of this is that Japan's trading partners, especially America, have never tired of complaining about its economic practices. Japan-bashing reached its most recent peak in the 1980s, when American politicians and businessmen blamed "unfair" competition for Japan's large trade surpluses. But similar complaints could be heard within a few decades of Commodore Perry's mission. The attitude was summed up by "Mr Dooley", a character created by Peter Finley Dunne, an American satirist, at the close of the 19th century: "Th' trouble is whin the gallant Commodore kicked opn th' door, we didn't go in. They come out."

Nowadays, although poor countries still want Japan (along with America and the European Union) to free up trade in farm goods, most rich-country complaints about Japan are aimed at its approach to macroeconomics and finance, rather than its trade policies. Japan's insistence on protecting bad banks and worthless companies, say its many critics, and its reluctance to let foreign investors help fix the economy, have prevented Japanese demand from recovering for far too long. Once again, the refrain goes, Japan is unfairly taking what it can get from the world economy—exports and overseas profits have been its only source of comfort for years—without giving anything back.

While these complaints have always had some merit, they have all too often been made in a way that misses a crucial point: Japan's economic miracle, though at times paired with policies ranging from protectionist to xenophobic, has nevertheless proved a huge blessing to the rest of the world as well. The "structural impediments" that shut out imports in the 1980s did indeed keep Japanese consumers and foreign exporters from enjoying some of the fruits of that miracle; but its export prowess allowed western consumers to enjoy better and cheaper cars and electronics even as Japanese households grew richer. Similarly, Japan's resistance to inward investment is indefensible, not least because it allows salvageable Japanese companies to wither; but its outward investment has helped to transform much of East Asia into a thriving economic region, putting a huge dent in global poverty. Indeed, one of the most impressive aspects of Japan's economic miracle is that, even while reaping only half the potential gains from free trade and investment, it has still managed to do the world so much good over the past half-century.

Setting an Example

Arguably, however, Japan's other big effect on the world has been even more important. It has shown clearly that you do not have to embrace "western" culture in order to modernise your economy and prosper. From the very beginning, Japan set out to have one without the other, an approach encapsulated by the saying "Japanese spirit, western things". How did Japan pull it off? In part, because the historical combination of having once been wide open, and then rapidly slamming shut, taught Japan how to control the aperture through which new ideas and practices streamed in. After eagerly absorbing Chinese culture, philosophy, writing and technology for roughly a millennium, Japan followed this with 250 years of near-total isolation. Christianity was outlawed, and overseas travel was punishable by death. Although some Japanese scholars were aware of developments in Europe—which went under the broad heading of "Dutch studies"—the shoguns strictly limited their ability to put any of that knowledge to use. They confined all economic and other exchanges with Europeans to a tiny man-made island in the south-western port of Nagasaki. When the Americans arrived in 1853, the Japanese told them to go to Nagasaki and obey the rules. Commodore Perry refused, and Japan concluded that the only way to "expel the barbarians" in future would be to embrace their technology and grow stronger.

But once the door was ajar, the Japanese appetite for "western things" grew unbounded. A modern guidebook entry on the port city of Yokohama, near Tokyo, notes that within two decades of the black ships' arrival it boasted the country's first bakery (1860), photo shop (1862), telephone (1869), beer brewery (1869), cinema (1870), daily newspaper (1870), and public lavatory (1871). Yet, at the same time, Japan's rulers also managed to frustrate many of the westerners' wishes. The constant tension between Japan's desire to measure up to the West—economically, diplomatically, socially and, until 1945, militarily—and its resistance to cultural change has played out in countless ways, good and bad, to this day. Much of it has reflected a healthy wish to hang on to local traditions. This is far more than just a matter of bowing and sleeping on futons and tatami, or of old women continuing to wear kimonos. The Japanese have also clung to distinct ways of speaking, interacting in the workplace, and showing each other respect, all of which have helped people to maintain harmony in many aspects of everyday life. Unfortunately, however, ever since they first opened to the West, anti-liberal Japanese leaders have preferred another interpretation of "Japanese spirit, western things". Instead of simply trying to preserve small cultural traditions, Japan's power-brokers tried to absorb western technology in a way that would shield them from political competition and protect their interests. Imitators still abound in Japan and elsewhere. In East Asia alone, Malaysia's Mahathir Mohamad, Thailand's Thaksin Shinawatra, and even the Chinese Communist Party all see Japan as proof that there is a way to join the rich-country club without making national leaders or their friends accountable. These disciples of Japan's brand of modernisation often use talk of local culture to resist economic and political threats to their power. But they are careful to find ways to do this without undermining all trade and investment, since growth is the only thing propping them up.

Japan's first attempt to pursue this strategy, it must never be forgotten, grew increasingly horrific as its inconsistencies mounted. In 1868, while western writers were admiring those bakeries and cinemas, Japan's nationalist leaders were "restoring" the emperor's significance to that of an imaginary golden age. The trouble, as Ian Buruma describes in his new book, "Inventing Japan" (see article), is that the "Japanese spirit" they valued was a concoction that mixed in several bad western ideas: German theories on racial purity, European excuses for colonialism, and the observation from Christianity that a single overarching deity (in Japan's case the newly restored emperor) could motivate soldiers better than a loose contingent of Shinto gods. This combination would eventually whip countless young Japanese into a murderous xenophobic frenzy and foster rapacious colonial aggression.

It also led Japan into a head-on collision with the United States, since colonialism directly contradicted America's reasons for sending Commodore Perry. In "The Clash", a 1998 book on the history of American-Japanese relations, Walter LaFeber argues that America's main goal in opening Japan was not so much to trade bilaterally, as to enlist Japan's support in creating a global marketplace including, in particular, China. At first, the United States opened Japan because it was on the way to China and had coal for American steamships. Later, as Japan gained industrial and military might, America sought to use it as a counterweight to European colonial powers that wanted to divide China among their empires. America grew steadily more furious, therefore, as Japan turned to colonialism and tried to carve up China on its own. The irony for America was that at its very moment of triumph, after nearly a century of struggling with European powers and then Japan to keep China united and open, it ended up losing it to communism.

A half-century later, however, and with a great deal of help from Japan, America has achieved almost exactly what it set out to do as a brash young power in the 1850s, when it had barely tamed its own continent and was less than a decade away from civil war. Mainland China is whole. It has joined the World Trade Organisation and is rapidly integrating itself into the global economy. It is part of a vast East Asian trade network that nevertheless carries out more than half of its trade outside the region. And this is all backed up by an array of American security guarantees in the Pacific. The resemblance to what America set out to do in 1853 is striking.

For both Japan and America, therefore, the difficult 150-year relationship has brought impressive results. They are now the world's two biggest economies, and have driven most of the world's technological advances over the past half-century. America has helped Japan by opening it up, destroying its militarists and rebuilding the country afterwards, and, for the last 50 years, providing security and market access while Japan became an advanced export dynamo. Japan has helped America by improving on many of its technologies, teaching it new manufacturing techniques, spurring on American firms with its competition, and venturing into East Asia to trade and invest.

And Now?

What, then, will the continuing tension between Japanese spirit and western things bring in the decades ahead? For America, though it will no doubt keep complaining, Japan's resistance to change is not the real worry. Instead, the same two Asian challenges that America has taken on ever since Commodore Perry sailed in will remain the most worrying risks: potential rivalries, and the desire by some leaders to form exclusive regional economic blocks. America still needs Japan, its chief Asian ally, to combat these dangers. Japan's failure to reform, however, could slowly sap its usefulness.

For Japan, the challenges are far more daunting. Many of them stem from the increasing toll that Japan's old ways are taking on the economy. Chief among these is Japan's hostility towards competition in many aspects of economic life. Although competitive private firms have driven much of its innovation and growth, especially in export-intensive industries, Japan's political system continues to hobble competition and private enterprise in many domestic sectors.

In farming, health care and education, for example, recent efforts to allow private companies a role have been swatted down by co-operatives, workers, politicians and civil servants. In other inefficient sectors, such as construction and distribution, would-be losers continue to be propped up by government policy. Now that Japan is no longer growing rapidly, it is harder for competitive forces to function without allowing some of those losers to fail.

Japan's foreign critics are correct, moreover, that its macroeconomic and financial policies are a disgrace. The central bank, the finance ministry, the bank regulators, the prime minister and the ruling-party politicians all blame each other for failing to deal with the problems. All the while, Japan continues to limp along, growing far below its potential as its liabilities mount. Its public-sector debt, for instance, is a terrifying 140% of GDP.

Lately, there has been much talk about employing more western things to help lift Japan out of its mess. The prime minister, Junichiro Koizumi, talks about deregulatory measures that have been tried in North America, Europe and elsewhere. Western auditing and corporate governance techniques—applied in a Japanese way, of course—are also lauded as potential fixes. Even inward foreign direct investment is held out by Mr Koizumi as part of the solution: he has pledged to double it over the next five years. The trouble with all of these ideas, however, is that nobody in Japan is accountable for implementing them. Moreover, most of the politicians and bureaucrats who prevent

competitive pressures from driving change are themselves protected from political competition. It is undeniable that real change in Japan would bring unwelcome pain for many workers and small-business owners. Still, Japan's leaders continue to use these cultural excuses, as they have for 150 years, to mask their own efforts to cling to power and prestige. The ugly, undemocratic and illiberal aspects of Japanese traditionalism continue to lurk behind its admirable elements. One reason they can do so is because Japan's nationalists have succeeded completely in one of their original goals: financial independence. The desire to avoid relying on foreign capital has underlain Japan's economic policies from the time it opened up to trade. Those policies have worked. More than 90% of government bonds are in the hands of domestic investors, and savings accounts run by the postal service play a huge role in propping up the system.

Paradoxically, financial self-reliance has thus become Japan's curse. There are worse curses to have, of course: compare Japan with the countless countries that have wrecked their economies by overexposing themselves to volatile international capital markets. Nevertheless, Japan's financial insularity further protects its politicians, who do not have to compete with other countries to get funding.

Theories abound as to how all of this might change. Its history ought to remind anyone that, however long it takes, Japan usually moves rapidly once a consensus takes shape. Potential pressures for change could come from the reversal of its trade surpluses, an erosion of support from all those placid postal savers, or the unwinding of ties that allow bad banks and bad companies to protect each other from investors. The current political stalemate could also give way to a coherent plan, either because one political or bureaucratic faction defeats the others or because a strong leader emerges who can force them to co-operate. The past 150 years suggest, however, that one important question is impossible to answer in advance: will it be liberalism or its enemies who turn such changes to their advantage? Too often, Japan's conservative and nationalist leaders have managed to spot the forces of change more quickly than their liberal domestic counterparts, and have used those changes to seize the advantage and preserve their power. Just as in the past, East Asia's fortunes still greatly depend on the outcome of the struggle between these perennial Japanese contenders.

Job Security, Too, May Have a Happy Medium

Louis Uchitelle

For more than a decade, many American economists have pointed to Europe and Japan as prima facie evidence that layoffs in the United States are a good thing. The economies in those countries were not nearly as robust as this country's. And the reason? Too much job security in Europe and Japan, the economists said.

American employers, in sharp contrast, have operated with much more "flexibility." Hiring and firing at will, they shift labor from where it is not needed to where it is needed. If Eastman Kodak is struggling to establish itself in digital photography, then Kodak downsizes and labor moves to industries and companies that are thriving—software, for example, or health care, or Wal-Mart Stores or Caterpillar.

This shuffling out of one job and into another shows up in the statistics as nearly full employment. Never mind that the shuffling does not work as efficiently as the description implies or that many of the laid-off workers find themselves earning less in their next jobs, an income roller coaster that is absent in Europe and Japan. A dynamic economy leaves no alternative, or so the reasoning goes among mainstream economists.

"Trying to prevent this creative destruction from happening is a recipe for less economic growth and less productivity," said Barry Eichengreen, an international economist at the University of California, Berkeley.

Starting in the mid-1990s, Europe and Japan did wallow in recession or weak growth while the American economy expanded at a spectacular clip. But no longer. Growth is slowing in the United States just as it speeds up in the 25-nation European Union and in Japan. Unemployment rates in those countries are also beginning to come down, suggesting that the American system is not the only route to full employment.

As the gaps close, does that mean that job security, in the European and Japanese style, is the right way to go after all? The question would be easier to answer if the European Union countries and Japan had stuck to their orthodox job security. They have not. On their way to revival, they adopted some of America's practices.

"A number of countries have found ways to make their labor markets more flexible, without sacrificing their greater commitment to a government role in equalizing incomes," said Paul Swaim, a senior economist at the Organization for Economic Cooperation and Development in Paris.

So the old dichotomy—insecurity versus security—is gradually giving way to a new debate. "It is obviously the right mix of security and insecurity that has to be achieved," said Richard B. Freeman, a labor economist at Harvard. "You can't protect people their whole working lives. That undercuts incentive. But you can't tell people they have no security at all."

The guideposts in this search for the right mix should not be just economic growth rates and unemployment levels. These are too often affected by business cycles. Many American economists, bent on demonstrating the payoff from layoffs, paid relatively little attention to the cyclical reasons for the underperformance of Japan and Europe.

"Sometimes we forget these cyclical forces," said Sanford M. Jacoby, an economic historian at the University of California, Los Angeles.

Japan and Western Europe flourished in the 1980s. And then the cycle changed. Japan plunged into a prolonged recession, brought on by the bursting of stock market and real estate bubbles, an overcautious central bank and a banking crisis. Europe also fell into the doldrums, partly because of the difficulties of organizing the European Union. Integrating East Germany into West Germany, Europe's strongest economy, did not help, either.

But now Japan is in the fifth year of an ever-stronger recovery, and this year, according to some forecasts, growth in the European Union may even exceed that in the United States, where the economy may be weakening in the sixth year of a recovery.

Cycles count. But so do labor policies.

In some European countries, employers are using temporary and part-time workers much more than they did in the past. That gives them leeway to expand and contract their work forces without having to add full-timers who are protected against layoffs. Similar protection exists in Japan, which also relies for "flexibility" on part-timers and temps.

If cost-cutting is necessary in Japan, there is a pecking order, says Yoshi Tsurumi, an economist at Baruch College in Manhattan and a consultant to Japanese companies. Dividends are cut first, then salaries—starting at the top. Finally, there are layoffs—if attrition is not enough to shrink staff.

"The matter of flexibility is important," Mr. Tsurumi said, "but the Japanese notion is to retrain and transfer people within an organization."

Elsewhere, France and Germany have eased job protection for employees of small businesses. Payroll taxes paid by employers have been cut for some low-income workers, increasing the demand for them.

And the Danish model is getting a lot of attention. Employers in Denmark are relatively free to lay off workers, but the state then steps in with benefits that replace 70 percent of the lost income for four years. Government also finances retraining and education, pressuring the unemployed to participate and then insisting that they accept reasonable job offers or risk cuts in their benefits.

The Danish government devotes 3 percent of the nation's gross domestic product to retraining, compared with less than 1 percent in the United States. And, of course, everywhere in Europe, the state pays for health insurance and for pensions that often encourage early retirement by replacing big percentages of preretirement income.

"What the Europeans and the Japanese understand is that modern economies can sustain social protections without killing the golden goose," said Jared Bernstein, a senior economist at the Economic Policy Institute in Washington.

That is an understanding that perhaps will take root among American economists and policy makers, deprived as they now are of their long-running contention that job security resulted in weak economic growth in Europe and Japan.

UNIT 7

Trends and Challenges: Institutional Change through Democratization, Globalization, or Supra-National Government?

Unit Selections

Key Points to Consider

- What are the changes that lead to democratization?

- How does globalization lead to institutional changes?

- How is the EU important?

- How is negative opinion different from value-bias in expressing Anti-Americanism?

- How useful are cultural explanations?

- How does culture explain value changes?

- What explains value changes?

Student Web Site
www.mhcls.com

Internet References

Commission on Global Governance
   http://www.sovereignty.net/p/gov/gganalysis.htm
Europa: European Union
   http://europa.eu.int
ISN International Relations and Security Network
   http://www.isn.ethz.ch
NATO Integrated Data Service (NIDS)
   http://www.nato.int/structur/nids/nids.htm
United Nations Environment Program
   http://www.unep.ch/

Units 1 through 6 describe the systematic treatment of the political behaviors of citizens, interest groups, parties, the executive, legislature, bureaucracy, and the judiciary in government. The discussions make clear the relevance of institutions in providing formal venues to regulate and regularize political behaviors so that they are clear-cut, comprehensible, constant and, thus, predictable. But, if political behaviors are influenced by institutions, it is also indisputable that they shape institutions. In this Unit, we examine the "what, how, and why" of institutional changes. In the process, we consider the extent to which political behaviors shape institutions.

What are institutional changes? Institutional changes refer to the creation or alteration of political organizations, conventions, or participation. They include modifications in the political control of an existing organization, as the article on Beijing censors reports. They may involve the creation of new political organizations, as indicated by the article on the EU. Or they may capture a change in political conventions, as described in the article on Anti-Americanism.

How do institutional changes occur? Institutional changes are brought on by a combination of the following: domestic demand, such as by citizens, interest groups, and the government; or new pressures, such as the need for political, social, and economic integration in response to globalization. Thus, the article on the Beijing censors points out that domestic demand by citizens has led to a change in information control under the Propaganda Department in China, the country's "information police" that outranks even government ministries (2007: 93–5).[1] The example is significant in two regards: first, it shows that even governments in authoritarian countries make institutional changes in response to the people's challenges and demands. Second, it reveals the potency of market forces, particularly in the form of capital, as a viable means to exercise challenge and bring about political or institutional change. Some may quarrel about the utility of market forces; there are arguments that anti-Americanism actually represents a "globalization backlash" against the role of the market forces in changing societies and political traditions. But the articles by international scholars Peter Katzenstein and

Robert Keohane, and Ronald Inglehart and Pippa Norris, assert that this argument is baseless and share the conclusion that "economic development generates changed attitudes" that fundamentally fuel institutional changes.

Institutional changes are also brought on by new pressures. Thus, Alberta Sbragia's article on the EU constitution notes that the economic, social, and political regional integration of European nations has been institutionalized in the past 50 years in response to political, economic, and social pressures from a changing world. She names several EU policies that are in place that have benefited those in and out of Europe, including development aid to poor countries, peacekeeping troops in Bosnia and Herzegovina, and a lower cost of living and travel for Europeans. Given the situation, one is pressed to ask: why was the EU constitution rejected? According to Alberta Sbragia, the rejection is from the public, whose reaction to the EU is largely from a domestic economic perspective rather than a supra-national, geo-political, or geo-economics argument. While her article deals with the set-back posed by the rejection of the EU constitution in France and the Netherlands, it is provocative primarily in its conclusion of the inevitability of such regional integration, rather than how such integration is achieved.

Why do institutional changes occur? The articles by Katzenstein and Keohane, and Inglehart and Norris emphasize the relevance of value or attitude changes to institutional changes. Thus, Inglehart and Norris point out that democratization in the Muslim world is supported or hampered by values over self-expression rather than on its cultural aptitude for democracy. Likewise, Katzenstein and Keohane argue that the anti-Americanism is most problematic when it goes beyond negative opinions and is, instead, based on value-bias against the U.S. This seems to be reiterated in the Sbragia article: her proposal that the EU constitution will likely be accepted if framed as a geo-political or geo-economics project that maximizes European influence shows that it is an issue of values rather than a fundamental rejection of EU institutionalization.

What about the role of culture in institutional changes? Although frequently cited as a reason for change or the lack of change, it is not a useful explanation of either political stability or institutional change. The articles by Inglehart and Norris, and *The Economist* on cultural explanations conclude that the term is imprecise and hinges on stereotypes rather than on realistic information. Thus, Inglehart and Norris point out that survey results show that, contrary to Huntington's assertion that "individualism, liberalism, constitutionalism, and human rights" are uniquely western values, survey results show that in Albania, Azerbaijan, Bangladesh, Egypt, Indonesia, Iran, Morroco, and Turkey, "92 to 99 percent of the public endorsed democratic institutions—a higher proportion than in the US (89 percent)." The article on cultural explanations also finds much to question regarding Huntington's assertion—for instance, if the European countries are lumped together as one culture even though they speak different languages, what is the rationale for separating Spain and Mexico, which speak the same language? And, is Catholic Philippines Western or Asian? As the article notes, such questions of detail matter because they fundamentally raise the question: how is culture defined?

Our survey of political behaviors and institutions across a wide net of countries returns full circle to this: institutional changes occur in response to demands for better or more representative venues within which citizens and government may interact. While onlookers may fault institutions or even countries for failing to be more accountable, representative, or just, it is primarily the demands of domestic constituents—the citizens—that will usher in and support changes. How the international community nurtures and supports such demands, without imposing our own preferences and impatience, is key to promoting stability in inter-nation relations.

Note

1. Susan Shirk. 2007. *China: Fragile Superpower.* New York: Oxford University Press.

Beijing Censors Taken to Task in Party Circles

JOSEPH KAHN

A dozen former Communist Party officials and senior scholars, including a onetime secretary to Mao, a party propaganda chief and the retired bosses of some of the country's most powerful newspapers, have denounced the recent closing of a prominent news journal, helping to fuel a growing backlash against censorship.

A public letter issued by the prominent figures, dated Feb. 2 but circulated to journalists in Beijing on Tuesday, appeared to add momentum to a campaign by a few outspoken editors against micromanagement, personnel shuffles and an ever-expanding blacklist of banned topics imposed on China's newspapers, magazines, television stations and Web sites by the party's secretive Propaganda Department.

The letter criticized the department's order on Jan. 24 to shut down Freezing Point, a popular journal of news and opinion, as an example of "malignant management" and an "abuse of power" that violates China's constitutional guarantee of free speech.

The letter did not address Beijing's pressure on Web portals and search engines.

That issue gained attention abroad after Microsoft and Google acknowledged helping the government filter information and Yahoo was accused of providing information from its e-mail accounts that was used to jail dissident writers. The issue will be the subject of Congressional hearings in Washington on Wednesday.

In addition to shutting down Freezing Point, a weekly supplement to China Youth Daily, since late last year, officials responsible for managing the news media have replaced editors of three other publications that developed reputations for breaking news or exploring sensitive political and social issues.

The interventions amounted to the most extensive exertion of press control since President Hu Jintao assumed power three years ago.

But propaganda officials are also facing rare public challenges to their legal authority to take such actions, including a short strike and string of resignations at one newspaper and defiant open letters from two editors elsewhere who had been singled out for censure. Those protests have suggested that some people in China's increasingly market-driven media industry no longer fear the consequences of violating the party line.

The authors of the letter predicted that the country would have difficulty countering the recent surge of social unrest in the countryside unless it allowed the news media more leeway to expose problems that lead to violent protests.

"At the turning point in our history from a totalitarian to a constitutional system, depriving the public of freedom of speech will bring disaster for our social and political transition and give rise to group confrontation and social unrest," the letter said. "Experience has proved that allowing a free flow of ideas can improve stability and alleviate social problems."

Some of the signers held high official posts during the 1980's, when the political environment in China was becoming more open. Although they have long since retired or been eased from power, a collective letter from respected elder statesmen can often help mobilize opinion within the ruling party.

One of those people who signed the petition is Li Rui, Mao's secretary and biographer. Others include Hu Jiwei, a former editor of People's Daily, the party's leading official newspaper; Zhu Houze, who once ran the party's propaganda office; and Li Pu, a former deputy head of the New China News Agency, the main official press agency.

Party officials and political experts say President Hu, who was groomed to take over China's top posts for more than a decade, has often attended closely to the opinions of the party's elder statesmen.

Mr. Hu is widely thought to favor tighter media controls. Party officials said he referred approvingly to media management in Cuba and North Korea in a speech in late 2004.

But he has also solicited support from more liberal elements. Last year Mr. Hu organized high-profile official ceremonies to mark the 90th anniversary of the birth of Hu Yaobang, the reform-oriented party leader who lost his posts in a power struggle and whose death in 1989 was the initial cause of the student-led democracy demonstrations that year. Some of the officials who signed the petition were close associates of Hu Yaobang.

The reaction against the shutdown of Freezing Point was organized by its longtime editor, Li Datong, 53, a party member and senior official of the party-run China Youth Daily. Mr. Li broadcast news of the secret order on his personal blog moments after he received it and has since mobilized supporters to put pressure on the Propaganda Department to retract the decision.

Under his stewardship, Freezing Point became one of the most consistently provocative journals of news and public opinion. It published investigative articles on sensitive topics like the party's version of historical events, nationalism and the party-run education system. Freezing Point ran opinion articles on politics in Taiwan and rural unrest in mainland China that caused a stir in media circles in recent months.

The cause cited for closing Freezing Point was an opinion piece by a historian named Yuan Weishi. He argued that Chinese history textbooks tended to ignore mistakes and provocations by leaders of the Qing Dynasty that may have incited attacks by foreign powers in the late 19th century.

Mr. Li often tussled with his bosses at China Youth Daily and officials at the Propaganda Department. But he has also cultivated support among the party elite. He often speaks supportively of President Hu and quotes extensively from the writings of Marx, who he says favored a robust free press.

He has maintained that the Propaganda Department had overstepped its authority by ordering Freezing Point closed, and he filed a formal complaint to the party's disciplinary arm.

"The propaganda office is an illegal organization that has no power to shut down a publication," Mr. Li said in an interview. "Its power is informal, and it can only exercise it if people are afraid."

He added, "I am not afraid."

Mr. Li scored an initial victory last week, when propaganda officials told China Youth Daily to draft a plan to revive Freezing Point, which had been formally closed for "rectification," Mr. Li and another editor at the newspaper said. Some media experts had predicted that the authorities would not allow Freezing Point to reopen, and the new order was treated as a signal that officials had misjudged the reaction to its closing.

Shortly after the contretemps at China Youth Daily broke out, the former editor of another national publication attacked the bosses who had replaced him, saying they had exercised self-censorship in the face of pressure from propaganda officials.

Chen Jieren, who lost his position last week as the editor of Public Interest Times, posted a letter online entitled "Ridiculous Game, Despicable Intrigue." The letter disputed his bosses' statement that he had been dismissed for "bad management skills" and said he had a struggled constantly against senior officials for the right "to report the truth with a conscience."

One recent issue of Public Interest Times mocked the poor quality of English translations on official government Web sites.

In a separate incident earlier this year, a group of editors and reporters at the party-run Beijing News declined to report for work after the editor of the paper, known for breaking news stories on subjects the Propaganda Department has ruled off limits, was replaced. Many of the protesters have since resigned, reporters at the newspaper said.

The resistance against censorship could signal a decisive shift in China's news media controls, already under assault from the proliferation of e-mail, text messaging, Web sites, blogs and other new forums for news and opinion that the authorities have struggled to bring under their supervision.

Even most of the major party-run national publications in China, including China Youth Daily, no longer receive government subsidies and must depend mainly on income from circulation and advertising to survive.

That means providing more news or features that people want to pay for, including exclusive stories and provocative views that go well beyond the propaganda fare carried by the New China News Agency or People's Daily. Few serious publications survive for long without subsidies if they do not have popular content, editors say.

"Every serious publication in China faces tough choices," said Mr. Li of Freezing Point. "You can publish stories people want to read and risk offending the censors. Or you can publish only stories that the party wants published and risk going out of business."

The EU and Its "Constitution"

Public Opinion, Political Elites, and Their International Context

ALBERTA SBRAGIA

The European Union is going about its regular business. It is putting forth proposals to keep the Doha Round alive, continuing to negotiate a major trade agreement with Mercosur in South America, keeping peace-keeping troops in Bosnia and Herzegovina, spending development aid in numerous poor countries, financially supporting the Palestine Authority while giving Israel preferential access to the EU market, investigating Microsoft's business practices, and battling over the reach and scope of an ambitious new legislative attempt to regulate the chemical industry. The EU Greenhouse Trading Scheme, the largest greenhouse emissions trading scheme in the world, is up and running. The European Central Bank is making monetary policy decisions while the euro makes up almost 20% of central banks' foreign currency holdings. The European Medicines Agency (EMEA) has called for suspending the sale of the children's vaccine Hexavac. The European Court of Justice, for its part, has recently declared illegal a high profile Italian law designed to prevent foreign take-over of Italian energy companies. And the commissioner for Health and Consumer Protection is playing a leading role in the EU's response to the threat of a pandemic of avian bird flu.

Meanwhile, EU citizens are enjoying the benefits of the EU in very direct ways—when they fly on a low cost airline, make a phone call which is far cheaper than it otherwise would have been, study abroad while receiving credit back at their home institution, cross national boundaries without passport or customs control, or use the euro in any one of the 12 EU member-states which have adopted it. Although the EU is often characterized as a regulatory rather than a welfare state (Majone 1996), it is responsible for many policy outputs which are generally popular.

The defeat of the EU Constitution[1] in French and Dutch referenda held in mid-2005 has not blocked the EU from carrying out its usual activities. Those are currently subject to the Treaty of Nice as well as the other treaties which have been ratified since 1958 and are still in force. Nor has it affected the kinds of benefits to which EU citizens have become accustomed. While there is angst and confusion about the future direction of the Union among political elites, it is important to note that the institutionalized machinery of governance which has evolved over nearly 50 years is in place and functioning. The fact that the Constitution's defeat did not alter the by now routine operations of policymaking highlights how embedded such policymaking is in the political life of an integrating Europe. The institutions of the European Union—the European Commission, the European Court of Justice, the European Parliament, the Council of Ministers, and the European Central Bank—are in place and doing the kind of substantive work they did before the Constitution was drafted.

Nonetheless, the Constitution's defeat is clearly an important moment in the history of European integration. For the first time, an agreement designed to further integration has been resoundingly defeated in two of the original six founding members of the European Union. Although supporters of the Constitution argue that the use of the referendum is an inappropriate mechanism for the approval of treaties, the referendum does enjoy a legitimacy which is difficult to negate. The impact of the "no" votes has been so great that many analysts argue the days of further integration in Europe are finished.

The medium to long-term impact of the Constitution's rejection, however, is far from clear. Even without the contingency endemic to international affairs, the Constitution's defeat very probably will have unanticipated consequences. And those consequences, in turn, may actually run counter to the predictions of those who argue that the future looks bleak for European integration.

Two basic arguments can be made regarding the implications for European integration of the Constitution's defeat. The first argues that the political context has changed so fundamentally that policymaking and the trajectory of further integration will be affected in irreversible ways. In that sense, the defeat is a strategic defeat for those who wish for Europe to move toward ever greater integration.

The second argues that, by contrast, this defeat will simply encourage Europe's political elites to continue the process of integration through means other than treaties put to a referendum. That process could include a new treaty focused on the institutional changes incorporated in the Constitution which would be submitted to parliamentary ratification only. More interestingly, however, it could also involve moving toward further integration by using the institutional instruments currently available under the Treaty of Nice—in spite of the fact that political elites supported the Constitution because they viewed those instruments as too weak to allow further integration. Both arguments can be justified.

The Constitution

The Constitution was clearly meant to drive integration forward. Although the "Constitution" was actually a constitutional treaty since it had to be ratified unanimously and could only be amended unanimously, it was viewed as the next major agreement which would lead both to more integration among the EU-25 and pave the way for further enlargement. It was written in a less intergovernmental fashion than had been previous treaties. Although national governments negotiating in an intergovernmental forum had the last word, national and (especially) European parliamentarians had an important role in shaping its content and direction.

The comparatively diverse group of participants in the Constitution-drafting process highlighted the Constitution's symbolic value. That symbolic value was in fact far greater than its actual substantive content would have warranted. And the question now stands—how much does its defeat matter?

Much of the EU Constitution was not new. It included "old" treaties which had been approved (at times in referenda in selected countries) and had been in effect for years. Those treaties will remain in effect. The defeat primarily affects proposed new institutional arrangements. Those included increasing the power of the European Parliament, establishing new voting weights for the various member-states, and strengthening the Union's external relations. It may, therefore, become more difficult, at the institutional level, to construct a more cohesive European Union in the global arena. Finally, enlargement will become more problematic, as the proposed institutional changes were designed to accommodate new members.

A Strategic Defeat?

There is no doubt that the defeats have re-framed the process of European integration in the minds of Europe's political class. There is currently a sense of indirection, of confusion, and of doubt as to where the grand project that the Six began with the Treaty of Paris in 1951 is going. The current climate is reminiscent of that which emerged after the Maastricht Treaty was approved by a margin of 1% in France in September 1992 and was only approved by the Danes in a second referendum in May 1993. At that time, too, the Commission was weakened, political elites were shaken, and the process of integration seemed much frailer than it had appeared only a few months earlier. The calls for full EU membership by the post-communist countries undergoing often difficult transitions to democracy added a kind of pressure which national leaders were at times reluctant to accept. Terms such as "a multi-speed Europe," "variable geometry," and

a "Europe a la Carte" entered the political as well as academic discourse about future paths which European integration might follow (Stubb 1996).

Of course, the EU recovered in a spectacular fashion from the Maastricht crisis. Although a great deal was written at the time about the caution that elites would need to demonstrate given the French public's reluctance to whole-heartedly endorse the next stage of integration, the European Union in 2005 looks very different from its pre-Maastricht incarnation. It created the new institutions called for in the Treaty and continued to become more important as a global actor. The European Central Bank was established, the euro was accepted by 12 of the 15 members, and, on the international stage, the EU was critical to the establishment of an important new international institution—the International Criminal Court—as well as to the successful conclusion of the Uruguay Round. It even began developing a European Security and Defense Policy. Thus, the question arises of whether the long-term implications of the Constitution's defeat will be as transient as were those of the narrow margin of victory in France (and the necessity of holding a second referendum in Denmark) during the Maastricht process.

The difference between Maastricht and the Constitution lies in the clear and unequivocal distinction between approval (however slim the margin) and defeat. Maastricht became the treaty in force—with its commitment to a single currency and a more united European Union acting on the global stage. Furthermore, it was a much smaller EU that had to deal with the aftershocks of the Maastricht debate—the then EU-12 could more easily regroup than the current EU-25 (soon to be 27).

The consequences of defeat could in fact be far more damaging than the consequences of a razor-thin ratification. The political momentum which has traditionally been so important for the movement toward further integration could be absent, for political leaders would be unwilling to act against public opinion. The lack of a "permissive consensus" on the part of electorates could lead to a protracted stalemate, paralysis, and a gradual drift away from the kind of goals and aspirations which are traditionally associated with further integration. In particular, the attempt to create a stronger global presence would be stymied, and the move toward bringing ever more policy areas under the EU umbrella would be stopped or even reversed. The role of the so-called Community method—which involves a key policymaking role for the supranational European Commission, the European Parliament, and the European Court of Justice—would be at best frozen. And further enlargement—beyond the accession of Romania and Bulgaria—would become impossible.

In a worst case scenario, the lack of commitment by political leaders to the European Union would gradually infect the EU's institutions, for the latter's effectiveness is in fact anchored in the willingness of national institutions and elites to support the overall project of integration by supporting its supranational institutions.

The view that the defeat of the Constitution will sap the political momentum from the Union privileges the role of public opinion in the process of European integration. It implicitly argues that the hitherto elite-driven process of integration has been fundamentally transformed. The role of a majoritarian representative institution—the national parliament—in ratifying treaties which advance European integration would have been diminished by the expression of voters engaged in direct democracy through the referendum. In fact, given the role of party government and party discipline in national parliamentary systems, the role of political parties would have been diminished.

Since the major political parties in Europe (whether in government or in opposition) have supported treaty ratification since 1958 and supported the ratification of the Constitution, the view that European integration will stall privileges public opinion *vis a vis* the opinions of governmental and party elites. In brief, the key support for integration—elite consensus—would become less powerful as an effective driving force.

The role of public opinion in European integration over the past 50 years has been ambiguous. The scholarly literature has come to varied conclusions, and in general scholars of European integration have focused on the role of elites in driving integration forward. Yet it is fair to ask how such an elite-driven process could sustain itself over so many decades. The liberalization of markets in particular would have been expected to lead to more contentious politics directed specifically against the EU than has been evident (Imig and Tarrow 2001; Gabel 1998; Sbragia 2000). Perhaps the underlying assumption of those who assume that public opinion should be expected to play a central role in the integration process was most pungently expressed by Herbert Morrison, deputy prime minister of Britain at the time when the British Cabinet rejected the invitation to join the European Coal and Steel Community. As Morrison summed up the issue, "It's no good. We can't do it. The Durham miners would never wear it" (cited in Gilbert 2003, 42).

If public opinion were indeed to significantly slow the pace of integration or re-shape its nature in the post-Constitution phase, it would have entered the stage as a significant factor relatively late in the process of integration. Given that elections to the European Parliament have been viewed as "second order elections"—based far more on national issues and political cleavages as opposed to EU-wide political debate—and that elites have enjoyed a "permissive consensus" which they have used to deepen integration, the strengthening of the role of public opinion in determining the course of European integration would represent a major new phase in this project.

The EU: A Geo-Economic/ Political Project?

Europe's political elites, however, may well continue the process of European integration, enlargement, and global integration *even if* key aspects of the Constitution are not ultimately resurrected in some fashion. This argument views the European Union as a key geo-economic/political project as well as a complex variant of a (con) or (semi) or (crypto) federation/federalism-constructing exercise (Sbragia 1993; Majone 2006).

It is quite possible that the EU's international dimension may well override the kinds of constraints imposed by public opinion. If the EU is viewed only or primarily as a domestic political system, the defeat of the Constitution would in fact be a strategic defeat. If the EU is also conceptualized as a geo-economic/political project, however, the defeat might well have unanticipated consequences which are far more conducive to further integration than might be evident in the short-term.

The beginning of the accession negotiations with Turkey in October in the face of widespread public hostility to Turkish membership symbolizes the determination of governments to carry out the promises they have already made to other international actors. Although governments opened the accession negotiations with Turkey after a good deal of conflict with each other and down-to-the-wire negotiations with the Austrian government (which wanted to leave open the possibility of a privileged partnership for Turkey rather than accession), what stands out is the fact that accession negotiations actually went forward as planned. A mere four months after the Constitution's defeat, the EU was not only back in business, but back in a very difficult kind of business. Although many analysts argue that Turkey will never actually join, the very fact of opening negotiations has triggered a process of long-term change within Turkey that makes the outcome less predictable than the skeptics admit.

In a similar vein, the active engagement of the EU in the Doha Round symbolizes the understanding by elites that Europe's economic well-being is nested within a larger—global—economic reality. Although French voters fear economic liberalization of the services sector, it is quite possible that at least some such liberalization will occur due to pressure from the Doha negotiations. The EU is enmeshed in a larger multilateral trading system, and the decisions made at that level affect it in ways which have not been well understood by either publics or political scientists.

I would argue that external challenges, although understudied in the EU literature, have always been very significant in influencing the evolution of European integration.[2] The Soviet threat and the evolution of the GATT in the 1950s, the impact of de-colonization on states' commercial interests in the 1960s, the changes in economic competitiveness in the 1980s, and the perceived need for greater military and political power during the Balkan crises of the 1990s have all been influential in the process. The dynamics of European integration have been embedded in the larger international environment, and that environment cannot be ignored in explaining the extraordinary depth of European integration.

More specifically, the implementation of the customs union in goods was supported by the GATT negotiations in the Kennedy and Dillon rounds (Langhammer 2005). The Single European Act which brought the single market to the EU was motivated in great part by the sense that European firms were falling behind their Japanese and American counterparts (Sandholtz and Zysman 1992) while the Maastricht Treaty was shaped in significant ways by the fall of the Berlin Wall and the end of the division of Europe. The restructuring of the Common Agricultural Policy was partially driven by the Uruguay Round negotiations (Patterson 1997). The movement toward a European Security and Defense Policy was at least partially a response to pressure from Washington (Howorth 2005) as well as to Europe's failures in addressing the tragedy of the wars in the Balkans.

External economic and security pressures will continue to exert a deep influence. While some of the most immediate pressures have been addressed by extending membership to the EU-15's neighbors, the enlargement process cannot keep meeting that challenge indefinitely. The WTO, the rise of China, changes in American grand strategy, and new security threats on the periphery of the Union will unavoidably push the European project in new directions as elites attempt to deal with emerging situations in world politics.

Some of the most significant institutional changes that the Constitution would have made were in fact designed to help the EU address foreign policy challenges in a more cohesive and effective way. Ironically, public opinion across the EU seems to favor a more unified global posture on the part of Brussels (German Marshall Fund 2005). Europe does not exist in a vacuum, and both elites and publics are aware of that basic fact. A more cohesive Euro-level foreign policy may therefore emerge even in the absence of the institutional changes that the Constitution would have produced. It is very likely that elites can pull mass publics with them in the area of foreign policy. In fact, the effort to strengthen the Union as a global actor can serve to link elites and publics more firmly than have economic policies of liberalization and regulation.

Economic integration, inevitably involving economic liberalization, is not as intuitively attractive as is a "stronger Europe on the world stage." Whether such liberalization can be successfully presented to voters as necessary for the strengthening of the EU as a geo-economic project is unclear, but it is possible that the "twinning" of European economic and foreign policy integration would help make economic liberalization more appealing.

The argument that an elite-driven process of integration—which incorporates party, governmental, and many business elites as well as national parliamentarians—has suffered a disruption but neither a strategic change of direction nor a strategic defeat downplays the role of public opinion as expressed in the defeat of the Constitution. It assumes that elites will in fact be able to move toward further integration. External events will provide support for further integration—such as recent events in the area of energy have demonstrated.

One of the unanticipated consequences of the Constitution's defeat in France and the Netherlands may be that integration will proceed in new ways. Just as the defeat of the European Defence Community in 1954 led to the European Economic Community, so too the need to circumvent public opinion (or at least not consult it directly) may lead to new forms of integration. The American executive, for example, has developed a host of ways to deal with international affairs which essentially circumvent or limit the role of Congress. Executive agreements and "fast track authority" for trade agreements (now known as trade promotion authority) both have been designed to allow the executive to have more flexibility in international than domestic affairs.

Second, cohesion in the foreign policy arena may develop more quickly than it has heretofore. Integration in foreign policy has lagged integration in "domestic" affairs given the member-states' concern with sovereignty. However, elites' desire to continue the process of integration coupled with the need to matter in a world in which not only the U.S. but also such countries as China and India will be important actors may provide the impetus for moving forward in that area. The role that the EU has played since 1958 in the GATT/WTO provides a useful precedent.

The defeat of the Constitution ironically may lead national leaders to move forward, develop new mechanisms to forge agreements without creating a context in which referenda are called, and actually become far more cohesive in foreign policy than would have been expected. One of the motivating forces for the Constitution was the desire on the part of national elites that the European Union should become a more effective global actor. The defeat of the Constitution will not necessarily defeat that desire, and external pressures will continue to entice national leaders to follow that road. Geo-economics and geo-politics have always provided a rationale within domestic politics for the insulation of representative institutions from direct constituency pressures. It is very possible that they will provide the same kind of rationale for the European Union.

If the EU is in fact framed or presented by elites as a geo-economic and geo-political project which will maximize European influence on the world stage and thereby help it respond to external events, it is quite possible that mass publics will become more supportive and that integration will move relatively rapidly in the one area that has been most resistant to Europeanization—that of foreign policy. Furthermore "sensitive" domestic areas clearly subject to external influences, such as energy, will become Europeanized far more quickly than one would expect.

The lack of institutional efficiency which the Constitution was supposed to remedy will undoubtedly make this process messier and more convoluted than the Constitution's backers would have liked. That same inefficiency will, however, allow the new accession states to play a role more similar to that which the EU-15 have played and give them a chance to make their mark in the shaping of the EU-25. If external pressures do indeed allow political elites to move integration forward, convince public opinion that such integration is acceptable, and help integrate the new accession states politically rather than simply institutionally, the defeat of the Constitution may be viewed quite differently 20 years from now than it is at present.

References

Gabel, Matthew J. 1998. *Interest and Integration: Market Liberalization, Public Opinion, and European Union.* Ann Arbor: University of Michigan Press.

German Marshall Fund of the United States et al. 2005. *Transatlantic Trends: Key Findings 2005.* Washington, D.C.: German Marshal Fund of the United States.

Gilbert, Mark. 2003. *Surpassing Realism: The Politics of European Integration since 1945.* New York: Rowman and Littlefield.

Howorth, Jolyon. 2005. "Transatlantic Perspectives on European Security in the Coming Decade." *Yale Journal of International Affairs* (summer/fall): 8–22.

Imig, Doug, and Sidney Tarrow, eds. 2001. *Contentious Europeans: Protest and Politics in the New Europe.* Lanham, MD: Rowman and Littlefield.

Langhammer, Rolf J. 2005. "The EU Offer of Service Trade Liberalization in the Doha Round: Evidence of a Not-Yet-Perfect Customs Union." *Journal of Common Market Studies* 51 (2): 311–325.

Majone, Giandomenico. 1996. *Regulating Europe.* New York: Routledge.

———. 2006. "The Common Sense of European Integration." Presented at the Princeton International Relations Faculty Colloquium, March 13.

Mayhew, David R. 2005. "Wars and American Politics." *Perspectives on Politics* 3 (September): 473–493.

Patterson, Lee Ann. 1997. "Agricultural Policy Reform in the European Community: A Three-Level Game Analysis." *International Organization* 51 (1): 135–165.

Sandholtz, Wayne, and John Zysman. 1989. "1992: Recasting the European Bargain." *World Politics* 42: 95–128.

Sbragia, Alberta. 1993. "The European Community: A Balancing Act." *Publius: The Journal of Federalism* 23 (summer): 23–38.

———. 2000. "Governance, the State, and the Market: What Is Going On?" *Governance* 13 (April): 243–250.

Stubb, Alexander C-G. 1996. "A Categorization of Differentiated Integration." *Journal of Common Market Studies* 13 (2): 283–295.

Notes

1. The "Constitution" was actually a constitutional treaty rather than a constitution as traditionally understood. However, the political debate in most countries used the term "Constitution" rather than "constitutional treaty," and I therefore shall use the term "Constitution" as well.

2. For a similar perspective on American politics, see Mayhew 2005.

ALBERTA SBRAGIA is director of the European Union Center of Excellence and a Jean Monnet Professor of Political Science at the University of Pittsburgh. She has chaired the European Union Studies Association and is particularly interested in EU-U.S. comparisons. Her current work focuses on the role of the EU in the field of commercial diplomacy and the global emergence of economic regionalism.

Anti-Americanisms
Biases as Diverse as the Country Itself

Peter J. Katzenstein and Robert O. Keohane

Arab reactions to American support for Israel in its recent conflict with Hezbollah have put anti-Americanism in the headlines once again. Around the world, not just in the Middle East, when bad things happen there is a widespread tendency to blame America for its sins, either of commission or omission. When its Belgrade embassy is bombed, Chinese people believe it was a deliberate act of the United States government; terror plots by native British subjects are viewed as reflecting British support for American policy; when AIDS devastates much of Africa, the United States is faulted for not doing enough to stop it.

These outbursts of anti-Americanism can be seen simply as a way of protesting American foreign policy. Is "anti-Americanism" really just a common phrase for such opposition, or does it go deeper? If anti-American expressions were simply ways to protest policies of the hegemonic power, only the label would be new. Before World War I Americans reacted to British hegemony by opposing "John Bull." Yet there is a widespread feeling that anti-Americanism is more than simply opposition to what the United States *does,* but extends to opposition to what the United States *is*—what it stands for. Critiques of the United States often extend far beyond its foreign policy: to its social and economic practices, including the public role of women; to its social policies, including the death penalty; and to its popular culture, including the flaunting of sex. Globalization is often seen as Americanization and resented as such. Furthermore, in France, which has had long-standing relations with the United States, anti-Americanism extends to the decades before the founding of the American republic.

With several colleagues we recently completed a book, *Anti-Americanisms in World Politics,*[1] exploring these issues, and in this short article we discuss four of its themes. First, we distinguish between anti-Americanisms that are rooted in opinion or bias. Second, as our book's title suggests, there are many varieties of anti-Americanism. The beginning of wisdom is to recognize that what is called anti-Americanism varies, depending on who is reacting to America. In our book, we describe several different types of anti-Americanism and indicate where each type is concentrated. The variety of anti-Americanism helps us to see, third, the futility of grand explanations for anti-Americanism. It is accounted for better as the result of particular sets of forces.

Finally, the persistence of anti-Americanism, as well as the great variety of forms that it takes, reflects what we call the *polyvalence* of a complex and kaleidoscopic American society in which observers can find whatever they don't like—from Protestantism to porn. The complexity of anti-Americanism reflects the polyvalence of America itself.

Opinion and Bias

Basic to our argument is a distinction between *opinion* and *bias.* Some expressions of unfavorable attitudes merely reflect opinion: unfavorable judgments about the United States or its policies. Others, however, reflect *bias:* a predisposition to believe negative reports about the United States and to discount positive ones. Bias implies a distortion of information processing, while adverse opinion is consistent with maintaining openness to new information that will change one's views. The long-term consequences of bias for American foreign policy are much greater than the consequences of opinion.

The distinction between opinion and bias has implications for policy, and particularly for the debate between left and right on its significance. Indeed, our findings suggest that the positions on anti-Americanism of both left and right are internally inconsistent. Broadly speaking, the American left focuses on opinion rather than bias—opposition, in the left's view largely justified, to American foreign policy. The left also frequently suggests that anti-Americanism poses a serious long-term problem for U.S. diplomacy. Yet insofar as anti-Americanism reflects ephemeral opinion, why should it have long-lasting effects? Policy changes would remove the basis for criticism and solve the problem. Conversely, the American right argues that anti-Americanism reflects a deep bias against the United States: People who hate freedom hate us for what we are. Yet the right also tends to argue that anti-Americanism can be ignored: If the United States follows effective policies, views will follow. But the essence of bias is the rejection of information inconsistent with one's prior view: Biased people do not change their views in response to new information. Hence, if bias is the problem, it poses a major long-term problem for the United States. Both left and right need to rethink their positions.

The view we take in the volume is that much of what is called anti-Americanism, especially outside of the Middle East, indeed is largely opinion. As such, it is volatile and would diminish in response to different policies, as it has in the past. The left is correct on this score, while the right overestimates resentment toward American power and hatred of American values. If the right were correct, anti-Americanism would have been high at the beginning of the new millennium. To the contrary, 2002 Pew polls show that outside the Middle East and Argentina, pluralities in every country polled were favorably disposed toward the United States. Yet with respect to the consequences of anti-American views, the right seems to be on stronger ground. It is difficult to identify big problems for American foreign policy created by anti-Americanism as such, as opposed to American policy. This should perhaps not be surprising, since prior to the Iraq war public opinion toward the United States was largely favorable. The right is therefore broadly on target in its claim that much anti-Americanism—reflecting criticisms of what the United States does rather than what it is—does not pose serious short-term problems for American foreign policy. However, if opinion were to harden into bias, as may be occurring in the Middle East, the consequences for the United States would be much more severe.

Anti-Americanisms

Since we are interested in attitudes that go beyond negative opinions of American foreign policy, we define anti-Americanism as *a psychological tendency to hold negative views of the United States and of American society in general.* Such negative views, which can be more or less intense, can be classified into four major types of anti-Americanism, based on the identities and values of the observers. From least to most intense, we designate these types of anti-Americanism as liberal, social, sovereign-nationalist, and radical. Other forms of anti-Americanism are more historically specific. We discuss them under a separate rubric.

Liberal anti-Americanism. Liberals often criticize the United States bitterly for not living up to its own ideals. A country dedicated to democracy and self-determination supported dictatorships around the world during the Cold War and continued to do so in the Middle East after the Cold War had ended. The war against terrorism has led the United States to begin supporting a variety of otherwise unattractive, even repugnant, regimes and political practices. On economic issues, the United States claims to favor freedom of trade but protects its own agriculture from competition stemming from developing countries and seeks extensive patent and copyright protection for American drug firms and owners of intellectual property. Such behavior opens the United States to charges of hypocrisy from people who share its professed ideals but lament its actions.

Liberal anti-Americanism is prevalent in the liberal societies of advanced industrialized countries, especially those colonized or influenced by Great Britain. No liberal anti-American ever detonated a bomb against Americans or planned an attack on the United States. The potential impact of liberal anti-Americanism would be not to generate attacks on the United States but to reduce support for American policy. The more the United States is seen as a self-interested power parading under the banners of democracy and human rights rather than as a true proponent of those values, the less willing other liberals may be to defend it with words or deeds.

Since liberal anti-Americanism feeds on perceptions of hypocrisy, a less hypocritical set of United States policies could presumably reduce it. Hypocrisy, however, is inherent in the situation of a superpower that professes universalistic ideals. It afflicted the Soviet Union even more than the United States. Furthermore, a prominent feature of pluralist democracy is that its leaders find it necessary to claim that they are acting consistently with democratic ideals while they have to respond to groups seeking to pursue their own self-interests, usually narrowly defined. When the interests of politically strong groups imply policies that do not reflect democratic ideals, the ideals are typically compromised. Hypocrisy routinely results. It is criticized not only in liberal but also in nonliberal states: for instance, Chinese public discourse overwhelmingly associates the United States with adherence to a double standard in its foreign policy in general and in its conduct of the war on terror specifically.

Hypocrisy in American foreign policy is not so much the result of the ethical failings of American leaders as a byproduct of the role played by the United States in world politics and of democratic politics at home.

It will not, therefore, be eradicated. As long as political hypocrisy persists, abundant material will be available for liberal anti-Americanism.

Social anti-Americanism. Since democracy comes in many stripes, we are wrong to mistake the American tree for the democratic forest. Many democratic societies do not share the peculiar combination of respect for individual liberty, reliance on personal responsibility, and distrust of government characteristic of the United States. People in other democratic societies may therefore react negatively to America's political institutions and its social and political arrangements that rely heavily on market processes. They favor deeper state involvement in social programs than is politically feasible or socially acceptable in the United States. Social democratic welfare states in Scandinavia, Christian democratic welfare states on the European continent, and developmental industrial states in Asia, such as Japan, are prime examples of democracies whose institutions and practices contrast in many ways with those of the United States.

Social anti-Americanism is based on value conflicts that reflect relevant differences in many spheres of life that are touching on "life, liberty and the pursuit of happiness." The injustice embedded in American policies that favor the rich over the poor is often decried. The sting is different here than for liberals who resent American hypocrisy. Genuine value conflicts exist on issues such as the death penalty, the desirability of generous social protections, preference for multilateral approaches over unilateral ones, and the sanctity of international treaties. Still, these value conflicts are smaller than those with radical anti-Americanism, since social anti-Americanism shares in core American values.

Sovereign-nationalist anti-Americanism. A third form of anti-Americanism focuses not on correcting domestic market outcomes but on political power. Sovereign nationalists focus on two values: the importance of not losing control over the terms by which polities are inserted in world politics and the inherent importance and value of collective national identities. These identities often embody values that are at odds with America's. State sovereignty thus becomes a shield against unwanted intrusions from America.

The emphasis placed by different sovereign nationalists can vary in three ways. First, it can be on *nationalism:* on collective national identities that offer a source of positive identification. National identity is one of the most important political values in contemporary world politics, and there is little evidence suggesting that this is about to change. Such identities create the potential for anti-Americanism, both when they are strong (since they provide positive countervalues) and when they are weak (since anti-Americanism can become a substitute for the absence of positive values).

Second, sovereign nationalists can emphasize *sovereignty.* In the many parts of Asia, the Middle East, and Africa where state sovereignty came only after hard-fought wars of national liberation, sovereignty is a much-cherished good that is to be defended. And in Latin America, with its very different history, the unquestioned preeminence of the U.S. has reinforced the perceived value of sovereignty. Anti-Americanism rooted in sovereignty is less common in Europe than in other parts of the world for one simple reason: European politics over the past half-century has been devoted to a common project—the partial pooling of sovereignty in an emerging European polity.

A third variant of sovereign-nationalist anti-Americanism appears where people see their states as potential great powers. Such societies may define their own situations partly in opposition to dominant states. Some Germans came to strongly dislike Britain before World War I as blocking what they believed was Germany's rightful "place in the sun." The British-German rivalry before the First World War was particularly striking in view of the similarities between these highly industrialized and partially democratic societies and the fact that their royal families were related by blood ties. Their political rivalry was systemic, pitting the dominant naval power of the nineteenth century against a rapidly rising land power. Rivalry bred animosity rather than vice versa.

Sovereign-nationalist anti-Americanism resonates well in polities that have strong state traditions. Encroachments on state sovereignty are particularly resented when the state has the capacity and a tradition of directing domestic affairs. This is true in particular of the states of East Asia. The issues of "respect" and saving "face" in international politics can make anti-Americanism especially virulent, since they stir nationalist passions in a way that social anti-Americanism rarely does.

China is particularly interesting for this category, since all three elements of sovereign-nationalist anti-Americanism are present there. The Chinese elites and public are highly nationalistic and very sensitive to threats to Chinese sovereignty. Furthermore, China is already a great power and has aspirations to become more powerful. Yet it is still weaker than the United States. Hence, the superior military capacity of the United States and its expressed willingness to use that capacity (for instance, against an attack

by China on Taiwan) create latent anti-Americanism. When the United States attacks China (as it did with the bombing of the Chinese embassy in Belgrade in 1999) or seems to threaten it (as in the episode of the EC–3 spy plane in 2001), explicit anti-Americanism appears quickly.

Radical anti-Americanism. We characterize a fourth form of anti-Americanism as radical. It is built around the belief that America's identity, as reflected in the internal economic and political power relations and institutional practices of the United States, ensures that its actions will be hostile to the furtherance of good values, practices, and institutions elsewhere in the world. For progress toward a better world to take place, the American economy and society will have to be transformed, either from within or from without.

Radical anti-Americanism was characteristic of Marxist-Leninist states such as the Soviet Union until its last few years and is still defining Cuba and North Korea today. When Marxist revolutionary zeal was great, radical anti-Americanism was associated with violent revolution against U.S.-sponsored regimes, if not the United States itself. Its Marxist-Leninist adherents are now so weak, however, that it is mostly confined to the realm of rhetoric. For the United States to satisfy adherents of this brand of radical anti-Americanism, it would need to change the nature of its political-economic system.

The most extreme form of contemporary radical anti-Americanism holds that Western values are so abhorrent that people holding them should be destroyed. The United States is the leading state of the West and therefore the central source of evil. This perceived evil may take various forms, from equality for women, to public displays of the human body, to belief in the superiority of Christianity. For those holding extreme versions of Occidentalist ideas, the central conclusion is that the West, and the United States in particular, are so incorrigibly bad that they must be destroyed. And since the people who live in these societies have renounced the path of righteousness and truth, they must be attacked and exterminated.

Religiously inspired and secular radical anti-Americanism argue for the weakening, destruction, or transformation of the political and economic institutions of the United States. The distinctive mark of both strands of anti-Americanism is the demand for revolutionary changes in the nature of American society.

It should be clear that these four different types of anti-Americanism are not simply variants of the same schema, emotions, or set of norms with only slight variations at the margin. On the contrary, adherents of different types of anti-Americanism can express antithetical attitudes. Radical Muslims oppose a popular culture that commercializes sex and portrays women as liberated from the control of men and are also critical of secular liberal values. Social and Christian democratic Europeans, by contrast, may love American popular culture but criticize the United States for the death penalty and for not living up to secular values they share with liberals. Liberal anti-Americanism exists because its proponents regard the United States as failing to live up to its professed values—which are entirely opposed to those of religious radicals and are largely embraced by liberals. Secular radical anti-Americans may oppose the American embrace of capitalism but may accept scientific rationalism, gender egalitarianism, and secularism—as Marxists have done. Anti-Americanism can be fostered by Islamic fundamentalism, idealistic liberalism, or Marxism. And it can be embraced by people who, not accepting any of these sets of beliefs, fear the practices or deplore the policies of the United States.

Historically Specific Anti-Americanisms

Two other forms of anti-Americanism, which do not fit within our general typology, are both historically sensitive and particularistic: elitist anti-Americanism and legacy anti-Americanism.

Elitist anti-Americanism arises in countries in which the elite has a long history of looking down on American culture. In France, for example, discussions of anti-Americanism date back to the eighteenth century, when some European writers held that everything in the Americas was degenerate.[2] The climate was enervating; plants and animals did not grow to the same size; people were uncouth. In France and in much of Western Europe, the tradition of disparaging America has continued ever since. Americans are often seen as uncultured materialists seeking individual personal advancement without concern for the arts, music, or other finer things of life. Or they are viewed as excessively religious and therefore insufficiently rational. French intellectuals are the European epicenter of anti-Americanism, and some of their disdain spills over to the public. However, as our book shows, French anti-Americanism is largely an elite phenomenon. Indeed, polls of the French public between the 1960s and 2002 indicated majority pro-Americanism in France, with favorable ratings that were only somewhat lower than levels observed elsewhere in Europe.

Legacy anti-Americanism stems from resentment of past wrongs committed by the United States toward another society. Mexican anti-Americanism is prompted by the experiences of U.S. military attack and various forms of imperialism during the past 200 years. The Iranian revolution of 1979 and the subsequent hostage crisis were fueled by memories of American intervention in Iranian politics in the 1950s, and Iranian hostility to the United States now reflects the hostile relations between the countries during the revolution and hostage crisis. Between the late 1960s and the end of the twentieth century, the highest levels of anti-Americanism recorded in Western Europe were found in Spain and especially Greece—both countries that had experienced civil wars; in the case of Spain the United States supported for decades a repressive dictator. Legacy anti-Americanism can be explosive, but it is not unalterable. As the Philippines and Vietnam—both highly pro-American countries today—show, history can ameliorate or reverse negative views of the United States as well as reinforce them.

The Futility of Grand Explanations

Often Anti-Americanism is explained as the result of some master set of forces—for example, of hegemony or globalization. The United States is hated because it is "Mr. Big" or because of its neoliberalism. However, all of these broad explanations founder on the variety of anti-Americanisms.

Consider first the "Mr. Big" hypothesis. Since the end of the Cold War, the United States has been by far the most powerful state in the world, without any serious rivals. The collapse of the Soviet bloc means that countries formerly requiring American protection from the Soviet Union no longer need such support, so their publics feel free to be more critical. In this view, it is no accident that American political power is at its zenith while American standing is at its nadir. Resentment at the negative effects of others' exercise of power is hardly surprising. Yet this explanation runs up against some inconvenient facts. If it were correct, anti-Americanism would have increased sharply during the 1990s; but we have seen that outside the Middle East, the United States was almost universally popular as late as 2002. The Mr. Big hypothesis could help account for certain forms of liberal and sovereign-nationalist anti-Americanism: Liberals criticize the United States for hypocrisy (and sometimes for being too reluctant to intervene to right wrongs), while sovereign nationalists fear the imposition of American power on their own societies. But it could hardly account for social, radical, elitist, or legacy anti-Americanism, each of which reacts to features of American society, or its behavior in the past, that are quite distinct from contemporary hegemony.

A second overarching explanation focuses on *globalization backlash*. The expansion of capitalism—often labeled globalization—generates what Joseph Schumpeter called "creative destruction." Those who are adversely affected can be expected to resist such change. In Benjamin Barber's clever phrase, the spread of American practices and popular culture creates "McWorld," which is widely resented even by people who find some aspects of it very attractive.[3] The anti-Americanism generated by McWorld is diffuse and widely distributed in world politics. But some societies most affected by economic globalization—such as India—are among the most pro-American. Even among the Chinese, whose reactions to the United States are decidedly mixed, America's wealth and its role in globalization are not objects of distrust or resentment as much as of envy and emulation. In terms of our typology, only social anti-Americanism and some forms of sovereign-nationalist anti-Americanism could be generated by the role of the United States in economic globalization—not the liberal, radical, elitist, or legacy forms.

A third argument ascribes anti-Americanism to cultural and religious identities that are antithetical to the values being generated and exported by American culture—from Christianity to the commercialization of sex. The globalization of the media has made sexual images not only available to but also unavoidable for people around the world. One reaction is admiration and emulation, captured by Joseph Nye's concept of soft power. But another reaction is antipathy and resistance. The products of secular mass culture are a source of international value conflict. They bring images of sexual freedom and decadence, female emancipation, and equality among the sexes into the homes of patriarchal and authoritarian communities, Muslim and otherwise. For others, it is American religiosity, not its sex-oriented commercialized culture, that generates negative reactions. Like the other arguments, the cultural identity argument has some resonance, but only for certain audiences. It may provide an explanation of some aspects of social, radical, and elitist anti-Americanism, but does not explain the liberal, sovereign-nationalist, or legacy varieties.

Each of the grand explanations probably contains at least a grain of truth, but none constitutes a general explanation of anti-Americanism.

The Polyvalence of American Society

American symbols are *polyvalent*. They embody a variety of values with different meanings to different people and indeed even to the same individual. Elites and ordinary folks abroad are deeply ambivalent about the United States. Visitors, such as Bernard-Henri Lévy, are impressed, repelled, and fascinated in about equal measure. Lévy dislikes what he calls America's "obesity"—in shopping malls, churches, and automobiles—and its marginalization of the poor; but he is impressed by its openness, vitality, and patriotism.[4] As David Laitin has noted, the World Trade Center was a symbol not only of capitalism and America but of New York's cosmopolitan culture, so often scorned by middle America. The Statue of Liberty symbolizes not only America and its conception of freedom. A gift of France, it has become an American symbol of welcome to the world's "huddled masses" that expresses a basic belief in America as a land of unlimited opportunity.

The United States has a vigorous and expressive popular culture, which is enormously appealing both to Americans and to many people elsewhere in the world. This popular culture is quite hedonistic, oriented toward material possessions and sensual pleasure. At the same time, however, the U.S. is today much more religious than most other societies. One important root of America's polyvalence is the tension between these two characteristics. Furthermore, both American popular culture and American religious practices are subject to rapid change, expanding further the varieties of expression in the society and continually opening new options. The dynamism and heterogeneity of American society create a vast set of choices: of values, institutions, and practices.

America's openness to the rest of the world is reflected in its food and popular culture. The American fast-food industry has imported its products from France (fries), Germany (hamburgers and frankfurters) and Italy (pizza). What it added was brilliant marketing and efficient distribution. In many ways the same is true also for the American movie industry, especially in the past two decades. Hollywood is a brand name held by Americans and non-Americans alike. In the 1990s only three of the seven major Hollywood studios were controlled by U.S. corporations. Many of Hollywood's most celebrated directors and actors are non-American. And many of Hollywood's movies about America, both admiring and critical, are made by non-Americans. Like the United Nations, Hollywood is both in America and of the world. And so is America itself—a product of the rest of the world as well as of its own internal characteristics.

"Americanization," therefore, does not describe a simple extension of American products and processes to other parts of the world. On the contrary, it refers to the selective appropriation of American symbols and values by individuals and groups in other societies—symbols and values that may well have had their origins elsewhere. Americanization thus is a profoundly interactive process between America and all parts of the world. And, we argue here, it is deeply intertwined with anti-American views. The interactions that generate Americanization may involve markets, informal networks, or the exercise of corporate or governmental power—often in various combinations. They reflect and reinforce the polyvalent nature of American society as expressed in the activities of Americans, who freely export and import products and practices. But they also reflect the variations in attitudes and interests of people in other societies, seeking to use, resist, and recast symbols that are associated with the United States. Similar patterns of interaction generate pro-Americanism and anti-Americanism, since both pro- and anti-Americanism provide an idiom to debate American and local concerns. Anti- and pro-Americanism have as much to do with the conceptual lenses through which individuals living in very different societies view America as with America itself. In our volume, Iain Johnston and Dani Stockmann report that when residents of Beijing in 1999 were asked simply to compare on an identity-difference scale their perceptions of Americans with their views of Chinese, they placed them very far apart. But when, in the following year, Japanese, the antithesis of the Chinese, were added to the comparison, respondents reduced the perceived identity difference between Americans and Chinese. In other parts of the world, bilateral perceptions of regional enemies can also displace, to some extent, negative evaluations of the United States. For instance, in sharp contrast to the European continent, the British press and public continue to view Germany and Germans primarily through the lens of German militarism, Nazi Germany, and World War II.

Because there is so much in America to dislike as well as to admire, polyvalence makes anti-Americanism persistent. American society is both extremely secular and deeply religious. This is played out in the tensions between blue "metro" and red "retro" America and the strong overtones of self-righteousness and moralism this conflict helps generate. If a society veers toward secularism, as much of Europe has, American religiosity is likely to become salient—odd, disturbing, and, due to American power, vaguely threatening. How can a people who believe more strongly in the Virgin Birth than in the theory of evolution be trusted to lead an alliance of liberal societies? If a society adopts more fervently Islamic religious doctrine and practices, as has occurred throughout much of the Islamic world during the past quarter-century, the prominence of women in American society and the vulgarity and emphasis on sexuality that pervades much of American popular culture are likely to evoke loathing, even fear. Thus, anti-Americanism is closely linked to the polyvalence of American society.

In 1941 Henry Luce wrote a prescient article on "the American Century." The American Century—at least its first 65 years—created enormous changes, some sought by the United States and others unsought and unanticipated. Resentment and anti-Americanism were among the undesired results of American power and engagement with the world. Our own cacophony projects itself onto others and can be amplified as it reverberates, via other societies, around the world.

Perhaps the most puzzling thing about anti-Americanism is that we Americans seem to care so much about it. Americans want to know about anti-Americanism: to understand ourselves better and, perhaps above all, to be reassured. This is one of our enduring traits. Americans' reaction to anti-Americanism in the twenty-first century thus is not very different from what Alexis de Tocqueville encountered in 1835:

The Americans, in their intercourse with strangers, appear impatient of the smallest censure and insatiable of praise. . . . They unceasingly harass you to extort praise, and if you resist their entreaties they fall to praising themselves. It would seem as if, doubting their own merit, they wished to have it constantly exhibited before their eyes.[5]

Perhaps we care because we lack self-confidence, because we are uncertain whether to be proud of our role in the world or dismayed by it. Like people in many other societies, we look outside, as if into a mirror, in order to see our own reflections with a better perspective than we can provide on our own. Anti-Americanism is important for what it tells us about United States foreign policy and America's impact on the world. It is also important for what it tells us about ourselves.

Notes

1. Peter J. Katzenstein and Robert O. Keohane, eds., *Anti-Americanisms in World Politics* (Cornell University Press, *2007*).

2. Philippe Roger, *The American Enemy: The History of French Anti-Americanism* (University of Chicago Press, *2005*).

3. Benjamin Barber, *Jihad vs. McWorld* (Crown, *1995*).

4. Bernard-Henri Lévy, *American Vertigo: Traveling America in the Footsteps of Tocqueville* (Random House, 2006).

5. Alexis de Tocqueville, *Democracy in America* (*1835*), *1965* edition, *252*.

The True Clash of Civilizations

Samuel Huntington was only half right. The cultural fault line that divides the West and the Muslim world is not about democracy but sex. According to a new survey, Muslims and their Western counterparts want democracy, yet they are worlds apart when it comes to attitudes toward divorce, abortion, gender equality, and gay rights—which may not bode well for democracy's future in the Middle East.

RONALD INGLEHART AND PIPPA NORRIS

Democracy promotion in Islamic countries is now one of the Bush administration's most popular talking points. "We reject the condescending notion that freedom will not grow in the Middle East," Secretary of State Colin Powell declared last December as he unveiled the White House's new Middle East Partnership Initiative to encourage political and economic reform in Arab countries. Likewise, Condoleezza Rice, President George W. Bush's national security advisor, promised last September that the United States is committed to "the march of freedom in the Muslim world."

> **Republican Rep. Christopher Shays of Connecticut: "Why doesn't democracy grab hold in the Middle East? What is there about the culture and the people and so on where democracy just doesn't seem to be something they strive for and work for?"**

But does the Muslim world march to the beat of a different drummer? Despite Bush's optimistic pronouncement that there is "no clash of civilizations" when it comes to "the common rights and needs of men and women," others are not so sure. Samuel Huntington's controversial 1993 thesis—that the cultural division between "Western Christianity" and "Orthodox Christianity and Islam" is the new fault line for conflict—resonates more loudly than ever since September 11. Echoing Huntington, columnist Polly Toynbee argued in the British *Guardian* last November, "What binds together a globalized force of some extremists from many continents is a united hatred of Western values that seems to them to spring

from Judeo-Christianity." Meanwhile, on the other side of the Atlantic, Republican Rep. Christopher Shays of Connecticut, after sitting through hours of testimony on U.S.-Islamic relations on Capitol Hill last October, testily blurted, "Why doesn't democracy grab hold in the Middle East? What is there about the culture and the people and so on where democracy just doesn't seem to be something they strive for and work for?"

Huntington's response would be that the Muslim world lacks the core political values that gave birth to representative democracy in Western civilization: separation of religious and secular authority, rule of law and social pluralism, parliamentary institutions of representative government, and protection of individual rights and civil liberties as the buffer between citizens and the power of the state. This claim seems all too plausible given the failure of electoral democracy to take root throughout the Middle East and North Africa. According to the latest Freedom House rankings, almost two thirds of the 192 countries around the world are now electoral democracies. But among the 47 countries with a Muslim majority, only one fourth are electoral democracies—and none of the core Arabic-speaking societies falls into this category.

> **. . . the real fault line between the West and Islam. . . concerns gender equality and sexual liberation. . . the values separating the two cultures have much more to do with eros than demos.**

Yet this circumstantial evidence does little to prove Huntington correct, since it reveals nothing about the underlying

The Cultural Divide

Approval of Political and Social Values in Western and Muslim Societies

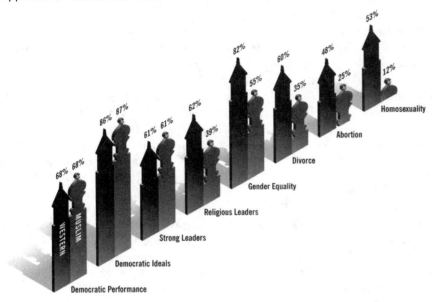

SOURCE: WORLD VALUES SURVEY, POOLED SAMPLE 1995-2001; CHARTS (3) BY JARED SCHNEIDMAN FOR FP

The chart above draws on responses to various political and social issues in the World Values Survey. The percentages indicate the extent to which respondents agree/disagree with or approved/disapproved of the following statements and questions:

Democratic Performance

- Democracies are indecisive and have too much quibbling. (Strongly disagree.)
- Democracies aren't good at maintaining order. (Strongly disagree.)

Democratic Ideals

- Democracy may have problems, but it's better than any other form of government. (Strongly agree.)
- Approve of having a democratic political system. (Strongly agree.)

Strong Leaders

- Approve of having experts, not government, make decisions according to what they think is best for the country. (Strongly disagree.)
- Approve of having a strong leader who does not have to bother with parliament and elections. (Strongly disagree.)

Religious Leaders

- Politicians who do not believe in God are unfit for public office. (Strongly disagree.)
- It would be better for [this country] if more people with strong religious beliefs held public office. (Strongly disagree.)

Gender Equality

- On the whole, men make better political leaders than women do. (Strongly disagree.)
- When jobs are scarce, men should have more right to a job than women. (Strongly disagree.)
- A university education is more important for a boy than for a girl. (Strongly disagree.)
- A woman has to have children in order to be fulfilled. (Strongly disagree.)
- If a woman wants to have a child as a single parent but she doesn't want to have a stable relationship with a man, do you approve or disapprove? (Strongly approve.)

Divorce

- Divorce can always be justified, never be justified, or something in between. (High level of tolerance for divorce.)

Abortion

- Abortion can always be justified, never be justified, or something in between. (High level of tolerance for abortion.)

Homosexuality

- Homosexuality can always be justified, never be justified, or something in between. (High level of tolerance for homosexuality.)

beliefs of Muslim publics. Indeed, there has been scant empirical evidence whether Western and Muslim societies exhibit deeply divergent values—that is, until now. The cumulative results of the two most recent waves of the World Values Survey (wvs), conducted in 1995–96 and 2000–2002, provide an extensive body of relevant evidence. Based on questionnaires that explore values and beliefs in more than 70 countries, the wvs is an investigation of sociocultural and political change that encompasses over 80 percent of the world's population.

A comparison of the data yielded by these surveys in Muslim and non-Muslim societies around the globe confirms the first claim in Huntington's thesis: Culture does matter—indeed, it matters a lot. Historical religious traditions have left an enduring imprint on contemporary values. However, Huntington is mistaken in assuming that the core clash between the West and Islam is over political values. At this point in history, societies throughout the world (Muslim and Judeo-Christian alike) see democracy as the best form of government. Instead, the real fault line between the West and Islam, which Huntington's theory completely overlooks, concerns gender equality and sexual liberalization. In other words, the values separating the two cultures have much more to do with eros than demos. As younger generations in the West have gradually become more liberal on these issues, Muslim nations have remained the most traditional societies in the world.

This gap in values mirrors the widening economic divide between the West and the Muslim world. Commenting on the disenfranchisement of women throughout the Middle East, the United Nations Development Programme observed last summer that "no society can achieve the desired state of well-being and human development, or compete in a globalizing world, if half its people remain marginalized and disempowered." But this "sexual clash of civilizations" taps into far deeper issues than how Muslim countries treat women. A society's commitment to gender equality and sexual liberalization proves time and again to be the most reliable indicator of how strongly that society supports principles of tolerance and egalitarianism. Thus, the people of the Muslim world overwhelmingly want democracy, but democracy may not be sustainable in their societies.

Testing Huntington

Huntington argues that "ideas of individualism, liberalism, constitutionalism, human rights, equality, liberty, the rule of law, democracy, free markets, [and] the separation of church and state" often have little resonance outside the West. Moreover, he holds that Western efforts to promote these ideas provoke a violent backlash against "human rights imperialism." To test these propositions, we categorized the countries included in the wvs according to the nine major contemporary civilizations, based largely on the historical religious legacy of each society. The survey includes 22 countries representing Western Christianity (a West European culture that also encompasses North America, Australia, and New Zealand), 10 Central European nations (sharing a Western Christian heritage, but which also lived under Communist rule), 11 societies with a Muslim majority (Albania, Algeria, Azerbaijan, Bangladesh, Egypt, Indonesia, Iran, Jordan, Morocco, Pakistan, and Turkey), 12 traditionally Orthodox societies (such as Russia and Greece), 11 predominately Catholic Latin American countries, 4 East Asian societies shaped by Sino-Confucian values, 5 sub-Saharan Africa countries, plus Japan and India.

Despite Huntington's claim of a clash of civilizations between the West and the rest, the wvs reveals that, at this point in history, democracy has an overwhelmingly positive image throughout the world. In country after country, a clear majority of the population describes "having a democratic political system" as either "good" or "very good." These results represent a dramatic change from the 1930s and 1940s, when fascist regimes won overwhelming mass approval in many societies; and for many decades, Communist regimes had widespread support. But in the last decade, democracy became virtually the only political model with global appeal, no matter what the culture. With the exception of Pakistan, most of the Muslim countries surveyed think highly of democracy: In Albania, Egypt, Bangladesh, Azerbaijan, Indonesia, Morocco, and Turkey, 92 to 99 percent of the public endorsed democratic institutions—a higher proportion than in the United States (89 percent).

Yet, as heartening as these results may be, paying lip service to democracy does not necessarily prove that people genuinely support basic democratic norms—or that their leaders will allow them to have democratic institutions. Although constitutions of authoritarian states such as China profess to embrace democratic ideals such as freedom of religion, the rulers deny it in practice. In Iran's 2000 elections, reformist candidates captured nearly three quarters of the seats in parliament, but a theocratic elite still holds the reins of power. Certainly, it's a step in the right direction if most people in a country endorse the idea of democracy. But this sentiment needs to be complemented by deeper underlying attitudes such as interpersonal trust and tolerance of unpopular groups—and these values must ultimately be accepted by those who control the army and secret police.

The wvs reveals that, even after taking into account differences in economic and political development, support for democratic institutions is just as strong among those living in Muslim societies as in Western (or other) societies [see box, The Cultural Divide]. For instance, a solid majority of people living in Western and Muslim countries gives democracy high marks as the most efficient form of government, with 68 percent disagreeing with assertions that "democracies are indecisive" and "democracies aren't good at maintaining order." (All other cultural regions and countries, except East Asia and Japan, are far more critical.) And an equal number of respondents on both sides of the civilizational divide (61 percent) firmly reject authoritarian governance, expressing disapproval of "strong leaders" who do not "bother with parliament and elections." Muslim societies display greater support for religious authorities playing an active societal role than do Western societies. Yet this preference for religious authorities is less a cultural division between the West and Islam than it is a gap between the West and many other less secular societies around the

A Barometer of Tolerance

Gender Equality and Democracy

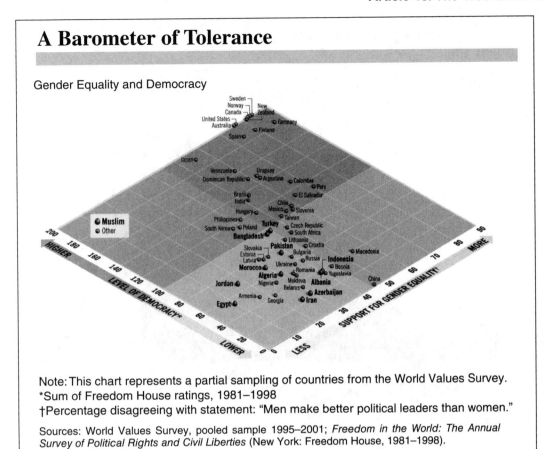

Note: This chart represents a partial sampling of countries from the World Values Survey.

*Sum of Freedom House ratings, 1981–1998

†Percentage disagreeing with statement: "Men make better political leaders than women."

Sources: World Values Survey, pooled sample 1995–2001; *Freedom in the World: The Annual Survey of Political Rights and Civil Liberties* (New York: Freedom House, 1981–1998).

globe, especially in sub-Saharan Africa and Latin America. For instance, citizens in some Muslim societies agree overwhelmingly with the statement that "politicians who do not believe in God are unfit for public office" (88 percent in Egypt, 83 percent in Iran, and 71 percent in Bangladesh), but this statement also garners strong support in the Philippines (71 percent), Uganda (60 percent), and Venezuela (52 percent). Even in the United States, about two fifths of the public believes that atheists are unfit for public office.

Today, relatively few people express overt hostility toward other classes, races, or religions, but rejection of homosexuals is widespread. About half of the world's populations say that homosexuality is "never" justifiable.

However, when it comes to attitudes toward gender equality and sexual liberalization, the cultural gap between Islam and the West widens into a chasm. On the matter of equal rights and opportunities for women—measured by such questions as whether men make better political leaders than women or whether university education is more important for boys than for girls—Western and Muslim countries score 82 percent and

55 percent, respectively. Muslim societies are also distinctively less permissive toward homosexuality, abortion, and divorce.

These issues are part of a broader syndrome of tolerance, trust, political activism, and emphasis on individual autonomy that constitutes "self-expression values." The extent to which a society emphasizes these self-expression values has a surprisingly strong bearing on the emergence and survival of democratic institutions. Among all the countries included in the wvs, support for gender equality—a key indicator of tolerance and personal freedom—is closely linked with a society's level of democracy [see box, A Barometer of Tolerance].

Muslim societies are neither uniquely nor monolithically low on tolerance toward sexual orientation and gender equality. . . . However, on the whole, Muslim countries not only lag behind the West but behind all other societies as well.

In every stable democracy, a majority of the public disagrees with the statement that "men make better political leaders than women." None of the societies in which less than 30 percent of the public rejects this statement (such as Jordan, Nigeria, and Belarus) is a true democracy. In China, one of the world's least

A Widening Generation Gap

Support for Gender Equality, by Age and Type of Society

*The 100-point Gender Equality Scale is based on responses to the following five statements and questions: "If a woman wants to have a child as a single parent but she doesn't want to have a stable relationship with a man, do you approve or disapprove?"; "When jobs are scarce, men should have more right to a job than women"; "A university education is more important for a boy than a girl"; "Do you think that a woman has to have children in order to be fulfilled or is this not necessary?"; and "On the whole, men make better political leaders than women do." The scale was constructed so that if all respondents show high scores on all five items (representing strong support for gender equality), it produces a score of 100, while low scores on all five items produce a score of 0.

Source: World Values Surveys, pooled 1995–2001

democratic countries, a majority of the public agrees that men make better political leaders than women, despite a party line that has long emphasized gender equality (Mao Zedong once declared, "women hold up half the sky"). In practice, Chinese women occupy few positions of real power and face widespread discrimination in the workplace. India is a borderline case. The country is a long-standing parliamentary democracy with an independent judiciary and civilian control of the armed forces, yet it is also marred by a weak rule of law, arbitrary arrests, and extra-judicial killings. The status of Indian women reflects this duality. Women's rights are guaranteed in the constitution, and Indira Gandhi led the nation for 15 years. Yet domestic violence and forced prostitution remain prevalent throughout the country, and, according to the wvs, almost 50 percent of the Indian populace believes only men should run the government.

The way a society views homosexuality constitutes another good litmus test of its commitment to equality. Tolerance of well-liked groups is never a problem. But if someone wants

Want to Know More?

Samuel Huntington expanded his controversial 1993 article into a book, *The Clash of Civilizations and the Remaking of World Order* (New York: Simon and Schuster, 1996). Among the authors who have disputed Huntington's claim that Islam is incompatible with democratic values are Edward Said, who decries the clash of civilizations thesis as an attempt to revive the "good vs. evil" world dichotomy prevalent during the Cold War ("**A Clash of Ignorance**," *The Nation*, October 22, 2001); John Voll and John Esposito, who argue that "The Muslim heritage. . . contains concepts that provide a foundation for contemporary Muslims to develop authentically Muslim programs of democracy" ("**Islam's Democratic Essence**," *Middle East Quarterly*, September 1994); and Ray Takeyh, who recounts the efforts of contemporary Muslim scholars to legitimize democratic concepts through the reinterpretation of Muslim texts and traditions ("**Faith-Based Initiatives**," FOREIGN POLICY, November/December 2001).

An overview of the Bush administration's **Middle East Partnership Initiative**, including the complete transcript of Secretary of State Colin Powell's speech on political and economic reform in the Arab world, can be found on the Web site of the U.S. Department of State. Marina Ottaway, Thomas Carothers, Amy Hawthorne, and Daniel Brumberg offer a stinging critique of those who believe that toppling the Iraqi regime could unleash a democratic tsunami in the Arab world in "**Democratic Mirage in the Middle East**" (Washington: Carnegie Endowment for International Peace, 2002).

In a poll of nearly 4,000 Arabs, James Zogby found that the issue of "civil and personal rights" earned the overall highest score when people were asked to rank their personal priorities (*What Arabs Think: Values, Beliefs and Concerns*, Washington: Zogby International, 2002). A poll available on the Web site of the Pew Research Center for the People and the Press ("**Among Wealthy Nations . . . U.S. Stands Alone in Its Embrace of Religion**," December 19, 2002) reveals that Americans' views on religion and faith are closer to those living in developing nations than in developed countries.

The Web site of the **World Values Survey** (wvs) provides considerable information on the survey, including background on methodology, key findings, and the text of the questionnaires. The second iteration of the A.T. Kearney/Foreign Policy Magazine Globalization Index ("**Globalization's Last Hurrah?**" Foreign Policy, January/February 2002) found a strong correlation between the wvs measure of "subjective well-being" and a society's level of global integration.

For links to relevant Web sites, access to the fp Archive, and a comprehensive index of related Foreign Policy articles, go to www.foreignpolicy.com.

---

to gauge how tolerant a nation really is, find out which group is the most disliked, and then ask whether members of that group should be allowed to hold public meetings, teach in schools, and work in government. Today, relatively few people express overt hostility toward other classes, races, or religions, but rejection of homosexuals is widespread. In response to a wvs question about whether homosexuality is justifiable, about half of the world's population say "never." But, as is the case with gender equality, this attitude is directly proportional to a country's level of democracy. Among authoritarian and quasi-democratic states, rejection of homosexuality is deeply entrenched: 99 percent in both Egypt and Bangladesh, 94 percent in Iran, 92 percent in China, and 71 percent in India. By contrast, these figures are much lower among respondents in stable democracies: 32 percent in the United States, 26 percent in Canada, 25 percent in Britain, and 19 percent in Germany.

Muslim societies are neither uniquely nor monolithically low on tolerance toward sexual orientation and gender equality. Many of the Soviet successor states rank as low as most Muslim societies. However, on the whole, Muslim countries not only lag behind the West but behind all other societies as well [see box, A Widening Generation Gap]. Perhaps more significant, the figures reveal the gap between the West and Islam is even wider among younger age groups. This pattern suggests that the younger generations in Western societies have become progressively more egalitarian than their elders, but the younger generations in Muslim societies have remained almost as traditional as their parents and grandparents, producing an expanding cultural gap.

Clash of Conclusions

"The peoples of the Islamic nations want and deserve the same freedoms and opportunities as people in every nation," President Bush declared in a commencement speech at West Point last summer. He's right. Any claim of a "clash of civilizations" based on fundamentally different political goals held by Western and Muslim societies represents an oversimplification of the evidence. Support for the goal of democracy is surprisingly widespread among Muslim publics, even among those living in authoritarian societies. Yet Huntington is correct when he argues that cultural differences have taken on a new importance, forming the fault lines for future conflict. Although nearly the entire world pays lip service to democracy, there is still no global consensus on the self-expression values—such as social tolerance, gender equality, freedom of speech, and interpersonal trust—that are crucial to democracy. Today, these divergent values constitute the real clash between Muslim societies and the West.

But economic development generates changed attitudes in virtually any society. In particular, modernization compels systematic, predictable changes in gender roles: Industrialization brings women into the paid work force and dramatically reduces fertility rates. Women become literate and begin to participate in representative government but still have far less power than men. Then, the postindustrial phase brings a shift toward greater gender equality as women move into higher-status economic roles in management and gain political influence within elected and appointed bodies. Thus, relatively industrialized Muslim societies such as Turkey share the same views on gender equality and sexual liberalization as other new democracies.

Even in established democracies, changes in cultural attitudes—and eventually, attitudes toward democracy—seem to be closely linked with modernization. Women did not attain the right to vote in most historically Protestant societies until about 1920, and in much of Roman Catholic Europe until after World War II. In 1945, only 3 percent of the members of parliaments around the world were women. In 1965, the figure rose to 8 percent, in 1985 to 12 percent, and in 2002 to 15 percent.

The United States cannot expect to foster democracy in the Muslim world simply by getting countries to adopt the trappings of democratic governance, such as holding elections and having a parliament. Nor is it realistic to expect that nascent democracies in the Middle East will inspire a wave of reforms reminiscent of the velvet revolutions that swept Eastern Europe in the final days of the Cold War. A real commitment to democratic reform will be measured by the willingness to commit the resources necessary to foster human development in the Muslim world. Culture has a lasting impact on how societies evolve. But culture does not have to be destiny.

From *Foreign Policy,* March/April 2003, pp. 63–70. Copyright © 2003 by the Carnegie Endowment for International Peace. Reprinted with permission. www.foreignpolicy.com

Cultural Explanations

The Man in the Baghdad Café

Which "civilisation" you belong to matters less than you might think.

Goering, it was said, growled that every time he heard the word culture he reached for his revolver. His hand would ache today. Since the end of the cold war, "culture" has been everywhere—not the opera-house or gallery kind, but the sort that claims to be the basic driving force behind human behaviour. All over the world, scholars and politicians seek to explain economics, politics and diplomacy in terms of "culture-areas" rather than, say, policies or ideas, economic interests, personalities or plain cock-ups.

Perhaps the best-known example is the notion that "Asian values" explain the success of the tiger economies of South-East Asia. Other accounts have it that international conflict is—or will be—caused by a clash of civilisations; or that different sorts of business organisation can be explained by how much people in different countries trust one [an]other. These four pages review the varying types of cultural explanation. They conclude that culture is so imprecise and changeable a phenomenon that it explains less than most people realise.

To see how complex the issue is, begin by considering the telling image with which Bernard Lewis opens his history of the Middle East. A man sits at a table in a coffee house in some Middle Eastern city, "drinking a cup of coffee or tea, perhaps smoking a cigarette, reading a newspaper, playing a board game, and listening with half an ear to whatever is coming out of the radio or the television installed in the corner." Undoubtedly Arab, almost certainly Muslim, the man would clearly identify himself as a member of these cultural groups. He would also, if asked, be likely to say that "western culture" was alien, even hostile to them.

Look closer, though, and the cultural contrasts blur. This coffee-house man probably wears western-style clothes—sneakers, jeans, a T-shirt. The chair and table at which he sits, the coffee he drinks, the tobacco he smokes, the newspaper he reads, all are western imports. The radio and television are western inventions. If our relaxing friend is a member of his nation's army, he probably operates western or Soviet weapons and trains according to western standards; if he belongs to the government, both his bureaucratic surroundings and the constitutional trappings of his regime may owe their origins to western influence.

The upshot, for Mr Lewis, is clear enough. "In modern times," he writes, "the dominating factor in the consciousness of most Middle Easterners has been the impact of Europe, later

of the West more generally, and the transformation—some would say dislocation—which it has brought." Mr Lewis has put his finger on the most important and least studied aspect of cultural identity: how it changes. It would be wise to keep that in mind during the upsurge of debate about culture that is likely to follow the publication of Samuel Huntington's new book, "The Clash of Civilisations and the Remaking of World Order".

The Clash of Civilisations

A professor of international politics at Harvard and the chairman of Harvard's Institute for Strategic Planning, Mr Huntington published in 1993, in *Foreign Affairs*, an essay which that quarterly's editors said generated more discussion than any since George Kennan's article (under the by-line "x") which argued in July 1947 for the need to contain the Soviet threat. Henry Kissinger, a former secretary of state, called Mr Huntington's book-length version of the article "one of the most important books . . . since the end of the cold war."

The article, "The Clash of Civilisation?", belied the question-mark in its title by predicting wars of culture. "It is my hypothesis", Mr Huntington wrote, "that the fundamental source of conflict in this new world will not be primarily ideological or primarily economic. The great division among humankind and the dominating source of conflict will be cultural."

After the cold war, ideology seemed less important as an organising principle of foreign policy. Culture seemed a plausible candidate to fill the gap. So future wars, Mr Huntington claimed, would occur "between nations and groups of different civilisations"—western, Confucian, Japanese, Islamic, Hindu, Orthodox and Latin American, perhaps African and Buddhist. Their disputes would "dominate global politics" and the battle-lines of the future would follow the fault-lines between these cultures.

No mincing words there, and equally few in his new book:

> Culture and cultural identities . . . are shaping the patterns of cohesion, disintegration and conflict in the post-cold war world . . . Global politics is being reconfigured along cultural lines.

Mr Huntington is only one of an increasing number of writers placing stress on the importance of cultural values and institutions in the confusion left in the wake of the cold war. He looked at the influence of culture on international conflict. Three other schools of thought find cultural influences at work in different ways.

- **Culture and the economy**. Perhaps the oldest school holds that cultural values and norms equip people—and, by extension, countries—either poorly or well for economic success. The archetypal modern pronouncement of this view was Max Weber's investigation of the Protestant work ethic. This, he claimed, was the reason why the Protestant parts of Germany and Switzerland were more successful economically than the Catholic areas. In the recent upsurge of interest in issues cultural, a handful of writers have returned to the theme.

It is "values and attitudes—culture", claims Lawrence Harrison, that are "mainly responsible for such phenomena as Latin America's persistent instability and inequity, Taiwan's and Korea's economic 'miracles', and the achievements of the Japanese." Thomas Sowell offers other examples in "Race and Culture: A World View". "A disdain for commerce and industry", he argues, "has . . . been common for centuries among the Hispanic elite, both in Spain and in Latin America." Academics, though, have played a relatively small part in this debate: the best-known exponent of the thesis that "Asian values"—a kind of Confucian work ethic—aid economic development has been Singapore's former prime minister, Lee Kuan Yew.

- **Culture as social blueprint**. A second group of analysts has looked at the connections between cultural factors and political systems. Robert Putnam, another Harvard professor, traced Italy's social and political institutions to its "civic culture", or lack thereof. He claimed that, even today, the parts of Italy where democratic institutions are most fully developed are similar to the areas which first began to generate these institutions in the 14th century. His conclusion is that democracy is not something that can be put on like a coat; it is part of a country's social fabric and takes decades, even centuries, to develop.

Francis Fukuyama, of George Mason University, takes a slightly different approach. In a recent book which is not about the end of history, he focuses on one particular social trait, "trust". "A nation's well-being, as well as its ability to compete, is conditioned by a single, pervasive cultural characteristic: the level of trust inherent in the society," he says. Mr Fukuyama argues that "low-trust" societies such as China, France and Italy—where close relations between people do not extend much beyond the family—are poor at generating large, complex social institutions like multinational corporations; so they are at a competitive disadvantage compared with "high-trust" nations such as Germany, Japan and the United States.

- **Culture and decision-making**. The final group of scholars has looked at the way in which cultural assumptions act like blinkers. Politicians from different

countries see the same issue in different ways because of their differing cultural backgrounds. Their electorates or nations do, too. As a result, they claim, culture acts as an international barrier. As Ole Elgstrom puts it: "When a Japanese prime minister says that he will 'do his best' to implement a certain policy," Americans applaud a victory but "what the prime minister really meant was 'no'." There are dozens of examples of misperception in international relations, ranging from Japanese-American trade disputes to the misreading of Saddam Hussein's intentions in the weeks before he attacked Kuwait.

What Are They Talking About?

All of this is intriguing, and much of it is provocative. It has certainly provoked a host of arguments. For example, is Mr Huntington right to lump together all European countries into one culture, though they speak different languages, while separating Spain and Mexico, which speak the same one? Is the Catholic Philippines western or Asian? Or: if it is true (as Mr Fukuyama claims) that the ability to produce multinational firms is vital to economic success, why has "low-trust" China, which has few such companies, grown so fast? And why has yet-more successful "low-trust" South Korea been able to create big firms?

This is nit-picking, of course. But such questions of detail matter because behind them lurks the first of two fundamental doubts that plague all these cultural explanations: how do you define what a culture is?

In their attempts to define what cultures are (and hence what they are talking about), most "culture" writers rely partly on self definition: cultures are what people think of themselves as part of. In Mr Hungtington's words, civilisation "is the broadest level of identification with which [a person] intensely identifies."

The trouble is that relatively few people identify "intensely" with broad cultural groups. They tend to identify with something narrower: nations or ethnic groups. Europe is a case in point. A poll done last year for the European Commission found that half the people of Britain, Portugal and Greece thought of themselves in purely national terms; so did a third of the Germans, Spaniards and Dutch. And this was in a part of the world where there is an institution—the EU itself—explicitly devoted to the encouragement of "Europeanness".

The same poll found that in every EU country, 70% or more thought of themselves either purely in national terms, or primarily as part of a nation and only secondly as Europeans. Clearly, national loyalty can coexist with wider cultural identification. But, even then, the narrower loyalty can blunt the wider one because national characteristics often are—or at least are often thought to be—peculiar or unique. Seymour Martin Lipset, a sociologist who recently published a book about national characteristics in the United States, called it "American Exceptionalism". David Willetts, a British Conservative member of Parliament, recently claimed that the policies espoused by the opposition Labour Party would go against the grain of "English exceptionalism". And these are the two components of western culture supposedly most like one another.

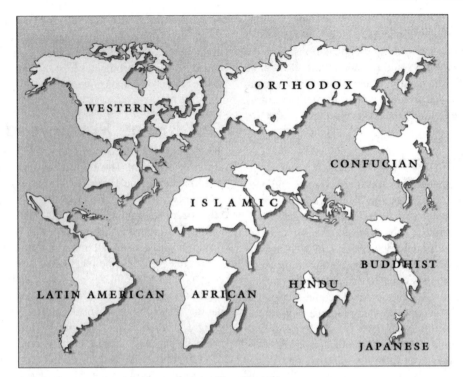

Figure 1   The World According to Huntington.

Source: Adapted by The Economist from "The Clash of Civilisations and the Remaking of World Order" by Samuel Huntington

In Islamic countries, the balance between cultural and national identification may be tilted towards the culture. But even here the sense of, say, Egyptian or Iraqi or Palestinian nationhood remains strong. (Consider the competing national feelings unleashed during the Iran-Iraq war.) In other cultures, national loyalty seems preeminent: in Mr Huntington's classification, Thailand, Tibet and Mongolia all count as "Buddhist". It is hard to imagine that a Thai, a Tibetan and a Mongolian really have that much in common.

So the test of subjective identification is hard to apply. That apart, the writers define a culture in the usual terms: language, religion, history, customs and institutions and so on. Such multiple definitions ring true. As Bernard Lewis's man in the Levantine café suggests, cultures are not singular things: they are bundles of characteristics.

The trouble is that such characteristics are highly ambiguous. Some push one way, some another.

Culture as Muddle

Islamic values, for instance, are routinely assumed to be the antithesis of modernising western ones. In Islam, tradition is good; departure from tradition is presumed to be bad until proven otherwise. Yet, at the same time, Islam is also a monotheistic religion which encourages rationalism and science. Some historians have plausibly argued that it was the Islamic universities of medieval Spain that kept science and rationalism alive during Europe's Dark Ages, and that Islam was a vital medieval link between the ancient world of Greece and Rome and the Renaissance. The scientific-rationalist aspect of Islam could well come to the fore again.

If you doubt it, consider the case of China and the "Confucian tradition" (a sort of proxy for Asian values). China has been at various times the world's most prosperous country and also one of its poorest. It has had periods of great scientific innovation and times of technological backwardness and isolation. Accounts of the Confucian tradition have tracked this path. Nowadays, what seems important about the tradition is its encouragement of hard work, savings and investment for the future, plus its emphasis on co-operation towards a single end. All these features have been adduced to explain why the tradition has helped Asian growth.

To Max Weber, however, the same tradition seemed entirely different. He argued that the Confucian insistence on obedience to parental authority discouraged competition and innovation and hence inhibited economic success. And China is not the only country to have been systematically misdiagnosed in this way. In countries as varied as Japan, India, Ghana and South Korea, notions of cultural determination of economic performance have been proved routinely wrong (in 1945, India and Ghana were expected to do best of the four—partly because of their supposed cultural inheritance).

If you take an extreme position, you could argue from this that cultures are so complicated that they can never be used to explain behaviour accurately. Even if you do not go that far, the lesson must be that the same culture embraces such conflicting features that it can produce wholly different effects at different times.

That is hard enough for the schools of culture to get to grips with. But there is worse to come. For cultures never operate in isolation. When affecting how people behave, they are always part of a wider mix. That mix includes government policies, personal leadership, technological or economic change and so on. For any one effect, there are always multiple causes. Which raises the second fundamental doubt about cultural explanations: how do you know whether it is culture—and not something else—that has caused some effect? You cannot. The problem of causation seems insoluble. The best you can do is work out whether, within the mix, culture is becoming more or less important.

Culture as Passenger

Of the many alternative explanations for events, three stand out: the influence of ideas, of government and what might be called the "knowledge era" (shorthand for globalisation, the growth of service-based industries and so forth). Of these, the influence of ideas as a giant organising principle is clearly not what it was when the cold war divided the world between communists and capitalists. We are all capitalists now. To that extent, it is fair to say that the ideological part of the mix has become somewhat less important—though not, as a few people have suggested, insignificant.

As for the government, it is a central thesis of the cultural writers that its influence is falling while that of culture is rising: cultures are in some ways replacing states. To quote Mr Huntington again "peoples and countries with similar cultures are coming together. Peoples and countries with different cultures are coming apart."

In several respects, that is counter-intuitive. Governments still control what is usually the single most powerful force in any country, the army. And, in all but the poorest places, governments tax and spend a large chunk of GDP—indeed, a larger chunk, in most places, than 50 years ago.

Hardly surprising, then, that governments influence cultures as much as the other way around. To take a couple of examples. Why does South Korea (a low-trust culture, remember) have so many internationally competitive large firms? The answer is that the government decided that it should. Or another case: since 1945 German politicians of every stripe have been insisting that they want to "save Germany from itself"—an attempt to assert political control over cultural identity.

South Korea and Germany are examples of governments acting positively to create something new. But governments can act upon cultures negatively: ie, they can destroy a culture when they collapse. Robert Kaplan, of an American magazine *Atlantic Monthly*, begins his book, "The Ends of the Earth", in Sierra Leone: "I had assumed that the random crime and social chaos of West Africa were the result of an already-fragile cultural base." Yet by the time he reaches Cambodia at the end of what he calls "a journey at the dawn of the 21st century" he is forced to reconsider that assumption:

> Here I was . . . in a land where the written script was one thousand two hundred years old, and every surrounding country was in some stage of impressive economic growth. Yet Cambodia was eerily similar to Sierra Leone: with random crime, mosquito-borne disease, a government army that was more like a mob and a countryside that was ungovernable.

His conclusion is that "The effect of culture was more a mystery to me near the end of my planetary journey than at its beginning." He might have gone further: the collapse of governments causes cultural turbulence just as much as cultural turbulence causes the collapse of governments.

Culture as Processed Data

Then there is the "knowledge era". Here is a powerful and growing phenomenon. The culture writers do not claim anything different. Like the Industrial Revolution before it, the knowledge era—in which the creation, storage and use of knowledge becomes the basic economic activity—is generating huge change. Emphasising as it does rapid, even chaotic, transformation, it is anti-traditional and anti-authoritarian.

Yet the cultural exponents still claim that, even in the knowledge era, culture remains a primary engine of change. They do so for two quite different reasons. Some claim that the new era has the makings of a world culture. There is a universal language, English. There are the beginnings of an international professional class that cuts across cultural and national boundaries: increasingly, bankers, computer programmers, executives, even military officers are said to have as much in common with their opposite numbers in other countries as with their next-door neighbors. As Mr Fukuyama wrote in his more famous book: the "unfolding of modern natural science . . . guarantees an increasing homogenisation of all human societies." Others doubt that technology and the rest of it are producing a genuinely new world order. To them, all this is just modern western culture.

Either way, the notion that modernity is set on a collision course with culture lies near the heart of several of the culture writers' books. Summing them up is the title of Benjamin Barber's "Jihad versus McWorld". In other words, he argues that the main conflicts now and in future will be between tribal, local "cultural" values (Jihad) and a McWorld of technology and democracy.

It would be pointless to deny that globalisation is causing large changes in every society. It is also clear that such influences act on different cultures differently, enforcing a kind of natural selection between those cultures which rise to the challenge and those which do not.

But it is more doubtful that these powerful forces are primarily cultural or even western. Of course, they have a cultural component: the artefacts of American culture are usually the first things to come along in the wake of a new road, or new television networks. But the disruptive force itself is primarily economic and has been adopted as enthusiastically in Japan, Singapore and China as in America. The world market is not a cultural concept.

Moreover, to suggest that trade, globalisation and the rest of it tend to cause conflict, and then leave the argument there, is not enough. When you boil the argument down, much of it seems to be saying that the more countries trade with each other, the more likely they are to go to war. That seems implausible. Trade—indeed, any sort of link—is just as likely to reduce the potential for violent conflict as to increase it. The same goes for the spread of democracy, another feature which is supposed to encourage civilisations to clash with each other. This might well cause ructions within countries. It might well provoke complaints from dictators about "outside interference". But serious international conflict is a different matter. And if democracy really did spread round the world, it might tend to reduce violence; wealthy democracies, at any rate, are usually reluctant to go to war (though poor or angrily nationalist ones may, as history has shown, be much less reluctant).

In short, the "knowledge era" is spreading economic ideas. And these ideas have three cultural effects, not one. They make cultures rub against each other, causing international friction. They also tie different cultures closer together, which offsets the first effect. And they may well increase tensions within a culture-area as some groups accommodate themselves to the new world while others turn their back on it. And all this can be true at the same time because cultures are so varied and ambiguous that they are capable of virtually any transformation.

The conclusion must be that while culture will continue to exercise an important influence on both countries and individuals, it has not suddenly become more important than, say, governments or impersonal economic forces. Nor does it play the all-embracing defining role that ideology played during the cold war. Much of its influence is secondary, ie, it comes about partly as a reaction to the "knowledge era". And within the overall mix of what influences people's behaviour, culture's role may well be declining, rather than rising, squeezed between the greedy expansion of the government on one side, and globalisation on the other.

The books mentioned in this article are:

Benjamin Barber. Jihad versus McWorld (Random House; 1995; 400 pages; $12.95).

Francis Fukuyama. The End of History and the Last Man (Free Press; 1992; 419 pages; $24.95. Hamish Hamilton; £20.) and Trust: The Social Virtues and the Creation of Prosperity (Free Press; 1995; 480 pages; $25. Hamish Hamilton; £25).

Lawrence E. Harrison. Who Prospers? How Cultural Values Shape Economic and Political Success (Basic Books; 1992; 288 pages; $14).

Samuel Huntington. The Clash of Civilisations? *Foreign Affairs* Vol. 72 (Summer 1993) and The Clash of Civilisations and the Remaking of World Order (Simon & Schuster; 1996; 367 pages; $26).

Robert Kaplan. The Ends of the Earth (Random House; 1996; 475 pages; $27.50. Papermac; £10).

Bernard Lewis. The Middle East (Wiedenfeld & Nicolson; 1995; 433 pages; £20. Simon & Schuster; $29.50).

Seymour Martin Lipset. American Exceptionalism (Norton; 1996; 352 pages; $27.50 and £19.95).

Robert Putnam. Making Democracy Work: Civic Traditions in Modern Italy (Princeton; 1993; 288 pages; $24.95 and £18.95).

Thomas Sowell. Race and Culture: A World View (Basic Books; 1994; 331 pages; $14).

Test-Your-Knowledge Form

We encourage you to photocopy and use this page as a tool to assess how the articles in *Annual Editions* expand on the information in your textbook. By reflecting on the articles you will gain enhanced text information. You can also access this useful form on a product's book support Web site at *http://www.mhcls.com*.

NAME: DATE:

TITLE AND NUMBER OF ARTICLE:

BRIEFLY STATE THE MAIN IDEA OF THIS ARTICLE:

LIST THREE IMPORTANT FACTS THAT THE AUTHOR USES TO SUPPORT THE MAIN IDEA:

WHAT INFORMATION OR IDEAS DISCUSSED IN THIS ARTICLE ARE ALSO DISCUSSED IN YOUR TEXTBOOK OR OTHER READINGS THAT YOU HAVE DONE? LIST THE TEXTBOOK CHAPTERS AND PAGE NUMBERS:

LIST ANY EXAMPLES OF BIAS OR FAULTY REASONING THAT YOU FOUND IN THE ARTICLE:

LIST ANY NEW TERMS/CONCEPTS THAT WERE DISCUSSED IN THE ARTICLE, AND WRITE A SHORT DEFINITION:

We Want Your Advice

ANNUAL EDITIONS revisions depend on two major opinion sources: one is our Advisory Board, listed in the front of this volume, which works with us in scanning the thousands of articles published in the public press each year; the other is you—the person actually using the book. Please help us and the users of the next edition by completing the prepaid article rating form on this page and returning it to us. Thank you for your help!

ANNUAL EDITIONS: Comparative Politics 09/10

ARTICLE RATING FORM

Here is an opportunity for you to have direct input into the next revision of this volume.
We would like you to rate each of the articles listed below, using the following scale:

1. **Excellent: should definitely be retained**
2. **Above average: should probably be retained**
3. **Below average: should probably be deleted**
4. **Poor: should definitely be deleted**

Your ratings will play a vital part in the next revision.
Please mail this prepaid form to us as soon as possible.
Thanks for your help!

RATING	ARTICLE	RATING	ARTICLE
	1. What Democracy Is . . . and Is Not		22. An Embattled Cristina Fernández de Kirchner
	2. Public Opinion: Is There a Crisis?		23. Iran's Tool Fights America's Stooge
	3. Advanced Democracies and the New Politics		24. Let Women Rule
	4. Referendums: The People's Voice		25. Equity in Representation for Women and Minorities
	5. Facing the Challenge of Semi-Authoritarian States		26. Judicial Review: The Gavel and the Robe
	6. People Power		27. Political Influence on the Bureaucracy: The Bureaucracy Speaks
	7. Bin Laden, the Arab "Street," and the Middle East's Democracy Deficit		28. Turkish Court Calls Ruling Party Constitutional
	8. What Political Institutions Does Large-Scale Democracy Require?		29. The Making of a Neo-KGB State
	9. Interest Groups: Ex Uno, Plures		30. Why Can't Uncle Sam Spy?
	10. Political Parties: Empty Vessels?		31. The Formation of State Actor-Social Movement Coalitions and Favorable Policy Outcomes
	11. Police Clash with Monks in Myanmar		32. Capitalism and Democracy
	12. Concerns Grow About Role of Interest Groups in Elections		33. China: The Quiet Revolution
	13. Venezuela Hands Narrow Defeat to Chávez Plan		34. A Confident New Country
	14. The Historic Legacy of Tony Blair		35. Japanese Spirit, Western Things
	15. Russia's Transition to Autocracy		36. Job Security, Too, May Have a Happy Medium
	16. Angela Merkel's Germany		37. Beijing Censors Taken to Task in Party Circles
	17. Iran's Conservative Revival		38. The EU and Its "Constitution"
	18. How Did We Get Here?		39. Anti-Americanisms
	19. In Quake, Apotheosis of Premier 'Grandpa'		40. The True Clash of Civilizations
	20. Japan's Upper House Censures Prime Minister		41. Cultural Explanations
	21. The Case for a Multi-Party U.S. Parliament?		

NO POSTAGE
NECESSARY
IF MAILED
IN THE
UNITED STATES

BUSINESS REPLY MAIL
FIRST CLASS MAIL PERMIT NO. 551 DUBUQUE IA

POSTAGE WILL BE PAID BY ADDRESSEE

McGraw-Hill Contemporary Learning Series
501 BELL STREET
DUBUQUE, IA 52001

ABOUT YOU

Name   Date

Are you a teacher? ❏ A student? ❏
Your school's name

Department

Address   City   State   Zip

School telephone #

YOUR COMMENTS ARE IMPORTANT TO US!

Please fill in the following information:
For which course did you use this book?

Did you use a text with this ANNUAL EDITION? ❏ yes ❏ no
What was the title of the text?

What are your general reactions to the Annual Editions concept?

Have you read any pertinent articles recently that you think should be included in the next edition? Explain.

Are there any articles that you feel should be replaced in the next edition? Why?

Are there any World Wide Web sites that you feel should be included in the next edition? Please annotate.

May we contact you for editorial input? ❏ yes ❏ no
May we quote your comments? ❏ yes ❏ no